ABOUT THE COVER PHOTO

The promise of silver and gold wealth drew early immigrants from Spain and, more briefly, from Portugal to the Americas. As the photograph of miners at La Rinconada reveals, gold has retained its luster despite the mine's location in southeastern Peru at an elevation some 17,000 feet above sea level. Unlike the poorly paid colonial laborers drafted from native villages to work at the famed Potosí mines, in today's Bolivia most workers at La Rinconada get their compensation from the practice of retaining fifty-kilogram sacks of ore once every several weeks. This type of remuneration is a form of wage supplement long employed in colonial mines in both Peru and Mexico. Like at the silver mills of the colonial era, the use of mercury in processing ore at La Rinconada results in mercury poisoning today.

Exploitation, Inequality, and Resistance

The United Nations launched the first International Women's Day in 1975. The March 8 holiday has since expanded globally in support of women's rights and gender equality and it has become widely recognized throughout Latin America. In 2017, feminist organizations staged a worldwide strike dubbed "A Day without a Woman" to protest persistent exploitation, inequality, and violence against women. In Bolivia, thousands of female workers and others participated by placing candles in a public square in the capital city of La Paz.

Exploitation, Inequality, and Resistance

*A History of Latin America
since Columbus*

MARK A. BURKHOLDER

MONICA RANKIN

LYMAN L. JOHNSON

New York   Oxford
OXFORD UNIVERSITY PRESS

Oxford University Press is a department of the University of Oxford.
It furthers the University's objective of excellence in research,
scholarship, and education by publishing worldwide.
Oxford is a registered trademark of Oxford University Press
in the UK and certain other countries.

Published in the United States of America by Oxford University Press
198 Madison Avenue, New York, NY 10016, United States of America.

Library of Congress Cataloging-in-Publication Data

Names: Burkholder, Mark A., 1943- author. | Johnson, Lyman L., author. |
    Rankin, Monica, 1972- author.
Title: Exploitation, inequality, and resistance : a history of Latin America
    since Columbus / Mark A. Burkholder, Lyman L. Johnson, Monica Rankin.
Description: New York, NY : Oxford University Press, 2018. | Includes
    bibliographical references and index.
Identifiers: LCCN 2016053838 (print) | LCCN 2016054309 (ebook) | ISBN
    9780199837618 (pbk. : alk. paper) | ISBN 9780190683818 (updf)
Subjects: LCSH: Latin America—History—To 1830. | Latin
    America—History—1830-
Classification: LCC F1412 .B97 2018 (print) | LCC F1412 (ebook) | DDC
    980—dc23
LC record available at https://lccn.loc.gov/2016053838

9 8 7 6 5 4 3 2
Printed by Webcom, Inc., Canada

FOR RMCLASISTAS, PRESENT AND FUTURE.

CONTENTS

LIST OF PRIMARY SOURCES

PREFACE

The words "exploitation," "inequality," and "resistance" bind together attitudes and actions that encapsulate much of Latin America's economic, social, and political history for more than half a millennium. Inequality and exploitation connote a relationship of power and dominance, in which an individual, institution, or country benefits disproportionately to the detriment of others. These two concepts describe the political structure and social organization of Latin America's many peoples. They characterize economic systems designed to profit the few and the conditions of forced and much free labor from the time of Columbus. But instead of considering exploitation and inequality as a component of "colonialism" and "neocolonialism"—imposed by outside forces onto Latin America as a victim—our examination recognizes both external and internal systems of mistreatment.

Some examples of exploitation and inequality in the following chapters include slavery and other labor systems, sexual and gender exploitation, an inequitable economic relationship with foreign countries, repressive political systems through dictatorship and military regimes, and an unequal diplomatic relationship with the United States and other powerful nations.

Despite deeply entrenched systems of injustice, Latin Americans remain notable for their resilience. Active and passive resistance to oppression and discrimination still persist in the twenty-first century. Examples of challenges to exploitation include native revolts and slave flights, unionization, the emergence of the Latin American women's movement, black market economies, the emergence of populism, and various forms of revolt and revolution.

This textbook tells the story of more than 500 years of Latin American history through the lens of exploitation, inequality, and resistance. The analysis in each chapter emphasizes these themes and makes explicit the ways earlier events continue to resonate in later years. Other common threads appear throughout the narrative that may help students examine the ideas of exploitation, inequality, and resistance more deeply. The book emphasizes that each country and/or region of Latin America has a unique story and character. But at the same time it demonstrates that the shared experience of Iberian rule created trends and themes that echo throughout the region, even after independence.

Iberian Institutions

Spanish and Portuguese rule laid important foundations for trends that emerged in official institutions as well as in cultural practices in later periods. The Iberian influence is particularly evident in themes such as the Catholic Church, education, administrative institutions, agriculture and economic development, labor institutions, the military, the corporatist nature of Latin American society, and corruption and law. The text also considers the contradictions inherent within many of the foreign and inherited ideas and institutions that form an integral part of Latin American history. These include debates about political systems such as monarchy versus republic, centralism versus federalism, and liberalism versus conservatism. Many of the debates regarding suffrage, women's roles and rights, and ethnicity and citizenship also derive from the cultural and political assumptions that took root during three centuries of European rule.

Identity

Various forms of identity emerged during the era of Iberian rule and continue to the present day. The text examines the origins of powerbrokers such as local caciques and regional *caudillos* and traces their influence as viceroyalties made the postindependence transition into more numerous countries. The book charts the importance of racial, corporate, cultural, political, and class identities by examining the early utilization of the casta system and its evolution after independence. It also considers the role of cultural forces such as literature, art, music, dance, sport, fashion, entertainment, and various modes of technology in shaping notions of regional and national identity. This approach allows an examination of the development and perpetuation of stereotypes both within and outside Latin America.

Global Context

National and regional histories do not exist in a vacuum; rather, they are intricately linked with the rest of the world. The first half of the text presents the Latin American region as part of the larger Iberian empires, taking into account both the role of the Americas in the broader scope of the conflicts that defined early modern European history and the international dimensions of developments within the Americas. Later sections of the text examine Latin American independence as part of an "Age of Revolution" in the Atlantic world and consider economic and cultural developments of the nineteenth century in the context of informal imperialism. Twentieth-century coverage presents national developments against the backdrop of the Great Depression, World Wars, and eventually the emergence of the Cold War. Taken together, all of these themes reinforce the text's focus on exploitation, inequality, and resistance while underscoring the importance of Latin America's Iberian foundations.

Our teaching experience confirms that most students arrive in entry-level courses on Latin America knowing little or nothing about the region's varied histories, societies, and economies. This holds true for the pre-Columbian civilizations, the three centuries of European rule, and the two subsequent centuries of political independence. In the 26 chapters that follow, we provide introductory students with a survey of Latin America written in readable, informative, and jargon-free prose. Appropriate generalizations and supporting evidence reveal both continuity and change in diverse societies, economies, and political and cultural systems from the arrival of Europeans to the present. Each chapter provides "Suggestions for Further Reading" to guide students who want to pursue a specific topic more deeply.

ACKNOWLEDGMENTS

Some years ago, Brian Wheel, who oversaw several editions of Burkholder and Johnson's *Colonial Latin America* for Oxford University Press, suggested to Lyman that he would be interested in receiving a proposal for an introductory survey of Latin American History from its origins to the twenty-first century. Lyman and Mark recognized that such a book required an authority on the twentieth century and agreed that Monica could provide the expertise needed. When Lyman's other commitments forced him to withdraw from the project, Monica agreed to write the chapters following independence in the early nineteenth century and she and Mark prepared the proposal that ultimately led to this book.

The first 13 chapters draw heavily upon *Colonial Latin America*; chapters 14-26 are completely original. Both Monica and Mark read and edited in detail each other's draft chapters and agreed to share any praise or blame bestowed on the final product.

We thank Charles Cavaliere who took over the editorship of this book for Oxford while we were revising the manuscript. His continued support has been extremely valuable as we brought the project to a close. We acknowledge the research support provided by Center for U.S.-Latin America Initiatives at the University of Texas at Dallas, and in particular the contributions of graduate assistant, Toni Loftin. Furthermore, we are grateful to the Denver Art Museum for the illustrations in the first half of the book.

Thank you also to Oxford University Press's reviewers Carlos A. Contreras of Grossmont College, Marcela Echeverri of Yale University, Scott Ickes of University of South Florida, Tamara J. Walker of University of Pennsylvania, Peter Klaren of The George Washington University, John R. Burch Jr. of Campbellsville University, Patricia Juarez-Dappe of California State University of Northridge, Teresita Levy of Lehman College, Eric Paul Roorda of Bellarmine University, and four reviewers who wished to remain anonymous for their critical and constructive reviews of the manuscript.

Additionally, we thank our spouses Carol Burkholder and Brian Rankin, along with Shiloh and Kyla Rankin, for putting up with the hassles involved in living with historians.

We dedicate the book to our colleagues of the Rocky Mountain Council for Latin American Studies, the oldest and most enjoyable multi-disciplinary professional body focused on Latin America in the United States.

Mark Burkholder, St. Louis
Monica Rankin, Dallas

MAPS

TABLES AND FIGURES

Map 0.1 Topographical Map of Latin America

Exploitation, Inequality, and Resistance

CHAPTER 1

The Eve of Atlantic Empires

CHRONOLOGY

c. 1325	Mexica begin to build Tenochtitlan
1415	Portuguese capture Ceuta in North Africa
1426–1521	Triple Alliance and Aztec Empire
c. 1438–1533	Inka Empire
1440s	Portuguese start transporting African slaves to Lisbon
1469	Marriage of Ferdinand of Aragon and Isabel of Castile
1483	Portuguese reach the Kingdom of Kongo in West Central Africa
1492	Fall of Granada; expulsion of Jews from "Spain"; first Castilian grammar published

Victory over Muslim Granada in 1492 concluded the Reconquest that Christians initiated in Iberia's northern mountains in the eighth century. In the Americas during the 1400s, militant Aztec and Inka empires emerged as successors to earlier high cultures. Meanwhile, the Portuguese established fortified trading posts on or near the West African coast, introduced increasing numbers of enslaved Africans into Europe, and made sugar plantations on their Atlantic islands synonymous with bondage. By the early sixteenth century, Iberians in the Americas had already initiated patterns of exploitation and inequality and sparked cases of resistance. Accompanied by political, economic, and social transformations, the subsequent conflicts, defiance, and accommodation spawned consequences that continue to the present day.

IBERIA

Over eight centuries, the Reconquest of Moorish Iberia influenced institutions, strengthened a hierarchical society, and bolstered the economies of the peninsula's four Christian monarchies—Castile, Aragon, Portugal, and Navarre. The Muslim

Kingdom of Granada's surrender to King Ferdinand of Aragon and Queen Isabel of Castile on January 2, 1492, ended a decade of war and increased the lands of the Crown of Castile. The final triumph convinced the victors that their God extended his favor to Castile in particular, a sentiment that conquistadors soon carried to the Americas.

Castile was the preeminent kingdom of the Iberian Peninsula, a landmass of nearly 225,000 square miles. More than triple the area of the Crown of Aragon's mainland realms—Aragon, Catalonia, and Valencia—Castile's population of perhaps 4 million underpinned its political and economic strength. Portugal, whose reconquest had ended in the thirteenth century, was home to a population of perhaps 1 million, slightly more than in the Crown of Aragon. Portuguese residents dominated the expanding trade along the northwestern and central coast of West Africa. Granada added some 200,000 inhabitants to the Crown of Castile after postwar Muslim emigration ended. The annexation of part of Navarre in 1512 provided another 120,000 inhabitants.

Castile, Aragon, and Portugal were hereditary monarchies marked by social, economic, and legal inequality. Below each ruler were a few titled aristocrats, many more untitled nobles (Sp. *hidalgos* and Port. *fidalgos*), an overwhelming majority of commoners, and some African slaves. The Castilian aristocracy constituted about 2 percent of the realm's total population in 1492, but owned or controlled 95 percent or more of the land. The wealthiest nobles enjoyed an opulent lifestyle most Castilians could only dream of emulating, and local elites dominated municipalities. Commoners included merchants, professionals, artisans, and servants, but most of them worked in the fields or tended livestock. Those who entered the clergy usually served at the parish level or became friars or monks in religious orders. Wives normally shared their husbands' social rank. A small number of women entered convents.

The nuptials of Ferdinand of Aragon and Isabel of Castile in 1469 and their later inheritance of the two crowns created the potential for political unification. However, the "Catholic Monarchs," as Pope Alexander VI titled them, ruled each realm separately by its traditional institutions, laws, taxes, and privileges. The king and queen, not shared institutions, united these patrimonial possessions.

Victory over Granada reinforced a "booty mentality" forged during the Reconquest. Warfare made available spoils, land, slaves, and the possibility of upward social mobility, all alluring to young, single men. Historically, the Crown of Castile rewarded vassals who served it, an approach that for centuries provided special benefits for cavalrymen and the military orders founded during the Reconquest. By the mid-twelfth century, inherited noble status was replacing status earned through valorous military service. Nobles received royal rewards that included inheritable land, grants of jurisdiction and fees from persons residing on their property, and legal privileges, one of which exempted them from a tax (*pecho*) that only commoners paid. Although it awarded nobles some properties and municipalities in Granada, the Crown retained control over the most important lands. Nonetheless, successful combatants gained parcels at least double the size of those bestowed on later settlers.

The foundation in Granada of new municipalities and the incorporation and reorganization of conquered ones strengthened both the importance of community life and a tradition of local government and privileges based on ancient municipal charters. Settlers received urban plots and access to land for farming and pasture within walking distance from their home. Everywhere, allegiance to family, birthplace, and residence outweighed attachments to larger administrative units, including kingdoms.

The Catholic Monarchs ruled without a fixed capital. Their extensive travels throughout Castile gave them extraordinary knowledge of the kingdom that facilitated effective administration. They emphasized the provision of justice and the historic essence of royal responsibility, introduced additional provincial officials (*corregidores*), and attracted men with university training in Roman law to royal service. Close administrative oversight bolstered tax receipts and reduced the monarchs' need to rely on the *Cortes*, or parliament of Castile, for revenue.

Victory in Granada brought Isabel a papal grant of royal patronage that gave the Crown unprecedented power over the Church in the newly acquired kingdom. Although she had less authority over clerics in Castile, the queen recognized that the Church there badly needed reform. Many monks and friars—the regular clergy—ignored their orders' rules and displayed an appalling lack of appropriate discipline. Diocesan clerics—the secular clergy—were in even worse shape; some parish priests failed to celebrate mass just four times a year. Isabel judiciously sought qualified candidates for high ecclesiastical positions and encouraged some mid-level bishops, abbots, and prebendaries to undertake reforms. Many clerics opposed the changes, including a substantial group of monks from Seville who emigrated to Africa with their mistresses rather than relinquish them. Nevertheless, religious orders turned toward their guiding principles. Internal reforms and external pressure stimulated the Franciscans in particular to participate enthusiastically in evangelization activities in Granada. Greater control over ecclesiastical appointments in Castile reinforced the Crown's ability to improve the secular clergy.

Victory over the Muslims increased royal determination to foster religious homogeneity based on Christianity. The Crown expelled unconverted Jews in 1492 and unconverted Muslims a decade later. The recently established (1478) Tribunal of the Inquisition vigorously pursued all "New Christians," converts (*conversos*) especially of Jewish lineage, whose commitment to their new faith seemed dubious.

Spaniards and resident Italians participated in Atlantic and Mediterranean trade. Genoese merchants resided in the river port of Seville after its reconquest in the mid-thirteenth century. Castilians cultivated wheat, olives, and grapes; raised livestock, notably sheep; and exported large quantities of wool and cloth. Merchants from outside the peninsula attended the trade fair at Medina del Campo, where Castilians sold wool, iron, mercury, salted fish, leather goods, and wine, among other products. Often they sailed north to trade in the Flemish city of Bruges. On Spain's northern coast, towns in Santander, Vizcaya, and Guipúzcoa in particular produced fishermen, sailors, and maritime traders.

On the eve of empire, Castile was a politically stable, prosperous, and growing kingdom. A hierarchical society received spiritual reinforcement from clerics who preached acceptance of this world and reward after death. The Christian population viewed the victory over the Kingdom of Granada as recompense, an unambiguous demonstration of their God's special favor, and an opportunity to proselytize. The Inquisition's success against *conversos* additionally signaled Christianity's growing strength as it became, to the Spaniards' way of thinking, ever more pure.

INDIGENOUS SOCIETIES IN "THE INDIES"

The year 1492 opened without fanfare in lands Europeans would soon call "the Indies," "the West Indies," "America," and the "New World." Most, if not all, of the indigenous population's distant ancestors had crossed Beringia (the temporarily passable land bridge connecting northeastern Russia and present-day Alaska), continued through an ice-free corridor, and subsequently dispersed throughout the Americas. Although water again covered this bridge approximately 12,500 years ago, evidence indicates that humans had reached southern Chile 2,000 to 6,000 years earlier. An archaeological team in Brazil claims to have discovered artifacts dating to more than 20,000 years ago. Debate about the antiquity of humans in the Americas has also revitalized discussion regarding how they arrived.

Although the predominant explanation supports initial human passage across Beringia, another hypothesis posits that maritime peoples originally from East Asia followed the "Kelp Highway" adjacent to the Pacific coast shoreline. These migrants survived thanks to numerous varieties of seaweed known as kelp that thrived in oceanic "forests" containing marine birds, edible shellfish, mammals, and fish. The early travelers may have left behind small populations that spawned settlements in coastal valleys and along rivers into the interior of the American continents. This argument could explain the early presence of humans in Chile, but archaeologists have yet to find evidence that corroborates it.

By the time Columbus reached the Indies, its 15 or more distinctive cultural centers were home to more than 160 linguistic stocks. Nomadic hunters, fishers, and food gathers, such as Chichimecas in the north of present-day Mexico and Caribs in the Lesser Antilles, comprised one group of indigenous cultures. Sedentary or semisedentary peoples included, for example, Chibchas or Muiscas in present-day Colombia and Guaraní in Paraguay. A few regions held densely populated sedentary civilizations: the Nahua and Mixtec-Zapotec in Mexico, Maya in Yucatan and Central America, and Inka in South America. Their nobles

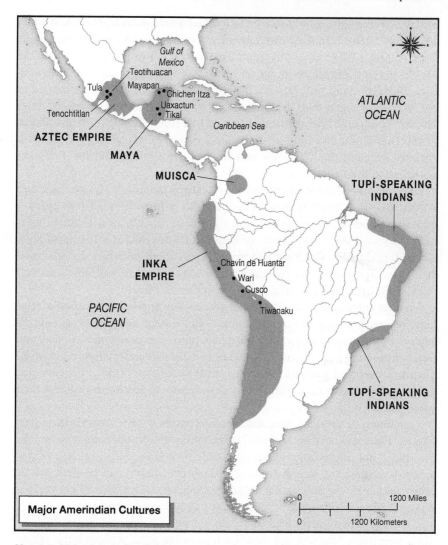

Map 1.1 Major Amerindian Cultures

and priests lived off the agricultural surplus of exploited laborers. All of these cultures lacked large domestic animals, wheeled vehicles, hard-metal tools (except for bronze used by the Inka), ships other than canoes and balsa rafts, and the plow.

The Nahua

The Nahua, a collective term for Nahuatl speakers in Central Mexico, included the Mexica or Tenocha in Tenochtitlan, an island capital in Lake Texcoco in the Valley of Mexico. They reached the fertile region in the mid-thirteenth century, initially serving existing city-states as exploited mercenaries and slaves. Around 1325, they constructed their own city, after dredging the lake and expanding its land. At first a tributary of Atzcapotzalco, the valley's dominant city-state, the Mexica became a kingdom about 50 years later. Creating a triple alliance with two other city-states on Lake Texcoco's shores, they defeated Atzcapotzalco in the 1420s and began their expansion. Led by the Mexica, the so-called "Aztec Empire" conquered and demanded tribute of peoples from the Pacific Ocean to the Gulf Coast and into southern Mexico. Several remaining independent enclaves included the Tlaxcalans southeast of Tenochtitlan and the Tarascans northwest of the capital.

Numerous ethnic city-states or *altepetl* existed in Central Mexico. Each had a ruler (*tlatoani*), a society marked by inequality, a main temple for its primary god, some kind of central market, and a group of subunits or constituent parts called *calpolli* divided into groups of households or wards. The 16 *calpolli* present at Tenochtitlan's founding had expanded to about 80 when the Spaniards arrived in 1519. The Mexica ruler and high priest at that time was Moteuczoma II (1502–1520), the most powerful sovereign in Central Mexico.

Nobles at the core of the Mexica aristocracy descended from the first Mexica king, reputedly a ruler of the semidivine Toltec lineage and heir to its political legitimacy. Known as *pipiltin*, they filled high offices, received a share of land and tribute from conquered regions, and had one official wife and multiple other wives. Their sons prepared at school to become either warriors or priests. The remaining nobles were elevated commoner warriors rewarded with lifetime nobility for their valor and success.

Commoners included long-distance merchants (*pochteca*) with their own *altepetl*, Tlatelolco, adjacent to Tenochtitlan. Although some became very wealthy, they dared not display their affluence outside their homes. Craftsmen, a second group of commoners, included feather makers, goldsmiths, and jewelers, among other specialists. The description of the great market at Tlatelolco by Bernal Díaz reveals the Spaniards' awe at the goods available and their orderliness.

Average commoners lived in urban *calpolli* but enjoyed access to land. Their sons trained for war and could be required to serve. Although the *calpolli* held land, this valuable resource passed from citizens to their heirs. Most commoners had to pay tribute, provide labor service for the nobles, and work for their *calpolli*. Sumptuary legislation underscored their status, prohibiting them from donning certain clothing or wearing sandals while walking on city streets. A lowly group of commoners included losers in wars who lived and labored on nobles' lands. They lacked access to *calpolli* land, but neither performed public duties nor paid tribute.

A small number of slaves, perhaps 5 percent of the population, completed Mexica society. Some had reached Tenochtitlan as tribute, others were in bondage as a penalty for a criminal offense, and an unknown number had sold themselves to pay off debt. Slaves could purchase their manumission and, unlike in the later African slavery, all indigenous children were born free.

Mexica women enjoyed substantial rights and responsibilities. They participated fully in many varied activities, but not in most public offices. Nonetheless, each *altepetl* made at least one female responsible for organizing and regulating women's activities. Parents approved, if they did not select, the men their daughters married, a practice that enabled them to parlay marriages into political alliances. Once wed, most wives' household responsibilities included preparing meals, cleaning, child care, spinning and weaving cloth, and embroidery. Outside the home they served as priestesses in the temples, sold cacao and other goods, delivered babies, cured the sick, weaved and embroidered, and supervised some activities in the markets. Although commoners engaged in these tasks more extensively than their noble counterparts, almost all women added to their family's material well-being and oversaw their households when husbands were on military duty. Their contributions provided an economic reason for Mexica men's interest in polygyny. Inheritance practice recognized women's numerous economic activities. Wives owned any possessions they brought to a marriage and could bequeath them and any inherited property.

All *altepetl* had numerous deities. Huitzilopochtli, God of the Sun and God of War, headed the Mexica pantheon and held the honor of having led them to the site where they built Tenochtitlan. To continue his movement across the skies as God of the Sun, Huitzilopochtli required a magical substance released by human sacrifices. Wars of expansion supplied the Aztec Empire with new lands, tribute, and some sacrificial victims. To ensure a supply of worthy prisoners for religious rituals, starting in the 1450s the Mexica fought the so-called "Flowery Wars." In them, two matched opponents engaged in hand-to-hand combat until one was captured or had taken flight.

The Mexica, in short, comprised a hierarchical society organized for war and dedicated to achieving victory. Through warfare, they sought to capture approximately 20,000 enemy warriors annually for sacrifices. All commoner boys not preparing to enter the priesthood attended local schools and began weapons handling at the age of 15. Success in warfare determined those who would advance through the military ranks and potentially obtain noble status for life. Valorous actions in battle alone provided the most highly desired symbols of success, such as jewels, shields, and elaborate capes. Failure on the battlefield brought a commoner shame and life as a carrier or porter; a cowardly noble lost his rank and its benefits.

The Inka

Parallel to the creation of the Aztec Empire, the Inka were rapidly extending their domain in South America from a small territorial base centered on their capital, Cusco. By 1530 their empire stretched about 3,000 miles from nearly the border between present-day Ecuador and Colombia to central Chile and held an estimated 9 million inhabitants.

Andean societies lived in mountain valleys at elevations between 9,800 and 11,200 feet, where inhabitants could grow potatoes and maize. Above them lay high, flat, grassy plains without extensive human settlement. There llamas and

Portraits of the first Inka royal couple, Manco Capac and Mama Ocllo, painted in late nineteenth-century Peru.

alpacas grazed; deposits of gold, silver, and copper could be found; and lakes served as headwaters for rivers used in irrigation. At a lower elevation, warmer but sparsely settled regions featured a climate suitable for growing coca, chili peppers, and varieties of fruit. Below these elevations were pasturelands in desert oases. These "vertical archipelagos," or distinct islands of differing economic potential, characterized land on the western slopes of the Andes. Access to each type of "island" was necessary to enjoy the full array of Andean flora and fauna.

The Inka applied the threat and, if necessary, the use of military force to propel their territorial growth. Once expansion from Cusco was underway, men from conquered lands composed most of the armies and normally served under professional Inka officers. After taking over an area, the Inka demanded that its commoner warriors participate in the next campaign. As incentives, they offered new soldiers the opportunity to avenge themselves against old enemies, share in the rewards of conquest, and have the prospect of fighting in future wars. Aside from Inka officers, the few professional soldiers were mercenary bowmen and the bodyguard of the Inka ruler drawn from the Cañari of modern Ecuador. Notably, the Inka executed few prisoners of war other than leaders and routinely returned prisoners to their homes. Inka officials supervised local chieftains (*kurakas*) and nobles who retained their positions, but sent their sons to Cusco for schooling and to serve as hostages. In contrast to the Nahua in Central Mexico, the Inka's use of human sacrifice was limited.

The Inka's organizational skills were their great advantage. By relying primarily on soldiers from a region adjacent to where they were fighting, they minimized the time away from home and avoided problems associated with different ecological zones. They also conscripted soldiers in a way that did not disrupt agricultural production. Especially valuable was their system of roads and supply. Some 10,000 miles of parallel highways in the mountains and along the coast connected to each other as necessary. Every few miles, rest areas and storehouses (*tambos*) provided food, clothing, and weapons maintained by labor drafts from nearby villages. Llamas served as both pack animals and a source of food. Couriers (*chasquis*) used the highways to carry messages with the aid of colored, knotted strings (*quipus* or *khipus*) that served as memory aids. This communication system allowed runners to convey messages from Cusco to the Pacific Coast near present-day Lima in three days. It also enabled Inka armies to move quickly to quell a revolt or other resistance.

The spread of Inka religion and the Quechua language contributed to integrating the empire, but Inka rule was too brief to yield effective assimilation. Resettlement helped to preserve peace by moving large numbers of troublemakers to other regions and replacing them with loyal settlers. Systematically stressing the benefits of peace, the Inka provided access to goods from varied ecological islands, thus enabling conquered peoples to secure otherwise unobtainable raw materials. For example, they distributed llama wool to all inhabitants of the empire and introduced llamas in regions that previously did not have them. Building on their predecessors' efforts, the Inka also promoted public works, especially large terraces and irrigation canals that increased agricultural production.

The Inka required a labor tax (*mita* or *mit'a*) for specific projects that included constructing fortresses and warehouses; fighting in wars; building and maintaining roads, storehouses, and inns; and planting and harvesting. One massive storage site on the frontier facing the Amazon Basin could store a million bushels of corn, potatoes, and other foodstuffs. Officials sent residents (*mitmaq*) to specific sites to serve as agents of acculturation for Inka values.

The principle of reciprocity undergirded social organization. Commoners in an *ayllu* or kin group provided service on the lands of their *kuraka* and local gods. In return, the *kuraka* provided the food and drink at festivals as well as goods received from the community's members (*mitmaq*) serving their turn in a distant island location. This reciprocity worked its way upward through the provincial governors to the Sapa Inka himself.

Birth and kin relations primarily determined social position. The son of a father in the governing class enjoyed access to goods and foodstuffs produced by others. Within a given province, the rank of kin groups (*ayllus*) determined the order of participating in feasts, worship, and the division of spoils of war. Thus, a hierarchical society extended downward from the Inka ruler to elders and *kurakas*, to commoners who belonged to *ayllus*, and finally to those (*yana*) who (or whose ancestors) had left their *ayllu* and labored for the empire and its nobles.

The Andean population of the central highlands lived in scattered administrative units rather than stable territorial entities as a result of the core-island form of organization. A group of *ayllus*, the basic kin group, formed a *waranqa*; multiple *waranqa* constituted a *repartimiento* (or tribe), the unit that became the original *encomiendas* after the Spanish conquest. When assigning labor service (*mita*), the Inka used units that ranged from 10 to 10,000 households.

Starting with the family, each social unit claimed its identity and lands on the basis of its tie to a recognized ancestor, who might be real or mythical. In above-ground tombs, the Inka kept mummified ancestors that were brought out for ceremonies and festivals, where they were fed, honored, and given gifts to ensure bountiful harvests and herds. Enormous in number, these *wak̓as* (*huacas*) took a wide variety of shapes. All of a social unit's deities needed to be worshiped and fed to ensure their households' well-being. Priests served and interpreted the *wak̓as*, overseeing proper behavior and ceremonies honoring them as well as maintaining a community's history. Mummies in the Atacama Desert along the coast of northern Chile predate the Inka Empire by more than 6,000 years and are more than twice as old as the earliest mummy found in Egypt.

The Nahua and the Inka were the two largest cultural groups the Spaniards would encounter in the Americas. Both had hierarchical social systems that meshed in many ways with what Castilians considered the natural order of society. Additionally, religion's centrality in these indigenous societies mirrored its importance throughout Iberia. Before they met either of these Amerindian societies, however, the Spaniards introduced the first Africans to the Americas.

AFRICA AND THE EARLY SLAVE TRADE

Contact between Iberians and Africans began centuries before Columbus reached the Indies. African gold traders were well known in markets of the Middle East and the lure of more direct access to the metal attracted Portuguese monarchs, other investors, and mariners beginning early in the fifteenth century. Starting on the continent's western coast, the Portuguese established armed trading posts (*feitorias*) located, when possible, on islands close to the mainland and staffed with state and private employees. Garrisoned trading posts and offshore locations were rational responses to Europeans' high mortality from malaria and yellow fever, endemic diseases of Africa. Additionally, they offered protection against native armies whose cavalry and metal weapons made them formidable opponents.

The Portuguese soon turned to Africa's existing slave trade as a source of wealth. Beginning in the 1440s, they conveyed enslaved Africans to Lisbon for sale. Before long, they also sold them as laborers in the growing sugar industry of Portugal's Atlantic island settlements, where their cultural traits made them more valuable than natives. Familiarity with metalwork and the production and use of metal tools, for example, made the Africans desirable laborers in the emerging plantation economy. Those sold in Europe often provided their owners with status as well as domestic labor. In some cases they even had prior knowledge of European religious practices.

Atlantic Africa in the Fifteenth Century

The Portuguese capture of Ceuta across the Strait of Gibraltar in 1415 opened the era of exploration, trade, conquest, and settlement for the Iberian kingdoms. By the late fifteenth century, Portuguese ships had coasted Atlantic Africa. When Bartolomeu Dias rounded the Cape of Good Hope in 1488, he identified the long-desired direct maritime route to India and its spices. The resulting Asian trade further reduced the Portuguese court's willingness to allocate significant resources to controlling the West African coast. Thus, merchants sailing from Lisbon used coastal intermediaries to tap into gold mined in the continent's interior and began to trade European goods for slaves, purchasing and exporting about 2,200 of them annually between 1480 and 1499. The Atlantic slave trade came to dominate relations between Africa and Europe, although for a century or more after the initial contacts, Portuguese and other European coastal traders also purchased goods that included cloth, salt, gold, iron, and copper. They paid local taxes and generally bowed to restrictions imposed by African rulers.

West Africa and West Central Africa, vast regions extending from the Senegal River to the southern reaches of Angola, were home to numerous rulers of variously sized states that competed for power and wealth. Language and other cultural differences frequently separated hundreds if not thousands of ethnic groups, although three principal linguistic zones prevailed: Upper Guinea, Lower Guinea, and West Central Africa. As in contemporary Iberia, local and regional identities—for example, Bambara, Hausa, Jolof, and Mandingo—dominated. The subjects of West African or West Central African polities were perhaps even less likely to consider themselves "Africans" than were Iberians to view themselves as "Europeans."

West Africa

By the mid-fifteenth century the expanding Songhay Empire had used military force to gain power in the lower Gambia and Senegal River areas of West Africa's interior. The rulers Sunni Ali (d. 1492) and Askiya Muhammad (d. 1538) revived the rich trade routes across the Sahara Desert. Songhay sovereigns needed to fuse the interests of a largely Muslim merchant class, crucial to the court, and a vast rural population tied to the kings in older royal rites and traditional religious practices. In a culture renowned for its learning, crafts, and merchants' success, the rulers' power rested on the army's loyalty and on the appointees sent to govern conquered peoples.

Although gold remained a crucial trade item, Songhay's currency was salt or cowries, mollusk shells used as money. Cloth, food, kola nuts, and slaves were also important trade items. Successful military campaigns enlarged the slave population and thereby allowed the empire to increase agricultural production. Visitors were impressed by the intellectual life of the capital Gao and Timbuktu, a manufacturing and commercial hub that became the major center of Islamic scholarship in the region.

The royal palace of the *oba* or king of Benin was adorned with brass plaques that told the story of court life. This plaque presents the figure of a nobleman wearing court regalia.

Numerous small states divided the West African coast in the late fifteenth century. Among them was the kingdom of Benin, located inland from the Niger River Delta. King (*Oba*) Ewuare established Benin's commercial and political power in the mid-fifteenth century and correspondingly reduced the authority of other rulers and chiefs. Early European visitors universally testified that the capital, Benin City, was large and prosperous because the kingdom's women produced beautiful cotton cloth, and its metal goods circulated throughout West Africa. Its merchants also controlled the regional trade in ivory and pepper. Even after the establishment of the Atlantic slave trade, cloth remained Benin's most important export.

Following initial contacts with the Portuguese, the *oba* sent an emissary to Portugal to learn about these strangers. The ambassador returned with rich gifts, some Christian missionaries, and a new group of Portuguese merchants. The king appreciated the utility of European firearms and perhaps thought the missionaries might also strengthen his power. Trade continued, but by 1570 Christian missionaries had failed to convert the *oba* and his court.

West Central Africa

To the southeast, the Kingdom of Kongo dominated a broad region with many linguistically related Bantu ethnic groups. When the Portuguese arrived in 1483, this great regional power had few local threats to its political ambitions. From the capital of Mbanza Kongo, the ruler, or *manikongo*, controlled numerous tributary states and direct dependencies through a bureaucracy composed mostly of kinsmen. A population of nearly 2.5 million lived in towns whose officials and merchants administered regional political life, collected taxes, and organized commerce. The economy relied on both an important metallurgical sector and a highly productive agriculture. The elites perceived that relations with the Portuguese might bring political benefits, such as desired trade goods, prestige, and enhanced spiritual power.

As in Benin, Kongo had a coherent, non-Islamic religious tradition. Nonetheless, contact with the Portuguese led the *manikongo* and his court to explore Christianity. Experimentation culminated in 1491 with the baptism of the royal heir, Nzinga Mbemba. As Afonso I, he became the *manikongo* in 1507 and ruled as a Christian until the 1540s. With royal encouragement, Portuguese missionaries sought converts across the kingdom and sent sons of important families to Portugal for religious instruction. Many returned fluent in Portuguese, but the new faith never completely replaced native religious traditions. Instead, the two melded into a unique local Christianity. Nonetheless, as the Portuguese presence grew and Christianity spread, the Kongo court began to lose power relative to both the increasingly aggressive and confident Portuguese and the kingdom's distant tributaries who perceived an opportunity to assert their own power.

Central to Kongo's decline was the growing importance of its slave trade to the rapidly expanding sugar sector in Brazil. The need for Portuguese allies helps to explain the Kongo elite's sanction of slave sales. Warfare became a staple of the region's political life as armies of Portuguese soldiers and far more numerous native allies campaigned relentlessly. Each battle and every victory added to the slave trade's volume because Kongo's elite required war captives to exchange with the Portuguese for the goods and missionaries that helped to support their political power. By the early sixteenth century, Kongo kings were complaining of the trade's destructiveness to Portuguese authorities and even appealing directly to the pope. But it was too late. The *manikongo*'s authority and the power of the capital declined while the slave trade roiled the interior and provoked constant warfare. By 1600, no African state had been more affected by Europeans' arrival than the Kongo, and nowhere in Africa had the slave trade become more important.

In regions of intense contact, African peoples incorporated elements of European culture, technology, and belief. Scholars refer to these regions as Atlantic Creole cultures. In the Kongo, for example, evangelization by Portuguese priests and African converts spread Christian belief and practice to areas outside administrators' direct control. The Portuguese recruited native military allies that, in turn, adopted European tactics, weapons, and hierarchies. At the same time, the Kongo elite and other African rulers of Portuguese allies sought access to language, religious instruction, and material goods as ways of strengthening their authority and status.

The Kongo and Angola, where Portuguese presence was strongest, were centers of Atlantic Creole culture, but the more distant Ndongo and Matamba participated in these cultural exchanges as well. Importantly, this meant that a large number of slaves shipped to the New World already had experience with central elements of European culture, including Christian belief, language, aesthetics, and material goods, before entering the Iberians' orbit. Once in the Americas, these prior experiences and adaptations facilitated the rapid development of slave communities.

Slavery was well established in most of Atlantic Africa centuries before Portugal seized Ceuta. Wealth rested heavily on the possession of slaves across the large empires of West Africa, as well as in Benin and other kingdoms. Most slaves were taken in wars against distinct ethnic groups with their own religious traditions. Rulers and other slave owners used this human property as administrators, soldiers, concubines, domestic labor, field labor, miners, and artisans, as well as various other occupations. Owners in sub-Saharan Africa also employed their chattel in a host of labors, such as producing agricultural products that included millet, cotton, wheat, and rice. In the western Sudan, slaves worked in gold mines and, in some desert sites, salt works. Owners used, sold, or traded the products of slave labor, and rulers taxed people rather than land, which was held collectively and not as private property. In the fifteenth century, war, raiding, and kidnapping in sub-Saharan regions enabled slavers to send annually an estimated 4,000 to 5,000 victims to Islamic regions of North Africa and the Middle East via routes along the eastern coast and the Red Sea and especially across the Sahara Desert.

The Early Atlantic Slave Trade

The Atlantic slave trade grew during the initial century of contacts between Africans and Europeans and would continue to do so into the eighteenth century. A low ratio of people to land in much of West Africa made control over labor a key to wealth. Coupled with extensive political fragmentation that resulted in ample potential slaves located within traveling distance, this low ratio goes far to explain the development of slavery in sub-Saharan Africa. Slaves were a part of Songhay trade and had become important to the West African regional economy as well by the time the Portuguese arrived. Backed by private investors, these merchants moved slowly down Africa's Atlantic coast, trading goods that included textiles; copper and brass wristlets and basins; horses, saddles, bridles, and other tack; iron bars; and cowries. As the fifteenth century progressed, the importance of slaves in this trade grew. Central to the gradual expansion of this commerce was the use of slave labor in southern Iberia and increasingly in the sugar plantations of the Azores and São Tomé.

Local political authorities initially constrained West Africa's slave traffic to Europe. Although human commerce was important in the Islamic world, rulers' restrictions limited it and meant that slaves flowed only slowly from the interior states to the coast. Similarly, Benin prohibited the export of enslaved males for centuries and thereby controlled the trade's growth. Nevertheless, it utilized human chattel in its own economy and allowed its importation from other African states. Although local rulers were eventually unable to control the mounting trade crossing the Atlantic, there is no doubt that the Portuguese lacked the military power to overcome their objections during the century after first contacts.

Despite slavery's pervasiveness and economic and cultural importance prior to the arrival of the Portuguese, the institution's historic place in African society differed in fundamental ways from the form that Europeans implanted in their American possessions. First, the Atlantic slave trade extracted a volume of slaves never previously witnessed in Africa. As this trade matured, numbers spiraled upward until peaking in the eighteenth century. Second, the distance that the trade carried its victims also necessarily altered the meaning of slavery, tearing families, ethnicities, and even polities apart by forcefully removing men and women from their native regions, cultures, languages, and religions and relocating them to the distant Americas. Finally, the Atlantic slave trade worsened the status of slaves relative to African customs, reducing legal protections and increasing owners' power over them.

Atlantic Africa and the Americas in the fifteenth century had many similarities. These included numerous ethnic states, kingship, frequent wars, hierarchical social structures with strong kinship bonds, multiple religions with prominent priesthoods, indigenous slavery, a variety of languages and dialects, and sedentary agriculture. But the consequences of contacts with Europe in the fifteenth and sixteenth centuries would be very different. Following the defeat of the Aztec and Inka, the Spaniards established direct rule in the Americas. Other than in the kingdom of Kongo, the Portuguese and other Europeans depended on the goodwill of local rulers to engage in trade until the nineteenth century. African political and military resources and the prevalence of malaria, yellow fever, and gastrointestinal ailments also slowed the foreigners' advance. Over time, however, the balance of power shifted to Europeans, as measured in the growing volume of slaves purchased. As a result of this cruel and exploitative trade, Africa made important demographic and cultural contributions to Iberian America.

Primary Source

The Market at Tlatelolco

The great market at Tlatelolco astonished Bernal Díaz del Castillo because of the variety of goods and the orderliness of their display. His only comparison was the fair at Medina del Campo, the entrepôt of Castilian trade with much of Europe.

SOURCE: Bernal Díaz del Castillo, *The True History of the Conquest of New Spain*, trans. Janet Burke and Ted Humphrey (Indianapolis, IN: Hackett, 2012), 208–9.

Each type of merchandise was by itself and had its place fixed and marked out. Let us begin with the merchants of gold, silver, rich stones, featherworks, cloths, embroidered goods, and other merchandise, including men and women Indian slaves; . . . Then there were other merchants who sold coarse clothing, raw cotton, and articles of twisted yarn, and cacao vendors, and in this way there were as many types of merchandise as there are in all of New Spain, arranged in the way it is in my region, which is Medina del Campo, where the fairs are held, . . . and those who sold cloaks of maguey fiber, ropes, and sandals, which are the shoes they wear and make from the same plant; and from the same tree, they make very sweet cooked roots and other sweet things. All were in one part of the market in their designated place. In another part were skins of tigers, lions, otters, jackals, deer and other animals, badgers and mountain cats, some tanned and others untanned, and other types of articles and merchandise.

Let us go on and talk about those who sold beans and sage and other vegetables and herbs in another part. Let us go to those who sold hens, roosters with wattles, rabbits, hares, deer, and large ducks, small dogs, and other things of that sort in their part of the marketplace. Let us talk about the fruiterers, of the women who sold cooked food, corn pudding, and tripe, also in their own part. Then every sort of pottery, . . . Then those who sold honey and honey paste and other delicacies like nut paste. Then those who sold wood, boards, cradles and beams, and blocks and benches, all in their own part. . . . There were many sellers of herbs and goods of other types.

SUGGESTIONS FOR FURTHER READING

Carrasco, David, and Scott Sessions. *Daily Life of the Aztecs*. 2nd ed. Westport, CT: Greenwood Press, 2011.

Coe, Michael D., and Rex Koontz. *Mexico: From the Olmecs to the Aztecs*. 7th ed. New York: Thames & Hudson, 2013.

Downey, Kirstin. *Isabella: The Warrior Queen*. New York: Talese/Doubleday, 2014.

Eltis, David. *The Rise of African Slavery in the Americas*. Cambridge and New York: Cambridge University Press, 2000.

Kamen, Henry. *Spain, 1469–1714: A Society of Conflict*. 4th ed. London: Longman Group, 2014.

Liss, Peggy K. *Isabel the Queen: Life and Times*. 2nd ed. Philadelphia: University of Pennsylvania Press, 2004.

Lovejoy, Paul E. *Transformations in Slavery: A History of Slavery in Africa.* 3rd ed. Cambridge: Cambridge University Press, 2011.

Lynch, John. *Spain 1516–1598: From Nation State to World Empire.* Oxford: Basil Blackwell, 1991.

Rostworowski de Diez Canseco, Maria. *History of the Inca Realm.* Translated by Harry B. Iceland. Cambridge: Cambridge University Press, 1999.

Thornton, John. *Africa and Africans in the Making of the Atlantic World, 1400–1800.* 2nd ed. Cambridge and New York: Cambridge University Press, 1998.

CHAPTER 2

Exploration, Columbus,
and Early Settlement

CHRONOLOGY

1492	Columbus undertakes first voyage and reaches "the Indies"
1493	Papal donation; Columbus's second voyage (1493–1496)
1494	Treaty of Tordesillas
1498–1500	Columbus's third voyage; distribution of Taíno to labor for Spaniards
1500	Pedro Alvarez Cabral lands on Brazilian coast
1501	Importation of African slaves begins in Caribbean
1502–1509	Nicolás de Ovando arrives with some 2,500 persons and administers Española, increasing gold production
1512	Laws of Burgos
1513	Blasco Núñez de Balboa crosses isthmus of Panama to Pacific Ocean
1518	Royal authorization to import slaves directly from Africa

In April 1492, King Ferdinand of Aragon and Queen Isabel of Castile sealed an agreement with the Genoese mariner Christopher Columbus. The contract stipulated both the responsibilities of the newly titled Admiral of the Ocean Sea and the rewards for him and the Crown of Castile if his proposed westward voyage reached the fabled lands of the Orient. With the expenses of war in Granada ended, the Catholic Monarchs could gamble on Columbus's proposal and provide some needed capital for the expedition. If he failed, the financial loss would be modest; if he succeeded, conversion of the lands' inhabitants would surely follow and perhaps enormous financial benefits as well. For a quarter of a century, the Crown and assorted Spanish adventurers focused their attention on the islands and adjoining mainland of the Caribbean. Were these lands and their peoples worth the Crown's investment? If so, what type of permanent presence should it establish? Only experience with the region's conditions and opportunities could provide answers. The Caribbean experiment was soon under way.

AN AGE OF EXPLORATION

Motivated by religious beliefs, the lure of potential financial gain, and political ambition, Iberian and other European mariners risked their lives on wide-ranging voyages of exploration and trade. The desire to spread Christianity, convert infidels, and
retake Jerusalem complemented a long-standing aspiration to conquer the Islamic
world. Rumors circulated of a Christian emperor in Africa who, if found, might
join in a two-front war against the Muslims. Gold from Sudan and exotic spices that
included pepper, ginger, cinnamon, and nutmeg from India and southeast Asia had
long arrived via Muslim merchants in Middle Eastern markets and Venetian traders
who transported the goods to Europe. The trade's high profits influenced Portugal
in particular to seek access to African gold, grain, and new fishing grounds.

The Portuguese followed their conquest of Ceuta in 1415 by setting up a
trading post and base for further exploration and exchange to the south. By 1475
they had explored the African coast between Cape Bojador and Benin and established fortified commercial depots as used by Italian merchants. They exchanged
European goods that included horses and riding equipment; cloth and hats;
saffron, wine, wheat, and salt; and lead, iron, steel, copper, and brass. In return, they
obtained gold, slaves, cotton, malagueta pepper, and other African items. Genoese
and Castilian merchants also entered this commerce, securing gold that contributed to an expansive Castilian economy.

The Portuguese Crown invested actively in exploration and trade. The monarch or another member of his family authorized voyages, selected the captains,
and divided the profits with them. The captains, in turn, split their share with their
crews. The ships carried enough soldiers to reinforce negotiation with African
rulers. In the early 1480s, King John II oversaw the construction of a fortified trading post at El Mina whose residents were royal employees and partners. Although
it existed without families, civil government, or a civilian community, the post's
success made it a model for subsequent Portuguese expeditions.

Precedents in Conquest and Settlement

Both Portugal and Castile had experience in conquest and settlement dating from
the early fifteenth century. Castile in 1402 launched an invasion of the Canary
Islands where a succession of nobles enjoyed lordship until Isabel reclaimed the
territories for the Crown in 1477. Portugal recognized the islands as Castilian in
the Treaty of Alcáçovas of 1479, and permanent conquest and settlement followed
on the three largest—Gran Canaria, La Palma, and Tenerife—between 1483 and
1496. The Castilian conquistadors captured natives and sold or retained them as
slaves. Entrepreneurs soon introduced sugar cane, but the natives' high mortality
led planters to import Africans to replace them.

The Portuguese responded to Castilian interest in the Madeira Islands by
sending an expedition to found permanent communities. Settlers started arriving

in the 1430s. After clearing forests and constructing terraces and irrigation canals, they began to grow grain and sugar cane. As sugar production expanded, planters imported African slaves to work on their plantations. Similarly, the Portuguese began to inhabit São Tomé about 1470, established sugar plantations, and employed slaves as laborers. The island subsequently became a center for the transatlantic slave trade. Thus, both Castilians and Portuguese exploited their islands through settlement and forced labor as opposed to the trading posts the Portuguese employed in Africa.

Columbus and the Enterprise of the Indies

Born in the international trading center of Genoa, Columbus started sailing in the Mediterranean as a teenager. Moving to Lisbon, he married the daughter of a Portuguese sea captain, sailed to Africa at least twice, made numerous voyages to the Madeira Islands, and traveled north by sea at least as far as England and Ireland. Maritime experience and novels of chivalry encouraged both his ambition for social elevation and his belief that he could reach Asia by sailing west. All he needed was a patron willing to finance a voyage. Royal advisors in Portugal and Castile, however, correctly believed the target destination was much farther from Iberia than the optimistic mariner claimed.

After initially failing to convince any European monarch to fund his dream, Columbus made a second pitch to Portugal's King John II. But the mariner was too late. Bartolomeu Dias's report of rounding Africa's Cape of Good Hope and thereby opening a sailing route to India dashed any hope of Portuguese investment. Returning to Castile, Columbus finally obtained support from King Ferdinand. With the Reconquest concluded, the king's treasurer convinced Queen Isabel that the potential benefits fully warranted the moderate investment requested.

The Catholic Monarchs agreed to a contract that promised Columbus abundant benefits if successful. In addition to "Admiral of the Ocean Sea," they named him governor and viceroy of the lands he reached. They also granted him the right to judge all commercial disputes there, receive one-tenth of the profits, and invest in subsequent expeditions in return for a corresponding share of the returns. Thus, the new admiral was to lead a voyage of exploration and trade that followed the Portuguese model used at El Mina; all men accompanying him would go as royal employees.

With three ships and about 90 men, Columbus departed from the small Andalusian port of Palos on August 3, 1492. After stopping at the Canary Islands for repairs and additional provisions, he sailed due west. Despite near mutinies, he sighted land on October 12, 1492, and, after disembarking, planted his monarchs' banners and claimed the island for the Crown of Castile. Which island he reached remains uncertain, although Samana Cay, Plana Cays, Grand Turk, San Salvador or Watling Island, and others claim the honor.

Columbus believed he had reached islands off the shore of India and consequently referred to the lands as "the Indies" and their inhabitants as "*indios*" or Indians, a misnomer that widespread usage has kept in continuous application for more than half a millennium. On the large island he named Española (Hispaniola), the admiral encountered an indigenous population that little resembled his fantasies. He initially described the Taíno (Arawak) as timid, guileless, generous, intelligent, and well-formed.[1] They engaged in simple agriculture, planting cassava on raised mounds of soil in quantities that met their needs but with no surplus to feed intruders.

Seeing that a Portuguese-style fortified trading depot was unfeasible, Columbus realized that he would have to erect settlements as in the Canaries and Madeiras. Nonetheless, he coasted various Caribbean islands in a futile effort to find gold roofs, silk, and spices. After the *Santa María* unexpectedly sank, he had to leave behind more than 40 men on Española in a fort constructed largely of lumber salvaged from the ship. Twelve Taíno occupied space on the returning *Niña* because the admiral wanted them to bolster his claims to the monarchs as well as to acquire facility in Castilian for future service as translators.

A difficult return voyage included an unintended stop in Lisbon and a meeting with John II, who nervously thought Columbus might have made contact with lands Portugal claimed. Proceeding to Barcelona, the admiral received a warm greeting from Ferdinand and Isabel and confirmation of his promised rewards. Although Columbus died believing that he had reached the outskirts of Asia, his presentation of a few natives, little gold, and various other articles triggered the monarchs' skepticism. Although they authorized a second expedition, they also approached Pope Alexander VI, a Valencian client of Ferdinand, for title to whatever lands Columbus had encountered or might in the future. Obligingly, the pope issued four bulls in 1493 that designated them as "islands and firm land" located in "the western parts of the Ocean Sea, towards the Indies." He drew an imaginary line about 400 miles west of the Azores and Cape Verde Islands; lands to the west would be Castilian and those to the east would be Portuguese. This carefully worded "papal donation" neither confirmed nor ruled out that Columbus had reached Asia.

John II protested strongly the pope's partition of the globe. To avoid a possible war, Ferdinand and Isabel agreed in the 1494 Treaty of Tordesillas to a demarcation located approximately 1,000 leagues west of the first. The new partition confirmed Portugal's right to territory in Africa and to the route to India around the Cape of Good Hope. Additionally, it gave the Portuguese a claim to Brazil, although no Europeans had yet reached it.

THE CARIBBEAN EXPERIMENT

Columbus's return from Española in 1493 aroused considerable interest. Although dubious of his claimed success, Ferdinand and Isabel appreciated that he had landed somewhere previously unknown to Europeans. Accordingly, in late May they endorsed a second voyage (1493–1496) with the dual purposes of converting the native population to Christianity and establishing a profitable royal commercial site that excluded private traders. In response, numerous adventurers and would-be conquistadors clamored to join the Genoese mariner on his new expedition.

When the admiral sailed in September, the fleet's 17 ships carried 1,200–1,500 men, including 7 Taíno who had survived their stay in Spain and perhaps 1 woman. Also accompanying him were about a dozen clerics, a few officials, a complement of seamen, and a variety of other initially enthusiastic voyagers because the Crown had agreed to pay all participants except the approximately 200 "gentlemen volunteers." Added to food shortages on Española, this provision meant that many men would remain in the Indies only briefly.

On landing, the admiral discovered that the Taíno had razed the tiny settlement and killed the 44 men left behind, probably in retribution for the sailors' demands for women and food. This early resistance to exploitation perhaps sobered, but did not discourage Columbus. He founded a new settlement, but immediately found that the men he had brought lacked interest in growing crops and raising livestock, things they could have done in Spain. Rather, they craved provisions and gold and insisted that the natives provide both. The Taínos' inability to do so quickly convinced many Spaniards to leave. Less than 10 weeks after the fleet reached Española, 12 ships embarked for Spain carrying an unknown number of early enthusiasts anxious to return to a place where wheat bread and wine were readily available.

Columbus appreciated his men's desire for familiar foods. In 1494 he requested from Spain large quantities of wheat, biscuit, wine, salted fish, and other Castilian victuals for them. For himself and his household, however, he also sought less pedestrian provisions appropriate to his new, elevated station. These included dates, jars of preserves, sugar, rice, good honey, fine oil, and ham.

The Spaniards' demands for food finally drove the Taíno to resist again in 1495. The intruders' superior arms, 20 fierce dogs, and cavalry proved victorious. The triumph enabled Columbus to enslave the losers and inaugurate a harshly enforced tribute system. Beyond any doubt, the Castilians were the conquerors and the local population the vanquished. Armed force and physical abuse displaced the initial cordiality.

The relations among Columbus, his companions, and the Crown were more complex. When the admiral sailed for Spain in March 1496, his two small ships carried 30 Indians and 225 Europeans, many of whom considered the Caribbean experiment a failure. Although other Spaniards remained in the Indies and continued to back him, the Catholic Monarchs suspended their partnership, ordered his accounts audited, and authorized other entrepreneurs to finance and send ships to South America.

The Portuguese model that the admiral was to impose had proved inadequate. Whereas a ship or two every several years sufficed to service Portugal's fortified trading posts, the more numerous Castilians in Española required frequent supplies and support. Starting in 1498, one or more ships arrived annually with goods and additional Spaniards.

The Crown directed Columbus on his third voyage (1498–1500) to abandon the idea of a trading post and to implement the model of settlement employed during the Reconquest. He was to create autonomous free towns complete with common and private lands, women and families, elected councils, and free and open marketplaces. The need for immediate change was disruptively obvious. Before the admiral reached Española, a revolt against his brother Bartolomé involved perhaps half of the settlers. Trying to buy off the rebels, Columbus pardoned and restored them to office, assigned free land grants, and agreed to give Spaniards distributions of natives (*repartimientos*) as servants and laborers. When he refused to establish the new towns and free markets the Crown had authorized and insisted on maintaining a company store, however, the settlers rebelled anew and protested to the monarchs. Many returned to Spain, emphatically rejecting the admiral's administration of the island.

Responding to the accumulated complaints, in 1499 Ferdinand and Isabel sent a new governor to the island to investigate. He promptly arrested Columbus, clapped him in irons, and dispatched him to Spain. Although the monarchs confirmed the admiral's honors, they never again allowed him to govern. By 1501 they ordered the 300 or so Spaniards remaining on Española to live in towns rather than dispersed in the countryside. Columbus's authority had effectively ended, although the monarchs permitted him a fourth and final voyage.

While Columbus explored the Caribbean and north coast of South America, the Portuguese focused on trade in India via the route around Africa's Cape of Good Hope. In 1500, a large fleet under Pedro Alvarez Cabral made a wide swing to the west and saw land that he claimed for Portugal under the terms of the Treaty of Tordesillas. The native population, as described by an official present, included unclad, "well built," men with "good faces" and "well-shaped noses" and equally nude native women and girls "not displeasing to the eye" that impressed the male Portuguese.[2] Cabral left two sailors behind to learn the language spoken by the Tupí and two other men apparently jumped ship to remain with the females they had met. The abundant availability of a profitable red dyewood shipped to Europe later provided the name "Brazil" (red like an ember) for the land reached so fortuitously.

Order and Prosperity

During the Spaniards' first decade on Española, it was questionable whether the rewards of transatlantic travel and settlement justified the expense and risk. The number of travelers to the island reflected the imaginative tales told in Spain, but the many who sailed back to Iberia confirmed its actual conditions. An irreversible turnaround began in 1502 when Governor Nicolás de Ovando, a knight of Calatrava, arrived with the largest expedition to date. It included 30 to 32 ships, 59 horses, and some 2,500 persons eager to participate in a rumored gold boom. As with his immediate predecessor, Ovando's appointment signaled the Crown's intention to assert control over its distant agents. The new administrator soon put both the previous governor and the leader of the earlier rebellions on a ship for Spain; a hurricane almost completely destroyed the 30-ship fleet and both men drowned.

Ovando's challenges were to assert control over mining, supply the industry with adequate labor, and obtain sufficient food for the Spaniards. His solution was to exploit the Taíno even more. Their recent rebellion gave him a pretext to order a punitive expedition. Following this, he established towns for Spaniards on the eastern portion of Española, away from the city of Santo Domingo, and let them supervise agricultural production. With the food problem resolved, he addressed the distribution of labor, an issue complicated by Spaniards who had married female chieftains (*cacicas*) and then demanded control over their people. Disallowing these claims, he expelled the protesters to Spain.

The governor's administrative skills enabled him to foster a productive mining system by 1504, run it smoothly, obtain the tax levied on gold, and demand efficiency and honesty from his subordinates. Onerous labor demands placed on the Taíno, however, disrupted their major communities. Despite orders to Christianize and treat their charges well, the recipients of native labor and tribute (*encomenderos*) devoted their attention to profiting from "their Indians." Whereas almost all Spaniards had access to at least a few Taíno in the early years of settlement, their rapidly declining numbers left ever more Spaniards without workers.

Perhaps one-third or more of Española's indigenous population died within five years of Columbus's initial arrival. The already diminished number fell to 60,000 in 1508 and to 20,000 or fewer by 1512. Almost every Spanish practice contributed to the demographic disaster. Harsh new labor and tribute demands, the expropriation of locally produced food, and new diseases, including perhaps influenza, between 1493 and 1496 created conditions so horrific that some Taíno committed suicide and others resorted to abortion and infanticide. Spaniards also experienced high mortality from epidemic disease, dysentery, malnutrition and even starvation, and intermittent warfare with the natives. The Dominican friar Bartolomé de Las Casas later asserted that more than 1,000 of the passengers who had arrived with Ovando perished from illness and inadequate food.

Although the Dominicans might lament the fate of fellow Spaniards, they protested vigorously against the settlers' abuse of the natives. Father Antonio Montesinos in 1511 rose to the pulpit and denounced the *encomenderos*: "you are in mortal sin, and live and die therein by reason of the cruelty and tyranny that you practice on these innocent people. . . . Why do you so greatly oppress and fatigue them, not giving them enough to eat or caring for them when they fall ill from excessive labors, so that they die or rather are slain by you, so that you may extract and acquire gold every day?"[3] When the good friar left the pulpit, the congregation engaged in such deprecations of him that the mass could scarcely be completed.

Faced with repeated reports of *encomenderos*' abuses, Ferdinand in 1512 issued the Laws of Burgos, the Crown's first attempt to provide justice for the indigenous population, albeit within a framework of exploitation. Already the settlers' self-serving descriptions had convinced officials in Spain to view the natives as indolent, inclined toward vice, and deficient in learning Christian virtues. The laws ordered *encomenderos* to provide their Indians with churches and access to clerics. The provisions also mandated that natives mine gold for five months a year and receive pay. Although forbidden to beat or trade their charges, many Spaniards ignored the laws' protective requirements. The Laws of Burgos stand as a monument to the settlers' exploitation of the rapidly disappearing Taíno population and laudable but unfulfilled royal intentions. Thus, from these early years of Spanish presence in the Americas, settlers demonstrated a propensity to ignore unwanted restrictions, but to obey enthusiastically laws that benefited them, for example, that natives were to provide labor.

The irreversible drop in the supply of indigenous laborers in the Caribbean led Ferdinand and Isabel in 1501 to allow the importation of African slaves. Initially, settlers purchased slaves introduced from Spain because Seville was second only to Lisbon as an Iberian market for them. Royal authorization in 1518 to import slaves directly from Africa simplified the process. In addition, settlers complemented their search for new sources of gold with raids on other islands and the mainland of Central America to enslave natives on the pretext they were cannibals.

Spaniards reached Puerto Rico and left some livestock in 1505. Juan Ponce de León occupied the island in 1508 and quickly became wealthy from the gold mined, but the preconquest population perished in little more than a decade. The occupations of Jamaica and Cuba began in 1509 and 1511, respectively. The current Bahama Islands briefly proved a ready source of indigenous slaves, but by 1513 they were entirely depopulated. Although the Spaniards also advanced toward the mainland of South and North America in their pursuit of gold, silver, and natives to enslave and sell, success was not automatic.

Trading expeditions reached the eastern coast of Venezuela and adjacent islands beginning in 1500 and turned a profit with pearls and enslaved natives. In contrast, expeditions to Central America starting in 1499 generally were most notable for the Europeans' suffering. Blasco Núñez de Balboa emerged as the effective, although unofficial, leader in Panama after gathering together the remnants of two unsuccessful forays. He not only crossed the isthmus and claimed the Pacific Ocean for the Castilian Crown, but also followed a policy of conciliation with the indigenous population and married a chieftain's daughter. Some settlers grew crops and traded with the natives. The arrival of Governor Pedro Arias de Avila, also known as Pedrarias, with an expedition of some 1,500 persons and the remarkable document known as the "Requirement," shattered this peaceful interlude. Read aloud at the beginning of each conquest in a tongue no natives could understand, the Requirement outlined the arguments for Castile's title to America. It ordered the puzzled listeners to acknowledge the Church as superior in the world, the pope as its high priest, and the monarch of Castile as its agent. Natives had to permit the gospel to be preached to them or become chattel. Moreover, they bore the responsibility for any subsequent battle, enslavement, and death that occurred. In short, the Requirement provided a legal justification for exploitation and served as a protocol for declaring war.

Pedrarias proved a disastrous administrator. He ordered the execution of Balboa on trumped-up charges in 1519 and supported slaving raids that ended the peace and goodwill made possible by the earlier leader. By that year, Havana had emerged as the center for further expeditions of exploration and settlement of North America, and the town of Panama that Pedrarias had established soon became a base for exploration and conquest to the south. In the same year, the Portuguese captain Ferdinand Magellan sailed under the Castilian flag to find a passage to the Pacific Ocean. Although the captain was killed en route, the Basque Sebastián del Cano completed the circumnavigation of the globe, arriving in 1522 at the port of San Lúcar de Barrameda, located down the Guadalquivir River from Seville.

By 1515, Diego de Velázquez, the lieutenant governor and the effective administrative head of Cuba, began to authorize expeditions to enslave replacements for the island's disappearing native population. In 1517 he sent Francisco Hernández de Córdoba to Yucatan with three ships laden with cassava bread, pigs, and trinkets to trade. The charge was to explore new lands and to enslave natives to pay for the ship Velázquez had provided. After sailing for three weeks, the ships reached Yucatan. Local inhabitants ambushed the conquistadors as they proceeded toward a large town. Before returning to Cuba, the expedition's losses included its leader. Informed of the pyramids, temples, towns, houses, and dress of the people and shown looted objects with some gold content, Velázquez promptly dispatched a second expedition under his relative, Juan de Grijalva. This foray coasted along the Gulf of Mexico to the mouth of the Pánuco River, several miles south of present-day Tampico. Before the explorer's return to Cuba, Velázquez authorized his secretary, Fernando Cortés, an *encomendero* with some gold mines, to explore, trade, and search for Grijalva and his men. The new expedition lacked authority to settle because the lieutenant governor was actively seeking that power for himself. Aware of Velázquez's growing concern about his voyage, Cortés prepared to sail before he could be stopped. With supplies and men from the Caribbean, he departed for Yucatan in February 1519 determined to conquer and found municipalities despite his instructions.

How many Spaniards went to the Indies between 1493 and 1519? Fewer than 5,500, of whom at least a fifth of the total, and perhaps about half, have been identified; among them were scarcely 300 females. Although some Spaniards married native women, this extreme disparity in numbers resulted in the mostly young and unwed males making offensive demands of native women. Officials' willingness during these early years to regard the offspring of these relationships as Spaniards and thus exempt from labor requirements placed on the indigenous did not mitigate the abuse native women experienced.

The Castilian Crown's initial uncertainty as to whether the lands claimed under the papal donation were worth the effort to conquer and settle disappeared as a result of Ovando's successful administration. Overlapping the mistreatment of Taíno on Española was exploration, trade, and the seizure and enslavement of natives on other islands and the northern coast of South America. Gold, pearls, slaves, and dyewood confirmed the economic benefits available. Although many Spaniards perished in the early years of exploration, conquest, and settlement, the disastrous use of *encomienda* and the appearance of diseases previously unknown in the Indies caused far greater mortality to the indigenous population. Emperor Charles V ordered an end to new grants of *encomienda* because of both the high

Primary Source

Description of the People Columbus First Met on Reaching an Island in the Caribbean

SOURCE: Ferdinand Colón, *The Life of the Admiral Christopher Columbus by His Son, Ferdinand*, trans. and ann. Benjamin Keen (New Brunswick, NJ: Rutgers University Press, 1959), 60–61.

Being a people of primitive simplicity, they all went about as naked as their mothers bore them; and a woman who was there wore no more clothes than the men. They were all young, not above thirty years of age, and of good stature. Their hair was straight, thick, very black, and short—that is, cut above the ears—though some let it grow down to their shoulders and tied it about their heads with a stout cord so that it looked like a woman's tress. They had handsome features, spoiled somewhat by their unpleasantly broad foreheads. They were of middle stature, well formed and sturdy, with olive-colored skins that gave them the appearance of Canary Islanders or sunburned peasants. Some were painted black, others white, and still others red; some painted only the face, others the whole body, and others only the eyes or nose . . . . They appeared fluent in speech and intelligent, easily repeating words that they had once heard.

native mortality associated with them and an unwillingness to allow in the Indies the creation of a powerful nobility similar to that in Castile. By the time his mandate reached Fernando Cortés in 1523, however, the conquistador leader had already awarded *encomiendas* that effectively nullified the ban. *Encomienda* accompanied Spanish conquest and settlement throughout the Indies, quickly entrenching the exploitation of natives that became a hallmark of Spanish rule.

NOTES

1. Letter from Columbus to Santangel taken from Cecil Jane, *Voyages of Christopher Columbus*, http://mith.umd.edu/eada/html/display.php?docs=columbus_santangel .xml&action=show (accessed August 13, 2013).
2. Bailey W. Diffie, *A History of Colonial Brazil, 1500–1792* (Malabar, FL: Krieger, 1987), p. 15.
3. Benjamin Keen, ed. and trans., *Readings in Latin-American Civilization, 1492 to the Present* (Boston: Houghton Mifflin, 1955), 87–88.

SUGGESTIONS FOR FURTHER READING

Clayton, Lawrence A. *Bartolomé de las Casas and the Conquest of the Americas*. Malden, MA: Wiley–Blackwell, 2011.
Deagan, Kathleen, and José María Cruxent. *Columbus's Outpost among the Taínos: Spain and America at La Isabela, 1493–1498*. New Haven, CT, and London: Yale University Press, 2002.

Fernández-Armesto, Felipe. *Columbus and the Conquest of the Impossible.* 2nd ed. London: Phoenix Press, 2001.

Las Casas, Bartolomé de. *An Account, Much Abbreviated, of the Destruction of the Indies.* Edited by Franklin W. Knight. Translated by Andrew Hurley. Indianapolis, IN: Hackett, 2003.

Phillips, William D., Jr., and Carla Rahn Phillips. *The Worlds of Christopher Columbus.* Cambridge: Cambridge University Press, 1992.

Sauer, Carl Ortwin. *The Early Spanish Main.* Berkeley and Los Angeles: University of California Press, 1966.

Seed, Patricia. *Ceremonies of Possession in Europe's Conquest of the New World, 1492–1640.* Cambridge: Cambridge University Press, 1995.

Studnicki-Gizbert, Daviken. *A Nation upon the Ocean Sea: Portugal's Atlantic Diaspora and the Crisis of the Spanish Empire, 1492–1640.* New York: Oxford University Press, 2007.

Thomas, Hugh. *Rivers of Gold: The Rise of the Spanish Empire, from Columbus to Magellan.* New York: Random House, 2003.

CHAPTER 3

Conquest and Failure on the Mainland

CHRONOLOGY

1519–1521	Fernando Cortés and conquest of Aztec Empire; Totonacs, Tlaxcalans, and other indigenous peoples ally with Spaniards
c. 1525	Death of Sapa Inka Huayna Capac during an epidemic, probably of smallpox
1527–1536	Disastrous expedition led by Pánfilo de Narváez with four survivors, including Álvar Núñez Cabeza de Vaca
1527–1532	Civil war between Atahuallpa and Huascar in Peru
1530–1535	Francisco Pizarro, conquest of the Inka, distribution of Atahuallpa's ransom; foundation of Lima
1536	Failed attempt to settle at Buenos Aires; Manco Inka leads rebellion in Peru
1538	Execution of Diego Almagro after military defeat by Pizarro's forces
1540–1541	Pedro de Valdivia founds Santiago, Chile; assassination of Francisco Pizarro
1541–1542	Mixton War in New Galicia
1542	New Laws issued
1552	Publication of *Destruction of the Indies* by Bartolomé de Las Casas
1570s	Spanish settlement of Philippine Islands
1580	Definitive settlement of Buenos Aires; Brazil emerges as leading sugar producer in the world

The conquests of the Aztec and Inka empires led by Fernando Cortés and Francisco Pizarro are among the best known episodes of Spain in America. Considering their small number, the conquistadors' successes initially seem incredible. Closer examination exposes the critical assistance of native allies and auxiliaries and the contributions of some black freedmen and slaves. It also reveals the limited geographical consequences of initial victories and the arduous continued effort required to "complete" the conquest of a given region. Finally, despite dreams of returning home rich, most conquistadors found their rewards place bound; wealthy and prominent in the Indies, they could transfer neither their sources of income nor their subsequently claimed nobility to Spain.

THE FALL OF THE AZTEC EMPIRE

Fernando Cortés, son of an Extremaduran noble (*hidalgo*), obtained enough education to work as a notary in Spain and then in Española, where he arrived in 1506. He participated in the conquest of Cuba led by Diego de Velázquez, received a good *encomienda*, and served as the governor's secretary. After authorizing Cortés to lead an expedition devoted to discovery and trade on the mainland, Velázquez had second thoughts. But he was too late to prevent the ambitious captain's departure on what he and a number of his men thought was also an enterprise of conquest and settlement.

Largely outfitted by his own funds, loans, and investments by expeditionaries, Cortés set sail in February 1519 with 11 ships, 16 horses, supplies, about 500 men, a few women, and some black slaves and Taíno. In Yucatan he made contact with coastal natives and ransomed Jerónimo de Aguilar, an Andalusian who had learned Yucatec Maya after being enslaved following a shipwreck in 1511. Aguilar's enslaved and tattooed shipmate, Gonzalo Guerrero, refused to join the Spaniards because he was a local military leader in a Maya village and married to an indigenous woman with whom he fathered the first known mestizos born in Mexico.

Shortly after defeating Maya forces on the Gulf Coast, the conquistadors received food, gold jewelry, and 20 young slave women, including one named Malintzin (baptized as Marina and also known as Malinche) who spoke Nahuatl and the Maya language. She initially collaborated with Aguilar to translate Nahuatl into Castilian, but quickly learned it herself and became indispensable to Cortés. Although still on the coast, the leader already considered Charles I, Castile's new monarch, sovereign of the entire land that, following the explorer Juan de Grijalva, he called "New Spain."

After accepting an alliance with the Totonac that confirmed the existence of native opposition to the Aztec Empire, in May 1519, the conquistadors founded the town of Vera Cruz. Its formally installed municipal government immediately elected Cortés to head an expedition inland, legal cover for his insubordination, if not treason, against Governor Velázquez. The town council and Cortés strengthened the leader's case for obtaining Charles I's approval by dispatching to Spain a ship carrying valuable gifts received from representatives of Moteuczoma II, the ruler of the Aztec Empire. After Velázquez's supporters failed in an effort to seize a ship and return to Cuba, Cortés ordered nine of the ships at anchor scuttled, carefully preserving their fittings and sails.

Proceeding to the large Totonac city of Cempoala, the Spaniards received representatives of the Aztec Empire on several occasions; Moteuczoma wanted information about the newcomers as well as confirmation that their tributary city-states were remaining loyal. Having sent word to the Mexica ruler that the Spaniards were proceeding to Tenochtitlan, Cortés's actions effectively forced the Totonac to support the invaders or face Aztec revenge. Accordingly, their new allies provided them with food and porters, but almost no warriors because they lacked a standing army.

En route to Tenochtitlan, the Spaniards barely escaped defeat in several days of battle with the Tlaxcalans. These bitter enemies of the Mexica ceased fighting in the belief that they could benefit from allying with the invaders. At Cholula, an Aztec ally and tributary, the Spaniards and their confederates launched what was subsequently described as a preemptive attack to avoid a trap, killing as many as 6,000 natives and replacing the ruler with one acceptable to the Tlaxcalans. It is likely that the Tlaxcalans were using Cortés and the Spaniards against their enemy. Regardless, the success warned other city-states that the foreign intruders and their allies possessed substantial military capability.

Tenochtitlan

Cortés led the invaders across the volcanic mountain chain that forms the southeastern boundary of the Valley of Mexico and looked down on the splendid complex of cities, lakes, and canals. For the first time, the conquistadors fully appreciated their momentous undertaking.

Members of the royal court and finally Moteuczoma himself met the Spaniards as they crossed the broad causeway into the capital. In an exchange of ritual gifts, the ruler stirred the Spaniards' cupidity by providing items of gold, presents he knew they valued most. He then personally led Cortés and his men to quarters in his father's palace.

The opulence and splendors of Moteuczoma's court impressed the Spaniards. Yet their precarious position in the heart of the Aztec capital was frightening. Cortés sought to strengthen his position by placing Moteuczoma under house arrest. This confinement provoked a crisis among the highest levels of Aztec society, already angered by their leader's failure to resist the invaders militarily. Once the unrivaled ruler of Mesoamerica's greatest empire, the hostage was now merely a pawn of the foreigners. But despite Moteuczoma's public signs of submission, Cortés could not be certain that the traditional political discipline of this authoritarian and hierarchical state would hold firm. Popular resistance might still erupt, and the Triple Alliance was fraying as a result of the emperor's hesitance to attack his captors.

From his first contacts with urban centers of coastal Mesoamerica, Cortés encouraged proselytization and sought to demonstrate the impotence of native beliefs. Repeatedly, he overrode Spanish clerics' advice to proceed slowly and avoid inflaming religious passions. Military victory whetted his efforts to promote Christianity and led to unrestrained assaults on indigenous sacred practices. Exuberant Spaniards drove native priests from temple precincts and threw down and defaced sacred ornaments. After cleaning the stains and stench left from human sacrifices and whitewashing a temple's interior, Spaniards replaced the stone image of Huitzilopochtli or another native god with a cross and the image of the Virgin Mary. Both invaders and the vanquished recognized the political significance of the conquerors' spiritual symbols replacing those of the Mesoamerican gods.

Threats to Cortés

News that a large expedition sent by Cuba's governor had arrived on the Gulf Coast complicated Cortés's plans, but he turned the threat to his advantage. Leaving a garrison in Tenochtitlan under Pedro de Alvarado, Cortés marched less than 250 men rapidly to the coast and in a night attack smashed the larger force of Pánfilo de Narváez. By treating the defeated men generously and promising great riches, he won most of them to his side. Heading to Tenochtitlan at once, he soon received distressing news: Mexica warriors had the Spaniards and their native allies under siege.

During a major religious celebration, Alvarado had ordered his men to attack an unarmed crowd in Tenochtitlan's central square. The assault killed many nobles, enraged the city's populace, and provoked a massive popular uprising. Although Alvarado later claimed that the natives had planned to use the celebration as cover for an assault on the reduced number of Spaniards, his brutal attack, like the massacre that Cortés had ordered at Cholula, remains one of the most controversial events of the conquest.

The Mexica let the Spaniards reenter the capital unopposed. Trapped where their horses and weapons offered reduced advantage, Cortés and his reinforced column soon felt the full brunt of the natives' rage. Finally, they led Moteuczoma onto the roof, hoping his people would end their attack at the sight of their once-mighty ruler. But the storm of stones, spears, and arrows continued unabated. According to the most widely accepted account, a stone struck Moteuczoma's head and led to his death three days later.

Convinced that defeat was imminent, Cortés resolved to flee under cover of darkness. His men prepared carefully to avoid detection, covering the horses' hooves with cloth and constructing portable bridges to span gaps in the causeway. Finally, they divided the loot collected since reaching Mexico. Especially the most recent arrivals loaded themselves with gold and silver, sacrificing physical mobility in flight for the promise of later social ascent. Their greed proved a deadly mistake.

The Spaniards' efforts to escape undetected failed and Mexica warriors attacked them from all sides before they had crossed the first causeway gap. All pretense of discipline collapsed under the onslaught. Cortés lost more than 400 Spaniards, 4,000 native allies, and many horses before the terrified remnant of his force reached the mainland. For good reason, the Spaniards called June 30–July 1, 1520, *La Noche Triste* (the sorrowful night). Confident of total victory, native warriors boasted they would soon sacrifice the invaders. As Spaniards looked back across the causeway, they could see captured compatriots being marched up the steps of Huitzilopochtli's temple for sacrifice. Bernal Díaz later related that more than half the Spaniards in Mexico had perished before the fleeing conquistadors reached sanctuary in Tlaxcala.

The terrible defeat proved only a temporary setback. The Tlaxcalans provided a safe haven while Cortés rested and resupplied his forces. After *La Noche Triste*, the Spanish leader realized that he must turn Tenochtitlan's location in the lake to his advantage. He ordered a fleet constructed that could sever the capital from its mainland supplies of food and water. Thirteen small brigantines were built and then disassembled. Once the Spaniards and their allies reached a canal near the shore of Lake Texcoco, they quickly reassembled, armed with artillery, and launched the vessels. Native armies recruited from Tlaxcala and other indigenous city-states joined the final assault on the detested Aztec capital.

Victory

Cortés divided his force into three columns that began to move up the broad causeways linking Tenochtitlan to the mainland. His brigantines immediately proved their value by defeating a large force of warriors in canoes. The city garrison's heroic resistance and the stoic suffering of a population denied adequate food and water by the blockade slowed the Spaniards' advance toward the city center. Consolidating their gains was initially difficult because the defenders nightly retook structures lost during the day. Accordingly, Cortés ordered his Indian auxiliaries to pull down the city's buildings to prevent their reoccupation.

The Spaniards also had an unexpected and valuable ally. A soldier who arrived with the Narváez expedition inadvertently introduced smallpox. Previously unknown in Mesoamerica, the disease devastated the indigenous population. In the confined space of a besieged city already weakened by starvation, the epidemic killed thousands of people, almost certainly more than died from wounds received in battle. Moteuczoma's successor, Cuitlahuac, was among the first victims. Following his death, authority passed to his eighteen-year-old brother, Cuauhtemoc. Because the foreign invaders suffered no apparent effects from the disease, the epidemic confirmed the natives' most pessimistic assessments of the impotence of their deities and of Spanish invincibility.

Finally, on August 21, 1521, the Spaniards and tens of thousands of indigenous allies breached the capital's last defenses, and the remaining warriors surrendered. Cuauhtemoc attempted to flee by canoe, but the crew of a brigantine captured him. Tenochtitlan, one of the grandest achievements of the Mesoamerican world, was little more than a pile of rubble. A newly constructed Mexico City would rise on its ruins.

Although victorious, the Spanish found the spoils disappointing. Valuable booty was unearthed in Tenochtitlan's ruins, but few conquistadors received the immediate gold, silver, and rich *encomiendas* they had expected. Their disillusion produced some ugly confrontations, and Cortés quieted his followers only with difficulty. To still these passions and provide a controlled outlet for his men's destructive energies, he encouraged and helped finance new expeditions to the south and west.

The surrender of Cuauhtemoc in 1521 effectively ended the Aztec Empire. Although the Spaniards continued to recognize the "natural rulers" of Mexico in the short term and the Tlaxcalans and other allies maintained some autonomy, the conquistadors and more recent arrivals from Spain and the earlier Caribbean settlements soon became the indisputable lords of the land. Many took Indian mistresses, and a few married Indian women. The translator Doña Marina, Cortés's mistress and the mother of his son, for example, became a respected member of the early Mexico City aristocracy and married a prominent conquistador. Mestizo children that resulted from the longer-lived unions often lived with their fathers in blended families that included legitimate Spanish siblings. They identified with their fathers' culture and religion and became an important bulwark of Spanish rule during later Indian rebellions.

Although the Spaniards never gave them adequate credit, native allies were largely responsible for the fall of the Aztec Empire. Indeed, they may well have believed that they were the victors and the Spaniards their pawns in another cycle of Mesoamerican wars. Tribute to Tenochtitlan ended and the Spaniards were a shield against attempted retaliation. By the mid-1520s, however, the newcomers were demanding more than alliances. They wanted dominance over native labor, tribute, and religious practices in New Spain and utilized *encomenderos*, Spanish officials, clerics, and local indigenous leaders to exact labor and tribute from their peoples. By the 1550s, Spanish authority and exploitation were firmly established in the densely populated central region of New Spain.

THE FALL OF THE INKA EMPIRE

Panama served as the staging ground for expeditions to what became Spanish South America. In 1526 and 1527, Francisco Pizarro, an experienced conquistador who held a decent *encomienda*, headed a foray toward Peru that found unmistakable signs of a high civilization. When Panama's governor denied him additional support, the frustrated leader journeyed to Spain. There, he met fellow Extremaduran Fernando Cortés and arranged a contract with the Crown to conquer and settle Peru. The agreement's terms favored Pizarro to such an extent that his junior associate, Diego de Almagro, almost withdrew from their partnership. Once calmed, however, the men prepared another attempt.

Begun on December 27, 1530, Pizarro's expedition landed north of Tumbes, Ecuador. Their arrival followed by several years the death of Sapa Inka Huayna Capac during an epidemic often described as smallpox. On reaching the city, the intruders found signs of a civil war fought between the armies of his sons, Atahuallpa and Huascar, to determine the new Inka. Augmented by several recently arrived small parties of Spaniards, the conquistadors traveled south about a hundred miles, founded the town of San Miguel de Piura, and left several dozen invaders there. About 60 horsemen and more than 100 men on foot proceeded southeast to Cajamarca near the location of Atahuallpa and his victorious army, estimated at some 80,000 men. After a display of horsemanship, Spanish emissaries convinced the Inka to meet Pizarro in the city's central square.

Atahuallpa entered Cajamarca with several thousand followers the next day, November 17, 1532. Ambushing them, the Spaniards captured the Inka, slaughtered countless warriors, and seized items of gold and silver. Atahuallpa observed their obsession for precious metals and offered to pay a ransom of one large room

Portrait of Francisco Pizarro painted long after the conqueror's death.

filled with gold and another with silver. Pizarro agreed, "provided he did no trea-son," to let the Inka go to Quito in return.

The Inka's three undefeated armies remained in place while his officials collected and delivered the gold and silver. When Almagro reached Cajamarca in mid-April 1533 with reinforcements and Hernando Pizarro, one of Francisco's brothers, returned from exploration and looting on the coast, Atahuallpa astutely began to doubt his promised release. Although the rooms were not yet filled, in June the Spaniards began to melt the treasure, save for the royal tax of 20 percent.

The precious metal available for distribution was enormous. Following standard practice, the conquistadors present at Atahuallpa's capture received the largest shares. The usual allocation to the footmen among the 168 "Men of Cajamarca" was almost 45 pounds of gold and 90 pounds of silver. Horsemen received double that amount, and captains pocketed considerably more. Francisco Pizarro's share was seven times that of a horseman.

Since Pizarro had declared the bargain fulfilled, Atahuallpa asked for his release. However, Almagro's men, recipients of token shares of the ransom, charged the Inka with treason; they wanted him dead to preclude any claim that later spoils were part of the ransom. With rumors circulating of 30,000 cannibals en route from Quito, Francisco Pizarro yielded.

Atahuallpa had no trial; declared guilty of treason, he was sentenced to be burned alive. Because he accepted Christianity, the Spaniards strangled him prior to immolation on July 26, 1533, and then buried him in an elaborate Christian service. The execution stunned the Inka's followers, but the local indigenous population felt relief that the civil war was truly over. Pizarro, moreover, was able to lead his enlarged force to Cusco as a liberator. In Spain, Charles I criticized Atahuallpa's execution; regicide set a bad example wherever it occurred.

With the Inka dispatched, the invaders advanced toward Cusco, a distance by air of some 750 miles. Pizarro and subsequent Spanish leaders in the conquests of Peru and Quito benefited from indigenous allies that included Cañari warriors. The Inka had conquered the Cañari in the late fifteenth century and Atahuallpa had ravaged their Ecuadorean province and killed many of their leaders during the civil war. Profoundly anti-Inka, Cañari, including those who had been resettled in Cusco and elsewhere, provided military services to the Spaniards for decades.

On the way to Cusco, Pizarro obtained recognition as the new Sapa Inka for Túpac Huallpa, the younger brother of Huascar, who had been murdered on Atahuallpa's order. Many Inka and other Andean peoples accepted his elevation as restoring a legitimate ruling line. The new Inka's death from an illness before reaching Cusco, however, forced Pizarro to find a replacement.

The Spaniards were victorious on the way to Cusco and, miraculously it seemed, an undefeated Inka army between them and the capital withdrew, allowing the conquistadors to enter the city on November 15, 1533. On the same day, Manco, another son of Huayna Capac, appeared. For Manco, the Spaniards' presence meant he was safe. For Pizarro, the newly identified Inka provided a puppet who enabled the invaders to enter Cusco as liberators.

Pizarro quickly sent Manco with indigenous warriors and some Spaniards to pursue one of Atahuallpa's remaining armies; Captain Sebastián de Belalcázar led a campaign to Quito that eliminated another. In March 1534, the conquistadors formally refounded Cusco as a Spanish municipality and Pizarro assigned *encomiendas*. Although the former Inka capital yielded slightly more treasure than Atahuallpa's ransom, the greater number of Spanish participants reduced the amount of individual shares and further inflamed Almagro and his adherents.

With Pizarro's encouragement, Almagro departed in August 1535 to conquer Chile with nearly 600 supporters, a few black servants, and more than 10,000 indigenous auxiliaries. The expedition proved a disaster. The Spaniards failed to find the gold and silver they sought and the exploited auxiliaries suffered from harsh treatment, inadequate clothing, lack of shoes, and unbearable cold and hunger. When they returned to Cusco, moreover, the remnants of Almagro's force immediately had to battle Manco's rapidly assembled army that was besieging Cusco as a result of Spaniards' abuse of native women and theft of property. Unfortunately for Manco, his forces dissipated when planting season began. The victorious Almagro claimed Cusco on the strength of Francisco Pizarro's promise, but Hernando Pizarro returned from Spain with a new grant that included the former Inka capital. Exasperated and angry, Almagro jailed Hernando and assumed control.

Francisco, who had left the highlands and founded Lima on January 5, 1535, agreed to let Almagro retain Cusco if he released Hernando. Once his brother was free, however, the duplicitous leader prepared for a civil war in which each side claimed to fight for the king. The decisive battle occurred at Las Salinas near Cusco on April 26, 1538. Pizarro's forces triumphed and executed Almagro. Although his son and followers revenged his death by assassinating Francisco in Lima on June 26, 1541, the arrival of the governor Cristóbal Vaca de Castro with an army soon ended their jubilation. Vaca de Castro defeated the forces of the younger Almagro and executed their leader. Despite chaotic political conditions in Peru continuing, Manco's assassination reduced the ongoing Inka threat in 1544, the year Blasco Núñez Vela reached Peru as its first viceroy.

The new executive arrived with the New Laws issued in 1542. Among its numerous provisions, the legislation sought to improve conditions for natives and bring *encomenderos* under royal control. Ominously, one provision stated that all persons involved in the conflicts between Pizarro and Almagro were to lose their *encomiendas*. If implemented, nearly all of Peru's most powerful Spaniards faced confiscation of their most prized possession.

The threat to *encomenderos* led many to join Gonzalo Pizarro in rebellion when Núñez Vela attempted to enforce the New Laws. In January 1546, the rebels defeated and killed the viceroy, the only time this happened in nearly three centuries of Spanish rule. With Gonzalo supreme, the Crown dispatched a new executive who skillfully induced numerous rebels' defections. Defeated in battle in 1549, Gonzalo suffered execution. Royal authority was finally entrenched, although Sapa Inka Túpac Amaru remained uncaptured until 1572.

CONTINUED CONQUEST

The Spanish conquest continued long after victory over the Aztec and Inka empires, but none of the many campaigns that followed encountered analogous civilizations. Cortés encouraged expeditions to southern and western New Spain. In the mid-1520s, his lieutenant Pedro de Alvarado, for example, led a force of several hundred Spaniards, thousands of Nahuatl-speaking allies and auxiliaries, some 2,000 Kaqchikel warriors, and probably a few blacks into Central America. This brutal invasion led to the enslavement of tens of thousands of natives, many of whom were subsequently exported to Peru.

Indigenous peoples in the west differed from the Nahua of Central Mexico. Divided among numerous independent ethnicities and distinct languages, they were fragmented politically and geographically and willing and able to fight. As a result, Spaniards found inapplicable the lessons learned in the Caribbean islands and conquest of the Aztec Empire. Both seizing a leader and trying to enlist native allies failed; unless enslaved, the indigenous refused either to serve or to provide tribute to Spaniards. Missionary efforts also proved futile. It took two decades to impose effective rule, and even then, the natives would turn to violence against the new overlords.

Death and the destruction of indigenous villages and property marked the initial Spanish foray in 1524. What followed was even worse. From 1530 to 1533, Nuño Beltrán de Guzmán, a Spanish official notorious for enslaving natives and trading them for livestock, led an enormous expedition: about 400 Spaniards, each with a native female cook; as many as 15,000 indigenous allies and auxiliaries from Central Mexico; thousands of pigs and sheep; arms and goods to trade; and other provisions and medicines. Guzmán founded four Spanish municipalities, including Guadalajara, but destroyed towns, reduced countless natives to bondage, and executed the indigenous ruler of Michoacan. A judicial review of his tenure in office (*residencia*) led to his arrest, jailing, and return to Spain, his career over.

In mid-1540, serious native resistance began with attacks on Spaniards and their slaves who resided north of Guadalajara. Led by the unconquered Cazcanes holed up in mountain fortifications, the warriors rebuffed Spanish attempts to overcome them, partly because the Spaniards could not trust locally recruited indigenous allies. Despite a devastating attack on Guadalajara, the Spaniards held firm. Victory, however, required the intervention of Viceroy Antonio de Mendoza with several hundred Spaniards and thousands of natives. Picking off rebel strongholds one at a time, Mendoza's forces ended the Mixton War in early 1542, but at high cost. Thousands of local natives fled, perished in battle, or committed suicide. Others suffered enslavement or execution, although the viceroy encouraged resettlement and rejected enslaving the Indians wholesale, as Guzmán had done. The New Laws of 1542 provided no effective relief and natives often refused to submit to *encomienda*, missionaries, or other Spanish institutions. Nonetheless, the region known as both New Galicia and the Audiencia of Guadalajara soon received a bishop and a high court, or *audiencia*. The discovery of silver at Zacatecas and an expansion of cattle on vacant lands emphasized that Spanish settlement was permanent.

The difficulties Spaniards experienced in New Galicia characterized their expeditions more than their rapid success in Central Mexico. Mobile natives used to warfare and unwilling to ally with the Europeans made conquest challenging and, when defeated, reduced the probability that victors would receive substantial, viable *encomiendas*.

The conquest and settlement of Chile also proved demanding. Diego de Almagro's initial expedition in 1535 turned out to be both a high-mortality disaster for the natives accompanying him and a great disappointment to the Spanish conquistadors, who found neither gold nor silver. Nonetheless, Pedro de Valdivia and his mistress, Inés de Suárez, left Cusco in January 1540 with a dozen Spaniards, perhaps 1,000 natives, and a few black slaves. He expanded his force en route and reached Chile intending to settle rather than merely plunder the natives.

Valdivia founded Santiago in early 1541. The city withstood a siege during his absence, in part because of Inés de Suárez's contributions, and remained a base for the Spaniards. Over the course of a decade, Valdivia founded other towns in Chile. He died in 1553 in a battle against Araucanian warriors led by his former groom, Lautaro, as they proceeded to drive the Spaniards from the town of Concepción. Valdivia's demise exemplified the fate of numerous Spanish leaders and far more of their followers.

REWARDS OF CONQUEST

Spaniards suffered the long, uncomfortable trip across the Atlantic anticipating benefits from exploration, conquest, and settlement. Most conquistadors remained wherever they considered the rewards sufficient. Inadequate compensation, in contrast, pushed men toward other expeditions in pursuit of success and appropriate recognition. As one later commented, "I say that the least of the conquistadors merited great reward, for at his own expense . . . he gave the king so great a world as this."[1]

The value of the rewards for conquest and settlement varied by region, but their nature was generally predictable. Even before Spaniards reached New Spain, they expected to receive *encomiendas* for their services. These grants of a local ruler and natives under his authority initially provided the recipient (*encomendero*) with labor and tribute in exchange for Christianizing "his Indians" and providing military service to the Crown, if requested. Land grants were common, but required a separate labor concession for optimal exploitation. *Encomenderos* also routinely secured municipal offices, for example, as aldermen. Occasionally the Crown granted a coat of arms, membership in a military order, and, in the singular cases of Fernando Cortés and Francisco Pizarro, a title of nobility. Aside from those present at Atahuallpa's capture in 1532, however, few conquistadors received substantial gold or silver, a circumstance that allowed a small number of Spaniards to profit disproportionately and left at least some of the remainder feeling exploited. Since cash and bullion were the only tangible benefits readily transferable to Spain, enjoying most rewards required residence in the region of conquest.

The "Men of Cajamarca" were unique in the quantity of precious metals they received. With gold and silver in hand, they had to determine whether they could live better as prosperous conquistadors in Peru or in Spain. Larger distributions to horsemen made them more likely than footmen to return to their homeland. Recipients of both a share of the ransom and an *encomienda* formed the initial base of the aristocracy in Lima, Cusco, and other Peruvian cities, where they enjoyed high status for the remainder of their lives. Awards of mines, land, and office further solidified their standing.

In contrast to bars of gold and silver distributed to the Men of Cajamarca and the victors at Cusco, Spanish conquistadors present at the fall of Tenochtitlan collected a pittance. Footmen received some 60 pesos and horsemen about 100, an amount roughly one-fifth the cost of a horse. In the conquest of New Granada, only the expedition led by Gonzalo Jiménez de Quesada obtained significant booty, more than 200,000 gold pesos and 1,630 emeralds. The gold amounted to perhaps one-seventh of Atahuallpa's ransom; an individual share totaled about 550 gold pesos and 5 emeralds.

SPECTACULAR FAILURES

The conquests of central Mexico and Peru fired the imaginations of would-be conquistadors and attracted immigrants from Spain as well as Spaniards previously located elsewhere in the Americas. Given the existence of the Mexica and the Inka, perhaps comparable civilizations or rumored cities of gold lay beyond the initial zones of exploration, conquest, and settlement. For generations, many Spaniards and other Europeans believed that a passage connected the Atlantic and the Pacific. Locating this mythical Strait of Anián would enable people and goods to sail to their ultimate coastal destination. And what civilizations might be found along such a route? Inspired by dreams of fabulous riches and novels of chivalry, Spaniards explored previously uncharted regions, often at the cost of high mortality.

An expedition led by Pánfilo de Narváez, a conquistador of Cuba, was especially catastrophic. Misfortune had already knocked in 1520 when he led 900 men to New Spain to gain control of the conquest. Blinded in one eye and captured, Narváez endured imprisonment while his men joined Cortés. Again embarking from Cuba, in 1528 Narváez took some 400 men, at least 10 women, and 80 horses to explore the northern Gulf Coast. Desertion, followed by a hurricane, native attacks, illness, and the inability either to rendezvous with remaining ships or to construct and sail vessels to New Spain, killed all but 4 of the remaining participants. The survivors, most notably Alvar Núñez Cabeza de Vaca, reached Mexico in 1536 after walking across much of today's southwestern United States. Narváez disappeared without a trace.

In 1540, the governor of New Galicia, Francisco Vázquez de Coronado, led a large expedition into an area of North America that reputedly had one of seven "cities of gold." A personal appointee of Viceroy Mendoza, he departed with more than 300 Spaniards, several Franciscans, a few black slaves, and 1,000 or more native auxiliaries. The effort failed miserably. Although they destroyed 13 Pueblo villages in present-day New Mexico, the would-be conquistadors had to repress an indigenous uprising and discovered no precious metals.

Calamity similarly marked efforts to explore and settle the southern end of America. Pedro de Mendoza reached the estuary of Río de la Plata in early 1536 with some 1,600 men and a few women. He founded the city of Buenos Aires on its western bank, but within 18 months more than 1,000 expeditionaries had perished from starvation, disease, and native attacks. Abandoning the enterprise, Mendoza sailed for Spain, but died en route. The remaining Spaniards fled Buenos Aires after an indigenous assault destroyed the city in 1541. They moved upstream more than 950 miles to the city of Asunción, Paraguay, founded in 1537 by Mendoza's deputy, Juan de Ayolas.

The Spaniards' success in conquests throughout the Indies rested on their beliefs, technology, native allies and auxiliaries, free and enslaved blacks, and other advantages. At their core, the conquistadors were groups of Indian fighters; few had formal military training or experience. They believed, however, that the Christian God of the Reconquest was on their side; alleged sightings of Saint James during battles expressed their certainty of divine support. They benefited, notably in Central Mexico and Peru, from Indian allies who provided warriors, provisions, and transportation. Although at times they thought they were manipulating the Spaniards, the natives' internal dissension and civil war played into the hands of the invaders. The participation of West African slaves and freedmen—black conquistadors in the view of the conquered—was also important. Technology too favored the invaders: steel swords and lances, metal helmets and armor, cannons, harquebuses, and crossbows provided at least initial advantages. War dogs and horses also deserve mention. A rider had the advantage of raining blows down on the enemy. Additionally, on reasonably level terrain, horses could cover distance much more rapidly than men on foot. Epidemic disease, notably smallpox, warrants emphasis because it killed large numbers of natives while largely sparing Spaniards, most of whom had gained immunization through exposure early in life. None of these reasons, or others that could be named, was individually responsible for Spanish success, but together they enabled the Spaniards to impose their rule on substantial portions of the American mainland.

BRAZIL

The Portuguese occupation of Brazil shared many characteristics with the Spanish experience in the Río de la Plata region. Brazil had no wealthy, urbanized native societies, and its early exploration and settlement lacked the drama of the expeditions led by Cortés and Pizarro. Its several million Indians comprised numerous nonsedentary and semisedentary cultures. Along the coast where the first contacts occurred, the newcomers encountered many large settlements, but none remotely like Tenochtitlan or Cusco. The natives' different languages and local tradition of armed conflict often permitted the Portuguese, and briefly the French, to establish alliances and gain a foothold.

Following Cabral's landing in 1500, initial relations between the Indians and Europeans were generally peaceful. At the time, Portugal was devoting its limited resources to the Far East, whose spices and silks found eager buyers in Europe. The Brazilian product with the largest market at first was a red dyewood, brazilwood, although tropical birds, animals, and some Indian captives found purchasers in Europe. Portuguese and, soon, French ships anchored along the coast and traded iron tools, weapons, and other European goods to the Indians. At first the natives eagerly cut and transported the heavy logs to the waiting ships. But competition between the Portuguese and French for dyewood placed unacceptable pressure on the workers and undermined the early barter economy. The attractiveness of European trade goods was limited, and the natives resisted labor demands that would fundamentally alter their culture. As a result, the Portuguese began to enslave them as a way to continue exploiting the profitable dyewood.

The creation of more permanent settlements and the introduction of sugar cultivation led to a rapid expansion of Indian slavery. Sugar was produced in Pernambuco in 1526 and launched successfully in São Vicente and Espirito Santo in the 1530s. Nearly constant war among the indigenous peoples provided the invaders with a ready opportunity to organize the supply of slaves. Previously, native warriors had slain their enemies on the battlefield, with the exception of a few captives kept for sacrifice and cannibalism. Now the labor needs of expanding European agriculture transformed these practices. The advent of new weapons and a new objective, procuring captives as a commodity for market exchange, promoted increased native violence.

Divided by ancient rivalries and vendettas, the Indians proved incapable of uniting to resist European settlement. Often, Tupí-speaking Portuguese "married" Indian women or lived with them in concubinage. This integration into the native elite further reduced the potential for native resistance. The *mameluco* children of these unions, especially in Bahia and São Paulo, later created a political and cultural bridge between independent Indian culture and the ascendant Portuguese-dominated society.

By the time that some indigenous groups tried to overthrow the encroaching new order in the 1550s, the European population, reinforced by *mameluco* kinsmen and a Crown finally willing to commit resources to Brazil, proved too strong. Although the Indians killed Brazil's first bishop and nearly destroyed the Portuguese settlements of Ilhéus, Espirito Santo, and Salvador, the action of the governor general Mem de Sá (1558–1572) turned the tide. Horses, firearms, metal weapons, and armor provided advantages that no amount of native heroism or military competence could overcome. Eventually, the Portuguese defeated the Tupinamba, the Caete, and the Tupinkin and, by the end of the sixteenth century, had pacified nearly the entire coast between Rio Grande and São Vicente. Although the French established a colony known as France Antarctique near present-day Rio de Janeiro in 1555, Mem de Sá captured their island fortress five years later. By the early 1570s, the Portuguese had eliminated resistance by French settlers and their Tupinamba allies on the nearby coast.

By the late sixteenth century, explorers had reached most of what became the effective territorial limits of the Iberian empires in America. The conquerors had defeated militarily or subordinated in the new European-dominated order nearly all native peoples they had encountered. They had accomplished this enormous undertaking, moreover, with mostly private resources and little government control. As each region fell to conquest and settlement, the Iberian monarchs turned to the task of imposing order and elaborating the institutions of government, church, and economy.

Primary Source

Conquistadors at Cajamarca

SOURCE: Pedro de Cieza de León, *The Discovery and Conquest of Peru*, ed. and trans. Alexandra Parma Cook and David Noble Cook (Durham, NC: Duke University Press, 1999), 241–5, passim.

Those who were present at Cajamarca are the following:

Horsemen The Governor Don Francisco Pizarro; Hernando Pizarro; Hernando de Soto; Juan Pizarro; Pedro de Candia; Gonzalo Pizarro; Juan Cortés; Sebastián de Belalcázar; Cristóbal de Mena; . . . [a total of 62]

These were the horsemen and they divided among them according to their deeds because some had endured more than others; 24,230 marks of silver were divided among them.

Footmen Those who had entered and were without horses are the following: Juan de Porras; Gregorio de Sotelo; García de Paredes; Pedro Sancho; Juan de Valdivieso; Gonzalo Maldonado; . . . [a total of 106]

These were the footmen, and fifteen thousand marks of silver and ounces were distributed among them, each taking according to his deeds and not all equally. When the silver was divided, the governor wanted to do the same with the gold, . . .

The treasure was divided so quickly, . . . that it caused envy among the Spaniards because those of Almagro grumbled . . . .

They say that each one of these shares amounted to 4,120 pesos of gold and 180 marks of pure silver for the footmen. To some they gave one share, to others three-quarters, and there were some who took half a share; consequently, some of the horsemen took two shares and others one and a half, according to their service and quality. But because they had so much money among so few, there was great gambling. Things were sold at very excessive prices. Many of them were well provided by important and beautiful ladies and had them as concubines.

NOTES

1. Alonso de Aguilar quoted in Peggy K. Liss, *Mexico under Spain, 1521–1566: Society and the Origins of Nationality* (Chicago: University of Chicago Press, 1975), 95.

SUGGESTIONS FOR FURTHER READING

Altman, Ida. *The War for Mexico's West: Indians and Spaniards in New Galicia, 1524–1550.* Albuquerque: University of New Mexico Press, 2010.

Avellaneda, José Ignacio. *The Conquerors of the New Kingdom of Granada.* Albuquerque, University of New Mexico Press, 1995.

Cortés, Hernán. *Hernán Cortés: Letters from Mexico.* Translated and edited by A. R. Pagden, with an introduction by J. H. Elliott. New York: Orion Press, 1971.

Díaz del Castillo, Bernal. *The True History of the Conquest of New Spain, 1517–1521.* Translated by A. P. Maudslay. New York: Farrar, Straus & Giroux, 1966.

Francis, J. Michael. *Invading Colombia: Spanish Accounts of the Gonzalo Jiménez de Quesada Expedition of Conquest*. University Park: Penn State University Press, 2007.

Hassig, Ross. *Mexico and the Spanish Conquest*. London and New York: Longman, 1994.

Hemming, John. *Red Gold: The Conquest of the Brazilian Indians*. Cambridge, MA: Harvard University Press, 1978.

Hemming, John. *The Conquest of the Incas*. New York: Harcourt Brace Jovanovich, 1970.

Léon-Portilla, Miguel (ed.). *The Broken Spears: The Aztec Account of the Conquest of Mexico*. 2007 revised edition. Translated by Lysander Kemp. Boston: Beacon Press, 2011.

Matthew, Laura E., and Michel R. Oudijk (eds.). *Indian Conquistadors: Indigenous Allies in the Conquest of Mesoamerica*. Norman: University of Oklahoma Press, 2007.

Restall, Matthew. *Seven Myths of the Spanish Conquest*. New York: Oxford University Press, 2003.

Restall, Matthew and Felipe Fernández-Armesto. *The Conquistadors: A Very Short Introduction*. New York: Oxford University Press, 2012.

Schwaller, John F. *The First Letter from New Spain: The Lost Petition of Cortés and His Company, June 20, 1519*. Austin: University of Texas Press, 2014.

Townsend, Camilla. *Malintzin's Choices: An Indian Woman in the Conquest of Mexico*. Albuquerque: University of New Mexico Press, 2006.

Velasco Murillo, Dana, Mark Lentz, and Margarita R. Ochoa (eds.). *City Indians in Spain's American Empire: Urban Indigenous Society in Colonial Mesoamerica and Andean South America, 1530–1810*. Brighton, Great Britain: Sussex Academic Press, 2012.

CHAPTER 4

Invaders Alter the Indies

Returning from the Indies in 1493, Columbus penned a publicity release to boast about his claimed success as well as to encourage Ferdinand and Isabel to fund a second expedition. Quickly translated from Castilian to Latin, the so-called "Letter to Santangel" soon appeared in at least nine editions from presses in Barcelona, Rome, Paris, and elsewhere. The multiple printings document the excitement that greeted the returned admiral. As further exploration clarified the Indies' enormous size, appreciation increased of the voyage's significance. No author surpassed the exuberance of the historian Francisco López de Gómara's declaration in 1552 that "the discovery of the Indies" was "the greatest event since the creation of the world," other than the life and death of Christ.[1]

Over time, the Indies' existence and Iberians' presence there stimulated intellectual debates as well as demographic and environmental changes. Europeans had to rethink previously accepted knowledge of the world's geography and the nature of its peoples. The inadvertent introduction of epidemic diseases previously unknown to indigenous populations resulted in horrific demographic disasters. The spread of Old World flora and fauna permanently altered both the Americas' landscape and the diet of many inhabitants. Climate and natural disasters also affected the environments in which the indigenous populations as well as Europeans, Africans, and the descendants of all three lived.

RETHINKING THE WORLD AND IDENTIFYING UNKNOWN PEOPLES

Columbus's return to Spain in 1493 stimulated cartographers, theologians, and lawyers to ponder his voyage's implications. Intellectual interest in previously unknown lands and peoples resulted in a revised world map printed in 1507 that portrayed for the first time North and South America and their relationship to other parts of the known world. The German mapmaker Martin Waldseemüller and his colleagues labeled the newly inserted "America" to honor the source of their information, a published letter by the Florentine navigator Amerigo Vespucci. The Italian believed, as Columbus never did, that the admiral and his successors had indeed reached a "New World," in Vespucci's phrase, a continent additional to those of Europe, Asia, and Africa that formed the previously "known" or "Old World" as Europeans understood it. Awareness of a "Fourth Part" of the world rendered earlier maps of earth obsolete. Its existence, moreover, provoked debates over the nature of the inhabitants and the consequences of birth and upbringing in a New World.

In the Indies, Europeans encountered humans whose countenance differed from their own. Unlike the bearded, light-skinned Spanish males, indigenous men were usually beardless, were rarely bald, and had darker skin. Moreover, they generally escaped the frequent digestive problems and stomach disorders that plagued Spaniards. Columbus initially described young Taíno men as "very well made, of very handsome bodies and very good faces . . . generally fairly tall," generous, gentle, and free from guile.[2] This favorable view of natives' disposition rapidly succumbed to widespread denigration. The Laws of Burgos issued in 1512 articulated the opinion of most Spaniards in the Indies that the natives were "inclined to idleness and vice," lacked "virtue," and were polygynous. One law specifically forbade Spaniards from calling any native a "dog," a reference to the term's widespread and insulting usage. Some later writers averred that the allegedly inferior stars and constellations of America bore at least partial responsibility for the natives becoming lazy inebriates. As a peninsular Dominican writing in the early seventeenth century commented, "The heavens of America induce inconstancy, lasciviousness and lies," "vices characteristic of the Indians."[3]

Medicine further clarified for Iberians the nature of the Indians. An ancient theory by the Greek Hippocrates held that the body's "humors"—heat, cold, black bile, and yellow bile—were affected by food, climate, and other "non-natural things" to produce different types of humans. The hot-tempered and irascible Spaniards earned the label "cholerics." In contrast, humoralists lumped together women and indigenous peoples either as emotional melancholics or as lazy "phlegmatics."

Spaniards in the Indies wanted to eat the preferred foods of Spain: wheat bread, wine, olive oil, familiar vegetables and fruits, and meat from sheep, pigs, and cattle. Rarely were they willing to remain in a region incapable of furnishing these items. If forced to do without these staples, the invaders ate in bad grace native foods that included maize, cassava, and potatoes; not surprisingly, they readily blamed the indigenous diet if they fell ill. Although the immigrants liked pineapples, tomatoes, and avocados, López de Gómara captured their overall disgust in 1552. The natives "eat porcupines, weasels, moths, locusts, spiders, worms, caterpillars, bees and ticks—raw, cooked, and fried. There is not a single thing that they will not guzzle, and it is all the more astonishing that they eat such dirty animals and bugs given that they now have good bread and wine, fruits, fish, and meat."[4] Speaking in Nahuatl, the Franciscan Bernardino de Sahagún informed a native audience that they should grow wheat; raise sheep, cattle, and pigs; and consume "that which the Castilian people eat, because it is good food." He noted, "May you not eat the flesh of dogs, mice, skunks, etc. For it is not edible."[5] In short, the indigenous population needed to adopt Spanish "customs" in diet. Additionally, they should wear modest clothing, learn Castilian, and embrace Christianity.

The question of whether the native peoples of the Indies were human—rational beings able to comprehend Christianity—received formal resolution in 1537. Pope Paul III issued a bull declaring "Indians are truly men . . . capable of understanding the Catholic faith" and should not "be deprived of their liberty or the possession of their property . . . ; nor should they be in any way enslaved."[6] Papal authority and some intellectuals' endorsement, however, failed to quell opponents who applied Aristotle's doctrine of natural slavery and consigned Indians to that status. The issue had important implications both for Spaniards' treatment of and demands on indigenous peoples and for the approach clerics employed to convert them. Indeed, a well-known Aristotelian authored a manuscript justifying war on the natives as necessary for conversion.

In April 1550, Emperor Charles V ordered conquest to stop, pending the outcome of deliberations over whether war conducted before conversion efforts was just. About four months later, a proponent of natural slavery, Juan Ginés de Sepúlveda, and the Dominican Bartolomé de Las Casas, a champion of the Indians and advocate of their peaceful conversion, presented their cases to a learned group of theologians and jurists. Despite weeks of hearings and months of intermittent discussion, the panel never reached a conclusion. Overall, however, the Crown's attitude toward the indigenous peoples proved paternalistic; their state of permanent childhood required royal protection. Moreover, in 1573 Philip II promulgated ordinances that spoke of "pacification" rather than conquest in any subsequent discoveries. New terminology, of course, did not alter the past. Conquistadors and settlers had already brought many of the most valuable areas of the Indies under royal rule and the resident native populations had disappeared in some regions and collapsed to a small fraction of their precontact size in others.

DEMOGRAPHIC DISASTER

Serious estimates of the indigenous population in the Americas on the eve of contact with Europeans and Africans range from an implausibly low 9 million to an equally dubious high exceeding 100 million. A reasonable estimate is between 35 and 55 million. Regardless of the initial total, demographers and historians concur that it soon plummeted as a result of contact with Iberians, other Europeans, and Africans. They disagree on the extent of demographic decline and correctly note that population losses varied by region and date.

Epidemics and Varied Patterns of Population Change

The indigenous peoples were what demographers term "virgin soil"—a population without previous exposure to a given disease. In this circumstance, a smallpox epidemic could have a mortality rate of 50 percent or higher, although the death toll was often less. Repeated claims that Europeans enjoyed a genetic immunity to the illness, however, remain unsubstantiated. Whereas in Spain smallpox was a childhood disease that provided survivors with lifetime immunity, in the Americas, it struck natives of all ages and left the suffering community without caregivers, thus increasing mortality rates.

The precontact population of the Americas plummeted everywhere that Spaniards, Portuguese, and Africans established themselves and in many places before their physical arrival. Although the overall result was catastrophic, even calamities vary in intensity. The worst case was extinction, an outcome evident in some parts of the Caribbean within decades of the Spaniards' appearance. Other regions experienced a slow reduction that continued beyond independence. Elsewhere, an initial abrupt decline gave way to reduced rates of mortality followed by stability, in some cases additional decline, and then growth.

The latter group included the peoples of central and southern Mexico, the Central American highlands, and the Andean zone of present-day Peru, Bolivia, and Ecuador. Within these broad areas, tropical, low-elevation coastal locations had far higher mortality rates than those in mountainous regions. In both Mexico and Peru, the indigenous population ultimately stabilized at less than 1 million persons and then began an upward trajectory. As the Mexican case illustrates, however, even relatively advantaged highlands could be left with less than 10 percent of their precontact population. Similarly, native populations in El Salvador, Honduras, and Nicaragua dropped precipitously, but with substantial differences between Chiapas and the coastal provinces of Guatemala, which lost perhaps 95 percent of their population by 1570. The demographic disaster profoundly affected Iberians' use of indigenous labor and resulted in their demand for slaves imported from Africa.

Contributing Causes of Population Loss

Epidemic disease was the primary source of population loss, but endemic illnesses also afflicted indigenous populations both before and after 1492. A hemorrhagic fever of New World origin might have been responsible for high mortality in New Spain in the sixteenth century and later. Other causes worsened the effects of disease, for example, warfare; abusive slavery and forced labor, especially in mines and as porters; torture; and general mistreatment. Some native women lost the will to reproduce or even live; the results included suicide, infanticide, abortion, and lower birth rates. Malnutrition and starvation followed the failure of subsistence agriculture and the conquerors' monopolization of available food. Spaniards also disrupted indigenous society by shipping natives to new locations and environments, as occurred, for example, when conquistadors sent Indian slaves from Central America to Peru. Coupled with exploitative Spanish institutions, the rupturing of local cultures further increased the rate of mortality.

At times, natives fled their homes to avoid Spanish demands; in other cases they resorted to subterfuge. On Española, some took refuge in a difficult mountainous region where they remained in rebellion for years. Maya in Yucatan at times left settled regions in favor of informal refugee communities in the bush. In Peru, large numbers of Indians gave up their access to *ayllu* land when they fled provinces subject to the Potosí labor draft (*mita*) and joined as outsiders (*forasteros*) communities exempt from this hated service. In today's Ecuador, *caciques* used various strategies to hide numerous natives and thereby prevent their registration on tribute lists.

ENVIRONMENTAL CHANGE

The notion that the Americas were a pristine landscape prior to the arrival of Europeans and Africans is nonsense, especially given the size of the indigenous population. Humans had cleared forests and planted and harvested crops; built villages, cities, and monumental architecture; constructed terraces, roads, and irrigation systems; and mined. Nonetheless, the environmental consequences that followed the arrival of Iberians and Africans were substantial in many locations and at times horrendous.

Two notable examples of the natives altering their environment come from the Valley of Mexico and Peru. In the former, a combination of vulnerability to flooding and the desire to expand food production resulted in a sophisticated hydrological system in the five connected lakes. The largest single project was construction of a dike 10 miles in length across Lake Texcoco to separate the salty northwestern half from the remainder, which included the Mexica capital of Tenochtitlan. This created a substantial area then developed for agriculture on expanded "chinampas," or artificial islands. Additionally, sluiced dikes enabled control of the water levels in the lakes, whereas causeways facilitated foot traffic to the shores. All together, about 60 miles of dikes, causeways, and aqueducts crisscrossed the lakes. The results included improved flood control and increased crops in an environment shaped by human intervention.

The Inka responded to their mountainous environment by building on the accomplishments of earlier empires. They expanded land reclamation by constructing additional terraces usually suitable for irrigated agriculture. Indeed, the name "Andes" that the Spaniards gave to the enormous mountain chain derived from the "andenes," or platforms that appeared as steps ascending and descending the mountains. Although almost half of the terraces were abandoned not long after the Conquest, many are still visible. Those in Peru, almost all constructed before the Conquest, provided about 2,300 square miles of cultivable land; another 1,900 square miles of terraces are on the Bolivian side of Lake Titicaca. The total of 2.7 million acres is more than half the size of the total land in the state of Massachusetts.

The Iberians' introduction of domesticated livestock altered and even transformed environments as grazing sheep, cattle, mule, and other quadruped populations expanded rapidly in number. The devastation of the Valley of Mezquital, a region north of Mexico City, illustrates the damage they could cause. In 1521, the region had forests, multiple sources of water used for irrigation, diverse vegetation, substantial maize production, and perhaps more than a million inhabitants. Spaniards introduced livestock—horses, cattle, sheep, and pigs—no later than the 1530s. Following Castilian practice that considered grass a common resource and permitted grazing on croplands after the harvest, owners sent their animals into natives' agricultural lands. Because cattle damaged crops, authorities banned them from the region in the 1550s, but allowed an estimated 4,000 sheep to remain. Although the region was still free of substantial environmental degradation, rapid changes were underway.

By 1579, the number of sheep had burgeoned to an estimated 4 million owned by both Spaniards and Indians. This increase followed high indigenous mortality from epidemic disease that made additional land available for grazing. Overgrazing at the expense of intensive irrigation agriculture allowed mesquite and other arid-zone plants to choke out native grasses by the 1570s. Although the number of sheep in 1600 had dropped to less than 3 million, pasture failure had reduced the land's carrying capacity. Requiring more land for their animals, wealthy owners expanded their properties or haciendas by buying out smaller-scale competitors. Environmental degradation by 1600 had transformed the once-verdant Valley of Mezquital into a region fit only for raising sheep and goats.

Mining precious metals also profoundly affected the environment. Commonly, miners found silver ore in an outcropping of rock and then followed its subterranean course. The digging and extraction processes produced piles of low-grade ore below the mouths of tunnels. Refining operations yielded enormous heaps of waste material known as slag that also changed the environment.

In New Spain, the discovery of silver at Guanajuato and Zacatecas attracted entrepreneurs and laborers who spawned new cities and introduced cattle, other livestock, wheat, maize, and other crops. They created transportation networks largely dependent on mules, but also on oxen where wagons could be used. These new enterprises required support from nearby pasture and cultivable land. In such locations, as with the "Rich Town" of Potosí in today's Bolivia, the buildings and requirements of municipal living permanently transformed the landscape.

Mercury mining at Huancavelica, Peru, affected the environment in several ways. Mercury posed a frightful health risk and contemporaries aptly considered the mines a "public slaughterhouse" in which laboring equaled a death sentence. In the early seventeenth century, up to two-thirds of the workers died from mercury poisoning, other illnesses, or accidents. Handling the ore in either a mine or at the furnaces, inhaling its poisonous gas, or absorbing it through the skin was often fatal. Additionally, workers frequently contracted pneumonia or were victims of cave-ins or other mining accidents. Conditions in the Santa Barbara mine were so bad that it was shut down to complete its first ventilation shaft. Despite the addition of two other shafts, the mortality rate stayed high. The soil of the region remains toxic today.

Mining resulted in deforestation and the construction of dams also changed the environment. Processing ore not only left unsightly slag heaps, but also allowed zinc, lead, mercury, and other toxic metals to leach into soil for centuries. An international scientific research team has determined that mercury pollution near Huancavelica began nearly 3,500 years ago when Andeans started to mine cinnabar, the mineralogical source of mercury, to produce the brilliant orange–red pigment vermillion that women used as rouge. Production reached its preconquest peak under the Inka, but the greatly expanded mining during Spanish rule intensified the associated pollution.

Climate and Natural Disasters

Drought, flooding, unseasonal frost, famine, earthquakes, hurricanes, and pestilence repeatedly afflicted Latin America both before and after Europeans arrived. These events heightened mortality and left a trail of material damage. Several years of famine following a major flood in the Valley of Mexico in 1450 exhausted the royal storehouses in Tenochtitlan. The most unfortunate families sold themselves and their children into slavery in distant locations spared from the disaster. In Inka Peru, storage facilities provided access to basic foodstuffs in good times and bad. The arrival of Spaniards established additional venues for natural disasters: new cities, mines and ore-processing mills, and rural properties used for livestock grazing and agriculture. Competing claims over access to water pitted landowners and native villages against each other and stimulated conflict within each group.

Earthquakes

Earthquakes were sufficiently terrifying that 21 were recorded for Mexico from 1455 to 1519. Spaniards first mentioned one that occurred in 1523. Chile has long suffered serious earthquakes, often accompanied by tsunamis. Between 1570 and 1796, 13 major quakes struck, including 3 in or near Santiago. One quake in 1751 severely damaged the cathedral in Concepción. Similarly, Peru has endured numerous earthquakes. A list published first in 1748 enumerated 16 "of the most remarkable" that struck Lima between 1582 and 1746. Most devastating were several in 1687 and one in 1746, both accompanied by tsunamis that inundated the capital's port of Callao. To explain the disaster in 1687, a cleric preached to an overflowing crowd in the cathedral that "God was very angry about our faults, and that which has him most annoyed is the nefarious sin which is practiced between members of the same sex, women with women, and men with men."[7] Guatemala also endured serious quakes, sometimes accompanied by volcanic eruptions. An earthquake and accompanying mudslide from the volcano Agua (now Hunahpú) in 1541 destroyed the capital city of Santiago de los Caballeros; it was rebuilt farther from the volcano as Santiago de Guatemala. The new city (now known as Antigua Guatemala) suffered from the combination twice in 1717 and again in 1751. In 1773, two catastrophic quakes brought another relocation of the capital city, this time to a nearby valley.

Volcanoes

Volcanic activity struck not only Guatemala. Ash also blanketed Arequipa, Peru, in 1600 when Huaynaputina, southeast of the city, erupted. The accompanying earthquakes worsened the situation and additional quakes in 1604 destroyed the reconstruction that had occurred. In 1601, the region's wine production was down 95 percent; adding insult to injury, the beverage was undrinkable. Popocatepetl, located a few miles from both Mexico City and Puebla, has erupted repeatedly since the Spaniards arrived and continues to do so. Numerous volcanoes were active in Ecuador during Spanish rule. Mt. Pichincha (the "boiling mountain") erupted many times from 1539 to 1660. The second eruption, in 1566, covered Quito with a yard of ashes and stones, but the last three caused more damage. At an elevation exceeding 19,300 feet, Cotopaxi, the highest active volcano in the world, has erupted on more than 50 occasions since 1738; an eruption in the 1740s destroyed the town of Latacunga and killed hundreds of people.

THE COLUMBIAN EXCHANGE

The term "Columbian Exchange," coined by Alfred W. Crosby, refers to the transfer of fauna, flora, and disease from the Old World to the New World and vice versa. Horses, cattle, sheep, goats, pigs, donkeys, chickens, dogs, cats, and rats reached Española with Columbus in 1493. At the same time, he brought sugar cane, cabbage, beets, limes, lemons, oranges, melons, onions, radishes, cucumbers, parsley, wheat, olive trees, and grape vines; the latter three failed in the island's climate, but thrived in more temperate mainland locations. Bananas arrived from the Canary Islands in 1516, and rice and numerous vegetables, fruits, and spices reached the Americas in the early 1500s as well. Oats, rye, lentils, and hemp dated from the 1500s and coffee appeared in the seventeenth century.

Europeans carried back from the Americas little in the way of native animals, but did introduce various types of beans, chili peppers, cocoa, corn (maize), peanuts, potatoes, pumpkins and squash, quinine, sunflowers, sweet potatoes, tomatoes, and vanilla, among other plants. They also developed several important exports from plants in the Indies: indigo (a blue dye), cacao, and tobacco. Manioc or cassava later became a major food source in Africa.

The desire to replicate the foods that they knew in Europe affected where most Spaniards settled in the Americas, locations that Crosby has labeled "neo-Europes" because their climates allowed the desired plants and animals to thrive. Crop yields were higher than in Europe, and longer and staggered growing seasons made fresh food available most of the year. From the combination of American and European foods came a diverse and nutritionally sound diet, often at a reasonable price.

Primary Source

Smallpox in Tenochtitlan, 1520

The arrival of smallpox in Tenochtitlan in 1520 initiated the devastation caused by epidemic diseases introduced by the invaders on the American mainland. The selection from a Nahuatl source poignantly describes the suffering that resulted.

SOURCE: Miguel Leon-Portilla, ed., *The Broken Spears: The Aztec Account of the Conquest of Mexico*, trans. Lysander Kemp (Boston: Beacon Press, 1992), 92–3.

While the Spaniards were in Tlaxcala, a great plague broke out here in Tenochtitlan. It began to spread during the thirteenth month and lasted for seventy days, striking everywhere in the city and killing a vast number of our people. Sores erupted on our faces, our breasts, our bellies; we were covered with agonizing sores from head to foot.

The illness was so dreadful that no one could walk or move. The sick were so utterly helpless that they could only lie on their beds like corpses, unable to move their limbs or even their heads. They could not lie face down or roll from one side to the other. If they did move their bodies, they screamed with pain.

A great many died from this plague, and many others died of hunger. They could not get up to search for food, and everyone else was too sick to care for them, so they starved to death in their beds.

Some people came down with a milder form of the disease; they suffered less than the others and made a good recovery. But they could not escape entirely. Their looks were ravaged, for wherever a sore broke out, it gouged an ugly pockmark in the skin. And a few of the survivors were left completely blind.

Moreover, the ready availability of acceptable food became an important selling point for settlers urging relatives to join them. A tailor writing his brother from Puebla in 1576 noted, "Work is paid well here. And food is cheap. For a *real* they give you 16 pounds of beef, or 8 pounds of mutton and 8 loaves of bread; they harvest wheat twice a year, and a bushel and a half is worth 4 *reales*."[8] About the same time, a resident of Tunja, New Granada, wrote, "The fertility of this land is so great that there is never any shortage of food, even for men who don't work."[9] What more could one want?

Two trends profoundly affected the landscape of the Indies. The first was the precipitous decline of indigenous populations from Mexico to Chile, a decline that increased the availability of arable land and pasture. The catastrophic drop in population, however, adversely affected the availability of labor and stimulated the importation of African slaves. Second, Spaniards benefited by occupying land that, in the most populated regions, the indigenous inhabitants had previously used for agriculture. There they introduced European flora and fauna that complemented native sources of food, food that the invaders and their descendants often disdained. These trends influenced both where Spaniards founded municipalities and where they remained.

NOTES

1. Quoted in J. H. Elliott, *The Old World and the New* (Cambridge: Cambridge University Press, 1970), 10.
2. Fernando Colón, *The Life of the Admiral Christopher Columbus by His Son Ferdinand*, trans. Benjamin Keen (New Brunswick, NJ: Rutgers University Press, 1959), 60.
3. Juan de la Puente quoted in Jorge Cañizares Esguerra, "New World, New Stars: Patriotic Astrology and the Invention of Indian and Creole Bodies in Colonial Spanish America, 1600–1650," *American Historical Review* 104, no. 1 (February 1999): 46.
4. Rebecca Earle, *The Body of the Conquistador: Food, Race and the Colonial Experience in Spanish America, 1492–1700* (Cambridge: Cambridge University Press, 2012).
5. Ibid., 165.
6. "Sublimus Dei," http://www.papalencyclicals.net/Paul03/p3subli.htm (accessed May 10, 2012).
7. Josephe and Francisco Mugaburu, *Chronicle of Colonial Lima: The Diary of Josephe and Francisco Mugaburu, 1640–1697*, trans. and ed. Robert Ryal Miller (Norman: University of Oklahoma Press, 1975), 318.
8. Quoted in James Lockhart and Enrique Otte, eds. and trans., *Letters and People of the Spanish Indies: The Sixteenth Century* (Cambridge: Cambridge University Press, 1976), 118–19.
9. Quoted in Earle, *Body of the Conquistador*, 107.

SUGGESTIONS FOR FURTHER READING

Alchon, Suzanne Austin. *A Pest in the Land: New World Epidemics in a Global Perspective.* Albuquerque: University of New Mexico Press, 2003.

Cook, Noble David. *Born to Die: Disease and New World Conquest, 1492–1650.* Cambridge and New York: Cambridge University Press, 1998.

Crosby, Alfred W. *The Columbian Exchange: Biological and Cultural Consequences of 1492.* 30th anniversary ed. Westport, CT: Praeger, 2003.

Denevan, William M. (ed.). *The Native Population of the Americas in 1492.* 2nd ed. Madison: University of Wisconsin Press, 1992.

Earle, Rebecca. *The Body of the Conquistador: Food, Race and the Colonial Experience in Spanish America, 1492–1700.* Cambridge: Cambridge University Press, 2012.

Livi Bacci, Massimo. *Conquest: The Destruction of the American Indios.* Translated by Carl Ipsen. Cambridge: Polity Press, 2008.

Melville, Elinor G. K. *A Plague of Sheep: Environmental Consequences of the Conquest of Mexico.* Cambridge: Cambridge University Press, 1994.

Miller, Shawn William. *An Environmental History of Latin America.* Cambridge: Cambridge University Press, 2007.

Miller, Shawn William. *Fruitless Trees: Portuguese Conservation and Brazil's Colonial Timber.* Stanford, CA: Stanford University Press, 2000.

Robins, Nicholas A. *Mercury, Mining, and Empire: The Human and Ecological Cost of Colonial Silver Mining in the Andes.* Bloomington: Indiana University Press, 2011.

Super, John D. *Food, Conquest and Colonization in Sixteenth-Century Spanish America.* Albuquerque: University of New Mexico Press, 1988.

CHAPTER 5

Tools of Empire: Administration

IMPERIAL ORGANIZATION FOR THE INDIES

The New World's enormity, diverse terrain, and distance from Iberia formed an immutable background against which the Castilian and Portuguese monarchs sought to establish and maintain their authority. Ambitious conquistadors in the Spanish possessions and early settlers there and in Brazil sought to become genuine aristocrats with seigniorial rights. Iberian rulers, in turn, opposed the emergence of powerful hereditary nobles living beyond their direct control. Both crowns expected their American realms to contribute directly to royal revenue. Additionally, their monarchs bore the responsibility to promote Christianization of the indigenous population. To address these challenges, they turned to royal officials and clerics who accompanied the expansion of New World settlement and for three centuries or more contributed significantly to the Indies' overall political stability.

Challenges of Time and Distance

Distance, slow oceanic travel, and the resulting unavoidable delays in communication between the New World and Iberia affected royal officials' ability to exercise authority in the Americas. Winds and currents normally made the outbound voyage from Iberia shorter than the return trip, but ships sailing from an Andalusian port to Santo Domingo or Cartagena averaged 51 days and to Panama or Veracruz 75 days. Sailing back to Spain required an average of nearly four months from Cartagena and several more weeks from Veracruz or Panama. Travel from Lisbon to Bahia took 70 to nearly 100 days; voyages to Recife were slightly shorter and to Rio de Janeiro slightly longer. Sailing from Belém, near the mouth of the Amazon, to Lisbon was easier than sailing to Bahia, thus making it more convenient to communicate with officials in Lisbon than with those in the Brazilian capital. Slave ships from Angola could reach any Brazilian port in the comparatively brief time of 35 to 60 days.

The round trip for a fleet sailing from Spain to the Indies usually required 14 or 15 months. Annual fleets in the late sixteenth and early seventeenth centuries helped maintain orderly, low-risk commerce and communication, but starting in the 1620s, the convoys sailed less frequently. Small mail boats provided supplemental service, but departed only intermittently in the 1500s and often only twice to four times a year in the 1600s.

The coastal locations of Brazil's major cities until the establishment of São Paulo facilitated communication with Lisbon. The interior sites of Mexico City and Bogotá, in contrast, required additional time for land travel. Rapid contact between Madrid and cities on the Pacific Coast side of the Andes was impossible. Travel from the mining center of Potosí to the Panamanian port of Portobello, for example, often took seven weeks or more.

The long lag time in communication with New World locations forced the Iberian courts to delegate greater authority to officials there than to their counterparts on the peninsula. At the same time, distance exacerbated the problem of overseeing these royal representatives. Substantial administrative flexibility resulted as officials far from their source of authority responded to local pressures and negotiated informally with resident elites.

Administering an Empire

The Indies' vastness, the presence of densely populated and advanced sedentary civilizations, and scattered rich mineral deposits led the Crown of Castile to move quickly to gain control over conquistadors, settlers, and indigenous peoples as successive expeditions added to its domains. Creating a variety of jurisdictions, the Crown modified institutions already proven in Spain to administer them. By 1535, it had named officials to oversee its political and financial interests, provide justice to settlers and natives, and supervise the allocation of resources—primarily native labor, land, mines, and offices. The territorial divisions and administrative structure in place by the 1580s experienced little modification until the eighteenth century.

Territorial Jurisdictions

The Castilian monarchs initially believed their sovereignty extended over the entirety of the American continents, except for Brazil. Nested within the Indies, as they termed this enormous territory, were the viceroyalties of New Spain (1535) and Peru (1542). With cores labeled kingdoms in recognition of the Aztec and Inka empires, the two viceroyalties also included lesser kingdoms, such as New Granada, and provinces, such as Chile, also referred to as presidencies, governorships, and captaincies general, depending on the chief executive's title. These large territorial units contained numerous provinces divided, in turn, into Spanish municipalities and Indian villages. Specific executives or corporate bodies oversaw each of these jurisdictions.

Decentralization characterized imperial organization. Administration in the Indies resembled a set of wheels with hubs in the *audiencia* and gubernatorial capitals and spokes extending to the municipalities. The Spanish court, in turn, formed the hub of a wheel whose spokes reached the capitals of each *audiencia* and gubernatorial jurisdiction. From this perspective, decentralization characterized imperial administration.

The Council of the Indies

The Council of the Indies bore responsibility for overseeing the Crown's interests in the New World from its foundation in 1524 until the early eighteenth century. Modeled on the older Council of Castile, the tribunal for the Indies oversaw every kind of government activity in the blended authority characteristic of Spanish administration. The council issued laws, recommended policies to the monarch, approved major expenditures in the Indies, and heard cases appealed from the American *audiencias* and the House of Trade. It arranged for *residencias*, the judicial reviews conducted at the conclusion of officials' terms of office, and occasional general inspections, or *visitas*. Additionally, it exercised royal patronage over the Church in the American realms and recommended candidates for most high-ranking royal positions there.

Councilors and crown attorneys formed the council's core. Initially, monarchs relied on men with university degrees in civil or canon law and prior service on a lower tribunal in Spain, but starting with Philip III (1598–1621), they also named nobles without these credentials, thereby facilitating favoritism and abuse. Moreover, until the eighteenth century, few councilors had personal experience in the New World. The Crown's failure to come to grips with basic personnel issues thus weakened the council's ability to provide high-quality oversight and administration. The delays inherent in committee deliberations, coupled with inescapably slow communication with the Indies, further reduced the tribunal's effectiveness.

Viceroys

The enormity and distance of the New World realms from Castile led the Crown to name viceroys, initially drawn from the high nobility, to oversee them and to provide a sense of royal presence. The foremost executives in the Indies, the viceroys of New Spain and Peru also routinely held the titles of president, governor, and captain general. Their many responsibilities included general administration; the imposition, collection, and disbursement of taxes; remittance of surplus revenue to Spain; construction and maintenance of public works; public order; defense against internal rebellions and foreign enemies; support of the Church; protection of the Indians; and exercise of patronage. At the same time, local elites and other high-ranking officials constrained viceroys' ability to act independently. Negotiation was routine into the eighteenth century. A viceroy could formally delay and contribute to a revision of directives from Spain by applying the formula *obedezco pero no cumplo* ("I obey [recognize the legitimacy of the order], but I do not execute" [implementation would have undesirable consequences]). Repeated failure to carry out royal mandates, however, invited conflict and judicial scrutiny during the *residencia*.

Audiencias and Lesser Jurisdictions

Smaller territorial units within the viceroyalties included provinces grouped into *audiencias*, each with an executive head (titled president, governor, and increasingly captain general) and a tribunal also called an *audiencia*. The number of these courts increased as the empire expanded. Each heard cases on appeal from throughout its jurisdiction; its judges (*oidores*) collectively advised the chief executive and individually served commissions as required. Provincial administration and justice within each *audiencia's* jurisdiction fell to officials variously called *corregidores*, *alcaldes mayores*, and governors. The Crown also founded royal treasuries near major mining and administrative centers and ports. Local officials, complemented at times by provincial officials and *audiencia* ministers, administered Spanish cities and towns as well as Indian villages and their adjoining hinterlands.

Native Sons, Radicados, and Outsiders

Most officeholders shared a myriad of social and economic ties with prominent families in their jurisdiction. Some were "native sons," men serving in the region of their birth, for example, a man born in Lima serving in Peru. Others were *radicados*, men born elsewhere who had become "rooted" in local society. Although "outsiders" or newcomers to a region regularly received royal appointments, those with lifetime tenure usually became *radicados* within a few years. Keenly sensitive to local needs and desires, *radicados* and native sons could often stall or otherwise frustrate the implementation of unpopular royal legislation as well as do favors for members of their networks. Although the Castilian Crown preferred to name outsiders, especially men born in Spain, to high-ranking positions, the sale of appointments in the seventeenth and early eighteenth centuries compromised this principle. Purchases by native sons and *radicados* gave local elites unprecedented access to power, both directly through securing offices and indirectly through family and economic ties to officeholders.

Map 5.1 Major Territorial Divisions in 1650

THE SALE OF ROYAL APPOINTMENTS
IN SPANISH AMERICA

The Crown correctly considered political, judicial, and fiscal positions central to its authority, revenue, and security. As European wars exhausted Spain's finances, however, the Crown gradually turned appointments to these offices into a source of revenue, starting with appointments to treasury posts and the tribunals of accounts in 1633 and expanding to those for provincial administrators—*corregidor*, *alcalde mayor*, and governor—in the 1670s. In the following decade, it initiated the systematic sale of *audiencia* appointments during time of war and by 1700 had even sold appointments to the office of viceroy.

The sale of appointments to *audiencia* and treasury offices, especially in the Viceroyalty of Peru, bore witness to the Indies' reduced dependency on Spain. Native sons considered service at home far more attractive than entering office elsewhere as an outsider and were willing to pay a premium for such an appointment. Sales thus increased the proportion of native sons in higher royal offices and diminished the Crown's effective authority over officeholders; since most of these purchasers were young, they clogged the lines of promotion and thus contributed to the number of *radicados*. Additionally, the purchase of an appointment, particularly if made with borrowed funds, forced the incumbent to secure not only a reliable income but also a profit on his investment. The temptation to resort to extralegal sources of income proved irresistible and also worked against the Crown's interest.

One important result of the sale of appointments and the evolution of an administration laden with native sons and *radicados* was an increasing compatibility and, indeed, blending among royal servants and local elites, although both groups spawned competing factions. Bureaucrats who borrowed money were not likely to enforce vigorously laws that harmed their creditors. Although the venal antecedents for this sensitivity to local interests are clear, the practical result was to increase officials' negotiation with local elites and thereby reduce the potential for dangerous conflicts between powerful interest groups in the New World and the distant metropolis.

MUNICIPALITIES

Castilians considered municipalities the boundary between themselves (*civilized* and Christian) and non-Iberians (*barbarians* and pagans). Urban space encapsulated Castile's civic values and was the location for secular and religious institutions. Although innumerable native villages and some impressive cities already existed in the Indies, conquistadors and settlers constructed urban centers where none had existed and rebuilt old ones as political statements of victory over the indigenous population. These new and refounded municipalities physically marked the invaders' territory and way of life.

Spaniards typically built cities and towns around a central core (*traza*) with a rectangular plaza (*plaza mayor*) at its heart. Regularly flanking it stood a church, a municipal council building, the office of the region's ranking royal representative, and retail shops. Located within the open rectangle were frequently a fountain that provided drinking water and a pillory (*picota*), a stone column that represented justice and served to display heads or bodies of executed criminals. Unlike in medieval European cities, walls and fortifications generally protected only ports. The large squares in Brazilian municipalities were not centered like the *plazas mayores* of Spanish American cities.

A municipality included the plaza, a residential core, and an often-substantial surrounding hinterland that extended to the boundary of the next town. The jurisdiction of seventeenth-century Buenos Aires, for example, stretched some

300 miles before meeting that of Córdoba. The Crown considered Mexico City's early boundary claim outrageous and reduced it in 1539 to a still-substantial 45 miles or so in each direction.

By 1574, Spaniards had founded some 30 municipalities in New Spain alone. Throughout the whole of Spanish America by 1580 were 225 towns and cities, including many that still serve as administrative centers. A half-century later, the total reached 331. In Brazil, Bahia (Salvador), Rio de Janeiro, and São Paulo existed by 1580, but even in the mid-seventeenth century, the colony counted only 6 cities and 31 towns, most located close to the coast.

Municipal Councils

Iberians found it more attractive to live in cities than in the countryside and normally chose to reside in the cities unless they were lured to a prosperous mining site. Locally born Spaniards (native sons) with aristocratic pretensions appreciated that urban settings offered the largest selection of potential spouses for themselves and their children. Peninsular Spaniards in royal service and commerce also availed themselves of these marital opportunities.

After founding a city or town, Iberians immediately created its ruling council, known as a *cabildo* or *ayuntamiento* in Spanish America and a *senado da câmara* in Brazil. Following the distribution of lots for homes and gardens, the councils established services in the public interest and for the regulation of community activities. For example, they represented the municipality and its citizens in dealings with royal officials; monitored weights, measures, and, in some cases, prices in the market; responded to external threats; oversaw public safety, holidays, and processions; dealt with the problems of providing potable water as well as trash and sewage disposal; and maintained a jail.

Propertied adult male citizens (*vecinos*) were eligible for election or appointment to the council's positions, although the royal official (*corregidor, alcalde mayor*, or governor) of the provincial capital normally chaired the meetings. Aldermen numbered from 4 to 6 for small towns to 12 or more for Lima and Mexico City. Each January 1, all municipal councils elected one or two judges of first instance (*alcaldes ordinarios*) to deal with malefactors. Depending on a municipality's size, its other offices could include a municipal standard bearer; an inspector of weights and measures; a collector of fines; a notary; an attorney; an overseer for city property; a sheriff or chief constable; and rural constables.

Municipal councils in Brazil were also the fundamental institution that administered cities, towns, and their surrounding jurisdictions. With both aldermen and judges, local government looked much like that in Spanish America, overseeing and regulating public services. The use of elections for aldermen soon distinguished Brazil's councils from those in Spanish America. In Salvador a complicated indirect electoral process annually selected three aldermen, two local magistrates, and a municipal attorney chosen from a list of eligible candidates.

Municipal councils frequently lacked adequate financial resources to address their many responsibilities. Fees charged for services, licenses, and use of common lands (*ejidos*) and other municipal property often proved insufficient.

Furthermore, royal restrictions on local taxation left the councils chronically short of funds to maintain streets, water, and bridges as well as to provide the ceremonies and public rituals that served to legitimize monarchical rule and demonstrate the councilmen's authority.

The Spanish Crown tried to establish and enforce the notion of separate and unequal "republics" for Spaniards and the indigenous population. Thus, it assigned Indians discrete districts (*barrios*) in Mexico City, Lima, and other cities, as well as distinct villages. This policy of segregation failed, however, and cities soon housed diverse populations of Spaniards, natives, blacks, and persons of mixed ancestry. Where black slaves and mulattoes were numerous, whites might comprise only a minority. Such was the case, for example, in Vera Cruz in 1570 and both Mexico City and Lima in the early seventeenth century.

Sale of Municipal Offices and Local Elites

Citizens under Spanish rule in the Indies initially elected their municipalities' officeholders, but soon the Crown began to name aldermen as a favor or reward for service. In 1558, the year after the Crown's "bankruptcy," Philip II transformed royal grants of municipal office into a source of royal income. Beginning with fee-collecting positions, most notably that of scribe/notary (*escribano*), saleable offices swelled to include all municipal posts except those of elective local magistrates. In many cases, the purchaser could assign a deputy to perform the actual work. Gradually, the Crown added the right to sell or bequeath the municipal posts to increase their value, forcing the owner to pay a tax on the sales. As the number of posts sold for a lifetime increased, subsequent grants gave the purchaser a second life or even perpetuity.

Philip III brought uniformity to the process in 1606 when he established a specific class of "saleable and renounceable offices" as a form of property in the Indies. This decision guaranteed that native sons throughout the empire could legally dominate the municipal councils and their elective positions of local magistrate. Prices varied by office, location, and date; at times, they could be exorbitant. In the city of Mexico, the peninsular merchant and financier Baltasar Rodríguez purchased the post of sheriff for the princely sum of 125,000 pesos. The prominent wholesaler and founder of the merchant guild (*consulado*) Diego Matías de Vera, a native of Seville, and his wife Ana de Ureña paid 250,000 pesos in cash for the mint's directorship and the right to bequeath it; at that time, a peon in Mexico earned one-quarter of a peso (2 *reales*) for a day's labor.

Since saleable and transferable offices were property, fathers could include them in daughters' dowries and thereby formally and easily incorporate peninsular sons-in-law into municipal oligarchies. Marriages by aldermen on Lima's city council reveal that peninsulars' entry into the elite via formal unions with locally born women (native daughters) increased in the seventeenth century. By sanctioning inheritance of municipal positions, the Crown ensured that native sons would frequently own the most desirable ones and hence effectively eliminated them as a source of clashes with peninsulars.

"Open" Town Meetings

Occasionally, an issue of widespread interest or concern led to an "open town meeting" (*cabildo abierto*). Modeled on precedents in Castile, this formal gathering brought together officials and municipal *vecinos* (household heads). For example, in Asunción, Paraguay, a *cabildo abierto* elected a governor when the incumbent died without royal provision of a successor. In 1590, the citizens of Potosí met to vote an additional contribution to the treasury of Philip II. In contrast, the residents of Quito angrily protested against that monarch's decision to extend to them the sales tax (*alcabala*) imposed earlier in Mexico and Peru. In response, Philip suspended the city council's right to elect local magistrates in 1593. The city finally regained the privilege in 1699, at least partly by offering the Crown a financial donation.

NATIVE COMMUNITIES

The sedentary majority of the Indies' indigenous population resided in communities of vastly different size and complexity. By far the largest precontact city in New Spain was Tenochtitlan, with a population estimated at some 200,000. Texcoco, the next largest city in the Valley of Mexico, had only 30,000 and Cempoala, not far from Veracruz, perhaps 20,000. At the other extreme were outlying villages dependent on a head town (*cabecera*); together they formed an *altepetl*, or city-state. In the same way that Castilians referred to themselves as *sevillanos* (from Seville) or *madrileños* (from Madrid), Mixtecs and other indigenous peoples referred to individuals as from a particular community, regardless of its size.

In the 1530s, the first viceroy of New Spain, Antonio de Mendoza, began to name Indian rulers and nobles as governors, local magistrates (*alcaldes*), and council members of villages. By the mid-sixteenth century, every head town in the Valley of Mexico had a governor and Spanish-style municipal council on which usually two Indian *alcaldes* and three or four aldermen held one-year terms. Unlike in Spanish municipalities, the local nobility annually elected village aldermen, although the viceroy could void the results. Although the Crown did not sell the post of alderman in native villages (pueblos), it did make the positions of constable and scribe/notary saleable and inheritable. Natives in Brazil lacked any comparable village government.

The *cabildo* members bore responsibility for collecting and paying the village's tribute and for meeting its labor quotas. Because of population losses, this made council positions so unattractive by the early seventeenth century that few men wanted to hold them. Although Spanish administrators tried to regularize native town councils and posts throughout New Spain in accord with the peninsular model, the selection of officials drawn from traditional noble families revealed the persistence of pre-Hispanic practices in some locations.

Depopulation fostered a crucial change—the consolidation of multiple sparsely peopled villages into single larger ones. Friars believed this would facilitate conversion and promote orderly living and sobriety. Royal officials, in turn, thought the new communities would simplify tax collection and administrative oversight. Spaniards looking to establish or expand their lands realized that consolidation would make available vacated property.

Termed *congregación* in Mexico, the process of forcing natives to move from hamlets into new Spanish-style villages (*pueblos*) began slowly in the 1550s, intensified later in the century, and was completed, at least in theory, in the early seventeenth century. Transplanted natives received house lots and access to property for growing maize. In Yucatan, as elsewhere in New Spain, the new villages copied the grid pattern that characterized Spanish settlement. Around the central plaza stood a church or convent, town hall, often a jail, and sometimes a school, especially in the eighteenth century.

The final effort at congregation encountered considerable indigenous resistance, especially when relocation would place a population in a different *altepetl*. Such displaced natives often contested with their feet, abandoning their new homes. Indeed, the long-term trend was dispersal rather than concentration as dependent villages sought independence by claiming they were head towns (*cabeceras*).

In Peru, the viceroy Francisco de Toledo (1569–1581) forced more than 1 million natives into numerous *reducciones*, the Andean equivalent of *congregación*. Although he wanted the new settlements to have 400 tributaries, the number varied substantially, probably in response to local conditions. In Charcas or Upper Peru, the process reduced 901 villages to just 44 new settlements, increasing their average size from 44 to almost 3,000 inhabitants. The amount of land per person was almost certainly less than before the mandatory consolidation.

The most celebrated reductions were the 30 Guaraní missions that the Jesuits established in the Alto Paraná basin of Paraguay. In Brazil, the Jesuits in particular employed a process analogous to that used in Spanish America to create a reduced number of villages known as *aldeias*.

Opposition to resettlement came, not surprisingly, primarily from affected indigenous communities. For example, in Peru they argued that their old lands offered better protection against intruding cattle and yielded larger crops. They also resisted their forced combination with natives from different ethnicities. The *reducciones*, moreover, often split village populations from their colonists located in another geographic zone. The imposition of the Potosí *mita* on the resettled population in Charcas's highlands profoundly affected the *reducciones*. Men anxious to avoid the forced service fled to other, often lower zones, where the hated mining *mita* was not in effect. Although some new villages survived, the inhabitants frequently returned to their original lands.

ADMINISTRATION IN BRAZIL

Portuguese administration in Brazil developed more slowly and modestly in scale than its Spanish American counterpart. Small concentrations of Portuguese resided in several coastal locations, although transportation challenges made communication between northern and southern settlements difficult. Furthermore, Brazil lacked both a powerful and ambitious group of conquistadors and any indigenous cultures comparable to the Mexica or Inka. Collectively, these conditions contributed to more decentralized oversight and fewer officials than in Spain's possessions.

Various offices in Portugal had administrative responsibility for Brazil. No equivalent to Spain's Council of the Indies existed until 1642, when the Braganza dynasty began a decade-long experiment by creating the Overseas Council charged with many similar functions. The *Desembargo do Paço* located in Lisbon oversaw judicial matters for Portugal and the empire, appointing, promoting, and reviewing the conduct of royal magistrates.

Initially, the Portuguese Crown sought to treat Brazil as part of the system of fortified trading posts it used in Africa and Asia. When French merchants began obtaining dyewood directly from the natives, however, John III (1521–1557) turned to permanent settlements. In the 1530s, he granted 12 men with good court connections hereditary captaincies extending inland from the Atlantic Coast to the Line of Tordesillas. These "donatary captains" received rights similar to those granted earlier in Portugal and the Atlantic islands. Each recipient was to settle and defend his captaincy in return for specified revenues, the right to grant land and name officials, and jurisdiction in most criminal and civil matters. The Crown retained several royal taxes and its monopoly over the dyewood trade. But with the exception of São Vicente and Pernambuco, the private-enterprise donatary system failed. Continued French pressure convinced John III to regain some of his alienated authority in a manner analogous to that employed by the Castilian Crown.

In 1549, John purchased the captaincy of Bahia from its owners and named a governor general to administer it. This political reorganization facilitated exploration, Indian campaigns, and settlement in the north, beginning in the 1570s. The Portuguese established themselves in Paraíba in the 1580s, Rio Grande do Norte in 1598, and Ceará in 1610. An expedition to expel a short-lived French settlement in Maranhão began in late 1615, and the Portuguese moved into Belém and the lower Amazon from 1616 to 1630.

As the chief executive in Brazil, the governor general (titled a viceroy in 1720) had responsibilities and restrictions similar to those of the Spanish American viceroys. He exercised general oversight of administration, defense, Luso–Indian relations, the treasury, the secular clergy, trade, and land grants. Legislation also circumscribed his activities in many ways. For example, it prohibited him from investing in trade or agriculture and allowed him to travel outside Bahia only with royal permission. Moreover, the Crown subjected him to a special investigation during his term in office and a review (*residencia*) at its conclusion, checks similar to the Spanish *visita* and *residencia*. Named to a three-year term, many governors general served longer, some more than two decades. Most came from Portugal's upper nobility and had been professional soldiers; none had been high-ranking clerics. As did their counterparts in Spain's America, usually governors general reached Brazil accompanied by kin and retainers eager to benefit from their patron's largesse.

Governors served as the commanders in chief of their captaincies and were responsible for protecting the natives and overseeing treasury and judicial offices. Like the governor generals, they acted under standing instructions and directives from Lisbon and endured the *residencia* and sometimes a *devassa*. The need to defend the exposed Atlantic Coast led the Crown to name seasoned military veterans with administrative experience as governors. Nearly all were born in Portugal; among the few Brazilians named, almost none served in his home province. It appears that Brazil did not experience the sale of governorships that plagued Spanish America.

In 1621, the northern captaincies of Ceará, Maranhão, and Pará were united as the State of Maranhão, whose separate administration continued until 1772. The remaining captaincies formed a single unit called the "State of Brazil." In subsequent territorial reorganizations, the Crown generally transferred jurisdiction from the governor general in Bahia to the governors in Pernambuco and Rio de Janeiro.

With the decision to assert royal control in 1549, John III superimposed a superior royal magistrate to handle appeals from municipal and donatary-named judges and to serve as the royal judge for the captaincy of Bahia. Not until 1609, nearly a century after the creation of the first Spanish American *audiencia*, did the Portuguese Crown establish a high court of appeals (*relaçao*) for Brazil in Salvador. Suppressed in 1626 after the Dutch seized the city, the court reopened in 1652 and remained the sole high court in Brazil until 1751 with the creation of a second in Rio de Janeiro. As in Spanish America, the judges had administrative and advisory responsibility in addition to judicial service. Their frequent outside assignments adversely affected the administration of justice and led to repeated complaints about its slowness.

The most professional bureaucrats in Brazil, members of the high court of Bahia came primarily from modest families of commoners. All had a university degree in law, almost invariably earned at Portugal's University of Coimbra, the only university in the Portuguese world empowered to confer degrees in civil and canon law. Unlike the open-ended appointments to *audiencias*, magistrates in Brazil received term appointments of six years, but some stayed longer, occasionally more than two decades. Protracted service routinely tied them more closely to the region they served. Frequent promotions to a court in Portugal, usually the High Court of Oporto, and the paucity of Brazilians named to the Bahia tribunal, however, meant that the judges' social and economic bonds to the region were less common and intense than those of their counterparts in Spanish America. Corruption, nonetheless, was typical, and magistrates in Brazil repeatedly engaged in commercial affairs and often sought to become landowners. Because most judicial appointees reached their posts in middle age, they arrived with a Portuguese spouse. Those born in the colony, not surprisingly, were most involved in local society and economy.

Except for the high executive and judicial posts and municipal council positions, virtually every office in Brazil could be obtained by purchase or royal concession. The key fiscal offices, for example, were proprietary, and the problems of graft and embezzlement experienced in Spanish America also plagued Brazil. The practice of farming out the tithe, customs duties, and other imposts to private tax collectors compounded the financial mismanagement.

The most impressive single feature of bureaucrats in the Iberian empires was the extent to which they were embedded in the region in which they served. Time after time,

---

Primary Source

Avoiding Conflict of Interest

SOURCE: Richard Konetzke, ed., *Colección de documentos para la historia de la formación social de His-panoamérica, 1493–1810, Vol. 1: 1493–1592* (Madrid: Consejo Superior de Investigaciones Científi-cos, 1953), 486–87.

Madrid, February 10, 1575.

The King. Because of *visitas* and *residencias* and other reports that have been sent and through experience, we have seen some problems as a result of marriages contracted by our Viceroys, presidents and civil judges, criminal judges, and crown attorneys of our high courts (*audiencias*) of the Indies, islands and Tierra Firme of the Ocean Sea, and their sons and daughters. It is desirable for good administration of justice that they be free of relatives and kin in their districts so that they can do their job, consider and resolve matters with complete integrity, and prevent any need or excuse for appeals and other recourses that would preclude their hearing cases. Our Royal Council of the Indies has seen and discussed this issue. In order to avoid these difficulties and so that our subjects and vassals may receive justice without offense, we have agreed to send this *cédula*, by which we prohibit and expressly forbid that from now on, until a new order is issued, or without our particular license, our viceroys, presidents, and civil judges, criminal judges, and crown attorneys of our high courts may not marry in their districts while they are serving. The same applies to their sons and daughters while these officials are serving. The punishment for not complying with this order is removal from office, and we will name another person to hold it. To ensure fulfillment of this *cédula*, we order that it be read in each and every one of our high courts with the president and civil judges, criminal judges and crown attorneys in attendance; our scribe of the chamber (*cámara*) and government will witness the event.

---

the crowns turned to newly appointed outsiders when they wanted to effect changes. Thus, they employed visitors to investigate abuses or the failure to implement specific legislation. The extent of innovation, however, was often modest. Deeply rooted local elites, of which high-ranked officials formed a part, proved resilient to challenge. When examined closely, so-called change and reform often turned out to be the old politics with a few new players. Yet it was precisely the flexibility and resilience produced by the fusion of individual bureaucrats' interests and those of other members of the elite in their district that reduced pressure within a system of bureaucratic rule.

Iberian municipalities and indigenous communities served as the primary environments for society and royal administration in the Indies. They provided the intersection of church and state at the local level, served as the primary arena for charitable institutions, and contributed substantially to the increasing self-sufficiency of the Indies evident already during the reign of Philip II (1556–1598). The crown attempted to segregate Spaniards and Indians within cities; it also restricted nonnative residence in indigenous villages. Despite these policies, municipalities in general and cities in particular provided the primary locations for ethnic diversity and miscegenation. Local governments also served as the mouthpiece of residents in response to royal decisions. For the indigenous population, the municipal council oversaw collective legal initiatives to retain or regain community assets, notably land and access to water.

SUGGESTIONS FOR FURTHER READING

Burkholder, Mark A., and D. S. Chandler. *From Impotence to Authority: The Spanish Crown and the American Audiencias, 1687–1808.* Columbia: University of Missouri Press, 1977.

Cañeque, Alejandro. *The King's Living Image: The Culture and Politics of Viceregal Power in Colonial Mexico.* New York and London: Routledge, 2004.

Herrera, Robinson A. *Natives, Europeans, and Africans in Sixteenth-Century Guatemala.* Austin: University of Texas Press, 2010.

Higgins, Kathleen J. *"Licentious Liberty" in a Brazilian Gold-Mining Region: Slavery, Gender, and Social Control in Eighteenth-Century Sabará, Minas Gerais.* University Park: Pennsylvania State University Press, 1999.

Hoberman, Louisa Schell, and Susan Migden Socolow (eds.). *Cities and Society in Colonial Latin America.* Albuquerque: University of New Mexico Press, 1986.

Horn, Rebecca. *Postconquest Coyoacan: Nahua–Spanish Relations in Central Mexico, 1519–1650.* Stanford, CA: Stanford University Press, 1997.

Kagan, Richard L. *Urban Images of the Hispanic World, 1493–1793.* New Haven, CT: Yale University Press, 2000.

Kinsbruner, Jay. *The Colonial Spanish-American City: Urban Life in the Age of Atlantic Capitalism.* Austin: University of Texas Press, 2005.

Lane, Kris E. *Quito, 1599: City and Colony in Transition.* Albuquerque: University of New Mexico Press, 2002.

Metcalf, Alida C. *Family and Frontier in Colonial Brazil: Santana de Parnaíba, 1580–1822.* Austin: University of Texas Press, 2005.

Mumford, Jeremy Ravi. *Vertical Empire: The General Resettlement of Indians in the Colonial Andes.* Durham, NC: Duke University Press, 2012.

Nader, Helen. *Liberty in Absolutist Spain: The Habsburg Sale of Towns, 1516–1700.* Baltimore: Johns Hopkins University Press, 1990.

Owensby, Brian. *Empire of Law and Indian Justice in Colonial Mexico.* Stanford, CA: Stanford University Press, 2008.

Ruiz Medrano, Ethelia. *Reshaping New Spain: Government and Private Interests in the Colonial Bureaucracy, 1531–1550.* Translated by Julia Constantino and Pauline Marmasse. Boulder: University Press of Colorado, 2006.

Schwartz, Stuart B. *Sovereignty and Society in Colonial Brazil: The High Court of Bahia and Its Judges, 1609–1751.* Berkeley and Los Angeles: University of California Press, 1973.

CHAPTER 6

Tools of Empire: The Church

Clerics and royal administrators were the face of Iberian power in the Indies. Nurtured by the Crown financially and legislatively, the Church preached obedience to the monarch and prospered into the early nineteenth century. Converting the Indians to Christianity was its initial priority, indeed, the underlying justification of the Iberian presence in the Indies. Municipal attractions, however, ensured that numerous clerics preferred to reside in cities and towns rather than in mission villages. Whereas Christianity in Western Europe was still a single faith—Catholicism—when Spaniards and Portuguese began to settle in the Americas, the Protestant Reformation soon split it into numerous new religions uniformly rejected by Iberian monarchs. Thus, the "Church" during the centuries of Spanish and Portuguese rule refers explicitly to the Catholic Church.

The Church in the Indies preached a single faith, but was not monolithic. A major divide separated the secular or diocesan clergy from the mendicant or regular orders and the Society of Jesus. The Franciscans, Dominicans, and Augustinians comprised the most important mendicants; they often stood at odds with the Jesuits as well as each other. The diocesan clergy was split between the upper clergy or hierarchy—archbishops, bishops, members of cathedral chapters—and the far more numerous lower clergy of parish priests and ordained clerics without a parish. Place of birth, family background, and social status subdivided all of these clerical categories.

THE EARLY CHURCH

Unlike later English and Dutch governments, the Spanish Crown insisted on evangelization, an effort that met its responsibility outlined in the papal donation of 1493. The first Spanish missionaries accompanied Columbus on his second voyage. Franciscans, Dominicans, and Augustinians in the early decades—and Jesuits subsequently—led the conversion effort and the accompanying instruction of natives. An impressive total of more than 15,000 friars and Jesuit priests arrived in the Indies during the centuries of Spanish rule. Even more were born and educated there.

Mendicant friars and Jesuit fathers employed conversion as the primary vehicle to draw indigenous peoples into the cultural orbit of the Spanish and Portuguese settlers. At the same time, they sought to shield the Indians from the Iberians' corruption, immorality, and exploitive labor demands. By imposing Christian beliefs, social practices that included monogamy, and political organization through a mission system, they also undermined the natives' potential for resistance and rebellion. These changes helped prepare the indigenous communities for integration into the emerging social, political, and economic order of the Indies.

In Spanish America, the Church also ministered to Spaniards, dominated their education, and provided social services that the Crown declined to shoulder directly. By the 1570s, the initial missionary commitment had waned notably. Royal policy favoring the secular clergy over the orders contributed to a shortage of dedicated clerics in the countryside as mendicants turned increasing attention toward the cities and prospered in that environment.

The Church consolidated its gains in the seventeenth century. Participating in nearly every dimension of life, it accumulated and displayed wealth with Baroque exuberance. As spiritual enthusiasm and utopian vision declined, ecclesiastical routine triumphed, although individual examples of clerical activism remained. The clergy's composition, moreover, began to change notably. By the early seventeenth century, native sons surpassed peninsular clerics numerically and firmly anchored the Spanish Church in the social fabric of cities and towns.

Royal Patronage

The royal patronage (*patronato real*) established the basis for the Spanish Crown's control over the Church. A series of papal bulls (1493–1508) clarified its responsibility to promote conversion as well as its substantial authority over religious, educational, and charitable institutions. Granted jurisdiction over the tithe collected on agricultural production and livestock, the Crown assigned this fundamental source of income to sustain the ecclesiastical hierarchy and the Church's physical facilities and activities. It also determined the founding of churches, convents, and hospitals and the appointment and payment of secular clerics. Additionally, it licensed and paid for clerics to sail to its New World possessions and inhibited their travel on arrival. No papal document could be sent to the Americas unless the Council of the Indies had certified that it did not infringe on royal patronage.

The Portuguese Crown exercised similar supervisory authority over the Church in its dominions under the *padroado* or patronage derived from papal bulls. The king controlled the creation of Brazilian bishoprics, the appointment of bishops, the movement of missionaries, and efforts to convert the Indians. The Portuguese Church, however, lacked the wealth and political power of its Spanish counterpart. The end of Muslim rule in Portugal in the thirteenth century had made the country's ecclesiastical history different from that of its neighbor. Still, the country's later expansion into North Africa and especially India increased the Church's crusading zeal and material rewards.

Mendicants and Missions: The Evangelical Effort

The conquests of the Aztec and Inka empires opened the most populous regions of the Indies to Christian evangelization. The arrival of 12 Franciscans in Mexico in May 1524 was the first contingent of an order that would lead the spiritual assault against native religious beliefs and practices. Dominicans, Augustinians, and, in some locations, Mercedarians soon joined the effort. All mendicants took vows of poverty, chastity, and obedience and committed to converting the Indians. Notably, Franciscans pursued the task with a millenarian belief that the second coming of Christ would follow their evangelization and creation of a primitive apostolic church.

The friars faced numerous obstacles. Dispersed residential patterns outside the urban centers made rapid conversion difficult. Superficial resemblances between native and Christian religious practices hindered presenting Christianity as new and distinct. The multitude of native languages posed a special problem. Friars addressed the obstacle by learning native tongues and employing interpreters who quickly made themselves indispensable assistants and links to other parishioners. Yet the friars also enjoyed some advantages.

The conquistadors' success transferred political power to the Spanish and endowed Christianity with great prestige. Victory over the Mexica and Inka had undermined their gods, deities the Spaniards considered the devil's representatives. Systematic and persistent destruction of indigenous religions and their priests followed. Prudence dictated that the natives, whatever their private beliefs, publicly comply with their conquerors' religion.

At first, the friars emphasized converting native chieftains and nobles who, they anticipated correctly, would bring their peoples into the Church. Baptizing natives obliged the Church to provide the sacraments of marriage, confession, communion, and confirmation that would enable new converts to live as Christians. Adult Indians, however, received only minimal instruction prior to baptism because Franciscan friars in particular focused their attention on educating children.

The young, the friars believed, would become the most effective proselytizers and advocates of Christian customs. Accordingly, they often took sons of chieftains into their convents as boarders and taught them in that environment. Basic numeric skills and learning how to speak, read, and write in Castilian constituted only part of the curriculum. Religious teaching centered on the sign of the cross, prayers, and core doctrines and beliefs of the Church, for example, the Ten Commandments, the seven sacraments, the seven deadly sins, and the importance of confession. In teaching Indian youth, friars utilized illustrated catechisms, pictures, and music. Baptized adult parishioners received instruction through repeating the catechism, listening to sermons, and attending classes in basic Christian doctrine.

The regulars founded villages (*pueblos*) to bring together Indians scattered throughout a region, segregate them from Europeans, and streamline conversion activities. Declining native population accelerated this process. The Augustinians proved particularly effective at establishing new villages complete with plaza, convent, hospital, water supply, and well-constructed residences. There the friars oversaw political and economic activities as well as religious affairs. By about 1600, Franciscans, Augustinians, and Dominicans in New Spain had established more than 250 communal residences for friars. In both Guatemala and Peru, Dominicans and Franciscans in particular established Christian *pueblos*.

A shortage of clergy, especially in remote villages, hindered evangelization. Fewer than 800 active friars resided in Mexico by 1559. In this environment, Indians combined traditional religious beliefs with Catholicism to produce local practices reflecting both sources. Additionally, regular and secular clergy fought repeatedly over jurisdiction in the *pueblos*. In remote locations, clerics frequently countenanced and at times participated in unorthodox religious activities as well as behavior that mocked their vows, including that of chastity. Not even a belief in the church's sanctity enjoyed universal acceptance. In 1611, a horrified district official in Michoacan discovered not only animals in a village church but also a local Portuguese merchant hanging cloth for sale from the crucifix and the altar in the sanctuary.

The shortage of clerics in isolated parishes facilitated imposters donning priestly garb and, presumably for a fee, providing a variety of sacraments. In a three-day period in 1565, one such charlatan celebrated two masses, heard the confessions of 100 Indians, and performed two marriages. When discovered, such frauds could be subjected to public whipping and exile from the region.

The mendicants usually introduced a lay confraternity (*cofradía*) into each indigenous community. The organization ensured the presence of mourners at members' funerals and sometimes provided a small amount of money for a widow and orphans. *Cofradía* events, especially its saint's day, enjoyed village-wide participation and joyous celebrations. The institution won rapid support and its officers typically became active associates of the friars and devotees of the Virgin Mary, whom the local elites considered their protector and a replacement for the traditional link between local gods and their lands. *Cofradía* officers often shared goals with the local friar. This partnership enabled them to become "*ladinos*" (Hispanicized Indians), which gave them more latitude to incorporate preconquest concepts into their Catholic faith. Confraternities thus emerged as a central institution and remained at the core of native communities' culture throughout the centuries of Spanish rule.

Indians frequently responded enthusiastically to evangelization. Religion had been central to indigenous life before the Conquest, and natives could not imagine existence without belief in the supernatural. In addition, they immediately recognized the Spaniards' veneration of clerics, the Cross, and images of the Virgin. The customary Spanish practice of erecting churches or at least placing crosses on pre-existing religious sites reaffirmed the locations' sacredness. In Mexico, Indian adoration of Our Lady of Guadalupe, who became the most celebrated image of the Virgin Mary, benefited from an earlier devotion to the native goddess Tonantzin. The natives perceived Guadalupe-Tonantzin as "God," much to the dismay of the Franciscans, who opposed the blended and overlapping religious beliefs and practices that came to characterize "Christianity" among the natives. Crediting Our Lady of Guadalupe with miraculous healings, Indians flocked to her sanctuary on a hill just north of Mexico City.

The Church's insistence on monogamy clashed with the polygyny common among Indian elites, especially in Mexico. Even after two generations, some Indians baptized during their youth and educated in Christian precepts still married one wife in the Church and kept other women as concubines, although this custom and resistance to monogamy faded away over time.

Among the most outstanding clerics in sixteenth-century New Spain was the Franciscan Vasco de Quiroga. He invested most of his own wealth in creating mission communities in Michoacan modeled on Sir Thomas More's *Utopia*. Natives held land communally and learned new skills based on European technology, but friars regulated their labor closely to prevent abuse. In addition to a church, the settlements provided hospitals and a wide array of social welfare benefits. Named the bishop of Michoacan in 1537, Quiroga continued to promote mission settlements. Both Jesuits and mendicants used this strategy successfully when the Christian frontier later moved north into Texas and California and south to the Río de la Plata region.

In Peru, the Dominican Vicente de Valverde and several other clerics accompanied Pizarro to Cajamarca. Franciscans and Mercedarians arrived before Atahuallpa's execution, and Augustinians appeared in 1551. However, friars in Peru failed to duplicate the intensive evangelization of New Spain's early decades. Although the disruption of civil war undoubtedly hindered efforts at conversion, it appears that the quality and enthusiasm of the early clerics in Peru paled in comparison to that of the friars in Mexico.

Religious orders spread throughout the Spanish empire, often advancing its boundaries of effective settlement. The Society of Jesus arrived in Peru in 1568 and New Spain in 1572. Quickly the Jesuits came to dominate elite education in the cities. In addition, the Society soon began to establish missions in numerous locations, from the northern frontier of Mexico to Paraguay. The first of the famous Guaraní mission villages in Paraguay was founded in 1610. By 1707, the region had 30 villages with nearly 100,000 Indians.

In Brazil, the Society of Jesus directed evangelization after Manoel da Nobrega and five other Jesuits reached Salvador in 1549; the few Franciscans already in Brazil had shown little interest in Christianizing the native population. Defeated Indians near Salvador provided the Jesuits' first converts. As in New Spain and Peru, European military successes enhanced Christianity's prestige and facilitated superficial conversion. The Jesuits concentrated the Indians in villages (*aldeias*) to maximize the evangelical potential of their small numbers. After 1557, when voluntary concentration failed, the fathers supported Governor Mem de Sá in crushing the remaining armed resistance. In 1560, more than 40,000 Indians resided in the Society's *aldeias* of Bahia alone, and by the end of the century, Brazil's 169 Jesuits controlled nearly all pacified natives. The missionaries promoted Tupí as a common language. In the *aldeias* they taught crafts, introduced new crops, and enforced European work habits and social practices—monogamy and an abhorrence of nudity, in particular. They also fostered European culture, especially music.

After the early achievements—mass baptisms and the creation of the first *aldeias*—the Jesuits realized the shallowness of the conversions. Old beliefs persisted, intermingled with Christian doctrine. By the 1560s, the fathers were venting their frustration in reports and letters. Recognizing the difficulty of converting adults, they increased their emphasis on close supervision and education of young males. When such converts denounced their elders for retaining ancient customs, the missionaries happily noted their achievement.

Missions provoked conflict between the Church and settlers. Miners, planters, and *obraje* owners coveted control over converts already accustomed to the discipline and organization of the missionaries and familiar with rudimentary European technology. Because Dominicans and Jesuits in particular worked to defend the Indians from exploitation and abuse, they continually found themselves in conflict with settlers. These pressures grew when epidemics drastically reduced the Indian population. In Brazil, for example, the Jesuit Antônio Vieira's efforts to protect the natives led to a revolt and the Society's temporary expulsion from Maranhão and Pará in 1661. Earlier, Jesuits working with the Guaraní in disputed borderlands that separated Brazil and Paraguay had armed their Indians against slave raiders from São Paulo. Forced to choose between the claims of the missionaries and those of wealthy elites in the Indies, the monarchs of both Spain and Portugal moved to restrict the Church's control over pacified Indian communities.

Portrait of San Ignacio Loyola, founder of the Society of Jesus (Jesuits)

Religious Orders in the Cities

In New Spain, mendicant orders began to emphasize placing religious houses in cities around 1570. A time of vigorous urban growth followed as Franciscans, Dominicans, Augustinians, Discalced Carmelites, and Mercedarians founded a total of 47 new houses by 1630. The Society of Jesus, which reached Mexico in 1572, also expanded rapidly as the fathers created *colegios* in numerous cities.

Painting of an anonymous Inka noblewoman identified as the first Christian convert in Peru. She was believed to have killed and beheaded a man who challenged her vow of celibacy. The image borrows heavily from the story of Judith, who was represented in Christian iconography with the head of an Assyrian general she killed to save her people.

Pizarro allocated lots to the Dominicans and the Franciscans when he founded Lima in 1535. In 1548, however, the only Franciscan convents in Peru were in Cusco, Lima, and Trujillo. A mission of Augustinians arrived in 1551. Including Mercedarians, in 1630 the mendicant orders and the Society of Jesus had 236 convents in Peru, Charcas, Quito, Buenos Aires, and Chile, with nearly 3,000 friars and fathers.

THE MATURE CHURCH

Secular or diocesan clergy made up the ecclesiastical hierarchy that extended upward from parish priests to cathedral chapters, bishops, and archbishops. Unlike mendicants—all of whom took vows of poverty and whose orders provided their subsistence—secular priests bore primary responsibility for their own financial security, an obligation that led them into numerous economic activities. Despite restrictions against engaging in wholesale or retail trade, crafts, and direct employment outside the Church, not all seculars complied.

Although present in Brazil from the first decades of Portuguese settlement, secular clergy had little influence. Indeed, the Jesuit Nobrega, a biased source to be sure, characterized the secular priests of Bahia as "irregular, apostates and excommunicates." When Bahia's first bishop arrived in 1552, he exhibited little interest in converting the natives. With fewer than 150 parishes, Bahia was Brazil's only diocese until 1676; elevated to archiepiscopal status in that year, by the late eighteenth century it had six suffragan bishoprics. Although the development of the episcopal structure accompanied an expansion in the secular clergy, approximately half of the bishops appointed in Brazil before 1800 were regulars.

In Spanish America, the establishment and spread of the episcopacy and growth in the secular clergy produced conflict with the regulars. At issue was control of the native population and its labor and income. The regulars, moreover, were justly proud of their accomplishments and loath to share the benefits with seculars, whom they considered inferior in ability and commitment. Antagonism was not limited to words. On one occasion in 1559, seculars raided the Dominican convent in Puebla, Mexico, sacked it, broke the prior's teeth, and departed with every valuable item.

Aware of the conflict between secular clergy and the orders, Philip II issued an ordinance in 1574 that increased the former's power and limited that of the latter. Eventually, secular priests took over many Indian parishes. Increasingly, mission activities by the Jesuits and the mendicants, when they occurred, took place in isolated frontier areas.

Tridentine Catholicism

The Council of Trent (1545–1563) provided the Church's response to Protestantism and a program for Catholic reform endorsed by the Spanish Crown. Its mandates sought to raise the quality of a clergy known for its ignorance, corruption, and even concubinage. For example, the council tried to promoted clerical education by ordering the creation of a seminary in every diocese. It regularized the liturgy and ceremonies and advocated the use of catechisms for instructing parishioners. It also determined what existing practices could be continued. The resulting "baroque piety" emphasized the hierarchical structure of society, communal activities, and the essential mediation of clerics and saints between individuals and God.

Among other things, Catholics encouraged numerous saints' feasts and celebrations, elaborate liturgy, popular devotions, and processions for funerals attended by all members of the deceased's brotherhoods or sodalities (*cofradías*). In 1640, one procession in Mexico City included 50 diocesan clergy and a dozen friars from each religious order, all paid for by the wealthy departed who wanted to associate himself and his family with spiritual splendor. For the rich, burial followed in a family crypt located either in the parish church or in that of a religious order; this placed the body in a privileged and consecrated setting that included sacred relics. To be wearing a Franciscan shroud, moreover, provided a form of indulgence that offered a reprieve from unspecified torments in Purgatory, according to believers.

Rich testators often created chantries to celebrate private memorial masses in perpetuity for their souls. The founder and immediate heir typically designated a family member as chaplain. This strategy retained in the family the income of the endowment, whether it had been established with cash, a gift of property, or an encumbrance on real property that pledged specified annual payments. Other pious works included the provision of dowries and burial funds and even the foundation of convents and colleges.

Baroque piety dominated Catholicism in Iberia and the Indies for more than two centuries. Ornate churches, opulent decoration in sanctuaries, elaborate funeral processions, extravagant saints' days, and the expanded creation of endowed chantries accompanied doctrinal decisions that affirmed the importance of intermediaries—clergy and saints—between believers, a single God, and heaven. Not until the latter half of the eighteenth century was there a serious challenge to these tenets.

An Economic Institution

By 1600, the Church was erecting the strongest economic base in the Indies. The expansion of commercial agriculture in New Spain, Peru, Central America, and Brazil produced unprecedented tithe revenues in the 1590s. Although the Jesuits led the way, the mendicant orders—save the Franciscans—also became active and successful landowners. In New Spain and Peru, the growth of mining and commerce after the Conquest era created excess capital that its owners dedicated, in part, to endow pious works.

As a major recipient of cash, the Church became the principal source of mortgages in the Indies, normally receiving a return of 5 or 6 percent on loans made in the sixteenth century. Because canon law forbade lending money at interest as usury, the mortgage's conditions stipulated that the recipient was buying capital instead. Not only did the Church's many branches comprise the primary fount of investment funds, but also their combined holdings made it the major owner of real estate.

Over time, its sources of revenue—tithes; fees paid for marriages, burials, and other services; gifts from the faithful; and pious works—enabled the Church and some individual clerics to become extremely wealthy. Both acquired urban and rural property. The Jesuits, most mendicant orders, and individual secular priests actively operated in the colonial marketplace, producing sugar, wine, textiles, pottery, and other products. In large cities, the Church was the most important landlord, renting property to both residential and commercial users. By employing part of its wealth and income to sustain cultural activities and welfare programs for the poor, the Church added substantially to the well-being of society.

Division Based on Place of Birth

Antagonism between Europeans and American-born clerics was an issue before the sixteenth century ended and persisted beyond independence in the early nineteenth century. Conflict focused on the highest positions, especially in the orders. European Spaniards (peninsulars) believed that Old World birth automatically made them superior to all men born in the Americas. This self-flattering characterization became a grave problem because the growing majority of native sons and other creoles threatened the peninsulars' dominance in their province's positions. The peninsulars responded by obtaining decrees that required mandatory alternation of elective offices between themselves and creoles (the *alternativa*). In mid-seventeenth-century Peru, only the Franciscans and Jesuits were not bound by this forced rotation. Beginning in the 1660s, however, the peninsular Franciscans sought, and in 1683 received, final approval to use the *alternativa*. Eventually the Franciscans in Brazil also applied the practice. Thus, the policy was the peninsulars' solution to their reduced numbers. It enshrined their continued officeholding within an order's province even when they were a small minority. More than an annoyance, this patent rejection of native sons enjoying the benefits of their majority repeatedly reminded them of Europeans' claims of superiority.

Less conflict troubled the diocesan clergy of Spanish America. American-born seculars repeatedly sought and at times secured high ecclesiastical offices. By 1640, 28 Peruvian creoles had been named archbishops (5) and bishops (23) in the New World. Although peninsulars filled almost all of these positions in the sixteenth century, creoles obtained about one-third of the total in the seventeenth century. By 1700, the 5 high-ranking prebends that constituted the cathedral chapters were a different story as native sons and other creoles enjoyed heavy representation.

The increase in native-son clerics in the seventeenth century and the Church's growing economic influence bound it to American soil in a way that the early focus on missionary activity had not. Nearly every household of the middle and upper sectors had relatives in one or more of the Church's branches. Religion had become ubiquitous in the Indies, and clerics pervaded local societies at the most fundamental level, that of the family.

The León Garavito y Illescas family illustrates this pattern. The peninsular Francisco de León Garavito prospered in Lima as a merchant, property owner, law professor, government attorney, and alderman. About 1574, he married Isabel de Illescas. The wealthy couple's sons included an *oidor* of the Audiencia of Panama, three Dominicans, a Jesuit, and a secular priest. Isabel's four sisters entered Lima's prestigious convent of La Encarnación early in the seventeenth century, and three of her daughters followed. All became nuns of the black veil, that is, full voting members of the house, and one was elected abbess.

Nunneries

The seven nuns of the Illescas and León Garavito families underscore the presence of women in ecclesiastical vocations as well as the inequality that permeated the nunneries. Convents established starting in 1540 enabled women to pursue a religious life, control their own affairs, obtain and provide education, and, in many locations, enjoy a comfortable existence. Protected from the demands of husbands and families, nuns often cultivated the arts and literature, providing a venue for the transfer of European culture. The majority of convents dated from 1570 and the number of nuns peaked in the seventeenth century. At their height, the 13 convents in Lima housed more than 20 percent of the city's women. Foundations occurred rarely after 1700; in Peru, at least, the number of nuns fell sharply beginning in the early eighteenth century.

The first convent in Brazil appeared in Salvador in 1677. Before then, small numbers of Brazilian women seeking a contemplative life entered convents in Portugal or the Azores. By the end of the eighteenth century, 3 more convents were available, but Mexico City, with 21 convents, still had proportionately twice as many nuns as Bahia.

Founded locally, the many religious orders for women in the Indies maintained only loose ties to Iberian establishments. Franciscan, Carmelite, Augustinian, and all other orders before the 1750s followed contemplative routines and lacked substantial educational or charitable roles. Nuns of the black veil, the most educated group of women in the Indies, made up the elite within each convent. Almost exclusively native daughters (locally born creoles), they entered religious life with sizable dowries and enjoyed the exclusive right to vote, serve in offices, and sing the canonical hours in the choir. In Bahia, the affluent heiress Ursula Luisa de Monserrat founded the Convent of Our Lady of Mercedes in 1735 and became its first abbess. Wealthy families commonly purchased or built quarters for their daughters and made specified donations to the houses. Although convents occasionally waived the required dowry—most frequently for young women of extraordinary musical ability—they enforced social prerequisites. In Lima's convents, for example, nuns of the black veil were daughters of socially prominent families and accordingly addressed as "Doña."

Many women in convents lacked family ties to the local social and economic elite. Nuns of the white veil served as housekeepers and performed various activities considered inappropriate for those of the black veil. Born into modest white and racially diverse families, their limited opportunities reflected the elite's perception of their social and economic inferiority. Still lower, poor, mixed-race women served the nuns of the white veil but could wear nuns' habits. With servants and black slaves also present, the convents in many ways mirrored the diverse society and inequality outside their walls.

Convents participated actively in economic life. Their residences, some occupying several city blocks, required constant repair and maintenance. Moreover, the nuns and their servants, who totaled nearly a thousand persons in some of Lima's larger convents in the seventeenth century, spent enormous sums for provisions and to provide outstanding music and accoutrements for their elite residents. In addition to their own residences and schools, nunneries owned urban property that they rented as a source of income. Wealthy convents earned capital by providing mortgages, mainly on urban properties. Unlike their male counterparts, however, the female orders normally did not engage in agricultural production.

The early presence and importance of the convents, the vigor of the Jesuits and the male mendicant orders, the size of the secular clergy, and the continued support of both residents and the Crown combined to make the Church in Latin America a powerful, wealthy, and influential institution. At times, individual clerics failed to observe their vows and connived with local officials, entrepreneurs, and landowners to exploit the Indians. A particularly horrific example was Juan Bautista de Albadán, a peninsular parish priest in Andean Peru who engaged in systematic sexual abuse of young Indian girls, gruesome torture of male opponents, and theft of his parishioners' property and labor. But the instances of abuse pale in comparison to the efforts of many clergymen to establish and maintain Christianity among the native peoples. A bastion of European culture and civilization, the Church in Latin America retained considerable strength throughout the centuries of Iberian rule.

THE INQUISITION

The Spanish Crown established tribunals of the Inquisition in Mexico City and Lima in 1569 and in Cartagena in 1610 to replace the Indies' earlier unsatisfactory episcopal or "apostolic" inquisitions headed by bishops. The fear of duplicitous converted Jews (*conversos*) had prompted the Inquisition's establishment in Spain in 1480. In the New World, the Crown authorized tribunals more to maintain the purity of the Catholic faith against heretical Protestant beliefs introduced by foreign interlopers. Nonetheless, once created, the New World tribunals periodically prosecuted "New Christians"—principally converted Portuguese Jews and their descendants—who persisted in their ancestors' faith. Their jurisdiction included Protestants and all non-Indians baptized as Christians.

The Holy Office in America paralleled its peninsular predecessors in organization and procedure. Normally a tribunal had two inquisitors, an expert who examined evidence for heresy, a prosecutor, a constable, a notary, and other officials, as necessary. In each province of its jurisdiction, investigators or commissaries who could be laymen or clerics, and lay agents, or *familiares*, arrested suspects and enforced its decrees. Although the first inquisitors were peninsulars educated in Spain, by 1640 at least one creole served on the tribunals in Mexico City and Lima. Thereafter, a sprinkling of Americans, including some native sons, secured appointments as long as the Holy Office existed.

A powerful body independent of civil and ecclesiastical hierarchies, the Inquisition unavoidably conflicted with both. Its agents' judicial privileges further enhanced the advantages of cooperation and encouraged the participation of wealthy citizens. The tribunal's policy of obtaining *familiares* well placed in local society guaranteed prominent support.

The Holy Office initiated a case after receiving a denunciation. Self-denunciation was possible, usually by an individual who anticipated lighter penance as a result, but generally a third party levied the charge. The accepted procedure was for the inquisitors to gather corroborating evidence before taking further action, a process that could drag on for years. When the evidence seemed conclusive, the tribunal's agents arrested and jailed the accused and sequestered his or her property for later auction as necessary to pay the costs of imprisonment.

Secrecy most distinguished the Inquisition's procedure from that of other tribunals. The accused remained in isolation while the case proceeded and sometimes died in confinement. Only a confession could bring absolution and reconciliation with the Church. Inquisitors repeatedly ordered the victim to confess, but initially did not inform the prisoner of the charge or identify the accuser. Although in many cases, perhaps most, the accused knew the reason for his or her arrest, a guiltless party faced formidable difficulties. Some strategies employed to demonstrate innocence included naming personal enemies or claiming inebriation or insanity.

The Inquisition prescribed punishment or penance at a private or public *auto de fé*, literally, an "act of faith." Here the condemned revealed remorse for their sins and professed hatred of heresy. Public *autos* were great spectacles that officials, clerics, nobles, and the general populace attended. During the centuries of Spanish rule, the Holy Office in America ordered death in fewer than a hundred cases, perhaps 1 percent of the total considered, all for nonrecanting heretics. Bigamy, blasphemy, and other transgressions against public morality became the tribunal's primary concerns. The principal sentences for such offenses included fines, flogging, confiscation of property, gagging, exile, and service on the galleys. Punishments became less severe as time passed. The largest *autos de fé* occurred by the mid-seventeenth century and subsequently the tribunals' importance diminished.

The Inquisition also exercised censorship in a frequently vain attempt to protect the literate populace from heresy and unorthodox ideas. Its officials searched arriving ships for prohibited literature, works listed on the Spanish *Index* of forbidden publications, and censored manuscripts before publication by a New World press. Although these activities limited the amount of protest literature that entered the Indies and slowed the publication of locally authored works, the censors' greatest interest lay in ecclesiastical materials.

Primary Source

Establishing the Inquisition in the Indies

Philip II communicated in January 1569 his decision to establish the Holy Office (Tribunal) of the Inquisition in the Indies. The document emphasizes both the monarchy's historic devotion to the Church and what the king believed to be a threat to Catholicism that only the Inquisition could address.

SOURCE: John F. Chuchiak IV, ed. and trans., *The Inquisition in New Spain, 1536–1820: A Documentary History* (Baltimore: Johns Hopkins University Press, 2012).

Having discovered and incorporated in our Royal Crown, by providence and the grace of God our Lord, the kingdoms and provinces of the Western Indies, Islands, and *Tierra Firme* of the Ocean Sea, and other parts, . . . [our glorious ancestors, faithful and Catholic children of the Holy Roman Catholic Church] put their great care in giving them the knowledge of the true God, and to strive to enlarge his Holy Evangelical law, and to conserve, free from errors and false and suspicious doctrines, and in their discoverers, settlers, children, and descendants of our vassals, the devotion, good name, reputation, fame, and the strength of care and fatigue they strove to enlarge and exalt. And because those who are outside the obedience and devotion of the Holy Roman Catholic Church, obstinate in errors and heresies, always strive to pervert and to separate from our Holy Catholic Faith, the faithful and devoted Christians, and with their malice and passion work with all effort to attract them to their wicked beliefs, communicating their false opinions and heresies, popularizing and spreading diverse condemned and heretical books; and the true remedy consists in turning aside and excluding all communication by the heretics and suspicious persons, castigating and extirpating their errors, shunning and obstructing what causes great offense to the holy faith and Catholic religion in those parts; and the natives that are perverted with the new, false, and reprobate doctrines and errors: the apostolic inquisitor general in our kingdoms and realms with the agreement of those of our Council of the General Inquisition and consulting with us, ordered and decided that the Holy Office of the Inquisition will be established and seated in those provinces.

Whether born in Iberia or the Indies, most Spaniards routinely supported the Inquisition rather than feeling personally threatened by it. *Castas* also found ways to turn the Holy Office to their advantage by claiming to be indigenous. Christians in general considered protection from heresy a worthy objective and actively reported persons who strayed too far from accepted morality. In an era in which formal political representation was absent, moreover, the Inquisition provided an alternative institution from which residents in the Americas could seek support for their own purposes, especially during its first century of existence. The political dimension of the Inquisition gave added importance to the repeated conflicts, often over seemingly trivial matters, that the inquisitors had with civil and ecclesiastical authorities.

Portugal established an effective inquisition only in 1547. Despite several tribunals in Portugal and one in Goa, none existed in Brazil. Occasionally the Portuguese Inquisition sent special agents to Brazil, but normally bishops, familiars, or other agents in the colony investigated persons accused of heresy or other offenses. Charges of bigamy, blasphemy, reading prohibited literature, and other infractions triggered investigations far more frequently than allegations of heresy. Persons considered guilty were shipped to Portugal for trial. The procedures employed were similar to those in Spain and Spanish America except that the Portuguese Inquisition may have been even harsher in its early years.

The Church provided for the spiritual life of a diverse and complex population, serving as a fundamental buttress of social stability and public order in both Spanish America and Brazil. It organized much of society's communal life through public celebrations associated with the religious calendar. By converting Indians and blacks to Christianity, it extended European cultural values; its leading role in education and public charity further emphasized its centrality in the lives of rich and poor alike.

SUGGESTIONS FOR FURTHER READING

Burns, Kathryn. *Colonial Habits: Convents and the Spiritual Economy of Cuzco, Peru.* Durham, NC: Duke University Press, 1999.

Charles, John. *Allies at Odds: The Andean Church and Its Indigenous Agents, 1583–1671.* Tucson: University of New Mexico Press, 2010.

Chuchiak, John F., IV. *The Inquisition in New Spain, 1536–1820: A Documentary History.* Baltimore: Johns Hopkins University Press, 2012.

Hyland, Sabine. *The Chankas and the Priest: A Tale of Murder and Exile in Highland Peru.* University Park: Pennsylvania State University Press, 2016.

_____. *The Jesuit and the Incas: The Extraordinary Life of Padre Blas Valera, S.J.* Ann Arbor: University of Michigan Press, 2003.

Lavrin, Asunción. *Brides of Christ: Conventual Life in Colonial Mexico.* Stanford, CA: Stanford University Press, 2008.

Mello e Souza, Laura de. *The Devil and the Land of the Holy Cross: Witchcraft, Slavery, and Popular Religion in Colonial Brazil.* Translated by Diane Grosklaus Whitty. Austin: University of Texas Press, 2004.

Melvin, Karen. *Building Colonial Cities of God: Mendicant Orders and Urban Culture in New Spain.* Stanford, CA: Stanford University Press, 2011.

Nesvig, Martin Austin (ed.). *Local Religion in Colonial Mexico.* Albuquerque: University of New Mexico Press, 2006.

Ramos, Gabriela. *Death and Conversion in the Andes: Lima and Cuzco, 1532–1670.* Notre Dame, IN: University of Notre Dame Press, 2010.

Saeger, James Schofield. *The Chaco Mission Frontier: The Guaycuruan Experience.* Tucson: University of Arizona Press, 2000.

Schroeder, Susan, and Stafford C. M. Poole (eds.). *Religion in New Spain.* Albuquerque: University of New Mexico Press, 2007.

CHAPTER 7

Language, Education, and Idolatry

CHRONOLOGY

1493	First European clerics reach the Indies
1527	First Franciscan novitiate founded in the city of Mexico
1536	First printing press arrives in the city of Mexico
1551	Crown authorizes "major" universities in city of Mexico and Lima
1562	Bishop Diego de Landa destroys hieroglyphic codices in Yucatan as sources of idolatry
1560s	Millenarian movement (Taqui Onqoy) in the central Andes
1568	Jesuits found *Colegio* of San Pablo in Lima
1570s	Native-son and other creole parish priests outnumber peninsular counterparts in the Archbishopric of Mexico
1582	Jesuits of Peru vote to prohibit mestizos from entering their society
1618	The *Colegio* of the Prince opens in Lima for young indigenous nobles
1676	Foundation of the University of San Carlos de Guatemala

INSTRUCTING THE NATIVES

Converting the indigenous population to Christianity justified Spain's presence in the Indies, but enormous challenges awaited the missionaries. Few in number, they encountered large native populations that spoke a daunting variety of languages and dialects. A friar conversant in Arawak on Española immediately discovered this linguistic knowledge was irrelevant in New Spain. If posted in Central Mexico, he had to master Otomi or Nahuatl, the language of the Mexica and a second language for many natives. But neither was useful among the monolingual Maya of Yucatan or Purepecha-speaking Tarascans of Michoacan.

On paper, the missionaries' utilization of native tongues for conversion and instruction appeared deceptively simple—learn the languages and use them to write catechisms, preach, quote the Bible, and convert the Indians. At least in theory, once the mendicants had met these objectives, secular clergy would take over the native parishes (*doctrinas*) and the friars could repeat the process among still-unconverted indigenous peoples.

In Mexico, the first Franciscans especially rose to the challenge, learned native languages, wrote bilingual dictionaries, and prepared works on the Catholic faith for other clerics' use. They also established schools and taught elite male youth the Castilian language, Christian doctrine, and Spanish values. The arrival of a printing press in 1536 helped to make supporting materials available. Between 1539 and 1580, more publications appeared in native tongues than in Castilian or in Latin. Nahuatl received the most attention because many native peoples understood it. Friars even taught it to establish a common language that would keep the natives separated from the corrupting influence of conquistadors and settlers.

An important question concerned whether to translate and publish the Bible in Nahuatl. Whereas Franciscan friars and Bishop Juan de Zumárraga favored doing so, Inquisition officials and conservative theologians in Spain disagreed. They argued that only an educated intermediary—an ordained cleric—could enable the laity to understand God's word. Spain's Supreme Tribunal of the Inquisition forbade any translation of the Bible other than Latin. When the book of Ecclesiastes appeared in an indigenous language, the Inquisition in Mexico banned it in 1577. Inquisitors considered that the risk of heresy outweighed any benefit resulting from such translation into a vernacular language.

Superficial resemblances that some native rites shared with Christianity intensified Spanish clerics' alarm over heresy. The regular clergy considered these similarities hindrances because they wanted to emphasize that the "true" faith's doctrine was very different from precontact "pagan" religious beliefs. Yet the desire to convert the natives regularly won out over inadequate linguistic ability and the resulting insufficient instruction. Indeed, without a deep understanding of a native language, the friars could realistically administer only baptism and marriage. Lacking appropriate knowledge, most "converted" Indians could adhere to these sacraments only superficially at best. Nonetheless, the early clerics generally succeeded in quickly eliminating human sacrifice, native temples, and the priests that tended them.

Although Charles V wanted the natives to learn Spanish, the religious soon opposed this directive, turning their attention to the study and the delivery of sermons in indigenous languages, for example, Quechua and Aymara in Peru. With support from subsequent monarchs, Nahuatl became a second language in Mexico for people who spoke, for example, Otomi, Tarasco, or Mixteca, as a first tongue.

The friars' protested against teaching Castilian on the grounds of insufficient time and personnel to dedicate even an hour or two daily to the task. More importantly, they realized that learning Castilian would promote Hispanicization and enable natives to communicate with Spaniards other than themselves. As a matter of policy, they wanted to keep the Indians segregated, considering other Europeans bad examples. This position made themselves indispensable intermediaries between natives and other Spaniards. Nonetheless, in New Spain by the mid-sixteenth century, draft labor requirements and local trade thwarted attempts at segregation; the relocation program of congregation also expanded the opportunities for interchange between settlers and Indians despite royal mandates to keep the two "republics" separate.

Clerics not conversant in a vernacular relied on interpreters. Fearing adverse consequences of this practice, the Provincial Church Councils held in Lima in the 1550s and 1560s mandated that clerics acquire their parishioners' language to reduce the need for go-betweens. Philip II ordered all parish priests in Peru to learn Quechua and established professorships to teach it at the University of San Marcos in Lima. Even this did not solve the problem because the faculty taught the dialect spoken by Cusco's Inka elite, and the Church used it in the trilingual catechism, confessional manual, and collection of sermons published in the mid-1580s. Since many Andeans spoke nonofficial versions of Quechua, clerics trained in the Cusco dialect could not address them intelligibly or understand their confessions. Rendering complex doctrinal points clearly in a native language that lacked appropriate synonyms proved another major hurdle. Repeatedly, Hispanicized Indians (*ladinos*) petitioned ecclesiastical courts to remove clerics unable to communicate effectively with their parishioners.

Friars' inadequate command of their parishioners' native language persisted in some locations for centuries as an incident in late eighteenth-century Guatemala illustrates. With the archbishop observing him, a Dominican proved unable to urge recipients of confirmation to wash their foreheads. Trying to help him, the prelate suggested that he give the instructions in their native tongue. The Dominican responded, "I already told them in their language, but they don't understand it."[1]

INDIANS IN THE CLERGY?

An alternative to training bilingual Spanish clerics was to educate Indians, teach them Castilian, and allow them to enter the priesthood. Accordingly, in 1536 Franciscans in New Spain opened the Colegio of Santa Cruz in Tlatelolco for young nobles. They sought to educate a Catholic laity, train a native clergy, and prepare linguists and translators who could assist illiterate natives in understanding scripture and the liturgy. Among other subjects, the students learned reading, writing, music, Latin, and philosophy. Some mastered Latin sufficiently to translate it into Castilian and Nahuatl. Despite, or perhaps because of, the students' excellence and trilingual training, the Dominicans opposed the project. Their objections led to the school's failure and their insistence brought the formal prohibition of Indian ordination from 1555 to 1591. Subsequently, unofficial discrimination ensured the natives' permanent inferiority in the Mexican Church. Inequality thus permeated the Church's practices, as it did society as a whole.

Despite the failure of the Colegio of Santa Cruz, attempts to educate Indian nobles persisted. Native elites welcomed this instruction because they fully understood the power of language and the opportunities that alphabetic literacy, mastery of Castilian, and the accompanying Hispanicization could provide for their sons. By the late 1540s, a Franciscan school in Merida, Yucatan, attracted numerous students. After a *cacique* acquired Latin, he, in turn, became a translator. Each new Franciscan mission opened a school for noble Maya boys who learned the Latin alphabet and the skills of reading and writing along with singing and praying. Alumni became scribes, choirmasters, *caciques*, and governors. Within a decade, alphabetized Maya appeared in land documents. Despite literacy in Castilian, however, for decades indigenous nobles continued to use hieroglyphic script as a form of resistance. Spanish clerics viewed natives' codices as sources of idolatry and, starting in the early 1560s, destroyed the ones they found. This hostile attitude encouraged nobles to perpetuate their documentation via alphabetic script that helped to mask its content.

By the close of the sixteenth century, friars tried to eradicate the use of hieroglyphics by educating commoners rather than nobles in Castilian. Accompanying this shift, Spanish officials sought to replace Maya village governments with Spanish municipal councils (*cabildos*) and to displace the traditional Maya elite from their most prominent posts, including that of *batab* or *cacique*. But elite Maya proved resilient and used their literacy to gain and retain possession of the councils' office of notary/scribe (*escribano*). Unlike Spaniards, they considered the position on par with the local governorship, a post that Spanish officials worked to remove from their possession with some success. As the friars' original enthusiasm succumbed to mundane pursuits, noble Maya *escribanos* trained their successors, perpetuating and effectively limiting literacy to villages' social and political elites.

In Lima, the *Colegio* of the Prince (*El Colegio del Príncipe*) opened in 1618 as a boarding school. It offered six years of study during which young indigenous nobles learned the Castilian language, music, and religious doctrine away from possible contamination by idolaters. The founders expected graduates to return to their home parishes, where they would assist *corregidores* and clerics. A similar institution opened in Cusco in 1621 to serve sons of Inka nobles in the region. *Kurakas* sent their heirs to these schools to strengthen their recognition as members of the elite worthy of education equal to that of Spaniards. This occurred despite a 1582 prohibition against ordaining either Andeans or mestizos, although the latter had learned their mother's native Quechua or Aymara along with the Christianity of their Spanish fathers. By the mid-seventeenth century, however, creoles had largely displaced the future *kurakas* in these schools. Most Andeans attended only to remain eligible to succeed their fathers in office. Royal orders starting in 1691 allowed ordination of Indian nobles and authorized them to solicit the same positions as Spaniards. But even this additional opportunity failed to fill the classrooms.

The early prohibition against Indian ordination meant the continued use of conversion methods employed by the early mendicants. Friars serious about evangelization learned the language spoken in their parish and used catechisms, pictures, music, plays, and interpreters to instruct not only unconverted natives, but also those who had received baptism before learning even the rudiments of Christianity. Initially, what Indians needed to know before receiving the sacraments—baptism, marriage, confession, penitence, communion, confirmation, and extreme unction—was itself a matter of bitter dispute. The Christian belief in monogamous marriage also posed a serious problem in societies in which elite males routinely took multiple wives.

Despite the bias and long prohibition against Indian ordination, additional possibilities for recruiting clerics existed. One was to provide the requisite education to mestizos, free mulattoes, and other *castas* who had grown up speaking a native tongue. By 1568, however, the Mercedarians, Franciscans, and Dominicans in Peru had prohibited mestizos from taking vows. The newly arrived Jesuits, in contrast, included them in their first class of novices, primarily because they knew native languages and customs. Among them was Blas Valera, the first mestizo Jesuit in the bishopric of Lima. The gifted son of a Spanish conquistador and an indigenous mother, Valera taught Quechua, but emphasized commonalities between Catholicism and Inka religious beliefs. Considered heretical, his approach led to his exile to Spain. In 1582, the Jesuits of Peru voted to permanently prohibit mestizos from entering their ranks because of their inability to abandon native customs. Additionally, they agreed to admit few native sons or other creoles. As expressed by Father José de Acosta, "Experience has shown that most of these [mestizos] impede the faith more with their corrupt customs than aid it with their skilled tongues."[2] Nonetheless, Acosta worked with Lima's archbishop Toribio de Mogrovejo at the Third Lima Council to approve the inclusion of mestizos, provided they be restricted to serving only in Indian parishes (*doctrinas*). The Mercedarians ultimately proved to be key supporters of mestizo ordination in Peru.

In contrast to Peru, the Church in Mexico never admitted mestizos to the ministry on a regular basis. In 1578, Philip II warned the archbishop against allowing them or other unsuitable candidates to enter holy orders. Later in the century, however, the Crown authorized the ordination of mestizos of legitimate birth, ability, and appropriate education. Although subsequent legislation ordered diocesan seminaries to admit a significant minority of mestizos and also Indians, primarily men of Spanish ancestry filled the clergy.

Native-Son Clerics

Qualified native sons and other creoles who had learned a native language from Indian nursemaids and household servants formed an important pool of potential clerics to serve in Indian parishes. Their bilingual skills gave them an advantage when the Crown emphasized the ability to use an indigenous tongue. Beginning in 1575, competitors for positions as parish priests in Mexico had to document their Old Christian ancestry (*limpieza de sangre*), validate by examination their skill in either Nahuatl or Otomi, and demonstrate knowledge of moral theology and administration of the sacraments. The language requirement complemented the 1574 Ordinance of Royal Patronage's reiteration that descendants of the conquistadors and early settlers were to be favored for appointments.

No later than the 1570s, native-son and other creole parish priests surpassed in number their peninsular counterparts in the Archbishopric of Mexico. The ranks of the locally born Spaniards continued to increase. By the early seventeenth century, more than 95 percent of the priests in the diocese of Guatemala had been born within its boundaries; this near monopolization continued for the remainder of Spanish rule. In Charcas, American-born priests began to outnumber peninsulars in the decade 1611–1620, and in the 1640s, native sons exceeded clerics from all other regions combined. In Cusco, creoles accounted for 85 percent of the secular parish priests in 1657. Since few diocesan clergy from Spain had any interest in serving poor rural communities, the royal policy of favoring native sons for parish benefices ultimately succeeded almost by default.

In the 1570s, debate about who should serve indigenous parishes (*doctrinas*) flared up in the Viceroyalty of Peru. The archdeacon of Quito's cathedral chapter complained that most peninsular friars could not speak their parishioners' language. At the same time, the appointment of Spanish-born mendicants limited bilingual sons of the conquistadors and early settlers from obtaining benefices. Complementing this criticism, the city's representative argued that native-son, secular clergy in the diocese should enjoy preference to clerics from Spain. A royal order in 1583 specified that diocesan priests should fill empty indigenous parishes in Peru, but mendicant protests led to the policy's suspension five years later.

Indios ladinos

Clerics unskilled in a native language relied on interpreters drawn from "*indios ladinos,*" Indians able to communicate easily in Castilian and bridge Spanish and indigenous cultures in word and often in dress. Such men served as *fiscal de iglesia,* every Indian village's most important parish office other than that of priest. The position carried extensive assignments in day-to-day operations and the authority to act for the priest in many nonsacramental capacities.

The priest would often charge the *fiscal* to teach children to read, write, and count in Castilian, collect fees from parishioners, and note transgressions by members of the flock. Whether of noble or commoner descent, the *ladino* learned church law and practice, court procedures, and legal sources useful in litigation. Abusive, exploitive, or simply incompetent clerics discovered at times that *indios ladinos* were employing their bilingual skills, knowledge, and positions against them. Moreover, some *fiscales de iglesia* in Peru used their positions to promote Andean religious practices in private while they appeared as the priest's assistant in public. Few, however, wrote in Quechua or other native languages, a notable difference from counterparts in Mexico, many of whom penned documents in Nahuatl.

Native assistants who filed suits against their parish priests often emphasized that the clerics exploited parishioners through mandatory "donations" and illegal business operations; collected fees for marriages, baptisms, funerals, and feasts;

and engaged in immoral behavior that included gambling, smoking before mass, and spending time with women. Furthermore, priests neglected their parish spiritually through failure to administer sacraments, such as providing last rites to a dying infant. Monolingual clerics in particular eschewed their obligation to teach Christian doctrine. In addition, the assistants complained about the priests' violent behavior toward them, such as subjecting them to whippings and sometimes shaming by cutting off their hair. Some priests sold appointments to parish offices, a practice that both enriched them and placed pressure on the purchasers to exploit other natives for personal gain. Between 1570 and 1618, the number of officials who worked only for a priest increased eightfold or more. This trend concerned the Crown because these officials avoided both taxation and service in labor drafts, thus providing an incentive to serve in parish positions and increase their number.

Preparation for the Secular Clergy

Whereas *encomenderos* could be illiterate—as many were—clerics needed to be able to read, write, and apply basic mathematical skills. As immigrants who had sought a better life for themselves, conquistadors and early settlers also wanted to provide benefits for their sons. The desire to qualify them for entry into religious orders, benefices, prebends, and prelatures, as well as royal positions, underlined the need for accessible formal education. In its absence, Spanish fathers arranged as best they could for their sons to learn the basic skills of literacy. Initially they hired private tutors or clerics to teach Latin because of its use in administering the sacraments, its role as the academic skill requirement for university admission, and its importance as the common language of intellectuals and many authors. Although a few wealthy peninsulars sent sons to Spain for their education, most fathers considered the cost prohibitive and supported the establishment of schools (*colegios*) and universities where they resided.

Prior to ordination, aspirants for the secular clergy needed to meet requirements that included legitimate birth and Old Christian ancestors, virtuous personal habits, literacy in Latin, and a formal education. Increasingly, candidates completed a baccalaureate degree and studied theology for four years. These credentials enabled them to pass a public examination in moral theology. A few priests also boasted advanced degrees, an asset when seeking a position on a cathedral chapter or as bishop.

Usually a candidate progressed from minor orders through the major orders of subdeacon, deacon, and presbyter or priest, the last allowing him to say mass. Licenses to hear confession, to administer baptism, last rights, and other sacraments, and to preach qualified the candidate for the priesthood. Ordination followed, generally when the candidate was in his early to mid-twenties, but did not guarantee he would assume a parish. Without the income of a benefice, many of the ordained served as assistants and temporary replacements for beneficed clergy and others became chaplaincy priests saying memorial masses.

FORMAL EDUCATION

Paper undergirded Spain's empire. The increase of university-trained lawyers or *letrados* in royal administration accompanied an expansion of positions in the Americas. This sixteenth-century upsurge in opportunities encouraged the growth of universities in Castile and their creation in the Indies. Implementation of the Council of Trent's more stringent requirements for clerical schooling spurred higher education to new heights. Prior to Trent, a literate young man with knowledge of basic prayers could enter the lowest level of the priesthood, but advancement required demonstrated mastery of Latin and the liturgy. Although bishops and archbishops had routinely founded cathedral schools, Trent charged them to establish a seminary in each diocese.

Frequently, religious orders provided schools for parishioners and other students. The Dominicans started some early *colegios* or secondary schools and even a university in Santo Domingo. The Franciscans founded the first of the regulars' novitiates in New Spain with studies in Latin grammar, philosophy, and theology for the preparation of new friars. As in Europe, the Society of Jesus provided educational institutions of exceptional importance for native-son elites. A few creole alumni continued their studies in Spain, but many more attended universities established in America.

The Jesuits specialized in making high-quality education available without cost to the students. Soon after arriving in a city, they would establish one or more schools. In Lima, they opened the *Colegio* of San Pablo in 1568. By the end of the sixteenth century, civil authorities awarded it a monopoly over instruction in the humanities, making it the official preparatory institution for the University of San Marcos. Jesuits taught the same curriculum in America as in Iberia and much of Europe, thus ensuring a comparable education. In addition, they offered instruction in Quechua. San Pablo grew to some 500 students in the early seventeenth century and served 1,000 or more boys annually between the 1660s and the 1760s. The Jesuit *colegio* in Bahia had 215 students by 1589 and offered a curriculum that extended from reading, writing, and arithmetic to the study of theology.

After completing San Pablo's course of study, students by 1592 could proceed to one of Lima's other educational institutions. The Royal *Colegio* of San Martín founded in 1582 was the Jesuits' most important facility in the City of Kings for the study of arts, grammar, and Latin. Students could enter at the age of 12 and remain until 24; some resided at the college and a few scholarships were available. Student matriculation at San Martín demonstrated, not surprisingly, that beginning in the late sixteenth century, native sons and other creoles always outnumbered peninsulars. Over time, the increased identification of the American-born pupils as nobles ("*dons*") documented a higher social status attributed to them, whereas the number of peninsular students declined.

The Royal *Colegio Mayor* of San Felipe, a residential facility established in 1592 under royal patronage, housed 16 young men pursuing work in arts, philosophy, civil or canon (Church) law, or theology. Its founder created San Felipe specifically for "sons, grandsons and descendants of conquistadors and settlers" of Peru and others of appropriate merit and service. Explicitly articulating social inequality, its constitution forbade the admission of persons from the lower class, those punished by the Inquisition, mulattoes and *zambos*, the offspring of Indians and blacks. Students pursuing a religious vocation could enroll in the Royal *Colegio*–Seminary of Santo Toribio, named for the future saint Toribio de Mogrovejo, who founded it in 1590 while he was the archbishop of Lima. The school offered programs in theology and sacred scripture; lay students could also study civil and canon law.

The municipal councils of the first viceregal capitals lobbied successfully for universities. Mexico City sought one in the 1530s and Viceroy Antonio de Mendoza supported the request. In January 1550, Lima requested that the recently created Dominican *colegio* be turned into a university. The Crown acceded and in 1551 authorized universities in both capitals to benefit "the sons of the citizens"; females had no opportunity for higher education anywhere in the Indies or Spain.

The Royal and Pontifical University of Mexico held its first classes in 1553, in part as a result of efforts by Archbishop Juan de Zumárraga, who had previously opened a seminary. The Royal and Pontifical University of San Marcos replaced its Dominican predecessor in the 1570s. Both offered degrees in the five faculties that characterized a "major" university: arts or philosophy, medicine, theology, and civil and canon law. Admission required proficiency in Latin—the ability to read, write, and understand it—because the faculty delivered lectures and made assignments in that language. The bachelor of arts degree was somewhat akin to a modern high school diploma and mandatory for subsequent study in every faculty.

In Spain, sons of poor *hidalgos* often attended universities. In contrast, students at the University of San Marcos often came from well-to-do families of local oligarchies that included *encomenderos*, owners of substantial properties, high-ranking officials, and wholesale merchants. Earning a degree in civil or canon law and approval to practice law before the *audiencia* required five years for the baccalaureate plus four years of postbaccalaureate training with an approved attorney. A small number of baccalaureate recipients subsequently secured a higher degree.

Eventually, every major city in Spanish America except Buenos Aires had a university under either royal auspices or a religious order. As a result, native sons ultimately enjoyed educational opportunity in numerous locations. In Guatemala, for example, Dominican, Franciscan, and Mercedarian friaries taught philosophy by the 1570s and at least the Franciscans offered scholastic theology by the following decade. The diocesan seminary to educate secular clergy opened in 1597 and the long-desired University of San Carlos de Guatemala followed in 1676.

An earned baccalaureate degree separated native-son and other creole recipients from nearly all peninsulars in both Castile and the Indies. Americans with the advanced licentiate and doctorate degrees stood out even more. Higher education thus enabled native sons to compete with peninsulars as well as among themselves. Graduates in theology, scripture, and canon law quickly availed themselves of employment opportunities in the Church.

The number of educated native sons and other creoles aspiring to ecclesiastical vocations increased, and the composition of the clergy changed. By the early seventeenth century, Spaniards born in the Indies had gained prominence in both the secular clergy and at least several of the regular orders. Although a few well-placed *castas* and Indians initially enjoyed limited educational opportunities, universities, colleges, and even primary schools later excluded them. Educators in Lima imposed this restriction in the 1640s, despite the Jesuits' resistance. The lack of a university in Brazil limited the number of native sons who obtained ecclesiastical positions.

Natives' Informal Acquisition and Use of Written Language

The formal educational system of *colegios* favored the sons of native rulers and nobles, but informal means of learning alphabetic writing existed as well. These included apprenticeships with native scribes/notaries (*escribanos*) and other local municipal officials and instruction by priests and their native assistants. Over the first century of Spanish rule, knowledge of alphabetic writing and appreciation of its importance, for example, in keeping records, extended beyond the indigenous ruling class. Ambitious commoners recognized opportunities to become interpreters, scribes/notaries, and priests' assistants for those with bilingual oral and written language skills. In Lima, the most important post an Indian could obtain was interpreter general to the Audiencia of Lima, a position that made him the intermediary between the court and native society. In New Spain, the ability to write alphabetically in Nahuatl or another indigenous language became necessary for village notaries and other officials. Since indigenous-language materials required translation into Castilian for use as evidence in court, every tribunal in New Spain used one or more interpreters.

CAMPAIGNS TO EXTIRPATE "IDOLATRY"

Despite initial claims of success, clerics in numerous locations of the Indies soon faced the disturbing reality that neither early nor continuous efforts to Christianize the Indians had yielded the anticipated results. Despite recitation of catechisms and prayers, in many places Indians continued at least some precontact religious practices. To eliminate what they identified as pagan customs and beliefs, clerics destroyed native "idols" along with related paraphernalia, historical sources, and records. In some cases, they resorted to horrendous torture and a wide repertoire of punishments. A guilty verdict in court meant that both the prosecutor and the defendant agreed that the latter had confessed to an idolatrous action, words, or belief. The accused convicted themselves through acknowledging that they had knowingly participated in forbidden practices.

The Franciscan Diego de Landa led a major sixteenth-century campaign of persecution against traditional religious practices in Yucatan. His extirpation efforts culminated in 1562 with an enormous *auto de fé* in which he ceremoniously burned some 20,000 idols and other items, including several dozen Maya codices.

Accused of usurping royal jurisdiction and the bishop's authority, Landa defended himself against charges of employing excessive harshness against the Maya. After a decade, he returned from Spain as Yucatan's second bishop. A new round of extirpation commenced, complete with torture, harsh punishments, summary judgments without appropriate judicial procedure, and more prosecutions than before. Faced with his relentless persecution, many Maya resisted by fleeing into the forest. The campaign abated only after Landa's death in 1579. In Peru, the first Council of Lima in 1551 launched a full-scale assault on surviving Inka religious activities. Declaring all Andeans who had died before the conquest to be in Hell, the council vigorously attacked the worship of *huacas* and ancestors. Priests and government officials henceforth destroyed *huacas* and burned mummies whenever possible, but natives resisted as well.

In the province of Huamanga, Peru, a nativist religious movement in the 1560s called on Andeans to purify themselves of their Christian teaching and return to their own gods and religious practices. Known as Taqui Onqoy, its adherents asserted that the *huacas*, angry at being deserted for Catholicism, had brought epidemics from which the only escape was a restoration of traditional religious beliefs. Itinerant dancers and preachers believed that a forthcoming life-or-death struggle between Europeans and Andeans would bring the demise of the former and all but the purified among the latter. Ominously, the leaders called on natives to refuse to pay tribute or serve in the labor drafts (*mita*). The Spaniards launched a two-year anti-idolatry campaign against this religion-based resistance that resulted in more than 8,000 arrests and the collapse of the movement.

Broadly defined idolatry, often found in conjunction with Christian beliefs and practices, stimulated extirpation campaigns until the mid-eighteenth century. Their undeniable harshness and cruelty can easily obscure the accompanying efforts to instill Christian beliefs and practices. Published guides directed extirpators to engage in intense daily teaching and preaching while also searching for evidence of idolatry. Despite continued problems of communication in local dialects, the priests employed a multipronged approach that included teaching doctrine, delivering sermons, and administering sacraments. They also used the catechism, music, pictures, and sometimes plays as they sought to instill Christian beliefs and practices to displace what they defined as idolatry.

In Yucatan, extirpation campaigns occurred in three periods: 1572–1579, 1636–1714, and 1716–1827. In the first, led by Bishop Landa, clerics optimistically believed that they could eliminate precontact religious practices. In the second, bishops largely turned over the campaign to the chief judge of the see's episcopal court; during this period, clerics continued to believe that they could eradicate an ever more broadly defined "idolatry." In the final period, the now-disillusioned clergy gave up on the possibility of uprooting traditional Maya idolatry and delegated extirpation to parish assistants who classified as idolatry all traditional Maya practices.

Mexico avoided the lengthy and repeated campaigns that occurred in Peru and among the Maya of Yucatan. Local priests engaged in attempts to eliminate

Primary Source

Abuse by Clerics

Jorge Juan and Antonio de Ulloa, two young peninsular Spaniards, accompanied a French scientific expedition to Ecuador in 1735 and spent some time in Peru before returning to Spain. At the request of the royal minister Marquis of Ensenada, they (primarily Ulloa) wrote a confidential report on conditions they had found, with particular emphasis on Peru. As part of a broad-brush condemnation of the behavior of royal and religious authorities, they outlined numerous abuses by clerics that included lewd behavior, living with concubines, operating a textile manufactory within the church building itself, and gouging the native population for administering sacraments. The selection below identifies clerical greed in providing burials.

SOURCE: Jorge Juan and Antonio de Ulloa, *Discourse and Political Reflections on the Kingdoms of Peru*, ed. John J. TePaske, trans. John J. TePaske and Besse A. Clement (Norman: University of Oklahoma Press, 1978), 109.

> If the clergy treat the Indians badly while they are still alive, they also treat them pitilessly when they die. In the first place they allow the bodies of the dead to be left in the streets, ripped apart by dogs, and devoured by vultures. Showing no compassion when they receive nothing for burial charges, they do not even provide a grave for the body. . . . If the deceased leaves some property, however, the priest ultimately becomes the sole heir, taking the dead man's oxen and sheep and despoiling his wife, children, and brothers of everything. Although the heirs might complain and their fiscal protector might demand an accounting, the priest protects himself by showing a bill for a memorial service, tolling the bells, and the Masses he has said for the dead man. Thus, he is absolved of their charges.
>
> The miserable condition of the Indians stems from their abuse at the hands of the clergy, the heavy burdens imposed on them by the corregidores, and the bad treatment they generally receive from Spaniards. To escape from oppression and to break the bonds of slavery, many have rebelled and fled to unconquered territory in order to continue in their barbarous, heathen ways.

what they considered idolatry, but the episcopacy refrained from launching the type of centrally directed campaigns employed in Peru. In any case, by the mid-eighteenth century, the vigor and rigor that the Church once applied to conversion and education had largely waned, save perhaps in some frontier regions. The Crown's reliance on the Church as a partner in the Indies had diminished as well.

The Church faced enormous obstacles in realizing its goal of converting the indigenous population of the Americas to Christianity. The Spanish Crown allocated resources to support evangelization and minister to the spiritual needs of all groups in society, but a paucity of clerics hampered its efforts. Despite the creation of schools, seminaries, and universities in the Indies and the use of printing presses to publish and reprint religious materials, clerics never fully met the challenge of multiple indigenous languages and dialects. Linking race, legitimacy, and place of birth to educational and employment opportunities limited the pool of potential clerics. Clerical abuse and exploitation as well as campaigns to extirpate idolatry served to alienate parishioners. Nonetheless, Post-Tridentine Catholic beliefs and practices modified by a multitude of local variations ultimately took root with a vast majority of the non-Iberian population of the Indies.

NOTES

1. Adriaan C. van Oss, *Catholic Colonialism: A Parish History of Guatemala, 1524–1821* (Cambridge: Cambridge University Press, 2002), 18.
2. Sabine Hyland, *The Jesuit and the Incas: The Extraordinary Life of Padre Blas Valera, S.J.* (Ann Arbor: University of Michigan Press, 2003), 69.

SUGGESTIONS FOR FURTHER READING

Borah, Woodrow. *Justice by Insurance: The General Indian Court of Colonial Mexico and the Legal Aides of the Half-Real.* Berkeley and Los Angeles: University of California Press, 1983.

Griffiths, Nicholas. *The Cross and the Serpent: Religious Repression and Resurgence in Colonial Peru.* Norman: University of Oklahoma Press, 1996.

Hyland, Sabine. *The Jesuit and the Incas: The Extraordinary Life of Padre Blas Valera, S.J.* Ann Arbor: University of Michigan Press, 2003.

Metcalf, Alida C. *Go-betweens and the Colonization of Brazil, 1500–1600.* Austin: University of Texas Press, 2005.

Mills, Kenneth. *Idolatry and Its Enemies: Colonial Andean Religion and Extirpation, 1640–1750.* Princeton, NJ: Princeton University Press, 1997.

Ramos, Gabriela, and Yanna Yannakakis (eds.). *Indigenous Intellectuals: Knowledge, Power, and Colonial Culture in Mexico and the Andes.* Durham, NC: Duke University Press, 2014.

Ruiz Medrano, Ethelia, and Susan Kellogg (eds.). *Negotiation within Domination: New Spain's Indian Pueblos Confront the Spanish State.* Boulder: University Press of Colorado, 2010.

Távarez, David. *The Invisible War: Indigenous Devotions, Discipline, and Dissent in Colonial Mexico.* Stanford, CA: Stanford University Press, 2011.

Yannakakis, Yanna. *The Art of Being In-between: Native Intermediaries, Indian Identity, and Local Rule in Colonial Oaxaca.* Durham, NC: Duke University Press, 2008.

CHAPTER 8

Economies and Trade

EARLY TRIBUTE

Castilian rulers assumed that Spaniards in their overseas realms would engage in economic production, participate in trade, and provide royal income. Early settlers took for granted the centrality of native labor and tribute; only the terms of exploitation required resolution. When conquistadors reached the American mainland, they expected to rely on *repartimiento/encomienda* and native slavery. Since the Crown had started to regulate labor, travel, and trade and secure tax revenue from mining, the potential benefits of the Indies looked promising.

Conquistadors and early settlers on the mainland initially sought gold, as had their predecessors in the Caribbean islands. A few proved successful, but silver was more plentiful, although less valuable. In general, Spaniards willingly advanced into unknown regions regardless of the perils, but most rejected the hard physical work of mining. Their behavior broadcast an intention to leave all unskilled labor to conquered peoples and African slaves.

Successful conquistadors expected appropriate rewards to cover their debts for arms and provisions as well as to provide a comfortable life. Bernal Díaz del Castillo groused years later that, after the distributions to the king and Fernando Cortés, "very little remained for each share, and because it was so little, many soldiers did not want to accept it."[1] Caribbean precedent emphasized reward with grants of indigenous labor and tribute, in short, an *encomienda*.

Charles V's instructions to Cortés in 1523 facilitated future exploitation by requiring natives to deliver "each year as much revenue and tribute as were given and paid until now to their priests and lords."[2] The emperor reasoned that "it is just and reasonable that Our pacified and obedient Indian vassals should serve Us and give tribute in recognition of Our sovereignty and labor which they owe Us as vassals."[3] He subsequently agreed, however, that for one generation, conquistadors and early settlers might receive *encomiendas* in exchange for Christianization and protection of their Indians against abuse.

In the 1520s, some Mixteca in *encomiendas* turned over gold that had adorned temples, palaces, and tombs as well as what they had panned or mined. Mostly, however, indigenous peoples supplied finished cloth, cotton, cacao, cochineal, maize, turkeys, and other foodstuffs, items that the *encomenderos* could sell in the markets of central Mexico. The introduction of wheat and silk expanded the tribute items collected in the 1540s. Raising livestock, especially sheep and goats, proved another source of income.

In Peru, Francisco Pizarro complemented the distribution of Atahuallpa's "ransom" with awards of *encomiendas* to supporters. Post-Cajamarca arrivals Cristóbal Pérez and his son received an allocation of labor and tribute that included some 1,500 Indians in the Colca Valley northwest of Arequipa. Pizarro conferred the grant in 1535 with an understanding that the recipients would use some of the labor for gold mining. *Encomenderos'* enthusiasm for profiting from "their Indians" far outweighed their interest in Christianizing them. In one of many attempts to end rampant exploitation and abuse of the natives, the Crown in 1563 prohibited *encomenderos* from living among their Indians.

Spaniards originally defined tribute as including personal service. Regularly ignoring prohibitions, they forced their Indians to serve as beasts of burden, construct buildings, and grow specified crops. The religious made similar demands and uncompensated native labor built the churches in Indian pueblos. Similarly, viceregal authorities insisted that natives provision the emerging city of Mexico. In the 1530s, *encomenderos*, officials, and clerics demanded labor for agriculture, raising stock, and mining. Tributaries constructed roads, canals, houses, churches, and other buildings, using materials they often had to furnish. They also transported merchandise, agricultural products, and personal effects. For young women, domestic service frequently included acquiescence to sexual demands.

In locales with a tradition of artisanal production, indigenous specialists could sometimes practice their craft. Imported black slaves also benefited from such prior knowledge. Spanish artisans trained and used indigenous and black apprentices in Old World methods that complemented their skills and increased their value. Women continued to weave cloth after the Spaniards' arrival, but much of their production flowed to *encomenderos* for subsequent sale.

THE EVOLUTION OF LABOR SYSTEMS

Expeditions to enslave natives spread from the Caribbean to the mainland. They turned some regions into wastelands, particularly where the indigenous population itself was the sole identifiable source of wealth. No location suffered more than Central America, where precontact slavery had long existed and Spaniards had gathered slaves even before 1519. The natives in Honduras rose against the intruders, thereby providing justification for seizing them as "slaves of war." The ubiquitous and brutal conquistador Pedro de Alvarado allegedly forced 1,500 of these captives to work in the region's mines. Preparing to depart for Peru, he authorized all of his men to take enslaved natives to that important market. In the decade before the New Laws of 1542 again banned native enslavement, Spaniards likely exported more than 100,000 and perhaps as many as 200,000 slaves from Nicaragua.

Although less important than in Central America, indigenous slavery imposed by conquistadors also scarred central Mexico and Andean Peru. Cortés and Nuño de Guzmán were but two leaders who captured numerous natives during their campaigns. In the northern Mexico frontier, war often served as a pretext for enslavement as late as the eighteenth century. When the natives refused to settle where Spaniards wanted, the latter attacked them and sold the captives for mining labor in Parral or elsewhere. Similarly, in distant Chile, soldiers considered a royal authorization of 1608 to enslave captives a license for enrichment. Although the Crown soon revoked this permission, dependence on forced native labor persisted.

The precipitous decline of indigenous populations that followed the arrival of ever more Spaniards and Portuguese stimulated repeated royal injunctions to treat the natives with Christian humanity. Spurred by the Dominicans in general and Fray Bishop Bartolomé de Las Casas in particular, Charles V tried again to terminate *encomienda* because its abolition would solve three interrelated problems: the need to protect the new Christian vassals from abuse; the continued desire to prevent the emergence of a genuine nobility modeled on that of Castile; and the political necessity of providing access to labor to settlers who arrived after the initial distributions.

The New Laws of 1542 ordered both an end to native slavery and the elimination of *encomienda* as an institution of labor and tribute on the death of current *encomenderos*. The laws also documented the royal desire to terminate a reward intimately related to high noble status in Spain. No officials were to reassign escheated *encomiendas*, that is, those that had reverted to the Crown. Additionally, the legislation promised to increase direct royal oversight of the indigenous population and thus implicitly encouraged later-arriving Spaniards to anticipate access to native labor. Unrewarded conquistadors and their sons expected to benefit from appointments as provincial officials (*corregidores*); widows and daughters might receive pensions assigned from the tribute of escheated *encomiendas*.

The New Laws enraged *encomenderos*. They envisioned their families and heirs deprived of the natives who provided status, income, and a source of capital to invest in mining, agriculture, livestock, commerce, and other means of income. In Peru, the legislation sparked a civil war between disaffected *encomenderos* and the Crown that ultimately resulted in the surrender and execution of Gonzalo Pizarro, his lieutenants, and several dozen other leaders. Royal officials sentenced some 350 rebels to galley service and exiled another 700 from Peru.

In New Spain, Viceroy Mendoza agreed to delay implementation of the New Laws following a show of opposition. The *encomenderos* sent a deputation to argue before the Council of the Indies that the Crown should both suspend the anti-*encomendero* provisions in the New Laws and grant *encomiendas* in perpetuity. Although they failed to gain these major concessions, they did obtain repeal of the prohibition against succession for a second generation. The Crown's retreat was tactical because it had established the principle that royal permission was necessary for additional extension of the grants. Furthermore, it separated labor from tribute and forbade the former being considered part of the latter.

The Crown's action opened the way for rotating labor drafts known in New Spain as *repartimientos* to provide workers in agriculture, mining, and other purposes considered in the public interest. In Peru, the subsequent assignment of workers for the silver mines and mills of Potosí institutionalized exploitation in a rotating draft labeled the *mita* (a Spanish term for an Inka institution known as *mit'a*) employed on an unprecedented scale. Drawing on 16 Andean provinces between Cusco and Potosí, in 1573 Viceroy Francisco de Toledo (1569–1581) created an annual draft that peaked at more than 13,000 tributaries assigned to serve one year of seven at the famous "red mountain" of present-day Bolivia. Other *mitayos* (*mita* laborers) would mine mercury at Huancavelica and silver elsewhere.

The continued decline of New Spain's indigenous population into the 1620s rendered labor drafts inadequate for estate owners (*hacendados*) with crops to plant, weed, and harvest. Turning to nearby villages, they hired seasonal laborers at higher wages than *repartimiento* workers received. When the Crown eliminated draft labor for agriculture in 1632, the transition to free wage labor was nearly complete and some workers already resided on haciendas. Employers sometimes tried to retain workers through debt peonage, but laborers often resisted by fleeing. Only in the nineteenth century did this form of servitude truly tie debtors to landed estates.

DOMESTIC ECONOMIES AND REGIONAL TRADE

Following a conquest, Spanish settlers received land grants for cultivating crops and raising livestock. The resulting agricultural and animal products underpinned domestic economies throughout the empire. Although the invaders insisted on raising and consuming wheat wherever possible, indigenous populations accustomed to growing maize continued to do so. Vital regional crops included potatoes, beans, and manioc. Also known as cassava and yucca, manioc was a dietary staple in the Bahia region of Brazil, where it was rendered into a starchy, filling flour through a process that removed deadly prussic acid. Animal husbandry arrived with the Spaniards except for camelids and guinea pigs in Peru and some turkeys and barkless dogs in Mexico. Indigenous populations preferred chickens to quadrupeds, perhaps because the latter damaged their crops.

Raising livestock soon became a major business. Producers supplied meat to Spanish cities through contracts with municipal councils. In Mexico City, the *cabildo* moved slaughterhouses away from central plazas in an effort to ensure that consumers could buy safe, accurately weighed, and fairly priced meat from legal and traceable animals. Stockmen resident on their ranches could butcher livestock for consumption by their families and employees. Additionally, authorities tried to prevent the slaughter of animals for tallow and hides to maintain adequate numbers of sheep and cattle. Initial high prices collapsed as livestock multiplied quickly where pasture was readily available. In the 1540s, a single *real* (about two days' wages for the poorest workers) purchased 32 pounds of meat in the city of Mexico. Pigs provided fresh pork on voyages between Spain and the Indies. Raised in large numbers, they made available meat and lard; cooks substituted the latter for the olive oil used in Spain. By the end of the sixteenth century, the Indian population in many parts of the Americas had developed a taste for animal protein.

Weaving cloth from cotton and, in Inka Peru, the wool of llamas was a long-established domestic activity. Because of the product's value and utility, Aztec rulers demanded standard measures of cloth as tribute. In Inka Peru, state warehouses stored both rustic and fine cloth for distribution. Although domestic production continued, Spaniards introduced manufactories known as *obrajes* that produced coarse cloth for local and even regional sale. Quito prospered until the late seventeenth century through embracing this type of production and distributed distinctive blue cloth to a large regional market that included the mining center of Potosí.

MINING: GOLD AND SILVER

Precious metals ensured royal interest in the Indies and attracted early conquistadors and settlers. Gold production in Española sealed the fate of its native population as *encomenderos* employed violent practices to hasten the yield and by 1530 had exhausted the sources. Atahuallpa's "ransom" and early looting by conquistadors accounted for much of Peru's gold before 1560. As in New Spain, its gold production paled next to that of silver. New Granada's yield varied considerably, but after 1560 it always surpassed that of any other part of Spain's America. As Table 8.1 indicates, Brazil proved the most important producer of gold in the Indies, exceeding all Spanish sources combined. After its discovery in the colony's interior in the 1690s, the precious metal provided successful miners and their merchant creditors with unprecedented prosperity until the mid-eighteenth century.

Table 8.1 Estimated New World Gold Production, 1492–1810[4]
(Millions of Silver Pesos of 272 Maravedís)

YEARS	BRAZIL	NEW GRANADA	NEW SPAIN	PERU	CHILE	OTHER	TOTALS
1531–1560	0.0	6.4	3.3	10.9	5.0		25.6
1561–1590	0.0	14.4	0.2	2.1	5.2		21.9
1591–1620	0.0	24.3	5.8	0.2	0.7		31.0
1621–1650	0.0	13.1	6.9	0.0	0.0		20.0
1651–1680	0.0	10.4	5.2	0.1	0.0		15.7
1681–1710	30.7	10.7	4.5	0.9	0.1		46.9
1711–1740	185.6	16.9	6.4	0.7	0.6		210.2
1741–1770	235.4	34.2	16.0	1.1	5.5		292.2
1771–1800	179.3	55.7	24.2	22.3	19.9		301.4
1801–1810	25.5	23.3	16.1	8.0	6.9		79.8
Totals	**656.5**	**209.4**	**88.6**	**46.3**	**43.9**	**55.3**	**1,100.0**

Silver

In Spain, the value of gold per unit of weight far exceeded that of silver. Although it required much more capital investment for mining and processing, however, silver quickly emerged as the most important single export for both New Spain and the two Perus (Peru and Upper Peru, or Charcas). The discovery of rich veins of ore at Zacatecas in 1546 turned Mexico into a major producer. From at least the 1560s into the early eighteenth century, Zacatecas was the kingdom's most important single source of silver, but receipts at its treasury office reveal that the region's level of production varied substantially.

Located high in the Andes in present-day Bolivia, Potosí's renown as a mountain of silver made it a byword for mining wealth in the sixteenth and seventeenth centuries. After a native revealed its silver ore to his *encomendero* in 1545, a rush of Spaniards hoping to strike it rich and numerous indigenous workers seeking employment quickly confirmed the site's potential. Although natives obtained silver by smelting, in the 1570s the amalgamation process that used mercury to separate the metal from ore arrived from New Spain. With Viceroy Toledo's creation of a labor draft (*mita*) and the mine owners' construction of reservoirs to provide waterpower in processing ore, silver production at Potosí boomed. After peaking in 1592, registered silver began a long decline that, despite occasional upticks, continued into the early eighteenth century. As in Zacatecas, the availability of mercury was key to output. Although mines at Huancavelica, located in Lower Peru, provided much of the mercury needed in the amalgamation process used to separate silver from ore at Potosí, its erratic yield forced the Crown to send the liquid quicksilver to Charcas from the mines at Almadén, Spain. In the seventeenth century, this diverted mercury from New Spain and caused a decline in the viceroyalty's silver production.

How much silver was produced? Based on tax records, Figure 8.1 reveals that the decade 1631–1640 had the highest empire-wide totals until the mid-eighteenth

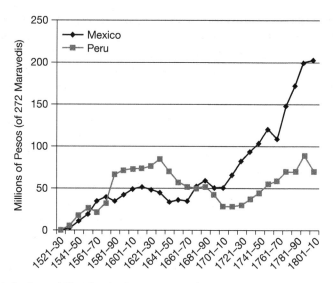

Figure 8.1 Registered Silver Production, 1521–1810[5] (in Millions of Pesos of 272 Maravedís)

century. In the 1670s, Mexican production finally surpassed that of Peru and Char-cas; the northern viceroyalty maintained its lead for the remainder of Spanish rule. Some non-Spanish sources suggest that actual production might have been the highest to date during the half-century 1661–1710.

Whatever the actual amount produced, silver was the leading export remitted to Spain. It enabled residents of the Indies to purchase textiles, tools, wine, paper, glass, and a variety of luxury and other goods carried by the fleets to Portobello and Veracruz, as well as silks, porcelain, spices, and other largely Chinese items carried from the Philippines to Acapulco on the Manila Galleon. Additionally, sur-plus tax revenue from the Indies reached Spain primarily in the form of silver. At its peak for the Habsburg period (1516–1700) during the reign of Philip II, American revenue accounted for about a quarter of the income received by the Crown of Castile.

SUGAR

Sugar gave Brazil an export whose importance rivaled that of silver for Mexico and Peru. Although gold and diamonds challenged its lead in the first half of the eighteenth century and tobacco, too, rose in prominence, the natural sweetener remained Brazil's most important export until coffee supplanted it in the 1830s. The profitability of sugar production in Iberia and the Atlantic islands—Madeira, the Azores, the Cape Verdes, the Canaries, and São Tomé—led Portuguese settlers to introduce sugar cane into Brazil soon after Cabral's landfall. By the 1580s, the combined output of the northeastern captaincies of Pernambuco—the most im-portant sugar region until the 1630s—and Bahia dominated production.

Sugar plantations (*engenhos*) required substantial capital to construct mills and purchase labor, but early profits funded expanded operations. Typically an *engenho's* mill processed both the owner's cane and, for a price, that of some *lavradores de cana*, cane farmers who were tenants, sharecroppers, renters, or independent landowners. This sound business practice enabled men with little capital to plant cane and, in good years, to profit handsomely. By spreading the risks and costs of planting, moreover, it gave the mill owner, who relied on credit, some protection against falling prices or a bad harvest. The relationship also allowed planters to benefit from economies of scale by investing in more efficient, large-scale crushing and refining capacity.

Engenhos varied in value according to the amount and quality of land, the number of slaves, and the condition of the mill and processing equipment. Livestock, transportation equipment, and residential facilities added further worth. Land and slaves required the most capital and fluctuations in slave prices could greatly affect profit.

Unlike gold and silver, sugar lacked intrinsic value. Bulky and perishable, the commodity required rapid handling when harvested and timely shipping to market and sale; storage costs could drain profits quickly. These requirements limited sugar plantations to coastal regions or along rivers with inexpensive transportation. The particularly advantageous Bahia Recôncavo, the area surrounding the Bay of All Saints, contributed substantially to its great success.

Slave laborers performed the tasks associated with sugar cultivation and processing under the supervision of whites, freedmen, or other slaves. *Engenhos* with 60 to 80 workers were most common in Bahian mills, and few had less than 40. Field hands invariably outnumbered all other slaves combined, although they were individually worth less than house slaves, artisans, skilled workers, or labor foremen.

Sugar production rose principally from plantation owners devoting more land and labor to it. The most important technological improvement was a three-roller vertical mill introduced early in the seventeenth century. Quickly adopted by planters, the less expensive, smaller, and faster mill surpassed in energy efficiency the earlier two-roller horizontal version. These advantages enabled some *lavradores* to open small operations and contributed to a near doubling of mills from 1612 to 1629.

Initially dependent on Indian slave labor, Brazilian sugar production grew rapidly in the sixteenth century. The importation of Africans increased after 1570 and sustained the industry's growth into the nineteenth century. Annual production rose from 6,000 metric tons in 1580 to 10,000 in 1610 and to between 15,000 and 22,000 in the 1620s, a level maintained for more than a hundred years.

A crisis for Brazilian planters began in the 1680s when foreign competitors in the Caribbean lowered sugar prices and drove up the cost of slaves. Despite some subsequent good years, Brazilian planters' overall position deteriorated, partly because gold mining in Minas Gerais increased the competition for slaves until

1750. Sugar's vulnerability to competition thus limited planters' control over their economic fortunes.

Bullion and sugar dominated exports from Spanish and Portuguese America. Tax revenue, governmental monopolies, and other fiscal measures associated with these products provided crucial support for the two crowns. Consequently, royal officials directly encouraged and promoted mining and the sugar industry and sought to safeguard their access to a steady supply of cheap labor and the safe shipment of silver, gold, and sugar to Iberia. Mining and the sugar industry tended to determine the cyclical behavior of the economies' market-oriented sector: When profits expanded, other areas of the economies grew. When profits fell, all of the economies tended to contract, reducing capital for investment and consumption.

The centrality of mining and sugar in the imperial economies separated them from other Indies' exports. Although each region of the New World tried to produce goods that would command an external market, no other products affected such large geographic areas or contributed so much to imperial finances. The fortunes of cacao in Venezuela, cochineal in Oaxaca, indigo in Central America, and hides in the Río de la Plata, to cite four examples, profoundly affected local and regional economies. But they provided modest revenue to the Spanish Crown and limited impact on other areas of the economy in comparison with silver. Not until the eighteenth century would such regional exports emerge from the long shadow of mining and assume a significant place in the imperial economy.

TRANSOCEANIC TRADE

Atlantic Trade

French corsairs' capture of ships that Cortés sent with treasure for Charles V in the early 1520s highlighted the risks in transatlantic shipping. The Crown's response in 1526 was to prohibit single ships from sailing to or from the Americas. The use of fast warships to protect the convoys began in the 1540s. The French occupation and destruction of Havana in 1555 stimulated a regularized fleet system and initial efforts to fortify the principal harbors where the convoys docked.

Spain's Fleet System

The Crown created the House of Trade in Seville in 1503 to oversee a Spanish monopoly over commerce with the Indies. By giving the merchant guild (*consulado*) of Seville control of wholesale trade to the Americas in 1543, Charles V completed the institutional framework for a trading system used into the eighteenth century. The restriction of legal trade to a single port facilitated tax collection and administrative oversight. Warships protected the fleets against foreign enemies. The system sought to make sailings predictable and to avoid, when possible, hurricane season in the Caribbean. The Crown also hoped to ensure regular profits for merchants by limiting market risk through equating supply to demand and thereby preventing gluts.

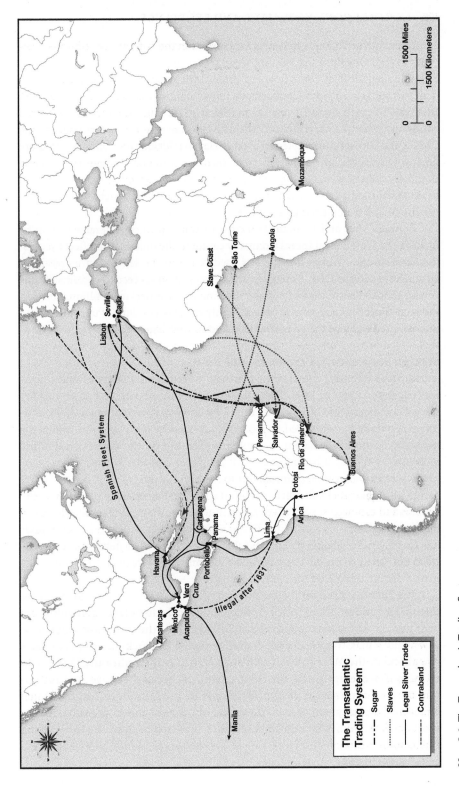

The Transatlantic Trading System

- – – – Sugar
- · · · · · Slaves
- ——— Legal Silver Trade
- – · – · – Contraband

Map 8.1 The Transatlantic Trading System

At its most effective, the system established in the 1560s rested on squadrons of six to eight warships that accompanied two distinct convoys from Spain. Officials intended the fleet (*flota*) to sail to Veracruz in May and the galleons (*galeones*) to depart subsequently for Cartagena de Indias, continuing to Nombre de Dios or, after 1597, Portobello, on Panama's northern coast. After merchants exchanged goods for precious metals and officials delivered tax revenue for remission to the Crown, the two fleets attempted to meet at Havana. Ideally, the combined treasure fleet would depart for Spain in May or early June, sailing through the Bahama channel, catching winds to the northeast, and continuing to the Azores and then to an Andalusian port. In practice, delays often plagued the system and increased the risk of loss from hurricanes.

Between 1581 and 1640, the two convoys sailed with considerable regularity. In 1628, the Dutch West Indies Company captured the only treasure fleet ever lost to enemy attack. Sailings became less predictable in the 1640s and increasingly erratic from 1650 to 1699. Nonetheless, the fleet system succeeded in terms of conveying goods safely to the Indies and returning with the declared bullion intact. At the same time, the convoys also proved highly effective conduits of undeclared and thus untaxed silver as the system succumbed to contraband trade.

Foreign Settlements, Privateers, and Pirates

Anticipating foreigners' interest in the Indies, Ferdinand and Isabel had sought the "papal donation" in 1493. Their premonitions proved correct. French corsairs started arriving in the Caribbean in the 1530s and occupied Havana in 1555. English expeditions first appeared in 1562 as traders led by John Hawkins. When the incoming Spanish fleet caught the captain and his ships near Veracruz, capturing more than 100 men, it became clear that Spaniards considered any foreign interlopers pirates and, if Protestant, subject to the Inquisition.

In 1572, Francis Drake successfully attacked the Panamanian port of Nombre de Dios and captured several silver-laden mule trains. Returning in the late 1570s, the "Sea Dog" tried his luck on the Pacific Coast before crossing the ocean, rounding Africa, and returning to England. Later expeditions left destruction in their wake but failed to produce the desired ransoms; both Drake and Hawkins ultimately died of disease off the coast of Panama.

The Dutch arrived on the north coast of Venezuela in 1599 to load salt for their fishing industry and to sell contraband goods. After earlier marauding expeditions on the Pacific coast, they established in 1621 the West Indies Company. Essentially a massive privateer operation designed to attack Iberian possessions in particular, the West Indies Company carried to the Indies the Dutch War of Independence against Spain (1568–1648). Its greatest success was to capture the Mexican treasure fleet near Havana in 1628. In the 1630s, the Dutch established a permanent base on the island of Curaçao and took Aruba. After a short occupation of Bahia, in 1624–25, they returned to Brazil in 1630, taking Pernambuco and remaining in its sugar-growing region until the Brazilians expelled them in 1654.

Overlapping with Dutch incursions, the French took Martinique and Guade-loupe, and England established its first permanent colonies on the North American mainland and seized several Caribbean islands including, in 1655, Jamaica. In sum, Spain's enemies had created a permanent presence in the Indies. For decades, their bases enabled the development of sugar-producing plantations based on slave labor, provided safe havens for pirates, and facilitated contraband trade.

In contrast to the early French corsairs, English "Sea Dogs," and Dutch "Sea Rovers" who typically returned to Europe after their assaults, pirates (sometimes in the guise of privateers commissioned by a government) resided primarily on Caribbean islands. A collection of disreputable fortune hunters, escaped prison-ers, shipwrecked sailors, and runaways, these buccaneers broadened their activi-ties from hunting pigs and cattle and selling smoked meat and hides to attacking mostly Spanish settlements. With the tacit support of English, Dutch, and French officials in the region, pirates of English provenance often operated out of Port Royal, Jamaica, a location that in the 1670s offered thirsty raiders taverns that included the Green Dragon and the Sign of Bacchus. French pirates and their in-ternational collaborators used Tortuga, a small island off the northwest coast of Española, as their major base.

The most notorious pirates included Henry Morgan (knighted Sir Henry for his success). In 1668, he led about 400 men in a surprise attack on Portobello, Panama, a triumph that netted 250,000 pesos and established his reputation for destruction and torture of prisoners. The following year, he attacked Maracaibo, Venezuela, and then managed to capture three Spanish ships laden with silver. After sacking Santa Marta and Río de la Hacha and Portobello again, in 1670 he marched some 1,500 men, including 500 Frenchmen from Tortuga, across the isthmus and attacked the city of Panama. Subsequently, the English government named him to repress the pirates of Jamaica, where he died a wealthy knight and lieutenant governor in 1688.

The capture and sack of Veracruz in 1683 by Lorenzo de Graaf and his con-federates exemplified the terror, devastation, brutality, and torture wrought by pirate expeditions. Having ferried nearly 4,000 hostages from the port to Sacri-ficios Island in the Gulf of Mexico, the pirates initially demanded a ransom of 1 million pesos to forgo burning the city to the ground; they ultimately settled for 150,000 pesos sent from Mexico City plus everything seized in Veracruz. This re-portedly included some 1,500 blacks and mulattoes because mobile treasure easily converted into cash.

The pirates' plunder of coastal towns of the Spanish Main and occasionally on the Pacific coast and their seizure of any ship that appeared an attractive prize also took a toll on foreign contraband traders. At last realizing that the benefits of trade surpassed the pleasures of pillage, the English, French, and Dutch governments started to suppress pirates in the mid-1680s and establish peace in the region. Symbolically, an earthquake and tsunami in 1692 destroyed Port Royal, a haven for some 1,200 buccaneers as well as a center for contraband trade in slaves, tex-tiles, flour, and other goods. The French government's use of pirates in the capture of Cartagena in 1697 was the last hurrah because the Treaty of Ryswick marked the end of most piracy in the West Indies. In this agreement, Spain ceded to France the western portion of Española, renamed Saint-Domingue, to which it annexed Tortuga, the small island already occupied in 1660. The French colony would become the foremost sugar producer in the Caribbean.

Fraud and Contraband

Smuggling and tax avoidance began to plague the fleet system by at least the early seventeenth century. A tax levied on imports and exports paid for the warships accompanying the convoys. Only 1.7 percent as late as 1585, the rate more than quadrupled following the celebrated English defeat of the Spanish navy in 1588. In the seventeenth century, it reached occasional peaks above 30 percent. High rates prompted more fraud that reduced tax yields and forced further rate increases to provide minimum protection. Underpaid officials with salaries frequently in arrears routinely accepted bribes, and the commanding officers of fleets regularly returned to Spain with considerable unregistered bullion. The Crown finally broke the cycle in 1660, when it terminated import duties on American commodities in exchange for an annual sum divided between merchants involved in the Atlantic trade and the treasury.

Contraband trade also occurred outside the fleet system. The establishment of Dutch, French, and English colonies in the Caribbean enabled their traders to sell directly to cooperative Spanish merchants and officials, especially on the northern coast of South America. Because foreign manufactures had increasingly replaced Spanish textiles as exports, eliminating the middlemen in Spain enabled foreign merchants to sell the same foreign goods at lower cost. This contraband destroyed the predictability of the American market and thus increased risks for wholesalers arriving on the fleets. When they found the Indies' markets saturated with illegal merchandise, Spanish merchants refused to invest in merchandise for another fleet until they thought the glut had disappeared. Their uncertainty rested on a real possibility of loss, despite serving primarily as fronts for foreign enterprises in the seventeenth century.

Contraband expanded as well when Portugal established Colônia do Sacramento in 1680. The fortified trading post sat opposite Buenos Aires on the northern coast of the estuary of the River Plate. A pawn in border disputes between Spain and Portugal, Colônia received African slaves and merchandise from British and Brazilian sources and supplied them to Buenos Aires and the interior as far as Potosí until it fell to Spanish arms for a fourth and final time in 1777.

Periodization of Spain's Trade with the Indies

The amount, value, and content of the Atlantic trade changed substantially over time. At first, conquistadors and settlers received from Spain nearly everything they needed to survive, purchasing goods with gold and silver. After a lengthy mid-century recession, the introduction of the fleet system and burgeoning silver production resulted in protracted growth from 1562 to 1592. Expanding exports

Table 8.2 Registered American Silver Production and Bullion Reaching Europe, 1661–1710[6] (in Silver Pesos of 272 Maravedís)

YEARS	REGISTERED SILVER PRODUCTION	BULLION REACHING EUROPE
1661–1670	90 million	157 million
1671–1680	105 million	141 million
1681–1690	116 million	143 million
1691–1700	101 million	136 million
1701–1710	111 million	119 million
Totals	**523 million**	**696 million**

of textiles and manufactured goods buoyed the trade even more. Despite rising prices, the appearance of English raiders in the Indies, and the armada's defeat in 1588, Atlantic commerce remained at a high level until the early 1620s, although at times it was surpassed by the Manila–Acapulco trade under way from the 1570s.

After a lengthy depression and significant decline in both sailings and tonnage, the value and volume of merchandise, almost all of foreign manufacture, finally began to rise after 1660. By that time, however, fraud and contraband trade, irregular sailings, and a loss of merchant confidence had disrupted the fleet system and left it in disarray. The galleons to Portobello, for example, sailed only four times between 1680 and 1700.

Bullion Reaching Europe, 1661–1710

Table 8.2 compares registered silver production with bullion that mercantile newspapers reported arriving in Europe from 1661 to 1710, the five highest consecutive decades since Spaniards reached the Americas. The difference—173 million pesos—represents fraudulent registration and contraband bullion, underscoring the extent of illegal commerce. Much of the bullion did not remain in Europe because merchants and trading companies sent it to the Far East to purchase silks, porcelains, spices, and other desirable imports.

The Transpacific Trade

The development of transpacific trade between the Americas and China via Manila rested on China's ability to provide comparatively inexpensive manufactured goods including silks, porcelain, jewelry, and other wares, as well as its seemingly insatiable demand for silver. Silver settled accounts everywhere and, because its market value in China far exceeded its value in Europe, especially until about 1640, foreign merchants could make astonishing profits on both Chinese exports and the exchange of silver for gold. Manila became the entrepôt where merchants from Mexico traded silver from New Spain and Peru for Chinese manufactures and gold. A Lima official explained the advantages in 1594: "A man can clothe his wife in Chinese silks for 200 real[e]s [25 pesos], whereas he could not provide her clothing of Spanish silks with 200 pesos."[7]

The Manila Galleon, authorized in 1593 to sail annually between Acapulco and the Philippines, brought to New Spain inexpensive Chinese silks, jewelry, and porcelains; cloves and nutmeg from the Molucca and Banda archipelagos in Indonesia; and other oriental items to the Mexican port. Faced with Lima merchants' efforts to obtain Chinese goods, and, when the galleons failed to sail, European merchandise in New Spain, the Crown outlawed all trade between the northern viceroyalty and Peru in the early 1630s. Notwithstanding the hopes of wholesale traders in Seville, this prohibition failed to force Lima's merchants to buy imported products only at Portobello.

Despite its illegality, around 1680 the trade among the Philippines, Mexico, and Peru started to expand significantly; its virtual autonomy from the convoy trade of the Atlantic has led one historian to label this trading zone of the Pacific "the American lake."[8] Indeed, the volume and value of the "semiformal" trade structure in the Pacific seriously affected Spain's transatlantic commerce. Since Peruvian merchants could buy Chinese textiles for a fraction of the cost of cloth carried by the galleons to Portobello, they readily purchased large quantities. In addition, they could procure inexpensive European merchandise in Acapulco; to supply this market demand, Mexican wholesalers ordered larger shipments via the fleet to Veracruz. Thus, Peruvian purchases in Acapulco strengthened the fleet system to New Spain while contributing significantly to the demise of the galleons to Portobello.

In addition to substantial amounts of silver and some gold, by the seventeenth century the Americas were exporting to Europe cochineal, hides, indigo, wool, emeralds, and pearls. Cacao became an important export from the mid-seventeenth century onward, and tobacco exports increased substantially starting in the 1680s. Lima merchants carried to New Spain not only silver and mercury, but also, by the late seventeenth century, significant amounts of cacao from Guayaquil and Peruvian wine.

The Indies' economies became increasingly independent of Spain in the seventeenth century. This resulted from robust agricultural and livestock production; substantial local artisanal goods; fraudulent trade and access to contraband carried by foreign merchants; and the semiformal commercial structure in the Pacific linking New Spain, Peru, and the Philippines that made available inexpensive Chinese textiles and porcelains. Mercury received from Peru and Spain was the most important import for New Spain's mining economy.

Brazil's Trade

Portugal exercised little control over Brazil's early economic development because initially it focused on the riches of the East Indies. Until the mid-seventeenth century, its monarchs allowed almost unrestricted trade between metropolitan and Brazilian ports. Although each captaincy had a port, those of Recife, Salvador, and Rio de Janeiro dominated the exportation of sugar. Portuguese participated in the trade, but English and especially Dutch shippers operating under Portuguese licenses eclipsed them in the sixteenth and early seventeenth centuries.

Spain had sought to regain control over the United Provinces of the Netherlands since their rebellion began in 1568. When Philip II attached Portugal and its possessions to his crown in 1580, he gave the Dutch a larger theater in which to operate. As a result, Philip III's effort to exclude them from trade with the Portuguese world in 1605 triggered Dutch retaliation by raiding ships carrying Brazilian sugar. During the Twelve-Years' Truce (1609–1621) between Spain and Holland, Dutch merchants conveyed sugar to numerous European markets including Amsterdam. Soon after the truce ended, the Dutch invaded Salvador in 1624–25 and occupied Pernambuco from 1630 to 1654. Faced with this unrelenting pressure, the Portuguese Crown turned to convoys. It chartered the Brazil Company in 1649 to protect Atlantic routes in return for a monopoly of the colony's most common imports—flour, olive oil, wine, and codfish—and the right to tax its exports. When the company failed to meet its obligations, the Crown took it over in 1664, enabling the convoy system to survive for another century. Fleets of a hundred vessels or so sailed with some frequency, although an English observer remembered an early convoy as "the pitifullest vessels that ever I saw."[9]

A separate African trade supplied slaves for Brazil's sugar industry. The Crown experimented with monopoly contracts, but in practice hardly regulated the trade, allowing merchants resident in the colony to organize and direct much of the exchange. This relatively lax oversight of the slave trade distinguishes the Portuguese commercial system from that of Spain. Brazilian merchants, moreover, participated more in offshore commerce.

British trade with Portugal and its American colony remained insignificant for several decades after sugar produced in England's Caribbean plantations supplanted that of Brazil. Beginning in the 1690s, however, the gold mining boom in Brazil rekindled its mother country's prosperity. By outlawing colonial manufactures and failing to protect its own, Portugal allowed British goods to capture the Brazilian market. In the mid-eighteenth century, British exports to Portugal valued at little more than 1.1 million pounds produced an annual favorable balance of trade of nearly 800,000 pounds. Although some historians attribute Britain's commercial ascendency to the Methuen Treaty of 1703 and its antecedents in addition to shifting European political rivalries, the country's early development of cotton textiles suitable for wear in the tropics proved more important.

Merchants

The earliest professional Spanish merchants in the Indies—as opposed to broad-based investors in trade—generally represented Seville's established mercantile families. Their ties of birth and marriage offered what contemporaries considered the strongest deterrent to unscrupulous behavior in the distant Indies. For a generation or more, most of them eschewed significant personal ties in the Americas, devoting themselves to wholesale and also often retail trade and providing credit to purchasers.

In the 1590s, wholesale merchants in Lima and the city of Mexico who engaged in the Atlantic trade obtained royal approval to establish *consulados* as their corporate base. Between 1590 and 1660, peninsular importers included many of the wealthiest businessmen in Mexico. They often married native daughters whose prosperous

Primary Source

The Labor Draft

The labor draft (*mita*) in Potosí is well known, but forced labor occurred elsewhere as well. The following selection describes its use in the Kingdom of Quito as related in the "confidential" report submitted by Juan and Ulloa.

SOURCE: Juan and Ulloa. *Discourse and Political Reflections,* 127–28.

> In those places where there are mines to be worked but no haciendas, some of the Indians perform mita service, while others are held in reserve to alternate in the work. In those corregimientos having both haciendas and mines, mita Indians are divided up and assigned both tasks. One group extracts ore from veins in the earth and the other farms and cultivates the land for raising crops. The corregimientos which have only haciendas or obrajes (as textile workshops are called there) use all mita Indians in these operations. There are also corregimientos with no mines where Indians perform no mita service because Negro slaves work the haciendas . . . .
>
> The mita requires all villages to provide a set number of Indians to work haciendas located in the Corregimiento. The same is done in the mines. When the mine owners register a strike, they obtain a mita concession to carry on their mining operations more effectively. The Indians should perform mita service for one year and then return to their villages. Since other Indians are available as replacements, they should be free of the mita obligation until their turn comes up again, but this method, clearly delineated in the law, is not followed. For the Indians, working as mita laborers for a mine owner or a hacendados is the same as working as a free man for the corregidores' enrichment, especially since the burden is the same under both systems.
>
> All the corregimientos in the province of Quito and those located to the south in the mountains of Peru have mitas.

fathers came from the ranks of merchants, royal officials, and landowners. Diversified investments held the key to their continued success, with land particularly attractive for its value as collateral. About half of their families remained wealthy into the third generation. Wholesalers' children and grandchildren often surpassed them in status, partly as a result of obtaining royal offices, often by purchase.

By 1700, Spain's American realms had long lost their primitive dependence on the metropolis. Most enjoyed self-sufficiency in food production and those without an adequate fiscal base, including Chile, Panama, Cuba, Florida, and Manila, received subsidies from the treasuries of Peru and New Spain. With Castile's production, trade, and treasury suffering, the balance of economic, but not political, power had shifted to the Americas. In Brazil's interior, gold discovered in the 1690s in Minas Gerais quickly affected not only the colony but also Portugal and England, its major trading partner.

NOTES

1. Bernal Díaz del Castillo, *The True History of the Conquest of New Spain*, trans. Janet Burke and Ted Humphrey (Indianapolis, IN: Hackett, 2012), 249.
2. Quoted in Hans J. Prem, "Spanish Colonization and Indian Property in Central Mexico, 1521–1620," *Annals of the Association of American Geographers* 82, no. 3 (September 1992), 445.
3. Quoted in Ann M. Wightman, *Indigenous Migration and Social Change: The Forasteros of Cuzco, 1520–1720* (Durham, NC: Duke University Press, 1990), 128.
4. John J. TePaske, *A New World of Gold and Silver*, ed. Kendall W. Brown (Leiden, The Netherlands: Brill, 2010).
5. Based on data in *ibid.*
6. Based on data in *ibid.*, especially p. 315.
7. Arturo Giraldez, *The Age of Trade: The Manila Galleons and the Dawn of the Global Economy* (London: Rowman & Littlefield, 2015), 153.
8. The phrase is from Mariano Ardash Bonialian, *El Pacífico hispanoamericano: Política y comercio asiático en el Imperio Español (1680–1784)* (Mexico: Colegio de México, 2012).
9. C. R. Boxer, *The Portuguese Seaborne Empire 1415–1825* (London: Hutchinson, 1969), 224.

SUGGESTIONS FOR FURTHER READING

Bakewell, P. J. *Silver and Entrepreneurship in Seventeenth-Century Potosí: The Life and Times of Antonio López de Quiroga.* Albuquerque: University of New Mexico Press, 1988.

Bakewell, Peter J. *Silver Mining and Society in Colonial Mexico: Zacatecas, 1546–1700.* Cambridge: Cambridge University Press, 1971.

Fisher, John R. *The Economic Aspects of Spanish Imperialism in America, 1492–1810.* Liverpool, UK: Liverpool University Press, 1997.

Fuente, Alejandro de la. *Havana and the Atlantic in the Sixteenth Century.* Chapel Hill: University of North Carolina Press, 2008.

Giraldez, Arturo. *The Age of Trade: The Manila Galleons and the Dawn of the Global Economy.* Lanham, MD: Rowman & Littlefield, 2015.

Hoberman, Louisa Schell. *Mexico's Merchant Elite, 1590–1660: Silver, State, and Society.* Durham, NC: Duke University Press, 1991.

Lane, Kris E. *Pillaging the Empire: Piracy in the Americas, 1500–1750.* Armonk, NY: M. E. Sharpe, 1998.

Lynch, John. *The Hispanic World in Crisis and Change, 1598–1700.* Oxford: Basil Blackwell, 1992.

MacLeod, Murdo J. *Spanish Central America: A Socioeconomic History, 1520–1720.* Revised ed. Austin: University of Texas Press, 2007.

Robins, Nicholas A. *Mercury, Mining, and Empire: The Human and Ecological Cost of Colonial Silver Mining.* Bloomington: Indiana University Press, 2011.

Schwartz, Stuart B. *Sugar Plantations in the Formation of Brazilian Society, Bahia, 1550–1835.* Cambridge: Cambridge University Press, 1985.

TePaske, John Jay. *A New World of Gold and Silver.* Edited by Kendall W. Brown. Leiden, The Netherlands: Brill, 2010.

CHAPTER 9

Societies of Caste and Class

After European settlement, societies in the Indies took shape and evolved within a context of profound demographic and economic change. The initial simplicity of a social order created by conquest proved unsustainable despite the efforts of the conquerors, churchmen, and early royal administrators. Many European immigrants' claim to high status, moreover, lacked justification through conquest. This combined with the arrival of enslaved Africans, Indians' plummeting population and forced relocation, and the rapid growth of a racially mixed populace to overwhelm the early social categories and economic arrangements.

Sixteenth-century Iberians accepted the inevitability of human inequality, supported hierarchy, and lacked any enthusiasm for promoting social mobility. They sought privileges rather than equality, believing that a properly ordered society concentrated power, wealth, and status in legally privileged groups at the top. Laws set forth the privileges (*fueros*) that nobles and clerics enjoyed and that distinguished them from the commoners who comprised more than 90 percent of Iberia's population. Corporate bodies including the Church, artisan guilds, and universities also had *fueros* that gave them judicial authority over their members.

These institutional arrangements and beliefs persisted in the Indies. But distance from Europe; the mixture of races, ethnicities, and cultures; and the at times tumultuous performance of regional economies created a more fluid and complex social ordering often identified as "societies of caste." Legislation and social discrimination classified as inferior the indigenous population, Africans and their American-born descendants, and *castas*, a term applied to persons of mixed-race parentage. Simultaneously, the ownership of substantial property created a presumption of white status, even when appearance suggested otherwise. The mixed-race children and grandchildren of conquistadors and Indian women moved in elite circles and married Europeans. Not biology, but wealth, lineage, occupation, and power or, alternatively, poverty and tributary status largely defined race. Yet culture, the mastery of Spanish or Portuguese, Christianity, mode of dress, diet, place of residence, and honor also contributed to racial and ethnic identity. By the late eighteenth century, total reputation (*calidad*) reclassified persons according to these characteristics. As a result, the "Spanish" and *casta* populations in particular expanded, although white elites continued to pride themselves on "pure" lineage as the basis for being "Spaniards."

In the male-dominated Iberian world, law and custom defined women as unequal to men and narrowly circumscribed acceptable female roles. Through often-violent relationships with native women, conquistadors and the men who followed them imposed domination from the start. Male clerics and bureaucrats articulated the patriarchal ideologies of Church and state. Fathers and then husbands restricted the lives of elite and middle-group women, whereas priests monitored the lives of females who chose the convent. No woman from a "decent" or propertied family could walk unescorted in the street, go to the market, hold a job, or visit a man alone without causing a scandal. A handful of wealthy and urban middle-class girls received private educations, but generally only elite widows could gain control over their assets and act as their own economic agents. Females who rebelled, fled their homes, defied sexual customs, or resisted imperious demands of fathers and husbands suffered virtual incarceration in convents, hospitals, or houses of refuge or seclusion (*recogimientos*). Nevertheless, differences in experience existed across the class structure.

Despite the male ideal of familial control, poor free and slave women led active but difficult lives as they engaged in numerous social and economic activities. Dominant in the daily markets, they ran small businesses in cities and towns; in rural areas they sometimes operated farms and ranches. Women often provided significant labor, capital investments, and entrepreneurial skills, particularly among the rural and urban working classes, where they headed many families. Few couples could survive on the earnings of the male head of household.

Securing an adequate income necessarily meant satisfying class and ethnic cultural norms and realizing individual and family ambitions for social status.

Among privileged groups, income levels allowed men and women to purchase distinctive discretionary items such as costly European or Asian textiles. The middle groups imitated these styles and fashions as best they could, always finding ways to distinguish themselves from those below them. The poor struggled to satisfy fundamental material needs: food, clothing, and shelter. But even the most impoverished families usually had a religious image or two in their homes.

The character of the Latin American economies, particularly the structural instability of the export sector, increased the vulnerability of all social classes. The profits of a merchant who imported European or Chinese textiles, the income of a muleteer, the wages of a weaver, and the ability of a sheep rancher to repay a loan reflected the volume of trade carried by Spanish ships, the productivity of silver mines, and demographic changes. Any alterations could redistribute income and opportunities among social classes.

THE ELITES

The immense distances separating major centers of wealth in Spanish America and Brazil precluded a single empire-wide elite emerging in either place. Rather, a local elite dominated the political, economic, social, and cultural life of each urban core and its surrounding rural area.

Heterogeneous and often interlocking mixes of ranchers, planters, miners, merchants, high-ranking churchmen, and bureaucrats regularly comprised local elites. Intermarriage and the incorporation of successive generations of newly successful entrepreneurs and royal appointees sent from Iberia constantly renewed their ranks. The elites' members generally pursued activities that crossed economic boundaries. Except for high-ranking bureaucrats and churchmen, the extent of wealth, influence, family, and social connections surpassed occupation in determining high status. In all Indies' elites, wealth meant power.

Early Iberian immigrants rarely came from distinguished families or could legitimately boast the Spanish title of *don* or the Portuguese *dom*. They typically assumed, however, that participation in conquest or settlement had elevated their social status. Their American-born heirs used these honorifics without apology, claiming their ancestors' ennoblement reflected service and contributions at their own expense to the expansion of royal domains. This assumption of de facto noble status (*hidalgo* in Spanish or *fidalgo* in Portuguese) reflected reality in the Indies. Exemption from tribute, considered the New World equivalent of the direct tax (*pecho*) commoners paid in Spain, served to confirm this claimed noble rank. Without qualification, Europeans believed themselves superior to Indians, enslaved and free Africans, and persons of mixed descent. Nevertheless, Indian nobles also gained recognition as *dons* as royal officials came to rely on them to collect taxes and organize labor drafts.

The wealthiest and most powerful settlers emulated Iberian nobles, demanding deference from inferiors, living in great houses surrounded by retainers, providing guests with lavish dinners, and, whenever possible, following Europe's

Portrait of Francisco de Orense y Moteuczoma, Count of Villalobos. Some marriages be-tween conquistadors and noble indigenous women created elite families that endured until the end of the colonial period. The young count was descended on his mother's side from Doña Isabel de Moteuczoma Tecuichpotzin, the main female heir of Moteuczoma.

fashions and styles. In Spanish America, a small number of local magnates, usu-ally of peninsular birth, secured titles of nobility that routinely passed to their native-son heirs. Although the wealthiest sugar planters in Brazil imitated the Portuguese aristocracy, few sought this elevation. A knighthood in the Spanish military orders of Santiago, Calatrava, or Alcántara or the Portuguese orders of

Christ, Avis, or Santiago confirmed an individual's nobility at a lower cost but could not be bequeathed.

In the Iberian world, *limpieza de sangre* or *limpeça de sangue*, the concept of blood purity or "unsullied lineage," defined Christian identity in general and elite identity in particular. Limited in Europe to the absence of Jewish or Muslim antecedents, this concept expanded in the Americas to exclude lineage connected to Africans or Indians other than Inka or Nahua royalty. In Brazil, the terms "infected blood" or "defect of blood" identified someone with Jewish or African antecedents and legitimated exclusion from elite organizations or marriages into prominent families. Thus, blood purity bestowed lifelong advantages to the offspring of Spanish or Portuguese parents.

Elite families frequently invested in both urban and rural enterprises. In the mature domains, many derived substantial wealth and status from large properties devoted to agriculture or grazing. They lived a traditional seigniorial life, commanding numerous free dependents and slaves. Nonetheless, estate owners often found their interests subordinated to those of wealthy merchants.

Large-scale rural enterprises depended on credit. With agricultural income concentrated after the harvest, landowners had to secure loans to cover expenses during the remainder of the year. Additionally, the unpredictable effects of droughts, pests, and changes in market conditions generated extraordinary debts that endangered the survival of their estates. Most rural elites, therefore, forged strong ties with the Church and the merchant community, the two major sources of credit. A small minority of the landed elite sought to perpetuate their family's wealth and prestige through the legal device of entail called *mayorazgo* (Spanish) or *morgado* (Portuguese).

Middle Groups

Interconnected families of powerful bureaucrats, clergymen, miners, merchants, and landowners, most claiming only European ancestors, dominated the settlers' societies. But the Iberian empires' longevity also depended on the loyalty and energy of the larger population of middle groups. Although elites viewed them as clients or dismissed them as rustics, they provided the muscles and sinews of the imperial structures. As retailers and peddlers, they connected imported goods with local consumers. As priests, teachers, and intellectuals, they extended the reach of the Catholic faith and the languages of Spain and Portugal. And in times of foreign threat or local rebellion, they provided fiscal resources and the leadership of the police and military forces that sustained the empires' existence.

Manufacturers, clerics, master artisans, retail merchants, and middle-ranking government officials sat atop the urban middle sector. Priests and bureaucrats enjoyed the most security because their status rested on institutional prestige and predictable, if often modest, incomes. The other groups depended on volatile market conditions to maintain their position in society. Members of the urban middle sector routinely imitated elite fashion and customs and attempted to protect their status and income via institutional guarantees.

Significant rural middle groups lived in some regions of the Indies. In the Viceroyalty of New Spain, for example, numerous small ranches and farms produced food and livestock for local markets in the Bajío, to the south in Oaxaca, and on the northern frontier. Some proprietors differed little from subsistence farmers, who in good years sold surplus to nearby consumers. More substantial properties concentrated on cash crops and employed seasonal laborers. Although such workers kept labor costs low, the scale of enterprise and limited local demand commonly restricted profits. As a result, few members of this group acquired the land and resources necessary to ascend into the elite.

The *lavradores de cana* of the Brazilian sugar zone perhaps best exemplified this social type. Although reliant on nearby plantations for refining and processing, these cane producers included some comparatively wealthy individuals who owned slaves and land. Others seemed little more than sharecroppers dependent on the owners of mills for refining. The high cost of land, slaves, equipment, and plants for refining limited their advancement. Although their place in the production process curtailed their profits during boom times, the *lavradores* had lower fixed costs and lower levels of indebtedness than planters and therefore had less risk of catastrophe during periods of falling prices. Throughout the productive cycle, but especially during the harvest, wives, daughters, and sons contributed crucial labor to *lavradores de cana*. Small, independent farmers and ranchers in Spanish America also relied on the work of family members.

THE BROAD BASE OF NEW WORLD SOCIETIES

During Spanish and Portuguese rule, most of Latin America's population—the rural and urban poor—lived lives constrained by material deprivation and violence. They harvested crops, cared for livestock, manufactured textiles, mined and refined silver and gold, and transported goods from place to place. Ethnically diverse, they included Indians, black slaves and freemen, and *castas*. Whether journeymen, market women, stevedores, soldiers, day laborers, beggars, prostitutes, or vagrants, they established themselves in the public spaces of cities and towns and constituted the most common inhabitants of jails. Indigent Spanish and *casta* males suffered mandatory military service and were among those inhabitants who received the harshest corporal punishments, such as mutilation and whippings.

Poverty and the routines of draft labor developed differently in urban and rural areas. Mandatory labor service characterized the countryside. The demands of the labor drafts, the frequent requirement that Indians pay tribute in cash, and the forced purchase of goods by Indian communities (*repartimiento de bienes*) in the Spanish kingdoms and provinces amounted to heavy burdens. In effect, indigenous laborers had to subsidize the farms, ranches, mines, and *obrajes* of the elite in return for wages that seldom met subsistence needs. In Brazil, the plantation economy depended on African slaves. Even in the absence of forced labor, few free agricultural workers, whether Indians, free blacks, or *castas*, could buy land or, if they were landowners, avoid domination by powerful owners of ranches and plantations.

Urban economies offered greater opportunities to large and diverse underclasses. The more successful included skilled journeymen, market people, peddlers, servants, soldiers, and sailors. At the bottom lived beggars, thieves, prostitutes, and the impoverished victims of accidents or diseases such as leprosy. Many slept in the streets or back rooms and struggled daily to buy food. Unemployment or illness could reduce them to begging.

Urban slaves in elite households typically lived in better surroundings than the multitude of free *castas* who sought work each day. Other slaves, notably those owned by persons of modest means, resided outside their owners' households and pursued employment on their own. A minority managed to acquire small amounts of property and purchase their freedom. Many female slaves participated in market activities; particularly in Brazil, these enterprising women dominated the urban marketplaces.

Indians

Under Spanish rule, earlier distinctions of culture and class among the highly urbanized and socially stratified indigenous societies of Mesoamerica and the Andes suffered reduction and at times virtual eradication. In Brazil, Chile, the Río de la Plata, and the Caribbean region of South America, Iberian settlers found village cultures or dispersed semisedentary populations. In such areas, settlers and royal officials viewed indigenous groups as potential enemies or prospective laborers.

The social compression of diverse indigenous cultures and societies began with the creation of the *indio*, or "Indian." Originally a racial description, Indian also became a cultural expression and, for the Spanish Crown, a fiscal category with defined obligations. Royal representatives of the Spanish and Portuguese crowns issued legislation that gave *indio* political and economic meaning. Spanish authorities placed them in the legal category of minors and the "wretched poor" (*miserables*), unable to defend themselves under normal judicial practices because of inadequate instruction in the faith. Accordingly, the Crown adopted policies to protect and defend them.

Mandates intended to ameliorate injustice, as in the New Laws of the Spanish realms, or to enrich the treasury, as in the imposition of tribute, blurred distinctions of culture and class. In Mexico, for example, tribute collection eliminated a long-standing division between commoners with and without access to communal land. Through employment by Spanish settlers, *yanaconas* in Peru escaped *mita* service and improved their status relative to *ayllu* members, who retained traditional property rights.

Chastened by the demographic tragedy of the Caribbean islands and committed to the Indians' conversion, the Spanish Crown sought to keep the native population separate from Spaniards, other than missionaries. Legislation barred whites and *castas* from Indian settlements and eventually forbade *encomenderos* from visiting their tribute populations. But this attempted social engineering soon collapsed. Epidemic disease, resettlement programs, and the growth of the market economy overwhelmed statutory isolation as increasing contacts with Europeans irrevocably altered native cultures.

Only the maintenance of long-established land rights enabled Indian communities to survive. Indigenous officials quickly learned to use the newly imposed legal system for redress of grievances, especially when close to royal judicial agents. Changes in the natives' approaches to using legislation affecting their lands illustrated just one consequence of their forced adaptation to Spanish institutions.

Throughout Spain's rule, the Indian population continuously flowed away from native communities toward Spanish cities and towns. Pushed by the demands of tribute and labor service and pulled by envisioned greater opportunity and independence, migrants worked as domestic servants, but often found only a hand-to-mouth existence as day laborers, ambulatory vendors, or employees in textile manufactories (*obrajes*). A small minority learned trades and became propertied workers. Whether successful or not, they contributed to a process of assimilation and cultural change that helped produce the multiethnic working class.

After the initial enslavement of natives in the coastal regions of Brazil, subsequent raids in the interior drove surviving Indian populations away from Portuguese settlements. The absence of a Brazilian equivalent of the *repartimiento/mita* also reduced the presence of natives in urban centers.

European rule substantially altered Indian communities, although many survived. Collective landholding practices proved remarkably resilient, despite population loss and the advent of market forces. Natives' oversight of numerous local affairs also continued in many regions, especially those distant from urban centers. Yet the precontact agricultural community lost vitality and relative abundance because of external demands for labor and land. In its place developed the impoverished peasant villages still visible in Latin America.

Blacks

Aspiring conquistadors and settlers reached the Indies in the 1490s accompanied by free, Hispanicized Africans (*ladinos*). Portuguese traders had introduced enslaved Africans in Lisbon and Seville starting in the mid-fifteenth century and elite families soon deemed owning one or more slaves as domestics an essential sign of their elevated status. Black slaves reached Española starting in 1503 and their direct importation from Africa was underway by the mid-1520s.

Both enslaved and free, the earliest Africans in the Indies spoke Castilian and typically attended their masters and employers as personal servants and auxiliaries. For a brief period, participation in military campaigns enabled some slaves to gain their freedom and, in limited cases, land. Most, however, continued to serve Spaniards, often assuming an intermediate position between their master or employer and the indigenous population as overseers and foreman of workers assigned to agricultural tasks, mining, and transporting goods.

Distant royal authorities failed to understand the new higher status that black agents of Spanish power held in a world of defeated indigenous societies. Consequently, they acted on the basis of ingrained prejudice and reports of blacks' aggressive actions. Promulgating unenforceable directives, they sought to prohibit most contacts between blacks and Indians, although no evidence indicates that blacks were more likely than Europeans to mistreat natives. Early punitive laws foreshadowed later efforts by Spanish and Portuguese officials to control and discipline a growing black population by mutilation, flogging, and brutal executions.

Owners, in turn, routinely resorted to corporal punishments. Ironically, slaves frequently suffered less severe punishment than free blacks because owners had a financial stake in protecting their property. Regardless of whatever material or political advantages blacks gained relative to Indians, the legal system always castigated their insubordination and crime harshly.

The African slave trade expanded following the Crown's abolition of most Indian slavery in 1542. By 1570, more blacks and mulattoes than Spaniards lived in Mexico City and, indeed, in New Spain as a whole. Soon after its regular slave trade ended in 1640, that kingdom's American-born (creole) black population, mostly free mulattoes descended from Africans and Indians, exceeded 115,000, more than triple the survivors of the Middle Passage from Africa. Between 1576 and 1700, Brazil received approximately 810,000 slaves and Spanish America about 310,000. These numbers permitted slaves' widespread use on sugar plantations, for example, in Brazil, coastal Peru, and southern Mexico, and in some mining activities, notably in extracting and processing gold in Brazil and in the Chocó region in New Granada starting in the late seventeenth century.

Elite families routinely confirmed their status by owning slaves for domestic service. Artisans frequently purchased and trained a slave or two in their craft, for example, as tailors, cobblers, masons, or blacksmiths. Shopkeepers employed free blacks and slaves as street vendors. Low-level royal and local officials often had one or more slaves, and some elite Indians also possessed them. Even poor widows might own a single slave whose daily earnings as an artisan, vendor, or day laborer covered modest expenses. The cultural distinctiveness of the African slave population and the social effects of harsh labor and brutal discipline promoted negative racial stereotypes. They also reinforced the effects of discriminatory legislation and racial prejudice brought from Portugal and Spain.

The Catholic Church, and especially the Society of Jesus, owned numerous slaves in Iberian America. However, it helped to restrain their ill treatment, particularly in cities, and to protect their marriages and family life. Participation in confraternities, Christian rituals, celebrations of saints' days, and processions also provided relief. The Church neither opposed the institution of slavery itself nor justified it based on the presumed inferiority of Africans and their American-born descendants, a common rationalization by Protestant denominations in the United States. Although institutionalized racial discrimination formed part of both civic and religious life, the Catholic Church recognized the essential humanity, the soul, of black slaves.

Acculturated slaves born in the Americas, especially those in urban centers, gained emancipation much more frequently than slaves imported from Africa (*bozales*). Portuguese and Spanish law provided a framework for determining a fair market value and the supervision of self-purchase. As a result, purchased manumissions became the most common road to freedom in both Brazil and Spanish America. Masters also freed slaves without payment, particularly their children by enslaved mothers, and the elderly, as an act of religious piety or a reward for exemplary service. Freed slaves then often saved to purchase the manumission of family members still in bondage. Indeed, the commitment and enterprise of black families fostered the rapid growth in the free black population as much as imperial laws and Catholic beliefs. Although manumission took place far more commonly in Latin America than in the British colonies, the majority of African slaves lived and died in bondage. Added to the stigma associated with slavery, free blacks, regardless of their achievements, continued to suffer from a broad array of discriminatory and restrictive legislation and prejudice.

Castas

A racially mixed population, a fundamental characteristic of contemporary Latin America, originated in the initial encounter of Spaniards and the indigenous population on Española and the Iberians' subsequent introduction of Africans. By the eighteenth century, real and imagined combinations of Indians, Spaniards, and blacks inspired a surfeit of labels for their offspring. The most important in Spain's America are listed in Table 9.1.

Racial labeling was fluid and flexible. Contemporaries often used the generic term *casta* for a mixed-race person identified as neither Spaniard nor Indian; thus, it applied to all free persons with any African ancestry or suspicion of it because of illegitimacy. A viceroy of Peru summarized the category in 1792 in the phrase "mulattoes, blacks, and other free *castas* of color."[1] "Mestizos" included free mulattoes, blacks, and other *castas* of color in the census of New Spain in 1793. In 1810, however, a summary of *castas* encompassed mestizos and all other persons of mixed ancestry. Although the labels originated to identify racial combinations, in practice they soon lost putative racial precision. Individuals often presented themselves as first one race and then another depending on circumstances because legislation endowed each of the major groups with distinct rights, obligations, and restrictions, underscoring their inequality.

By the mid-sixteenth century, whites' offspring with Indian women became increasingly known as mestizos. Royal officials considered young mestizo males particularly troublesome, especially those living with neither parent, and subjected them to restrictive legislation. In a bow to their paternal lineage, however, they exempted mestizos from paying the tribute demanded of the indigenous. The censuses of New Spain in 1742 and 1793 and Peru in 1790 listed the number of mestizos as second only to Indians.

Table 9.1 Racial Mixture

PARENT	PARENT	OFFSPRING
Spanish	Indian	Mestizo
Spanish	Black	Mulatto
Indian	Black	Generally *zambo* in Peru; mulatto in New Spain and Central America; also *pardo*
Casta (mixed)	Any combination of Indian, black, or Spaniard	*Casta*; often applied to all persons not fully Spanish or indigenous; *pardo* if one parent of African ancestry

Spain and Portugal adhered to the "law of the womb." This stricture meant that children followed the civil state (free or slave) of their mother. Black males' progeny with Indian women, unlike those with enslaved black women, provided the beginnings of a free black population that expanded rapidly from Afro-Indian

Portrait from Eighteenth-Century Mexico City of the Young Daughter of a Free Black Woman and a Spaniard. Discriminatory sumptuary laws barred free black women from wearing rich garments and expensive jewelry. The intention was to install a clear boundary between white women and *castas*.

unions. By the mid-seventeenth century, free Afro-Mexicans in New Spain were the largest Afro-mestizo population in the Indies. In Yucatan as well, free, mixed-race Afro-Yucatecans outnumbered slaves by 1600 and continued to increase during Spanish rule. Located between the Maya and the Spaniards, their middle position typified their relative ranking throughout Spain's mainland possessions.

In Santiago de Guatemala, possessing one or more mulatto slaves (mulattoes in Guatemala included persons with any African heritage) enabled the Spanish elite to distance themselves from other citizens (*vecinos*). The wealthiest house-holds had dozens of residents that included family members; Spanish, mestizo, and mulatto offspring; retainers, servants, and slaves living together and sleeping "under the same roof, regardless of status or race."[2] One result was an ongoing expansion of the *casta* population. By the 1650s, the racially mixed common folk were almost twice as numerous as Spaniards and Indians combined. Continued blending made the majority of the population indistinguishable from each other in terms of appearance. As a result, after about 1670, contemporaries extended to all *castas* the term *ladino*, originally applied to Hispanicized Indians.

For mulattoes and free blacks, service in the local militia offered a route to social advancement. Starting in 1540, the Crown ordered settlers to form militia companies to provide for their own defense. Too few Spanish males of appropriate age to serve in such units led administrators to look for soldiers in the indigenous and free colored populations. A century later, the militia of Santiago de Guatemala had separate companies composed of mulattoes and blacks in most of its districts; by the eighteenth century, mulatto officers commanded all of these units. Mesti-zos and nonmulatto *castas* also served in the city's Spanish infantry companies. Indeed, Spaniards filled only the cavalry unit. In Lima in 1680, Indians, free mulat-toes, and free blacks comprised a majority of the infantry companies. Additionally, Indians manned two cavalry companies and mulattoes manned one.

Throughout the Indies, free blacks and mulattoes joined militias both for potential social advancement and for possible exemption from tribute. In the 1620s, the colored militia of Lima secured this relief for their service and loyalty in the face of Dutch threats. By 1650, soldiers in the *pardo* militia company of Campeche, their counterparts in Merida, and some free black and mulatto militia-men in northern Peru received exemption. In New Spain, most militia units won this benefit in the closing decades of the seventeenth century.

Free colored militia officers in New Spain started to receive the military *fuero* in the late seventeenth century. The Crown extended these privileges to all militia-men in the late 1760s, but in the 1790s the viceroy took steps to end free coloreds' service in the militia. He also integrated companies, assigning both white and nonwhite soldiers to them. This eliminated benefits that *pardo* units had enjoyed and forced competition between colored and white soldiers. In Yucatan, however, most free colored units remained in existence.

Both integrated religious confraternities (*cofradías*) and those specifically es-tablished for slave and free blacks and mulattoes started to appear in the sixteenth century. They made available mutual assistance, charity, funerals, and sometimes aid to widows and orphaned children. Their fiestas and other activities provided an organized focus for developing and maintaining community and networks amid the socializing. Thus, they simultaneously attracted blacks and mulattoes to the Church and enabled them to utilize the Christian calendar for their festivities.

The demographic consequences of racial mixture and identification based on an overall evaluation of individuals' "quality" or status appear in counts from the late eighteenth and early nineteenth centuries. In the large province of Caracas, Venezuela, as well as in New Granada, *castas* totaled just less than half of the population. Including slaves raised the African-descended population to a majority. In contrast, the indigenous outnumbered the remainder of the population in Peru and New Spain. Persons identified as mixed race (mestizos and *castas*) in Peru together were roughly double the number of Spaniards. In New Spain, the mestizo category included all persons of mixed race (Indo- and Afro-mestizos) and also outnumbered the Spaniards. In Cuba, free people of color, a classification that encompassed all racial blending, constituted about 20 percent of the island's population in both 1791 and 1810.

FAMILY: THE FOUNDATION OF SOCIETY

The family formed the basic social unit during Spanish and Portuguese rule. Race, gender, wealth, and occupation contributed to an individual's position in the social structure, but his or her importance rested within the framework of a broadly defined family. More than blood relatives, "family" in this context included the relations created by marriage and alliances through the selection of godparents, the arrangement called _compadrazgo_ in Spanish and *compadrio* in Portuguese. Appreciating an extended family's political activities and social and economic objectives thus provides a better understanding of the settlers' world over time than chronicling an individual's successes and failures.

The advantages, or burdens, of familial associations had a longitudinal character because families achieved and asserted status across successive generations. Lineage, social and legal privileges, and service to the Crown contributed to individual family members' place in society. Accordingly, aspiring men and women, especially of the elite, worked to elevate their families' reputations as platforms for both their own ambitions and those of their kin and heirs. Government officials and other propertied groups, such as urban professionals, similarly protected and enhanced family reputation.

Indians emphasized the extended family as much as Iberians. Like settler elites, indigenous nobles prided themselves on their lineages and exploited the benefits of familial connections and resources. Long after the Conquest, native elites normally married within their own rank, maintaining social distance from those below them. But commoners also exercised control over marriage decisions. The strength of indigenous kinship groups enabled Indian communities to maintain land rights and provide assistance during droughts and other difficult economic times, in short, to survive, despite heavy demands that included tribute and labor.

The experiences of the mixed population, the *castas*, defy generalizations. Although some Spanish and Portuguese settlers married Indian women during and immediately following the Conquest, many more lived in less formal arrangements.

Mixed children from these relationships raised within their fathers' households shared their desire to advance familial ambitions. The indigenous mothers and their offspring served as important cultural intermediaries who transmitted language, customs, technologies, and folkways back and forth between themselves and the Europeans. When not recognized by their fathers and when separated from their mothers' communities and traditional rights, orphaned or abandoned mestizos often sought to survive in cities and towns. These locations increasingly became the focus of an emerging *casta* culture that combined elements of indigenous, European, and African practices and beliefs.

By the mid-sixteenth century, Church officials and royal authorities increasingly assumed illegitimate birth for *castas*. Indeed, most of the mixed population struggled to survive as rural or urban laborers or as artisans and petty retailers. They often lacked connections to kinship groups and thus had little opportunity to elevate their household's standing as the elite did. Nevertheless, they could turn honesty, hard work, or courage to advantage in the neighborhood or village.

Marriage

The Spanish and Portuguese crowns and the Catholic Church considered the sacrament of marriage between a man and a woman the only acceptable basis for a family. The richest and most influential men in the Indies, of course, normally sought to wed younger women of their own culture and class; their offspring benefited most from their parents' social position and fortune. Although formal dissolution or divorce terminated a few marriages, union for life, if not love, underlay Spanish and Portuguese matrimonial practices and the accompanying elaboration of the extended family.

Marriages most commonly united couples from the same or adjoining ethnicities and social classes, but Iberian males frequently engaged in less formal but sometimes enduring relationships with Indian, black, and *casta* women. Although deeply held prejudices associated with differences in color or culture limited marriages across ethnic boundaries for elites, such biases did little to slow the development of informal unions and the rate of miscegenation. Some Spanish and Portuguese fathers, however, granted legal recognition to their illegitimate mixed-race children, an action that improved their status.

Because *castas* largely lacked access either to traditional Indian landholding rights or to full participation in the Spanish economy, they tended to marry at rates lower than that of other groups. Less constrained by family preferences, *casta* men and women sought mates, established families, and wed in response to their own needs and resources.

Black slaves entered formal unions with less frequency than did the free population. The sexual imbalance in the slave trade, impediments inherent in bondage, and often masters' active opposition worked to inhibit marriages among their chattel. Urban slaves wed more frequently than did those on plantations or farms, but the obstacles in most places limited matrimony to a minority of males and a somewhat larger percentage of females. Consequently, many slave families forged long-term relationships unsanctified by the Church.

The Family as an Economic Unit

Elite families in both Spanish America and Brazil routinely emphasized their Iberian origins to distinguish themselves from persons they considered social inferiors. High-ranking officeholders frequently depended on their connections in Iberia for favors and worked hard to maintain and enhance these ties. But most leading families in the sixteenth century traced their social ascendancy to a single conquistador or settler or sometimes to the efforts of several close relatives, for example, the Pizarro brothers, rather than to European connections. In Spanish America, the windfalls of the age of conquest, early mining discoveries, political offices, *encomiendas*, and the accumulation of urban and rural real estate often combined to form the foundations of family prestige and power. Brazilians followed a similar pattern, but the smaller indigenous population, the absence of an early mining boom, and comparatively few royal administrative positions slowed the growth of elite family wealth. In both cases, leading families sought to perpetuate their status by diversifying their holdings through investment in trade, agricultural and pastoral activities, and other enterprises appropriate to the region of residence. But these fragile economic underpinnings often left the remnants of early elite families in difficult straits by the seventeenth century.

Few descendants of the first *encomenderos* in Spanish America bequeathed resources equal to their own inheritance. The growth in international trade and the decline in Indian populations transformed social and economic structures. Mining also proved unreliable, since a rich vein of silver could unexpectedly become exhausted. As a result of this turmoil, few prominent families in the seventeenth century traced their origins to conquerors, *encomenderos*, or early miners.

After about 1640, the pace of territorial expansion slowed in many areas of Spanish America and subsequent periods of economic depression and stagnation hindered new families' access to the upper levels of the social order. At the same time, fiscal constraints limited the growth in royal offices; family members received only inheritable municipal positions from their forebears. Although generally poorer than their parents, heirs rarely declined in status precipitously, and marriage alliances with other select families could shore up the privileges and social eminence of a prominent family.

In seventeenth-century Brazil, in contrast, expansion into the interior, the growth in the sugar industry, and, at the end of the century, the discovery of gold and other precious minerals provided more opportunities to accumulate wealth and improve social status than were then available in the Spanish dominions. Huge cattle ranches spread throughout the Brazilian northeast. In São Paulo, in the south, the wealth of the elite expanded rapidly as a result of growing exports of Indian slaves taken in raids in the interior and agricultural products, such as wheat, rum, and sailcloth. Here, as in the Spanish kingdoms and provinces, economic diversification and control of political offices helped protect prominent families against the adverse effects of inheritance and economic volatility. Despite these time-tested strategies, some elite families declined or disappeared completely. Others died out after two or three generations because of infant or child mortality or because heirs either chose not to marry or failed to produce offspring. Still others descended into middle groups of the white population as a result of financial reverses or a surfeit of heirs.

Childhood was viewed as anticipation of adult life. In this eighteenth-century portrait of young Joaquín Sánchez Pareja Narváez, he is posed in a military uniform with a rifle.

WOMEN IN THE SOCIETIES AND
ECONOMIES OF THE INDIES

Within the parameters established by race and social standing, gender played the most important role in determining an individual's place in the patriarchal society of early Latin America. The activities of men and women, and thus husbands and wives, reflected distinct opportunities and responsibilities. Although varied by region, they rested on the Iberian and indigenous heritages. Men held all civil offices, made political decisions, and dominated the most lucrative economic activities. They generally performed the heavy manual labor in fields and mines, constructed buildings and ships, worked on roads, and transported goods as carriers, muleteers, and seamen. Males provided military service and held all ecclesiastical posts, except those in female convents. And they alone could secure a higher education, join a *consulado*, or, in most cases, enter an artisan guild.

The social and economic reality of life in the Indies, however, exhibited far more complexity than this description of a largely male-dominated society. Below the elite, women frequently worked outside the home. Brazil's sugar estates and smaller cane farms depended on the labor of both slave and free women throughout the production cycle, but especially during the harvest. Small independent farmers and ranchers also relied on the labor of wives and daughters because few produced enough income to hire temporary workers. Retail sales in many urban and rural markets and mining camps depended largely on women, who sold thread, brooms, and other handicrafts and produced and sold sweets, bread, pastries, and alcoholic beverages.

Women also held an important place in manufacturing, providing skilled labor in textile production. Female guilds appeared in Mexico City as early as the sixteenth century. Some women worked in textile and ceramic factories. Even artisan trades that ostensibly prohibited female participation benefited from women's labor. Poorer masters unable to afford the set wages of journeymen or the expense of an apprentice used their wives and children to prepare raw materials and maintain tools. Despite regulations that required a woman to remarry an eligible guild member to keep her deceased husband's shop open, widows often became effectively independent master artisans without license. Females of this class frequently supplemented family income by taking in washing, renting rooms, or working as domestics.

The capital investments, labor, and entrepreneurial skills of women proved particularly significant in less privileged groups. Additionally, they held marginal, and sometimes dangerous, positions in medicine and religion as curers, potion makers, fortune-tellers, and spirit mediums. Few families in the rural and urban working classes could survive on only the income earned by the male head of household because the cost of basic necessities almost invariably exceeded the income of any single worker, whether peon, cowboy, weaver, cobbler, blacksmith, or carpenter.

African slaves contributed a second stream of women for domestic labor. Nearly every elite family owned black slaves, the majority of them often females who cleaned, cooked, made clothes, and provided almost all essential household services.

Indeed, dowries often included slaves because "decent" households required their skills. Females in bondage as slaves secured freedom through manumission more frequently than males, purchasing it at market value with money earned in their off hours. Their broad engagement in the economy, especially in cities, made them primary agents of cultural change for their community. Like indigenous women who served in Spanish and Portuguese households, slaves faced the possibility of sexual exploitation. As a result, such women found themselves coerced participants in the emergence of mixed populations and the forging of new cultural identities that blended traditions of indigenous America, Africa, and Europe.

THE CULTURE OF HONOR

Spanish and Portuguese immigrants brought to the Americas a fundamental concern for honor, the recognition and defense of individual and family position in the social hierarchy. It allowed society to sort out the Indies' incredibly complex relationships of wealth, class, gender, race, and culture through sensitivity to shame, jealousy of others' success, and a desire to be the object of others' envy.

Honor preoccupied elite families. They paid close attention to every interaction: competition for offices and rewards, business dealings of all kinds, marriages of children, the selection of godparents, and even seating arrangements at public dinners. Honor determined one's equals and inferiors. As such, it controlled who was invited into a home, who stood and who sat, who kept a hat on and who removed it. Disagreements over the order in which administrative groups, clerics, and officials marched through the streets during celebrations of feast days or the coronation of kings produced lawsuits that lasted years. If individuals or groups allowed themselves to be treated as inferiors without protest or revenge—if they failed to react appropriately to challenges to their honor—they lost status. The competing claims to honor and precedence both arranged society hierarchically and potentially destabilized it.

Although elite families viewed honor as unique to their class, concern for it permeated the social order. Members of the urban middle sector such as physicians, lawyers, and even master artisans came eventually to assert their honor in legal proceedings and, on occasion, in violent confrontations with those who presumed to insult them. Men of humble circumstances, journeymen and day laborers, explained violent assaults in terms of the need to answer an insult or as an effort to avoid shame. Even slaves, society's most vulnerable group, held a clear regard for reputation and, when offended, displayed a willingness to find remedy in violence or sometimes in the courts.

The basic social unit in the Indies, the extended family carried the most significance for the elite. As each region achieved economic and social maturity, its leading prominent families intermarried and incorporated through marriage successful newcomers, normally peninsular males, into their midst. Although the timing varied, this establishment and consolidation of kin networks took place in settings as diverse as Recife, Salvador, Santiago, Lima, Popayan, Guatemala, and Puebla.

Primary Source

Foreigners' Comments on Chile and Peru's Inhabitants, 1710s

In 1717, an English press published *A Voyage to the South-Sea* by the French engineer Amédée Frezier. The work was a translation of Frezier's 1716 account in French of his travels in Chile and Peru between 1712 and 1714; a Spanish translation finally appeared (in Chile) in 1902. In addition to describing geographic features, minerals, animals, plants and agriculture, fortifications, military forces, trade, and religious practices, Frezier commented on the inhabitants and their races, colors, customs, and dress. The following selection (spelling and capitalization modernized) illustrates his commentary as well as translator's additions that would appeal to an English audience's anti-Spanish bias.

SOURCE: [Amédée] Frezier, *A Voyage to the South-Sea, and along the Coasts of Chili and Peru, in the Years 1712, 1713, and 1714* (London: Jonah Bowyer, 1717), 68, 187, 202, 219.

The "natural color [of the native population in Chile] is dark, inclining to copper-color, wherein they differ from the mulatto's, which proceeds from a mixture of whiteness and blackness: This color is general throughout all America, as well North as South; whence it is to be observed, that it is . . . a particular affection of the blood, for the descendants of the Spaniards, who are settled there, and married to Europeans, and have continued unmixed with the Chileans, are of a finer and fresher white and red, than those in Europe, tho' born in Chile, fed almost after the same manner, and commonly suckled by the natives of the country."

"The blacks they carry thither from Guinea, or Angola, do also retain their natural color from Father to Son, when they keep to their own kind."

About mulattoes: "Those poor people, like all the other Creolian Spaniards, that, is the mixed races . . ."

About the Peruvian savant Pedro de Peralta: "a creole or mongrel Spaniard of Lima."

"Both men and women are equally inclined to be costly in their dress; the women not satisfied with the expense of the richest silks, adorn them, after their manner, with a prodigious quantity of lace, and are insatiable as to pearls and jewels, for bracelets, pendants and other ornaments; the fashion whereof, which amounts to very much, ruins the husbands and the gallants. We saw ladies who had about them above the value of 60,000 pieces of eight in jewels: they are generally beautiful enough, of a sprightly mien, and more engaging than in other places; and perhaps one part of their beauty is owing to . . . [their contrast with] the mulattas, blacks, Indians, and other hideous faces, which are the most numerous throughout the country."

Indian societies also maintained familial ties, although epidemics, forced relocation, and voluntary migration worked against their perpetuation. The centrality of family was hardest on the free mixed-race population. The prevalence of illegitimacy among the early generations in particular made impossible the kind of kinship ties and support common to the majority of society. But as the number of persons of mixed ancestry increased, they, too, conformed to the ideal of the extended family.

NOTES

1. Viceroy Francisco Gil de Taboada y Lemos to Conde de Aranda, November 5, 1792, in María Pilar Pérez Cantó, *Lima en el siglo XVIII: Estudio socioeconómico* (Madrid: Ediciones de la Universidad Autónoma de Madrid, 1985), 193.
2. Christopher H. Lutz, *Santiago de Guatemala, 1541–1773: City, Caste, and the Colonial Experience* (Norman: University of Oklahoma Press, 1994), 46.

SUGGESTIONS FOR FURTHER READING

Bennett, Herman L. *Colonial Blackness: A History of Afro-Mexico.* Bloomington: Indiana University Press, 2010.

Cope, R. Douglas. *The Limits of Racial Domination: Plebeian Society in Colonial Mexico City, 1660–1720.* Madison: University of Wisconsin Press, 1994.

Gauderman, Kimberly. *Women's Lives in Colonial Quito: Gender, Law, and Economy in Spanish America.* Austin: University of Texas Press, 2003.

Johnson, Lyman L., and Sonya Lipsett-Rivera (eds.). *The Faces of Honor: Sex, Shame, and Violence in Colonial Latin America.* Albuquerque: University of New Mexico Press, 1998.

Katzew, Ilona. *Casta Painting: Images of Race in Eighteenth-Century Mexico.* New Haven, CT, and London: Yale University Press, 2005.

Kellogg, Susan. *Law and the Transformation of Aztec Culture, 1500–1700.* Norman: University of Oklahoma Press, 1995.

Martínez, María Elena. *Genealogical Fictions: Limpieza de Sangre, Religion and Gender in Colonial Mexico.* Stanford, CA: Stanford University Press, 2008.

McKinley, Michelle A. *Fractional Freedoms: Slavery, Intimacy, and Legal Mobilization in Colonial Lima, 1600-1700.* Cambridge and New York: Cambridge University Press, 2016.

Metcalf, Alida C. *Family and Frontier in Colonial Brazil: Santana de Parnaíba, 1580–1822.* Berkeley and Los Angeles: University of California Press, 1992.

Powers, Karen Vieira. *Women in the Crucible of Conquest: The Gendered Genesis of Spanish American Society, 1500–1600.* Albuquerque: University of New Mexico Press, 2005.

Restall, Matthew. *The Black Middle: Africans, Mayas, and Spaniards in Colonial Yucatan.* Stanford, CA: Stanford University Press, 2009.

Robins, Nicholas A. *Of Love & Loathing: Marital Life, Strife, and Intimacy in the Colonial Andes, 1750-1825.* Lincoln: University of Nebraska Press, 2015.

Socolow, Susan Migden. *The Women of Colonial Latin America.* Cambridge and New York: Cambridge University Press, 2000.

Twinam, Ann. *Purchasing Whiteness: Pardos, Mulattos, and the Quest for Social Mobility in the Spanish Indies.* Stanford, CA: Stanford University Press, 2015.

———. *Public Lives, Private Secrets: Gender, Honor, Sexuality, and Illegitimacy in Colonial Spanish America.* Stanford, CA: Stanford University Press, 1999.

Vinson, Ben, III, and Matthew Restall (eds.). *Black Mexico: Race and Society from Colonial to Modern Times.* Albuquerque: University of New Mexico Press, 2009.

CHAPTER 10

Living in an Empire

European conquest and settlement irreversibly altered the New World's architectural environment. The conquerors' cathedrals, convents, administrative buildings, and private residences soon replaced or complemented the palaces, pyramids, elevated plazas, and ball courts of the indigenous elites. Both the surviving traditions and the imported European architectural forms helped create the context for the evolution of societies under Spanish and Portuguese rule.

The architectural progression appeared most clearly in central Mexico and Peru, where large urban and ceremonial centers existed before European contact. In regions outside the great Andean and Mesoamerican civilizations, Spaniards founded new towns unencumbered by the architectural legacies and city plans of the Indian past. Eventually, however, common features in construction and town planning appeared throughout Spanish America. Because its indigenous peoples had not constructed urban centers, Brazil's experience resembled that of Spain's peripheral provinces in the Indies.

URBAN AND RURAL ENVIRONMENTS

City Foundations and Plans

Concentrations of natives, nearby agricultural resources, and a climate similar to what they knew in Europe attracted Spaniards who asserted political authority and then imposed a new urban landscape. In regions without sedentary agriculture and urbanization, missionaries and civil authorities created towns to organize and control the indigenous population. If necessary, they forcibly concentrated the Indians both to facilitate Christianization and to compel participation in the emerging monetary economy. In each case, Spanish and Portuguese settlers implanted their own concepts of urban social organization, architecture, and city planning, although elements of indigenous experience survived.

Spaniards founded nearly 100 cities and towns before 1550, and many of the major urban centers of modern Spanish America existed by 1600. From the outset, the Spanish Crown promoted urban planning that placed a grid pattern around a large plaza at a municipality's core. The rectangular public space served as a marketplace, hosted religious and secular ceremonies, and displayed a pillory, gallows, or other symbol of royal justice. In major administrative centers, for example, Lima, Mexico City, Bogotá, and Santiago de Guatemala, the cathedral, viceroy or governor's palace, and city council building bounded the plaza. Lesser municipalities, relocated Indian populations, and mission communities offered fewer and smaller public structures at their core.

Brazilian towns generally developed more spontaneously, and fewer than 40 cities and towns, almost all within a few miles of the Atlantic coast, took shape before 1650. Nevertheless, important cities usually had a grid pattern at the center and, like towns and villages, a plaza complete with pillory. Their coastal locations made Brazil's major commercial and administrative cities vulnerable to attack. Defensive walls and other fortifications often influenced the direction of urban growth.

By 1630, Spanish America's larger municipalities displayed a durable rank order established initially by demography, physical resources, and commercial activity. Spanish immigrants first settled near dense Indian populations, an attraction the *encomienda* system reinforced. Rich mineral deposits promoted rapid population growth in Potosí, Zacatecas, and other mining centers. The commercial activity of port cities like Cartagena, Havana, and, to a lesser extent, Portobello and Veracruz drew civilians as well as military garrisons.

This rapid proliferation of urban centers, however, failed to produce strong economic ties among Spanish America's major cities. Generally, economic and political structures linked them more closely to Seville, and later Cádiz and Madrid, than to each other. The prominence of sugar exportation in the Brazilian economy from the mid-sixteenth to the early eighteenth centuries defined even more sharply this pattern of isolation and initial dependence on the metropolis.

The City

The rectilinear core of American cities emphasized European culture and architecture. The cathedrals and richest convents had no rivals, and few secular buildings compared favorably with those in Iberia. Although large and well built, the vice-regal palaces in Lima and Mexico City lacked the architectural interest of Europe's great palaces. Government policy in Brazil prohibited the construction of unnecessarily expensive residences and office buildings.

The central plaza served as an arena for a host of public spectacles. Numerous civil and religious processions concluded with a mass at the cathedral. These festivities reflected the inequality inherent in the social hierarchy, with prelates, high-level officials, and knights of the military orders enjoying places of honor. Deviation from this expected system of preferment provoked protests and even litigation. Commercial and artisan corporations maintained a similar hierarchy. Bullfights, *autos de fé*, and public executions also drew enormous crowds to the plaza.

The ostentatious display by affluent citizens impressed European visitors. Most elite occupied well-furnished, spacious, two-story dwellings built of cut stone or brick, often with interior patios and attached carriage houses and stables. Even the richest merchants sold goods at retail in the first-floor rooms of multistory homes and the corner rooms of single-story buildings. Homeowners not directly involved in trade or manufacture frequently rented space to small shopkeepers and artisans. The result routinely intermixed commerce, manufacture, and residences throughout America's Iberian cities.

The majority of the poor, mostly Indians, *castas*, and free blacks, lived away from the central plaza in crowded, ill-furnished rooms located in sprawling impoverished districts (*barrios*) that generally lacked the orderliness of the city's grid. Small, mud-colored adobe houses fronted directly on the street. Only parish churches and poorer convents afforded architectural relief from the monotonous and squalid landscape. Yet significant differences in status and material conditions could be found. Some poor Spaniards, usually recent immigrants, lived among the *castas*. Skilled artisans and a small number of traditional indigenous political authorities represented the upper end of the neighborhood social pyramid. Below them came market gardeners, laborers, porters, and petty merchants. At the bottom resided Indians temporarily drawn to the city as *repartimiento* workers or engaged in voluntary, unskilled day labor. Most men and women wore their entire wardrobes on their backs, although the more fortunate also owned an extra shirt or a poncho that could double as a blanket. The relatively high cost of housing, particularly lodging adequate for family life, forced many young men and women to defer marriage and childbearing. Crowded conditions also made working-class women and children much more vulnerable to intimidation, sexual assaults, and common insults. In this environment, husbands and fathers found themselves defending their family's honor with fists or knives.

By the eighteenth century, members of the elite sought opportunities to display their wealth. This Mexican woman's dress is made from costly imported cloth, and she is posed next to a harpsichord for her portrait. The false beauty mark near her right eye was another common affectation.

Suburban districts (*barrios*) typically housed the most unsanitary, dangerous, and noisy urban businesses. Slaughterhouses and tanneries that exuded noxious odors, corrals that serviced local and long-distance freight businesses, and bakeries and brick makers' kilns that posed fire threats broke up impoverished neighborhoods. Numerous gaming and drinking establishments provided some pleasure and diversion. Although the choice varied by region, the urban poor consumed enormous amounts of *pulque, chicha,* rum, wine, and other alcoholic beverages. Endemic poverty and political powerlessness spawned drunkenness and related acts of violence, which indelibly marked the urban landscape.

Rural Settlements

Both small towns and dispersed rural settlements formed living environments in the countryside. Most traditional villages inhabited primarily by Indians lacked a grid pattern and large-scale religious or secular buildings; a general store vied with the church as the social focus. Residential construction depended on adobe and local timber. Houses typically featured a single room and a separate kitchen constructed of less substantial material.

By the early seventeenth century, large estates increasingly dominated much valuable countryside in many parts of Latin America. Often painstakingly amassed over years through numerous small grants, purchases, bequests, and usurpations of native land, the haciendas enabled their lay and ecclesiastical owners to profit by selling agricultural and pastoral products. Location, climate, and access to labor, however, affected both what the properties could produce and whether the market would be primarily local, regional, interprovincial, or international. The most heavily capitalized large estates employed slave labor and primarily exported to the international market. Sugar plantations (*engenhos*) developed in Brazil after the mid-sixteenth century and served as a model for the later Spanish counterparts (*ingenios*) in the Caribbean. Plantations also frequently produced tobacco, indigo, and cacao. Less capitalized estates, variously termed *haciendas* or *estancias* in Spanish America and *fazendas* in Brazil, grew wheat and other grains or raised livestock. Location frequently limited their products to sale in nearby markets, that they sought to monopolize.

On plantations, most slaves shared meager quarters, although some had single-family housing. Barracks helped to prevent runaways but severely hampered the development of family life. Impoverished material conditions restricted slaves' daily activities and forced isolation limited their access to religious and secular instruction. Collective forms of expression, such as the lay brotherhoods available in towns, could not be regularly sustained in the harsh work environment of the plantation.

In regions of low population density, *haciendas, estancias,* and *fazendas* provided the physical focus for social life as well as production. The owner's large house dominated the *hacienda*'s residential core, which might also include shops for one or more blacksmiths, potters, and carpenters. Although some wealthy estates maintained a chapel, resident priests were seldom present. The largest properties covered many square miles and had outlying corrals, line shacks, and some dispersed housing for tenants.

Small ranches and farms of frequently poor freeholders and tenants shared the rural landscape with *haciendas*, plantations, and, at times, Indian villages and missions. Isolated and usually minimal family housing lay scattered along the northern frontier of New Spain, in the southern *pampa* of the Río de la Plata, and in the interior grazing area (*llanos*) of Venezuela.

The architectural environment of Latin America helped shape and control a diverse mix of competing social groups. As in the most populous preconquest indigenous societies, settlers' planning and urban architecture contained a political message: Their cities asserted and sustained the authority of the white elites. Monumental architecture of the city center served to awe and intimidate the masses. When used for *autos de fé*, bullfights, and executions, the central plazas helped direct the energies and anger of the masses toward safe symbolic targets.

At another level, the physical settings provided by houses, taverns, shops, gaming establishments, and small manufacturers operated more subtly. They helped to fashion the values of family and class that arose from the inequalities imposed by the economy and Iberian social attitudes. The physical environment sometimes shaped and sometimes reinforced perceptions of race and gender, decisions about marriage and childrearing, and feelings of solidarity with or alienation from coworkers. More than places to reside and work, the urban and rural living environments reflected both the highest aspirations and the deepest despair present in the Indies.

Disasters

Devastating natural and manmade disasters periodically struck Latin America, afflicting particularly their societies' poorest and most vulnerable sectors. Earthquakes, hurricanes, and flooding brought tragedy to individuals, families, and, at times, cities and entire regions.

Earthquakes repeatedly caused terror and extensive destruction. Although the 1687 quake severely damaged Lima, the quake in 1746 resulted in even worse material losses and 1,300 deaths. The accompanying tsunami destroyed the port of Callao and left only some 200 survivors of a population that had numbered roughly 4,000. The furious storm sank 19 ships in the harbor and deposited 4 others on land. Major earthquakes also repeatedly plagued Chile, as well as Quito and other Ecuadoran sites. Destructive seismic activity afflicted Mesoamerica, too. Among the most devastating blows, two quakes of 1773 led to the transfer of Guatemala's capital to a new site.

Europeans knew about hurricanes' destructive power in the Caribbean from the time of Columbus. The hastily built town of Santo Domingo suffered severe damage in 1502 when winds ripped through its wooden structures. Despite the use of some stone in its reconstruction, the city experienced serious damage again in violent storms of 1508 and 1509. Cuba did not escape hurricane damage either. Ferocious hurricanes struck repeatedly between 1519 and 1558, causing destruction across the island. In October 1768, another killed more than 1,000 people, nearly leveled the city of Havana, and obliterated more than 50 ships in the bay.

The most notorious flooding during Spanish rule occurred in the Valley of Mexico. As the lakes silted from erosion caused by deforestation, Mexico City's excessive water problem worsened. Finally, after damaging inundations in 1604 and 1607, the viceregal government initiated a monumental project to reduce the lakes, but the drainage tunnel (*desagüe*) opened in late 1608 proved inadequate. In 1629, the worst flood in New Spain's history left the capital under water for four years. As a stopgap measure, native labor drafts turned the tunnel into an open trench and then maintained and expanded it until independence. Completion of the lakes' drainage awaited the late nineteenth century.

DAILY LIFE

Life in the Indies displayed extremes of social position and wealth on the one hand and the great disparity between rural and urban environments on the other. For the rural majority, only religious activities and occasional secular celebrations broke the tedium. The richer and more complex life of ritual and social interaction of the largest precontact indigenous cultures subsided as the effects of epidemic disease, miscegenation, and the penetration of the market economy forged postconquest rural culture. Urban dwellers experienced more frequent and varied entertainment than did rural residents, but most of them, too, lived a precarious existence marked by a long working day, minimal diet, and poor health. Crime and violence threatened urban and rural residents alike. Elites alone had access to the array of pleasures available, but less advantaged groups could enjoy religious celebrations as well as drinking, music, games, and gambling, among other diversions.

Work

From an early age, most people in the Indies spent the daylight hours engaged in manual labor in return for generally abysmal compensation. The struggle for survival consumed their energies, and Sundays and holidays alone offered respite. The special requirements of planting and harvesting could cancel even these unpaid breaks. Indians and other free rural laborers routinely toiled 10 to 12 hours a day, often for more than 300 days a year. Indian employees in the textile *obrajes* of Ecuador labored from 6:00 AM to 6:00 PM six days a week, except for an annual seven-week interval when they could sow, weed, and harvest their own fields. In the early seventeenth century, *mita* laborers had their workweek reduced from six to five days, but an oppressive quota system repeatedly extended their toil beyond the theoretical 12-hour shifts. Slaves, particularly on sugar plantations, frequently worked even more.

As in Europe at the same time, wages paid to the majority of free workers rarely exceeded the subsistence level, and men assigned to a *mita* or *obraje* often earned substantially less. Such minimal compensation reinforced the social order based on inequality. Considering nonwhites their inferiors, Spaniards and Portuguese believed that exploitive wages represented just and appropriate remuneration. They also maintained that the low pay that kept the workers mired in poverty encouraged productivity and discouraged idleness. Despite extreme fluctuations in the price of maize and other basic foodstuffs, wages generally remained stable in each category of employment after the mid-seventeenth century.

Urban manual laborers received higher cash wages than their rural counterparts, but usually faced greater living expenses for their housing, food, and

Native, African, and European traditions contributed to the development of music, dance, and games in Spain's America.

clothing. Cities, however, offered more opportunities for employment as artisans, retailers, or workers in a variety of services with better compensation. The concentration of wholesale merchants, successful landowners, clerics, and royal officials contributed to a rich and colorful social life in urban areas.

Clothing

Clothing revealed status in the Indies just as it did in Europe. Early commentators noted the contrast between commoners' attire and the finely woven and decorated cotton and woolen garments worn by indigenous nobles in central Mexico and Andean Peru. In general, simple design and shape characterized all indigenous clothing before the Iberians introduced steel shears. The new tool enabled tailors to produce trousers, shirts, and other items favored by European males. Moreover, the rapid expansion of bands of sheep soon made wool widely accessible, whereas imported cloth from Europe and later silk from China added variety and fineness to the selection of fabrics available.

Iberian attitudes reinforced the use of European-style clothing. Yielding to clerics' demand for modest dress, Indian males soon wore long pants, shirts, and jackets or vests, sometimes under a native tunic. Native women's garb changed less, although skirt length increased. After the alterations in indigenous clothing, Spanish authorities required natives to wear garments of the same design generation after generation. Free and slave black and mulatta women suffered interference with their dress as well. Sumptuary legislation ineffectively banned them from wearing woolens, silk, and lace of gold and other colors.

Although most people wore homespun clothing or items made from cheap textiles manufactured in *obrajes*, the well-to-do provided a market for European and East Asian textiles that thousands of tailors and seamstresses turned into more stylish attire. Visitors often commented on the luxurious apparel exhibited by all classes. In the early eighteenth century, a French engineer remarked that Lima's women had "an insatiable appetite for pearls and jewels, for bracelets, earrings and other paraphernalia, which saps the wealth of husbands and lovers."[1] A passion for lavish clothing established rich textiles as the single most important import throughout the centuries of Spanish and Portuguese rule.

Diet

Culture, taste, habit, availability, and price determined the composition of diet. European plants and animals quickly came to supplement indigenous staples that included maize, beans, squash, and chilies in Mesoamerica; potatoes and quinoa in the Andes; and manioc in the Caribbean zone and Brazil. Europeans, Indians, and Africans altered their diets and tastes to incorporate previously unknown or expensive foods and obtained additional variety and protein as a result. Regional products, moreover, gave Latin American meals a distinctly different flavor from the fare found on Iberian tables.

Maize remained the dietary staple of the indigenous population of Mesoamerica after contact and enjoyed continued consumption elsewhere. However it was served, it provided up to 90 percent of the calories in an Indian's diet in the seventeenth century. The rural *casta* population similarly depended on this vital food. Numerous varieties of beans also continued as a major source of protein, and squash, pumpkins, and gourds added calories and nutrients. Whether consumed raw or in sauces, chili peppers and tomatoes contributed vitamins and flavor.

Domesticated European animals made available the most notable postconquest additions to foodstuffs. Chickens, pigs, sheep, and cattle thrived in the New World and offered unprecedented amounts of protein. Indians prized eggs, and chickens soon became intrusive residents in most villages. Pork and mutton also won favor. Beef, in contrast, gained popularity more slowly, perhaps because the Indians associated cattle with the destruction of their crops. By the eighteenth century, however, residents in northern New Spain and in most of Brazil and the Río de la Plata often consumed beef.

Africa also contributed to New World cuisine. Bananas, kidney beans, and okra followed in the wake of the slave trade. Although Africans' fare generally lacked adequate calories and nutrition, they sought to imitate the dishes of their homelands whenever possible. The legacy of these traditions survives in the recipes of modern Cuba and especially Brazil.

Wheat remained the principal dietary ingredient of Europeans and their creole kin. Affluent households served only white bread, considering the dark variety a poor person's food, as in Spain. A prosperous male consumed daily at least two pounds of bread, four ounces of meat, some vegetables, and oil or fat. In the seventeenth century, even country stores in Mexican mining towns far from the capital stocked shrimp, oysters, honey, lentils, spices, bananas, vinegar, salt, sugar, chocolate, beans, cheese, garlic, molasses, lard, and figs.

Unlike Indians, Iberians and other advantaged groups acquired most of their protein from meat. Favorites in the Spanish possessions included mutton and pork; in mid-eighteenth century Lima, only peninsulars regularly ate beef. Cooks used lard extensively in cooking, a custom begun before domestic olive oil became readily available. Proximity to the Pacific Ocean also enabled Lima's residents to enjoy fresh fish instead of the salted cod common in Europe and on transatlantic voyages. Crayfish from the adjacent River Rimac added another source of protein.

In Brazil, Chile, Venezuela, and the Río de la Plata region, European livestock, especially cattle, proliferated, making beef consumption common. By the early eighteenth century, slaves in Brazil received small amounts of dried beef from the *pampas* region and *sertão*, or fresh beef, from nearby ranches of the interior. Most Brazilian planters reduced expenses by allowing their slaves to cultivate garden plots. Some produced a surplus to sell to other slaves or in the local market. The very poor, beggars, and prisoners seldom consumed protein, relying almost entirely on the nutrients provided in bread.

Fruit and vegetables supplemented bread and meat in the European diet. As a dessert or a snack, sweetmeats enjoyed widespread popularity throughout the Indies. Slave and free black women produced and sold sugared sweets and pastries in all of Brazil's major cities.

Beverages accompanied and at times supplanted food. By the eighteenth century, chocolate sweetened with vanilla, cinnamon, and sugar had become the most popular nonalcoholic beverage in much of Spanish America. In South America, creoles in particular drank yerba maté, or Paraguayan tea. Alcoholic beverages frequently complemented meals and consumers imbibed them liberally at other times as well. Spaniards brought a taste for wine from Iberia and imported the beverage in large quantities. Although soon prohibited in New Spain, domestic production of wine followed settlement quickly, especially in the favorable climates and soil of Peru, Chile, and the Mendoza region of the Río de la Plata. Brandy emerged as the beverage of choice in the late seventeenth century because of its greater potency and superior traveling characteristics. Soon it became the poor man's luxury among urban laborers, cowboys, and even slaves.

Whereas well-to-do Spaniards drank good wine and brandy, most of society imbibed less pretentious intoxicants. These included *chicha*, a beer made from corn, in the Andes and *pulque*, derived from the maguey or century plant, in Mexico. *Aguardiente de caña*, a potent, distilled beverage, became a favorite in Brazil, Paraguay, the Caribbean Islands, New Granada, and other locations where sugar cane grew. In postconquest central Mexico, alcohol consumption increased as commoners escaped traditional taboos regarding *pulque* and gained access to imported wine. Indians there considered drinking to stupefaction acceptable in ritual situations and Andean peoples also expected to imbibe alcohol during comparable events. Heavy consumption of alcohol, in short, characterized New World society, as in preindustrial Europe. The masses especially consumed great quantities as they sought temporary relief from the daily misery in their lives.

Appetite Suppressants: Tobacco and Coca

An appetite suppressant, tobacco accompanied both diet and the consumption of alcohol. Smoked and snuffed by natives, it immediately caught Europeans' attention. Over time, smoking rolled tobacco became commonplace and eighteenth-century observers commented that men and women of all races and economic status enjoyed cigarettes and cigars. The coca shrub cultivated for centuries in the Andes prior to the Spanish conquest provided leaves that also suppressed appetite. Whereas the Inka nobility had enjoyed the privilege of chewing the leaves accompanied by a little ash, the Spanish conquest enabled the broader populace to participate and coca use rapidly became widespread. Miners at Potosí used the leaf to help them work longer hours and combat the effects of altitude. Chewing coca in the Andes has remained popular to the present day, and cocaine, its high-intensity derivative, has a world market.

Illness and Medicine

Epidemic diseases introduced from Europe and Africa repeatedly swept through mainland Latin America. The most prominent killers included smallpox, measles, typhus, influenza, pneumonic plague, and pestilential fevers. Poor sanitation practices, inadequate water supplies, and a general absence of sound hygiene promoted disease and poor health. The streets of large cities served as running sewers filled with human and animal excrement. Slaughterhouses discarded their waste where dogs and other scavengers could carry it near the houses. The city councils of Buenos Aires and other towns regularly repeated prohibitions against leaving the dead bodies of slaves and livestock carcasses in the street. Few residents had access to safe wells. Although some larger cities had aqueducts, most inhabitants bought water from peddlers or used sometimes-contaminated rainwater collected in ceramic or wooden tubs. Poor personal hygiene compounded the dangers inherent

The threat of early death was ever present. Elite families sometimes memorialized the premature deaths of their children. In this painting by an unknown Mexican artist, the body of Don Tomás María Joaquín Villaseñor y Gómez is surrounded by symbols of religious faith.

under these conditions. Few people bathed regularly; only the more affluent enjoyed the luxury of soap and clean clothes on demand.

Against these grave health threats, contemporary medical practices provided little relief. Nor did medical practitioners—physicians, phlebotomists or bleeders, surgeons, and "curers" who relied on folk medicine—offer effective healing for the host of other ailments. Rheumatic and other fevers, stomach ailments, catarrh, syphilis, abscesses, and tumors weakened the population and frequently brought premature death. The techniques and medicines at hand, moreover, made it virtually impossible to treat serious injuries successfully. As a result of these inadequacies, most people in the Indies spent much of their lives ill or in pain.

Unlike all other medical practice, females almost exclusively delivered babies, although wealthy women in larger cities often sought assistance from a licensed surgeon as well. Midwives routinely lacked formal training or approval, and most relied more on superstition than anatomical knowledge. As in Europe, the deadly combination of frequent pregnancies and poor medical practice in the Indies made complications in childbirth a leading cause of death for women.

Inadequate opportunities for formal medical instruction and practitioners' generally low status resulted in few physicians. The universities in Mexico, Lima, and Guatemala together probably conferred fewer than 1,000 medical degrees in the centuries before independence; graduates typically established their practices in urban centers. Because Brazil lacked a university, Portuguese immigrants or colonials trained in Europe constituted its physicians.

Poverty and disease go hand in hand because the conditions creating the first produce an environment conducive to the second. Widespread poverty, an inadequate diet, hard labor, and unsanitary conditions at work and home resulted in both high mortality and lower labor productivity. For most inhabitants of the Indies, life offered few pleasures and fewer rewards.

Crime and Punishment

Crime and violence accompanied Iberians' settlement of the New World and remained permanent features of daily life. Authorities tried to address cases of robbery, assault, and homicide, but normally paid less attention to violations of legislation intended to protect Indians and slaves from physical and financial abuse. One ongoing preoccupation involved consumer fraud, particularly by bakers and other food vendors. Settlers, moreover, proved adept at conniving with underpaid officials to swindle the government, for example, through evading taxes and customs duties.

A paucity of law enforcement officials and divided jurisdiction meant that royal authorities failed to detect most crime. Within rural Indian villages, local leaders dealt with robbery, adultery, and rape. On the plantations and large ranches of Brazil and Spanish America, landowners or their agents exercised de facto judicial authority, usually administering corporal punishment. The death penalty remained a prerogative of the state and the comparatively rare cases of homicide, sedition, and aggravated assault required royal judges to intervene. Local and royal officials in cities, in contrast, dealt with the full spectrum of crime.

Thieves found urban centers irresistible with their unlit streets and insufficient night patrols. Assault with a deadly weapon often meant with a butcher or household knife. Assailants and victims tended to be young males and frequently family members, neighbors, or fellow workers.

Civil authorities administered exemplary public punishments to remind the populace that robbery, violent acts, and other crimes could bring severe retribution. Judges routinely ordered terms of hard labor in *obrajes*, port facilities, the galleys, or the military. They discriminated in the use of lashings, sparing only Spaniards from corporal punishment. Executions took place less frequently in Spain's possessions and Brazil than in the English colonies. This difference arose both from the Iberian legal systems' receptivity to pleas of extenuating circumstances and from an appreciation that dead offenders could provide no labor.

Entertainment

Daily life in urban areas offered variety and excitement far removed from the routine of the countryside. Bells in churches and convents marked the hours. Processions honoring religious holidays mixed with civic celebrations to add color, sound, and festive enjoyment. The concentrations of wealth in the largest cities enabled expenditures for public display and spectacles impossible elsewhere and beyond the imagination of villages. Even the funerals of rich residents became public events.

Public spaces helped to define urban life. In Spanish America, plazas hosted executions, bullfights, military parades, public *autos de fé*, jousting on horseback with cane spears, and religious and civil processions and fiestas of all sorts. Vendors hawked fruit, sweetmeats, beverages, ices, and other items. On crowded, dirty streets passed ambulatory vendors, mules laden with goods, persons going to and from work, horse- and mule-drawn coaches and chaises, wives and servants on daily shopping trips, and children working, playing, or, in the case of some young boys, going to school.

Public festivals entertained rich and poor alike. Although every municipality, parish, guild, and brotherhood honored the day of its patron saint, large cities held the most frequent and lavish fiestas. Mexico City celebrated more than 90 festivals a year in the late 1600s. Into the eighteenth century, extravaganzas marked a new viceroy's entrance into the city; the ceremonial oath to a new monarch also elicited spectacular display. A huge triumphal arch identified the venue. Entertainment included bullfights, mock jousts, military demonstrations, and fireworks that continued for hours. Parades featured native dancers and musicians as well as elaborately decorated floats depicting historic events.

The eight-day Corpus Christi celebration took place annually. In the viceregal capital, the festival featured a procession accompanying the Eucharist through the streets and plays performed outdoors to accommodate crowds of spectators. In the late seventeenth century, magnificent parades included clerics, professors, students, civic groups, government officials, and religious brotherhoods. Artisan guilds provided carefully constructed floats, giants, a dragon, huge heads, small devils, costumed dancers, decorated carts, and special altars of silver. This central religious festival brought together the populace of Mexico City as it emphasized that all persons shared a common religion, regardless of birth, social position, or economic means. Immensely expensive, the celebrations attracted huge audiences from the urban population as well as numerous onlookers from surrounding villages and towns. Each celebration formed a script that expressed the official ideologies of Church and state. The events' organizers thus took enormous care to arrange participating groups hierarchically and to confirm traditional authority through rituals.

The humble as well as the wealthy participated in fiestas. The day after an elaborate official celebration honoring the birth of Prince Baltasar Carlos in 1629, petty retailers in Lima decorated their stalls with hangings and flowers and the city's central plaza with trees and 14 large figurines. Throngs of persons from all walks of life gathered in the afternoon to celebrate, and fireworks enthralled the city that night. Over several weeks, grocers, hatters, tailors, shoemakers, silversmiths, merchants, and guilds of confectioners sponsored fiestas, many complete with bullfights and pyrotechnics. Smaller cities and towns offered similar entertainment on a reduced scale. Indian villages routinely invested their scarce resources in celebrating feast days and secular holidays.

Workers in all locales enjoyed the informal drinking, gambling, singing, and dancing that accompanied fiestas. Bullfights and cockfights could attract hundreds of spectators. When only brief periods separated holidays, for example, Christmas, New Year, and Epiphany or Twelfth Night, workers in Chihuahua treated themselves to an extended two-week vacation rather than returning to work. On the weekends, too, mineworkers, whose employment required a three-hour walk from the town, often extended their Saturday and Sunday entertainment beyond the weekend and celebrated "Saint Monday," despite their employers' opposition.

Although city life centered on public spaces, families also entertained at home. The elite's favored residential amusement combined playing cards and gambling. Participants included nearly anyone with pesos to lose and some high-ranked officials converted their homes into virtual gaming parlors. The lower classes also displayed a passion for betting. Few cantinas and taverns (*pulquerías*) failed to offer the opportunity to wager on cards, dice, and games of chance or skill. Here accusations of cheating or unexpected losses could degenerate into brawls and knife fights. Despite periodic royal and clerical efforts to ban cockfights, they too provided a venue for diversion and public gambling for rich and poor alike throughout the Americas.

Death and Dying

A high mortality rate plagued the Indies as well as Iberia and elsewhere at the time. Childbirth took a heavy toll on women, and infant death often followed. Epidemic diseases repeatedly ravaged villages, towns, cities, and even entire regions. In an era before antibiotics, modern sanitation, and workplace safety regulations, early death was common.

Whenever possible, clerics administered last rites to dying parishioners and then conducted funeral services. For many Indian families, a Christian burial became the most onerous financial liability they faced, in part because of the priest's exploitive fees. Charges for some native interments in the bishoprics of La Paz and Cusco exceeded what a manual laborer earned for 50 days of work. As in Iberia, elite families sought burial in chapels and the floors of cathedrals, convents, and parish churches to display their social status and be near images of saints.

Populous cities had to deal with a substantial volume of cadavers. In the late eighteenth century, few days passed without a burial in Lima's cathedral, although attendants simply deposited nonelite corpses in common vaults. The frequent reopening of burial sites spread a stench from bodies' decomposition that not even extensive incense could mask. The belief that foul-smelling air carried disease, the so-called miasma theory, convinced enlightened critics that interments should take place outside of cities. Although the Crown ordered the cessation of church burials and the creation of new suburban cemeteries in 1787, it took decades in some places for the innovation to bear fruit.

A wealthy and prudent adult usually left a will. After invoking God or the Trinity, the document routinely contained a profession of religious faith, a declaration of sound mental health, a designation of a burial site, a statement of the testator's desire for eternal life, and a provision for one or more cycles of posthumous masses to speed the soul's journey through purgatory. When financially possible and sometimes when inadvisable, the testator established endowments to pay a cleric, often a male relative, to say such masses in perpetuity. To regulate the practice of leaving part of one's estate to the Church, or even all of it in the absence of related heirs, the Crown prescribed conditions for such a bequest. Nonetheless, over time the Church gained an enormous amount of land and income from deceased Christians.

Work, illness, tiresome meals, and inadequate compensation marked the lives of most persons in the Indies. With few possibilities of significant improvement, only occasional fiestas broke the routine. In contrast, elites could purchase both imported and locally produced luxury goods. They enjoyed varied diets and ample entertainment. The divergence in daily life for nobles and commoners in Nahua, Inka, Spanish, and Portuguese society before the era of conquest persisted in the Americas. Local elites' material and social existence bore little resemblance to the hardship that weighed on most of society.

Primary Source

A Fiesta in Guatemala

Fiestas provided Indian villagers the opportunity to sing, dance, and drink (in short, to party) annually in honor of their local saint and on other occasions as well. The English Dominican Thomas Gage spent some years in Mexico and Guatemala before returning to England, renouncing his order, and encouraging Oliver Cromwell to launch a major attack on Spain's possessions in the Americas. In the following selection of *The English-American . . . or, A New Survey of the West India's . . . (London, 1648)*, he describes a village in Guatemala celebrating its saint's day.

SOURCE: J. Eric S. Thompson, ed., *Thomas Gage's Travels in the New World* (Norman: University of Oklahoma Press, 1958), 243.

There is no town in the Indies great or small, even though it be but of twenty families, which is not dedicated thus unto our Lady or unto some saint, and the remembrance of that saint is continued in the minds not only of those that live in the town, but of all that live far and near, by commercing, trading, sporting, and dancing, offering unto the saint, and bowing, kneeling, and praying before him.

The Indians of the town have their meetings at night for two or three months beforehand, and prepare for such dances as are most commonly used amongst them, and in these meetings they drink of both chocolate and *chicha*. For every kind of dance they have several houses appointed, and masters of that dance, who teach the rest that they may be perfected in it against the saint's day. For the better part of these two or three months the silence of the night is unquieted with their singing, their holloaing, their beating upon [drums and using as trumpets] the shells of fishes, their waits, and with their piping. And when the feast cometh, they . . . are that day well apparelled with silks, fine linen, ribbons, and feathers according to the dance. They begin this in the church before the saint, or in the churchyard, and . . . [for] eight days, they go drinking from house to house, where they have chocolate or some heady drink or *chicha* given them. All those eight days the town is sure to be full of drunkards. If they are reprehended for it, they will answer that their hearts rejoice with their saint in Heaven, and that they must drink unto him that he may remember them.

NOTES

1. Amadeo Frézier, *Relación del viaje por el mar del sur (1716)* (Caracas: Biblioteca Ayacucho, 1982), 191, cited by Rebecca Earle, "'Two Pairs of Pink Satin Shoes!!' Race, Clothing and Identity in the Americas (17th–19th Centuries)," *History Workshop Journal* 52 (Autumn, 2001): 192, n. 15.

SUGGESTIONS FOR FURTHER READING

Bauer, Arnold J. *Goods, Power, History: Latin America's Material Culture.* Cambridge and New York: Cambridge University Press, 2001.

Boyer, Richard. *Lives of the Bigamists: Marriage, Family, and Community in Colonial Mexico.* Albuquerque: University of New Mexico Press, 1995.

Curcio-Nagy, Linda A. *The Great Festivals of Colonial Mexico City: Performing Power and Identity.* Albuquerque: University of New Mexico Press, 2004.

Donahue-Wallace, Kelly. *Art and Architecture of Viceregal Latin America, 1521–1821.* Albuquerque: University of New Mexico Press, 2008.

Juan, Jorge, and Antonio de Ulloa. *A Voyage to South America.* The John Adams Translation. Tempe: Arizona State University Press, 1975.

Mangan, Jane E. *Trading Roles: Gender, Ethnicity, and the Urban Economy in Colonial Potosí.* Durham, NC: Duke University Press, 2005.

Martin, Cheryl English. *Governance and Society in Colonial Mexico: Chihuahua in the Eighteenth Century.* Stanford, CA: Stanford University Press, 1996.

Miller, Robert Ryal (ed.). *Chronicle of Colonial Lima: The Diary of Josephe and Francisco Mugaburu, 1640–1697.* Norman: University of Oklahoma Press, 1975.

Ramos, Frances L. *Identity, Ritual, and Power in Colonial Puebla.* 2nd ed. Tucson: University of Arizona Press, 2012.

Ramos, Gabriela. *Death and Conversion in the Andes: Lima and Cuzco, 1532-1670.* South Bend, IN: University of Notre Dame Press, 2010.

Taylor, William B. *Drinking, Homicide, and Rebellion in Colonial Mexican Villages.* Stanford, CA: Stanford University Press, 1979.

Villa-Flores, Javier. *Dangerous Speech: A Social History of Blasphemy in Colonial Mexico.* Tucson: University of Arizona Press, 2006.

Villa-Flores, Javier, and Sonya Lipsett-Rivera (eds.). *Emotions and Daily Life in Colonial Mexico.* Albuquerque: University of New Mexico Press, 2014.

Viqueira Albán, Juan Pedro. *Propriety and Permissiveness in Bourbon Mexico.* Translated by Sonya Lipsett-Rivera and Sergio Rivera Ayala. Wilmington, DE: Scholarly Resources, 1999.

Walker, Charles. *Shaky Colonialism: The 1746 Earthquake–Tsunami in Lima, Peru, and Its Long Aftermath.* Durham, NC: Duke University Press, 2008.

CHAPTER 11

Expanding Empires

Spain's America and Brazil expanded in multiple ways from the late seventeenth to the early nineteenth century. Population grew and missionaries, military units, and miners founded new settlements in frontier regions. Mining production and royal income reached unprecedented levels; agricultural and pastoral exports increased; both legal and contraband trade flourished; and the Crown strengthened its authority. A harsh geopolitical reality stimulated much of this multifaceted expansion. Great Britain's naval strength, trade, and empire exceeded that of Spain, and frequent war between the two imperial powers proved costly.

War stimulated Spain to spend more on its army and navy. Additional income came from increasing taxation, improving revenue collection, and stimulating production and trade. The umbrella of British protection, in contrast, provided Portugal and Brazil with access to African slaves, British textiles, and manufactured goods in exchange for Portuguese wine and Brazilian gold in particular. But as the American Revolution demonstrated, overseas wars were expensive and efforts to impose new taxes could foster insurrection. Ongoing abuse of slaves also posed a risk, as Haiti's successful revolution revealed. Protest and conspiracy occurred in Spain's America and Brazil as well.

THE SPANISH EMPIRE FROM THE LATE
SEVENTEENTH CENTURY TO THE 1750S

Territorial Loss and Expansion

From the mid-seventeenth century, Spain both lost territory in the Americas and extended its reach into regions it had largely ignored. The Dutch, English, and French effectively voided its original claim to the Indies by establishing colonies in the Caribbean and on the North American mainland during the seventeenth century. The loss of Jamaica (1655) and other islands accelerated contraband trade in and around the Caribbean, although the worst pirate depredations had ended by 1700. The French possession of the western third of Santo Domingo by treaty in 1697 highlighted the American dimension of European conflicts. Far to the south, in 1680 the Portuguese erected the fortified trading post of Colônia do Sacramento opposite Buenos Aires.

The War of Spanish Succession (1702–1713) confirmed Philip V, the Bourbon grandson of France's Louis XIV, as king of Spain and the Indies, facilitated cooperation with France, and continued enmity with Britain for a century. Early in the conflict, Portugal and England signed the Methuen Treaty (1703) that solidified a commercial relationship that lasted into the 1800s. By the Treaty of Utrecht (1713), England obtained for 30 years a monopoly on the introduction of African slaves and commercial rights in Spain's empire, thereby easing the way for more extensive contraband trade.

The creation of new military garrisons and missions strengthened Spain's American defenses against real and potential threats. The Jesuits established missions in northwestern New Spain as far north as Arizona. Following a disastrous loss to Indian rebels in the Pueblo revolt of 1680, Spaniards resettled New Mexico in the 1690s. In Texas they founded missions and garrisons in the early 1720s.

St. Augustine's successful resistance against the English during the War of Spanish Succession and the War of Jenkins' Ear (1739–1748) emphasized the Florida stronghold's value in New Spain's defensive perimeter. In the latter war, the British destroyed Portobello in 1739, but failed to duplicate the feat in Cartagena two years later.

Brazil's most significant territorial expansion occurred in the interior after prospectors discovered gold in the mid-1690s and diamonds in the 1720s. Minas Gerais and then Goiás proved remarkable mining regions that attracted thousands of ambitious immigrants from Portugal and employed large numbers of African slaves. Exploration and effective settlement had moved Brazil's claims far west of the line established by the Treaty of Tordesillas.

Increased Royal Authority

Victory in the War of Spanish Succession enabled Philip V (1700–1746) to lessen the monarchy's traditional emphasis that justice was the essence of kingship in favor of a more modern vision: the monarch should be an administrator who increased royal control and encouraged economic expansion and his subjects' well-being. Philip imposed Castilian law, institutions, and taxes on the realms of the Crown of Aragon, a harsh penalty for their support of the Habsburg candidate. Abolishing their historic *fueros* and multiple *Cortes*, the monarch terminated the monopoly of offices that native sons of Catalonia, Aragon, and Valencia had long enjoyed. He sought to implement more centralized authority in Madrid; uniformity, tighter control, and increased efficiency in royal administration; a reduction in privileges antithetical to royal financial and political interests; and improved conditions for economic advancement.

Philip introduced secretaries of state, also known as ministers, to provide him with direct advice and to assume many responsibilities previously assigned to councils. Thus, in 1717 he transferred much of the Council of the Indies' former portfolio to the new minister of the Indies. Additionally, he selected as viceroys military officers he knew personally and whose rank reflected demonstrated merit, efficiency, and a willingness to execute orders rather than inherited social status. Nonetheless, only in the mid-eighteenth century did the Crown stop selling appointments to *audiencia*, treasury, and provincial administrator positions in the Indies, a troublesome carryover from Habsburg to Bourbon rule.

The definitive creation of the Viceroyalty of New Granada in 1739 proved the most important administrative reorganization in the Americas during Philip's reign; the new unit combined today's Colombia, Ecuador, Panama, and Venezuela. His successor, Ferdinand VI (1746–1759), abolished the Audiencia of Panama.

Ferdinand relied for much of his reign on the marquis of Ensenada. Intent on strengthening royal authority in the Indies as well as Spain, the powerful minister ended the sale of appointments and implemented the intendant system throughout Spain. He also promoted regalism, the expansion of royal power over the Church in particular, and in 1749 reinvigorated a long-dormant secularization program that replaced mendicants in Indian parishes with secular clergy. Beginning in New Spain and Peru, this initiative expanded in 1753 to the remainder of the Indies.

Demographic Expansion

Population growth throughout the Indies continued a pattern begun about 1650 except in Peru, where it followed a major epidemic of 1719–20. Brazil's population increased nearly 50 percent between 1700 and 1750 because of the enormous importation of African slaves for labor in mining regions and on sugar plantations and, to a lesser degree, Portuguese immigration to the mining zone. By 1715, the number of slaves had reached some 30,000 in Minas Gerais. Slaves constituted the majority of a population of about 40,000 in Minas Novas within three years of the initial gold strike.

Registered Production of Silver and Gold

Registered silver and gold production in Spain's America attained unprecedented totals by the mid-eighteenth century. After a lengthy depression, silver production in New Spain first surpassed that of the two Perus (Lower and Upper Peru, or Charcas) in the 1670s (see Figure 8.1) and increased every decade from the 1710s until the 1760s, when it dipped to 107 million pesos. In the two Perus, output dropped from the 1640s to a nadir of 27 million pesos in 1711–1720 before climbing to more than 57 million pesos in the 1760s, a little more than half of Mexico's total.

Tax revenue sent to Castile anticipated Mexico's displacement of the Perus in silver production. Although the latter had remitted double New Spain's contribution in the 1650s, it sent less in the 1660s and scarcely exceeded 10 percent of New Spain's 5.3 million pesos by the 1740s. The northern viceroyalty dispatched more than 16 million pesos to Spain in the following decade, in addition to subsidizing several Indies' locations; Peru remitted none. Small wonder that the Crown focused more attention on Mexico.

Registered gold production in New Granada surpassed 4 million pesos in value in only three decades between 1631 and 1710, but output rose from the 1690s and exceeded 11 million pesos from 1751 to 1760. Brazilian production began in the 1690s and peaked at almost 94 million pesos in 1741–1750 before declining to 72 million in the following decade.

Commerce

Spain's convoy system struggled for much of the seventeenth century. Between 1660 and 1700, the galleons sailed to Cartagena and Portobello only a dozen times and the fleet reached Veracruz on just 17 occasions. Foreign goods filled the vessels' hulls, ridiculing the Crown's original vision of Spanish ships carrying Castilian merchandise to a captive American market. To sustain New Spain's vital silver production, the Crown had to send mercury to Vera Cruz not only on the fleet, but also on any other ships sailing from Spain to the port.

Despite irregular convoys, the value of Spain's exports to the Indies began to rise after 1660 and more than doubled by the mid-1690s. After a decline during the early years of the War of Spanish Succession, tonnage started increasing in 1709 and, when not disrupted by war, generally climbed into the 1790s.

The Crown had always authorized occasional single ships to carry goods to the Indies and permitted two small vessels to sail annually from Seville to Buenos Aires beginning in 1618. Nonetheless, it refrained from making major changes to the fleet system until the eighteenth century. In 1701, Philip allowed French ships to stop at ports in the Indies for repairs and provisions, but not to trade. The authorized activities, however, opened the door for substantial illicit commerce on the Pacific coast as merchants began to sail routinely around Cape Horn. The Utrecht settlement gave England both unprecedented legal access to the Indies' markets and permission to construct facilities for the African slave trade that masked more contraband.

Forced by its European enemies to resurrect the fleet system in 1720, the Crown subsequently expanded the use of "register ships," single, licensed vessels that initially sailed directly from Cádiz to designated Atlantic ports. This intentionally undercut the convoys because it challenged their high transportation costs and lowered prices at the trade fairs at Portobello and, in some years, at Jalapa, Mexico. Demonstrating both speed and dependability, between 1739 and 1756, register ships handled almost all legal trade between Spain and the Indies.

Emulating its international rivals, Spain chartered monopoly companies to handle trade and eradicate contraband from specified regions. The most successful was the Guipúzcoana or Caracas Company established in 1728, although constant friction between Venezuelan cacao planters and company officials led to a brief rebellion at mid-century. As a result of the company's efforts, Venezuela at last became fiscally self-sufficient and remitted royal revenue to Spain.

The expansion of transatlantic trade reflected growing colonial population, production, and purchasing power. At the same time, more regular shipping induced producers of agricultural and pastoral products to increase their output. Economic prosperity in regions ill served by the fleet system boosted the importation of expensive goods. Thus, the Río de la Plata, Chile, Venezuela, and Central America, areas long on the periphery of imperial commerce, were expanding economically before the 1760s. The Río de la Plata, in particular, also benefited from shipping to Chile, and mining areas of Upper Peru imported textiles, slaves, iron, and other items in exchange for bullion. In Chile, the renewal of gold production in the 1690s strengthened an economy already profiting from substantial wheat exports to Lima.

Contraband bullion that merchants and their agents sent to Europe buttressed the expansion of trade. Officials estimated in 1698 that the admirals' ships alone for the two convoys carried 21 million pesos of unregistered gold and silver. Their observation documented significant bullion production and commercial growth during the reign of Charles II. However, the royal treasury in Madrid benefited little, receiving at most 3 percent of the registered bullion in the 1680s. Military expenditures and subsidization of otherwise insolvent regions, such as Panama, Cuba, Florida, and the Philippines, drained a significant amount of royal revenue produced in the Indies.

Territorial, demographic, and economic expansion characterized the Indies between the 1680s and the British capture of Havana in 1762. Spain had to exploit exports more efficiently and enlarge American markets if it were to participate again as a great power in European affairs. Reliance on register ships, especially after 1740, marked the first major alteration in Spain's transatlantic trading system since the introduction of protected convoys in the sixteenth century.

The innovation initiated a course that finally led to the formal abolition of the fleet system for New Spain in 1789. By that date, however, the Crown had long ceased relying on halfway measures and ad hoc defensive responses to strengthen the empire economically and militarily. Building on the Indies' growing economic base, the Crown expanded a conscious and persistent policy of enhancing royal authority and American revenues to replace the earlier piecemeal and inconsistent efforts. In Brazil, gold production peaked in the decade ending in 1750 and the Portuguese Crown turned its attention to extracting additional income from trade and the exportation of sugar and other agricultural products.

THE REFORMS OF CHARLES III

On August 11, 1762, the British entered Havana after a campaign begun in early June. The victory reflected not only a successful military strategy but also the crippling effects of a hurricane and interminable rain, food shortages, and seasonal fevers on both the defenders and their anticipated reinforcements from elsewhere in Cuba. Yellow fever, an expected silent ally, arrived too late; the feared malady struck the British forces after the Spanish commander had surrendered.

Unable to control the weather or epidemics, the Spanish Crown answered Britain's humiliating capture of Havana with measures to invigorate its authority, trade, and revenue. Although the Peace of Paris (February 10, 1763) freed Cuba from British occupation, royal advisors anticipated another war with its despised enemy. Fears that a loss of empire would follow drove Charles III to pursue more ambitious, costly, and comprehensive alterations than his predecessors. The Crown focused mainly on the military, royal administration, bullion production, trade policy, enhanced revenue, and control of the Church. Handpicked inspectors known as visitors general received broad authority to introduce changes in both personnel and policy. They became instrumental in determining and implementing royal initiatives that, in Peru and New Granada, contributed to armed resistance.

Expanded Armies and Reorganized Militias

The preservation of empire demanded a stronger, more expensive military. Beginning in Cuba and spreading throughout the American possessions, the Crown turned to a combination of trained officers and soldiers sent from Spain and reorganized militias. The latter would have heavy local participation, including native-son officers, but a peninsular would supervise each unit's training. Although it offered unprecedented access to a military *fuero* and other perquisites, the Crown attracted fewer volunteers than needed because the armies offered low pay, harsh discipline, and poor prospects for advancement. Consequently, it filled the ranks with alcoholics, gamblers, vagabonds, and convicted criminals who often received defective weapons and late pay; as a result, the military failed to become an honored and prestigious institution. Moreover, despite draining immense amounts of royal revenue, it remained underfunded and, in many locations, required external subsidies to maintain a semblance of solvency.

Royal Administration

Charles III sought to replace Habsburg decentralization by integrating Spain and the American realms into a more uniform, efficient, and effective administrative system better able to exploit the resources of the Americas. As was true in Portugal and Brazil under the marquis of Pombal, more centralized authority characterized royal efforts to tighten control over administrators and local elites as well as to expand its power over the Church.

Changes in royal administration for the Indies took place in both Spain and the Americas. Recognizing the empire's growing importance, the Crown in 1773 declared the Council of the Indies equal to that of Castile and gave its members matching salaries. It also began to advance and retain the elevated council ministers who had spent significant time in the Americas or in positions in Spain that gave them relevant expertise, for example, in the House of Trade. As a result, by the 1790s the Council of the Indies had an unprecedented number of ministers with American experience and expertise, many of them veterans of service on one or more New World *audiencias*.

In another striking change, the peninsular ministers of the Indies who served from 1754 to 1790 had New World experience. José de Gálvez, the most important, reached New Spain in 1765 as a powerful visitor general. There, he changed personnel, oversaw expansion and settlement in northwestern New Spain, organized the fledgling tobacco monopoly into a major source of royal income, and promoted silver production through reducing the price of mercury and offering tax incentives to mine owners. Named minister of the Indies and governor of the Council of the Indies in 1776, he served until his death in 1787. His early actions included dispatching peninsular visitors general to Peru, Chile, and New Granada to increase royal revenue. He also used his positions to discriminate against native sons seeking high-ranking royal and ecclesiastical positions.

The Crown expanded the number of ministers on the *audiencias* and created three new tribunals in the 1780s (Buenos Aires, Caracas, and Cusco). Nevertheless, it continued to favor peninsulars for the tribunals as it had done since ending the sale of appointments in 1750. As a result, from 1751 to 1808, creoles, including but few native sons, constituted less than a quarter of the new ministers named, a substantial decline from the years 1687 to 1750.

In 1777, the Crown imposed a major territorial reorganization by placing roughly today's Argentina, Uruguay, Paraguay, and Bolivia in the empire's fourth viceroyalty, that of Río de la Plata. The measure eviscerated the viceroy of Peru's authority, jurisdiction, and financial resources, especially since Potosí and other mining centers of Upper Peru fell under the new administrative unit. Simultaneously, the change underscored the new region's economic dynamism and the military importance of Buenos Aires and Montevideo. On a smaller scale, the Crown responded similarly to the economic growth of Venezuela, elevating it to the status of a captaincy general and creating the Audiencia of Caracas.

The introduction of intendants constituted the Crown's most ambitious administrative innovation. Established throughout Spain in 1749, Charles III initiated the

French-inspired system in Cuba soon after the island returned to Spanish control. By 1787, intendancies existed throughout the mainland save for New Granada. Peninsulars secured more than 90 percent of appointments to the new post between 1764 and 1808. Charged with extensive responsibilities that included oversight of revenue collection, these powerful and well-paid officials provided a new level of administration between an *audiencia*'s chief executive and district officials, now labeled subdelegates rather than *corregidores* or *alcaldes mayores*. The miserable salaries paid to most subdelegates contributed heavily to the system's frequent failure. Receiving only a small percentage of the tribute collected in their jurisdictions, many subdelegates resorted to illegal activities, including the notorious *repartimiento de bienes*, to augment their compensation.

Bullion Production

Registered silver and gold production increased from the 1760s to the end of the century and, in some places, beyond. The growth of New Spain's output rested on tax incentives, an adequate supply of mercury from Almadén, and significant capital investment in mining by wholesale merchants shifting resources out of Atlantic trade. Record-level production followed in every decade starting in the 1770s. To stimulate increased output from the Andean mines, the Crown reduced the tax on silver from 20 to 10 percent in 1736. This started a turnaround in registered production at the Potosí treasury, ending a long decline. Coupled with the output of other Upper Peruvian mines and substantially increased production in Lower Peru, the total amount of silver from the Andean mining regions peaked in the final decade of the century. Mercury from Almadén rescued the industry from the dire implications of the collapse of Huancavelica's major mercury mine in the 1780s.

"Free Trade within the Empire"

To expand Atlantic commerce and raise revenue, the Crown initiated what it labeled "free trade" between Spain and the Indies, ending the monopoly Cádiz and the members of its merchant guild (*consulado*) had enjoyed. The new policy began cautiously in 1765 with Spanish merchants in designated ports permitted to send goods on Spanish ships to Cuba and several other Caribbean islands; products from these destinations, in turn, could be exported to Cádiz, Barcelona, or seven other Iberian ports. Building on success, the Crown extended the policy to include Louisiana and then several mainland ports in Yucatan and New Granada. In 1778, it authorized all South American kingdoms and provinces except Venezuela, still under the Caracas Company's monopoly, to trade directly with 16 ports in the mother country. Venezuela and New Spain finally entered the new system in the late 1780s. Reductions in duties and the removal of some restrictions on commerce within the empire opened trade further. Under the free trade policy, the value of legal imports from the metropolis perhaps doubled, whereas the value of exports from the Indies to Spain increased substantially more.

The Indies imported printed cottons, linens, silks, and other textiles manufactured in Catalonia and elsewhere in Spain; brandy (*aguardiente*) and wine; olives, figs, and nuts; and other goods. European merchandise originating outside Spain, especially endless varieties of textiles from France, continued to be reexported, especially from Cádiz, in large quantity.

Revenue

The Crown's revenue measures included greater use of royal monopolies, notably those of tobacco and some alcoholic beverages. In New Spain, the tobacco monopoly proved a money machine, yielding 3–5 million pesos of profit annually for decades. The Crown also emphasized enforcement of existing and modified tax levies such as the sales tax (*alcabala*) and customs duties, and replaced tax farmers with royal officials. Additionally, it took steps to increase silver and gold production. By the closing decades of the century, revenues received from the Indies averaged 8 to 9 million pesos annually, about 20 percent of the Crown's total income. Notably, this amount complemented the sums expended in the Indies and the Philippine Islands.

Regalism

In strengthening royal authority, the Crown reduced the privileges and temporal power of the Church. A partner of the Habsburg monarchs, the Church witnessed the Bourbon kings slowly tightening their control over the clergy. The new emphasis especially affected the mendicant orders, as the secularization of Indian parishes under Ferdinand VI demonstrated. The shift also reflected the influence of Spanish "Jansenists," an informal branch of Catholicism that emphasized an interior piety and deplored the extravagance associated with Baroque or post-Tridentine Catholicism.

Through its use of royal patronage, a power expanded significantly in Spain through an agreement (concordat) with the pope in 1753, the Crown named pro-reform bishops who supported greater royal authority over the Church in general, but particularly over the orders. These prelates would act firmly in their dioceses and implement the king's directives.

In its most extreme regalist action, the Crown expelled the Society of Jesus from both Spain and the Indies in 1767, a step Portugal and France had taken earlier. Several reasons influenced the decision to remove more than 5,000 peninsular and creole Jesuits: disapproval of their primary allegiance to the pope; a belief that the society had amassed extraordinary wealth; pent-up hostility over the Jesuits' long refusal to pay tithes; and a suspicion that they had established an independent state in their Paraguayan missions. The Jesuits' alleged culpability in a riot in Madrid in 1766 provided the immediate pretext for the expulsion, not least because the disturbance had caused Charles III to flee the city and dismiss his powerful but hated Italian minister, the marquis of Esquilache. After an investigation, the Crown expelled the Society and seized its assets, although its plan to sell all of them proved impossible. Additionally, the government had to address the disruption the Jesuits' forced exodus left in education in both Spain and the New World. Nonetheless, the action powerfully warned all religious orders that the Crown could also expel them.

Continued Demographic Expansion and Social Change

Demographic growth continued in both Spain's America and Brazil after the mid-eighteenth century. By 1800, the former's population reached an estimated 12.6 million and the latter's more than 2 million, about a third of whom were slaves. In Spain's mainland possessions, the indigenous outnumbered the rest of society in Mexico, Guatemala, Ecuador, and the two Perus. In every region, both the minority of whites and persons of mixed ancestry were increasing in number. Miscegenation was evident throughout the empire with mestizos, mulattoes, *pardos*, and other *castas* present everywhere and constituting the most numerous racial group in Colombia, Venezuela, and Chile.

The expansion of the number of whites throughout the Indies reflected natural increase, immigration from Spain, and the greater use of *calidad* in determination of an individual's status and identity. An examination of *calidad* in Orizaba, Mexico, clearly documents the mutability of racial classifications. Of just over a thousand non-Indians linked in two censuses, 330 had a different *calidad* in 1791 from that in 1777; 260 of them moved up the social ladder, whereas the status of 70 declined. The change was particularly evident in the elevation of *castas* to Spanish status.

The Crown responded to such social advancement by promulgating legislation that empowered parents to deny children under the age of 25 permission to marry based on the alleged "unequal," that is, lower, status of the prospective spouse. By explicitly exempting blacks, mulattoes, and others considered *castas*, the 1778 law offered protection to white and Indian parents. Its sole sanction—disinheritance of the offending child—however, had real meaning only for families with significant property to bequeath. Only in 1805 did the Crown prohibit marriages between persons of recognized noble status and blacks and mulattoes. Although willing to allow individuals to gain privileges and status recognition through payment of a fee, the limitations the Crown placed on marriage demonstrated its emphasis on obedience, its willingness to intervene in personal relationships, and its abhorrence of unequal marriages that challenged the more significant disparities inherent in a social structure built on inequality.

In a little more than a century, Spain's American realms expanded significantly in settled territory, population, bullion production, and other exports. The Crown increased its authority over the Church and made royal administration in the Indies more responsive through the careful selection of peninsulars and systematic discrimination against native sons for high-ranking positions. Nonetheless, the elites in the Indies continued to support the Church and Crown, despite the example of the American Revolution and the acceptance by many in the literate population of reliance on critical reason, experimentation, and other ideas associated with the Enlightenment.

BRAZIL IN AN AGE OF EXPANSION

Substantial gold deposits unearthed in the mid-1690s inaugurated a boom in the Brazilian interior and moved the viceroyalty's economic center southward. The discovery of diamonds three decades later added further attraction to Minas Gerais and other mining regions. Rapid population growth followed and led the Portuguese Crown to enlarge Brazil's bureaucracy. New transportation networks and commercial relations developed to supply the mining camps. The region's prosperity placed pressure on the established sugar-producing areas of the northeast by introducing price inflation and greater competition for labor and capital, although the value of sugar exports continued to exceed that of gold. The transfer of the viceregal capital from Salvador to Rio de Janeiro in 1763 culminated a series of administrative changes that reflected the southern regions' increased economic and political importance. It also meant explicit recognition of heightened tension with Spain along Brazil's border.

But boom slipped into depression as gold production descended steadily after peaking in the early 1750s. The interior's days of glory passed quickly, and the coastal provinces enjoyed a renewed prosperity by the early 1780s. Bolstered by the importation of unprecedented numbers of slaves and improved market conditions, sugar production expanded rapidly in the 1790s, a beneficiary of the Haitian Revolution that ended the former Saint-Domingue's dominance. The greater demand for tobacco, cotton, rice, coffee, indigo, and cacao also contributed to coastal Brazil's renewed economic vitality. New government policies helped stimulate this recovery and channel benefits to Portugal.

Administration

The growth of mining centers far from established settlements forced the Portuguese Crown to create new administrative, judicial, and treasury districts. The first step was to subdivide the immense territory previously under the governor and captain general of Rio de Janeiro into smaller units. In 1709, the Crown carved out of Rio's jurisdiction a new captaincy general, which it split in 1720 into São Paulo and Minas Gerais. The formation of two additional units, Goiás and Mato Grosso, in 1748 and a further reorganization in the early 1770s gave Brazil nine captaincies general and nine subordinate captaincies.

In 1752, Rio de Janeiro became home to Brazil's second colonial high court (relaçao). The great distance separating the frontier mining camps from the old administrative centers led to the partition of captaincies into judicial districts (comarcas) that, for example, divided both Minas Gerais and Bahia into four districts. In each district, judicial committees formed by the governor, the senior treasury official of the captaincy, and the senior judge of the comarca administered justice.

Administration in Brazil centered on towns. By formally elevating mining camps to townships, the Crown committed itself to providing at least skeletal royal administration. The simultaneous extension of land grants and other privileges to these new municipalities and their officials encouraged further settlement of the interior. Beginning in 1693, the foundation of new towns promised to improve law and order and to streamline the collection of royal revenue. Although creating municipalities and introducing administrative institutions strengthened royal control in Minas Gerais, little effective oversight existed in the sparsely inhabited captaincies of Mato Grosso and Goiás.

New treasury offices emerged as a central feature of these administrative changes. Each major mining area received a mint that weighed gold, extracted the

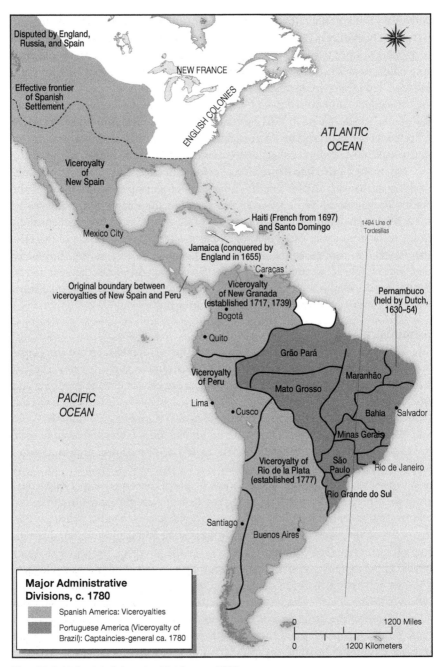

Major Administrative Divisions, c. 1780

Disputed by England, Russia, and Spain

NEW FRANCE

Effective frontier of Spanish Settlement

ENGLISH COLONIES

ATLANTIC OCEAN

Viceroyalty of New Spain

Haiti (French from 1697) and Santo Domingo

1494 Line of Tordesillas

Mexico City

Jamaica (conquered by England in 1655)

Caracas

Original boundary between viceroyalties of New Spain and Peru

Viceroyalty of New Granada (established 1717, 1739)

Pernambuco (held by Dutch, 1630–54)

Bogotá

Quito

Grão Pará

Viceroyalty of Peru

Maranhão

Mato Grosso

PACIFIC OCEAN

Lima

Cusco

Bahia   Salvador

Minas Gerais

Viceroyalty of Rio de la Plata (established 1777)

São Paulo

Rio de Janeiro

Rio Grande do Sul

Santiago

Buenos Aires

Major Administrative Divisions, c. 1780

Spanish America: Viceroyalties

Portuguese America (Viceroyalty of Brazil): Captaincies-general ca. 1780

0   1200 Miles

0   1200 Kilometers

Map 11.1 Major Administrative Divisions, c. 1780

royal fifth, and cast the remainder into bars. In addition, the Crown tried to limit access to the mining areas to collect taxes on imports. The usual royal monopolies of salt, wine, and olive oil comprised another source of revenue. Taken together, these imposts, the tithe, and local taxes contributed not only to increased royal revenues but also to the exorbitant cost of living in the mining zones.

The Crown sought to tighten its grip on Brazil under the powerful Sebastião José de Carvalho e Melo, who dominated affairs of state from 1750 to 1777. Elevated as marquis of Pombal in 1769, he understood that Portugal's fortunes rested on Brazil's prosperity. Accordingly, he pursued collecting and increasing the colony's tax revenues, expanding its economy and trade with the metropolis, and securing its defenses, particularly in the lands adjoining Spanish America.

Under Pombal, the Ministry of the Navy and Overseas Territories, established in 1736, gained control over Brazilian affairs. It oversaw general policy implementation and proposed high-ranking civil, military, and ecclesiastical appointments to the king. Pombal also amplified the authority of the Board of Trade created in 1755 to develop Portuguese industry and reduce the kingdom's reliance on British imports. Its greater scope led in 1788 to a more descriptive title: the Royal Board of Trade, Agriculture, Factories, and Navigation from this Kingdom and all her Dominions.

A new royal treasury founded in 1761 centralized accounting for Portugal and the empire. Headed by Pombal himself as inspector general, this agency consolidated the supervision of revenue collection and expenditure. The Crown then engaged in fiscal reorganization by creating during the 1760s and 1770s treasury boards in each captaincy general. Within their jurisdictions, the boards oversaw the activities of all departments of the royal exchequer.

The Church

The stronger and more centralized Portuguese monarchy of the eighteenth century acted repeatedly to reduce the power of the Church, its foremost institutional rival. As in Spain, under Pombal the government broke the long-standing tradition of equal and complementary authority exercised by Church and state.

The rapid economic and demographic expansion of Brazil's interior gold-mining regions lacked a parallel extension of clerical influence and authority. The first friars on the scene focused heavily on smuggling gold, leading the Crown to ban all religious orders from Minas Gerais in 1711. No subsequent campaign, however, attracted secular clergy to the region. Efforts to eliminate greedy priests' extortionate practices, by paying clerics from the royal treasury and limiting the fees charged for the sacraments, proved ineffective. In fact, these policies kept the Church from establishing itself as securely in the mining zone as it had in northeastern Brazil during the first stages of settlement.

The expulsion of the Society of Jesus from Brazil in 1759–60 demonstrated the Portuguese Crown's ability to destroy its opponents. Solidly entrenched in the colony when the Crown signed the Treaty of Madrid in 1750, the fathers' opposition to this agreement and exaggerated rumors of their wealth provided two reasons for its expulsion. Added to Pombal's outrage at their hostility to the creation of a joint-stock company to exploit the resources of Brazil's interior, the government's case for expelling the Jesuits from Portugal and the empire seemed sufficient. After seizing all Society properties, the Crown sold some rural estates but maintained others as royal domain. Churches passed to the secular clergy, and colleges often became government or military facilities. Because of the Society's central role in education, the expulsion had a chilling effect on Brazil's cultural life. The diversity and scale of the Jesuits' holdings also meant that the government's action affected farming, ranching, sugar production, and urban real estate. The Crown then turned its attention toward the assets of the remaining orders. It seized the rich cattle ranches and other property of the Mercedarians and forced other orders to lend it money in exchange for government bonds. Coupled with the state's lukewarm support for the secular clergy, these actions toward the Jesuits and other regular clergy significantly weakened the Church in Brazil.

PROTEST, POPULAR INSURRECTIONS, AND CONSPIRACIES

Violent popular uprisings scattered throughout Spain's American possessions between the mid-eighteenth century and 1808 typically employed the language of traditional Spanish law and Catholic theology as justification. In Brazil, conspiracies appeared in two distinct locales. None of these insurrections or conspiracies, however, provided direct connections to the later wars of independence.

Administrative corruption, new and increased taxes, and high prices, especially for food and drink, provoked occasional popular violence and mob action throughout the centuries of Spanish rule. At times, conflict among civil officials, clerics, and their supporters ignited the illegal use of force and served to define political objectives. The scale and duration of the uprisings increased during the eighteenth century and several directly threatened Spain's authority.

The administrative and fiscal changes associated with the Bourbons fanned the political character of popular protest. This occurred especially when the Crown imposed new or increased taxes or collected old ones more efficiently. Levies that affected consumer staples, for example, the creation of new monopolies involving tobacco and, in Venezuela, cacao, proved particularly prone to sparking popular antipathy. Such transfers of the tax burden from the mining sector and Atlantic trade to staples of everyday consumption directly affected the popular classes.

Quito provides an example. Decades of decline in the local textile industry adversely affected the whole of society. In 1765, members of Quito's elite and popular classes united to force the government to withdraw a program to increase and collect taxes more effectively. The coalition soon split along class and ethnic lines, however, and in the resulting atmosphere of fear and mistrust, all sides welcomed the arrival of royal troops in 1766. Lingering plebeian mistrust doomed an elite rebellion in 1809.

Spanish authorities in New Granada faced another popular political protest. To fund defense against possible English attack, a visitor general not only raised the *alcabala* and prices of tobacco and brandy, but also restricted tobacco cultivation to a designated area. In 1781 these changes combined with the effects of bad harvests and an epidemic to produce rebellion. The participants in this *comunero* revolt came from the middle and lower sectors of provincial society and included *castas* and natives. When a force numbering in the thousands marched on the almost defenseless capital of Bogotá, Archbishop Antonio Caballero y Góngora, representing the Bogotá elite, appeared to surrender to most of the dissidents' demands. But once the armed *comuneros* dispersed, loyal troops reestablished control. Although a small rebel force rejected the settlement, its defeat soon followed and royal authorities executed its leader.

Armed resistance to Spanish rule increased in the eighteenth century among exploited indigenous Andeans. Well over 50 uprisings occurred from the 1740s to the 1770s. Large-scale resistance began in Upper Peru in 1778. Two years later, in Lower Peru, a local *kuraka*, generally known as Tupac Amaru II, led a much bigger uprising near Cusco composed of Quechua groups supported by some creole and *casta* allies. Despite early successes, the rebels failed, and in May 1781 the government brutally executed the captured leader, his wife, and many family members. The focus of conflict shifted back to Upper Peru and continued until 1783, by which time perhaps 100,000 had died in the rebellions. Despite their military failure, the protests forced the end of the *repartimiento* of merchandise in Peru and ultimately brought about the establishment of the Audiencia of Cusco.

Conspiracies in Brazil

As in the Spanish dominions, imperial reforms and, after 1776, news of first the American and later the French Revolution combined to initiate a period of political unrest in Brazil. In 1789, Portuguese authorities uncovered a conspiracy that included members of the elite, intellectuals, and military officers in Minas Gerais. The conspirators' libraries included works by Voltaire and other popular *philosophes* as well as copies of the Articles of Confederation and American state constitutions, confirming their owners' admiration for the Enlightenment and American Revolution. The wealthiest schemers' active participation resulted from their massive debts to the Portuguese treasury. For them, an end to Portuguese rule appeared the only alternative to impending financial doom. Officials discovered the plotters before they could take action and arrested them. Social eminence, economic resources, and the questionable actions of the captain general saved all but one of the conspirators and their silent partners from death. The government hanged and beheaded Joaquim José da Silva Xavier, a military officer known as Tiradentes (toothpuller) for his part-time work.

In the late 1790s in Salvador, Bahia, authorities discovered a conspiracy led by free mulattoes, mostly artisans and a few soldiers; some whites and a small number of slaves allegedly supported the plotters as well. The French and Haitian revolutions influenced the leaders of this conspiracy. When interrogated, one of them said, "All [Brazilians] would become Frenchmen, in order to live in equality and abundance. . . . And that the difference between white, black and brown would be extinguished."[1] The implication of this sentiment for a society in which whites made up only one-fifth of the population stirred the authorities to action. They executed four leaders and punished other participants. Regardless of their

Primary Source

"In Worse Condition Than Slaves"

District officials' forced distribution (*repartimiento*) of merchandise to Indians in their jurisdiction enabled many to get rich within five years. Originally construed to ensure that natives had access to tools and other necessities, district officials quickly added a wide variety of merchandise, whether they needed the items or not. The Spanish Crown introduced the intendant system and outlawed the *repartimiento* in an attempt to end the abuses often associated with this system. The following is a small sample of the authors' discussion of *repartimientos* in South America.

SOURCE: Juan and Ulloa, *Discourse and Political Reflections*, 78–82 passim.

> Repartimientos consist of [the forced distribution of] mules, merchandise from Europe and the Indies, and food.... All the corregidores belonging to the Viceroyalty of Peru have to go to Lima to get their permits and applications for buying goods from the viceroy.... [There] corregidores obtain their stock for distribution here. They get the needed goods from the warehouse of some merchant on credit at a very high rate of interest.... Because the corregidor has no cash to pay for his purchases, he is obliged to submit to the wishes of the individual who sells him the merchandise on credit. At the same time, he must borrow money from the merchant to buy the consignment of mules needed for the trade in his corregimiento. [Once he takes office, the corregidor] goes about at his whim assigning each Indian the quantity and type of goods he wishes. Prices are set arbitrarily.... Of the many abuses connected with repartimientos ..., the mule repartimiento is the worst.... Normally the corregidor charges forty pesos for each mule [for which he usually paid 14 to 16 pesos].... In view of all this, who can deny that the Indians are in worse condition than slaves?

birthplace and individual grievances, the white merchants, planters, and officials of Bahia believed that their self-interest required the maintenance of the slave system and racial discrimination.

Brazilian gold complemented a profitable sugar trade to make Brazil the means for Portugal's rapidly expanding trade with Britain; an era of unprecedented prosperity followed until the 1750s. Immigration from Portugal increased, and the importation of African slaves continued apace. Then, declining gold and diamond production pummeled the Brazilian economy, and the catastrophic earthquake of 1755 shattered Lisbon. The future marquis of Pombal quickly emerged as Portugal's most powerful politician and instituted a series of reforms that improved tax collection in Brazil, reduced Portugal's reliance on British imports, and anticipated Spain in expelling the Society of Jesus. By the 1780s, economic recovery in the sugar industry and the growth of cotton exports brought renewed prosperity. The economic expansion in the eighteenth century made Brazil, not Portugal, the more dynamic partner in an increasingly inverted colonial relationship.

NOTES

1. Kenneth Maxwell, *Conflicts and Conspiracies: Brazil and Portugal, 1750–1808* (Cambridge: Cambridge University Press, 1973), 220.

SUGGESTIONS FOR FURTHER READING

Andrien, Kenneth J. *The Kingdom of Quito, 1690–1830: The State and Regional Development.* Cambridge: Cambridge University Press, 1995.

Brading, D. A. *Church and State in Bourbon Mexico: The Diocese of Michoacán, 1749–1810.* Cambridge: Cambridge University Press, 1994.

Burkholder, Mark A. *Spaniards in the Colonial Empire: Creoles vs. Peninsulars?* Malden, MA: Wiley–Blackwell, 2013.

Eissa-Barroso, Francisco A. *Early Bourbon Spanish America: Politics and Society in a Forgotten Era (1700–1759).* Leiden, The Netherlands: Brill, 2013.

Grieco, Viviana L. *The Politics of Giving in the Viceroyalty of Rio de la Plata: Donors, Lenders, Subjects, and Citizens.* Albuquerque: University of New Mexico Press, 2014.

Johnson, Sherry. *Climate and Catastrophe in Cuba and the Atlantic World in the Age of Revolution.* Chapel Hill: University of North Carolina Press, 2011.

Kuethe, Allan J., and Kenneth J. Andrien. *The Spanish Atlantic World in the Eighteenth Century: War and the Bourbon Reforms, 1713–1796.* Cambridge: Cambridge University Press, 2014.

Maxwell, Kenneth R. *Pombal: Paradox of the Enlightenment.* Cambridge: Cambridge University Press, 1995.

McFarlane, Anthony. *Colombia before Independence: Economy, Society, and Politics under Bourbon Rule.* Cambridge: Cambridge University Press, 1993.

Paquette, Gabriel B. *Enlightenment, Governance, and Reform in Spain and Its Empire, 1759–1808.* New York: Palgrave Macmillan, 2008.

Patch, Robert W. *Maya and Spaniard in Yucatan, 1648–1812.* Stanford, CA: Stanford University Press, 1993.

Prado, Fabrício. *Edge of Empire: Atlantic Networks and Revolution in Bourbon Río de la Plata.* Berkeley and Los Angeles: University of California Press, 2015.

Rosenmüller, Christoph. *Patrons, Partisans, and Palace Intrigues: The Court Society of Colonial Mexico, 1702–1710.* Calgary: University of Calgary Press, 2008.

Serulnikov, Sergio. *Revolution in the Andes: The Age of Túpac Amaru.* Durham, NC: Duke University Press, 2013.

Stein, Stanley J., and Barbara H. Stein. *Apogee of Empire: Spain and New Spain in the Age of Charles III, 1759–1789.* Baltimore: Johns Hopkins University Press, 2003.

Taylor, William B. *Magistrates of the Sacred: Priests and Parishioners in Eighteenth-Century Mexico.* Stanford, CA: Stanford University Press, 1996.

TePaske, John J. (ed. and trans. with Besse A. Clement). *Discourse and Political Reflections on the Kingdom of Peru by Jorge Juan and Antonio de Ulloa.* Norman: University of Oklahoma Press, 1978.

Walker, Charles F. *The Tupac Amaru Rebellion.* Cambridge, MA: Belknap Press of Harvard University Press, 2014.

CHAPTER 12

The Age of Independence (I)

After two decades of disastrous rule by Charles IV in Spain, France's emperor, Napoleon Bonaparte, forced the Spanish royal family to abdicate the throne in May 1808. This unprecedented event initiated Spain's war of independence against French rule and quickly raised questions about the relationship between Spain and its American realms. News of the abdications and the resulting fight for survival in Spain provoked varied responses in the Indies. These ranged from the advocacy of political autonomy and the creation of ruling juntas (committees) to insurgent campaigns and declarations of independence. The defeat of the French, the return of King Ferdinand VII, and his abolition of the constitution in 1814 triggered a period of harsh repression.

COLLAPSE

When Charles III died in 1788, Spain and the empire enjoyed relative prosperity and adequate royal income. These disappeared during his son's 20-year reign, however. Disaster ensued and efforts to create the integrated empire of Spain and the Indies sought by Charles III foundered. Virtual bankruptcy plagued the monarchy and growing debt drained the treasury in Mexico City. The British navy had almost eliminated Spain's fleet, and neutral countries' trade with the Indies had replaced free trade within the empire. Many Spaniards in both hemispheres viewed scornfully the *ménage à trois* of Charles IV, Queen Luisa, and the royal favorite Manuel Godoy, Prince of the Peace. The long slave rebellion that produced independent Haiti in 1804 added a fear of social revolution in plantation zones with substantial slave populations. In 1807, moreover, the invasion by a French army forced Portugal's royal family and court to sail to Brazil under British protection. Another French army reached Madrid in the spring of 1808. Finally, soon after Ferdinand VII replaced his father as monarch following two riots in Aranjuez, both he and Charles IV abdicated at Napoleon's insistence. The emperor then named his brother José king of Spain and the Indies.

The French Revolution and the wars and political change it spawned brought about this set of catastrophes. Except for 1802–1804, Spain was at war from 1793 to 1808; its American possessions paid a high price. Mandates for cash contributions from the Indies began immediately and intensified over the next 15 years. In an 1803 treaty, Napoleon demanded Spain pay France large monthly subsidies as a contribution to its military expenses. Charles IV responded by extending to the Americas an edict that required the Church to collect outstanding mortgages and then to remit the proceeds to the royal government. Forced to contract an enormous loan from a French firm in 1805, the Crown used as collateral all royal incomes of Spain, the customs revenues collected in Cádiz, and the treasuries of Mexico City, Lima, Cartagena, and Buenos Aires. Residents in the Indies correctly understood that Charles would ruin the empire to enable Spain's survival. Active citizens in the American realms increasingly endorsed the idea that they should have more autonomy from an incapable monarchy.

A POLITICAL REVOLUTION

on's forced abdications of Charles IV and Ferdinand VII in Bayonne, ance, in the spring of 1808 provoked an unexpected reaction. Despite growing discontent with Spanish rule, few Americans equated autonomy with independence from Spain. Rather, following the invasion of the mother country, they demanded independence from France. Refusing to accept José I as king, Spaniards everywhere rose to defend their monarch and the Catholic religion. Patriots in Spain quickly formed provincial juntas claiming to rule in Ferdinand's name until his return to the throne. In September, a Central Junta composed of representatives of the provincial committees convened as a general government of resistance to the invaders, whose armies in Spain continued to grow.

The Central Junta faced formidable challenges: retention of the Americas, prosecution of the war against the French, and maintenance of the new alliance with Britain that provided essential military support in the Iberian Peninsula. Although the Spanish government of resistance called for viceroyalties and captaincies general of the Indies to elect representatives to join it, none arrived in time to serve. Despite an astonishing victory over a French army in July 1808, euphoria faded into deep pessimism as the invaders pushed southward. Fleeing to the Isle of León adjacent to Cádiz, the Central Junta appointed a Council of Regency to assume its responsibilities. With some 300,000 French troops in Spain and its own legitimacy in doubt, the Regency convoked an elected representative, unicameral *Cortes*.

From its first meeting in September 1810, the Cortes of Cádiz claimed sovereignty and deliberated with American deputies present. Although it failed to satisfy their hopes for immediate equal representation based on population, the *Cortes* did write a liberal charter that created a modern constitutional monarchy for what it termed "the Spanish Nation"—all "Spaniards" in Spain and the overseas provinces. The unprecedented constitution of 1812 declared that sovereignty rested with the nation rather than the monarch and explicitly separated executive, legislative, and judicial powers. Additionally, it mandated individual rights, an elected *Cortes*, and freedom of the press on political matters. The creation of a new institution termed the provincial deputation allowed for considerable autonomy within each intendancy in Spain and the Indies. Numerous elections preceded and followed the promulgation of this remarkable document, sealing a political revolution.

In the Indies, announcements of the abdications, French invasion, and formation of multiple patriotic juntas in Spain shocked the population. Immediate widespread declarations of loyalty took tangible form in cash remitted to the metropolis. Napoleonic agents sent to enlist American support for José failed dismally. Although citizens favoring greater political autonomy argued for establishing their own juntas modeled on those in Spain, royal authorities successfully repressed initial attempts to replicate them. Joined by peninsular merchants, most high-ranking officials and clerics accepted the Central Junta as legitimately representing the captive monarch. When it resigned in favor of the Regency in early 1810, however, autonomists resurfaced. They formed juntas in Ferdinand's name in Buenos Aires, Caracas, Bogotá, and other cities and quickly expelled nonsupportive high-ranking royal officials. Many citizens in the empire willingly voted for representatives to the Cortes of Cádiz and endorsed the pursuit of autonomy in that forum. In contrast, a small number of dissidents advocated a complete break with Spain.

EARLY INSURRECTIONS IN SPANISH AMERICA

The French occupation and resulting instability in Spain opened the door for insurrections in the Indies. These uprisings overlapped transatlantic political experimentation that included juntas, an elected *Cortes*, and a constitution that transformed the expectations of many active citizens. Despite different chronologies, similar characteristics present in multiple theaters included an active press, localism and regionalism, economic crisis, insurgency and counterinsurgency, and leadership that usually included native sons—American Spaniards (creoles) participating in their home districts.

Spreading Revolutionary Ideas through News and Propaganda

Revolutionary ideas from the 13 English mainland colonies of North America circulated in print, including in the official *Gazeta de Madrid*, and by word of mouth in Spanish America even before the American Revolution. Second-generation revolutions introduced radical ideas from France and, more ominously, Haiti. The crisis of 1808 birthed new publications and the *Cortes* of Cádiz approved freedom of the press and included it in the constitution of 1812.

In applying the constitution, some Spanish officials in America used the free press to spread royalist propaganda. Others suspended the policy's implementation from fear that uncensored papers and pamphlets would encourage subversion. Such repression had limited effect because incendiary tracts printed in rebel areas circulated widely. Additionally, publications from Spain reported debates employing the very language that inspired revolutionaries in the Indies: "popular sovereignty," "liberty," "equality," "elections," and "independence."

The early military conflicts pitted loyalists against variously titled patriots, secessionists, rebels, and insurgents. Initially, both sides claimed to fight for Ferdinand VII. It soon became clear, however, that stimuli for many participants included acquiring loot, personal animosities, social and economic improvement, and the desire for local and regional control. Shifted allegiances, frequent amnesties, and high desertion rates became routine. Set-piece battles occurred rarely between armies that fielded few soldiers when compared to contemporary European standards.

REBELLION IN THE SPANISH EMPIRE'S PERIPHERY

The expansive regions of the empire's periphery responded quickly to the imperial crisis of 1808–1810. Less embedded in the traditional networks of the empire and faced with the imperative of getting perishable exports to market, Venezuela, Chile, and Buenos Aires and its hinterland formed juntas as a way to solve their economic and fiscal problems.

Localism and Regionalism

Long-standing tensions existed between administrative capitals that had a strong peninsular presence, for example, Lima, Mexico City, and Buenos Aires, and their distant, native son–dominated political dependencies. Competition between Buenos Aires and Montevideo as well as between Bogotá and Cartagena, for example, colored responses to the imperial crisis. American cities and towns pointed to the many juntas in Spain to justify their claims of provincial autonomy. The Viceroyalty of Río de la Plata exemplified this autonomist sentiment, but similar conflicts occurred elsewhere.

Informed that a Council of Regency claimed authority in Spain, many of Buenos Aires's most prominent citizens met as a *cabildo abierto* on May 25, 1810, and created the Provisional Governing Junta of the Provinces of Río de la Plata. As all earlier juntas in the Spanish monarchy had done, the new body swore allegiance to Ferdinand VII as its rightful monarch. Taking advantage of its recently claimed autonomy, the junta immediately used the opportunity to settle old scores and soon expelled from Buenos Aires the viceroy and other royal officials. The capital and most of today's Argentina would never again be under Spanish control.

Although Buenos Aires demonstrated its de facto independence from Spain, it failed to retain the outlying regions that had comprised the Viceroyalty of Río de la Plata. The new rulers repeatedly launched unsuccessful military campaigns against future Bolivia, Paraguay, and Uruguay. Despite the capital's efforts, Uruguay refused to yield; Paraguay formally asserted its independence in 1811; and the viceroy of Peru reattached the future Bolivia to Peru. At last, the province of Buenos Aires and its remaining regional allies declared independence in 1816.

New Granada also fragmented quickly. Between June 14 and August 10, 1810, Cartagena, Cali, Pamplona, El Socorro, Santa Fe de Bogotá, and Santa Marta formed separate juntas claiming to rule in Ferdinand's name. Some juntas sought local autonomy, whereas others, like Cartagena, declared complete independence. Still others remained royalist. The chosen course often reflected long-standing antipathies toward neighboring cities and the opportunity to remove potential opposition.

In Caracas, advocates of local rule emerged and formed a junta quickly. The belief that the captain general favored a French victory in Spain and widespread antagonism to most ministers on the Audiencia of Caracas fed antipeninsular sentiment. The junta quickly expelled them and then refused to recognize the legitimacy of the Regency in Spain. With considerable justification, it claimed that the

Central Junta lacked authority to delegate its sovereignty to this appointed body. In response, the Regency declared the Caracas junta in rebellion and imposed a blockade of La Guaira, Venezuela's major port. This prompted the irritated body to send agents to England seeking support. The mission failed, but the emissaries did elicit the interest of Francisco de Miranda, an aging advocate of Spanish American independence.

On July 5, 1811, rebels secured a declaration of independence from a recently installed congress and initiated a short-lived federalist First Republic that quickly learned that Caracas did not equate to Venezuela. Spanish troops supported loyalists from other regions and soon defeated the Republic's forces, imprisoning and exiling Miranda to Spain, where he died in prison. Following this defeat, the future "liberator," Simón Bolívar, fled Venezuela to Cartagena de Indias in the temporarily independent New Granada.

From Cartagena, Bolívar launched a particularly brutal campaign into Venezuela, declaring in 1813 "war to the death" against any European who refused to aid actively the insurgency. With native-son support, he successfully entered Caracas, where he oversaw the creation of a centralized republic. But in 1814, the loyalist *caudillo* José Tomás Boves emerged victorious in the brutal and relentless civil war with the backing of *casta* cowboys from the interior plains (*llanos*) of Venezuela.

The capitals of the empire's South American periphery initially swore loyalty to Ferdinand VII, pledging to provide him a safe haven should he be unable to return to Spain. But they also utilized the opportunities created by the French invasion of Spain to open their ports to foreign merchants. Although it was not a universal desire in the empire, by 1810 securing free trade constituted an immediate objective in Buenos Aires, Caracas, and Santiago, Chile. Having significantly increased their exports under free trade within the empire, these areas needed continued access to external markets to avoid economic collapse.

REBELLION IN THE OLD VICEROYALTIES

In the old viceroyalties of New Spain and Peru, long-established elites including both native sons and peninsulars responded differently to the cataclysmic events in Spain. The municipal council of Mexico City claimed to represent the whole of New Spain. When word arrived of the royal abdications and French invasion, the aldermen quickly asserted their desire for a junta to rule until Ferdinand VII returned to his throne. Because the viceroy seemed amenable to the idea, peninsular merchants in league with their compatriots on the Audiencia of Mexico deposed him. The cabal immediately secured a pliant replacement and maintained control of the organs of viceregal government. Between the coup and the associated repression of outspoken autonomists, opponents found themselves reduced to clandestine plotting. One conspiratorial circle included the native-son parish priest Miguel Hidalgo.

Word of the plot reached a new viceroy, who arrived from Spain in late August 1810. Informed of their imminent arrest, Hidalgo and his associates advanced to September 16 the initiation of their rebellion. Claiming the viceregal government planned to deliver Mexico to the French, they called for its overthrow and pledged to keep New Spain free of Napoleonic rule. Hidalgo successfully ignited the Indian population of his parish of Dolores, but the hope of gaining significant native-son support vanished within days. When the curate's ill-disciplined followers, estimated at some tens of thousands, looted the rich mining city of Guanajuato and massacred its European and American Spaniards, the fear of racial war drove whites in the viceroyalty to oppose the revolt. Within several months, loyalist forces had the priest and his remaining supporters on the run. Captured, defrocked, and executed, Hidalgo later became the symbol of Mexican independence.

Within weeks after the Hidalgo Revolt began, guerrilla bands started disrupting communication between Mexico City and Querétaro. They also harassed traffic on the vital link between the capital and Vera Cruz, reducing the loyalists to immense, slow, and expensive armed convoys. Unrelenting insurgency and counterinsurgency forced much of the population to live in fear for a decade. Using terror, summary justice and execution, and "blood and fire" to gain their ends, rebels committed atrocities against Spaniards from the outset. Loyalists responded in kind. After executing and decapitating Hidalgo and his chief associates in 1811, they sent the severed heads on tour throughout the region that had supported the rebellion and then displayed the skulls in iron cages located at the corners of Guanajuato's granary.

Insurgents and bandit gangs, often composed of demobilized soldiers, easily dispersed and disappeared into the general population of a town or region. To counter these tactics, royalists in Mexico used "flying detachments" of some 300 mounted troops. They swept through insurgent territory to seize arms, horses, and livestock; to capture persons identified as rebels; and, on occasion, to destroy completely towns that supported them. Following public executions, loyalists regularly issued pardons or amnesties, which allowed insurgents to change sides repeatedly.

José María Morelos, a *casta* priest who had studied with Hidalgo, inherited the insurrection. He successfully trained an army, won some battles, occupied a substantial portion of Mexico, and outlined a constitution. His capture and execution in 1815 ended the most organized and persistent rebellion in New Spain, but guerrilla bands and bandits kept the loyalists focused on counterinsurgency throughout much of Mexico for the remainder of the decade.

The presence of a strong viceroy and the cooperation of the Lima elite prevented the creation of a junta in Peru. Moreover, memory of the Tupac Amaru Revolt in the early 1780s raised the specter of a political shift that could give the majority Indian population heightened status and transfer the viceroyalty's political center from Lima to Cusco. No sign of serious rebellion disturbed loyalist rule until August 1814, when rebels in the old Inka capital called for the implementation of the constitution of 1812. Initially unaware that Ferdinand VII had nullified the charter, insurgents gained control of several cities in Lower and Upper Peru.

After a loyalist force took Cusco and executed the uprisings' leaders in early 1815, both Perus remained in Ferdinand's hands until the following decade.

Crisis and Transformation of the Imperial Economy

Disrupted by neutral trade because of war with England, Spain's traditional trans-atlantic commerce suffered further after the French invasion of 1808. Within five years, American markets had few Spanish products but ample goods from Britain. Moreover, Spanish ships carried little of the Indies' exports. Largely under the sway of Cádiz's powerful merchant guild that repeatedly provided them with money, Spain's governments of resistance refused to allow British merchants to trade legally in the Indies. Nonetheless, many royal officials in the Americas disregarded this policy. They understood that only such trade could meet consumers' demands, address serious fiscal needs, and facilitate the export of their jurisdiction's perishable products including cacao, cochineal, indigo, and hides.

Foreign trade and the resulting revenue from customs duties failed to enable either royal administrators or their revolutionary opponents to meet fiscal obligations. But the trade did ruin local commercial interests by destroying traditional patterns of credit and exchange. Put simply, American exports suffered from both the consequences of war and more mundane causes. Damage, flooding, and loss of workers dramatically reduced silver mining in New Spain. Having peaked in the 1790s, Peruvian silver production continued to decline. Additionally, rebellions reduced Venezuela's cacao exports, New Granada's gold mining, and New Spain's cochineal production. Already failing in 1808, Spain's imperial economy based on trade restrictions suffered almost complete destruction well before New World patriots achieved political independence.

PORTUGAL AND BRAZIL IN AN ERA OF REVOLUTION

The departure of the royal court from Portugal put its empire on a unique course. In the absence of its monarch, the country began to accommodate to the new order. Then, in 1808, word of the uprisings in Spain sparked a popular revolt and the formation of patriotic juntas. Aided by substantial British military support, Portuguese volunteers cleared Napoleon's forces from most of the kingdom. New French invasions in 1809 and 1811 caused extensive property damage and perhaps 250,000 Portuguese deaths. The war's significant destruction of the nation's already weak transportation system caused commerce to suffer. Expelling the French encumbered the Portuguese treasury with debt and left the economy in crisis.

John VI, the king after 1816, decided to remain in Brazil and elevate it to the status of an equal kingdom, actions that created dissatisfaction in Portugal. As regent in John's absence, the British general William Carr Beresford's consistent sacrifice of Portuguese commercial interests also prompted a rising tide of opposition. Even before the first French invasion, Portuguese merchant houses had lost Atlantic market share to Brazilian merchants who now competed directly in the African slave trade and related commerce. The court's relocation to Rio de Janeiro further strengthened the colonial interests. In 1810, John VI agreed to a commercial treaty that revoked prohibitions on manufacturing in Brazil and opened it to direct trade with friendly nations, especially Great Britain. This covenant confirmed the arrival of a new era. Despite legislation designed to benefit Portuguese merchants and shippers, the old monopolistic system had ended. Trade between Brazil and Portugal plummeted as exchange between the colony and Britain increased. As was the case with Spain, Portugal's empire had crumbled as an economic unit.

Political and economic subordination to Britain and anger over the monarch's decision to remain in Brazil stimulated a potent liberal opposition in Portugal, particularly among urban intellectuals, military officers, and merchants in port cities. Despite little sympathy for liberalism, some aristocrats in rural areas also disliked the regency.

Brazilian Independence

John's arrival in Rio de Janeiro dramatically changed Brazil's political life and economy. Access to the court and the possibility of gaining a title of nobility drew elite into his orbit. Although many Brazilians came to resent the recent arrivals' arrogance and privileged status, this anti-Portuguese sentiment did not seriously undermine support for the ruler.

As the prince regent and king, John VI moved quickly to address some long-standing grievances. He opened Brazil's ports to free trade, dropped some import duties, and removed the prohibition of local manufactures. The court also helped stimulate production by dramatically elevating the demand. More than 20,000 Portuguese and thousands of other European immigrants arrived in the city of Rio de Janeiro between 1808 and 1822. As the capital's population rose toward 100,000, the market expanded for housing, food, and Brazilian manufactured goods. Even the urban masses experienced small improvements in employment and wages.

Maintaining the royal court required substantial revenue. Whereas local producers largely paid the additional expenses through taxation, Portuguese émigrés held the highest administrative and military offices with enviable salaries and luxurious lifestyles provided by royal patronage. Despite general prosperity, some members of the Brazilian elite came to resent paying this forced subsidy. By yielding to British pressure and agreeing to restrictions on the slave trade, John lost support among sugar, cotton, and coffee producers. As the cost of slaves rose and the price of agricultural exports fell following Europe's return to peace in 1815, political unrest spread in Brazil's agricultural sector. Furthermore, the cost of armed intervention in Uruguay in 1811 and 1816 also proved unpopular. A military uprising in Pernambuco in 1817 underscored the dissatisfaction. The rebels attempted to create a republic, but it failed in less than three months.

Events in Portugal contributed more to Brazil's destabilization than local concerns and republicanism. The 1820 Riego Revolt forced Ferdinand VII to accept the restoration of the constitution of 1812 in Spain and triggered a successful rebellion in Portugal. As the movement spread, liberal political leaders in Lisbon and Oporto established juntas and sought John VI's return. Meanwhile, the Portuguese garrison in Rio de Janeiro forced the king to reorganize his ministry and to accept the creation of juntas and the formulation of a liberal constitution. Although he initially resisted the pressure to do so, John finally returned to Portugal in 1821. Despite his earlier fears, he only had to live briefly with the recently established constitutional order. In 1823, the restoration of Ferdinand VII to absolute power in Spain stimulated a conservative military revolt in Portugal supported by important elements within the Church hierarchy and the aristocracy. The constitutional government quickly fell, and John again ruled without formal political constraint.

When John departed from Brazil on July 26, 1821, he left his 22-year-old son Pedro as regent. The monarch's exodus and the presence of a regent in Rio de Janeiro made Brazilians more self-consciously aware of their differences from Iberian Portuguese. The *Cortes* meeting in Lisbon fed this growing sense of Brazilian distinctiveness by recreating the commercial system as it had existed in 1807 and reinforcing the American garrisons with Portuguese troops. As Portugal reasserted its domination, seven Brazilian delegates to the *Cortes* fled Lisbon rather than accept the Portuguese constitution of 1822.

Events now moved quickly. In response to intense pressure, including a petition signed by 8,000 persons, Pedro refused the *Cortes*'s order to return to Portugal. He purged the army in Brazil of officers and soldiers unwilling to swear allegiance to him and denied troops sent from Europe permission to land. The appointment of José Bonifácio de Andrada e Silva placed a wealthy and experienced Brazilian opposed to dramatic political or social change at the head of a cabinet. The break with the metropolis and continuation of a monarchical form of government as insurance against the chaos that had engulfed the Río de la Plata became inevitable. Although Portuguese dominated the cabinet numerically, all agreed with José Bonifácio on maintaining Pedro in Brazil in defiance of metropolitan authority.

In May 1822, the Constituent Assembly created in Rio de Janeiro decided that Pedro would hold the title of perpetual protector of Brazil. Moreover, only his prior approval would make decrees of the Portuguese *Cortes* enforceable. In June, the assembly required all government employees to swear support for Brazilian independence. Finally, it ordered the provincial governments to prevent individuals appointed by the Portuguese *Cortes* from taking office. Brazil had unofficially become independent.

While the prince was traveling in São Paulo, his wife met with the Council of State to inform them that the Portuguese *Cortes* planned to send troops to Brazil because it now regarded Dom Pedro and his advisors as traitors. At the urging of José Bonifácio, Pedro declared independence on September 7, 1822, and became the new country's first emperor. The British government guaranteed the declaration's bloodless success by warning Portugal that it would not tolerate European military intervention in Brazil.

Primary Sources

The Constitution of 1812 and War to the Death

The most notable accomplishment of the Cortes of Cádiz was writing a liberal constitution that included among its many provisions limited monarchy, a clear division of legislative, executive, and judicial authority, freedom of the press, and a broad suffrage. Numerous American deputies participated in drafting the document and it contributed to the formulation of constitutions by both emerging independent countries in Spain's erstwhile empire and Portugal.

Spanish Constitution of 1812

Title 1, Chapter 1 "Of the Spanish Nation"

Art. 1. The Spanish Nation is the reunion of all Spaniards of both hemispheres.

Art. 2. The Spanish Nation is free and independent, and is not nor can be the patrimony of any family or person.

Art 3. Sovereignty resides essentially in the Nation, and therefore so does this [the Nation] have the exclusive right of establishing fundamental laws.

Art. 4. The Nation is obligated to conserve and protect by wise and just laws civil liberty, property, and the other legitimate rights of all individuals that comprise it.

Chapter 4 "Of Spanish citizens"

Art. 18. Citizens are those Spaniards that by both lines trace their origin to the Spanish dominions of both hemispheres, and are citizens in whatever municipality of those same dominions.

Bolívar's Declaration of "War to the Death"

Issued at a time of bloody destruction by rebels and royalists alike, Simón Bolívar's decree of war to the death defined peninsular Spaniards as enemies of the independence for which he was fighting unless they actively supported it. Neutrality for them was impossible.

SOURCE: *El Libertador: Writings of Simón Bolívar*, ed. David Bushnell, trans. Frederick H. Fornoff (New York: Oxford University Press, 2003), 115–16.

Bolívar's Decree to Venezuelans of War to the Death against Peninsular Spaniards
June 15, 1813
Any [peninsular] Spaniard who does not join our fight against tyranny to further this just cause, actively and effectively, will be regarded as an enemy and punished as a traitor to the country and consequently put to death without appeal....

[Americans] You may count on absolute immunity regarding your honor, your lives, and your property: the mere title of Americans will be your guarantee and your safeguard....

Spaniards and Canarians, even if you profess neutrality, know that you will die unless you work actively to bring about the freedom of America. Americans, know that you will live, even if you are guilty.

SUGGESTIONS FOR FURTHER READING

Adelman, Jeremy. *Sovereignty and Revolution in the Iberian Atlantic*. Princeton, NJ: Princeton University Press, 2006.

Archer, Christon I. (ed.). *The Wars of Independence in Spanish America*. Wilmington, DE: Scholarly Resources, 2000.

Barman, Roderick J. *Brazil: The Forging of a Nation, 1798–1852*. Stanford, CA: Stanford University Press, 1988.

Blanchard, Peter. *Under the Flags of Freedom: Slave Soldiers and the Wars of Independence in Spanish South America*. Pittsburgh, PA: University of Pittsburgh Press, 2008.

Dym, Jordana. *From Sovereign Villages to National States: City, State, and Federation in Central America, 1759–1839*. Albuquerque: University of New Mexico Press, 2006.

Earle, Rebecca A. *Spain and the Independence of Colombia, 1810–1825*. Exeter, England: University of Exeter Press, 2000.

Eastman, Scott. *Preaching Spanish Nationalism across the Hispanic Atlantic, 1759–1823*. Baton Rouge: Louisiana State University Press, 2012.

Hawkins, Timothy. *José de Bustamante and Central American Independence: Colonial Administration in an Age of Imperial Crisis*. Tuscaloosa: University of Alabama Press, 2004.

Johnson, Lyman L. *Workshop of Revolution: Plebeian Buenos Aires and the Atlantic World, 1776–1810*. Durham, NC: Duke University Press, 2011.

Lynch, John. *San Martín: Argentine Soldier, American Hero*. New Haven, CT, and London: Yale University Press, 2009.

Lynch, John. *Simón Bolívar: A Life*. New Haven, CT, and London: Yale University Press, 2006.

Marks, Patricia H. *Deconstructing Legitimacy: Viceroys, Merchants, and the Military in Late Colonial Peru*. University Park: Pennsylvania State University Press, 2007.

Racine, Karen. *Francisco de Miranda: A Transatlantic Life in the Age of Revolution*. Wilmington, DE: Scholarly Resources, 2003.

Rodríguez O., Jaime E. *"We Are Now the True Spaniards": Sovereignty, Revolution, Independence, and the Emergence of the Federal Republic of Mexico, 1808–1824*. Stanford, CA: Stanford University Press, 2012.

———. *The Independence of Spanish America*. Cambridge: Cambridge University Press, 1998.

Walker, Charles F. *Smoldering Ashes: Cuzco and the Creation of Republican Peru, 1780–1840*. Durham, NC: Duke University Press, 1999.

CHAPTER 13

The Age of Independence (II)

SPAIN LOSES ITS MAINLAND EMPIRE

The path of Spain's loyalist possessions in America changed starting in 1814. Multiple elections, constitutional government, and access to a free press had altered many citizens' expectations since Ferdinand VII's abdication in 1808. Several regions had even declared independence. But Spain's victory against Napoleonic France allowed the reactionary monarch to reinstate the institutions and conditions in place before his exile. Despite some initial successes, the government's reliance on military force ultimately alienated former supporters in the empire. The wheel took a final turn in 1820 when rebellion in the metropolis precluded sending additional troops to the Indies and produced three years of constitutional rule. Independence triumphed throughout mainland America by the mid-1820s.

The Failure of Absolutism

A disastrous Russian campaign forced Napoleon to withdraw troops from the Iberian Peninsula. The final enemy forces departed in early 1814 and Ferdinand VII returned to widespread acclamation. "The Desired One" followed a leisurely course to Valencia, where military officers assured him of the army's support if he restored Spain's government to its state in 1808.

Buoyed by popular enthusiasm, the monarch promptly abrogated the constitution of 1812, reestablished Old Regime institutions, and, insofar as possible, reinstated the officials who were serving in May 1808. His claim of sovereignty and resumption of absolute authority put in bold relief the rights and political institutions developed in "the Spanish Nation" during the French occupation. Before this cataclysmic event, elites in both "these and those" realms (Spain and the Indies), like the rest of society, showed unquestioned loyalty to the Bourbons. But Napoleon's invasion had altered allegiance to royal rule. To defeat the French, liberals had fomented a political revolution that divided monarchists into constitutionalists and absolutists. In the Indies, many native sons had responded enthusiastically to elections, open political discussion, and the prospect of autonomy while rejecting more radical ideas of republics and independence.

Ferdinand's return recast politics in Spanish America. His suppression of representative government, freedom of the press, and other political guarantees increasingly moved elite opinion beyond the pursuit of autonomy within the "Spanish Monarchy" toward independence, a position whose adherents had appeared in a few places as early as 1810. Rejecting reform and compromise, the king embarked on the perilous course of applying military force to impose order. This pushed elites in "pacified" regions a step closer to independence. Property loss and harsh royalist reprisals in Venezuela, New Granada, Chile, and New Spain affected numerous elite families and undermined their earlier espousal of Spain's continued rule.

Ferdinand's policy failed. The cost of sending and maintaining troops in the Americas exceeded what normal revenues could support. Already deeply in debt in 1808, royal treasuries throughout the Indies 10 years later suffered almost total insolvency from accumulated deficits. Wartime destruction and the breakdown of established commercial links between Spain and the Indies had taken their toll. Yet despite flooded mines, diminished commerce, and the government's virtual bankruptcy, it took a decade after Ferdinand's return from his gilded captivity for independence to reign triumphant throughout the American mainland.

Spanish South America: Borderless Campaigns of Conquest and Liberation

Military conflicts between loyalists and separatists often expanded beyond a single kingdom or province in much of Spanish South America. José de San Martín and Simón Bolívar, the two greatest leaders of the immense region's independence movements, believed that the fledgling countries' security required an independent Peru. This strategic vision privileged liberating the viceroyalty. Given its elites' fear of social revolution since the Tupac Amaru revolt in the early 1780s, the two leaders relied on armies originating elsewhere on the continent.

Ferdinand's restoration enabled him to dispatch military forces in an attempt to reestablish Spanish control of the Indies. The arrival in 1815 of a large military expedition in Venezuela under General Pablo Morillo and the threat of still another army being sent elsewhere in the Indies emphasized the independent states' vulnerability. The general's forces entered Caracas in May 1815 and by October had pacified most of New Granada. To pay for this costly venture, Morillo confiscated and sold the property of well-known republican leaders and their noncombatant supporters. This harsh policy proved counterproductive as the native-son elite started to view independence as the best guarantee of their property.

The arrival of Spanish reinforcements in northern South America stalled Simón Bolívar's bloody campaign and forced the liberator to flee. He escaped to Jamaica, where he penned the famous "Jamaica Letter" detailing his vision of an independent Spanish America. He also spent time in the former French colony of Haiti, where its president, Alexandre Petion, provided him with needed supplies and moral support, using the opportunity to secure the liberator's promise to emancipate slaves.

Returning to Venezuela, Bolívar established himself in the *llanos* where he came to terms with José Antonio Páez, a *casta* cattle trader. The liberator's army also benefited from a large number of British adventurers, including a few veterans of the Napoleonic wars. A congress held in Venezuela's interior town of Angostura in 1819 optimistically declared the union of Venezuela, New Granada, and Ecuador in the Republic of Colombia—what historians often label Gran Colombia—and named Bolívar president. Even as the congress met, however, the leader had inaugurated an audacious military campaign that would determine the future of New Granada. With a mobile military force composed of the interior's cowboys (*llaneros*), Bolívar crossed the Andes and advanced toward Bogotá. Not far from the capital, his victory at Boyacá in 1819 effectively liberated most of present-day Colombia.

Despite Bolívar's success in the northern reaches of South America, substantial Spanish possessions to the south remained loyal to Ferdinand VII. The formal declaration of independence by the United Provinces of the Río de la Plata in 1816 left the future countries of Chile, Peru, and Bolivia in royalist hands. General San Martín believed that the only way to conquer Peru was via Chile.

Supported by political allies in Buenos Aires, San Martín used Mendoza, located on the eastern side of the Andes in present-day Argentina, as a base for recruiting and training an army. Augmented with a few Chileans, most notably Bernardo O'Higgins, San Martín's force crossed the Andes and liberated Chile in 1818. With O'Higgins' support as the new country's president, in 1820 the general sailed north with an army. The fleet commanded by Admiral Thomas Cochrane landed in Pisco, Peru, south of Lima. San Martín bided his time, believing that his presence would stimulate the Peruvians in Lima to declare independence and welcome his army. Cochrane, however, wanted to pay his men and ultimately sailed back to Chile with all the treasure he could collect, leaving the general and his army stranded. By this time, however, a new political environment in Spain provided an unanticipated opportunity for American patriots.

Liberal Rule in Spain and Its Consequences

On January 1, 1820, Major Rafael Riego launched a military revolt in southern Spain among troops gathered for another large expedition to the Americas. The revolt's success forced an angry Ferdinand VII to accept constitutional rule and prompted the final disintegration of Spain's mainland American empire. With no army to dispatch, Spain's new liberal government ordered its commanders in the Indies to arrange ceasefires with the separatists. In New Granada, General Pablo Morillo met with Bolívar to orchestrate a truce and then departed for Spain, leaving the remaining royalist forces in northern South America under weak leaders.

The final military campaigns in South America occurred between 1820 and 1825. Although it took some time to defeat all pockets of royalist resistance in the north, armies under Bolívar and his lieutenants, José Antonio Páez and Antonio José de Sucre, proved unstoppable. Páez's victory at Carabobo in 1821 signified the liberation of Venezuela. Sucre's success in present-day Ecuador the following year confirmed that it would indeed join the Republic of Colombia created in 1819.

Without fighting a major battle in Peru, San Martín pressured Lima's leading citizens to declare independence from Spain in July 1821. But the general failed to extend his authority into the interior, still controlled by an undefeated army under the viceroy's command. With the invading force disintegrating from desertion and the new government in Lima essentially bankrupt, San Martín sailed to Guayaquil, Ecuador, and sought Bolívar's support. Resigning as "protector" soon afterward, San Martín went into self-imposed exile, leaving Bolívar and Sucre to complete the liberation of the two Perus. Victories at Junín and Ayacucho in 1824 eliminated the royalist government and its army in Peru. During the following year, Sucre's triumphs in Upper Peru resulted in independent Bolivia, so named in honor of the great leader of independence. The last South American bases loyal to Spain surrendered in 1826.

New Spain: The Collapse of Empire

Independence in New Spain followed a different course than in South America. After the Riego Revolt, New Spain responded enthusiastically to Ferdinand's proclaimed allegiance to the constitution of 1812. The viceroy quickly restored provincial deputations and hundreds of constitutional municipal governments; elections identified deputies to the *Cortes* in Madrid. This last opportunity for autonomy within the Spanish Nation, however, proved fruitless.

In 1821, the separatist solution triumphed under the leadership of Agustín de Iturbide. The native son had proven himself among the most effective officers in Mexico's loyalist forces when they had fought against Hidalgo and Morelos. With no reinforcements available from Spain, the officer consulted with well-regarded autonomists and conservatives in the capital. Gaining acquiescence from the future president, Vicente Guerrero, the most prominent patriot leader, Iturbide issued a formal call for Mexico's complete self-rule in the Plan of Iguala.

A masterful compromise, this document gained support that secured Mexico's independence while protecting the interests of the army, the Church, and resident peninsulars. Separatists obtained their major objective while conservatives approved an end to the threats against special privileges posed by the *Cortes* in Spain. In an attempt to maintain a conservative executive, the plan unrealistically offered the throne of independent Mexico to Ferdinand VII. The newly arrived Spanish liberal and surrogate viceroy (*jefe político superior*), Juan O'Donojú, supported Mexican autonomy and agreed to the Plan of Iguala in the Treaty of Córdoba. This sealed independence without a major battle.

After Spain refused to accept the treaty, officers and soldiers organized popular demonstrations that led to the creation of a Mexican empire and Iturbide's coronation as Emperor Agustín I. Within a year, however, the empire collapsed, undercut by political divisions and fiscal crises. Following a brief exile in Europe, Iturbide returned to Mexico, where he suffered immediate execution.

The Kingdom of Guatemala, the Spanish dominion that would later become the modern countries of Guatemala, Honduras, Nicaragua, El Salvador, and Costa Rica, remained generally peaceful during the early stages of insurrection in Mexico. Efforts to implement the constitution of 1812 initiated conflict between liberals and conservatives, but not open warfare. This changed with Mexico's independence. Although some Central Americans proposed separation, most local governments accepted incorporation into the Mexican Empire. Nevertheless, with Iturbide's departure, the former Kingdom of Guatemala became an independent federal republic, with only Chiapas joining Mexico.

SOCIETIES AT WAR

The wars of independence in mainland Spanish America lasted for more than a decade, in part because the patriots lacked the critical foreign support that France and Spain had provided in the American Revolution. The conflicts in Spanish America also occurred over a geographical expanse that dwarfed the smaller region involved in what became the United States. Nonetheless, tens of thousands of men and women participated in the wars either directly or indirectly, and movement from one region to another was common.

American Leaders

The most influential insurgent leaders, almost all native sons and other creoles, ranged from men born in the 1750s to students born in the 1790s and came from varied occupations and social backgrounds. They included the professional advocate of independence Francisco de Miranda in Venezuela, the parish priest Miguel Hidalgo in New Spain, and Cornelio de Saavedra, a militia officer and member of the first junta, in Buenos Aires. *Casta* José Antonio Páez traded cattle in the interior plains of Venezuela before independence; he subsequently became president of his homeland. The mestizo parish priest José María Morelos in New Spain suffered execution in 1815. Among the few leaders with significant military experience before 1810 were Gervasio de Artigas in future Uruguay and Iturbide in Mexico.

The two most acclaimed leaders of insurrection embodied heroism on a grand scale. "The liberator" Simón Bolívar, aristocratic, wealthy, charismatic, and persistent, appreciated the need to defeat Spanish loyalists in all of South America. His weaknesses included impatience for administrative work and sometimes unreliable military skills. "The protector" San Martín, a royalist officer who fought against the French in two wars and ultimately retired from the Spanish army as a lieutenant colonel, also understood the big picture. He had excellent organizational and tactical skills and effectively instilled discipline. The inability to gain the independence of Peru with forces overwhelmingly drawn from Argentina and Chile proved his biggest failure.

Armies

Although insurgent armies often had strong local roots, both separatists and royalists frequently depended on recruits from distant areas. Stationed throughout the Indies, forces loyal to the Crown numbered about 35,000 in 1800, including some 5,500 peninsulars. The 41,000 troops sent from Spain between 1811 and 1818 had an immediate impact, but desertions, disease, and battlefield casualties quickly diminished their number. The willingness of the locally born to fight for the king would determine the mainland empire's survival or dissolution.

Patriot armies also depended on both local recruits and volunteers drawn from a wide area. In January 1817, San Martín commanded an army that incorporated political exiles from Chile, cowboys from the pampas, and numerous former slaves and freedmen from Buenos Aires. Similarly, Bolívar led troops enlisted in New Granada to combat Spanish forces in Venezuela. He later returned to New Granada to fight the Spanish loyalists with an army largely recruited in Venezuela. Along with his chief lieutenant Sucre, Bolívar then led a mixed force of Venezuelans, New Granadans, and the few remaining elements of San Martín's Argentine and Chilean army to liberate Lower and Upper Peru.

Service in either loyalist or patriot military units could facilitate upward social mobility for the poorest members of viceregal society. Slaves and free blacks confirmed their value to both sides. In 1821, nonwhites made up at least 60 percent of the royalist army in Venezuela and an overwhelming 85 percent of the royalist forces in Peru. Free and enslaved blacks and *pardos* also constituted the majority of insurgent troops in many other regions. Whatever the exact number, almost all slaves who served on either side of the conflict gained their freedom.

Indigenous troops fought as both loyalists and insurgents in the Andes and parts of New Spain as well. Spanish officials and other loyalist groups organized resistance to juntas pressing toward independence, thereby providing indigenous communities an opportunity to bargain for more power in exchange for military service. Voting in repeated elections to select representatives for the *Cortes* allowed Indians to participate directly in the political revolution supported by liberals and by many loyalists. Although both the *Cortes* of Cádiz and some patriot leaders abolished tribute and called for an end to Indians' other long-standing obligations, these burdens often survived in disguised form decades after independence.

Desertion and Disease

The practice of using soldiers far from their homes reduced desertion, but swelled mortality rates because of disease, change of climate, and unsanitary living arrangements. In Veracruz, recurrent epidemics of yellow fever killed thousands of Spanish soldiers en route to New Spain's interior. Between 1815 and 1821, General Morillo and other royalist officers in Venezuela and coastal New Granada lost some 90 percent of their peninsular soldiers, most from disease and other medical problems. Foreign soldiers fighting under Bolívar experienced similar extreme mortality rates. Of the nearly 7,000 Irish, English, and other foreign adventurers who enlisted in Bolívar's army between 1816 and 1825, almost half died of disease or while on campaign. Although 4,500 Argentines and Chileans accompanied San Martín to Peru in 1820, a scant 100 remained to fight at Ayacucho in 1824.

Women in the Midst of War

Women routinely suffered the consequences of civil war—often poverty and widowhood—without visible benefits. Hostilities reduced them to penury, required them to abandon their homes, and subjected some to robbery and rape by soldiers. Many witnessed the conscription or even execution of brothers, fathers, and husbands. With large numbers of men enlisted in loyalist or patriot armies, women regularly bore the burden of overseeing businesses, farms, and ranches, in addition to their traditional obligations of managing households and children.

Some free and slave women actively participated in the conflicts. Although the First Republic refused the offer of 21 women from Barinas, Venezuela, to join the republican army in 1811, it used the patriotic gesture to inspire others. Slave women embraced the opportunities presented by war to serve as cooks, servants, nurses, and camp followers, among other occupations, in the hope of gaining freedom. The mestiza Juana Azurduy of Chuquisaca, Upper Peru, worked with her husband to enlist men and weapons for the cause of independence. She also led troops in battle and cared for the wounded.

An educated minority of women participated in the lively debates that determined the future of their region. Others served as spies, attended meetings, delivered correspondence, cared for the wounded, and raised and donated funds. Women often aided recruitment and gathered information, accompanied husbands in military service, and, on one occasion, smuggled a printing press to the insurgents. These services involved substantial risk; in New Granada alone, royalists executed more than 50 women and imprisoned many others.

Manuela Sáenz, Bolívar's mistress, numbered among the most celebrated women in the republican ranks. She participated as a soldier in the battles of Junín and Ayacucho in Peru, gaining promotion to captain after Junín. In New Spain, Josefa Ortiz de Domínguez, the wife of the *corregidor* of Querétaro, contributed to the Hidalgo Revolt by informing conspirators that the government knew of the planned rebellion.

SOCIAL CHANGE

Independence introduced significant social change, although elements of the past persisted. Racial identification of baptized infants and their parents ended. Native sons at last gained the highest positions in the government and military. Transition to local control in the Catholic Church took much longer, with Europeans still occupying some episcopal positions at the end of the nineteenth century. Greater complexity marked the social consequences of economic transformation. Nearly everywhere, wealth became the primary indicator of social status. The emergence of export-led economies elevated the status of those who owned large estates and successful mines. British and other European merchants and investors resident in Latin America served as vectors of social and cultural change.

In many areas, locally born elites tied to export agriculture used mounting riches to assert political and cultural power. As a result, their social norms and manners gained wider acceptance, leading in Argentina, Brazil, and other countries to the adoption of a romanticized version of the large rural estate as a national cultural ideal. Nevertheless, even where enterprises in the countryside came to dominate national economies, the richest ranchers, plantation owners, and mine owners maintained opulent households in the major cities, as had their predecessors before independence. Despite the political and economic revolutions that had transformed Latin America, metropolitan centers continued to hold sway.

Cities also served as unpredictable social and cultural laboratories where native-born migrants from towns and villages mixed with temporary European residents and, after the 1830s, with increased numbers of immigrants. At the upper levels of these societies, commercial and professional sectors embraced fashions and ideas from abroad, even while they patriotically objected to foreign governments' aggressive exertion of economic, diplomatic, or military power. The middle and laboring classes experienced significant cultural change. The native-born population sampled and adapted new foods, sports, and political ideas while immigrants assimilated via language, political mobilization, and marriage with local women. This mounting foreign influence helped generate a reciprocal, sometimes defensive interest in regional history. New cultural expressions included heroic depictions of the indigenous past and literary and musical evocations of allegedly authentic national themes and customs. These two powerful phenomena weakened the still-important influence of inherited Iberian traditions.

Upward social mobility followed independence, despite ongoing discrimination against mixed-race men and women. Service in revolutionary armies by *casta* officers improved their social status. By the 1850s, some dark-skinned men had secured political and economic power, and a handful had become presidents. Although racism and cultural and color prejudices continued in every independent Latin American country, all experienced some social change. Particularly in rural areas, the discriminatory social order imposed initially by conquest and the African slave trade persisted. As economies began to grow again in the 1830s and 1840s, increased numbers of foreign immigrants arrived in Latin America, with Argentina, Brazil, and Uruguay receiving the most. Their presence complicated the social order, especially in urban areas.

GOVERNMENT AND POLITICAL LIFE

Substantial changes in government and political life followed independence. In Brazil, the presence of a Portuguese prince in Rio de Janeiro eased the transition. Although monarchy would survive until 1889, a constitution installed in 1824 restricted the emperor's power. Spanish America experienced a more dramatic and comprehensive political transition. Aside from Mexico's abortive experiment, the new countries abandoned the monarchical system that had provided legitimacy and continuity over three centuries. The victors also abolished nearly the entirety of the viceregal order and its agents; few experienced high officials retained posts much after independence.

Between 1810 and the late 1820s, juntas, constituent assemblies, and congresses wrote foundational laws and constitutions as frameworks for government; New Granadans drafted some 20 different codes by the end of 1815, a majority for city-states such as Cartagena. Following explicit declarations of independence, most separatists in Spanish South America supported constitutional republics.

Although monarchism found its supporters during the struggle for independence—San Martín and Iturbide being the most important—the political leadership in independent Spanish America generally acknowledged republican principles. The Spanish political revolution of 1808–1812 had altered the nature of political identity by transforming subjects into national citizens; independence accentuated this difference. The achievements of Spanish liberalism—freedom of the press, regular elections, and the Iberian world's first written constitution—helped set the agenda for the new governments. As a result, first-generation constitutions, many inspired by the constitution of 1812, affirmed the sovereignty of the people, created representative institutions, and sought to define individual rights. Nearly everywhere, the presence of elected representatives legitimized governments. Impressively, new constitutions defined voting rights more broadly than in the United States. Almost all free, adult males, but not women or slaves, initially received the right to vote. Over time, however, elites adopted property and literacy requirements to limit the suffrage of the poorest and most vulnerable, especially the indigenous population and former slaves.

Generous definitions of citizenship and voting rights did not guarantee democratic practices. O'Higgins, Bolívar, Páez, and Sucre, among others, accepted and exercised political authority and administrative power outside the limits established by constitutions. Representative institutions lost their importance as newly independent countries confronted centrifugal political threats. Local and regional loyalties destroyed Bolívar's vision of a Gran Colombia, subverted Central America's union with Mexico, and frustrated the re-creation of a United Provinces of the Río de la Plata. In many cases, strongmen exercised real power. For their legitimacy these *caudillos* relied on their clients and elite patronage rather than elections and formal institutions. Some called themselves liberals, others conservatives, but few accepted formal constitutional limits to their authority. The many important *caudillos* included Juan Manuel de Rosas of Argentina, Diego Portales of Chile, José Antonio Páez of Venezuela, and Antonio López de Santa Anna of Mexico. Contemporary admirers considered them "great men," but these leaders' political importance owed less to their merits than to the relative diminution of centralized power and the reduction of state resources during the 1820s and 1830s. Although they often slowed the pace of institution building, *caudillos* frequently promoted actively the political integration of the masses in national political life.

Despite women's many important contributions during the independence struggles, the first constitutions excluded them from active citizenship and the right to vote and hold office. New civil codes went still further in strengthening male authority in public life and the family. Even in poor households with disenfranchised adult males, fathers and husbands enjoyed legal authority over their wives and daughters that made them, in effect, agents of the state. Legislation defined married women as minors and compelled them to accept their husbands' authority. Widows alone had some financial and legal independence, gaining the right to sign contracts and control their own property. Thus, women's legal rights expanded only slowly. Not until 1860, for example, did single mothers and widows in Mexico obtain the right to direct their own families the way male family heads did.

The state maintained economic importance after independence, although limited resources reduced and constrained ambitions. Only the government of Brazil retained a pre–independence era ability to influence the allocation of resources. Even in this case, Great Britain's preponderant position as a trading partner limited the government's freedom of action. Politicians in London rather than Rio de Janeiro, for example, made the initial decisions that eventually ended the slave trade.

Nevertheless, the government remained countries' largest single employer and consumer. Thus, it could expand or restrict consumption and production through budgetary decisions. In general, all Latin American nations lagged far behind Europe and the United States in providing an environment suitable for commercial and industrial investment. In some cases, Latin American governments established central banks and promoted the creation of insurance companies in imitation of practices in Europe and the United States. But limited scope resulted in their rapid failure. New national monetary systems also proved less stable than the former reliance on silver coinage. In Argentina, for example, paper money quickly fed inflation; copper coins produced a similar result in Brazil. Unpredictable government policies and fluctuating markets encouraged investment in real property rather than in more risky enterprises.

After independence, the political importance of armies grew as civilian authority declined. Although current or former officers often held executive power, they did not militarize political life. In an era of civil war, regional secessionism, and ideological conflict, political peace could result only from the efforts of strongmen capable of organizing and asserting armed force. However, few successful leaders of this period politicized or even professionalized the armed forces. Páez, the Venezuelan revolutionary era military hero and later president, reduced the regular army to 800 men in 1838. Rosas, the Argentine *caudillo* of the 1830s and 1840s, refused for 15 years to increase the nominal pay of officers and enlisted men, despite inflation. Increasingly important regional militias and other irregular armed forces, not politicized regular armies, changed political life in Latin America. Often accompanied by violence, this new military phase resulted from a breakdown in public order and weakened central authority that tended to elevate the relative political weight of even small, poorly armed military forces at the provincial level.

The status of the Church became a bitterly divisive issue in the decades following independence. This conflict began with the Bourbon monarchs' efforts to subordinate the Church to secular authority, a process underscored by the expulsion of the Jesuits from both Portuguese and Spanish realms. Clerical immunity from secular jurisdiction in criminal and civil cases, the use of sanctuary, and the control of patronage remained unresolved when viceregal rule ended. New conflicts over secular education, religious freedom, and Church wealth effectively established the boundaries that separated conservatives and liberals after independence. Finally, the papacy's efforts to reassert patronage rights in Latin America proved an incendiary issue, as new political elites sought to create a compliant and supportive episcopal structure. In many nations, Mexico and Colombia, for example, these struggles proved to be major obstacles to the development of stable national governments.

Achieving independence fostered a reevaluation of Spanish rule. For nearly three centuries, the Crown and its vassals in the Americas referred to their lands as "kingdoms" and "provinces," not "colonies." In contrast, foreign authors routinely applied the term colonies to Spain's America, and from the 1760s Spanish publications increasingly employed it. Such references became more common from 1808 to 1814 with the publication of proclamations, political tracts, and *Cortes* debates. Progressively, native sons and other creoles endowed colonies with a derogatory character that reflected a rapidly expanding antipeninsular and anti-Spain sentiment.

Primary Source

Bolívar's Frustration

By the year of his death, 1830, Simón Bolívar had lost the optimism of his earlier years. A letter he wrote to Juan José Flores encapsulates his frustration.

SOURCE: *El Libertador: Writings of Simón Bolívar*, ed. David Bushnell., trans. Frederick H. Fornoff (New York: Oxford University Press, 2003), 146.

> Use the past to predict the future. You know that I have ruled for twenty years, and I have derived from these only a few sure conclusions: (1) America is ungovernable, for us; (2) Those who serve revolution plough the sea; (3) The only thing one can do in America is emigrate; (45) This country [Ecuador] will fall inevitably into the hands of the unrestrained multitudes and then into the hands of tyrants so insignificant they will be almost imperceptible, of all colors and races; (5) Once we've been eaten alive by every crime and extinguished by ferocity, the Europeans won't even bother to conquer us; (6) if it were possible for any part of the world to revert to primitive chaos, it would be America in her last hour.

In the 1820s, Americans introduced a deprecating neologism—*coloniaje*—to encapsulate the period of Spanish rule. Thus. independence transformed kingdoms and provinces into colonies, a term that still exudes a pejorative flavor.

Independence marked an important transition in the history of Latin America. In political and economic terms, the region became both more dynamic and more vulnerable than in what contemporaries disparagingly labeled the "colonial era." The difficult transition to republican institutions, a broader participation in political life, and increased economic volatility fed regional instability. Underlying these changes lay the inherited inequality of vestigial social and economic structures. Nevertheless, by the end of the nineteenth century every nation in Latin America had become richer, more democratic, and more fluid socially than prior to independence.

SUGGESTIONS FOR FURTHER READING

Adelman, Jeremy (ed.). *Colonial Legacies: The Problem of Persistence in Latin American History.* New York: Routledge, 1999.

Anna, Timothy E. *Forging Mexico 1821–1835.* Lincoln: University of Nebraska Press, 1998.

Haber, Stephen (ed.). *How Latin America Fell Behind: Essays on the Economic History of Brazil and Mexico, 1800–1914.* Stanford, CA: Stanford University Press, 1997.

Hünefeldt, Christine. *Paying the Price of Freedom: Family and Labor among Lima's Slaves, 1800–1854.* Translated by Alexandra Minna Stern. Berkeley and Los Angeles: University of California Press, 1994.

Jacobsen, Nils. *Mirages of Transition: The Peruvian Altiplano, 1780–1930.* Berkeley and Los Angeles: University of California Press, 1993.

Larson, Brooke. *Trials of Nation Making: Liberalism, Race, and Ethnicity in the Andes, 1810–1910*. Cambridge: Cambridge University Press, 2004.

McFarlane, Anthony. *War and Independence in Spanish America*. New York: Routledge, 2008.

Ringrose, David R. *Spain, Europe, and the "Spanish Miracle" 1700–1900*. Cambridge: Cambridge University Press, 1996.

Stevens, Donald Fithian. *Origins of Instability in Early Republican Mexico*. Durham, NC: Duke University Press, 1991.

Uribe-Uran, Victor M. (ed.). *State and Society in Spanish America during the Age of Revolution*. Wilmington, DE: Scholarly Resources, 2001.

Walker, Charles F. *Smoldering Ashes: Cuzco and the Creation of Republican Peru, 1780–1840*. Durham, NC: Duke University Press, 1999.

CHAPTER 14

Colonies to Nations

Independence was just the first step in a long struggle that Latin American countries faced in the nineteenth century. Three centuries of Spanish rule left in their wake long-standing traditions that influenced political institutions as well as economic and social networks. Politically, Latin American independence leaders debated how best to make the transition from rule by a European monarch to sovereign statehood. The mercantilist system that had restricted trade had also limited opportunities for economic growth. A social system based on racial discrimination, corporate bodies, and legal privileges for a few created a climate ripe for conflict. Exploitation and inequality that had characterized the centuries under European rule carried over into the nineteenth century.

Map 14.1 Latin America in 1830

More than a decade of war took a toll on the economies of soon to be sovereign states. The fighting disrupted mining, agriculture, and trade, and new governments struggled to find a path to financial solvency in the 1820s. Government revenues plummeted, paving the way for enormous foreign debt and general instability. The emergence of dominant personalities throughout Latin America had characterized the independence era and most new countries owed their existence to the leadership of these individuals. The most prominent included Simón Bolívar in the former viceroyalties of New Granada and Peru, Bernardo O'Higgins in Chile, and Agustín de Iturbide in Mexico. But although they served as bulwarks for fragile resistance movements, their political ambitions also created the potential for conflict.

A a Brazilian planter on his horse, followed by two males slaves carrying his wife, and a female slave balancing a bundle on her head. This illustration is taken from Henri Koster's 1817 travelogue of Brazil. Koster, a Portuguese coffee-grower, wrote extensively about his observations of slavery and life in northeastern Brazil.

Disputes arose regarding the way to structure new governments; civil wars, coups d'état, and general unrest became constant. Many areas of Latin America attempted to form a system of government under a loose federation, but by the 1840s the failed efforts had fractured into smaller countries. One notable exception was Brazil, which achieved independence in 1822 but remained under a monarchy of Portuguese royal lineage until 1889. The institution of slavery persisted there as well. Favored by political and economic consistency, Brazil maintained relative stability throughout the nineteenth century.

ECONOMIC AND FISCAL CONSEQUENCES OF INDEPENDENCE

The newly independent countries of Spanish America in almost every case began their existence with economic devastation. The fiscal stresses of Spain's wartime expenses exceeded regular sources of revenue and the new states inherited substantial domestic debt. Quickly, they also assumed foreign obligations beyond their means. "Free trade" initially had widespread appeal and new governments quickly opened ports to foreign merchants, particularly those from Britain. Although the quantities initially were smaller because of wartime destruction, the nature of exports remained unchanged as precious metals and agricultural products proved almost the only goods with international markets. Additionally, independence brought the disintegration of the empire's monetary union; new governments issued underweight coinage of inferior fineness even before the fighting ended. Inflation, deflation, and currency manipulation, all experiences that Spain had suffered and transmitted to the Indies, continued.

Production and Trade

New Latin American governments inherited an economic system defined by the mercantilist structures put in place during three centuries of colonial rule. The production of raw materials through mining and agriculture continued as the basis for Latin American economies, but the wars for independence disrupted many local operations and trade networks. A decline in production was most evident in the mining sector in the new countries of Mexico, Peru, Bolivia, Colombia, and Chile. Conflict resulted in flooded and caved-in mines, deteriorated and destroyed equipment, and a shortage of leather as well as mercury, the indispensable agent for processing low-grade ore. Silver production plummeted, particularly in Peru and Mexico, where it declined 44 percent in the decade following Hidalgo's revolt. In once-profitable Potosí, a precipitous decline also occurred as a result of war. Notable improvement did not take place until the 1860s. Gold production in Colombia and Chile also fell after 1810. Mining output continued to decrease throughout the 1820s, affecting government revenue as well as domestic and international trade.

Independence opened access to gullible European investors, who believed the only problem with Latin America's mining sector was that Latin Americans controlled it. Convinced a fortune awaited them, British financial backers created joint-stock companies to exploit mines in Mexico, Peru, and Bolivia. Nearly all foreign mining companies founded in the early 1820s, however, failed in 1824–25. For the first time, mine owners had to purchase mercury in the international market at prices that had doubled between 1810 and 1819. Added to other expenses, the cost of mercury served to reduce, if not eliminate, profits.

A downturn in the agricultural sector was another economic consequence of the independence era. Insurgents and counterinsurgents destroyed cropland and seized livestock and draft animals, which drove numerous small farmers to abandon their operations and cease producing goods for urban markets and miners. Commercial agriculture took a beating and a renewed focus on subsistence farming reduced specialization. Large enterprises on haciendas in Mexico suffered, and landowners in Colombia found the removal of slaves to build and repair roads still another handicap.

Throughout Spanish America, independence destroyed the last shreds of Spain's long-claimed trade monopoly. Although exports comprised a small portion of mainland Spanish America's total production, native-son merchants had long chafed under Spain's commercial policies. After independence, governments reduced prohibitions on trade to and from anywhere in the world, a policy they labeled free trade, but one that was definitely not free from taxes.

The U.S. merchants seized the opportunities provided by more open trade regulations after independence, often building on connections that had emerged as a result of neutral trade policies in the final decades under Spanish rule. British merchants, who had a long tradition of introducing contraband goods into Latin America, quickly established legal trade networks. By the mid-1820s, British commerce with Spanish America was worth nearly $60 million, whereas U.S. trade was worth $24 million.

Government Revenues

Revenues were a shambles throughout Spanish America as new governments inherited the consequences of the Crown's concerted efforts to increase income for war and treaty commitments in Europe. What happened in the mainland's richest realm illustrates the catastrophic fiscal circumstances that plagued new governments. Revenue in the treasury in Mexico City plummeted nearly 80 percent between 1809 and 1823; in 1830, it was still less than half of the 1809 figure.

Securing adequate revenue proved difficult. In efforts to curry popular support, numerous governments decided to eliminate the tobacco and *aguardiente* monopolies. Although these had provided substantial income, the populace hated them because they raised the cost of the small pleasures of smoking and drinking. Consequently, efforts to restore them were unpopular and, in Mexico, the reestablished monopoly for tobacco never again significantly added to the government's resources.

Tribute

Rising tribute in the eighteenth century reflected an expanding Indian population and more assiduous collection and remission to royal treasuries. Abolished by insurgents and royal governments alike, this tax was reinstated in those regions where it had been a significant source of income. It remained, often under a new name, until its final abolition in the mid-nineteenth century. Tribute collected under the euphemistic description "*contribución única*" constituted the Peruvian government's largest single source of income until about 1850. In Central America, the state government of Guatemala in 1825 restored the tax in practice, although not in name, and even extended it to all citizens. Exploitation of and discrimination toward the indigenous population continued after independence.

Customs Duties

Customs duties held a prominent but rarely leading place among regular sources of royal income, ranking behind government monopolies in New Spain and monopolies and tribute in Peru. With taxes related to mining falling rapidly and consumers' hatred of the tobacco and *aguardiente* monopolies, new governments turned to taxation of foreign trade. The goal was to find duties that would keep foreign merchants actively trading but not drive local producers and manufacturers out of the market. Peru, for example, initially lowered import duties to 20 percent of the goods' declared value, but in 1826 raised them to 80 percent on items that competed with local products, favoring jobs over income. Soon after independence, taxes on trade became the major source of revenue for most, if not all, new governments.

Government Debt

The implications of turning an enormous de facto customs union into multiple states were staggering as each country created its own monetary and tax systems. The antipeninsular campaign that characterized much patriot propaganda drove out significant capital during and after independence. The number of peninsulars who fled with their capital to Cuba, Puerto Rico, Spain, and even France is unknown, but one estimate suggests that commercial capital in Spanish America declined by more than 90 percent from 1800 to 1826.

Royal governments' enormous domestic debt in the American dominions antedated independence, but the new countries quickly added external obligations. In 1824 and 1825, Mexico secured two foreign loans totaling about 32 million pesos. Peru borrowed nearly 10 million pesos from abroad in 1822 and 1825. The republics of Colombia, Chile, and the United Provinces of the Río de la Plata also contracted foreign obligations in the early 1820s. Tragically, aside from Brazil, every Latin American country that obtained a foreign loan in the 1820s defaulted before 1830. As a result, for many years none of them could again tap European sources for financial assistance.

CENTRALISM OR FEDERALISM?

One of the most immediate dilemmas the first postindependence Latin American leaders faced was how to structure new governments. Those who had been strongly influenced by the Enlightenment, the example of the U.S. revolutionary experience, or the 1812 Constitution of Cádiz tended to favor some form of a republic with a representative government. A wave of new constitutions in the 1820s reflected this preference for limited forms of democracy, but some new states initially preferred to maintain a more autocratic system that closely resembled the monarchical form of government that had successfully maintained order throughout the colonial period. The two largest and most populous countries, Brazil and Mexico, turned to monarchy initially, although the latter's experiment quickly failed.

Even before the wars of independence drew to a close, Latin American leaders debated the merits of a strong central government versus greater local or regional autonomy. Some advocated centralism—a system of government in which political authority is concentrated under a strong central government, often dominated by an authoritarian executive. Others favored more local autonomy through provincial governments only loosely affiliated through a relatively weak central government. In nineteenth-century Latin America, the system of maintaining local or regional autonomy became known as federalism. This nomenclature is not to be confused with the emergence of the Federalist Party in the newly independent United States in the late eighteenth century. There, federalism under its official party framework came to represent a strong central government, particularly in the interest of establishing an effective fiscal system.

In Latin America, debates about centralism and federalism complicated the new countries' early attempts at establishing borders. In later decades, firm beliefs and disagreements over the merits of a strong central government versus local autonomy guided political party formation, at least in part. Leaders also shaped political party foundations around emerging concepts of conservatism and liberalism—competing ideologies that clashed over maintaining colonial systems of privilege and social order versus casting aside those traditions in favor of defending individual rights. Such disputes frequently generated bitter conflict. At times, these led to civil war and contributed to the chaos and instability that plagued Latin America repeatedly in the nineteenth century.

Attempts at Federation

The jurisdictional borders that had marked viceroyalties and *audiencia* districts during the colonial period often became new countries' boundary lines by default during and after independence. In Spanish America, military campaigns evolved into government formation and the first political entities emerged in the form of loosely affiliated federations. A common political, cultural, and linguistic heritage made unification under some type of a federated system a logical choice. But political leaders soon discovered that these connective commonalities could not surmount the challenges of the postindependence world. Difficult geography and poor transportation isolated some regions from their neighbors, making political unification untenable. Disputes surrounding economic priorities such as natural resources and trade routes also threatened initial attempts at political unity. But provincial elites who sought to preserve and expand local authority presented an even more pressing challenge.

The inclination to establish federations with a high degree of regional autonomy is evident in the examples of the United Provinces of Río de la Plata in the Southern Cone as well as Gran Colombia and the Peru–Bolivia Confederation in northern South America. The former Viceroyalty of New Spain offers additional case studies with the early attempt to form a Mexican empire and the later establishment of the United Provinces of Central America. In each of these examples, attempted federations soon failed in the face of internal rivalries, economic instability, and the drive to maintain provincial control.

United Provinces of Río de la Plata

Starting in 1810, leaders in Buenos Aires sought to maintain authority over the Viceroyalty of the Río de la Plata established in 1777. Their inability to do so quickly became clear as Paraguay broke away and established its independence in 1811. After repeated failed attempts to dominate present-day Argentina, Bolivia, and Uruguay (known at the time as the Banda Oriental), leaders in Buenos Aires settled for a loose confederation that declared sovereignty in 1816 as the United Provinces of the Río de la Plata. The constituent parts, however, had little in common. Although Buenos Aires became its capital, the United Provinces adopted a federalist structure that allowed a high degree of regional autonomy. Conflict surfaced almost immediately, primarily surrounding trade policies that established the capital city as the exclusive port of transit for imports and exports.

Internal infighting kept the United Provinces in a state of disarray, but external threats eventually brought about the federation's disintegration. In a continuation of earlier border disputes, Brazil laid claim to the Banda Oriental and repeatedly invaded it in the 1810s. By 1821, Brazilian forces had occupied the region and renamed it the Cisplatine Province. Leaders in Buenos Aires refused to recognize this claim and in 1825 the three-year Cisplatine War erupted. While the United Provinces and Brazil fought over the disputed territory, leaders in Montevideo sought political autonomy and independence. British mediation in 1828 finally ended the war with an accord that recognized the Eastern Republic of Uruguay as an independent nation. Persistent tension between the province of Buenos Aires and the other members of the United Provinces continued beyond the mid-nineteenth century.

Gran Colombia

At the behest of Simón Bolívar, in 1819 the Congress of Angostura sought to unite the regions that had comprised the former Viceroyalty of New Granada. The resulting Republic of Colombia—known today as Gran Colombia—initially encompassed the newly independent New Granada and Venezuela. Ecuador joined the republic in 1822 after its liberation. Bolívar firmly believed that, despite the three regions' geographic divisions and rivalries, a political union would ensure their most stable future. He led the military efforts that spearheaded his Gran Colombian vision while Francisco de Paula Santander worked to create political institutions to govern the federation.

Regional differences and political rivalries surfaced in 1821 as leaders from Venezuela and New Granada sought to write a constitution for Gran Colombia. They debated intensely the merits of a strong centralist governing system versus a more loosely structured federalist model. The resulting charter established a highly centralized government, although many regional elite hoped to adopt a more federalist model once the Spanish military threat ended. Bolívar, named president in 1819, retained that position and held near-dictatorial powers; Santander became vice president. The central government filled all provincial offices and, in times of military threat, the president could claim extraordinary powers—a stipulation deemed necessary with Ecuador, Peru, and the future Bolivia still under Spanish rule.

Framers of the constitution considered themselves liberal and adopted measures to ensure individual rights. They ended Indian tribute and passed a law of free birth that eventually would eliminate slavery. They also sought to establish a system of public education funded by the proceeds of confiscated Church properties. Nonetheless, many of the constitution's provisions demonstrated the delegates' apprehension of the masses and a system of inequality persisted. They mandated indirect elections for national executive and legislative positions and limited suffrage through property and income requirements.

The Gran Colombian experiment proved short lived—doomed to failure by rivalries among the remaining independence leaders and persistent clashes over centralism versus federalism. When Peru and Bolivia finally obtained independence in the mid-1820s, calls for greater regional autonomy began to grow louder. Furthermore, Venezuelan elite had long complained that Gran Colombia's centralist administrative structure favored New Granada. When Bolívar attempted to consolidate authority even further and assumed dictatorial powers in 1828, Venezuela seceded. Ecuador also withdrew in 1830. The three provinces that had once comprised Gran Colombia became three independent countries. Bolívar declined to serve as president of the Republic of New Granada and instead resigned from public life. Having failed to achieve his goal of establishing a united federation of former Spanish colonies, the disillusioned Liberator died in December 1830.

Peru–Bolivia Confederation

Bolívar helped to secure independence for the region encompassed by present-day Bolivia and Peru. True to his principles, he hoped to see the two Andean regions united as a single independent entity. Although he served as the president of both Bolivia and Peru until 1826, local political elite in each state favored autonomy over a confederation. After Bolívar's death, Andrés de Santa Cruz, who shared the Liberator's vision, rose to power in Bolivia. He invaded neighboring Peru in 1835 and declared the Peru–Bolivia Confederation. Under a new centralized constitution, he assumed dictatorial control as its supreme protector. Although individual presidents of the autonomous states maintained local control, they reported to Santa Cruz; but the dictator's repressive tactics earned him many rivals. A Chilean invasion designed to settle long-standing trade disputes precipitated the confederation's demise. Its component parts began to declare independence while Chilean forces continued to advance. Santa Cruz escaped into exile in 1839 as the Peru–Bolivia Confederation disintegrated.

Mexican Empire

The Plan of Iguala stipulated that independent Mexico would operate as a constitutional monarchy, a more conservative form of government than most insurgents had envisioned. As Emperor Agustín I, Iturbide ruled over an enormous empire only precariously held together by colonial tradition. The new country encompassed most of the former Viceroyalty of New Spain, reaching north into the present-day U.S. southwest. To the south, it included present-day Guatemala, El Salvador, Honduras, Nicaragua, and Costa Rica.

The personal and institutional loyalties that had bound the Spanish Indies to the Crown did not carry over to the Mexican Empire. To showcase the new state's power and legitimacy as well as to reduce dissent, Iturbide attempted to buy the loyalty of influential bureaucrats and select military leaders. He spent exorbitant amounts of money on dressing up the royal court with all the accoutrements of a European imperial setting, despite a shortage of revenue and a severely damaged economy. Additionally, Iturbide censored the press and imprisoned suspected dissidents, specifically targeting liberal deputies in Mexico's newly formed congress. His despotic tactics provoked an outcry among liberals and conservatives alike. When he dissolved congress, the growing wave of anti-Iturbide sentiment quickly turned into a groundswell and soon the emperor fled into exile.

Iturbide's departure enabled more liberal-minded politicians to step in and impose their vision. Mexico became a federal republic uncder the constitution of 1824 with a governing system that drew on the Spanish Constitution of 1812 as well as the model of the United States. This structure reflected the preferences of early federalist and liberal leaders, although it maintained the traditional privileges of the Catholic Church. Guadalupe Victoria, who had achieved prominence during the independence insurgency, became Mexico's first president.

United Provinces of Central America

The political divisions that had plagued the Mexican Empire were also evident in Central America. In the weeks following Iturbide's abdication, representatives from present-day Guatemala, Costa Rica, Nicaragua, El Salvador, and Honduras convened in Guatemala City, declared independence from Mexico, and formed the United Provinces of Central America. With the capital in Guatemala City, the five provinces maintained a high degree of autonomy. A constitution modeled after the 1812 Constitution of Cádiz abolished slavery, established limited suffrage, and maintained protection for the Catholic Church. Each province elected its own local president; a single executive and legislature governed the federal republic.

The governing structure produced conflict almost immediately as the ongoing bickering between liberals and conservatives became more intense. A contested election in 1825 brought the Salvadoran Manuel José Arce to power as the federation's first president, but factional infighting soon erupted in civil war. The liberal Honduran Francisco Morazán ended the dispute in 1829 and won the presidency the following year, but his efforts to institute a series of sweeping anticlerical reforms provoked further animosity. A coalition of conservative landowners, church leaders, and indigenous peasants in Guatemala led by Rafael Carrera rebelled against Morazán's regime. Individual provinces began to secede as the central government moved to take control of customs revenue, a measure deemed necessary to allow the ailing federation to recover from its debilitating struggles. By 1839, the United Provinces of Central America had broken up into five sovereign countries.

CAUDILLOS

In the midst of instability and chaos immediately following independence, a distinct type of political leader emerged. The *caudillo* was a strongman, an authoritarian leader who used a combination of charisma and coercion to acquire and maintain control. Some *caudillos* held power at the national level as elected presidents or as dictators who rose to office by force. Others were local and regional leaders who might or might not have aspired to higher positions of authority. In some areas, *caudillos* provided a sense of order and stability and at times they enjoyed considerable popular support. In other regions, competition among rival strongmen created obstacles to peace and stability, often leading to local armed conflict and even nationwide civil war.

The complex and often contradictory nature of the colonial political system created an environment that allowed *caudillos* to thrive in newly independent countries. For three centuries, the Spanish Crown had provided justice and mediated among contending parties. It recognized that its dominions' distance from Spain required some flexibility and allowed officials to employ "*obedezco pero no cumplo*" as a pragmatic approach to shelving laws incompatible with the realities where they served. Nonetheless, the inclination to disregard royal mandates often led to conflict among local officials exacerbated by overlapping jurisdictions and a convoluted hierarchy of authority. The Crown, through its representatives in Spain and the Indies, served as the final arbiter of jurisdictional and legal disputes. When the wars of independence removed the monarch as the ultimate political authority, the *caudillo* emerged to fill the resulting power vacuum.

Caudillos with military backgrounds sought to establish themselves as great leaders on the battlefield and often played up their martial contributions as evidence of dedication to the nation. They routinely cultivated a reputation as being larger than life and capable of the impossible, such as killing wild animals with their bare hands or emerging victorious on the battlefield while being outnumbered 100 to 1. Their personal charm enabled them to attract a loyal following; these "folk *caudillos*" enjoyed widespread popular support. Many descended from wealthy rural elite families, owned large landed estates, and could use their position as *hacendados* to raise and support their own armies. As power brokers of the early nineteenth century, *caudillos* relied on a culture of patronage that predated independence. When personal charm failed, however, they did not hesitate to employ repression and intimidation to ensure compliance. As a result, many operated outside the law. Their personal dictates could easily supersede the formalities outlined in early constitutions.

Caudillos frequently embraced no particular ideology, falling into all political camps and changing sides when it seemed advantageous. As postindependence politicians struggled to define political formalities such as procedures for succession to office and the composition of the electorate, *caudillos* often turned to armed uprising as a way to rise to power. Competition among political rivals remained fierce. Consummate patriots, most *caudillos* genuinely wanted to do what was best for their region or country, but were unalterably convinced that their personal leadership was a sine qua non for moving it forward. As a result, they tended to emerge in times of crisis, and critics could easily interpret their actions as merely a personal quest for power.

Juan Manuel de Rosas in Argentina

In Argentina, Juan Manuel de Rosas proved the quintessential *caudillo* who played a pivotal role in leading the still inchoate nation after independence. The son of a wealthy landowning family in Buenos Aires province, he rose to power by allying with other regional *caudillos* in an environment marked by nearly constant conflict between centralists and federalists. Rosas vigorously opposed Unitarios, who wanted a strong central government that would favor the port city of Buenos Aires. He supported Federales who advocated preserving provincial autonomy. Elected governor of Buenos Aires province in 1829, he ruled with the support of other *caudillos* but often resorted to repression and fear. Rosas persecuted enemies, relying on a violent extralegal enforcement squad known as La Mazorca to maintain order and at least the illusion of compliance to the Federales. Many Unitarios fled into exile in Uruguay and Chile, where they stayed until his enemies eventually drove the *caudillo* from power in 1852.

Juan Facundo Quiroga from La Rioja province provides an outstanding example of a regional *caudillo* and an early ally of Rosas. He earned a reputation for ruthlessness as rumors of his military exploits on the Argentine pampas became legendary. A strong defender of federalism, he gained the confidence of many other provincial leaders. Although some assumed he would eventually rise to national leadership, his promising political future threatened other rivals. Quiroga was eliminated in 1835, possibly on the orders of Rosas himself. Domingo Sarmiento's *Facundo: Or Civilization and Barbarism* later immortalized the provincial *caudillo*'s brutal tactics. One of Argentina's most well-known pieces of nineteenth-century literature, it relates the story of the regional strongman and offers a harsh criticism of the brutality of *caudillismo*. Part of a larger body of oppositional writing, it represents an important strategy Unitarios used to resist the Rosas regime.

Caudillismo's Heirs to Gran Colombia

After the dissolution of Gran Colombia, strong *caudillos* emerged in Venezuela and New Granada. As a military hero and political leader in Caracas, General Páez spearheaded the revolt in 1830 that restored Venezuela's independence. He led the country either as president or indirectly as the political muscle behind a series of conservative presidents throughout much of the 1830s and 1840s and returned to power formally once again in 1861. A horseman of the *llanos*, Páez fit the *caudillo* mold of the rough-and-ready military leader. He combined repressive tactics with personal charm and cooperation to bring order to the country. By providing some stability to Venezuela, Páez managed to attract foreign investment and make modest improvements to the nation's economy.

In New Granada, regional *caudillos* jockeyed for power following the central government's introduction of liberal reforms. Small, isolated uprisings of provincial military leaders eventually escalated into the War of the Supremes (1839–1842). From antiliberal origins, the conflict evolved into a defense of regional autonomy under the banner of federalism, an allegiance that had far-reaching political ramifications. By the end of the decade, the factions that emerged during the war gave rise to the country's first formal political parties.

Antonio López de Santa Anna in Mexico

One of Latin America's best known and most picturesque *caudillos* was Antonio López de Santa Anna, who rose to power in Mexico in the decades following independence. The son of a creole *hacendado* in Veracruz, Santa Anna initially fought in the Spanish army against the insurgents. In 1821 he rallied behind Iturbide's Plan of Iguala, but subsequently supported his ouster and the establishment of the Mexican Republic under the constitution of 1824. A prominent army officer, he staved off an attempted Spanish invasion in 1829, enhancing his reputation as a brave and capable military leader. Elected president in 1833, he almost immediately left the job of governing to his vice president, Valentín Gómez Farías. A committed liberal, Gómez Farías began implementing a series of sweeping reforms intended to curb the power of the military and the Church. Urged by the conservative elite to take action, Santa Anna reassumed power, dissolved congress, and replaced the republic with a more centralized authoritarian system governed by the "Seven Laws," a surrogate constitution.

Invariably relying on his personal charisma and reputation as a military hero to justify his accession to power, Santa Anna ruled Mexico at least 11 times between 1833 and 1853. During these years, he led the army on several occasions against forces from France, Texas, and the United States. Initially, he demonstrated the lack of ideological affiliation characteristic of many *caudillos*, appearing to change his position according to political expediency. But after 1835, Santa Anna regularly aligned himself with centralist and conservative interests, believing that a strong authoritarian government that protected the privileges of powerful institutions was the best way to bring order and stability to the country. Despite suffering devastating military defeats and repeatedly being forced into exile, he continued to return to power, often at the behest of supporters in conservative political circles. Santa Anna's long and turbulent political career illustrates the complex and contradictory nature of *caudillismo* and it underscores the protracted instability that plagued Latin American countries in the early decades after independence.

Rafael Carrera in Guatemala

A mestizo of humble origins, Rafael Carrera rose to power in Guatemala by defying the liberal leaders of the United Provinces of Central America and building a support network among wealthy landowners, Church leaders, and the rural indigenous population. Unlike many *caudillos*, Carrera initially possessed little military experience. But when a series of rebellions erupted in Guatemala against the government of the United Provinces, he helped to unite various rebel movements in the countryside. In 1838, he captured the capital city and installed a new government. He continued to resist incursions by the United Provinces and by 1840 had successfully separated Guatemala from the federation and consolidated political power for himself.

Carrera remained in power until his death in 1865, his longevity in part the result of a broad coalition of support. Identifying with the peasantry, he issued some modest measures to promote racial equality, even while supporting land tenure laws that allowed rural elite to encroach on indigenous communal property. His staunchly conservative policies preserved the privileged position of the Catholic Church and wealthy landowners, whose loyalty was fundamental to shoring up his authority. Like other Latin American *caudillos*, Carrera did not hesitate to use repression to silence dissent, earning a reputation for brutality and cruelty. In true *caudillo* fashion, he suspended elections in 1854 and declared himself president for life. He justified his tactics and dictatorial policies as necessary to defend Guatemala's national interests. Under his rule, the country achieved some modest economic growth, thanks to the expansion of coffee exports. Carrera also successfully defended Guatemala against attempts by Mexico at annexation and repelled repeated efforts by neighboring Central American nations to reconstitute the United Provinces.

Challenges that new countries faced in the early nineteenth century often derived from the legacies of Spanish rule. Although many early leaders rejected absolutism and instead embraced rising notions of republicanism, they repeatedly exhibited an impulse to form federations along colonial administrative lines. As regional rivalries simmered and geographic realities kept early federations physically fractured, debates surrounding federalism and centralism frequently turned violent and threatened governments' stability. Federalism was often popular with factions not in power and caused confusing and shifting alliances. Within two decades, attempts at forming loose federations had failed and smaller states began to take shape, although boundary disputes persisted.

Remnants of Spanish structures of authority can also be seen in the emergence of *caudillos* who stepped in to fill the power void left after the removal of royal and viceregal rule. Internal conflict and continued threats from abroad allowed *caudillismo* to thrive, but constant power struggles among competing strongmen often contributed to persistent instability.

Although the new countries pursued different paths, a number of commonalities are evident throughout the first half of the nineteenth century. Most attempted to implement some form of representative government, usually through constitutions modeled after that of the United States and Spain's 1812 charter. Nevertheless, powerful *caudillo* rivalries frequently rendered null the extremely limited suffrage, and political equality remained elusive. Widespread efforts to abolish slavery largely prevailed, although alternate forms of exploitative wage labor often replaced it, particularly in areas with a large indigenous population. National economies remained shaky for decades, often frustrating attempts to introduce direct taxation. Although no country reestablished the Inquisition, the Catholic Church and the military retained enormous influence.

Primary Source

Born in Campobasso, Naples, in 1774, Orazio Attellis inherited the title of marquis of Sant'Angelo, which he incorporated into his name as Santangelo. Immigrating to the United States in 1824, he immediately obtained citizenship and subsequently accompanied his son to Mexico. Caught up in factional politics, in 1826 and 1835 he suffered what he termed "illegal and unjust banishments from Mexico . . . both the work of a corrupt and ruthless ministry" as a result of "having dared to defend the honor and interests of my adopted country." The "Statement of Facts" alleges that he is "merely the victim of the stupidity of one Mexican President, and of the treacherous and base wickedness of another." His description of Antonio López de Santa Anna exudes the frustration and vitriol that the *caudillo* provoked among his enemies.

SOURCE: Orazio de Attellis Santangelo, *Statement of Facts Relating to the Claim of Orazio de Attellis Santangelo, a Citizen of the United States on the Government of the Republic of Mexico* (Washington, DC: Peter Force, 1841), 145–46, https://books.google.com/books?id=UOhYAAAAMAAJ&pg=PA80&lpg=PA80&dq=%22Orazio+Attellis%22&source=bl&ots=SaBKqN8f6M&sig=id_eVC_UNVVrGMyQlpuQqessr6E&hl=en&sa=X&ved=0ahUKEwirsfr86vLJAhVQ6WMKHRynDxsQ6AEIHjAA#v=onepage&q=Mexico&f=false (accessed December 23, 2015).

For these considerations, for the present, I, Orazio de Attellis Santangelo, do publicly declare, loudly pronounce, firmly assert, conscientiously swear, and irrevocably decree:

1st. That Antonio Lopez de Santa Anna is a **liar, a coward, a scoundrel, an imposter, a traitor, a disgrace to mankind**.

2dly. That should the Mexican nation ever place him again, or suffer him to place himself again, at her head, she ought and must be deemed to be, from the oldest to the youngest, from the richest to the poorest, from the strongest to the weakest of her citizens, nothing but a pitiful gang of stupid, ignorant, demoralized, debased fools.

3dly. That all Governments in the world, which may be so unprincipled as to engage at any time, in the least intercourse with Antonio Lopez de Santa Anna, as the *chief*, under whatever title, *of the Mexican nation*, should be looked upon as entirely destitute of honor, and worthy only of the execration of their subjects, and of the contempt of all reasonable beings.

4thly. That this my sovereign and irrevocable decree shall be translated into French, the universal language of diplomacy, and circulated as far as possible, all over the globe.

October 22, 1841
Orazio de Attellis Santangelo.

SUGGESTIONS FOR FURTHER READING

Arrom, Silvia Marina. *Containing the Poor: The Mexico City Poor House, 1774–1871.* Durham, NC: Duke University Press, 2000.

Blanchard, Peter. *Slavery and Abolition in Early Republican Peru.* Wilmington, DE: Scholarly Resources, 1992.

Caplan, Karen. *Indigenous Citizens: Local Liberalism in Early National Oaxaca and Yucatan.* Stanford, CA: Stanford University Press, 2009.

Chambers, Sarah C. *From Subjects to Citizens: Honor, Gender, and Politics in Arequipa Peru, 1780–1854.* University Park: Pennsylvania State University Press, 1999.

Connaughton, Brian F. *Clerical Ideology in a Revolutionary Age: The Guadalajara Church and the Idea of the Mexican Nation, 1788–1853.* Translated by Mark Alan Healey. Calgary, Alberta: University of Calgary Press, 2003; Boulder: University Press of Colorado, 2003.

Ducey, Michael T. *A Nation of Villages: Riot and Rebellion in the Mexican Huasteca, 1750–1850.* Tucson: University of Arizona Press, 2004.

Earle, Rebecca. *The Return of the Native: Indians and Myth-Making in Spanish America, 1810–1930.* Durham, NC: Duke University Press, 2008.

Fowler, Will. *Santa Anna of Mexico.* Lincoln: University of Nebraska Press, 2009.

Guardino, Peter. *The Time of Liberty: Popular Political Culture in Oaxaca, 1750–1850.* Durham, NC: Duke University Press, 2005.

Lynch, John. *Argentine Caudillo: Juan Manuel de Rosas.* Lanham, MD: Rowman & Littlefield, 2001.

_____. *Caudillos in Spanish America, 1800–1850.* Oxford: Clarendon Press, 1992.

Salvatore, Ricardo D., Carlos Aguirre, and Gilbert M. Joseph (eds.). *Crime and Punishment in Latin America: Law and Society since Late Colonial Times.* Durham, NC: Duke University Press, 2001.

Woodward, Ralph Lee, Jr. *Rafael Carrera and the Emergence of the Republic of Guatemala, 1821–1871.* Athens, GA: University of Georgia Press, 1993.

Zahler, Reuben. *Ambitious Rebels: Remaking Honor, Law, and Liberalism in Venezuela, 1780–1850.* Tucson: University of Arizona Press, 2013.

CHAPTER 15

Nation-State Formation

CHRONOLOGY

1840	Liberal Party formed in Venezuela
1846–1848	Defeat in the Mexican–American War results in Mexico ceding half of its territory to the United States
1850	Colombia abolishes slavery and the right of indigenous people to own land
1853	Constitution of 1853 in Colombia spurs liberal reform
1853	Santa Anna sells a 29,670-square-mile portion of Mexico's northern frontier to the United States for $10 million in a sale known the "Gadsden Purchase"
1854	Revolution of Ayutla—liberal coalition forces Santa Anna from office for the last time
1854	Venezuela abolishes slavery
1855–1857	William Walker stages a coup in Nicaragua and declares himself president; he is ousted two years later by the Central American army
1855–1857	Benito Juárez declares the Ley Juárez ends the Church and military *fueros*; Miguel Lerdo de Tejada drafts the Ley Lerdo that prevented the Catholic Church from owning land not used for religious purposes
1857	Constitution of 1857 in Mexico solidifies reform laws, abolishes slavery, establishes freedom of speech, the press, and assembly, and calls for protection of individual liberties
1858–1863	Federal War in Venezuela between the Liberal Party and Conservative Party results in 200,000 deaths
1858–1860	War of Reform between liberals and conservatives in Mexico; liberals emerge victorious and Juárez returns to the presidency
1862–1867	French Occupation of Mexico; conservatives in league with Napoleon III in France conspire to install Archduke Maximilian of Habsburg as emperor in Mexico
1863–1880	Radical Republic in Colombia; characterized by aggressive liberal reforms that significantly weakened Church power
1864	Archduke Ferdinand Maximilian of Habsburg arrives in Mexico
1864–1870	War of Triple Alliance pits Paraguay against Brazil, Argentina, and Uruguay
1867	Maximilian and his generals, Miguel Miramón and Tomás Mejía, are captured, tried, and executed in Mexico
1867	Blue Revolution in Venezuela where conservatives attempt to reclaim power
1868–1878	A nascent independence movement led by creole elites in Oriente Province in Cuba sparks the Ten Years' War

By the middle of the nineteenth century, Latin American governments began moving away from the early volatility of *caudillo* rule. Evolving from previous frameworks that had borrowed heavily from the United States and the Spanish Constitution of 1812, mid-century liberals more clearly articulated a political platform. They largely sought, often unsuccessfully, to correct imbalances in society and among institutions that endured from the era of Spanish rule. Corporate bodies, particularly the Church, became a primary target. As liberals adopted strategies and theories to strengthen the nation, they emphasized the role of the individual and the primacy of private property. Although widespread enthusiasm for free trade in the early 1820s waned, the notion of comparative advantage persisted even as governments adjusted tariff policy to the new economic realities. Formal political parties eventually emerged, but often only after intense conflict between adherents of competing ideologies. Conservatives pushed back against liberal reform and civil wars often ensued. Despite rhetoric among liberal leaders that paid lip service to the notion of equality, the masses often remained apart from debate over government policies. The struggles of the rural poor continued and their conditions arguably deteriorated as almost everywhere land concentration known as latifundia assumed increased importance. Urban conditions also changed little, despite population growth in cities that had long served as administrative and economic hubs. Everywhere the patriarchal structure of households maintained its grip.

POLITICS AND PARTIES

The transition from colony to nationhood challenged leaders throughout Latin America. The political uncertainty and social instability that followed the wars for independence intensified throughout the rest of the nineteenth century. Much of that turmoil reflected competing ideological currents of liberalism and conservatism that attracted the ruling elites and defined their attempts to shape the path to nationhood. Over time, formal political parties emerged as conflict intensified between those who advocated deeply rooted colonial traditions and those who promoted change and an abstract notion of progress. The struggle between conservatives and liberals perpetuated an environment in which the use of force often imposed political change. In many countries, coups d'état, isolated revolts, and even protracted national civil wars replaced presidents more often than democratic elections. Amended or even new constitutions followed these illegal transfers of power as the incoming ruling elite sought to impose their rigid vision of nationhood. Only the Spanish Caribbean and Brazil escaped the ideological turmoil that surrounded political divisions in Spain's former mainland possessions. Brazil maintained an emperor of Portuguese descent until 1889, whereas Cuba and Puerto Rico remained Spanish colonies until 1898.

Political Views

Although local circumstances defined the specifics of liberal and conservative political platforms at the national level, the underlying ideological foundations were essentially the same throughout Latin America. Issues related to governing structures, the Catholic Church, and the social order continued to divide politicians. In general, remnants of the colonial elite who had benefited under Spanish rule favored conservative movements. Some of them had resisted independence, fearing that the elimination of monarchy would create a power vacuum and result in social upheaval. Especially regions with large indigenous or African populations experienced such concerns.

On the one hand, after independence, many conservative elites sought a strong, centralized government with a powerful executive and little to no regional autonomy. Only such rule, they believed, would strengthen the new nations against both internal turmoil and outside attack—whether from neighboring countries, the United States, or European powers. Numerous revolts, wars between Latin American countries, and attempted foreign invasions intensified these concerns.

Liberals, on the other hand, considered any form of government reminiscent of colonial rule an obstacle to progress. They embraced the notion that change and forward thinking could improve the human experience. Influenced by eighteenth-century Enlightenment thought, the American and French revolutions, and the constitution of 1812 in particular, they believed that sovereignty resided in the people. Consequently, most envisioned independent nations as sovereign republics under some version of constitutional democracy. Many of the earliest liberal constitutions called for a separation of Church and state and created a complex system of checks and balances to prevent the consolidation of political authority in a centralized executive. Although espousing enlightened egalitarianism made for a powerful political platform, many of these leaders hailed from the elite and generally created a system of government that retained significant inequality. Thus, liberal governments routinely limited suffrage rights to wealthy, educated, largely white males by imposing literacy and property ownership requirements.

Social Views

Conservatives and liberals diverged profoundly in their prescriptions for organizing society. Conservatives favored the traditional blend of race and class that had ordered social relations for several centuries. They believed in an ethnic hierarchy that placed white Spaniards above the mixed races and above black and indigenous populations. In their view, the economic exploitation and social inequality that characterized the pre-independence era also served to maintain order. As military officers, members of the episcopacy, or descendants of the colonial nobility, powerful conservatives sought to continue the legal privileges (*fueros*) of long-standing corporate institutions.

Liberals viewed the social order differently from their conservative counterparts. At its core, social liberalism made the individual the cornerstone of a strong nation, a focus that reflected Enlightenment thought as well as the U.S. model. Indeed, many nineteenth-century Latin American constitutions drew heavily from that of the United States. For example, liberals subscribed to the notion that in thriving sovereign republics, a strong and direct connection existed between the individual and the state. The privileged corporations remaining from Spanish rule hindered this critical linkage. Thus, liberals feared that the Church, the military, and other entitled groups would command loyalty ahead of identification with the nation. Accordingly, they wanted to abolish *fueros* and promoted policies aimed at reducing corporate power and influence. During the nineteenth century, liberal reform attempts often sought to eliminate the judicial practices that protected clerics and the military from civil prosecution.

Other reforms sought specifically to curb the prominence of the Catholic Church as the main arbiter of the social order. Increasingly aggressive laws empowered the state to assume many functions historically provided by the Church. For example, the state created a civil registry to record births, marriages, and deaths—acts that the Church had long exalted as sacraments. Liberals considered this secularization of major life events vital for building a viable nation. They also worked to wrest formal education from Church control, arguing that a lay system of schooling was one of the most important ways in which the government could oversee and influence its citizens. Through such reforms, liberals intended to reduce the Church's influence and to prevent it from interfering in the developing relationship between the individual and the state.

Land Reform

A particularly contentious clash with the Catholic Church occurred when liberal governments enacted land reform. Inspired by the notion of the "Jeffersonian Republic," leaders in Mexico, Colombia, Paraguay, and elsewhere passed laws prohibiting corporate ownership of property. The U.S. president Thomas Jefferson had envisioned an idealistic model of a sovereign republic made up of small-scale farms. He argued that private property owners—particularly those whose livelihood was tied to agriculture—would make the most responsible citizens. Latin American liberals promoted a similarly romanticized vision of the agrarian sector as a cornerstone of nationhood and individual property owners, not corporate bodies, formed the basis of a responsible citizenry. Thus, liberal land reforms stipulated that only individuals could own property. Their authors knew full well that the Catholic Church had remained the largest single landowner after independence. The land reform decrees established legal mechanisms by which the state could take control of valuable ecclesiastical real estate, thereby curbing Church influence by reducing its wealth while fattening government coffers.

Economic Views

As in the social and political realms, liberals sought to move their countries away from the economic structures that had dominated during Iberian rule. Although the introduction of free trade within the empire had provided merchants with more choices, the mercantilist policy of limiting the colonies to legal commerce with the metropolis remained until independence. Such restrictions had fomented discontent among exporters of hides, dyes, cacao, and other agricultural products in the peripheral colonies in particular. Their complaints contributed to early interest in autonomy and even independence in some regions, such as Venezuela and Buenos Aires. Subsequently, ruling elites often embraced more open trade and economic systems.

Economic liberalism of the nineteenth century rested on a laissez-faire economic model that implied freedom from government regulation and interference. Latin American merchants demanded the right to trade directly and legally with other countries and to expand commercial networks in ways that mercantilism had prohibited. Leaders generally believed that economies freed of cumbersome trade restrictions would best stimulate national growth. Accordingly, most of the new nations opened their ports to foreign trade, although specific policies varied by country. The British in particular took advantage of the emerging opportunities in South America and Mexico. Large countries with vast natural resources received the most British commercial attention, but smaller countries attracted foreign trade as well.

The laissez-faire economic model called for nations to produce and export goods in which they held a comparative advantage—usually commodities that they could make available at a low cost relative to their trade partners. As a leader in the Industrial Revolution, the British correctly viewed Latin America as both a profitable source of raw materials and a largely untapped market for finished goods. With meager manufacturing and industrial development, Latin American nations held a comparative advantage in the production of raw materials through agriculture and mining. As the nineteenth century progressed, Latin American nations found themselves unequal trading partners in a system that favored industrialized economies.

Paraguay: An Exception

Paraguay stands as an important exception to liberal and conservative struggles in the nineteenth century. Under Spanish rule, this frontier, interior region had served primarily as a buffer zone between Brazil and the Spanish territories in Río de la Plata. It emerged as an isolated but independent country in 1811 after leaders in Asunción refused to form a federation with the United Provinces of Río de la Plata and instead declared independence. Because of its location, Paraguayan elite faced persistent threats of encroachment, violence, and instability in the early decades after independence. Two prominent leaders, Dr. José Gaspar Rodríguez de Francia and Carlos Antonio López, ruled Paraguay throughout much of the nineteenth century and kept the nation insulated from the rest of the world.

Dr. Francia's role in shielding Paraguay from the expansionist aims of Buenos Aires generated loyalty and confidence in his leadership among the political elite of Asunción. In 1816, congress named him dictator for life. Strongly influenced by the Enlightenment, Francia introduced some of the most liberal social policies in Latin America. He also abolished ecclesiastical *fueros* and redistributed Church properties to small farmers.

Paraguay defied the trends of economic liberalism and free trade that characterized its neighbors. Instead of relying on the export of commodity goods to generate economic growth, Francia encouraged agricultural diversification. Under his leadership, Paraguay became self-sufficient in food production. He kept the country isolated from Europe and the rest of Latin America and allowed only limited foreign trade.

Francia's leadership brought political stability and a strong national economy, but it came at the expense of personal freedoms. As supreme dictator, he ensured complaisance by silencing dissent and arresting potential enemies, many of whom were tortured or simply disappeared. The dictator's death in 1840 paved the way for Carlos Antonio López to take power.

Although López maintained many of his predecessor's despotic and isolationist tendencies, he took steps to modernize the economy, developed transportation and communications infrastructure, and improved the education system. Always distrustful of Brazil and Argentina, the ruler devoted considerable resources to expanding the armed forces, which he placed under the direction of his son, Francisco Solano López. Ironically, it was the presence of a strong military that contributed to forcing Paraguay out of isolation. Solano López assumed the presidency on his father's death in 1862 and two years later the nation found itself at war against Brazil, Argentina, and Uruguay. Only after Paraguay's devastating defeat in the War of the Triple Alliance in 1870 did a formal political party system emerge.

MEXICO AND LA REFORMA

Conflict between liberal and conservative leaders in Mexico turned unusually violent in the 1850s. After decades of near-constant discord between competing factions, liberal leaders seemed to prevail following Antonio López de Santa Anna's brief final presidency (1853–1854). The once-powerful *caudillo* had led the nation through civil wars, foreign invasions, and other disruptions in the tumultuous years following independence. After devastating defeat in the U.S.–Mexican War (1846–1848) cost the nation half of its territory, opponents forced Santa Anna into exile. Meanwhile, the humiliated country's social and political conditions deteriorated. Moderately liberal presidents tried to stabilize the country, but faced growing hostility from powerful conservative leaders with important military connections. In 1853, they invited Santa Anna to return from exile and direct the country. The aging *caudillo*'s supporters included Lucas Alamán, a particularly articulate proponent of conservative philosophy and among the founders of Mexico's Conservative Party in 1849.

Santa Anna's last period in office proved especially disastrous for his country. Armed with near-dictatorial powers granted by his allies, the *caudillo* squandered the limited resources available in the national treasury and declared himself "most serene highness." To address the government's financial woes, in 1853 he sold a valuable portion of Mexico's northern frontier in a transaction known in the United States as the Gadsden Purchase. The questionable sale of additional territory to an enemy only five years after the transfer forced by the Treaty of Guadalupe Hidalgo further inflamed nationalist sensitivities. Even Santa Anna's conservative allies soon lost patience with the elderly dictator, opening the door for a liberal coalition that drove him from office for good in 1855 through the Revolution of Ayutla.

With Santa Anna finally out of the picture and conservative leaders seemingly discredited, Mexican liberals set about to impose their ideological vision on the nation. The new laws that liberal politicians believed would transform the way society functioned gave this era the name *la Reforma*. Among the numerous changes, three bold reforms defined their agenda. The Juárez Law at last ended the *fueros* that clerics and the military had enjoyed for centuries. The Iglesias Law eroded Church authority even further by establishing a civil registry for recording births, marriages, and deaths. In addition, the law prohibited the clergy from charging the poor for the sacraments.

The Lerdo Law also attacked the Church, but its implications went far beyond it in seeking to end most land ownership by corporate bodies. Since the Church remained a major property owner, liberals expected the Lerdo Law to diminish its wealth and power, while allowing the state to profit from the confiscation and sale of its real estate. Many liberals firmly believed that private property formed the foundation of a strong society. They expected the measure to create a new agrarian class based on family-owned small farms. But unintended consequences followed the law's promulgation, demonstrating that liberal arguments about equality and individual rights frequently did not extend to the masses. Few landless peasants could afford to buy even a small plot of land and, as a result, wealthy large landowners and political allies of liberal leaders purchased much of the Church's property at auction. Furthermore, the Lerdo Law removed the legal protections that for centuries had enabled indigenous villages to own and use communal agricultural lands known as *ejidos*. This property also became available for purchase at auction. The forced sales further concentrated landownership into vast estates known as latifundios held by a small number of wealthy families. Additionally, it created a large labor pool of landless Indians available for exploitation.

Constitution of 1857

The liberal constitution of 1857 institutionalized the reforms introduced in the Juárez, Iglesias, and Lerdo Law. Modeled largely on the charter of 1824, the document called for protection of equality and individual liberties, including free speech, the right to assembly, and an uncensored press. It abolished slavery, repealed titles of nobility, and included provisions for a system of free and obligatory education. Together with the preceding reform laws, the new constitution became a strong and direct articulation of the liberal philosophy.

Mexico's reform laws understandably raised the ire of religious leaders, but they also distressed many others who feared that curtailing the power of the Catholic Church could threaten their spiritual well-being. Prominent clerics capitalized on these sentiments. They forbade the faithful from accepting the reform laws and the subsequent constitution and threatened excommunication to any congregant who did not abjure its most contentious provisions. The conflict between liberals and conservatives culminated in a violent civil war (1858–1860) that tore the country apart and further destabilized it. A liberal victory in this War of the Reform secured Benito Juárez's claim to the presidency. But the conflict had caused significant damage and taken a serious toll on Mexico's infrastructure and economy. More important, it left a greatly divided population and paved the way for a devastating period of foreign intervention in the 1860s as conservatives sought to regain power.

COLOMBIA AND LIBERAL REFORM

In Colombia, a new generation of liberals came of age in the mid-nineteenth century and advocated sweeping reforms to transform society and economy. The violent War of the Supremes (1839–1842) had personally affected many of them and they drew inspiration from the ideals of equality, fraternity, and liberty. Like their counterparts in the rest of Latin America, the young liberals attacked lingering colonial practices and beliefs. These had prevented the previous generation of leaders from bringing about a truly prosperous society and a strong nation based on democratic principles. Political power vacillated in the late 1840s as more extreme liberals and conservatives promoted increasingly polarized visions of the nation's future.

A first wave of liberal reform began in 1850 with legislation that abolished slavery and ended the ability of indigenous communities (*resguardos*) to own land. Other reforms sought to reduce the power of the central government by granting more fiscal authority to provincial authorities and dividing some provinces into smaller administrative entities to allow for even greater local autonomy. In keeping with the economic ideas of nineteenth-century liberalism, Colombian leaders also abolished the government's monopoly over tobacco in an effort to expand the commodity's export. Conservative leaders backed this measure as well, marking a rare instance in which both sides agreed. Bipartisan cooperation similarly made the Province of Panama—territorially and administratively a part of Colombia until the turn of the twentieth century—a free trade zone.

By 1851, liberals held a majority of the seats in congress and the presidency in the person of General José Hilario López. Their platform became the framework for the constitution of 1853, and unprecedented reform efforts persisted throughout the 1850s. The measures that López initiated continued under his successor, José María Obando. These included universal suffrage for adult, literate males and additional land reform targeting indigenous *resguardos*.

As in Mexico, the enhanced scope of reforms in Colombia provoked a backlash that eventually resulted in a conservative resurgence in 1858, followed by a brief civil war in 1860. But by 1861, the once-conservative former president, Tomás Cipriano de Mosquera, had triumphed over his former allies. An era of liberal dominance known as the Radical Republic (1863–1880) began with the passage of a new constitution that reinforced reforms from the previous decade. The government went after the Church, attacking its privileges, gaining administrative powers over it, and outlawing religious orders. The Mosquera Decrees called for the seizure and sale of ecclesiastical real estate to encourage private property ownership. Changes implemented during the Radical Republic gave state governments even greater autonomy and reduced the presidential term to two years.

Declining commodity exports along with general unease of the devoutly Catholic population over the anticlerical reforms created a climate ripe for a conservative takeover. In 1878, a new era, known as the Regeneration, abruptly ended the steadfast liberalism of the Radical Republic. Having abandoned the former ruling party, Rafael Núñez marked this ideological reversal by abrogating the constitution of 1863 and promulgating a new charter in 1886. He also overturned the anticlerical measures imposed by previous administrations, instituted literacy requirements for voting, and worked to strengthen the power of the central government and the executive, in part by extending the presidential term to six years.

LIBERALS AND CONSERVATIVES IN CENTRAL AMERICA

The framework of the United Provinces of Central America initially rested on early concepts of liberalism. But conflict between liberal and conservative interests quickly surfaced, as Francisco Morazán became president in 1830 and pursued a wide array of reforms. Ideological disputes evident in the federation's central government also manifested at the provincial level. With Morazán's backing, José Felipe Mariano Gálvez attempted to institute modest reforms in Guatemala, including measures to curtail the power of the Church. José Rafael Carrera quickly quashed these early efforts, and his revolt eventually led to the dissolution of the United Provinces.

Guatemala and Honduras experienced a prolonged period of conservative rule following their secession from the federation. In Nicaragua, intermittent civil war between opposing ideological elites plagued the nation until the 1850s, when desperate liberals invited the U.S. filibuster William Walker to intervene. His attempted takeover discredited them and conservative leaders prevailed until the 1890s.

Costa Rica's experience with political conflict in the nineteenth century provides a unique case study. An isolated and sparsely populated province within the Spanish empire, Costa Rica had contributed relatively little to the royal treasury. It developed an early sense of autonomy and lacked a traditionalist elite that might form the basis of a conservative movement. As a result, liberal leaders rose to power fairly easily in the decades following independence.

In the 1840s, an elite landowning class tied to the cultivation and export of coffee emerged as a powerful ruling bloc. These *cafetaleros* promulgated two constitutions that codified many of the social and political practices of nineteenth-century liberalism. Costa Rica's governing charters established protections for basic individual liberties and set up a framework for public education. The use of indirect elections along with gender, literacy, and property restrictions limited political participation. Furthermore, power often changed hands as a result of armed conflict among competing *cafetaleros*. Despite considerable infighting, Costa Rica's coffee presidents agreed on basic liberal principles that guided policy, particularly in the middle decades of the nineteenth century. Export-oriented agriculture, especially of coffee, allowed the *cafetaleros* to begin funding public works and other social projects. These activities included expanding public education, establishing incipient public health programs, and constructing communications and transportation infrastructure.

VENEZUELA

Party politics began to emerge in Venezuela under the *caudillo* José Antonio Páez. He brought the country much-needed stability by forming vital alliances with potential rivals and using repression when necessary. The high demand for Venezuelan coffee exports produced impressive economic growth in the 1830s, but collapsed by 1840, causing the *caudillo*'s delicate network of support to start disintegrating. His policies had favored the Catholic Church and other conservative interests. Liberal elite bolted, creating a formal Liberal Party led by Antonio Leocadio Guzmán and supported by José Tadeo Monagas and his brother, José Gregorio. The party advocated federalism, but initially failed to articulate a clear platform. In 1846, Páez supported the election of José Tadeo Monagas for president, anticipating the handpicked successor would continue to cater to conservative interests. But within two years, the new executive had forced Páez into exile and removed his supporters from the government.

José Tadeo and José Gregorio Monagas alternated in the presidency for the next decade, ruling in an increasingly dictatorial fashion. They strengthened the power of the executive and silenced political opposition by restricting free speech and censoring the press. The economy declined during their rule as further deterioration in the export market compelled them to engage in irresponsible deficit spending. They passed some laws promoting liberal ideals, such as the abolition of slavery and the elimination of the death penalty. Nevertheless, their corrupt spending, overt despotism, and attacks on personal liberties had alienated some erstwhile supporters. When the Monagas brothers in 1858 attempted to impose constitutional reforms that would extend presidential power even further, a coalition of liberal and conservative leaders overthrew them.

The solidarity by common opposition to the Monagas brothers proved transitory. The persistence of competing ideologies, now represented by formal political parties, became evident as liberals and conservatives failed to agree on a governing system to replace the dictatorship. Long-standing debates over centralism versus federalism resurfaced with members of the Liberal Party favoring a federalist system of provincial autonomy, accompanied by an expansion of the electorate and protections of individual freedoms. Members of the Conservative Party sought to maintain traditional social hierarchies and believed only a strong central government could ensure stability. Bitter hostilities between the two parties erupted in the Federal War—a five-year conflict that cost as many as 200,000 lives. Power changed hands several times during its course and Páez attempted to return to the presidency in 1861 to restore order.

Liberals eventually claimed victory in 1863 and installed a new constitution that established federalism and called for numerous liberal social reforms, such as voting rights, free speech, and public education. Nevertheless, unrest continued as leaders in Caracas soon discovered that the loose governing system allowed regional *caudillos* to thrive at the expense of national stability. A series of uprisings plagued Venezuela in the coming years as conservatives attempted to regain power in the Blue Revolution of 1867 and the Monagas clan reentered the political scene. The political seesawing between liberals and conservatives only ended in 1870 when Antonio Guzmán Blanco initiated a lengthy rule.

SOCIETY AND CULTURE IN THE MID-NINETEENTH CENTURY

Rural life continued to define much of Latin American society throughout the nineteenth century, and poverty persisted in the countryside. As in earlier centuries, Indians and *castas* constituted the bulk of the labor force there. A few peasants farmed their own lands, but most worked on large estates as latifundia expanded. Generally, entire families contributed to agricultural production. Boys began working in the fields at an early age, and domestic service initiated young girls into the rural workforce. Children of impoverished families had limited educational opportunities. Furthermore, growing debt peonage trapped future generations in a vicious cycle of grueling work and inheritable indebtedness. Few indigent peasants could escape unending exploitation.

Women attended to livestock, assisted with labor in the fields during planting and harvesting, and contributed to household income by selling a variety of wares. They peddled food and drink, such as *pulque* in Mexico and *chicha* in the Andes. During slow periods, they wove cloth and produced other household goods for market. The patriarchal nature of peasant society limited their freedoms to some extent. Nevertheless, at times a woman with family living nearby could rely on male relatives to intervene on her behalf in cases of marital problems. Local authorities might take into account her reputation as a dutiful and obedient wife when she appealed for their help with domestic disturbances. She could leave her husband only in extreme cases of spousal cruelty.

On large estates, *hacendados* exercised virtually unchecked power over their workers. They maintained social order by requiring their workers to adhere to a strict moral code and disciplining them for infractions. A husband could expect severe punishment for treating his wife with brutality, providing women a degree of protection. But at the same time, some landowners and supervisors resorted to sexual harassment and even forcible rape to exert control over female laborers. Throughout the nineteenth century, the isolation and economic importance of latifundia offered poor peasants little reprieve to the injustices of the countryside.

Cities

The poor also struggled in Latin American cities and children routinely worked to contribute to the family income. Boys, some no more than 10 years of age, labored for meager wages in shops, mills, and emerging factories. Young girls frequently became domestic servants. Almost always, children constituted a central part of the informal labor market. As in the countryside, young people in urban areas also suffered exploitation, receiving paltry wages and enduring treacherous and unhealthy conditions. Municipal authorities viewed vagrant children as a threat to orderliness and passed numerous laws to control their behavior. Nevertheless, evolving ideas of republicanism raised expectations for the role of the state in caring for the poor and protecting children, in particular. Governments joined charitable societies in operating orphanages and poorhouses designed to care for destitute youth. Some of the most desperate parents abandoned children at these facilities temporarily, hoping to reunite the family after a period of hardship had passed.

Nonelite women's experiences in urban environments varied across time and place, but shared some notable commonalities. Many worked in domestic service, either as live-in housekeepers or cooks or by taking in laundry, sewing, and ironing. Over the course of the nineteenth century, the relative number of domestics declined as other types of employment became available, such as working in factories in newly industrializing centers like Mexico City and Buenos Aires. In larger and smaller cities alike, women continued to comprise the majority of street vendors. They sold their wares on foot or on mules and used large pottery jars to haul water, milk, and other liquids. In Lima, black women dominated street vending.

Compared to their rural counterparts, women in urban areas enjoyed more independence and freedom of movement. But such liberties could also create more insecurity because they often lacked the family and community relationships that provided support in the countryside. Women in cities often established informal social and economic networks with each other, and their growing access to income could provide them leverage in their relationships with men. At the same time, employment status might also dictate the extent to which a woman could control her own sexuality. Men continued the centuries' old practice of abusing their domestic servants with impunity. Women of little means often turned to prostitution to support themselves.

During the course of the nineteenth century, new opportunities arose for elite and middle-class women. Legislators and intellectuals considered these females' roles as mothers and moral guides important to nation building. A number of liberal regimes adopted civil codes that granted women rights and protections within the domestic sphere. Nevertheless, long-standing gender roles proved recalcitrant and many of those new laws reinforced a system of gender inequality. As society secularized, concerns about regulating women's morality and status as legal actors shifted from the Church to the state.

Cultural Development

After independence, distinct Latin American literary styles began to take shape through autobiography and the letters and treatises of high-profile figures such as Simón Bolívar. Writers also penned *costumbrista* essays, a diverse genre that included satiric and social commentary and an emphasis on local custom. Popular poetry included Argentine *cielitos* and Mexican *corridos*, a form of epic lyric poetry, which emerged during the 1830s. Verse stories, such as *Martín Fierro* (1872), by José Hernández, remained popular until the late nineteenth century. Narrative forms were not always clearly defined, as demonstrated in Domingo F. Sarmiento's *Facundo* (1845), which combined biography with biting social commentary on the clash between barbarism and civilization. A relative latecomer to Latin America, the novel became more common in the latter half of the century. Romance novels such as *Amalia* (1851), by the Argentine writer José Mármol, and *María* (1867), by the Colombian author Jorge Isaacs, divulge nationalist and political anxieties through the struggles of their protagonists.

A man and woman performing a *fandango*, or folk dance, onstage at a theatre in St. Iago (Santiago de Cuba). This watercolor drawing is from William H. Meyer's diary of his travels in to Cuba and the Bahamas from 1838 to 1839.

Other forms of culture and entertainment included the theater and the circus. Circuses provided entertainment to the public, featuring puppetry, acrobatics, jugglers, and clowns. In Mexico, clowns regaled the crowd with poetry to thank them for their patronage. A type nationalist theater originated during the mid-century in Argentina. José J. Podestá, a former circus performer, founded the *teatro gauchesco* and showcased plays based on the lives of the cowboys of the pampas. In Cuba, *teatro bufo* (clown theater) became popular and featured Cuban characters and local themes. Performances often contained satirical content that criticized the Spanish colonial administration.

Primary Source

The eminent Mexican politician José María Luis Mora wrote prolifically on his vision of the Mexican nation and the need for a liberal foundation of government. He emphasized the need to safeguard individual liberties and to fight against tyranny.

source: José María Luis Mora, *Obras sueltas de José María Luis Mora, Ciudadano Mejicano. Revista Politica. Credito Publico* (Paris: Libreria de Rosa, 1837). Reprint, Breinigsville, PA: Nabu Press, 2010.

They deceive themselves and mislead governments when they try to convince them that the method of containing these threats is to impede individual liberty. Public indignation, which is the precursor to all of these acts, is agitated in such a way that it cannot be obscured. In a moderately educated populace, where it might be suspected that an innocent suffers, a heightened interest is taken in that victim of circumstance, and injustices are made public and strongly scrutinized. When this happens, discontent and alarm spread quickly throughout all levels of society ... and because of it, all social bonds are destroyed and men exist in a barbaric state of nature.

We would never advise the people to partake in a similar situation, but they are moved to adopt it instinctively and without deliberation.... The irrepressible wrath of a mutinous people results in the most horrendous havoc: it is clarified in our legal thinking and rejected by it as violent and ignominious, and those who have usurped that most august ability, and those party leaders who, betraying their duties, have no less thought that by upholding public liberty they have wickedly sacrificed the interests of a despicable and favored criminal; like those honorable men, their faithful representatives, who have managed to have sacrificed everything, even their existence and political reputation, for the public good, and the national good ...

Then take heed, all you who preside over the destinies of people. The French Revolution is a practical and recent example of which you must not lose sight; it demonstrates that *never has public authority attacked the rights of free men with impunity, and that the first step taken against individual well-being becomes the unfailing precursor to the ruin of the nation and the government.*

SUGGESTIONS FOR FURTHER READING

Burke, Janet, and Ted Humphrey (eds.). *Nineteenth-Century Nation Building and the Latin America Intellectual Tradition.* Indianapolis, IN: Hackett, 2007.

Bushnell, David, and Neill Macaulay. *The Emergence of Latin America in the Nineteenth Century.* 2nd ed. Oxford: Oxford University Press, 1994.

Delpar, Helen. *Red against Blue: The Liberal Party in Colombian Politics, 1863–1899.* Tuscaloosa: University of Alabama Press, 1981.

Gudmundson, Lowell. *Costa Rica before Coffee: Society and Economy on the Eve of the Export Boom.* Baton Rouge: Louisiana State University, 1986.

Hale, Charles A. *Mexican Liberalism in the Age of Mora, 1821–1853.* New Haven, CT: Yale University Press, 1968.

Hamnett, Brian. *Juárez.* London: Longman, 1994.

Hunefeldt, Christine. *Liberalism in the Bedroom: Quarreling Spouses in Nineteenth-Century Lima.* University Park: Pennsylvania State University Press, 2000.

Mahoney, James. *The Legacies of Liberalism: Path Dependence and Political Regimes in Central America.* Baltimore: John Hopkins University Press, 2001.

O'Connor, Erin. *Mothers Making Latin America: Gender, Households, and Politics since 1825.* Hoboken: Wiley, 2014.

Peloso, Vincent C., and Barbara A. Tenenbaum (eds.). *Liberals, Politics, and Power: State Formation in Nineteenth-Century Latin America.* Athens, GA: University of Georgia Press, 1996.

Rodríguez, O. Jaime E. (ed.) *The Divine Charter: Constitutionalism and Liberalism in Nineteenth-Century Mexico.* Lanham, MD: Rowman & Littlefield, 2005.

Saeger, James S. *Francisco Solano López and the Ruination of Paraguay: Honor and Egocentrism.* Lanham, MD: Rowman & Littlefield, 2007.

Sanders, James E. *Contentious Republicans: Popular Politics, Race, and Class in Nineteenth-Century Colombia.* Durham, NC: Duke University Press, 2004.

Soifer, Hillel David. *State Building in Latin America.* Cambridge: Cambridge University Press, 2015.

Wasserman, Mark. *Everyday Life and Politics in Nineteenth Century Mexico: Men, Women, and War.* Albuquerque: University of New Mexico Press, 2000.

Williams, John Hoyt. *The Rise and Fall of the Paraguayan Republic, 1800–1870.* Austin: University of Texas Press, 1979.

Zimmermann, Eduardo. *Judicial Institutions in Nineteenth-Century Latin America.* London: University of London, Institute of Latin American Studies, 1999.

CHAPTER 16

Early Foreign Wars and Interventions

1855	Callahan Expedition; Texas Ranger James Hughes Callahan pursues the Lipan Apache into Mexico and burns the town of Piedras Negras, Coahuila
1855–1857	William Walker stages a coup in Nicaragua and declares himself president; he is ousted two years later by the Central American army
1860	William Walker returns to Central America to reclaim Nicaragua, but is captured by the British and executed by Honduran authorities
1861	Dominican Republic becomes a Spanish protectorate
1861	Convention of London, signed by Spain, Britain, and France, called for seizure of Mexico's customhouse in Veracruz in response to Juarez's call for the suspension of payment of foreign debts
1862–1867	French occupation of Mexico; Napoleon III, with the help of Mexican conservatives, sends in troops to reestablish a monarchy and restore the power of the Catholic Church
1862	Battle of Puebla where Mexican troops, led by Porfirio Díaz, defeated the French at Puebla; it did not stop the French occupation of Mexico
1863–1865	War of Restoration expels Spanish from the Dominican Republic
1864	Austrian archduke Ferdinand Maximilian of Habsburg and his wife, Charlotte, arrive in Mexico; Maximilian is installed as Emperor Maximilian I of Mexico
1865	Second Republic established in Dominican Republic
1864–1870	War of the Triple Alliance between the Empire of Brazil and the Republic of Argentina and Republic of Uruguay against Paraguay
1867	Napoleon III withdraws French troops and Maximilian I is captured and executed by Juarez's troops
1879–1883	War of the Pacific between Chile against Bolivia and Peru over territorial boundaries and mining claims
1883	Treaty of Ancón ends War of the Pacific

As newly independent countries struggled to find stability amid internal turmoil, national leaders also found themselves challenged further by a near-constant threat of military invasion. Political strife among competing factions vying for power made the nations vulnerable to interventions from abroad. Oftentimes, *caudillos* and other leaders, having only recently risen to power, found themselves scrambling to mobilize a military force to defend against foreign invasion or to fight alongside a neighboring ally. Other times, governments faced an invading foreign army while trying to deal with threats by internal enemies to depose them. To make matters worse, poorly defined national boundaries created easy targets for antagonists' expansion. A lack of transportation and communications infrastructure made isolated frontier regions difficult to defend. Consequently, many nations faced destructive and protracted wars as ambitious neighbors laid claim to their land in attempts to shift national boundaries.

Other challenges arose as European nations saw postindependence instability in Latin America as an opportunity to claim land or recolonize. Spain, in particular, long refused to recognize the sovereignty of its former possessions and attempted to invade Mexico and the Dominican Republic. France also engaged in multiple colonization schemes. Nevertheless, the most serious threats of intervention came from the United States, where ideas of Manifest Destiny as a religious duty took hold in the middle of the nineteenth century. The U.S. emergence as a military and economic power coincided with the worst episodes of internal upheaval in Latin America. Prominent politicians seized these opportunities to expand U.S. territory in Mexico and Central America.

Nearly all those powers involved in Latin America's foreign wars from independence through the early 1860s had one objective in common: the acquisition of territory either in the form of a colonial possession or as a result of a redrawn border. And nearly every foreign intervention in the first part of the nineteenth century resulted in at least a temporary imperial occupation or a significant change in the recognized boundary between neighboring nations.

The constant threat of foreign intervention further exacerbated the already volatile nature of national politics for many young Latin American nations. Political rivals competing for power blamed their foes for the ensuing crises. Mobilizing a national army put an enormous strain on treasuries struggling to grow from customs duties related to the limited profits of commodity exports. Soldiers often went into battle poorly armed, malnourished, and stricken by disease. Invading forces also tended to advance with little regard for preserving the landscape in their path. Damaged roads and ports as well as abandoned fields and mines often brought exports to a halt. Military defeat on the battlefield frequently translated to political ire within governing circles. Countless leaders found themselves the target of military coups, *pronunciamientos*, and other methods of overthrow—some mere attempts, but some successful.

INTER-AMERICAN WARS

War of the Triple Alliance

Competition for trade and economic dominance led to a series of regional conflicts among Brazil, Argentina, and Uruguay in the decades following independence. The Guerra Grande, a civil war in Uruguay from 1838 to 1851, eventually resulted in foreign intervention by neighboring Brazil and Argentina along with France and Great Britain. In Uruguay, political factions emerged representing rural agricultural interests, led by Manuel Oribe, and urban intellectuals, led by José Fructuoso Rivera. Allies in the struggle for independence, the two leaders found themselves in opposing camps as early ideological divisions surfaced and Rivera overthrew President Oribe in 1838. Rivera and his supporters formed the liberal Colorado Party, supported by France, Great Britain, and Brazil. Oribe's backers created the conservative Blanco Party and established an alliance with the Argentine *caudillo* Juan Manuel de Rosas. Conflict between the two parties continued for more than a decade, sustained largely by the involvement of foreign allies. The downfall of Rosas in Argentina eventually weakened the Blancos and allowed the Colorados to take control in 1852. The victors maintained a strong alliance with the government of Pedro II in Brazil, and the monarch intervened repeatedly on their behalf.

When Brazilian forces helped to depose the Blanco president Atanasio Aguirre in 1865, Paraguay's *caudillo* Francisco Solano López reacted in defense of the Uruguayan conservatives. In reality, the dictator of the landlocked nation viewed the conflict as a way to shift the regional balance of power in his favor and to secure Paraguayan access to seaports.

Solano López sent forces into Brazil and Argentina and the two nations reacted by joining with Uruguay in the Treaty of the Triple Alliance. Although the country lacked allies, Paraguay had the advantage of a large army that in the early days of the war won many decisive victories. But as the Triple Alliance nations had the chance to mobilize, Solano López's advantages began to dissipate. The war among the South American nations lasted for five years and resulted in a massive loss of life on both sides. By 1870, more than half of Paraguay's population had perished, including a disproportionate number of men. Despite heavy fatalities and expense, the Triple Alliance forces had triumphed and forced Paraguay to cede parts of its territory to Brazil and Argentina. These nations emerged from the war as regional powers with modernized armies; Paraguay was not only smaller, but also still without a seaport.

War of the Pacific

Chile fought against Peru and Bolivia in the War of the Pacific, a conflict that eventually defined disputed national boundaries. Equally important, it resolved contested claims over large deposits of nitrates and other valuable natural resources in the Antofagasta region of the Atacama Desert. Bolivia had claimed the region after independence, but the Andes formed a physical barrier that effectively isolated the Antofagasta region from the remainder of the country. Easier access from the south prompted Chilean leaders to secure a series of treaties and resource-sharing agreements that gave its companies extraction rights. When Bolivia attempted to nullify the agreements in 1878, Chile responded by invading Antofagasta. Because of a defensive alliance with Bolivia, Peru immediately rose to its neighbor's aid. A full-scale naval war began in April 1879, followed quickly by a Chilean ground invasion of Peru. In 1881, Lima fell and a protracted occupation of Peru's capital eventually forced the country's leaders to harsh terms of peace. The Treaty of Ancón ended the War of the Pacific in 1883. Bolivia ceded the Antofagasta region to Chile and Peru gave up parts of its southern territory as well. Bolivia lost access to the Pacific and thus become permanently landlocked. The new boundary also gave Chile control over the mineral-rich Atacama Desert, which contributed to the country's impressive economic growth at the end of the nineteenth century.

DIRECT INTERVENTION AND TERRITORIAL ACQUISITION (1830S–1860S)

The United States and the Monroe Doctrine

As early as 1813, Thomas Jefferson and other prominent leaders had introduced the notion of the "Western Hemisphere idea," insisting that a unique set of characteristics set the Americas apart from Europe. Ten years later, the Monroe Doctrine formalized this idea and guided Latin America's relationship with the United States for the rest of the nineteenth century. Devised by U.S. Secretary of State John Quincy Adams and articulated by President James Monroe in his 1823 State of the Union address, this first major foreign policy statement for Latin America stipulated that the United States would not tolerate European attempts to recolonize any area of the Americas. By the time Monroe made his pronouncement, the wars of independence in Latin America had reached their final stages. Brazil had declared independence from Portugal in 1822 and most former Spanish colonies either had secured self-rule or were close to defeating the last royalist forces. The notable exceptions of Cuba and Puerto Rico in the Caribbean remained under Spanish rule until 1898.

The idea behind the Monroe Doctrine originated with the British foreign minister George Canning, who suggested a joint policy backed by both the United States and Great Britain. His country's long-standing interest in trade with Latin America seemed to be the motivation behind the proposal. He worried that the Spanish and French might attempt to recolonize areas of the Americas and again impose trade restrictions inimical to British interests. Leaders in the United States agreed with the spirit of the policy, but chose to articulate a unilateral position.

Monroe based the doctrine largely on the idea that common political and cultural systems united the Americas and set them apart from imperialist powers in Europe. He outlined the notion of "separate spheres" and rejected in advance any European powers establishing new colonies in the American sphere. Indeed, the doctrine considered any attack against Latin America a threat against the United States. To round out the idea of separate spheres, Monroe also pledged that the United States would not interfere in the internal affairs of European powers.

The Monroe Doctrine received mixed reaction throughout Latin America and around the world. The British generally favored the policy since it corresponded to their aim of securing open trade. Most European powers ignored the proclamation at first and Spain and France attempted to acquire colonies despite the doctrine. In truth, the United States lacked the power to enforce the doctrine throughout most of the nineteenth century and did not actively intervene to prevent numerous incursions by European powers. Only after 1870 did U.S. leaders begin invoking the Monroe Doctrine directly and flexing military muscle to prevent European armed actions in what they considered their hemisphere.

Early Spanish and French Interventions in Mexico

Spain long refused to recognize the sovereignty of its former colonies on the American mainland. As the largest, most profitable, and longest held mainland possession, Mexico continued to hold a strong attraction to the Crown. It represented the apogee of Spain's imperial power and that symbolism led royal advisors to fantasize about its recovery. Mexican leaders knew that the nation's sovereignty would remain vulnerable as long as the Spanish Crown withheld diplomatic recognition. President Guadalupe Victoria (1824–1829) interpreted Spain's continued presence in the Caribbean as a threat and ordered several naval attacks against its patrols near Cuba.

In 1829, a Spanish fleet of 40 ships and more than 3,000 men arrived off the coast of Tampico to attempt the reconquest of Mexico. President Vicente Guerrero, who had held office only a few months, sent Santa Anna to repel the invaders. After several weeks, disease and the effects of a hurricane along the coast expedited a Mexican victory. This success came to symbolize a finale to the Mexican struggle for independence, although Spain stubbornly withheld diplomatic recognition until 1836.

Mexico's troubles with foreign invasion did not end with Santa Anna's victory. In the midst of near constant coups d'état (*golpes*) and other civil unrest, armed conflict often left substantial destruction of personal property in its wake. Private citizens generally had little recourse to obtain reparations. In the 1830s, a French baker and other French citizens in the capital beseeched their government to compel Mexico to pay damages for losses incurred as a result of looting and other violence. In 1838, the French cited these claims along with outstanding debt obligations as a reason to blockade ports along the gulf in what became known as the "Pastry War." French troops seized the customs house at Veracruz and occupied the city in an attempt to collect compensation. In a pattern that he would repeat

Map 16.1 U.S. Acquisition of Mexican Territory

numerous times in subsequent years, Santa Anna reentered the national scene to lead the Mexican military in defending Veracruz against the invaders. Eventually the French agreed to a negotiated payment offered by the Mexican government, but not before Santa Anna suffered serious injury that required the amputation of his leg. The loss of his limb became a metaphor for the sacrifice the *caudillo* repeatedly reminded the country he had made for it.

MANIFEST DESTINY

The Texas Revolution

In addition to early incursions from European powers, Mexico had to confront threats inherent in the imposing proximity of the United States. In the early nineteenth century, the national territories of both countries included large stretches of sparsely populated frontier lands, with Mexico's northern border stretching far into the present-day U.S. Southwest. Even before Mexico achieved independence, U.S. leaders became interested in western expansion and particularly eyed Mexico's northern territory. First negotiating with the Spanish Crown and later with the Mexican government, Stephen F. Austin secured land concessions allowing settlers in the far northern agricultural province of Coahuila y Tejas. Throughout the 1820s, U.S. citizens moved into Texas—some with legal approval, others as illegal squatters. By 1830, such settlers had become a majority in the region. Mexican laws required them to abolish slavery and practice Catholicism, but officials in the distant national capital could only loosely enforce these measures.

Conflicts regarding federalism and centralism shook the delicate relationship between U.S. settlers in Texas and the Mexican government. In 1835, Santa Anna attempted to diminish the autonomy of Mexican states by replacing the constitution of 1824 with the *Siete Leyes*. Texans rebelled in response to this effort to impose centralism, and other regions of Mexico appeared to be on the brink of revolt as well. Santa Anna led an army of more than 6,000 to quell the uprising in the north and make it an example that would deter other areas from defying the central government. Local Texas leaders declared independence and mobilized militias to wage war against Mexico. After months of fighting, Santa Anna's forces laid siege to the Alamo fortress in San Antonio. Following a two-week standoff, Mexican forces attacked and killed nearly all of the approximately 200 defenders who had taken refuge inside—an episode that became a symbol of Texas pride and a legend that continues to resonate among the state's most ardent patriots.

Despite his victory, Santa Anna could not sustain his success. Rebel forces under the leadership of Sam Houston defeated his army at the decisive Battle of San Jacinto in April 1836 and soon captured the *caudillo*. Santa Anna signed the Treaties of Velasco, granting Texas independence in exchange for having his life spared. Nevertheless, he later reneged, refusing to recognize Texas sovereignty. Acrimony simmered between Mexico and the new republic for the next 10 years. The lack of a clear resolution to the Texas Revolution eventually contributed to the war between Mexico and the United States that began in 1846.

U.S.-MEXICAN WAR

The loss of Texas in 1836 left the Mexican political system in even greater disarray. In the subsequent decade, the presidency changed hands at least 13 times, primarily among conservative politicians who maintained a commitment to centralized authority. Diplomatic dilemmas with the United States further complicated Mexico's internal politics during this time of extreme political volatility and factional competition for power.

U.S. presidential politics in 1844 had important ramifications for its neighbor. At the time, the concept of Manifest Destiny increasingly seduced politicians in the United States. Since the conclusion of the Texas Revolution, they had debated the option of annexing the former Mexican territory. But its inclusion would have upset the balance between free and slave states that U.S. leaders had so fiercely maintained for decades. For that reason, many avoided taking a strong stand on the fate of Texas. Nevertheless, the Democratic candidate, James K. Polk, appealed to nationalist zeal and incorporated territorial expansion and annexation into his political platform. His presidential victory ensured that Mexico would soon become part of an expansionist strategy.

In 1846, Polk negotiated a favorable resolution with the British over the Oregon Territory and hoped to use a similar strategy to negotiate with Mexico. The primary issues were the U.S. annexation of Texas in 1845, which Mexican leaders refused to recognize, and a boundary dispute. Texas claimed the Rio Grande as the border, but Mexican officials argued for the Nueces River to the north. Polk also wanted to buy several Mexican ports along the Pacific. In 1846, he approved $15–$25 million to purchase the ports and sent John Slidell to negotiate. As expected, the emissary received a cool reception. Mexican leaders suspended the talks and expelled Slidell from the country as soon as U.S. intentions became clear. Moreover, the Mexican president maintained his country's refusal to recognize the annexation of Texas.

War broke out after U.S. troops occupied the disputed area between the Nueces River and the Río Grande and engaged in minor skirmishes with Mexican forces. This provided the needed provocation and Congress approved a declaration of war on May 13. With U.S. armies in the country, Santa Anna returned to Mexico from exile and led the nation's defensive forces. Despite devastating losses in the north, he reclaimed the presidency.

By September 1847, General Winfield Scott and his army had reached Mexico City and begun a lengthy occupation. The Treaty of Guadalupe Hidalgo signed on February 2, 1848, formally terminated the war. Under its terms, Mexico ceded nearly half of its national territory to the United States, land identified today as the states of California, Arizona, New Mexico, Nevada, Utah, and parts of Colorado. In addition, Mexico recognized the U.S. annexation of Texas. In exchange, the United States agreed to pay Mexico the original sum proposed before the war began, but this monetary compensation did little to assuage the understandable animosity many Mexicans felt toward their northern neighbor.

SANTA ANNA DECLINING A HASTY PLATE OF SOUP AT CERRO GORDO.

Santa Anna's retreat at the Battle of Cerro Gordo where his wooden leg and military chest containing $11,000 in gold fell into the hands of U.S. soldiers. Santa Anna is chased by Winfield Scott, who offers the Mexican general "a hasty plate of soup," a reference mocking Scott's penchant for comfortable appointments during military campaigns.

Stirring resentment even further, Santa Anna negotiated the Gadsden Purchase with the United States in 1853. During this last stint as ruler of Mexico, the *caudillo* saw the sale of territory as a way to replenish the national treasury, severely depleted as a result of costly wars and internal misspending. The United States paid Mexico $10 million for a 29,670-square-mile swath of territory that makes up the southern portion of the current states of Arizona and New Mexico. The backlash in Mexico over this sale contributed to growing discontent with and the *caudillo* and eventually led to his final overthrow in 1855.

FILIBUSTERS

Some incidents of foreign intervention in the nineteenth century unfolded without direct military involvement. As had occurred immediately prior to and during the independence period, between the 1830s and the 1860s numerous U.S. adventurers known as filibusters set out on unsanctioned quests to annex parts of Latin American nations. Although they often claimed to act on behalf of the U.S. government, its officials did not formally recognize their activities. The northern Mexican border was a hotbed of filibuster infiltrations, but such incursions also took place in Cuba and Central America.

Veterans of the U.S.–Mexican War found it hard to return to civilian life and filibustering provided a continuation of military adventure and camaraderie. Many of them joined campaigns in Cuba. Filibustering also attracted Freemasons, whose anti-Catholic views coincided with expeditions to free Latin Americans from the yoke of oppressive governments and the Catholic Church.

One of the most active and well-known U.S. adventurers, William Walker launched an invasion of Sonora and Baja California in northern Mexico in 1853 with the intent to establish an independent republic. He named himself president and successfully recruited hundreds of troops and investors from both sides of the border. Nevertheless, within a few short months the ambitious filibuster had lost the majority of his private army to desertion and the Mexican military had driven him back into the United States.

Despite his resounding failure, Walker's actions found a great deal of support among the U.S. public. He stood trial for violating neutrality laws, but a friendly jury readily acquitted him. Undeterred by his lack of success, he set his sights on Central America in 1855. Taking advantage of a factional dispute that had led to a violent civil war, Walker formed an alliance with Nicaraguan liberals based in the city of León. He launched an invasion of the troubled Central American republic and secured the conservative stronghold of Granada. With the blessing of his allies, the filibuster declared himself president—a move that the administration of the U.S. president Franklin Pierce eventually recognized.

Despite his relatively easy victory in Nicaragua, Walker's success in Central America lasted only briefly. Leaders in neighboring nations grew concerned that he would expand his imperialist ambitions. In addition, he enacted many controversial policies that began earning him enemies. He reversed Nicaragua's antislavery laws, began encouraging U.S. colonization, and made English the official language. In a particularly ill-advised move, Walker denied Cornelius Vanderbilt shipping rights across the isthmus. The American tycoon took revenge by funding a coalition of opposition forces. With external resistance mounting and his local support fading, Walker eventually surrendered himself to the U.S. Navy and went back to the United States in 1857. The audacious filibuster returned to Central America in 1860, intent on resuming his claim over Nicaragua. The British quickly captured him and happily turned him over to Central American authorities. Hondurans executed him by firing squad.

Other filibuster adventures included Narciso López's ill-fated attempts to invade Cuba and overthrow the Spanish in 1850 and 1851. The Venezuelan's initial expedition ended in retreat and the second in disaster. Spanish troops captured and imprisoned López, garroting him at the fortress near Havana Bay. The López affair transfixed American newspaper audiences, who eagerly awaited news of the filibuster's exploits.

SPAIN AND THE DOMINICAN REPUBLIC

The threat of foreign invasion continued after the filibusters' demise. In the 1860s, Spain successfully reestablished imperial control over the Dominican Republic, which had already endured several tumultuous decades following Haiti's independence. In 1822, the Haitian president Jean-Pierre Boyer sent an invading army across the border, drove the Spanish out of Santo Domingo, and inaugurated an occupation that lasted until 1844. The new leaders sought to weaken the Catholic Church, but the policies they imposed upset much of the remaining colonial elite. Eventually, resistance to the Haitians coalesced under the banner of La Trinitaria—a name that paid tribute to the Church. After a struggle lasting more than five years, the rebels defeated the Haitian forces and created an independent Dominican Republic complete with a constitution and Bill of Rights modeled after those of the United States.

For 20 years, political control alternated between two competing *caudillos*, Pedro Santana and Buenaventura Báez, who justified autocratic rule as the best safeguard against another Haitian invasion. Individually they pursued protection by a foreign patron to defend their country's national interests. After protracted negotiations with Spain, France, and the United States, in 1861 Santana finally allowed Spain to administer the Dominican Republic as a protectorate.

Resistance formed immediately against Santana's leadership and the Spanish incursion, but infighting initially prevented the emergence of a consolidated opposition. An organized revolutionary movement took shape in 1863 when José Antonio Salcedo declared independence and assumed the leadership of rebel forces in the War of Restoration. Fighting continued for nearly two years before the Spanish withdrew in 1865, allowing the victors to found the Second Republic.

FRENCH INTERVENTION

Shortly after the War of Reform ended in 1861, Mexico's external debt problems resurfaced. The liberals' tenuous victory had left Benito Juárez in power but drained the national treasury. Unable to pay the army or civilian government employees, the president suspended payments to the country's creditors in an attempt to allow national income to recover. Britain, Spain, and France responded with the Convention of London, which called for the coalition to seize Mexico's customs house in Veracruz. The partners planned to confiscate this major source of revenue and apply it to the debt. Although the accord specifically stated that the coalition would not occupy the country, the French Army, acting under orders from Napoleon III, quickly abandoned the guarantee and embarked on a full-scale takeover.

The French emperor capitalized on the deep political rifts that had plagued Mexico since independence and allied with Mexican conservatives still reeling from defeat in the War of the Reform. The staunchest reactionaries embraced the French occupation as a new opportunity to impose a monarchical government, restore a conservative social structure, and reinstate the power and privileges of the Catholic Church. Indeed, the initially overwhelming support from their Mexican allies lulled French military leaders into anticipating an easy victory in the city of Puebla, a conservative stronghold. But Juárez had resolved to make a strategic stand there and the Mexican Army, under the command of General Ignacio

Zaragoza and future president Porfirio Díaz, turned back the invaders in a surprising victory on May 5, 1862—a feat commemorated today in Cinco de Mayo celebrations in both Mexico and the United States.

Although symbolic as a token of national pride, Mexico's early victory in Puebla did not portend things to come. Mexico's conservatives rallied and Napoleon III fortified his army with 30,000 reinforcements. As in the War of the Reform, Juárez found himself on the run, fleeing the capital, escaping to San Luis Potosí, and trying to govern the nation. In Mexico City, a provisional government composed of prominent conservatives collaborated with Napoleon III to install a European monarch. They settled on Ferdinand Maximilian of Habsburg, the archduke of Austria and brother of Emperor Franz Josef. Persuaded by a cadre of conservative elite that the Mexican people eagerly awaited him, the archduke sailed for the Americas with his young wife, Charlotte, to become Emperor Maximilian I. The royal couple arrived in Veracruz in 1864 and began the hazardous journey to the capital over rugged terrain. Expecting a well-developed nation and warm welcome, they found instead a primitive countryside and a population decidedly hostile toward them.

On arriving in the capital, the new emperor and his bride installed themselves in Chapultepec Castle—once a residence of Aztec rulers and the site of one of the last major battles between the U.S. Army and young Mexican military cadets during the U.S.–Mexican War. The castle carried historic and nationalistic significance and Maximilian incorporated it into a broad strategy of attempting to inject himself into a sense of Mexican national identity.

Despite the emperor's best efforts, a majority of Mexicans never embraced him. Persistent conflict between liberal and conservative factions kept the country divided and politically unstable. Led by Benito Juárez, liberals had set up an alternate governing structure and refused to recognize Maximilian as Mexico's legitimate ruler. To make matters worse, the emperor personally favored liberalism and began instituting policies that angered prominent conservatives, some of whom had initially invited him to rule. Indeed, Maximilian dashed his allies' hopes by refusing to reverse most of the liberal reforms that they despised. He even attempted to push through measures directed at helping the nation's poor. Despite his sincere efforts to transform Mexico into a workshop of nineteenth-century liberalism, Maximilian failed to win the support of Juárez or other liberals. Placed in power by a foreign army, he suffered an eradicable stain in a country slowly developing a sense of nationhood.

Maximilian's predictable demise occurred in 1867. By that time, the U.S. Civil War—which had kept the guardian of the Monroe Doctrine distracted—had ended. Juárez began receiving vital military and financial aid and U.S. leaders exerted considerable pressure on Napoleon to withdraw French troops. Of equal if not greater importance, Prussia threatened France's border. Discretion triumphed at last, and Napoleon withdrew Maximilian's military backing. The emperor and a small group of remaining allies quickly found themselves on the run. Captured by Juárez's forces, they died by a firing squad on June 19, 1867.

SOCIAL AND CULTURAL IMPACT OF WAR

Wars and foreign invasions sowed destruction and increased political instability in Latin America. Although "intervention" more accurately describes some of the smaller conflicts, the persistence of even minor cases of armed foreign interference usually had a devastating effect. Lengthy and violent wars involved large numbers of people both off and on the battlefield and reinforced lingering social inequalities. Often the poorest members of society filled the ranks of hastily formed military units. Their conscription left behind wives and children, who struggled to meet their basic needs. The physical devastation of war also proved costly. Invading armies frequently destroyed already meager infrastructure; their presence disrupted agricultural and mining production and halted trade. New governments struggling to increase revenue saw exports stagnate until late in the nineteenth century.

Recruiting soldiers for national armies further burdened already strained populations, as did high casualty rates. An estimated 15,000 to 25,000 Mexicans died during the two wars with the United States alone. Chilean deaths exceeded more than 2,000 in the War of the Pacific, and Bolivia and Peru lost troops totaling approximately five times that number.

The aftermath of the War of the Triple Alliance offers a striking case of the devastating social effects of nineteenth-century armed conflict. The war decimated Paraguay. Estimates indicate as many as 300,000 died of a total population of roughly 500,000. Warfare killed entire families, from lineages that dated to the founding of the capital Asunción. Few men with political experience survived the war and law enforcement virtually disappeared. The imbalanced ratio of women to men reached 50 to 1 in the countryside and 3 to 1 in the capital because the scant number of surviving adult males often traveled to neighboring countries in search of employment. Poor sanitation during the postwar period facilitated epidemics that included smallpox and yellow fever; these further ravaged the population. As social mores deteriorated and sexual morality declined, prostitution, gambling, and banditry became hallmarks of postwar society.

By 1870, efforts to restore order and revive agriculture had begun. Government leaders attempted to relocate displaced people to abandoned lands and passed measures to curtail vagrancy. New elementary schools opened in Asunción and elsewhere to support compulsory education and to instill national consciousness in young people. Religious instruction and the prohibition of the Guaraní indigenous language in these facilities became part of a larger framework to shape a sense of Paraguayan identity. The opening of a public library and a national museum contributed to reviving intellectual and cultural life in the capital.

WAR, NATIONALISM, AND NATIONAL HEROES

Their destructive effects notwithstanding, wars also often contributed to emerging nationalism. Duty in official armies rather than the smaller militias loyal to *caudillos* helped foster a sense of belonging to the more expansive entity of "the nation." Furthermore, identifying a collective enemy outside their borders helped Latin Americans set themselves apart from neighboring countries as well as the imperialist powers in Europe or the United States. Many Latin American governments embraced national flags with symbols intended to foster a common sense of identity. Additionally, the use of national anthems followed independence or foreign wars in many countries. Subsequent armed conflict often inspired later composers to alter lyrics and incorporate new feats of heroism.

The need to promote patriotism in the midst of large-scale wars produced an environment ripe for the creation of national heroes. The U.S.–Mexican War left such a legacy when cadets of the military academy attempted to defend Chapultepec Castle from General Scott's invasion of Mexico City. According to historical lore, six young boys leapt to their deaths from the castle walls rather than surrender to the encroaching troops. Reportedly, Juan Escutia wrapped himself in the flag before hurling himself from the rampart to prevent the banner from falling into enemy hands. Later historical investigation has called into question the supposed exploits of these "Niños Heroes." Nevertheless, over time, government leaders have disseminated and memorialized the patriotic tale. A grand monument, built more than a century later, now stands at the base of the castle where the cadets reportedly met their demise.

The Central American coalition that thwarted William Walker's incursion in Nicaragua gave rise to Costa Rica's most prominent national hero. In a decisive 1856 battle against the filibuster's forces, a humble drummer boy named Juan Santamaría sacrificed himself by charging into a barrage of bullets and setting fire to a building where the enemy forces had fortified themselves. His actions helped the Central American resistance fighters secure a victory, but his bravery resulted in his death. Like many such legendary figures, Santamaría became a symbol of Costa Rican integrity and national valor, largely as a result of stories retold and at times exaggerated in the years that followed. Scant historical evidence exists to support these accounts, but belief in them persists. By the end of the century, the Costa Rican government began heralding him as a patriotic hero and declared the anniversary of his death a national holiday. Today, monuments to Juan Santamaría stand in many areas of the country and the international airport in San José bears his name.

NATIONALISM AND THE WRITTEN WORD

The War of the Triple Alliance gave rise to satirical graphic periodicals in Paraguay that mocked the nation's enemies and helped contribute to a sense of unity among the population. During Mexico's ill-fated wars with Texas and the United States, soldiers often relieved the tedium and frustration that accompanied military service by composing poems and songs that poked fun at national leaders. A satirical press also emerged during the conflict and provided an important outlet for expressing disillusion with Mexican politicians and acrimony toward enemy invaders. The Chilean Army looted and removed of thousands of books and manuscripts from Peru's national library and deposited them in the national library in Santiago. This event stimulated nationalism in Peru and remained a source of conflict between the two countries for more than a century. Only in 2007 did the Chilean government return some 3,700 historical manuscripts in an effort to improve relations with its northern neighbor.

Literature, newspapers, and pamphlets also furthered emerging nationalism. In the early nineteenth century, Latin Americans primarily imported publications of high culture from Europe, but the price of books relegated them to luxury status available almost exclusively to professionals and the well-to-do. Consequently, as early as the independence era, Mexican elites looked for ways to unify an ethnically and linguistically diverse population. The serial novel, a relatively new literary form, facilitated a broader dissemination of ideas and commentary to a larger audience. Published in both installments in newspapers or as a stand-alone book delivered to subscribers, this vehicle cost less and reached a wider segment of Mexican society. The early chapters of the first of these novels, José Joaquin Fernández de Lizardi's *El periquillo sarniento* (*The Mangy Parrot*) appeared in 1816. Its revolutionary commentary and nationalistic ideals attracted not only critics of royal government, but also censors who stymied the release of the entire work until 1831. New literary associations like the Academia de San Juan de Letrán collaborated to "Mexicanize" the written word and to make literary expression more widely accessible. In addition to serial novels, academia writers published poetry, novellas, and theater reviews in popular periodicals (*revistas*). In 1845, *El fistol del Diablo*, widely considered Mexico's second novel, appeared. Its author, Manuel Payno, fought against the U.S. invasion in the state of Puebla, and the war provides a backdrop to the plot, which repeatedly showcases the distinctiveness of daily life in the nation. Also at this time, Justo Sierra O'Reilly published serialized historical novels, primarily set within the racial diversity of the Yucatán. In his narratives, society's rejection of a mulatto protagonist serves as a metaphor for the ethnic ambiguity that hampered the formation of a coherent Mexican identity. Framed as a critique of the colonial legacy, Sierra's works contributed to the growing genre of nationalist literature.

The French Intervention in Mexico and the brief Spanish incursion in the Dominican Republic comprised the final serious attempts by foreign powers to intervene in the Americas or to invade with the purpose of territorial acquisition or recolonization. Some border conflicts persisted, but the threat of overt imperial intrusion dissipated after 1870. Violent foreign wars had devastated populations, ravaged economies, and exacerbated existing inequalities. Although they jeopardized Latin American stability, they also strengthened emerging nationalistic sentiments, often reflected in the creation of national heroes and in literary expression.

Primary Source

As the emperor of Mexico, Maximilian I desperately attempted to present his reign as part of a nationalist narrative, but his patriotic gestures held little sway among Mexican liberals. His independence-day speech invokes ideas of unity, sacrifice, and historic heroes.

SOURCE: Samuel Basch, *Recollections of Mexico: The Last Ten Months of Maximilian's Empire*, ed. and trans. Fred D. Ullman (Wilmington, DE: SR Books, 2001), 16–17.

Mexicans!

This is the third time that I celebrate our great and glorious Feast of Brother-hood with your enthusiastic participation.

On this day of patriotic memories, my heart makes me speak freely and openly to my fellow citizens and take part with them in the general celebration. Fifty-six years have passed since the first call to resurrections. By now, Mexico has already been fighting for a half century for independence and peace. Those who love their country must be impatient because such a period of time seems very long. However, for the history of a people that is being formed, this is merely the difficult learning period that every nation must endure until it is great and pow-erful. For a nation, there is no triumph without struggle and blood, no political development, no permanent progress.

The first period of our history teaches us to be ready for sacrifice. It also teaches us unity and a firm belief in the future.

I hope that all loyal friends of our country will energetically support this great job of regeneration, each in his own sphere of activity. Then my work will not have been in vain and I will cheerfully continue along the difficult road that I have set out on. May you have confidence and goodwill so that we may, one day, enjoy the fruits of the peace and happiness that we are all longing to see.

Regardless of all difficulties, I still firmly stand on the spot to which the will of the Nation has called me. I will not falter in my duties because a true Habsburg will not leave his post, certainly not in the moment of danger.

The majority of the Nation has chosen me to defend its holy right against the enemies of order, of property and of true independence. The Almighty must protect us because it is a holy truth that the voice of the people is the voice of God. This was demonstrated in wonderful ways in the days of the first national rebel-lion! And thus it will be shown at the rebirth of the Nation.

The ghosts of our heroes look down upon us. Let us follow their immortal example without hesitation and without fear, so that we may reach the enviable goal, namely, the independence which their blood has sanctified, secured and crowned.

Mexicans! Long live independence and the beautiful memories of our im-mortal martyrs.

SUGGESTIONS FOR FURTHER READING

Acree, William G., and Juan Carlos González Espitia. *Building Nineteenth-Century Latin America*, Nashville, TN: Vanderbilt University Press, 2009.

Brown, Charles. *Agents of Manifest Destiny: The Lives and Times of the Filibusters*. Chapel Hill: University of North Carolina Press, 1980.

Cunningham, Michele. *Mexico and the Foreign Policy of Napoléon III*. New York: Palgrave, 2001.

Henderson, Timothy J. *A Glorious Defeat: Mexico and Its War with the United States*. New York: Hill & Wang, 2008.

Hurtado, Albert L. "Empires, Frontiers, Filibusters, and Pioneers: The Transnational World of John Sutter." *Pacific Historical Review* 77, no. 1 (February 2008): 19–47.

Leuchars, Christopher. *To the Bitter End: Paraguay and the War of the Triple Alliance*. Westport, CT: Greenwood Press, 2002.

May, Robert E. *Manifest Destiny's Underworld: Filibustering in Antebellum America*. Chapel Hill: University of North Carolina Press, 2002.

Murphy, Gretchen. *Hemispheric Imaginings: The Monroe Doctrine and Narratives of U.S. Empire*. Durham, NC: Duke University Press, 2005.

Sater, William F. *Andean Tragedy: Fighting the War of the Pacific, 1879–1884*. Lincoln: University of Nebraska Press, 2007.

CHAPTER 17

Progress and Modernization

By the 1870s, the incessant clashes between liberal and conservative interests that had plagued much of Latin America since independence began to abate. In most countries, powerful alliances of liberal elites consolidated power and implemented policies to expand trade, modernize infrastructure, and strengthen the state. These oligarchies marked a shift away from the volatile personalism and tyranny that characterized earlier leaders; the new style merged *caudillismo* with formal political party frameworks. Ruling regimes generally considered themselves "liberal" and they relied on new social theories to outline a strategy for development. Positivism and the quest for "order and progress" guided Latin American government policies at the end of the century. The expansion of education in Argentina and the abolition of slavery in Brazil attest to the leaders' commitment to positivism and progressive ideals. But other policies deviated substantially from the tenets of liberalism. The poor, the indigenous, and other marginalized groups saw their standing deteriorate. Long-standing practices of exploitation and systems of inequality continued and, for some, became worse. Development strategies favored the economic enterprises of the oligarchs, allowing them to expand their influence and to justify limiting democracy.

OLIGARCHIES

Liberal oligarchies in many, but not all, countries of Latin America consolidated political power by the late nineteenth century. They often owned the essential resources—such as mining and agriculture—that formed the foundation of their nations' wealth. Economic policies that consolidated land tenure, promoted open trade, and fostered a reliance on the export market had enabled these small groups of families to accumulate great wealth and to solidify their political authority.

Oligarchic elites continued and even strengthened policies that had benefited them. New and revised constitutions bolstered the framework of liberal republics over conservative political models, even as political leaders embraced increased centralized authority under a strong executive. Generally, these oligarchies endorsed a more representative franchise, although frequently limiting suffrage to males who owned property. Social policies also followed outlines provided in earlier liberal party platforms. The ideas of Herbert Spencer provided a justification based on biology for the oligarchs' belief that whites' greater ability to adapt and progress made them superior to mixed and indigenous populations.

Liberals' advocacy of private land ownership over that of corporate bodies quickened the pace of land reform and concentrated even more property in the hands of a few, to the detriment of the Catholic Church and indigenous communities. The oligarchies also sought to create a favorable investment climate for attracting foreign capital to support the rapid modernization of infrastructure and economic production. Railroad and telegraph line construction began in earnest, as did efforts to upgrade roads and port facilities. As a result, many Latin American nations significantly improved their economies, rapidly expanded the production and export of primary goods, and fostered even greater fortunes for their elites.

But these changes came at a real cost. By the end of the nineteenth century, conditions for the poor had deteriorated and foreigners controlled substantial amounts of the nations' economic resources.

ARGENTINA'S LIBERAL OLIGARCHY

In Argentina, lengthy political conflict marked the relationship between the major urban center of Buenos Aires and the provinces. Juan Manuel de Rosas, the *caudillo* who dominated the future nation from 1829 to 1852, maintained his political power through a limited and controlled electorate. He promoted conservative policies that favored the Church and the military, but also adhered to political and economic formulas that distinguished him from otherwise similarly minded contemporaries. His most serious challenges often surfaced from commercial policies that favored the port and province of Buenos Aires over potential rivals in other regions.

Opposition began to emerge in the 1830s, even as Rosas's regime captured, silenced, and forced into exile a majority of his critics. A rising group of young, liberal intellectuals began speaking out against the dictatorial nature of the *caudillo*'s government. Among them, like-minded writers—including Esteban Echeverría, Domingo Faustino Sarmiento, Juan Bautista Alberdi, Miguel Cané, and Bartolomé Mitre—published essays, poems, and short stories questioning the government's barbaric tactics. They formed a literary salon and published *La Moda*, a weekly magazine that became a vehicle for their protest. Their writings argued that Rosas's tyranny engendered an uncivilized and backward society that imperiled national development. This "Generation of 1837" posed a serious philosophical challenge to the dictator by advocating both a new approach to government and changes in social and economic policies to civilize and modernize the nation. Rosas dealt with the dissent in typical fashion, censoring the writers' publications and forcing them into exile. From neighboring Chile and Uruguay, the critics continued to exert influence, and their writings contributed to Rosas's downfall. Importantly, their theories portended the subsequent consolidation of Argentina's liberal oligarchy.

In 1852, an alliance of disaffected provincial *caudillos* and ever-present Unitario enemies finally overthrew Rosas and soon convened a constitutional convention. The resulting constitution of 1853 established a democratic government with a strong legislature intended to preclude permanently a return to dictatorship under a strong executive. The charter also granted considerable power to the interior provinces, a provision that prompted Bartolomé Mitre and other liberal leaders in Buenos Aires to reject the document. The rift that separated Buenos Aires from the rest of the country ended in 1861 and Mitre became president the following year. His term initiated an era of liberal consolidation characterized by the pacification of the countryside and sustained economic growth. The government actively encouraged European immigration, reflecting the earlier dictum of Juan Bautista Alberdi, "to govern is to populate." The subsequent administration of Domingo Sarmiento continued these efforts and intensified measures to increase access to education.

The Teatro Colón (Columbus Theatre) in Buenos Aires, Argentina. Opened in 1908, the Teatro Colón is renowned for its acoustics and eclectic architectural design reflecting French–and Italian–inspired elements.

Collectively known as the "Generation of 1880," Argentina's ruling oligarchy coalesced in the new National Autonomist Party. During the final decades of the nineteenth century, the country's economy continued to expand; its leaders measured progress by urban growth, material wealth, and the adoption of new technologies. Architectural design and new construction gave Buenos Aires a European feel.

Beginning in the 1870s, European immigration helped to transform Argentina from a rural and agricultural nation to one focused on its growing and modernizing capital. Immigrants came primarily from Italy and Spain, but a smaller and also influential group of Ashkenazi Jews arrived from Eastern Europe. By 1895, almost 350,000 people in Buenos Aires, some 52 percent of the population, had migrated from outside of Argentina.

The vast numbers of new arrivals in the capital gave rise to *conventillos*, a type of urban tenement. *Conventillos* had few windows, one street entrance, the barest of amenities, and tiny rooms measuring about 12 by 12 feet with 9- to 14-foot ceilings. One tenement could house up to 300 to 400 people under appallingly crowded conditions. Single men shared rooms and a lack of space required them to sleep in shifts. Married women often earned an income by sewing, rolling cigars, or taking in laundry. From this environment arose a unique working-class culture that engendered negotiation, cooperation, and solidarity. Early tango music provided one form of entertainment associated with *conventillos'* working-class culture.

MEXICO

Mexico's era of liberal oligarchy began with the restored republic in 1867, a result of Benito Juárez's defeat of Maximilian, the French, and the discredited conservatives. The leader had effectively claimed the presidency twice starting in 1858 when the onset of the War of Reform had compelled President Ignacio Comonfort to resign. The civil war and the subsequent French intervention, however, had forced the beleaguered Juárez to spend much of that time in hiding—attempting to rule the nation far from the capital city. In the absence of competing claimants, Juárez began his first full presidential term in 1867 and immediately began implementing the liberals' political and social vision for the country with the help of important allies that included Porfirio Díaz, one of his most trusted military leaders. Sebastián Lerdo de Tejada, the administration's secretary of foreign relations whose brother had introduced aggressive land reform in the 1850s with the Lerdo Law, also played a prominent role. Other key supporters included Gabino Barreda, the secretary of education, and Matías Romero, the secretary of the treasury. Imbued with a relatively strong sense of cohesion, the liberal cohort oversaw profound political and social transformations.

During Juárez's third term, his administration devoted considerable resources to improving Mexico's transportation infrastructure to facilitate external trade and encourage economic growth. Leaders emphasized the production of primary resources through mining and agriculture. New tax laws created a more attractive economic climate for potential mining investors and the rate of *ejido* privatization and redistribution accelerated. Similar policies continued under the subsequent administration of Sebastián Lerdo de Tejada, who became president after Juárez died in 1872, just a few months into his fourth term. The government oversaw the completion of a vital railroad line connecting Mexico City to Veracruz, launched other railroad projects, and exponentially increased the number of telegraph lines throughout the country.

The consolidation of liberal political control also stimulated education reform as both Juárez and Lerdo directed a vast expansion of public school construction. Access to education varied considerably by region, and tradition and economic need forced many parents to keep their children out of school so they could work and contribute to the family income. Nonetheless, the two liberal leaders' education programs revealed a major social and cultural shift in government circles.

The successes achieved by the Juárez and Lerdo administrations belied serious rifts among Mexico's liberals. Early cracks in the veneer of political unity emerged when Juárez decided to run for a fourth presidential term in 1871. Many of his allies, including prominent members of his administration, opposed that decision, citing "no reelection" as a principal pillar of a strong republic. The two most outspoken challengers, Lerdo and Díaz, both ran for the presidency against Juárez in an attempt to thwart his pursuit of what they labeled "indefinite reelection." The once seemingly unified Liberal Party splintered among Juáristas, Lerdistas, and Porfiristas. When none of the three candidates won an outright majority of the votes, Juárez's allies in congress intervened to award him a fourth term. Díaz reacted by mounting an unsuccessful armed offensive against the president. In 1872, Lerdo took office following Juárez's sudden death, but the issue of reelection resurfaced four years later when he decided to seek a second term. Once again, Díaz rebelled, this time successfully with the Plan of Tuxtepec. When Lerdo fled the country, Díaz claimed the presidency.

One of the great ironies of Porfirio Díaz's career lies in his emphasis on the principle of no reelection in his armed seizure of office. He quickly abandoned this seemingly firmly held belief and, save for a four-year interregnum of his close ally, Manuel González (1880–1884), ruled Mexico for more than three decades, during which he regularly secured reelection.

THE AGE OF GUANO IN PERU

Peru's consolidation of liberal models in the last half of the nineteenth century rested on the emergence of the guano industry. The droppings of bats and seabirds, guano became the basis of natural fertilizers around the world after the German scientist Alexander von Humboldt publicized its nutritive properties following a visit to South America. The Peruvian government made guano a state monopoly in 1841 and negotiated a lucrative contract with a British company. Ramón Castilla—president from 1845 to 1851 and 1855 to 1862—benefited from the trade's expansion. He suppressed opposition, imposed law and order, and stabilized the nation's finances; and his alliances with other powerful liberal politicians allowed him to push through social and economic policies that benefited the oligarchy.

The government invested substantial income derived from the guano industry in infrastructure and social programs. Railroad construction began modestly in the 1850s, but foreign investors fostered significant expansion in the following decade. Castilla and his allies used guano profits to improve primary schooling and to make education more widely available. Notably, Castilla ended the Indian head tax that had replaced the colonial tribute system and abolished slavery in 1854, using guano income to compensate slave owners. These reparations enabled landowners to begin modernizing production as a way to cope with the loss of forced labor. The abolition of slavery had unintended consequences as well. Free blacks often became tenant workers on large estates as part of a system of debt peonage that persisted into the twentieth century. Additionally, in the two decades following the abolition of slavery, approximately 100,000 Chinese immigrants arrived in Peru to work, initially as contract laborers and subsequently in a type of indentured servitude on large estates, in the guano industry, and in railroad construction. The profits generated by these exploited laborers expanded the wealth of the oligarchs and helped to heighten their influence over national development.

COFFEE ELITE IN CENTRAL AMERICA

Liberal oligarchies in Central America developed from the wealthy coffee exporters who came to dominate the political and economic landscape of Guatemala, Costa Rica, El Salvador, and Nicaragua. In these countries, the elite sought to modernize society and usher in progress through political control and a series of liberal reforms.

In Guatemala, the *caudillo* Rafael Carrera's exiled opponents returned to support an eventual liberal takeover by General Justo Rufino Barrios in 1871. Barrios and other liberal dictators wanted to transform society; they professionalized the military and made modest expansions to education. They also attacked the Church, abolishing the tithe, requiring the secularization of marriage and other major life events, and passing land reforms that permitted the confiscation and auction of Church properties. Communal indigenous landholdings suffered forced sale as well in a related attempt to modernize the economy that ultimately benefited the emerging coffee elite and foreign investors. Subsidies to planters and projects to improve roads and ports also encouraged the expansion of coffee exports. In 1877, the Guatemalan government turned to William Nanne to build a Guatemalan railroad. His brief involvement in this endeavor set the stage for increased foreign involvement in Guatemala's railroad industry and foretold the eventual dominance of the United Fruit Company in the country's economy.

A Costa Rican coffee elite had emerged earlier in the nineteenth century, but personal rivalries among the *cafetalero* presidents had resulted in decades of infighting and barracks coups. A more cohesive liberal oligarchy, led by Tomás Guardia, consolidated control in the 1870s and oversaw a period of stability and economic growth. Known as "the Olympians," Guardia and his associates referred to themselves as the "priests of progress." They implemented measures intended to modernize the nation, primarily through renovating the coffee export economy. Identifying woefully inadequate transportation and communications as crucial obstacles to progress, in 1871 Guardia invited the U.S. railroad tycoon Henry Meiggs to launch construction of a rail line between the capital city of San José and the Atlantic Coast. Meiggs's nephew, Henry Meiggs Keith, initiated the project and Costa Rica's national debt expanded rapidly as difficult mountainous terrain slowed progress and forced the government to contract a series of unfavorable foreign loans intended to finance the rail line's completion. Keith's brother, Minor Cooper Keith, took over the failing project in 1883 and negotiated a new contract with the Costa Rican government—one that gave him the authority to restructure the country's foreign debt. He also received complete control over the nation's railway in addition to a land grant that amounted to 7 percent of Costa Rica's national territory.

"Progress at any cost" seemed to be the guiding principle of the Central American elite. Liberal measures ostensibly designed to promote modernization often benefited the nations' oligarchs at the expense of the masses. And many economic policies had the unintended consequence of exposing Central America to foreign exploitation; Costa Rica's contract with Minor Keith had particularly far-reaching ramifications. The mogul's extensive landholdings and monopoly control over the railroad allowed him to expand his commercial activities to include the cultivation and export of bananas. That enterprise became the predecessor to the United Fruit Company, the U.S.-based company that played a pivotal role in Central American economic and political developments throughout much of the twentieth century.

POSITIVISM

As the holy grail of modernization increasingly influenced the ideological foundation of liberal regimes, many leaders began incorporating new social theories gaining popularity in Europe. The tenets of positivism proved especially attractive when applied to economic and social policies in the late nineteenth century. Originally introduced by the French philosopher Auguste Comte, positivism argued that logic, reason, and empiricism should form the basis of knowledge. Rooted in the Enlightenment, positivism favored scientific observation and experimentation, rejecting superstition and speculation. Liberal oligarchies began to see positivist social models as the best way to understand and modernize the nation. "Order and progress" became the catchphrase for the ultimate goals of oligarchic regimes; the pursuit of modernity often came at a high price.

Latin American liberal elite embraced and adapted positivist theories to fit local realities. Of particular concern was how to incorporate the masses into notions of progress when large impoverished populations of indigenous and people of color complicated the social landscape. But Comte provided an answer. Positivism argued that all human intellectual development passed through three stages—starting with a theological stage in which religion and superstition informed knowledge and ending with a scientific stage. Different societies would progress through the developmental stages at different rates; transition to the final stage indicated when they had attained the basis of a modern society. Influenced by this approach, Latin American oligarchs believed that the elite were entering Comte's third stage, but that the masses, still languishing in the first stage, were holding the rest of society back. Accordingly, the leaders devised policies to accelerate underclasses' development and thereby enable a more rapid pace of modernization.

MEXICO

Porfirio Díaz's 34-year rule in Mexico, commonly referred to as the Porfiriato, exemplifies the transition from liberal theories of society and government to those of positivism. Díaz seized power by force, primarily as a response to his predecessor's violation of the ideal of no reelection. Once in office, he justified his three decades of rule by advancing Comte's positivist theories. He also surrounded himself with like-minded advisors, the *Científicos*, who eagerly sought ways to apply this allegedly more scientific view of society in Mexico.

As early as 1867, Gabino Barreda introduced a concept eventually embraced by positivist thinkers not only in Mexico, but also in all of Latin America—that of order and progress. Mexico's *Científicos* viewed the general turmoil that plagued their country in the 1870s as the greatest barrier to national development; as a result, many Porfirian policies sought to correct this problem to achieve progress through modernization.

The underclasses—namely the rural and urban poor—bore the brunt of these policies. The Porfirian elite believed that securing foreign capital offered the most effective way to modernize the country; they sought investors to finance expansion of transportation and communications infrastructure and improve the nation's mining and agricultural output. Decades of political infighting, foreign invasion, and general instability had left many areas of Mexico in a state of disarray. Bandits thrived without effective law enforcement in the countryside, and sanitation problems in large cities facilitated the spread of contagious diseases. The visible signs of extreme poverty throughout the nation testified to the widening disparity in living conditions between the haves and the have-nots. Although Mexico's elite had already reached modernity, positivism's highest level, the *Científicos* believed that the primitive state of the underclasses, languishing on the doctrine's lowest rung, prevented the entire country from achieving true progress.

Wed to such principles, Díaz undertook to impose order so that Mexico could attain economic and social advancement. He strengthened the rural police force started during Benito Juárez's rule to enforce order in the countryside. By dispatching them, as well as the army, to allegedly lawless regions, the Porfirian regime managed to bring rural banditry under control. At the same time, the *rurales* developed a reputation for harsh tactics—a reputation that may or may not have been warranted, but that certainly served as a deterrent.

Díaz also sought to improve foreigners' impressions of urban areas by significantly upgrading the drainage and sanitation systems in Mexico City. His administration also passed a slew of laws to regulate cemeteries and the disposal of dead bodies. Officials in large cities throughout the country passed ordinances governing the habits and appearance of the urban poor in an attempt to impress foreign businessmen. Paralleling the maintenance of order in the countryside, the government took steps to attract foreign investors. *Científicos* cleaned up government finances, restructured the nation's debt, and pared down government bureaucracy. New policies provided tax incentives and subsidies—usually in the form of land grants—to foreign companies willing to invest in industrial enterprises. This collaborative relationship between the Díaz administration and foreign investors revived the mining industry, improved transportation and communications infrastructure, and directed new investment to fledgling industries such as oil and manufacturing.

BRAZIL

The rise of positivist thought in Brazil at the end of the nineteenth century coincided with a move away from slavery and a growing desire to abolish the monarchy. Little had changed politically in the country since it declared independence from Portugal in 1822. Descendants of the Portuguese ruling dynasty—first Pedro I and then his son, Pedro II—had retained monarchical control in Brazil while the landed oligarchy exerted significant influence over the nation's political and economic direction. Changes in population and the economy, however, had altered the country.

Brazil's economy continued to rely primarily on slave labor during most of the nineteenth century, although the importance of the institution gradually decayed in the last half of the century. A shift in agricultural production from sugar cane in the northeast to coffee in the south began in the 1820s as global demand for the commodity grew. By mid-century, Brazil was growing more than half of the world's coffee supply; this boom in production initially brought about a surge in imported African slaves to work on the new coffee plantations. But Brazil abolished the slave trade in 1850 in response to international abolitionist pressures, and a gradual dismantling of African slavery in the country began. Within two decades, the dwindling slave labor supply compelled coffee planters to adopt modern agricultural techniques and to begin relying on a paid labor force. The 1871 Law of the Free Womb offered manumission to those born after that date and the 1884 Sexagenarian Law emancipated slaves over the age of 60. Complete abolition occurred in 1888 with the passage of the Golden Law.

The flourishing coffee farms in the south emerged as a mainstay of agricultural production, and provincial governments recruited European immigrants to work as agricultural colonists, or *colonos*. Under state or private sponsorship, some 250,000 immigrants came to Brazil in 1882 under an exploitative form of indenture that required a specified length of servitude. Other immigrants from Germany, Italy, and Poland and Basques from Spain settled in the south after 1880, also providing labor for large-scale coffee cultivation following the use of slash-and-burn methods to clear jungle and forests.

Benefiting from new manufacturing and service activities in growing urban areas, by the 1880s, an emerging middle class began to question the political status quo. The shift of economic power to the coffee-growing region of São Paulo and the emergence of incipient modern industries also brought demands for bringing the country up to date and allowed an emerging republican movement to thrive. Progressive-minded professionals and other intellectuals in numerous provinces initially formed political clubs as a venue for exchanging new ideas. Soon, formal Republican parties replaced local clubs and their influence broadened to the national level as well. These political bodies proved fertile ground for positivist ideas. Members saw both slavery and monarchy as obstacles to progress. In the 1880s, Republican platforms began merging with the agendas of military officers, many of whom fully accepted the positivist prescription for Brazil's future.

Benjamin Constant, a professor at the National Military Academy, played a prominent role in interpreting positivist philosophy according to Brazil's unique circumstances and spreading those ideas to military cadets in the classroom. The growing middle class, which included military officers, particularly embraced positivist ideas because family status had long defined traditional society and those not born into privilege found few opportunities for advancement. The military class and other mid-level professionals interpreted positivism's emphasis on order and scientific principles as an attractive alternative for organizing society. Constant allied with Manuel Deodoro da Fonseca and in 1887 the two created the *Clube Militar* in Rio de Janeiro, which allowed them to recruit like-minded military officers and organize their opposition to the government more formally.

In 1889, a small force led by Deodoro deposed Pedro II and declared the Republic of Brazil. Deodoro became the country's first president, and two years later a new constitution incorporated many positivist ideas. The republic's early leaders promoted industrial development, invited European immigration, and sought to expand education. The national flag, adopted in 1889, features the words "ordem e progresso" (order and progress) emblazoned across the center as a tribute to the intellectual foundations of the Brazilian republic.

VENEZUELA AND THE *GUZMANATO*

In Venezuela, an era of sustained stability began with the regime of Antonio Guzmán Blanco in 1870. The *caudillo* rose to power following the long period of civil war between liberals and conservatives marked by the Federal War and the Blue Revolution. As president, he ruled for 18 years in a nearly uninterrupted dictatorship known as the *Guzmanato*. Espousing theories of modernization, the *Guzmanato* became defined by the trappings of progress. The dictator brought regional *caudillos* under control and implemented liberal reforms to strengthen the state and diminish the power of the Catholic Church. He oversaw a stabilization and expansion of the economy as increased revenues allowed him to improve the nation's ports, roadways, and railroads. He invested in education and embarked on beautification projects in major cities. National monuments and new public buildings inspired by European architecture gave the illusion of modernity.

Political and economic stability accompanied by the visual markers of progress allowed Guzmán Blanco to attract loans and foreign investments and earned him the moniker "the Illustrious American." But the veneer of modernity masked underlying weaknesses and his policies did little to correct the exploitation and social inequality that kept much of the population in poverty. The dictator took advantage of economic growth to line his own pockets and the majority of the country never benefitted from the progress he brought to Venezuela. Furthermore, although part of a late generation of *caudillos*, the ruler maintained order by the same reliance on personalism and repression that had characterized earlier Latin American strongmen. Much of the seeming stability and progress achieved during the *Guzmanato* came to a halt after a coup ousted the dictator in 1888.

PERU

Many Peruvian political and intellectual elite turned to positivism after the nation's devastating defeat by Chile in the War of the Pacific. A merchant oligarchy emerged from the Civilista Party founded in 1872 with the goal of promoting electoral reform and economic modernity; this group exercised enormous influence in Peruvian society in the late decades of the nineteenth century. Early initiatives included infrastructure development—such as the expansion of the railroad and coastal port renovations—and some education reforms. Typical of Latin American elite at the time, President Manuel Pardo and other party leaders embraced scientific reasoning as a way to modernize the nation. In particular, they adopted a "civilizing mission" toward the nation's indigenous peoples, viewing that population's widespread illiteracy and poverty as evidence of a developmental gap in society. Civilista leaders opened Indian schools with the intention of "Hispanicizing" indigenous youth through instruction in Spanish and the teaching of modern and civilizing trades. Reinforcing the ruling elite's perception of an "Indian problem," a native peasant rebellion erupted in the Huaylas province on the heels of the War of the Pacific. The uprising further convinced Peruvian positivists that achieving order and progress required assimilating and civilizing the indigenous population.

Many Peruvian leaders argued that the nation's native peoples lacked patriotism and blamed them for the nation's defeat by Chile in the war. Manuel González Prada, Clorinda Matto de Turner, and other intellectuals generally agreed with this assertion, but ultimately pointed to enduring mistreatment and exploitation of the indigenous as the root cause of the nation's developmental shortfalls. Nevertheless, national policy in the late nineteenth century continued to look to assimilation and civilizing measures to resolve the so-called Indian problem. Like positivist leaders elsewhere in Latin America, Peruvian politicians encouraged European immigration as a way to elevate the nation and "dilute" the native population.

Other modernizing efforts took shape as government leaders attempted to address fiscal problems. Peru had unwisely relied on foreign borrowing and commodity revenue during the guano age and had printed money during the war with Chile. The resulting significant debt led President Andrés Avelino Cáceres to negotiate the Grace Contract in 1889. The agreement created the Peruvian Corporation, a group of British creditors who forgave Peru's fiscal liabilities in exchange for command over the nation's railroad industry. Monetary stability and economic growth resulted, but at the cost of allowing substantial foreign control over Peru's resources.

SOCIAL LIMITS OF PROGRESS

Liberal oligarchs and positivist elite often pointed to heightened stability, economic growth, and the expansion of modern infrastructure to argue that their formulas for national progress worked. Indeed, after decades of stagnation following independence, exports from Peru and Brazil nearly doubled between 1850 and 1870; those from Argentina and Chile had tripled by 1890. During the Porfiriato, Mexican mining exports alone jumped 650 percent. By the end of the century, vast networks of roads and rail lines connected formerly remote areas of Latin America to booming urban centers and newly modernized ports. In 1890, Brazil had more than 8,000 kilometers of rail lines and Mexico boasted more than 11,000 kilometers. Populations grew dramatically, fueled in many areas by successful strategies to encourage immigration. In the 100 years following independence, more than 6 million immigrants settled in Argentina and more than 4 million relocated to Brazil. Modern urban centers with architectural features that rivaled some European cities became emblematic of liberalism's and positivism's alleged success.

But such measures of development also belied numerous structural weaknesses and social inequalities that eventually exposed the thin veneer of progress. Economic growth often came at the expense of pervasive foreign control of national resources and new infrastructure. This trend often gave outside interests enormous influence over national politics and allowed them to export substantial profits instead of reinvesting them in Latin America. The concentration of land in latifundia continued—sometimes in the hands of foreign owners, other times in the hands of national elite. The continued ascendency of large estates squeezed out communal landholdings by indigenous peoples and created an ever-growing class of agrarian peasants often trapped in exploitative debt peonage.

A majority of the masses in Latin America remained tied to the countryside, but as urban centers emerged, rapid populations in cities brought a host of problems. A lack of sanitation and public services created numerous health crises. Crowded and dirty housing facilities fostered the spread of disease, and hazardous conditions in the rudimentary manufacturing sector put workers at risk. Positivist regimes attempted to make modest improvements in social welfare programs by building orphanages, hospitals, prisons, and asylums. But attempts to control prostitution in Mexico, Argentina, and Brazil used purportedly scientific reasoning to hold female sex workers responsible for moral decay and the spread of disease. Resulting regulations ultimately served to marginalize nonelite women. The elite had long associated crime and poverty with alcohol consumption, and they passed ordinances to restrict the consumption of inexpensive spirits as a way to police the masses. Positivist criminology sought scientific explanations for deviant behavior, using biology to connect crime to race and poverty. All too often, dominant social theories asserted that science justified the persecution and exploitation of the poor.

Whereas positivists claimed to favor an open political system, many relinquished this principle in favor of economic progress and social stability. In Argentina, Brazil, and Peru, a type of limited oligarchic democracy emerged. In Mexico, Guatemala, and Venezuela, a more autocratic system of enlightened despotism prevailed. Positivist leaders in these countries often resorted to violence and violated individual rights to maintain order. In all cases, restricted electoral participation meant that political decisions fell to a small number of elite.

Some regimes achieved measurable advancements in education at the end of the nineteenth century. The efforts of Sarmiento and others in Argentina helped to expand the number of schools by the end of the century, but only limited access in the countryside endured. Education also expanded in Mexico under Díaz, although by the end of his regime Mexico had a scant 12,000 schools to service a population of more than 15 million. But leaders in these countries, as elsewhere, often devised advancements in education as a way to civilize the masses and force them to adopt preferred indicators of civilized society. In many instances, positivists' propensity for showcasing modernity merely disguised the inequalities of the underclasses instead of offering relief. By the end of the century, most of the population remained illiterate and in poverty; contagious diseases and high rates of infant mortality prevailed; and the exploitation of rural peasants and urban workers endured.

The consolidation of rule under liberal oligarchies that believed in positivism brought political stability and economic growth. By the end of the century, relatively smooth transitions of power among the governing elite had replaced violent civil wars. Stability allowed Latin American leaders to attract foreign investors, whose capital helped fund massive infrastructure projects and contributed to widespread modernization efforts. But major social changes also took root. The development of a new manufacturing sector in rapidly growing cities gave rise to an urban labor class, fueled in some countries by an influx of European immigrants. The intensification of latifundia in the countryside left even more landless peasants under the exploitation of large estates. Social and political inequalities persisted. As populations increased, so, too, did the expectations of electoral rights, even as oligarchs limited political participation. The paradox in nineteenth-century development—that it benefited a select few and excluded the masses—set the stage for populism in the coming decades.

Primary Source

José María Ramos Mejía was an Argentine historian who embraced a scientific approach to studying society. His ideas epitomized the positivist trends that became prominent throughout Latin America.

SOURCE: Oscar Terán et al., *Positivismo y nación en la Argentina: con una selección de textos de J. M. Ramos Mejía, A. Alvarez, C. O. Bunge y J. Ingenieros* (Buenos Aires: Puntosur, 1987), 92–94.

In our political biology, the modern multitudes have not yet embarked on their true function. They are like a still-evolving larva, or better yet, an embryo that appears to maintain a *static* state awaiting the next stage of development. As I stated, there are no properly political multitudes (except in very rare and well-known exceptions), because among other reasons, there does not exist the passionate ardor of political sentiment, the love of a flag tied to the welfare of life, sectarian hatred, class or caste rage. Since it does not form freely, and are no problems which impassion and determine its constitution, which we usually see in the streets, more so than multitudes, are artificial groups, composed of operatives without enthusiasm, led by their bosses in those socialist comedies that often depict reckless *businessmen*; dependent laborers who on the threat of losing their modest jobs may express a false enthusiasm. They do not weigh in the elections, from which emanated the force that caused old England to transform itself without revolutions and upheavals. Diluted *demonstrations*, as we call these motley meetings of the kind, candidates without elections and weary musicians, many of their members will vote against what they endorsed, or inflame with their presence and their cries the ambition of the adversary they vilified in meetings the day before.

. . .

It is also true that all these hoodlums: alcoholics, vagrants and idlers who populate the police stations are, so to speak, the *harbingers* of misery, wayward birds from sea, trumpeting far off lands. But they need to go about so that this city becomes irritated through the teeth because of this disgrace.

SUGGESTIONS FOR FURTHER READING

Barman, Roderick J. *Citizen Emperor: Pedro II and the Making of Brazil, 1825–1891*. Stanford, CA: Stanford University Press, 1999.

Beezley, William H. *Judas at the Jockey Club and Other Episodes of Porfirian Mexico*. 2nd ed. Lincoln: University of Nebraska Press, 2004.

Bethell, Leslie. *The Abolition of the Brazilian Slave Trade*. Cambridge: Cambridge University Press, 2009.

Foster, David William. *The Argentine Generation of 1880: Ideology and Cultural Texts*. Columbia: University of Missouri Press, 1990.

Gootenberg, Paul. *Imagining Development: Economic Ideas in Peru's "Fictitious Prosperity" of Guano, 1840–1880*. Berkeley: University of California Press, 1993.

Graham, Richard, Thomas E. Skidmore, Aline Helg, and Alan Knight. *The Idea of Race in Latin America, 1870–1940*. ACLS Humanities E-Book (Project). Austin: University of Texas Press, 1990.

Haber, Stephen, Armando Razo, and Noel Maurer. *The Politics of Property Rights: Political Instability, Credible Commitments, and Economic Growth in Mexico, 1876–1929*. Cambridge: Cambridge University Press, 2003.

Hale, Charles A. *The Transformation of Liberalism in Late Nineteenth-Century Mexico* Princeton, NJ: Princeton University Press, 1989.

McCreery, David. *Development and the State in Reforma Guatemala, 1871–1885*. Athens, OH: University of Ohio, 1983.

Nouwen, Millie Lewis. *Oy, My Buenos Aires: Jewish Immigrants and the Creation of Argentine National Identity*. Albuquerque: University of New Mexico Press, 2013.

Nuccetelli, Susana, *A Companion to Latin American Philosophy*. Malden, MA: Blackwell, 2013.

CHAPTER 18

The Age of Informal Imperialism

The nature of foreign interventions in Latin America began to change in the final decades of the nineteenth century. Prior to the 1880s, interventions and foreign conflicts had generally arisen from boundary disputes or other attempts to acquire territory. Such wars contributed to decades of instability throughout the region and often worsened the political infighting that plagued struggling governments. After 1880, foreign interventions became less about territorial acquisition and instead resembled the "new imperialism" evident in other parts of the world. In Latin America, the United States came to dominate by employing economic power, supplemented by selective use of military force, to impose a type of "informal imperialism" that contrasted markedly with that of European rivals.

The altered nature of interventions in Latin America also signified the rise of the United States as a regional and world power. As its dominance grew, so did the country's flagrant paternalism and racism in many of its interactions with its southern neighbors. The ascendency of U.S. commercial influence provided considerable leverage in swaying Latin American political elite; and leaders in Washington began invoking the Monroe Doctrine in unprecedented ways. Oftentimes, new treaties and constitutions codified the U.S. role as "protector" and provided a legal rationale for lengthy military occupations. Such involvement in Latin America reinforced a disproportionate power relationship that became a part of the expansion of U.S. hegemony worldwide. It also had a substantial social and cultural impact because the U.S. presence in Cuba and Panama helped to usher in significant improvements in health and sanitation. Cultural reactions to "Yankee imperialism" inspired Latin American writers to pen numerous critiques that also fueled an ever-increasing antagonism toward the United States.

NEW ATTITUDES IN THE UNITED STATES

With the major exception of territorial acquisition in Mexico and the ill-fated adventures of filibusters before the 1860s, direct military intervention in Latin America marked a shift in U.S. foreign policy. Indeed, from the beginning of the Civil War through the 1880s, the American public as well as government leaders had remained relatively isolationist. During that time, public opinion favored expansion, but many denounced forcibly taking foreign land. Opponents of slavery, in particular, had decried Polk's decision to invade Mexico. Henry David Thoreau, Ralph Waldo Emerson, and other prominent literary figures condemned the war on moral grounds and a persistent wariness of imperialism unfolded. Many politicians and citizens believed it violated foundational tenets of American historical character—namely independence, democracy, and a rejection of colonialism. They viewed the lack of formal colonies as a distinctive and important difference that distinguished the United States from European rivals.

Furthermore, after the Civil War, national leaders focused on internal economic and technological advances; they limited further territorial expansion to the northwestern lands purchased from the British in the 1840s and the new western possessions acquired after the war with Mexico. Internal development and ample land within its borders provided the United States the same advantages that European powers gained from colonies—access to raw materials and markets for finished goods. An immense and seemingly sparsely populated territory to the west facilitated the expansion of industrial production.

In the 1880s and 1890s, attitudes in the United States began to shift toward a more active foreign policy. A worldwide industrial revolution under way in manufacturing, transportation, and the dissemination of information had created global competition for raw materials such as iron ore, minerals, timber, and foodstuffs. As profound transformations realigned trade networks, the enduring belief in restrictive mercantilist models faded and laissez-faire approaches to economic policy gained favor. Simultaneously, industrializing nations competed more intensely for both resources and markets.

In Latin America, the British emerged as the leading trade partner almost immediately after independence and broadened considerably this initial economic dominance after 1850. In the United States, settling western territories, maintaining a political balance over the institution of slavery, and eventually fighting a violent and protracted civil war kept leaders distracted while the British expanded their grip on Latin American markets. Their investors funded many of the infrastructure improvements undertaken by liberal oligarchic regimes, and merchants made important inroads with industrial goods. By 1870, the British provided more than 30 percent of both imports and exports throughout Latin America, and that figure continued to increase toward the end of the century. German and French interests offered the most serious competition, but they accounted for only 10–20 percent in their most important markets of Brazil and Argentina. The prominence of this investment and trade encouraged Latin American elite to adopt European fashion, food, and recreational activities as markers of high culture during the era of positivism.

Economic penetration in Latin America formed part of a larger strategy among Europe's industrializing nations as they contended for global supremacy. Whereas the British and French had long competed for markets and colonies, political unification in Germany and Italy enabled these countries to begin pursuing overseas colonization. Japan and Russia also expanded their reach. By 1900, imperial powers controlled roughly one-fifth of the world's territory. As colonies in Asia and Africa provided industrializing nations with cheap labor and raw materials, U.S. political and business leaders took notice. They worried that the nation would fall behind in the dynamic global market without comparable access to colonies.

The U.S. concern about competition intensified with the settlement of the western territories. In 1890, the U.S. Census Office had declared that a discernible frontier no longer existed in the U.S. West. Three years later, the historian Frederick Jackson Turner presented his "frontier thesis," in which he considered the impact that the final settling of these lands would have on American culture. He argued that the frontier had become a fundamental part of American character by providing both opportunity and challenge. Americans had to develop strength, inventiveness, and an adventuresome spirit to overcome the obstacles posed by savage and unsettled lands. Turner and others worried that the closing of the frontier would bring a crisis in American character—a crisis that involvement beyond U.S. borders might mitigate.

Other U.S. leaders began to promote greater attention to foreign policy out of a belief that the country's political and economic system and values were superior to all others. Consequently, the United States had a moral obligation to share them with uninformed and less fortunate areas of the world. Intellectuals provided support for this conviction. Herbert Spencer's theories of social Darwinism found traction among many public figures, who promoted the idea of a U.S. civilizing mission in the nonindustrialized world. Rudyard Kipling's poem, "The White Man's Burden," exemplified these attitudes, as did the writings of the aspiring sociologist William Graham Sumner. Adherents of these racist and largely Protestant notions believed that, because of its ethnic composition and cultural history, Latin America desperately needed the guidance of a civilized society. Not surprisingly, these devoted disciples of American exceptionalism concluded that the United States alone could provide the necessary tutelage.

A final argument that propelled a shift in attitudes toward foreign relations in the United States was "national greatness." Influential intellectuals and politicians, including Brooks Adams, Alfred Thayer Mahan, Henry Cabot Lodge, and Theodore Roosevelt, argued that great civilizations arose through military expansion and heroic actions. Some insisted that only armed confrontation against an external enemy could imbue the sense of national unity still lacking decades after the Civil War. The appeal of these theories in the late nineteenth century laid the foundations for an informal U.S. imperialism that opened Latin America to further exploitation.

EXPANSION OF U.S. TRADE

Following the Civil War, the United States became increasingly reliant on foreign trade to fuel economic growth. Overall exports tripled between 1870 and 1900, prompting businessmen and politicians to consider more closely the colonial expansion of rival countries. To stymie the growing European interests in the Western Hemisphere, many U.S. leaders began looking to Latin American markets. Because of the proximity, trade with the Caribbean islands, Mexico, and Central America grew considerably. By the end of the century, the United States provided more than 60 percent of those countries' imports and had also become the leading market for their raw materials.

The administration of Ulysses S. Grant made several bold overtures toward expanding U.S. influence in the Caribbean. Prior to the Civil War, pro-slavery interests had favored the U.S. acquisition of Cuba and Santo Domingo (today's Dominican Republic); after the war, these pressures resurfaced as Caribbean trade expanded. In 1870, Grant negotiated an annexation treaty with Dominican leaders and justified his actions as a way to bolster national security as well as U.S.

economic influence in the region. He argued that Santo Domingo would provide inexpensive goods for the U.S. public and become a market for the growing manufacturing sector. He also asserted that the annexation would allow the United States to exert influence in other areas of Latin America, specifically to bring an end to slavery in Cuba and Puerto Rico. Although Grant invoked the Monroe Doctrine as a legal rationale for expanding U.S. territorial possessions in Latin America, his annexation treaty failed to win Senate support.

VENEZUELA AND THE BOUNDARY DISPUTE

The major shift in U.S. attitudes toward involvement in foreign affairs became evident in the simmering border dispute between Venezuela and Guyana (British Guiana at the time). The British had taken over the colony on Venezuela's eastern border in 1803 after a long period of Dutch rule, and conflict over the boundary arose immediately. Those squabbles worsened when the Venezuelan government protested the results of a British survey to mark the official border in 1840. Discoveries of gold deposits in the disputed territory intensified the conflict, but the South American nation's civil wars prevented the two sides from reaching a diplomatic resolution. In 1877, Venezuela appealed to the United States to arbitrate the dispute as a way to protect U.S. trade interests in the region. Although such mediation had become a favored strategy for negotiating diplomatic disputes, U.S. leaders hesitated to challenge the British and refused to become involved.

Just 10 years later, the United States displayed a substantially different attitude. Continued imperialist maneuvers by European rivals alarmed many leaders who worried that those expansionist aims would challenge the claims of the Monroe Doctrine. When Venezuela severed diplomatic relations with Great Britain in 1887, the first administration of President Grover Cleveland tried to convince the European power to accept U.S. arbitration. British leaders resisted those pressures until 1895, when hemispheric diplomacy took on new urgency under Cleveland's second administration.

Despite being disregarded for much of the nineteenth century, the Monroe Doctrine took on new life. And the Western Hemisphere idea—delineating distinct spheres separating Europe and the Americas—reemerged. William L. Scruggs, the former ambassador to Venezuela, published a treatise entitled *British Aggression in Venezuela, or the Monroe Doctrine on Trial* that invoked the tenets laid out in 1823; he distributed it to members of Congress and other politicians. Cleveland took a position similar to that of Scruggs, and in 1895 his secretary of state, Richard Olney, delivered a lengthy dispatch defining the U.S. position to the British government. The secretary invoked the Monroe Doctrine and stated that the United States would consider it oppressive and injurious if Britain refused to submit to U.S. arbitration in the border dispute with Venezuela.

Olney's statement boldly interpreted Monroe's original position, applying the long-standing foreign policy for the first time to European colonies that predated it. He brazenly asserted U.S. dominance throughout the Americas. When the British flatly rejected his demands, Cleveland issued a bellicose message to Congress, essentially championing the Venezuelan position and threatening a military response. Public opinion and the U.S. media generally supported this combative stance and the British not only agreed to arbitration, but also conceded to Olney's new broad interpretation of the Monroe Doctrine. Although a final resolution in 1899 ultimately favored the British, the diplomatic jockeying and assertions of U.S. hegemony that characterized the episode illustrate the way the United States was reshaping the Western Hemisphere idea. The rhetoric of U.S. dominance also served as a precursor for the new informal imperialism emerging in U.S.–Latin American relations.

CUBA

Cuba pursued independence within the atmosphere of increasing jingoism and greater attention to foreign policy in the United States. Spain had retained both Puerto Rico and Cuba since the early 1500s. After the metropolis lost its mainland possessions, the latter island had come to symbolize the greatness of the Spanish imperial system. Plantation agriculture, supported by a large slave labor force, had long been the backbone of the Caribbean economy. The Haitian Revolution initiated the dismantling of Española's plantation economies, but enabled Cuba's sugar industry to achieve unprecedented success. Additionally, the Spanish Crown altered its trade restrictions, allowing Cuba to trade more openly with foreign nations. Most prosperous planters remained content, despite their fear of a slave uprising, and showed no interest in their island gaining independence in the early 1800s.

Slavery and the Ten Years' War

Incipient talks of separation from Spain emerged as the planter elite responded to transatlantic abolitionist movements gaining momentum in the 1840s. Although the Crown had officially abolished the importation of new slaves in 1817, Africans had continued to reach Cuba via illegal trade networks. Many of the island's elite, moreover, scorned the Spanish Crown for succumbing to British pressure to ban the slave trade. With the rising costs of owning chattel an increasing burden, many planters worried that the termination signaled a first step toward eventual abolition. Some turned to leaders in the U.S. South, hoping to join the union as a slave state.

The outbreak of the U.S. Civil War temporarily ended thoughts of annexation and also affected the Cuban economy. As southern plantations in the United States fell into ruin, demand for Cuban sugar grew, tying the island's economic well-being ever closer to U.S. markets. The Civil War also affected slavery in Cuba. Emancipation in the United States motivated international abolitionist groups to continue urging Spain to end the forced labor system in its remaining colonies. In Cuba itself, the Reformist Party established in the 1860s demanded tariff reform and a host of measures to modernize the island's economy, not the least of which included a gradual elimination of the slave trade.

Anti-slavery advocates in Cuba offered the first real challenge to Spanish rule when Carlos Manuel de Céspedes launched a rebellion in the eastern part of the island. His 1868 *Grito de Yara* served as the colony's declaration of independence and began the ill-fated Ten Years' War. Céspedes and many planters who supported him freed their slaves and created an army. He quickly established a provisional government and drafted a constitution that formalized numerous economic reforms and explicitly called for the abolition of slavery. Céspedes also wanted the United States to annex Cuba. While the U.S. government remained silent about the uprising and the issue of annexation, the revolutionary leader's supporters in the United States raised money and provided aid to the Cuban independence movement.

The issue of annexation split the rebellion's principals and led to infighting. Eventually, the war reached a stalemate and in 1878 most insurgent leaders signed the Treaty of Zanjón, which conceded some of the reforms they had been seeking. The accord also granted freedom to slaves who had fought on behalf of the rebellion and conferred amnesty to members of the revolutionary army. Although the treaty did not end Cuban slavery, it marked a major turning point in the abolitionist cause. Pressure began to mount to terminate completely the forced bondage. In 1880, the Spanish government passed a law that called for gradual emancipation after an eight-year *patronato*, or apprenticeship. A revised law in 1886 ended the *patronato* and abolished slavery for good.

Cuban Independence

The quest for independence continued after the Ten Years' War. Rebel leaders who had refused to accept the Treaty of Zanjón had fled into exile abroad, where many resumed their efforts to free their homeland. Three of the exiles—José Martí, Máximo Gómez, and Antonio Maceo—joined together in 1895 to launch a new offensive against the Spanish in eastern Cuba. Although Martí perished a mere six weeks into the fighting and Maceo a year later, the rebellion gained strength under Gómez and other leaders. Primarily using guerrilla tactics, the Cuban rebels quickly took control of the eastern portion of the island.

As guerrilla warfare spread throughout the Oriente province, Spanish officials ordered General Valeriano Weyler to defeat the insurgency swiftly. The general understood that distinguishing belligerents from innocent civilians posed one of his greatest difficulties. Furthermore, many Cubans refrained from participating as combatants, but contributed indirectly by providing supplies and aid to the rebels. To confront these challenges in regions with a particularly strong guerrilla presence, Weyler relocated residents to rudimentary and ill-equipped internment camps. There, more than 100,000 Cubans died of disease, neglect, and starvation, an outcome that brought heavy criticism of the general. The insurgency and Spain's counterinsurgency campaign devastated the population, catching many innocent bystanders in the fighting. The guerrilla war, moreover, caused the island's economy to falter. Although Weyler succeeded in slowing the rebel advance, the independence movement continued to gain ground.

As word of Spanish atrocities appeared in the press, the U.S. public reacted contemptuously toward what many perceived as tyrannical and despicable acts. Media moguls sensed an opportunity to sell newspapers by highlighting sensationalistic stories in a strategy that became known as yellow journalism. The *New York Journal*, under the direction of William Randolph Hearst, and its competitor *The New York World*, under the guidance of Joseph Pulitzer, provided graphic details of Spanish atrocities that at times were extreme exaggerations or even complete fabrications. Yellow journalism convinced some readers to press for U.S. military involvement, but prominent businessmen worried that trade disruptions would worsen if the United States became involved. They urged U.S. leaders to stay out of the conflict.

President Grover Cleveland had maintained a neutral stance toward Cuba, but as his term came to a close and William McKinley succeeded him, the official position toward the war began to change. McKinley demanded that Spain curb General Weyler's actions, backing his words with the threat of armed intervention. A few months later, General Ramón Blanco replaced Weyler and abruptly ended his repressive tactics. Although the Spanish government also granted Cuba greater political autonomy in an effort to end the rebellion peacefully, its measures had little effect because independence leaders vowed to settle for nothing less than complete sovereignty.

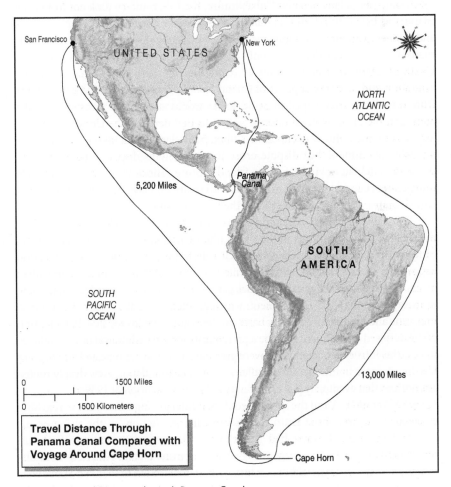

Map 18.1 Travel Distance through Panama Canal

In January 1898, McKinley ordered the warship USS *Maine* to anchor in Havana harbor as a demonstration of military strength and to protect U.S. property on the island should the need arise. Just a few weeks later, the *Maine* mysteriously exploded. War hawks in the United States insisted that the Spanish had mined the harbor in a cruel and inhuman act and demanded vengeance. The president wanted to avoid armed confrontation and offered to purchase Cuba, but when Spain rejected the proposal, Congress declared war. The campaign began as a dual offensive against Spanish strongholds in the Caribbean and in the Pacific. U.S. naval operations successfully took control of Guam and the Philippines in August 1898; by the end of the year, the Spanish had also formally relinquished Cuba. Under the peace terms, Spain turned over control of Guam and Puerto Rico to the United States; and the United States purchased the Philippines for $20 million. Although the Teller Amendment, a provision passed by the U.S. Congress in conjunction with the declaration of war, guaranteed Cuba's independence, the particulars of that status provoked much debate in the coming years.

While politicians debated Cuba's future, the U.S. military took control of the island and began to rebuild its damaged or destroyed infrastructure. New roads and bridges facilitated economic recovery, as did repairs and improvements to railroads. Occupation leaders also confronted the deadly tropical diseases and other health problems that had become epidemic during the conflict. They improved sanitation and, with the support of Cuban health experts, eliminated yellow fever from the island. They hoped these advances would attract U.S. investors to Cuba and reinforce the growing economic networks that tied it to the United States.

During the military occupation, Cuban politicians began taking steps to form a viable government, but dispute arose immediately as disparate factions competed to articulate a vision for the island's future. Those who wanted complete independence found themselves at odds with rivals who favored annexation by the United States. Pressures coming from the United States complicated the debate.

U.S. leaders had long assumed a paternalistic attitude toward Cuba. Public statements and media portrayals of the island often reflected racist attitudes and an assumption that Cubans were incapable of self-rule. In 1901, a constitutional convention approved a charter that allowed the United States considerable influence in Cuban affairs. Occupation leaders exploited delegates' relative impotence and required them to incorporate the Platt Amendment, which granted the United States the right to intervene and to establish military bases on the island. Cubans resisted, but adoption of the despised amendment became a prerequisite for the withdrawal of U.S. military forces. This intrusion on national sovereignty paved the way for repeated and flagrant U.S. interference in internal Cuban affairs. From this foundation grew deeply rooted animosities that eventually played out in the Cuban Revolution of 1959.

The War of 1898 and the subsequent U.S. military occupation had far-reaching consequences throughout Latin America. Earlier predictions of the rising dominance of the United States had materialized. Fear of armed intervention and resentment at growing U.S. hegemony came to dominate Latin America's relationship with its northern neighbor. Victory over Spain also left the United States with overseas possessions, which facilitated an expanded military and economic presence throughout the hemisphere and in the Pacific Ocean as well. The Philippines, Guam, Puerto Rico, and Guantanamo Bay in Cuba became the sites of strategic military installations in the twentieth century. Together with Hawaii, which the United States annexed in 1898, these islands formed a ring of defense bases around the Western Hemisphere. This enhanced armed presence allowed the United States to exert enormous influence as it embarked on an era of informal imperialism in Latin America. Without resorting to outright conquest or colonization, the rising global power could easily flex its muscle to suppress potential opposition to friendly regimes or to coerce the compliance of recalcitrant ones. Over the next 30 years, a pattern of armed intervention and economic interference emerged, breeding bitterness and hostility in increasingly exploited populations. More broadly, the new network of U.S. possessions encircling the hemisphere represented part of a larger strategy in the U.S. drive to become a major military power in the coming years.

PANAMA

As U.S. leaders were consolidating the nation's influence in Cuba, another brazen display of informal imperialism took place in South America. Theodore Roosevelt, who subscribed to theories touting war as a path to national greatness, had resigned his post as assistant secretary of the Navy to lead a volunteer unit in the war against Spain. He saw firsthand the challenges a two-ocean war posed to the maritime forces. Sending naval ships from the Philippine theater in the Pacific to the Cuban theater in the Caribbean required sailing an extra 8,000 miles to round Cape Horn at the tip of South America—a delay with strategic implications. After he became president in 1901, Roosevelt sought a solution to these military transportation concerns. Furthermore, U.S. leaders had long desired a quick and less expensive way of moving ships between the Atlantic and Pacific oceans to facilitate oceangoing trade. The new military bases in Cuba, Hawaii, Guam, and the Philippines made more efficient interoceanic transportation all the more urgent.

The United States was not the first foreign power to show interest in a transisthmian canal. Aware of the expense and risk of transporting silver and other merchandise by river or via mule on miserable roads across the Isthmus of Panama, the Spanish Crown had considered the possibility of building a canal there as early as the sixteenth century. The narrowest stretch of land between the Caribbean Sea and the Pacific Ocean cut through Panama. A large lake draining into the Caribbean Sea via the San Juan River made Nicaragua a viable alternative as well. The Spanish never pursued the canal project, and Panama continued to serve as an important site for interoceanic land transport for more than two centuries.

Following independence, new trade opportunities with Latin America prompted U.S. and European leaders to consider financing a transisthmian canal. In 1850, the U.S. and British governments signed the Clayton–Bulwer Treaty, which prevented either country from undertaking such a project unilaterally in Nicaragua. Since at that time neither country had sufficient resources to build a canal, the idea of a Central American interoceanic waterway languished for several decades. In 1879, a French company initiated a new project in Panama, a former province of the Viceroyalty of New Granada and part of what became the Republic of Colombia. Ferdinand de Lesseps, who had overseen the construction of the Suez Canal, led the endeavor, but a series of logistical and design problems bankrupted the company in 1889. For the next decade, French investors lobbied the United States to purchase and complete the abandoned project. As the Spanish–American War drew to a close, U.S. leaders became increasingly enamored by the potential benefits of an interoceanic canal. With vocal encouragement from Roosevelt, Congress approved moving forward with the Panamanian project in 1902.

U.S. Secretary of State John Hay negotiated with the Colombian government to allow the United States to build a canal in the Panamanian province. The 1903 Hay–Herrán Treaty would have given the United States construction rights and granted it control of lands around the waterway in exchange for $10 million plus a $250,000 annuity after nine years. But the violent Thousand Days' War (1899–1902) left Colombia's political system in shambles and its government desperate for revenue. Consequently, its senate rejected the treaty, hoping to extract more favorable payment terms with further negotiations.

Meanwhile, local discontent had been brewing in Panama. Rugged and inhospitable terrain kept the Panamanian province culturally and geographically isolated from the rest of Colombia and made land travel between them virtually impossible. Although the isthmus served as a land passage route between the Caribbean Sea and the Pacific Ocean, much of the proceeds from transit tolls ended up in government coffers in Bogotá. On several earlier occasions, the province's leaders had entertained ideas of secession, but concessions by the Colombian government had forestalled any real attempts at independence. Ironically, when efforts at peaceful conciliation failed, it was U.S. forces that put down separatist insurgencies in 1885 as part of a bilateral military accord with the Colombian government. But with Colombia's rejection of the Hay–Herrán Treaty, Roosevelt resolved to negotiate directly with local political leaders in Panama.

Angry and frustrated with the Colombian senate's refusal to move forward with the canal, Panamanians welcomed U.S. involvement. A separatist movement formed under the leadership of Dr. Manuel Amador, who secured the support of the Roosevelt administration. U.S. gunboats anchored off the Panamanian coast to prevent the Colombian military from putting down the insurgency. Revolutionary leaders declared Panama's independence from Colombia in November 1903 and the United States immediately recognized the new nation.

The Hay–Bunau–Varilla Treaty, finalized in less than two weeks, allowed the United States to begin construction of the Panama Canal in May 1904. The treaty guaranteed Panama the same payment terms that Colombia had rejected and created the Canal Zone under U.S. control spanning five miles on each side of the waterway. In addition to the favorable leasing terms, the United States demanded special provisions that permitted armed intervention in Panamanian affairs when deemed necessary to protect U.S. interests in the Canal Zone. Although some

Panamanian leaders resisted such a concession, they reluctantly acquiesced when it became clear that, without it, the United States would withdraw support of the secessionist movement. A new constitution, written under the direction of U.S. delegates in 1904, further codified the right of intervention, effectively making Panama a protectorate of the United States.

U.S. experts arrived immediately and took over operations of the failed French company. Despite numerous setbacks and serious challenges, the canal project moved forward over the next decade and spawned numerous social and economic transformations within Panama. As in Cuba, medical experts worked to eradicate the multitude of tropical illnesses that plagued the workforce. Dr. William Gorgas successfully identified mosquitos as the transmitters of malaria and initiated a rigorous fumigation campaign that reduced the disease's death rate to less than 1 percent by 1910. Medical experts eradicated yellow fever as well, mitigating at least some of the health and safety risks suffered by construction workers. The canal endeavor also necessitated improvements to the Panamanian railroad, which had fallen into a state of disrepair. Project leaders from the United States recruited tens of thousands of workers, primarily from the West Indies, but also from Europe and Asia. Sustaining a workforce that at its peak numbered more than 40,000 required investments in infrastructure, housing, social services, and recreational activities in the Canal Zone. Such facilities varied in quality and were generally segregated by race. The Panama Canal opened to interoceanic traffic in 1914.

INTELLECTUAL RESPONSE TO IMPERIALISM

As the nature of U.S. informal imperialism became evident, a strong reaction arose throughout Latin America. Growing resentment threatened the vitality of the Western Hemisphere idea that had originated with the Monroe Doctrine in the early nineteenth century. Political leaders grew suspicious of U.S. intentions and correctly feared that increased economic dependence on the United States created the potential for economic exploitation. Racist and degrading depictions of Latin Americans that became common in U.S. cultural expressions fueled resentment and gave rise to "Yankeephobia" among intellectuals and the masses alike. Some of the most articulate expressions of anti-imperialism and resentment toward the United States came from Latin American literary figures. As early as the 1890s, Latin American authors were penning scathing critiques of U.S. assumptions of hemispheric superiority. The Cuban writer José M. Céspedes and the Chilean writer Alberto del Solar published eponymous rebukes of the Monroe Doctrine. Others resented the tendency of their countrymen to emulate foreign culture. Eduardo Prado expressed his disappointment with the tendency of some Brazilian elite to emulate American republicanism in his 1893 *American Illusion* (*A Ilusão Americana*).

José Martí, an early proponent of Cuban independence, represents a precursor to the crescendo of condemnations that arose at the turn of the century. Exiled for his participation in the Ten Years' War, Martí spent time in the United States and wrote about his observations. He admired the idea of the "self-made man" and marveled at the country's technological advancements. But he also deplored defects he perceived in the American character, namely deeply entrenched racism, widespread anti-intellectualism, and the blind pursuit of wealth. Moreover, his writings predicted the impending threat of U.S. imperialism. Although he ardently supported Cuba's independence from Spain, he warned that Latin America risked replacing subjugation under a European country with subordination to the United States. His 1891 essay "Nuestra América" (Our America) challenged prevailing concepts of the Western Hemisphere idea through which U.S. leaders envisioned the Americas united under U.S. guidance. Instead, Martí called for Latin American solidarity in the face of looming commercial and economic expansion by the northern neighbor. He articulated a formula for pan-American identity reminiscent of the ideals embraced by Simón Bolívar, underscoring the common cultural and political heritage shared among former Spanish possessions. Martí also criticized what he considered the Latin American elite's adoption of foreign ideas and mimicry of North American political systems.

The Nicaraguan poet and writer Rubén Darío offered a similar critique of rising U.S. imperialism. Best known for his contribution to the *Modernismo* movement, his literature underscores the value of Latin American culture and represents a response to the changes that modernity introduced at the turn of the century. His *Cantos de vida y esperanza* (*Songs of Life and Hope*, 1905) illustrates his concerns with the threat posed by U.S. imperialism, especially with respect to Latin American culture. Also a champion of Latin American solidarity, Darío argues that the newly emerging world power to the north can no longer be seen as benign.

In Uruguay, response to the emergence of the United States as a hemispheric and global power came from the writings of José Enrique Rodó. Using personalities and themes from Shakespeare's *The Tempest*, the essayist, educator, and politician penned *Ariel* in 1900 as an indictment of North American cultural barbarism and an allegory of the contrasts between U.S. and Latin American character. The figure of Calibán embodies the materialism and worship of technology prevalent in the United States, whereas Ariel personified the idealism and spiritual values of Latin America, derived from its Spanish roots. Rodó disparaged the rise of U.S. imperialism and called on Latin Americans to create their own intellectual life rather than imitating that of their northern neighbor.

ROOSEVELT COROLLARY TO THE MONROE DOCTRINE

U.S. involvement in Cuban and Panamanian independence set the stage for its diplomatic relationship with the rest of Latin America for much of the twentieth century. Roosevelt faced intense backlash, not only from Latin American political and intellectual leaders, but also from other parts of the world. Critics accused him of using gunboat diplomacy to position the United States as a global policeman. For his part, the hawkish president remained unapologetic for his interventionist tactics. He fell back on the adage "speak softly and carry a big stick," suggesting that, although it preferred peace, the United States would be ready and willing to use force if necessary. The phrase quickly became a slogan to describe Roosevelt's foreign policy. The president reinforced his stance toward Latin America in 1904, when he stated in an address to Congress that the United States had a right and an obligation to intervene in Latin America in instances of "flagrant wrongdoing or impotence." He applied the Monroe Doctrine to U.S. actions in Cuba, Venezuela, and Panama and interpreted the policy as giving the United States the authority to act as an international police. Additionally, he characterized U.S. military interventions as a last resort when Latin American governments were unwilling or unable to protect U.S. interests.

The president's articulation of this foreign policy became known as the Roosevelt Corollary to the Monroe Doctrine and subsequent administrations called on it to justify military occupations in Latin America and the Caribbean in the 1910s and 1920s. During that time, U.S. policy became known as "dollar diplomacy" for its assumption that economic supremacy could bring the region more fully under control. Latin American indebtedness to European lenders was of particular concern, and a series of bilateral treaties established a "protectorate" relationship among the United States and Cuba, the Dominican Republic, Haiti, Nicaragua, and Panama. Such agreements invoked the spirit of the Roosevelt Corollary to prevent imprudent Latin American nations from falling under European control. But "protection" often meant military occupation.

A Cartoon from the Magazine Puck with Uncle Sam Dressed as Santa Claus, Handing out Toys and Money to a Boy Who Represents Panama while Other Children, Labeled "Colombia, Venezuela, Nicaragua, San Domingo," Look on Empty-Handed Political cartoons often portrayed Latin American nations as ill-behaved dark-skinned children in need of guidance, reflecting paternalistic U.S. foreign policy.

Primary Source

Ulysses S. Grant offers several reasons for the acquisition of San Domingo (Dominican Republic), including the island nation as a new homeland for former slaves, as well as its strategic value in the Caribbean. His arguments reflect the attitudes of the United States toward Latin America, as well as concerns in the post–Civil War era.

SOURCE: Ulysses S. Grant, *The Papers of Ulysses S. Grant*, Volume 20: November 1, 1869–October 31, 1870, ed. John Y. Simon (Carbondale: Southern Illinois Press, 1995), 74–76, http://digital.library.ms-state.edu/cdm/compoundobject/collection/USG_volume/id/22041/rec/1.

> Memorandum [1869–1870] Reasons why San Domingo should be annexed to the United States. It is an island of unequaled fertility. . . . Tobacco, tropical fruits, dyes, and all the imports of the equatorial region, can be produced on these lands.— San Domingo is the gate to the Carib[b]ean Sea, and in the line of transit to the Isthmus of Darien, destined at no distant day to be the line of transit of half the commerce of the world. It has but a sparce population and that in entire sympathy with our institutions, anxious to join their fortunes to ours. . . . Caste has no foot-hold in San Domingo. It is capable of supporting the entire colored population of the United States, should it choose to emigrate. The colored man cannot be spared until his place is supplied, but with a refuge like San Domingo his worth here would soon be discovered, and he would soon receive such recognition as to induce him to stay: or if Providence designed that the two races should not live to-gether he would find a home in the Antilles. . . . San Domingo is weak and must go some where for protection. Is the United States willing that she should go elsewhere than to the herself [seek protection from a foreign power]? Such a con-fession would be to abandon our oft repeated "Monroe doctrine." San Domingo in the hands of the United States would make slave labor unprofitable and would soon extinguish that hated system of enforced labor. To-day the United States is the largest supporter of that that institution. . . . In case of a Maratime War it would give us a foothold in the West Indias of inestimable value. Its acquisition is carry-ing out Manifest destiny. It is a step towards daring Europe all European flags from this Continent.*

> *The original contains a number of misspellings and imperfections, which the authors of this text let remain.

In the first three decades of the twentieth century, U.S. armed forces intervened repeatedly in Central America and the Caribbean, actions routinely justified as necessary to protect U.S. commercial interests and to protect Latin America from outside (European) interference. In some cases, troops moved in only briefly to oversee elections or to protect U.S. commercial stakes during threats of instability. In instances of protracted occupation, leaders cited protection for U.S. investments and for Latin American interests as justification. A 19-year occupation in Haiti started in 1914, and an 8-year occupation began in the Dominican Republic 2 years later. Marine forces landed in Nicaragua in 1912 to tame hostilities in the midst of a civil war; a contingent force remained until 1933. In Cuba, a U.S.

military presence strove to maintain peace in Cuba for 3 years following the over-throw of Tomás Estrada Palma in 1906; a 5-year intervention began in 1917 to protect U.S. economic interests on the island.

The Roosevelt Corollary complemented the emergence of informal imperial-ism using the notion of protecting commercial enterprises as leverage to influ-ence the internal affairs of Latin American nations. But this 1904 expansion of the Monroe Doctrine merely formalized an unequal power relationship that had been materializing through direct and indirect interventions for decades. By the turn of the century, leaders in Washington had made clear that they considered Latin America part of a Western Hemisphere commanded by the United States. Military actions in Cuba in 1898, followed by numerous incursions in Central American and the Caribbean in the early twentieth century, underscored these attitudes. Although such interventions allowed the United States to establish a powerful military presence throughout the Caribbean and the Pacific Ocean, they fostered strong resentment to Yankee imperialism throughout Latin America.

SUGGESTIONS FOR FURTHER READING

Bulmer-Thomas, Victor. *The Economic History of Latin America since Independence.* 3rd ed. Cambridge: Cambridge University Press, 2014.

Guyatt, Nicholas. "America's Conservatory: Race, Reconstruction, and the Santo Domingo Debate." *The Journal of American History* 97, no. 4 (March 2011): 974–1000.

Hassett, John J., and Braulio Muñoz. *Looking North: Writings from Spanish America on the U.S., 1800 to the Present.* Tucson: University of Arizona Press, 2012.

Hoganson, Kristin L. *Fighting for American Manhood: How Gender Politics Provoked the Spanish–American and Philippine–American Wars.* New Haven, CT: Yale University Press, 1998.

LaFeber, Walter. *The New Empire: An Interpretation of American Expansion, 1860–1898.* Ithaca, NY: Cornell University Press, 1998.

Langley, Lester D. *The Banana Wars: United States Intervention in the Caribbean, 1898–1934.* Lanham, MD: SR Books, 2002.

McCullough, David. *The Path between the Seas: The Creation of the Panama Canal, 1870–1914.* New York: Simon & Schuster, 1977.

Pérez, Louis A., Jr. *Cuba between Empires, 1878–1902.* Pittsburgh, PA: University of Pittsburgh Press, 1998.

Ramos, Julio. *Divergent Modernities: Culture and Politics in Nineteenth-Century Latin America.* Durham, NC: Duke University Press, 2001.

Renda, Mary A. *Taking Haiti: Military Occupation and the Culture of U.S. Imperialism, 1915–1940.* Chapel Hill: University of North Carolina Press, 2001.

Rodó, José Enrique. *Ariel.* Translated by Margaret Sayers Peden. Austin: University of Texas Press, 1988.

CHAPTER 19

Early Populism

1928	José Carlos Mariátegui publishes *Siete ensayos de interpretación de la realidad peruana* (*Seven Interpretive Essays on Peruvian Reality*), which called for a native-led socialist revolution to restore an authentic Peruvian nationalism
1928	Composer Carlos Chávez, whose works incorporate indigenous instruments and themes, named director of the Mexican National Conservatory
1930	Uruguay hosts and wins first Féderation Internationale de Football Association World Cup title in soccer
1931	Nellie Campobello publishes her experimental novel set in Northern Mexico, *Cartucho*
1932	Women granted the right to vote in Uruguay

The economic growth and social changes of the late nineteenth century gave rise to a new type of political leadership that would evolve and continue to the present. Known as "populism," it merged the charisma and strong personality of the *caudillo* with new realities of electoral politics in the twentieth century. Populists did not espouse a single, uniform ideology. Rather, they catered to a wide variety of needs among a large and disparate populace, appealing to the "masses" with compelling messages and promises. Their supporters came from nonelite groups, primarily in cities, who felt alienated from economic progress. Persistent inequalities in the emerging industrial labor sector made cities a prime target for populist leaders. Urban workers and a growing middle sector made up of students, professionals, intellectuals, and some businessmen represented varied interests and demands. Seeking to balance them successfully, populist politicians exploited constantly shifting needs and altered their platforms as necessary.

POPULIST RESPONSES

Liberal oligarchies and positivist leaders succeeded in establishing relative political and economic stability, but this major accomplishment also created an environment ripe for populism. The appearance of this new type of politics around the turn of the century addressed the significant changes of the preceding decades. A rising birth rate and the arrival of millions of European immigrants—particularly in the southern cone—induced rapid population growth after the 1850s and contributed to economic development. Urban expansion ensued as rural migrants and foreign-born workers filled the ranks of the incipient industrial and manufacturing sectors. Cities became sites for the cultivation of new ideas, some of which—anarchism, socialism, and Marxism—accompanied the immigrants. An exploitative labor market coupled with deplorable living conditions in urban areas prompted new attempts to foster worker activism and solidarity.

International conditions also contributed to the propagation of early populist ideas. Trade disruptions caused by World War I hit Latin American countries particularly hard. Declining export revenues and rising prices devastated low-wage earners in particular, and labor union activism increased as a result. Workers' developing class consciousness combined with an emerging middle sector's expanding clout to fundamentally alter Latin American society. Populist leaders capitalized on these changes and attracted political support from numerous manual laborers and white-collar workers.

The new political approach took two different forms. Political populism packaged the charm of an alluring personality and proved most successful in the southern cone—Uruguay, Argentina, and Chile. In these countries, leaders leveraged support from the masses to push for sometimes radical social and political reforms. Initial efforts by dynamic individuals created a foundation for a more corporatist version of populism that would become common by the 1940s. In contrast, revolutionary populism characterized Mexico's responses to late nineteenth-century changes. Instead of rallying behind a charismatic figure, the masses rebelled in what became a 10-year revolution.

Although populist movements catered to unique national circumstances, they typically included electoral reform; social justice issues such as welfare, labor, and education; and economic and cultural nationalism. An evolving sense of community identity and civic engagement frequently emerged at the same time. Women's movements and labor activism, for example, took shape in major cities. Changing recreational practices often reflected both the influence of immigrants and class-consciousness. Aesthetic and literary expressions revealed how intellectuals and artists grappled with these profound social adjustments.

POPULISM AND THE LABOR MOVEMENT

Growing numbers of laborers suffered exploitation and inequality in the workplace while enduring injustices in social and political systems that had traditionally favored the elite. Inchoate unions emerged in the early twentieth century and populist politicians often allied with their leaders to build a coalition of popular support.

In South America, immigrants from Italy and Spain in particular introduced anarchosyndicalism to industrial urban centers. Anarchism emphasized the inherent oppression within established political structures and encouraged the mistreated masses to seek solutions outside of formal state affiliation. This model of activism resonated with noncitizen immigrants and others excluded from political participation. Anarchist labor organizers mobilized these marginalized groups in Brazil, Argentina, and Uruguay and provided a platform for demanding improved workplace conditions. Some of South America's earliest unions resulted from their efforts: these included the Regional Argentine Workers' Federation and the Brazilian Workers' Confederation. Socialism influenced other labor unions as they forged alliances with formal political parties. In Chile, the Workers' Socialist Party established in 1912 gave rise to the first national labor federation. In Argentina, socialism inspired the formation of the General Workers' Union, which became particularly influential among workers in the nation's interior.

Labor unions based on anarchosyndicalism appealed to early populist leaders, and the relationship between them foreshadows strategies Latin American leaders would employ in later decades. Despite limited formal affiliation prior to the 1930s, many unions had influence far beyond their membership base. For political leaders seeking an electoral mandate, the growing working class represented an untapped pool of potential voters. Populists' reliance on personal dynamism and informal ties made anarchosyndicalist unions an especially attractive source of support. Labor leaders in these associations sought to protect and expand workers' rights, but eschewed a formal relationship with the state or established political parties. An unofficial partnership with a populist politician based on mutual interest thus suited their needs.

The relationship between unions and populist leaders was not always smooth. Anarchosyndicalists generally preferred collective action and labor stoppage as a strategy for obtaining change. In high-profile strikes, populist politicians could boost their popular support by arbitrating in favor of workers. But when work stoppage became detrimental to the national economy, many of them did not hesitate to use force. Moreover, union bosses had to demonstrate loyalty to a populist political party to win its leadership's support; labor groups affiliated with the opposition often faced suppression by armed forces. After 1917, the relationship became even more precarious as the Russian Revolution inspired a more extreme leftist turn in parts of Latin America. As some workers embraced communism and labor unrest increased, populist leaders applied escalating levels of violence to restore social control.

EARLY POPULISM IN SOUTH AMERICA

Uruguay

Uruguay initiated the Southern Cone's experiment with populism. The election of José Batlle y Ordóñez as president in 1903 followed a shift from military to civilian rule that left lingering conflicts between the nation's two ruling parties. As the representative of the landowning elite, the Blanco Party had dominated politics for much of the nineteenth century. But its influence began to wane as the population of Montevideo and other urban areas increased. Batlle y Ordóñez rose to prominence in Uruguay's liberal Colorado Party, which drew its principal support from these centers. As a young journalist, he criticized his country's military government; later, as a politician, he sought to consolidate the masses. Like many Latin American populists dependent on personal charm, his general reform program came to bear his name, becoming known as Batllismo.

In his first presidency, Batlle y Ordóñez faced an uprising by the Blanco Party. The Colorados triumphed in a brief civil war, and he rallied considerable popular support for sweeping reforms. During two terms (1903–1907; 1911–1915), he implemented some of Latin America's most progressive social legislation. Subsequent administrations continued the momentum for change and a new constitution in 1917 consolidated and expanded the programs he had initiated. The charter established the secret ballot and a congressional representation system that guaranteed minority parties a minimum number of seats proportional to the number of votes received. Other political reforms expanded the electorate by removing voting restrictions for males and, in 1932, granting women's suffrage.

Batlle y Ordóñez rejected the ideas of social Darwinism and positivism that had guided national policies in earlier decades. His concern for the poor led him to introduce social justice measures to improve the plight of the urban masses. Favoring the separation of church and state to secularize society, he reduced the church's historic role in education. Additionally, he legalized divorce and created mechanisms that empowered a woman to seek formal dissolution without her husband's assent. Although it remained severely limited throughout most of Latin America, divorce became more socially acceptable in Uruguay during the 1920s. Batlle y Ordóñez also attempted to implement land reform and break up the latifundia system that defined the countryside, but those efforts met stiff opposition from the pro-Blanco rural elite.

Departing from the liberal economic models still predominant in Latin America, Batlle y Ordóñez's nationalistic economic policies bordered on revolutionary. He pushed for regulations to allow greater state control over the economy and began to impose protectionist trade measures to encourage the development of local industries. He also nationalized the banking industry, public utilities, ports, and the railroad, which the British had constructed and controlled. Thus, Uruguay became one of the first countries to experiment with state-led economic growth, an approach that would become common later in the twentieth century.

In subsequent years, the nation mandated free, public high school education and became one of the first countries to introduce an eight-hour workday and a six-day workweek. Uruguay also enacted a minimum wage, ordered workers' compensation for injuries incurred on the job, and created an incipient system of social security. Other labor reform measures provided specific protections to underage and female workers. The constitution of 1917 included numerous safeguards of individual rights and banned the death penalty. A new ministry of labor oversaw issues dealing with workers' rights.

Batlle y Ordóñez's social and political coalition relied heavily on the support of workers along with the middle class, and this alliance facilitated the emergence and strengthening of workers' syndicates in later decades. In Uruguay, anarcho-syndicalism began gaining traction after World War I and resonated with the nation's immigrant population. Unions remained relatively small and narrowly focused in the 1920s, but their foundational activities under early populism allowed a more robust and influential movement to thrive in the 1940s and 1950s.

Argentina

Early populism in Argentina followed sweeping electoral reform backed by President Roque Sáenz Peña in 1912. An ardent nationalist and outspoken opponent of U.S. imperialism, he ostensibly represented the oligarchy through the National Autonomist Party, which had dominated politics since the 1870s. But he came from a growing faction that opposed the limited electorate and fraudulent elections that had allowed the party to remain in power. The Roque Sáenz Peña Law introduced a secret ballot and created a system of proportional representation. Its centerpiece extended suffrage to all adult male citizens and required them to vote. Although neither women nor the rapidly growing number of noncitizen immigrants received the right to vote, the expanded electorate changed the nature of Argentine politics and the National Autonomist Party disintegrated in the absence of widespread appeal. In 1916, the opposing Radical Civic Union consolidated popular support around Hipólito Yrigoyen, who won the presidency after promising a variety of benefits to the masses.

Following the passage of the Roque Sáenz Peña law, voter turnout strengthened and continued to grow as Yrigoyen enjoyed ever-increasing middle-class support. In 1918, he intervened through executive decree on behalf of university students in Córdoba who sought to reform and democratize university administration. This action not only imposed drastic and much-needed change in Argentine higher education, but also eventually spilled over to university reform movements throughout Latin America. Despite this notable success, the president employed more questionable strong-arm tactics in other areas. Since his party's failure to win a legislative majority threatened his populist efforts, the president frequently invoked executive privilege to oust opposition provincial governors. His authoritarianism eventually alienated many elites, including some prominent members of his own party.

Initially backed politically by the middle sector, Yrigoyen passed some social justice reforms, including rent controls, a minimum wage, and an eight-hour workday. Presenting himself as a "man of the people," he regularly met with ordinary citizens in his home and office. People approached him directly looking for favors and seeking government jobs. The bureaucracy expanded considerably as Yrigoyen offered employment and other favors in return for political loyalty, a practice known as clientelism that became a favorite populist strategy.

Yrigoyen at first sought to befriend the working class and developed good relationships with many exploited labor groups. Influential anarchosyndicalist groups had frequently clashed with government security forces in the years leading up to his election. In a strategy known as *obrerismo*, the president reached out to Argentine-born workers and specifically targeted second-generation immigrants to build a political coalition. He intervened on behalf of striking Buenos Aires railroad workers and forced the companies to comply with union demands. But often he limited his backing to labor disputes that would attract new supporters and to those unions whose moderate tactics did not disrupt the national economy.

Yrigoyen's benevolence toward the labor movement rarely extended to unions affiliated with rival political groups. He often blamed socialist or anarchist agitators when work stoppage or labor protest became overly militant. When faced with a strike by metalworkers in 1919, the president resorted to outright repression. Clashes between striking employees and police escalated into a week of riots and mob violence known as the Tragic Week. Yrigoyen terminated the conflict by ordering the military to end it with force.

Female laborers in Argentine cities often faced particularly deplorable conditions in food-processing plants, in textile and garment factories, and in domestic service. Growing numbers of women entered these sectors, particularly on the heels of an economic decline beginning in 1913. Nonetheless, their presence in the workplace induced controversy because some perceived it as endangering their health and morality as well as threatening to male employment. But societal attitudes eventually changed, in no small part because of the rise of feminism in the early twentieth century. Professional middle-class women pioneered this development, first as a political question and then as an issue of civil rights and education.

Early Argentine feminism helped bring the plight of women laborers to public consciousness, so much so that unions incorporated some of the most serious concerns into their platforms. Although Yrigoyen's populism failed to extend democratic reforms to women, labor groups found they could augment their ranks by considering ways to alleviate gender inequality and female exploitation in the workplace. Argentine socialist unions and eventually the Socialist Party became vital champions of emerging concepts of feminism. Activists like Alicia Moreau campaigned for suffrage on the grounds that many women earned an income and paid taxes. Socialist unions sought higher wages for female workers and their protection against unfair male competition. In 1912, the Tenth Argentine Socialist Party Congress advocated several workplace reforms for women that included a minimum wage and an eight-hour working day.

Incorporating large numbers of immigrants and workers into a populist coalition helped to shape evolving concepts of nationalism in Argentina. Similar strategies emerged in commercial matters as well. Yrigoyen did not pursue economic nationalism as vigorously as Batlle y Ordóñez in Uruguay, but he did take modest steps to place vital resources under state control. The president maintained Argentine neutrality during World War I, when an increased international demand for foodstuffs, notably beef and wheat, fueled a growth of exports and helped boost the economy. At the same time, the disruption of imported manufactured goods allowed for some new domestic production, a harbinger of the "import substitution" favored by many Latin American countries in later decades. So the nation would benefit from the discovery of petroleum in 1907, Yrigoyen formed the world's first state-owned oil company in 1922.

A Precursor to Populism in Chile

Chile's political and economic experiences did not follow the same trends that propelled populism in nearby countries, but a precursor movement did emerge there in the 1920s. The country lacked the large-scale immigration of its Southern Cone neighbors and enjoyed relatively stable economic expansion tied to the foreign-owned mining industry. In the early decades of the twentieth century, declining mortality rates and a boom in migration from rural areas propelled impressive population growth in cities—some doubling in size between 1891 and 1925.

Nitrate mining sectors in the north remained important but a shift in political influence took place as a new middle sector emerged and formal labor groups organized in urban areas. An accompanying change ended the legislature's dominance that had provided structure and consistent access to power for the nation's elite. The move away from this privileged cronyism occurred when Arturo Alessandri became president in 1920; within a decade, a directly elected strong executive had replaced legislative power.

Often labeled a "precursor" to populism in Chile, Alessandri exhibited a charismatic campaign style and attempted to introduce political and social reform. A gifted orator, he quickly gained a loyal following of supporters by appealing directly to nitrate miners, urban laborers, and the middle sector. During his first term in office, the president sought to protect workers and to bolster civil rights for women, but a stalemate with the legislature hindered these early efforts. Nevertheless, like most of his populist contemporaries, he turned to force if labor agitation turned militant or threatened to disrupt the national economy.

Ousted by the military in 1924, Alessandri returned the following year to codify political and legislative changes in the constitution of 1925. The new charter fundamentally altered Chile's governing system in an attempt to prevent future gridlock and to stymie potential abuses of power. It also outlined numerous social justice measures that provided welfare guarantees and gave workers the right to organize. Nevertheless, factional infighting among national leaders stalled the constitution's implementation and a coup replaced the president again in 1927. Military leaders censored the press, restricted political freedoms, curtailed labor union activities, and ignored many of the recently passed social justice measures. The constitution of 1925 took effect only after Alessandri resumed power in 1932.

The Alianza Popular Revolucionaria Americana in Peru

Peru's early experience with populism followed a different path. The political activist Victor Raúl Haya de la Torre founded the Alianza Popular Revolucionaria Americana while in exile in 1924. He derived initial support from Peru's rural sector, particularly plantation workers and small farmers in the country's export sector. Like other early populist movements, the Alianza Popular Revolucionaria Americana worked to build a broad coalition of support among students, workers, and intellectuals, although the party suffered a large degree of political persecution in its early years. Its leaders spoke out against the imperialist turn in Latin America in the early twentieth century and they advocated embracing national control over economic resources.

SOCIAL AND CULTURAL DYNAMICS

Populism's Shortcomings

Even as early reform-minded leaders worked to build broad popular coalitions, their policies typically left out women and the rural poor. Patriarchy continued to shape gender relations in Latin America society and the roles of wife and mother persisted as the ideal of feminine fulfillment. Populist politicians provided only limited support for a feminist movement that surfaced in the early decades of the twentieth century. Indeed, the responses to this wave of activism reflected the distinct challenges inherent in Latin America's gender history.

Primarily middle-class women comprised the organizations that campaigned for an expansion of their rights. In addition to suffrage, feminists sought legal protections for working mothers, moral reforms to curb vices such as prostitution and alcoholism, and revisions to civil codes that imposed legal restrictions on wives. They formed alliances with other advocacy groups around the world and participated in international women's conferences that took place as early as 1910 in Argentina and 1916 in Mexico. But these feminists also identified with and emphasized the primacy of motherhood as a foundation of their culture, a position that found a more receptive audience among male authority figures. Although philanthropic women's groups played a prominent role in Latin American feminism, many of their activities championed family welfare before political rights.

Religion also featured prominently in debates surrounding the feminist movement. Some leftist politicians opposed suffrage for women, fearing that their strong connection to the Catholic Church would benefit political opponents. Many countries granted voting rights to women only after conservatives endorsed them, normally in an attempt to bolster support for the right. In 1929, Ecuador became the first Latin American country to extend the franchise to women, a testimony to conservative politicians' efforts to combat socialism's growing influence.

Despite politicians' growing awareness of the diverse needs of the masses at the turn of the century, most women's situations remained largely unchanged. Although females in the middle sectors obtained expanded access to education, poor women everywhere saw few improvements to their daily circumstances. Indeed, the challenges associated with immigration and rapid population growth exacerbated the desperation and destitution that many experienced in urban slums.

Economically marginalized women in cities often resorted to prostitution out of desperation, but society as a whole viewed their poverty, medical problems, and presumed moral decay as threats to the nation. Foreign-born women in particular frequently turned to the sex trade, a trend that brought accusations of "white slavery" from international groups who pressured Latin American governments to end the exploitation of European women. But this characterization belies the fact that attitudes toward prostitution included a racial component. Women of color worked alongside poor European women in Brazil's sex trade and suffered frequent injustices as society blamed them for disease, crime, and general disorder in growing cities.

Women of Russian and Austro-Hungarian descent constituted approximately 60 percent of legally registered sex workers in Buenos Aires before 1920. Their presence prompted vigorous debates over public health, irregularities in the enforcement of the law, and the exploitation of poor women. Socialists insisted that government leaders pass stricter regulations in the 1920s and growing concern over women's exploitation ended legalized prostitution in 1934.

Early populists likewise tended to overlook the needs and demands of the poor in the countryside. The nineteenth-century expansion of latifundia continued after 1900, enabling a small number of powerful, landowning elite to profit at the expense of the rural masses. In response to the few opportunities for advancement in the agrarian sector, some peasants migrated to cities, where they joined the growing urban poor. Others continued to endure the exploitative working conditions that accompanied latifundia. As the twentieth century opened, wealthy foreigners constituted much of the landowning class and Latin America's economic reliance on export commodities compelled national leaders to cultivate a partnership that would favor the rural elite. Ignored by populists, indigenous communities in particular subsisted in deteriorating conditions.

Despite the relative fecklessness of national politicians, some rural leaders resisted inequalities and sought to address land problems at the local level. In Colombia, Manuel Quintín Lame led two armed insurrections in attempts to reclaim *resguardo* lands for indigenous communities. He united other like-minded leaders in the "Quintada" uprising, and he often invoked memories of native repression under Spanish rule to rally the rural masses. Mapuche-descended Manuel Aburto Panguile led a similar campaign in Chile. Both rebels drew on the common underlying current of capitalist exploitation to explore alliances with labor unions and leftist political parties. Colombian labor activists organized the ill-fated 1928 banana workers' strike in Ciénaga against the United Fruit Company. Armed forces violently dispersed a crowd of 4,000; the grisly massacre that ensued is portrayed in Gabriel García Márquez's acclaimed novel *One Hundred Years of Solitude*. The leftist affiliation proved ineffective for land reformers in the early twentieth century. Aside from Mexico, no Latin American country considered meaningful efforts at land reform until the 1950s. But Marxist militancy among early indigenous groups presaged the rise of the extremist guerrilla movements in later decades, particularly in remote regions of the Andean highlands.

Social and Cultural Changes

By the twentieth century, the large waves of immigration in South American cities had stimulated a growing social and cultural cohesiveness. Foreign-born and second-generation residents in Argentina formed civic clubs and neighborhood associations. These organizations stimulated a strong sense of community and many of them became loosely affiliated with Yrigoyen's Radical Party. Rising literacy rates and the increasing availability of newspapers and magazines engaged residents and gave them access to a common fund of information.

Recreational activities reflected both the influence of immigrant culture and the importance of local sociability in working-class neighborhoods. New arrivals to Latin America brought visions of domestic comforts that helped to shape cultural preferences in their communities. The local cuisine of Southern Cone countries began to resemble that of Southern and Eastern Europe. Argentines incorporated many Italian-style foods, whereas German and Asian cuisine affected Brazilian eating patterns. Chinese immigrants in Peru also shaped dietary practices there.

Italians in Buenos Aires introduced *lunfrado*, a type of slang used by criminals and in brothels, into the local language. Such expressions evolved and changed in meaning over time, and *lunfrado* words found their way into popular plays as well as tango and other folk music. The new lexicon also influenced journalists and literary genres through *costumbrista* writing and naturalist novels. The Argentine author Roberto Arlt used it in his 1926 novel *El juguete raiboso* and in his *Aguafuertes porteñas* in the daily *El Mundo* during the late 1920s.

British immigrants introduced soccer, or *fútbol*, to South America and the sport soon became popular. As an activity that required few material objects, soccer offered a way for even the poorest residents to form a sense of community. Informal matches often sprang up between different barrios and fostered a feeling of belonging, either in victory or in defeat. Member-based clubs provided the origin of professional soccer teams that later gained nationwide appeal. In 1926, the European-led Féderation Internationale de Football Association founded the World Cup and chose Uruguay to host the first tournament four years later. France, Belgium, Romania, and Yugoslavia represented Europe, whereas Argentina, Brazil, Bolivia, Chile, Mexico, Paraguay, Peru, and the United States represented the Americas. The Uruguayan team approached its role as host seriously, going into isolation two months before competition and adhering to a strict curfew. This dedication paid off and the team went undefeated throughout the tournament, eventually beating Argentina in the final match before a crowd of 93,000. The victory sparked days of celebrating and the Uruguayan government declared a national holiday.

Even as a relative cohesiveness emerged through recreation and popular culture, rapidly growing immigrant populations in urban areas also provoked strife. Native-born residents across socioeconomic sectors often blamed the recent arrivals for the crime, poverty, and moral decay that accompanied urban expansion. Although immigrants contributed substantially to growth and prosperity, satirists and the press repeatedly depicted them as greedy, degenerate, and unwashed. Nativist responses in Buenos Aires reinforced symbols of *argentinidad* such as the gaucho. Ironically, immigrants' eagerness for cultural integration led them to form their own gaucho clubs. Second- and third-generation immigrants eventually found avenues for upward mobility; many moved out of commerce and into other professions, including law, politics, and medicine. The military also offered immigrants' sons and grandsons a path to social and economic advancement.

REVOLUTIONARY POPULISM

Mexican Revolution

In Mexico, the social tensions that worsened during the Porfiriato erupted in a lengthy revolution beginning in 1910. Violence originally arose in response to Porfirio Díaz's authoritarianism and his jailing of Francisco Madero, an advocate of political reform who attempted to challenge the dictator for the presidency.

Shortly after Díaz's victory in a no longer contested election, Madero escaped to San Antonio, where he strategized with would-be allies across Mexico and issued a general call to arms. A defining feature of the Mexican Revolution that followed was its widespread popular nature. Marginalized and neglected groups that had suffered under Díaz's vision of positivist progress rose up in the early days of the revolution to force out the old regime. They sought to replace Porfirian rule with an economic, social, and governing system that would restore and protect their well-being.

The popular appeal that enabled the Mexican Revolution to spread so quickly also created serious challenges for its early leaders. In the south, Emiliano Zapata led peasants who had suffered under Porfirian land tenure policies. In the north, Pascual Orozco and Francisco (Pancho) Villa assembled armies of the dispossessed rural poor who quickly overran strategic federal garrisons. The first phase of the revolution—the removal of Díaz from power—concluded in less than six months. After Villa and Orozco dealt a devastating defeat to federal forces at the Battle of Ciudad Juárez in May 1911, the aged dictator fled into exile in Paris.

Although many disparate groups coalesced to overthrow Díaz, their tenuous alliance quickly disintegrated once the dictator fell. In the revolution's second phase, the victorious rebels needed to replace the old Porfirian system with new institutions. But the diverse interests of factional leaders precluded agreement on

The revolutionary leader Emiliano Zapata (front row, center) at the Hotel Coliseo in Mexico City on June 23, 1911. His brother, Eufemio Zapata, is to his right. Zapata's popular image of rebellion and resistance endured after the Mexican Revolution, eventually inspiring the Zapatista Army of National Liberation in the 1990s.

the best course of action. Nine more years of fighting followed as various disputes escalated into convoluted and at times illogical civil wars.

Elected president after a brief interregnum, Madero focused much of his immediate attention on reforming the political process and attempting to appease elite *Científicos*, hacendados, bureaucrats, clerics, and foreign investors who had benefited under Díaz. Initial supporters grew impatient with the slow pace of social reform for agrarian peasants and urban workers. Soon the beleaguered president faced uprisings led by his former allies—Zapata in the south and Orozco in the north. These rebellions, combined with counterrevolutionary movements directed by supporters of the old Porfirian regime, eventually resulted in Madero's downfall. General Victoriano Huerta, whom the president had sent to suppress the revolts, betrayed him. Carried out in collaboration with counterrevolutionaries and backed by the U.S. ambassador, the Huertista coup started with 10 days of brutal combat on the streets of Mexico City. It culminated in Madero's assassination on February 22, 1913. Huerta assumed the presidency but lacked political support from former Madero allies, who correctly considered him a dictator. He also faced the enmity of President Woodrow Wilson, who saw the general's violent rise to power and "government of butchers" as contrary to the United States' purported defense of democracy. Consistent with the attitudes of informal imperialism and the concurrent interventions taking place in Central America and the Caribbean, the U.S. leaders eventually attempted to undermine Huerta's rule. Naval ships intercepted an arms shipment bound for Mexico and occupied the port of Veracruz for seven months in 1914. An anti-U.S. backlash ensued and even Huerta's sworn enemies in Mexico denounced the action.

The assassination of Madero and return to dictatorship spawned new waves of violence and instability as revolts sprang up in various regions of the country. Venustiano Carranza, Alvaro Obregón, and Pancho Villa joined together against Huerta as "constitutionalists" and fought in the north. Although not formally a constitutionalist, Zapata also rebelled in the south. This second wave of revolutionary violence tore through Mexico until Huerta fled into exile some 18 months later. But combating the dictator's presence had been the strongest tie that bound the revolutionary factions together; his departure failed to bring peace to the battle-torn nation. Instead, many of Carranza's former allies turned against him when he declared himself president. A complex factional civil war erupted that ravaged the countryside for the next two years. An attempt to convene a peace conference at the Convention of Aguascalientes in 1914 produced a new alliance system. Obregón joined forces with Carranza to support his presidency and to advocate retaining the political, economic, and social framework established in the constitution of 1857. Villa and Zapata insisted on a major restructuring of Mexican society and formed an alliance against them.

Extreme violence and near anarchy became the norm as the demands of war tore families apart and destroyed much of the nation's infrastructure. Mining and manufacturing declined and agricultural output slowed considerably as the war destroyed crops, disrupted transportation networks, and diverted manpower to the battlefield. Local villages suffered tremendously as most adult males either joined one of the various armed factions or suffered forcible conscription by military bands advancing through the countryside. Those left behind in small towns fell victim to looting and pillaging by invading troops of revolutionaries. Some women accompanied husbands and other family members and became camp followers, providing domestic services, tending to the wounded, and offering sexual companionship. Several revolutionary armies called on women to become *soldaderas*, or female soldiers who fought alongside men. The civil war's staggering demographic consequences scarred the nation. Nearly 900,000 Mexicans fled into the United States to escape the violence. Casualty estimates, although imprecise, indicate that somewhere between 1 million and 3 million Mexicans were killed between 1910 and 1920; the country's total population dropped from 15.2 to 14 million.

By 1916, momentum had shifted in Carranza's favor as a series of destructive confrontations checked Zapata's army in the south and Obregón won impressive victories in the north. While battling the federal army, Pancho Villa also became the target of a protracted, but ultimately unsuccessful, U.S. intervention when General John J. Pershing led a punitive expedition to hunt down the elusive revolutionary after his destructive raid on Columbus, New Mexico. With the more radical forces of Villa and Zapata in retreat, Carranza attempted to consolidate his authority by convening a constitutional convention. But delegates insisting on major structural change triumphed over his vision of a more moderate governing document.

The constitution of 1917 eventually incorporated many demands by the more extremist factions of the revolution to end exploitation and rectify inequalities. These included an extensive program of land reform and one of the most progressive statements of workers' rights anywhere in the world at that time. Other measures legislated by populists elsewhere in Latin America also appeared in Mexico's constitution: free and obligatory public education, an incipient system of social welfare, efforts to curtail the influence of the Catholic Church, support for labor, and initial steps to promote economic nationalism. The constitution also outlined political reforms that embraced the concept of no reelection and a commitment to universal male suffrage; women gained the right to vote only in the 1950s. Despite the document's sweeping provisions, postrevolutionary leaders enacted social justice measures inconsistently and promising implementation often became a strategy politicians used in building coalitions rather than addressing social realities.

The revolution constituted a defining moment in twentieth-century Mexico and permeated multiple forms of cultural expression. A new literary genre, known as the novel of the revolution, took shape in the 1920s starting with the publication of Mariano Azuela's *Los de abajo* (*The Underdogs*, 1915). This seminal work narrates the exploits of a band of revolutionaries and portrays their disillusionment with the revolution. Other writers followed suit, often using autobiography and testimonials to create a national literature committed to social consciousness. Martín Luis Guzmán's *El águila y la serpiente* (*The Eagle and The Serpent*, 1926) depicts the civil strife during the revolution between competing factions after Madero's overthrow and assassination; his *La sombra del caudillo* (*The Shadow of the Chief*) critiques the pervasive corruption in national politics in the 1920s. Nellie Campobello (1900–1986) is the only female novelist of the revolutionary canon. Her 1931 *Cartucho* employs an experimental style that quotes *corridos* and incorporates *estampas* (lithographic prints) into a text that depicts the regional concerns of the author's birthplace in northern Mexico.

INDIGENISMO

Indigenismo in Mexico

Mexico stood alone among Latin American nations in its attempt to address the needs of indigenous communities through land reform. But political and intellectual leaders throughout the hemisphere did consider ways to integrate the role of native people into a cohesive cultural narrative. *Indigenismo*—the celebration of select characteristics of indigenous culture and heritage—became prominent in the first half of the twentieth century. Taking root in countries with large Indian populations, it fit nicely into the nationalist rhetoric of emerging populist movements. The philosophy moved beyond some of the racist social theories of the late nineteenth century, and its proponents sought ways to incorporate natives and mixed-race populations into an ever-evolving sense of national identity.

In Mexico, Porfirian leaders had already showcased the preconquest era by erecting a monument to the Aztec hero Cuauhtémoc along the capital city's main boulevard. During the revolution, intellectuals and military commanders adopted similar strategies in their attempts to unite a bitterly divided nation. Small-scale efforts—often merely symbolic and rhetorical—highlighted the heroic contributions of mestizos and those of Indian descent, who made up the bulk of revolutionary armies' foot soldiers. As early as 1913, Jorge Vera Estañol, a member of Huerta's administration and a former Porfirian education minister, began formulating social theories and national policies inspired by *indigenista* ideas. With the president's support, he introduced nascent rural education programs intended to modernize and assimilate the Indians into the rest of society. This included sending teachers into the countryside, where many people did not speak Spanish and followed lifestyles connected to native culture through diet, dress, and other daily practices.

The notion of incorporating the indigenous population into a prescribed construct of national identity took on new vigor after 1920, when Alvaro Obregón became president and named José Vasconcelos the minister of education. Vasconcelos firmly believed in the value of schooling to achieve national unity, but also understood that traditional programs would not serve adults—many of whom were illiterate and did not speak Spanish. Defining education broadly, the Obregón administration hired muralists to decorate public spaces with nationalistic portrayals of the country's history. The most prominent artists associated with this movement—Diego Rivera, David Alfaro Siqueiros, and José Clemente

Orozco—gained international reputations and collectively became known as *"los tres grandes."* Other artists included Jean Charlot, Dr. Atl, and Roberto Montenegro.

The muralists' early works presented a pictorial account of the nation's history, highlighting the strength of pre-Columbian civilizations and emphasizing the contributions of the masses during the revolution. For his part, Vasconcelos penned *La Raza Cósmica* (*The Cosmic Race*), the most influential treatise on Mexican national identity. Published in 1925, the book articulated a nationalist philosophy to match the visual message of the muralist movement. The author celebrated the various cultures whose combination formed contemporary Mexicans and argued that the strongest attributes of the region's indigenous and Iberian heritage elevated Latin Americans to a superior "cosmic race" that would eventually integrate all others.

In addition to the muralist movement, *indigenismo* informed composers, photographers, and other artists. Inspired by indigenous instruments, melodies, and rhythms, the musical composer Carlos Chávez (1899–1978) composed *El fuego Nuevo* (*New Fire*, 1921) and *Sinfonía India* (*Indian Symphony*, 1936) to reflect the changes in Mexican culture after the revolution. Named the director of the Mexican National Conservatory in 1928, his series of concerts for workers—*Concierto para Trabajadores* (1930) and *Sinfonía Proletaria* (1934)—display his political sympathies.

Indigenismo in the Andes
A similar intellectual trend developed in Peru, where Cusco became the epicenter of *indigenista* revivalism in the 1920s. Intellectuals there promoted the ancient center of Inca culture as the "true" capital over Lima while endorsing the supremacy of the Quechua language. Luis Valcárcel directed the Peruvian Mission of Inca Art; a troupe of Incan musicians, dancers, and thespians affiliated with that institution toured throughout Latin America. Martín Chambi, considered the first indigenous Latin American photographer, established the "Cusco School" of photography. His ethnographic approach highlighted the concerns of the *indigenista* movement through images of daily life in provincial villages.

The early writings of José Carlos Mariátegui applied Marxist theory to the plight of Peru's indigenous people. Referring to Latin America as "Indo-America," he celebrated the communal landholding traditions of pre-Columbian Andean civilizations. His best-known work, *Seven Interpretative Essays on Peruvian Reality* (1928), argued that European colonization destroyed both the indigenous system of "agrarian communism" and the underlying culture of native societies. Mariátegui believed this so-called indigenous communism to be far superior to what he considered a feudal model of society imposed by the Spanish and maintained after independence. Ultimately, he called for a native-led socialist revolution to restore his notion of authentic Peruvian nationalism. The Alianza Popular Revolucionaria Americana also promoted the ideals of *indigenismo* and Mariátegui initially aligned with many of the party's positions.

In Ecuador, Pio Jaramillo Alvarado's *El indio ecuatoriano* (*The Indian in Ecuador*) (1922) decried that country's system of debt peonage, known as *concertaje*.

Primary Source

Roque Sáenz Peña, the author of Argentina's electoral reform, articulated his populist political vision in a speech to open the 1911 legislative session.

SOURCE: Roque Sáenz Peña, *La reforma electoral; y, Temas de política international americana: selección de escritos discursos y cartas, con una noticia biográfica y varias notas* (Buenos Aires: Editorial Raigal, 1952), 106–109.

I pressed to instill reality into suffrage, and the government over which I preside is clearly on track to that national aspiration, fulfilling its compulsory role. It is not a personal vote which they expressed, it is in fact, a deed imposed upon us by the new spirit of the State which the Republic has achieved virtually through its expansion. Suffrage is a part of the guarantees that governments must acknowledge and a right to be exercised by the voters, and you cannot unfold its terms without the legal act disappearing and giving birth to fiction. It is not enough, then, for citizens to vote, if the powers that be do not recognize their will. Breaking the harmony of this pairing, it is necessary to inquire as to the reasons that have brought us to abstinence, but this analysis is a laborious process without a verdict, without an end, without a judge, I perceive this as such a sterile endeavor as wanting to find the end of a circle. In my view, it is sufficient for the government to do its part so citizens can make their part, I am convinced that this is a combined effort that should unite us patriotically, to pursue righteous solutions in elections encouraged by the people.

The author viewed exploitative labor practice as Ecuador's most critical social justice problem and a hindrance to economic development. His writings denounced the unequal land distribution that disenfranchised entire native communities. Borrowing from Vasconcelos' philosophy, Jaramillo advocated the assimilation of indigenous people into the mestizo population.

Dynamic changes in the social and economic fabric in many Latin American countries propelled an array of populist trends in the early decades of the twentieth century. Population growth, an expanding electorate, and evolving demands in urban areas prompted a new generation of charismatic leaders to build political coalitions based on mass appeal. Reaching out to labor groups and immigrant populations, these politicians often benefited from reforms that extended the franchise. Support from new constituencies gave populist presidents in Uruguay, Argentina, and Chile leverage to introduce social justice measures that protected workers and improved living conditions in urban areas. In Mexico, the masses rose up against the exploitation of the Porfirian regime in a violent revolution; the constitution produced in 1917 reflected many of the same populist trends under way in South America.

Social and cultural movements displayed the complexities of Latin American society after the turn of the twentieth century. New forms of recreation and artistic expression emerged as immigrant populations influenced local preferences and nationalist interpretations reconsidered the significance of the indigenous past. Although overlooked by national reform efforts, women found a voice through feminist organizations and campaigned for inclusion in national politics. By the 1930s, these dramatic experiences transformed Latin American society and fundamentally altered expectations.

SUGGESTIONS FOR FURTHER READING

Alba, Victor. *Politics and the Labor Movement in Latin America*. Stanford, CA: Stanford University Press, 1968.

Alexander, Robert Jackson, and Eldon M. Parker. *A History of Organized Labor in Uruguay and Paraguay*. Westport, CT: Praeger, 2005.

Barr-Melej, Patrick M. *Reforming Chile: Cultural Politics, Nationalism, and the Rise of the Middle Class*. Chapel Hill: University of North Carolina Press, 2001.

Conniff, Michael L. *Populism in Latin America*. 2nd ed. Tuscaloosa: University Alabama Press, 2012.

Coronado, Jorge. *The Andes Imagined: Indigenismo, Society, and Modernity*. Pittsburgh, PA: University of Pittsburgh Press, 2009.

Dawson, Alexander Scott. *Indian and Nation in Revolutionary Mexico*. Tucson: University of Arizona Press, 2004.

García, María Elena. *Making Indigenous Citizens: Identities, Education, and Multicultural Activism in Peru*. Stanford, CA: Stanford University Press, 2005.

Gilly, Adolfo. *The Mexican Revolution*. New York: New Press, 2006.

Guy, Donna J. *Sex & Danger in Buenos Aires: Prostitution, Family, and Nation in Argentina*. Lincoln: University of Nebraska Press, 1991.

Hahner, June Edith. *Emancipating the Female Sex: The Struggle for Women's Rights in Brazil, 1850–1940*. Durham, NC: Duke University Press, 1990.

Klarén, Peter Flindell. *Peru: Society and Nationhood in the Andes*. New York: Oxford University Press, 2000.

Knight, Alan. *The Mexican Revolution*. Vols. I & II. Lincoln: University of Nebraska Press, 1986.

Lavrin, Asunción. *Women, Feminism, and Social Change in Argentina, Chile, and Uruguay, 1890–1940*. Lincoln: University of Nebraska Press, 1995.

Miller, Francesca. *Latin American Women and the Search for Social Justice*. Hanover, NH: University Press of New England, 1991.

Soto, Shirlene. *Emergence of the Modern Mexican Woman: Her Participation in Revolution and Struggle for Equality, 1910–1940*. Denver: Arden Press, 1999.

Vanger, Milton I. *Uruguay's José Batlle y Ordoñez: The Determined Visionary, 1915–1917*. Boulder, CO: Lynne Rienner, 2009.

Vaughan, Mary Kay, and Stephen Lewis. *The Eagle and the Virgin: Nation and Cultural Revolution in Mexico, 1920–1940*. Durham, NC: Duke University Press, 2006.

Walter, Richard J. *The Socialist Party of Argentina, 1890–1930*. Austin: University of Texas Press, 1977.

CHAPTER 20

Depression and World War

CHRONOLOGY

1928	Argentina's Hipólito Yrigoyen overthrown in a military coup
1929	Women's suffrage in Ecuador
1930	Onset of Great Depression
1930	Getúlio Vargas becomes president of Brazil in military coup
1932	Hoover begins withdrawal of troops from Nicaragua
1932	Women's suffrage in Brazil
1932	Women's suffrage in Uruguay
1933	Franklin Delano Roosevelt initiates "Good Neighbor Policy," which repudiates the Roosevelt Corollary, encourages trade, and espouses nonintervention toward Latin America
1934	Women's suffrage in Cuba
1936	United States signs nonintervention treaty with Panama
1936	Inter-American Conference for the Maintenance of Peace held in Buenos Aires
1937	Lázaro Cárdenas nationalizes the railroads in Mexico
1937	David Toro Ruilova confiscates properties of the Standard Oil Company in Bolivia
1937	Getúlio Vargas declares a state of emergency in Brazil, canceling elections and initiating the *Estado Novo*, the New State, consolidating authority in a centralized government
1938	Lázaro Cárdenas nationalizes the Mexican petroleum industry
1938	U.S. State Department establishes Division of Cultural Relations to improve relations with Latin America
1939	Women's suffrage in El Salvador
1940	United States establishes the Office of the Coordinator of Inter-American Affairs to promote hemispheric unity against Axis influence
December 1941	Japanese attack Pearl Harbor, bringing the United States into World War II
1942	German submarines sink two Mexican oil tankers in the Gulf of Mexico; Mexico joins the Allies in World War II
1942	Bracero Program begins; brings Mexican workers to alleviate primarily agricultural labor shortage in United States during wartime
1942	Women's suffrage in the Dominican Republic

1943	Mexican director Emilio "El Indio" Fernández releases *Flor Silvestre* (*Wild Flower*) and *Maria Candelaria*, which feature the beauty of the countryside and incorporate an *indigenista* sensibility
1945	Mexico's Squadron 201 participates in the liberation of the Philippines
1945	Women's suffrage in Panama
1945	Getúlio Vargas resigns Brazilian presidency
1946	Juan Domingo Perón wins the presidential elections in Argentina; his wife, Evita, becomes a popular figure in Argentine public life
1947	Women's suffrage granted in Argentina
1951	Juan Domingo Perón wins reelection in Argentina
1952	Evita Perón dies from cancer
1955	Juan Domingo Perón overthrown in military coup and goes into exile

Major worldwide events disrupted the nascent wave of populism that emerged in Latin America in the early twentieth century. The onset of the Great Depression in 1930 hit Latin America hard and had repercussions that extended far beyond the region's economy. Political crises accompanied market collapse and gave rise to a wave of "depression dictators," who justified their autocratic rule as a way to bring stability during a time of economic decline. These leaders abandoned the open markets and laissez-faire liberalism that had guided trade and commercial policies in the nineteenth century. World War II caused further turmoil in Latin America as security concerns and the threat of Nazi and fascist subversion guided national and hemispheric policies. These disruptions facilitated the emergence of a distinctive brand of populism, as leaders often consolidated support through a combination of authoritarianism and nationalist appeal. *Indigenismo* and other inward-looking cultural expressions enjoyed widening allure, and new mass media technologies in radio and film helped to promote distinct national imaginaries. Improved diplomatic relations with the United States ushered in a new era of economic cooperation that tied the region closer together and contributed to major cultural shifts throughout Latin America.

THE GREAT DEPRESSION IN LATIN AMERICA

Economic Responses

The Depression's immediate impact was catastrophic. Markets collapsed; many crops failed and some rotted in fields. Mining slowed and in many areas production ceased. Global commerce declined 60 percent and U.S. and European trading partners erected high tariff barriers. Demand for commodity exports dropped, which caused prices to fall precipitously. Plummeting national incomes meant Latin American countries could neither afford imports nor continue payments on outstanding debts; many defaulted as a result. The enormity of the Depression ended the economic liberalism that had defined the nineteenth century. Laissez-faire trade and open markets failed the test of sudden worldwide decline. With

Latin American leaders arguing that the region needed an alternative, new economic models began to emerge.

Latin America responded to the global crisis with economic nationalism. Many leaders contended that their nations needed to become more self-sufficient and to protect domestic interests above all else. Some of the most extreme policy changes appeared in Mexico and Bolivia, where government leaders expropriated properties held by foreign entities and placed major industries under state control. In the spirit of revolutionary reform, Mexico in the 1920s had already initiated nationalization of some banks and utilities companies. The populist president Lázaro Cárdenas accelerated the trend when he took over the railroads in 1937 and the petroleum industry the following year. In both instances, he justified expropriation as a way to defend Mexican workers in grievances against foreign companies. When his presidency ended in 1940, Cárdenas had nationalized more than 50 industries. He also drastically accelerated the pace of land reform with a preference for returning communal properties to indigenous villages in the form of *ejidos*. The Bolivian president David Toro Ruilova confiscated the properties of U.S.-based Standard Oil Company in 1937. He also gave the government more control over the country's valuable mining industry. Nationalizations in the 1930s portended an even more drastic trend of state control of national economies in Latin America after World War II.

Cultural Responses

Cultural responses in the 1930s reflected Latin America's reactions not only to the Great Depression but also to the destruction and violence of World War I. Preceding the economic crisis, the first large-scale "industrial" war brought a level of carnage never before seen or imagined. The advent of the machine gun, chemical weapons, and armored vehicles produced massive human casualties. New communications and transportation technologies enabled the rapid movement of large numbers of troops and paved the way for unprecedented levels of battlefield slaughter. These horrific results led intellectuals around the world to question the credibility of long-standing institutions. Latin Americans, who had held up European culture as the height of sophistication in the late nineteenth century, now rejected its example. Many leaders began to look inward for new models of cultural and political greatness. As a result, the incipient expressions of nationalism that had begun to coalesce in the 1920s intensified after 1930.

Intellectuals, artists, and political leaders throughout Latin America incorporated the themes of *indigenismo* into their dialogues about national grandeur. In literature, writers began showcasing Indians in important ways. They described the exploitation of native workers on rural haciendas and struggles with corrupt church officials, while glorifying the virtue of long-held indigenous cultural practices. Visual artists continued the trends established by Mexico's muralist movement and showcased the elites' abuse of the Indians. The Ecuadoran Eduardo Kingman and the Peruvian José Sabogal joined the ranks of Mexico's *los tres grandes* in painting visual images that called attention not only to social injustices, but also to the strength of indigenous character.

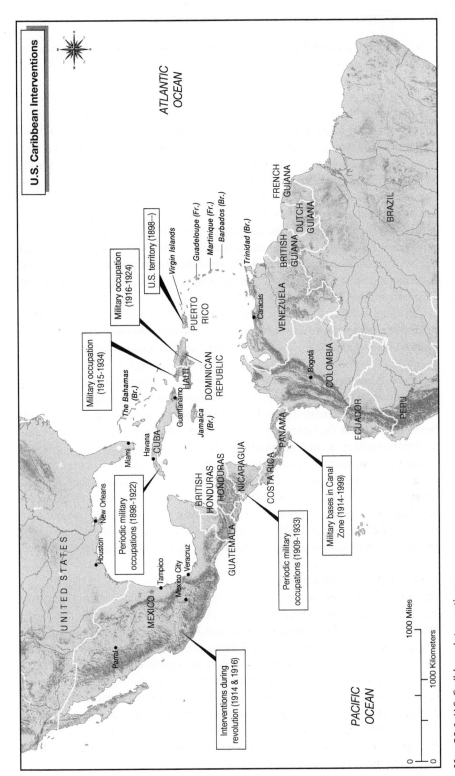

Map 20.1 U.S. Caribbean Interventions

U.S. Caribbean Interventions

ATLANTIC
OCEAN

FRENCH
GUIANA

BRITISH
GUIANA

DUTCH
GUIANA

BRAZIL

U.S. territory (1898–)

— Guadeloupe (Fr.)

— Martinique (Fr.)

— Barbados (Br.)

Military occupation
(1916–1924)

Virgin Islands

PUERTO
RICO

Trinidad (Br.)

VENEZUELA

Caracas

COLOMBIA

Bogotá

Military occupation
(1915–1934)

The Bahamas
(Br.)

HAITI

DOMINICAN
REPUBLIC

Guantánamo

Jamaica
(Br.)

ECUADOR

PERU

Havana

CUBA

Miami

PANAMA

Periodic military
occupations (1898–1922)

New Orleans

BRITISH
HONDURAS

HONDURAS

NICARAGUA

COSTA RICA

Military bases in Canal
Zone (1914–1999)

Houston

UNITED STATES

Tampico

GUATEMALA

Mexico City

Veracruz

MEXICO

Periodic military
occupations (1909–1933)

Parral

Interventions during
revolution (1914 & 1916)

PACIFIC
OCEAN

0   1000 Miles

0   1000 Kilometers

The idea of a Latin American race that José Vasconcelos had introduced in the 1920s gained even more appeal in the coming decades. Other Latin American intellectuals began to promote the notion of *mestizaje* as a way to understand ethnic identities. They argued that the virtues of race mixing should be celebrated and that mestizos represented the strongest attributes of European and indigenous heritage. In Mexico, President Cárdenas embarked on a program of comprehensive land reform for Indian and mestizo peasants that emphasized a return to communal landholding. Changes in education promoted a nationalist agenda by suggesting that rural Indians must become mestizos to be Mexican. Manuel Gamio, an intellectual who contributed to early discussions of *indigenismo* alongside Vasconcelos, served as the minister of education under Cárdenas and helped to craft a rural education program inspired by *mestizaje*. Such programs sought to preserve indigenous traditions deemed to have value, while modernizing rural Indians to eradicate negative traits. As the revolutionary government appropriated cultural nationalism, the theory of *mestizaje* moved increasingly to consider only European and Indian elements in Mexico's racial past.

In countries with a long and deeply ingrained history of slavery, intellectuals and artists tried to resolve debates about race and identity by embracing the contributions of African heritage. The Cuban writer Nicolás Guillén used poetry to celebrate a "Cuban color" as one born of *mestizaje* and reflecting a spiritual and cultural communion between Africa and the Americas. The Brazilian sociologist Gilberto Freyre argued that African influence permeated every aspect of society to the extent that "social race" or "cultural race" had replaced classification based on skin color. Freyre insisted that the intermingling of African, European, and indigenous cultures had created an egalitarian society in which racial discrimination did not exist.

Although *indigenismo* and *mestizaje* represented an improvement over positivism and other philosophies that dominated the nineteenth century, they also had drawbacks. Cultural and educational programs in Mexico often portrayed European contributions as inherently superior to those of the indigenous. And Freyre's depiction of Brazilian history described a benign system of slavery in which a benevolent patriarch supervised joyous subordinates who made up a kind of extended family.

The Rise of Depression Dictators

The potential openings for electoral reforms that seemed to surface with early populists quickly disappeared after 1930. Military coups, rebellions, and other forms of democratic disruption afflicted Latin America as a political consequence of economic hardship. Depression dictators became the norm throughout the region; even elected leaders turned to autocratic strategies to try to restore stability. Extreme conservatives often drew inspiration from the rise of fascism in Europe and attempted to impose similar structures to stifle leftist activism among the poor and the working class. Such leaders feared the rising influence of political parties and labor unions affiliated with socialism and communism.

Venezuela was under the dictatorship of Juan Vicente Gómez (1908–1935); upon his death, autocratic rule remained under his successor, Eleazar López

Table 20.1 Depression-Era Dictators

COUNTRY	LEADER	YEARS IN OFFICE
Brazil	Getúlio Vargas	1930–1945. 1951–1954
Argentina	Agustín P. Justo	1932–1938
Peru	Luis Sánchez Cerro	1930–1933
	Oscar Benavides	1933–1939
Chile	Arturo Alessandri	1920–1924, 1925, 1932–1938
Honduras	Tiburcio Carías Andino	1933–1949
Guatemala	Jorge Ubico	1931–1944
El Salvador	Maximiliano Hernández Martínez	1931–1944
Nicaragua	Anastasio Somoza	1936–1947
Cuba	Fulgencio Batista	1933–1944, 1952–1959
Dominican Republic	Rafael Leonida Trujillo	1930–1961

Contreras (1935–1941). Colombia escaped this trend as Liberal Party presidents won regular elections between 1930 and 1946. An attempted right-wing coup failed in Costa Rica and that country maintained civilian rule. Mexico also avoided outright dictatorship, although postrevolutionary leaders established a political party in 1929 that took on some authoritarian characteristics. It became the Institutionalized Party of the Revolution after several name changes and dominated the presidency for the rest of the twentieth century.

LATIN AMERICA AND THE WORLD

Good Neighbor Policy

Interventions by the United States in the late nineteenth and early twentieth centuries had bred an understandable environment of distrust and resentment. After 1930, U.S. leaders began to reconsider the hegemonic approach that had historically defined foreign relations in the hemisphere. The position taken by most Latin American nations in World War I illustrated the depth of diplomatic resistance in the region. Only Cuba, Panama, Haiti, Nicaragua, Costa Rica, Honduras, Guatemala, and Brazil had formally declared war and allied with the United States. All of these, except Brazil, were either formal protectorates or host to powerful U.S. economic interests. Others, including the Andean nations, Uruguay, and the Dominican Republic, broke diplomatic relations with Germany and its allies only as a token gesture. Mexico, geographically closest to the United States and with a shared border of nearly 2,000 miles, remained neutral. In fact, as the Mexican Revolution was in its most destructive phase, German leaders attempted to lure the country into an alliance of convenience against the United States. They hoped that such an agreement would force the U.S. military to deploy defensive resources in the Western Hemisphere and thereby reduce its potential for fighting in Europe. In the now famous Zimmerman telegram, Germany offered to help Mexico reclaim the U.S. Southwest in exchange for assistance in keeping the United States out of the war.

U.S. leaders understood that the lack of strong Latin American allies in World War I could have resulted in disastrous consequences. President Herbert Hoover initiated a new policy of goodwill and nonintervention toward Latin America. The administration of Franklin Roosevelt formalized the more conciliatory tenor under the Good Neighbor Policy, which became the cornerstone of his diplomatic strategies in Latin America throughout the 1930s and World War II.

The Good Neighbor Policy professed a commitment to nonintervention. Marking a major break from past strategies in Latin America, U.S. leaders repudiated the Roosevelt Corollary and restored the original meaning of the Monroe Doctrine. Already in 1932 Hoover began withdrawing U.S. troops from Nicaragua and took steps to end the U.S. military occupation of Haiti. That commitment to good neighborliness continued under Roosevelt as he resisted appeals to intervene in civil unrest in Cuba. In 1936, he signed a new treaty with Panama that effectively relinquished U.S. rights to intervene in that country's internal affairs. When Cárdenas nationalized the Mexican petroleum industry two years later, Roosevelt turned to negotiation, resisting self-serving demands by U.S. oil magnates for military action.

The more amicable approach to diplomacy extended far beyond the U.S. pledge of nonintervention. Economic measures introduced under the umbrella of the Good Neighbor Policy sought to ease some of the burdens Latin American nations faced as a result of decreased commerce and declining national incomes. In 1934, the Roosevelt administration created the Export–Import Bank to finance U.S. trade with select countries. By the end of the decade, much of the bank's effort focused on providing assistance to Latin American nations. Furthermore, within the context of the Great Depression and following the disastrous consequences of the U.S. protectionist reaction in the Smoot–Hawley Tariff, the Roosevelt administration secured the right to negotiate reciprocal tariff reductions with favored nations. The Reciprocal Trade Agreements Act passed by Congress in 1934 allowed the president to lower import taxes unilaterally up to 50 percent. Over the next six years, the Roosevelt administration secured bilateral treaties with 16 Latin American countries, resulting in an immediate 80 percent increase in trade.

In an attempt to cultivate an image of the United States not tied to intervention or dollars, the new diplomatic approach also included a cultural component. Although small at first, this arm of the Good Neighbor Policy established a vital foundation for future educational, artistic, and intellectual programs that built on important precedents in Latin American cultural affairs. For decades, private U.S. citizens had spearheaded initiatives to promote a greater awareness across the Western Hemisphere. Groups promoting pan-Americanism became active in major cities throughout the United States and sponsored educational and exchange programs to cultivate mutual understanding. U.S. delegates introduced a cultural convention at the Inter-American Conference for the Maintenance of Peace in Buenos Aires in 1936. Two years later, the State Department created the Division of Cultural Relations, institutionalizing government efforts to improve relations with Latin America in what became known as "soft diplomacy." Although the cultural arm of the Good Neighbor Policy was underfunded and achieved few tangible results in the 1930s, it set the stage for larger, more effective programs that became an archetype of U.S. diplomacy in the hemisphere during World War II.

Latin America in World War II

World War II marked a highpoint of cooperation in the inter-American system as the United States and the Allied Powers eventually enjoyed overwhelming support from Latin American nations. As hostilities surfaced in Europe in the late 1930s, most Latin Americans favored neutrality—viewing the impending world war as an overseas conflict that did not affect the Western Hemisphere in meaningful ways. Furthermore, extreme ideologies found some appeal among Latin Americans in the 1930s, especially as the economic consequences of the Depression escalated. The nationalist component of fascism and Nazism made sense to many Latin Americans on the eve of World War II. Large communities of immigrants from Germany and Italy, particularly in some regions of South America, complicated national loyalties even further. German spies and propagandists began infiltrating the region after the rise of the Nazi Party in 1933. They established a strong presence in Brazil and Argentina, but nearly every Latin American nation experienced some subversion. By the end of the decade, Nazi agents had successfully engendered some degree of sympathy and support for the Axis Powers.

The international scene had changed significantly in the decades following World War I. Unlike the previous global conflict, when most Latin American countries remained neutral, World War II quickly drew them into the struggle. Despite the appeal of fascist ideologies among some of the region's middle and upper classes, many people viewed those extremist movements as a threat. Republican refugees fleeing the Spanish Civil War and vulnerable German leftists attempting to escape the Nazi scourge sought safe haven in Latin America. Their influence complemented rudimentary propaganda campaigns sponsored by the British and French governments and generated some skepticism toward the growing Axis menace. Furthermore, Latin Americans generally responded favorably toward Roosevelt's Good Neighbor Policy, and the more cordial turn in U.S. diplomacy eventually helped to propagate an atmosphere of support for the Allies.

The broad commitment to neutrality among Latin American countries ended with the Japanese attack on Pearl Harbor in December 1941. Seeing the aggressive Axis offensive unfold within the Western Hemisphere convinced many Latin Americans that all of North and South America was at risk. Within five days of the attack, most Caribbean and Central American nations had declared war against Germany, Italy, and Japan, whereas others broke diplomatic ties. Mexico and Brazil issued war declarations of their own about six months later. By the end of the conflict, all Latin American nations had either declared war or severed diplomatic relations with the Axis Powers. But at times, the difficulties of winning over some of those nations to the Allied side left U.S. leaders juggling delicate diplomatic scenarios in an effort to secure the hemisphere.

Argentine leaders waited until 1945 to declare war and caused the Allies considerable concern. As home to large numbers of Italian immigrants and with close cultural ties to Germany and Spain, Argentina enjoyed enormous profits from wartime trade as a neutral nation. Its government proved to be highly sympathetic to European fascism, particularly after the army took over in a military coup in 1943. Many officers found the structure and order under fascist rule to be particularly attractive and expected to benefit from favorable trade terms with Germany and Italy after the war ended. These pro-fascist inclinations concerned leaders in other Latin American nations, and they put considerable pressure on the Argentine government at a series of Inter-American meetings throughout World War II.

Chilean leaders also proved reluctant to join the Allies until late in the war, in part because they feared the United States would not be able to guarantee protection of the nearly 2,700-mile coastline against possible attack from Japan. In many areas of Latin America, the government's official stance in support of the United States did not match the overall demeanor of the population. In Ecuador, Peru, and Guatemala, the threat of infiltration by Nazi espionage rings remained throughout the war. Charged by the Roosevelt administration with rooting out Axis saboteurs, the Federal Bureau of Investigation's agents covertly investigated German nationals and other suspected Nazi sympathizers in each Latin American country. They provided detailed reports on individual citizens as well as groups considered a threat to hemispheric security.

As an extension of the Good Neighbor Policy, the Roosevelt administration created a new bureau dedicated to U.S.–Latin American relations after the outbreak of war. Under the leadership of Nelson Rockefeller, the Office of the Coordinator of Inter-American Affairs (OCIAA) operated from 1941 until 1945. Its overall objectives included securing the hemisphere from Axis penetration, promoting inter-American economic networks, and cultivating greater cultural understanding. The creation of the coordinator's office marked a unique moment in U.S. foreign policy in general and in Latin America diplomacy in particular. Latin America was the only region of the world with one central U.S. bureau overseeing all diplomatic activities. The office only existed for the duration of the war and had neither a predecessor nor a successor. Notably, the OCIAA sponsored cultural activities throughout the United States as well in an effort to educate the American people on the charm and sophistication of their neighbors to the south. The bureau's unique role illustrates the importance of Latin America in U.S. wartime strategies and also affirms how strongly the Roosevelt administration promoted the Good Neighbor Policy.

During its brief existence, the OCIAA embarked on a zealous information campaign to convince the Latin American population that the Axis Powers were evil and that the Western Hemisphere could prosper under the guidance of the United States. Through radio, film, and print material, the bureau produced wartime propaganda intended to win support for the Allies. More subtle messages also promoted cultural exchange by showcasing the rhetoric of the Good Neighbor Policy. They introduced the idea of "the American way of life," a general notion that a victory in World War II could bring a U.S. middle-class lifestyle to all of the

School children in Corpus Christi, Texas participating in educational activities as sponsored by the Office of the Coordinator of Inter-American Affairs (OCIAA). Posters from the National Railway of Mexico and the Mexican Tourist Association depicting fisherman from Patzcuaro and dancers from Oaxaca can be seen in the background. The OCIAA encouraged the formation of pan-American clubs across the United States for both children and adults.

Americas. Other agency programs facilitated economic and commercial exchange with the intent of securing trade networks within the hemisphere during and after the war. Education and public health programs marked an effort to address some of the long-term needs of the poor in Latin America.

As the war drew to a close, President Harry S. Truman dissolved the OCIAA and other government agencies absorbed its functions. Despite a short life span, the bureau left a lasting legacy. Much of its propaganda promoted the U.S. middle-class standard of living as the goal to which all Latin Americans should aspire. The imagery of consumer goods combined with the shortages resulting from the war created a demand for appliances, automobiles, clothing, and other material goods during and after the conflict. In the immediate aftermath of World War II, a growing middle class became visible throughout Latin America. Its spending habits fueled a demand for markers of U.S. popular culture in the last half of the twentieth century, and U.S. films, music, fashion, food, and other products became increasingly popular.

Latin American Contributions to the War

Although Latin American nations escaped the large-scale military mobilization that occurred in the United States, the region did contribute significantly to the Allied war effort. Agricultural and industrial facilities in Latin America produced vital raw materials including tin, copper, oil, rubber, quinine, cotton, and foodstuffs. Rockefeller's office helped to negotiate bilateral treaties to facilitate trade in some of the most essential wartime resources. Furthermore, the OCIAA devised preclusive buying agreements in which the United States guaranteed minimum purchases and set prices for many specified exports that had previously gone to Axis Powers. For their part, Latin American leaders froze prices and at times suppressed organized labor to minimize strikes and other potential economic disruptions.

In 1942, the Roosevelt administration reached a bilateral agreement with Mexican leaders to set up a guest worker initiative. The Bracero Program was intended to offset the enormous labor shortage created by the massive military mobilization in the United States. Braceros labored primarily in agricultural fields, although some worked in the railroad industry. Popular among U.S. employers, the program continued long after the war drew to a close. By the time the program ended in 1964, more than 4.5 million Mexican workers had participated in it.

Most Latin American governments took early steps to limit the infiltration of potential Axis saboteurs. In 1941, the U.S. government published a "blacklist" of more than 1,800 pro-Axis individuals and companies in Latin America and restricted their ability to do business with U.S.-based firms. Some Latin American leaders cooperated closely by monitoring and deporting German and Italian nationals and other Axis sympathizers—many of whom were sent to detention facilities in the United States. Governments confiscated properties and businesses of detained Axis nationals and often made those assets available to the United States to assist in the war effort. Throughout 1941, numerous Latin American nations seized Axis-owned merchant ships and used them to deliver goods to the Allied Powers. The Mexican government appropriated the assets of the Bayer pharmaceutical company the following year and Brazil took over operations of the German-owned Condor Airlines.

Uniquely, Mexico and Brazil sent armed forces overseas to fight in the war. Mexico's Squadron 201 participated in the air battles that liberated the Philippines in 1945. The Brazilian navy helped to patrol the Atlantic Ocean in the face of Nazi submarine threats and the country dispatched ground forces to fight on the battlefields of Italy. Other nations cooperated by welcoming U.S. military training missions to supplant German and Italian military advisors. U.S. aid to Latin America evolved to include military equipment and other supplies under the Lend–Lease Program. By the end of the war, the United States had granted $500 million in Lend–Lease aid to 18 Latin American nations. In exchange, Brazil, Mexico, Central America, and countries on the west coast of South America allowed the United States to establish temporary military air bases on their territory.

CHANGES IN POPULISM

Early populists in Latin America achieved expanded electorates and initiated some social reform prior to the 1930s. But struggles to overcome remnants of the politically dominant liberal oligarchies limited their success. Moreover, the support base of early populists, comprising vastly different social groups, often formed fragile alliances. Consequently, leaders frequently made conflicting promises in an attempt to appeal to different constituencies. Their subsequent inability to deliver on these incompatible commitments compromised their relationships. The onset of the Great Depression and then World War II interrupted the early movement and changed the way populist leaders would operate. The need to survive the economic crisis and secure the Western Hemisphere from the Axis threat prompted a wave of autocratic rule even as a surge in industrialization expanded the working class.

Depression dictators reshaped the relationship between the state and the popular masses. At the same time, vocal groups attempted to mobilize in many Latin American countries, demanding political inclusion, improvements in working conditions, and the right to organize. The most prominent leaders to emerge from this era ruled as "authoritarian populists" and governed in dictatorial fashion. Yet they also incorporated the labor sector into a populist framework of support, acknowledging working-class grievances and establishing legal mechanisms for handling persistent inequalities.

The methods used to address the needs of laborers depended on each nation's political and social context. Where landowners had sufficient economic and political power to get their candidates elected, populist leaders often struggled. In Brazil and Chile, for example, the rural elite remained relatively strong throughout the 1930s and 1940s. In these countries, national leaders often succeeded in demobilizing urban workers and repressing existing labor movements. Where *hacendados* had lost economic and political influence, however, working classes had more room for maneuver. In both Argentina and Mexico, populist leaders officially recognized unions and partnered with labor leaders to institute various reforms, although only state-sanctioned unions benefited under this model.

Authoritarian populists sought to limit the power of the landed oligarchy while preventing the rise of anarchist and socialist influences that had surfaced in the early decades of the twentieth century. Most turned to a corporatist structure as an alternative to the radical ideologies that they believed threatened national stability. Under corporatism, major interest groups collaborated to oversee economic and social well-being of the country in an attempt to prevent class divisions from taking hold. Establishing formal relationships with distinct sectors allowed government leaders to boost popular appeal. State-sanctioned corporations generally included industry, military, civil servants, and agriculture. The Institutionalized Party of the Revolution, which emerged as Mexico's institutionalized political party, adopted this model and favored only the interest groups that established formal affiliation through the party's corporatist sectors. In this way, the social and political structure maintained a system of inequality as unaffiliated interest groups were left out of populist programs.

Authoritarian populists renewed and expanded the nationalist stance taken by their predecessors in earlier decades. Anti-imperialist rhetoric became widespread among political and intellectual leaders at the turn of the century. After the onset of the Depression, many Latin Americans roundly rejected foreign control of natural resources and nationalist arguments increasingly took on an economic tone.

Mid-century authoritarian leaders expanded the protectionist efforts introduced by early populists and began moving toward the state-sponsored structuralism and import substitution industrialization that would dominate after World War II. Their economic strategies reinforced the idea of a populist coalition between the popular masses and the middle sector, specifically tying industrialists and laborers together under a common interest group. A strong state and the prominence of a charismatic leader remained fundamental to this model.

Getúlio Vargas in Brazil

In Brazil, where the landowning classes were large and powerful, populism experienced a difficult start. During the Old Republic, from the end of the monarchy in 1889 until 1930, the coffee elite in São Paulo controlled the country's political system. They brokered a power-sharing agreement with the cattle-ranching elite from Minas Gerais. Carefully selected leaders from the two provinces alternated terms as president in a political compromise that became known as *café com leite* (coffee with milk), a moniker referring to the agricultural activities that formed the basis of each region's economy.

Some signs of discontent appeared in the 1920s as a small but growing group of intellectuals began to question the extreme gap between rich and poor. They argued that Brazil needed to modernize and to develop a self-sustaining economy that would meet the needs of all citizens. In 1922 and again in 1924, a small group of army officers rebelled against the government to demand political and social reforms. Although it failed initially, the *Tenentes* Movement—named for the lieutenants who participated in the rebellion—indicated that dissenting voices were gaining momentum.

Early conflict culminated in 1930 as Brazil struggled to manage the economic crisis fostered by the dramatic drop in the price of coffee, the nation's principal export. Economic turmoil and political infighting among the nation's elites created a volatile environment and the *café com leite* ascendancy ended in a relatively peaceful coup that brought Getúlio Vargas to power. From the state of Rio Grande do Sul, Vargas was a political outsider at the national level. He enjoyed a high degree of support from the masses, but his dictatorial style made him the quintessential authoritarian populist. He initially took power by force, aided by many of the military officers who had comprised the *Tenentes* movement. He later eliminated a potential electoral threat in 1937 by declaring a state of emergency and canceling elections. He proclaimed the *Estado Novo*, a government characterized by highly centralized authority and backed by a new constitution.

Vargas held power until 1945, largely as a result of support from the military, but he built a wide popular coalition as well. He embarked on a program of dramatic industrialization and flew the banner of economic nationalism, constantly warning of the dangers of foreign control over the country's resources. In 1943, the opening of the state-owned Volta Redonda steel plant launched a new era of heavy industry in Brazil. He expanded social welfare programs and portrayed himself as the "Father of the Poor." Relying heavily on the support of workers to reinforce his populist coalition, Vargas legalized labor unions and introduced a host of benefits including a pension system, workers' compensation, and safety and wage regula-tions. Nevertheless, he outlawed strikes under the *Estado Novo* and did not hesitate to use repression to maintain strong state control over the labor movement. Mount-ing pressure from Brazilians demanding democracy led to his overthrow in 1945, but Vargas returned to power after winning the presidency in 1950. He continued to support labor reform and accelerated the pace of economic nationalism. Facing a public scandal that associated him with an assassination attempt against a political opponent, Vargas committed suicide in 1954. Economic nationalism and state-led development continued in earnest under Juscelino Kubitschek (1956–1961).

The Perón Era in Argentina

Argentina's military heavily influenced the nation's populist experience in the 1930s and 1940s. As in Brazil, the Depression devastated the economy and eroded public confidence in the president. A military coup overthrew Hipólito Yrigoyen, who had been elected to a second term in 1928. That action ushered in an era of ultracon-servative, pro-elite rule that resorted to voter repression. A growing organized labor movement became increasingly vocal in opposing the government and in 1943 a small group of military officers led another coup. Among its leaders was Colonel Juan Domingo Perón, who took a position as head of the labor department.

Perón's connection to the working class gave him enormous political lever-age in Argentina's evolving society. Like in other Latin American countries whose economies had embraced manufacturing, between 1935 and 1945 the number of industries in Argentina had doubled, as had the workforce itself. And unlike in earlier decades, laborers in the 1940s were mostly native born, which meant they could vote and participate fully in the political system. Many were women and large numbers had migrated from rural areas to the major cities. Most were gen-erally unhappy with their working conditions, wages, and social status. They felt alienated and discriminated against as they saw the nation's elite prosper while they found few opportunities for upward mobility.

Perón sensed the laborers' profound dissatisfaction and also understood that, by virtue of sheer numbers, the working class could be mobilized into a formi-dable political force. He and his new bride used discontent in the labor sector to their advantage. Eva Perón, or Evita as she became known by Argentines, was a radio actress claiming a proletarian background who defied social conventions by taking an active public role in her husband's political career. The couple coined the term *descamisados* to give a sense of worth and identity to workers who rallied around them, and Perón capitalized on divisions within the national labor union. He backed its members in strategic circumstances, such as supporting a general strike in the meat-packing industry and pushing through social reform legislation to extend real benefits to the working class. With widespread support from orga-nized labor, Perón positioned himself to run for president.

Traditional political parties were rightly suspicious of Perón, as was the U.S. government. The U.S. ambassador, Spruille Braden, described Perón as the most powerful and most dangerous person in Argentina and worked behind the scenes to encourage a coalition of political parties to oppose him. Braden even published

Consultation among the American Republics with Respect to the Argentine Situation, nicknamed the "Blue Book," in an ill-advised attempt to influence the 1946 presidential election. The book alleged involvement by Perón and other Argentine military officials with the Axis Powers during World War II, but despite the powerful interests that opposed him, the labor minister's political base grew. When government leaders arrested him, workers began to organize demonstrations to secure his release. Encouraged by Evita, who rallied supporters through radio broadcasts, tens of thousands of *descamisados* descended on Buenos Aires. Their efforts were successful and Perón won the presidency.

President Juan Domingo Juan Domingo Peron of Argentina and his wife, Eva Duarte de Peron, on the grounds of their country estate in San Vincente, 35 miles outside of Buenos Aires.

Ruling as a quintessential populist, Perón spoke in nationalistic terms, emphasizing the prominence of Argentina over the broad concepts of capitalism and communism that dominated international debates. With the help of his wife, he came to symbolize the distinctiveness of Argentina. Indeed, Evita gave regular public addresses portraying her husband as the paternalistic figure who would never turn his back on the nation. She established the Eva Perón Foundation, which administered many social welfare programs for the poor. Additionally, she helped to secure women's suffrage in 1947, adding large numbers of new voters to her husband's political base. The president's popularity rose as a strong postwar economy allowed him to expand social services. Real wages, workers' pensions, and access to health care increased. In a nationalist vein typical of populists, Perón expropriated foreign-owned railroad and utilities companies and placed them under government control.

Opposition to Perón began to mount after he won reelection in 1951. Like many mid-century authoritarian populists, he relied increasingly on repression to silence dissent. Furthermore, the nation's economic growth during the early years of his presidency had stalled, causing middle- and upper-class Argentines to distance themselves from his policies. After the tragic death of Evita to cancer in 1952, Perón became even more heavy handed. Overthrown by a military coup in 1955, he was forced into exile, but his legacy persisted. Nationalistic economic policies continued and Peronism as a political and social movement remained firmly entrenched and became increasingly radicalized.

WOMEN'S SUFFRAGE

During the Depression and continuing through the 1950s, attitudes toward feminism often reflected strategies to mobilize women as a political force rather than bring meaningful improvements to their lives. Supporting female suffrage broadened the populist base Vargas was building in Brazil; dictators in Cuba and the Dominican Republic used it as a way to legitimize their dictatorial regimes. But after World War II, energetic feminist movements often accompanied a return to democracy and resulted in an expansion of voting rights. The end of the Ubico dictatorship in Guatemala coincided with extending the franchise to women, and Rómulo Betancourt and the Acción Democrática granted women's suffrage in Venezuela during a brief period of democracy in 1947. Perón ended military rule in Argentina, and the 1948 revolution in Costa Rica abolished that nation's army while introducing a host of social reforms. In both countries, female suffrage accompanied these changes.

Although Cárdenas advocated full political rights for women in the 1930s, Mexico did not extend the franchise until much later. As a populist, Cárdenas shrewdly recognized the growing influence of women's leagues and the need to consolidate their influence under the aegis of the government rather than the Catholic Church. During his administration, the revolutionary party granted "working women" the right to vote in its plebiscites and a suffrage amendment to the constitution nearly passed in 1938. Nevertheless, Mexican women did not receive the vote until after World War II.

Table 20.2 Date of Women's Suffrage in National Elections

YEAR	COUNTRY
1929	Ecuador
1932	Brazil
1932	Uruguay
1934	Cuba
1939	El Salvador
1942	Dominican Republic
1945	Guatemala
1945	Panama
1947	Argentina
1947	Venezuela
1949	Chile
1949	Costa Rica
1950	Haiti
1952	Bolivia
1953	Mexico
1955	Honduras
1955	Nicaragua
1955	Peru
1957	Colombia
1961	Paraguay

MASS MEDIA AND A NATIONAL IMAGINARY

Advances in communications technology brought profound cultural changes to Latin America, expanding and eventually overtaking the public reach enjoyed by print media. Prior to the 1950s, broadcast media provided news and entertainment to an ever-growing audience through radio and film. Since these technologies also allowed populist leaders to disseminate their messages more broadly, they incorporated broadcast communications into their political strategies.

Radio arrived in the 1920s and initially operated as a state-run enterprise in many countries. Over the next two decades, private national industries emerged, often linked to large commercial broadcast companies in the United States. In the early years, radio programs targeted cities, where electricity and other necessary infrastructure were better developed. The growing populations in those areas also provided a larger market for the predominantly nationalist and populist themes of early programming. As the number of stations and broadcasting range expanded, the radio industry contributed to the creation of a "national imaginary." A shared cultural vision began to emerge as mass media standardized not only the content of programs, but also language, jokes, and other cultural references.

The growth of broadcast media helped to advance the emergence of new icons and genres of music and dance. Tango originated in the brothels and dance halls of Buenos Aires's tenement neighborhoods in the late nineteenth century. The music and dance style reflected the combination of cultures that came together in the city's outer districts—countryside *gauchos*, European immigrants, and the Afro-American influence remaining from earlier decades.

Tango remained a cultural expression of the masses until it became popular in Europe after 1910. Within a decade it had gained worldwide appeal, popularized by the radio and film industries. Between 1920 and 1950, it experienced a "golden age" as Argentines embraced the dance and its distinctive musical accompaniment as an embodiment of national culture. In the 1940s, Juan and Evita Perón's populist message compelled many to associate them with the tango's humble origins. Several composers and directors wrote music and films tying the Peróns and tango together.

Samba underwent a similar transformation in Brazil as a result of new technologies and populist design. Originating from music and dance associated with African slaves and *candomblé* rituals, popular samba took shape in the urban slums of Rio de Janeiro in the last half of the nineteenth century. Its style evolved to include other influences as well, reflecting the hybrid culture that was emerging in the hillside slums (*favelas*) on the outskirts of the city. The distinctive dance and music genre eventually became associated with Brazil's *carnaval*, and samba schools played a prominent role in energizing the costumes, parades, and other public performances that distinguish the festival. An intentional formulation of nationalist character in the 1920s coincided with and facilitated the popularization of samba. The process accelerated even further under Vargas's *Estado Novo*; Brazil's populist leader relied on the emerging broadcast industry to shape cultural expressions of "the nation." He often reached out to popular artists, coordinating public performances and inviting them to visit the presidential residence. Radio and film became a vital part of his strategy for disseminating a sense of Brazilianness through samba and other icons.

The film industry also developed in the early twentieth century and contributed to the creation of a national imaginary, with the earliest motion pictures appearing in the 1890s. Driven largely by U.S. and European cinema companies, early cinema focused on the larger markets in Mexico, Argentina, and Brazil. As in radio, motion pictures appeared first in urban areas with larger audiences and better infrastructure, whereas people in smaller towns relied on itinerant projection crews to bring films to more remote areas. National cinematic industries developed, often in collaboration with moviemakers in Hollywood; the 1930s to the 1950s marked the golden age of Latin America film. The Mexican movie industry, bolstered by technical and financial assistance from the OCIAA during the World War II, became a transnational phenomenon throughout the Western Hemisphere. The Good Neighbor Policy and U.S. cultural diplomacy during wartime facilitated contact between Hollywood and Latin American artists, helping to perpetuate numerous genres and popular icons beyond national borders.

In Mexico, a variety of film styles, including *comedias rancheras, cabareteras*, (dance hall), family melodramas, and folkloric *indígena* stories, became popular. The golden age of film also gave rise to stars such as Pedro Infante, Jorge Negrete, Pedro Armendáriz, María Félix, and Dolores del Río. The comedic actor Cantinflas (Mario Moreno) brought his *pelado* (tramp) character and

Table 20.3 Film Premiers, Select Countries

COUNTRY	FIRST CINEMATIC PREMIER	FIRST LOCALLY PRODUCED FILM
Argentina	1896	1910
Brazil	1896	1898
Uruguay	1896	
Mexico	1896	1897
Chile	1896	1902
Guatemala	1896	
Peru	1897	1911
Cuba	1897	1898
Venezuela	1897	1897
Colombia	1897	1905
Ecuador		1950

ADAPTED FROM ANNETTE KUHN AND GUY WESTWELL, *OXFORD DICTIONARY OF FILM STUDIES* (NEW YORK: OXFORD UNIVERSITY PRESS, 2012).

verbal gymnastics to the silver screen with movies like *Ahí está el detalle* (*There's the Point,* 1940), a satirical look at Mexico's elite. Movies explored the pressures of modernization on the family and urban poverty in melodramas like *Cuando los hijos se van* (*When the Children Leave,* 1941) and *Nosotros los pobres* (1947).

The director Emilio "El Indio" Fernández imbued his movies with an *indigenista* sensibility and pioneered the Mexican "look." A veteran of the revolution and an actor himself, Fernandez established his artistic and nationalist vision through *Flor Silvestre* (*Wild Flower,* 1943) and *Maria Candelaria* (1943). Assisted by his cinematographer, Gabriel Figueroa, Fernández's style emphasized the landscape's picturesque beauty. His movies illustrated the conflicts within Mexican society between the indigenous and mestizo, with an emphasis on the value of the indigenous to the fabric of the nation.

Carmen Miranda rose to prominence in the 1930s as one of Brazil's most prominent entertainers. Raised in a working-class area of Rio de Janeiro, she became emblematic of Vargas's populist message during the *Estado Novo.* Radio stations played her renditions of popular Brazilian sambas, making them part of the national culture and identity advocated by the president. She moved to the United States in 1939 to appear on Broadway and to star in Hollywood films, but found herself typecast in roles of the exotic Brazilian bombshell. Miranda's onscreen persona generally lacked depth and Brazilians accused her of becoming "Americanized."

The Great Depression and World War II gave rise to new trends that would guide Latin American development after 1950. The rejection of European cultural and economic models in the 1930s converged with rising nationalism and helped to validate the strengthening of the state under authoritarian populism. An expansion of economic nationalism in the postwar years had widespread repercussions for the rest of the twentieth century. Furthermore, cooperation between Latin American nations and the United States presaged a new paradoxical turn in hemispheric relations, as Cold War tensions frequently surfaced alongside the adoption of U.S. symbols of popular culture.

Primary Source

In the spirit of the Good Neighbor Policy, the OCIAA attempted to craft wartime messages that would appeal to Latin Americans to support the Allied Powers. An internal memorandum from 1944 outlines strategies that involved portraying U.S. citizens as humble and friendly neighbors and emphasizing the cultural similarities between the United States and Latin America.

SOURCE: Office of the Coordinator of Inter-American Affairs Public Opinion Memo, May 1944, NARA, RG 229, Entry 126, Content Planning, Box 1459.

1. A presentation of life in the U.S. to the Latin American should be made with this in mind. We do *not* want to impress him with our gadgets, our bank accounts, our drive to success, even as examples of what he may also have. We *do* want to show him the inventive genius behind the gadgets, the pioneering spirit behind our drive to success, the wider interests made possible by our bank accounts. The average U.S. neighbor is at heart a simple hard-working, movie and church-going fellow who is actively interested in new things . . . . Above all, he is simpatico. The Latin American desperately wants to know him. Introduce him.

2. The United States interest in Latin America is a great phenomenon of the past few years. We are listening to Latin American music, wearing huaraches to the beach; millions of us are learning Spanish. We are reading books about Latin America. We are going there on our vacations.

3. This exchange of interest is a forerunner of our appreciation and adoption of the best in each other's language, customs, habits, methods. And this ability to add to what we have is what we mean by cultural growth. It contrasts with the German "Kultur" which is subtraction and decay, which is not simpatico.

. . .

Motion pictures, radio programs, and various other mediums should all bear this theme in mind when portraying life in the U.S.—our *similar cultural aspirations*.

We must remember that we are not selling heroes to Latin America: we are selling the average man who, like the average Latin American, is hard to put to pay his bills, anxious to better things for his family, to understand more clearly the world he lives in."

SUGGESTIONS FOR FURTHER READING

Alexander, Robert J. *A History of Organized Labor in Argentina*. Westport, CT: Praeger, 2003.

Archibald, Priscilla. *Imagining Modernity in the Andes*. Lewisburg, PA: Bucknell University Press, 2011.

Bethell, Leslie, and Ian Roxborough. *Latin America between the Second World War and the Cold War: 1944–1948*. Cambridge: Cambridge University Press, 1992.

Burke, Peter, and María Lúcia G. Pallares-Burke. *Gilberto Freyre: Social Theory in the Tropics*. New York: Peter Lang, 2008.

Doremus, Anne. "Indigenism, Mestizaje, and National Identity in Mexico during the 1940s and the 1950s." *Mexican Studies/Estudios Mexicanos* 17, no. 2 (Summer 2001): 375–402.

Drinot, Paulo, and Alan Knight (eds.). *The Great Depression in Latin America*. Durham, NC: Duke University Press, 2014.

Dulles, John W. F. *Sobral Pinto, "The Conscience of Brazil:" Leading the Attack against Vargas (1930–1945)*. Austin: University of Texas Press, 2002.

Frank, Gary. *Juan Perón vs. Spruille Braden: The Story behind the Blue Book*. Landham, MD: University Press of America, 1980.

Friedman, Max Paul. *Nazis and Good Neighbors: The United States Campaign against the Germans of Latin America in World War II*. Cambridge: Cambridge University Press, 2003.

Gellman, Irwin F. *Good Neighbor Diplomacy: United States Policies in Latin America, 1933–1945*. Baltimore: Johns Hopkins University Press, 1979.

Green, David. *The Containment of Latin America; A History of the Myths and Realities of the Good Neighbor Policy*. Chicago: Quadrangle Books, 1971.

Hammond, Gregory. *The Women's Suffrage Movement and Feminism in Argentina from Roca to Perón*. Albuquerque: University of New Mexico Press, 2011.

Hayes, Joy Elizabeth. *Radio Nation: Communication, Popular Culture, and Nationalism in Mexico, 1920–1950*. Tucson: University of Arizona Press, 2000.

Kampwirth, Karen (ed.). *Gender and Populism in Latin America: Passionate Politics*. University Park: Pennsylvania State University Press, 2010.

Karush, Matthew B. *Culture of Class: Radio and Cinema in the Making of a Divided Argentina, 1920–1946*. Durham, NC: Duke University Press, 2012.

King, John. *Magical Reels: A History of Cinema in Latin America*. New York: Verso, 2000.

Leonard, Thomas M., and John F. Bratzel. *Latin America during World War II*. Lanham, MD: Rowman & Littlefield, 2007.

Malloy, James (ed.). *Authoritarianism and Corporatism in Latin America*. Pittsburgh, PA: University of Pittsburgh Press, 1977.

McCann, Bryan. *Hello, Hello Brazil: Popular Music in the Making of Modern Brazil*. Durham, NC: Duke University Press, 2004.

Ramírez Berg, Charles. *The Classical Mexican Cinema: The Poetics of the Exceptional Golden Age Films*. Austin: University of Texas Press, 2015.

Rock, David (ed.). *Latin America in the 1940s: War and Postwar Transitions*. Berkeley: University of California Press, 1994.

Sadlier, Darlene J. *Americans All: Good Neighbor Cultural Diplomacy in World War II*. Austin: University of Texas Press, 2013.

Schoultz, Lars. *Beneath the United States: A History of U.S. Policy toward Latin America*. Cambridge, MA: Harvard University Press, 1998.

Tota, Antonio Pedro, and Daniel Joseph Greenberg. *The Seduction of Brazil: The Americanization of Brazil during World War II*. Austin: University of Texas Press, Teresa Lozano Long Institute of Latin American Studies, 2009.

Vaughn, Mary Kay. "Modernizing Patriarchy: State Policies, Rural Household, and Women in Mexico, 1930–1940." In *Hidden Histories of Gender and the State in Latin America*, edited by Elizabeth Dore and Maxine Molyneux, 194–214. Durham, NC: Duke University Press Books, 2000.

CHAPTER 21

Onset of Cold War

1952	Marcos Pérez Jiménez becomes dictator of Venezuela and embarks on modernization of Caracas
1953	Women gain the vote in Mexico
June 1954	U.S.-supported military coup in Guatemala deposes Árbenz, who flees into exile
1958	Protestors in Caracas mob vice president Richard Nixon's motorcade
1969	Four-day Soccer War between Honduras and El Salvador

After World War II, security concerns in the Western Hemisphere changed from fears of Nazism and fascism to anxieties over the spread of communism and the ascendancy of the Soviet Union. The United States took the lead in disparaging policies and interest groups that seemed to embody vaguely conceived tenets of "the left." But the upheavals that accompanied the Depression and World War II had left a lasting impact on Latin Americans. A fervently nationalist orientation in economic models took hold as state-sponsored development and protectionist trade policies became the norm. These strategies yielded some initial growth through import substitution industrialization (ISI) and improved the standard of living for middle-class consumers. But the benefits of this economic expansion did not extend to large sectors of the population and growth proved unsustainable in the long term.

The onset of the Cold War and the increasingly nationalist basis of Latin American economic models led to a major shift in the region's relationship with the neighbor to the north. As one of two world superpowers, the United States wielded disproportionate influence in the Western Hemisphere. Its leaders became ever more adamant that Latin American nations toe the line of anticommunism throughout the 1950s. The economic aid and cultural collaboration that had characterized the relationship during World War II gave way to new security concerns. In some countries, leftist and nationalist interests pushed back against U.S. pressure—at times with devastating consequences. Most notably, the United States helped to orchestrate a coup to overthrow a democratically elected leftist leader in Guatemala in 1954. That endeavor became a model for future covert strategies to fight communism in the rest of Latin America.

LEFTISM IN LATIN AMERICA

The first leftist political parties in Latin America formed in the early decades of the twentieth century and included a wide spectrum of ideological beliefs. From the beginning, critics often lumped together ideas stemming from communist, socialist, and other Marxist-inspired groups under the overarching label of "the left." Political opposition frequently considered the broad array of leftist ideas synonymous with communism. But leftism in Latin America emerged from diverse origins. Areas that experienced large waves of European immigration in the late nineteenth century, such as Argentina, Brazil, and Uruguay, saw the rise of an internationally tied, urban working-class movement through anarchosyndicalism. In other countries, communist movements took root in the rural masses. Like the early populist movements, communist parties initially developed as an alternative to the ruling oligarchies that dominated the political structures of the late nineteenth century. Commonly inspired by the popular mobilization within the Russian Revolution of 1917, early communist movements in Latin America sought to challenge authoritarian governing models. They also aspired to reject the Eurocentric capitalist economic system that had created vast inequalities in late nineteenth-century society.

The appearance of these movements immediately concerned U.S. leaders. Many Marxist-inspired groups rallied around the cause of anti-imperialism in response to various U.S. interventions in the early twentieth century. Agustín Farabundo Martí led such an initiative in El Salvador with the intent of introducing Marxist solutions to improve the lives of the country's rural poor. Backed by indigenous peasants, he started a rebellion against the nation's dictator in 1931. Government forces eventually captured and executed Martí and carried out a systematic massacre of tens of thousands of his supporters (known as *La Matanza*) after the uprising failed. A similar movement arose in neighboring Nicaragua when Augusto César Sandino rebelled against a U.S. military occupation of that country in 1927. He was killed in 1934 by Anastasio Somoza García, a military general who became a U.S.-backed dictator a few years later.

Unlike Martí, Sandino rejected the ideological tenets of communism and saw himself instead as a nationalist liberal. Nevertheless, leaders in Washington viewed both figures as evidence of a rising tide of communist infiltration in Latin America. But their deaths made them martyrs against U.S. imperialism in the eyes of their supporters. In later decades, both men became icons of nationalism and resistance to U.S. intervention as well as eponyms for the Farabundo Martí National Liberation Front and the Sandinista National Liberation Front during the Cold War.

U.S. leaders also viewed early moves toward economic nationalism as a form of communism. The nationalizations of major industries carried out by populist leaders caused particular concern. State-run industries emerged first in Uruguay and Argentina; Bolivia's expropriation of major oil installations followed in the 1930s. President Lázaro Cárdenas's nationalization of the railroad and oil industries in Mexico evoked a major outcry in the United States as industry owners and the media aggressively labeled his administration socialist. Such reactions to emerging leftism in Latin America in the early twentieth century began a long and important trend of U.S. leaders equating anti-Americanism with communism.

The Great Depression commenced just as the workforce in Latin America was growing and becoming more mobilized. The economic crisis caused by the fall in world markets created an environment ripe for communist parties, and many Latin American governments responded with repression. The Venezuelan government declared the party illegal and the Peruvian government banned the American

Popular Revolutionary Alliance along with the Peruvian Communist Party in the early 1930s. State control over the labor movement grew throughout Latin America during the 1930s, particularly as national leaders feared an association between labor groups and the growing influence of international communism.

Despite growing concerns over communist parties and socialist-oriented policies in the early twentieth century, U.S. and Latin American leaders considered fascism and other far-right movements the gravest ideological threat until after World War II. In fact, leftist movements around the world united as the Popular Front to fight fascism during the war. As a result, leftist-inspired organizations made significant gains during the war. Communist-affiliated artist groups in Mexico were the first to create antifascist propaganda in the late 1930s, even before more formal propaganda campaigns by the U.S. and Mexican governments. Particularly after the Soviet Union joined the Allied Powers in 1941, the position of the Popular Front in Latin America and around the world strengthened considerably. By 1946, communist parties existed in every country in Latin America and exerted considerable influence in labor unions.

POSTWAR ECONOMIC TRENDS

The relationship between the United States and Latin American nations shifted after World War II as U.S. leaders focused their attention on postwar recovery efforts in Europe along with combatting the spread of Soviet influence. The economic and cultural collaboration present in U.S.–Latin American diplomatic strategies during the war began to crumble, although Latin American leaders campaigned for a continuation of the wartime direct economic assistance and market guarantees. But even before World War II drew to a close in 1945, U.S. leaders made it clear that direct economic aid would end with the Allies' victory. Accordingly, they instructed Latin American nations to create a welcoming environment to encourage U.S. direct investment. This change, however, encouraged some leaders in the region to begin looking inward and developing more protectionist economic policies.

The Economic Commission for Latin America and the Caribbean

After World War II, leaders from the Allied Powers devised new strategies to prevent the type of global conflict that had led to such destruction. One central initiative was the creation of the United Nations, and Latin American leaders played an important role in its formation. Delegates from 20 nations and the United States gathered in Mexico City for the Inter-American Conference on War and Peace in February 1945. The resulting Treaty of Chapultepec established the framework for regional cooperation in matters of security and set the stage for the eventual foundation of the Organization of American States in 1948. In April 1945, they met again at the United Nations Conference on International Organization in San Francisco and became part of the 51 founding members of the United Nations. Thus, Latin American participation in postwar peacekeeping efforts included a commitment both to international cooperation and to regionalism through these newly formed organizations.

In addition to issues of hemispheric security, Latin American leaders looked to alliances in the area of economic development. Debates regarding trade and economic policy at the Mexico City Conference revealed deep divisions. U.S. delegates called for an elimination of the economic nationalism that had surfaced under early populist regimes; those from Latin America saw a need to alter inequalities in the economic paradigm that had left the region vulnerable in the wake of the Great Depression.

In 1948, the Economic and Social Council of the United Nations established the Economic Commission for Latin America. The Caribbean was later added as a specific designation and the commission became known as ECLAC, or by its Spanish acronym, CEPAL (Comisión Económica para América Latina y el Caribe). Its main objective was to facilitate economic development in the region and its leaders became instrumental in guiding the adoption of industrialization and trade strategies in Latin America in the decades following World War II.

The commission's first director, the Argentine economist Raúl Prebisch, used his position to press for a new model of economic development for Latin American and other developing nations. In terms of world trade, he argued, industrialized countries constituted the "center," and producers of raw materials made up the "periphery." Although global commerce tied the center and periphery together, industrialized nations enjoyed disproportionately larger benefits from that relationship. Not only were the finished goods exported by center nations valued higher, but their prices also rose more quickly than those of the agricultural goods and raw materials traded by nations on the periphery. This imbalance, according to Prebisch, kept periphery nations in a perpetual state of underdevelopment.

Prebisch's theories helped to engender new schools of thought among economists and policy makers in Latin America who sought to end the cycle of disparity and poverty that conventional economic models had seemed to produce. Broadly labeled structuralism, this new set of arguments called on national governments to become directly involved in economic development through state-led industrialization. Prebisch and other leaders of CEPAL specifically wanted national governments to participate actively in the economy in three ways: (1) placing manufacturing in heavy industry under state ownership; (2) facilitating an expansion of manufacturing in other industries; and (3) intervening in the economy to alter the balance of trade.

Import Substitution Industrialization

In the 1930s, the failure of the comparative-advantage model based on agriculture seemed obvious. As a consequence, many Latin American leaders were looking for an alternative to open markets and export-oriented monoculture even before the outbreak of World War II. They wanted to develop an economic base that would provide a reliable source of national income and facilitate consistent growth in productivity. During the war, direct-aid packages from the United States had provided technical and financial resources that enabled an increase in existing production and allowed the development of new industries to support the Allied war effort. Vital infrastructure projects, such as the improvement and expansion of highways, railroads, ports, and airfields, also resulted from strategic cooperation with the United States. Furthermore, favorable trade policies guaranteed prices and a market for many materials produced in Latin America and provided much-needed financial stability. Thus, the war years allowed Latin American economies to grow and to begin developing a more diversified and industrial economic base that provided a springboard for a dramatic expansion of industry in Latin America after 1945.

In the following decades, the region increasingly turned to ISI—an economic model that emphasized developing local industries to produce durable consumer goods for a local upper- and middle-class market. Under this model, Latin American nations hoped to reduce imports of high-priced consumer goods, such as large appliances and automobiles, by encouraging industrialists to manufacture those types of products and by encouraging consumers to purchase locally produced goods.

Since Latin American nations traditionally had not fostered durable consumer goods industries, government leaders repeatedly intervened in the economy in an effort to support the new manufacturing focus. Trade policies created high tariffs to protect new local industries by making imports of competing goods more expensive. National development banks provided financing and steered investments to preferred sectors. Governments created subsidies and tax incentives to allow new industrialists to maximize profits; and fiscal policy kept exchange rates overvalued to make machinery and other capital goods cheaper to import. Many Latin American governments created state-owned industries, or parastatals, in sectors such as energy, transportation, communications, petrochemicals, and steel. Those enterprises then subsidized the cost of industrialization by providing materials and resources necessary for manufacturing at a low price.

Consequences of Import Substitution Industrialization

On the surface, industrialization policies seemed to work as many measures of economic growth trended upward throughout the 1950s. The largest Latin American nations were the most successful; Mexico and Brazil developed some heavy industry and began diversifying exports. Even smaller nations expanded their manufacturing capacity and the gross domestic product of Latin America as a whole tripled between 1950 and 1970.

But overall growth came at a cost because import substitution development strategies significantly affected the relationship of Latin American governments with the labor and agricultural sectors. Economic policies privileged industrial development and regulations aimed to help new manufacturing enterprises maximize profits. Cheap, reliable labor comprised a vital component of this equation. During World War II, workers had come under tight government control. They often had made important concessions, such as wage increases and collective

Table 21.1 Gross Domestic Product Growth of Select Countries

	1950–1960	1960–1973	1973–1981	1950–1981	1981–1990	1950–1990
Argentina	2.8	4.0	1.2	2.9	−0.6	2.1
Brazil	6.8	7.5	5.5	6.8	2.3	5.8
Chile	4.0	3.4	3.6	3.6	2.5	3.4
Colombia	4.6	5.6	4.5	5.0	3.9	4.8
Peru	5.5	4.8	3.8	4.8	−1.7	3.3
Venezuela	7.6	4.7	−0.1	4.4	0.6	3.5
Small countries	3.6	5.4	4.3	4.5	1.2	4.3

ADAPTED FROM RICARDO FRENCH-DAVIS, "THE LATIN AMERICA ECONOMIES, 1950–1990," IN LESLIE BETHELL (ED.), *CAMBRIDGE HISTORY OF LATIN AMERICA, VOLUME VI, LATIN AMERICA SINCE 1930, ECONOMY, SOCIETY AND POLITICS, PART I ECONOMY AND SOCIETY* (CAMBRIDGE: CAMBRIDGE UNIVERSITY PRESS, 1994), 189.

work stoppage, in the interest of national and hemispheric security during war-time emergency. The close relationship between labor groups and populist leaders, such as Juan Perón in Argentina and Getúlio Vargas in Brazil, set the stage for a more cooperative working class and incomes increased for highly skilled laborers. But those workers with low skill levels generally saw their real wages plateau or even decline, whereas the elite and growing middle class secured the profits. Keeping wages low for urban workers required Latin American leaders to provide economic concessions to maintain the support of unions. Populist leaders in particular used subsidies for rent, food, and other day-to-day expenses as a way to meet workers' expectations while ensuring profits for industrialists.

Government subsidies and high levels of regulation negatively affected the agricultural sector. The rapid development of new industries precipitously expanded cities throughout Latin America. Urban migration increased the numbers of people forced to purchase basic foodstuffs because they could no longer grow their own. Whereas greater demand for agricultural goods would normally lead to rising prices, government-imposed price controls served to subsidize the cost of food and ease the financial burden on the working class, thereby ensuring a more favorable standard of living in the cities. But the resulting drop in agricultural profits discouraged farmers from producing. Large numbers of farmers abandoned the fields and relocated to cities, where they joined the ranks of the expanding urban working class. In many countries, the reduced food supply forced government leaders to import and subsidize food to feed the growing population in cities. In a reversal of the comparative-advantage economic models that had defined the nineteenth century, many Latin American countries now imported foodstuffs while attempting to support an industrial sector.

Import substitution policies eventually generated a host of other problems. Government interference in the economy did little to create an entrepreneurial class. State-owned enterprises dominated in heavy industry, but in other areas of the economy, power remained in hands of the elite. Furthermore, in most areas of Latin America, import substitution measures exacerbated inequality and those living below the poverty line saw their income and their standard of living deteriorate. Many new government incentives penalized the very poor and those whose livelihood was not tied to manufacturing. Furthermore, rampant corruption plagued many areas as public officials accepted payoffs for government contracts, import licenses, and other favors.

With limited growth, the weaknesses of the import substitution model soon became evident. Even the largest Latin American nations began to exhaust ISI possibilities within a decade. After building new industrial sectors to replace previously imported products, national leaders discovered that they needed alternate methods to expand markets and ensure continued growth. Presidents Eduardo Frei in Chile and Juscelino Kubitschek in Brazil adopted a two-pronged strategy of reforming the agricultural sectors while promoting the expansion of nontraditional exports. Such schemes often involved turning to multinational corporations, which allowed new infusions of investments, expertise, and capital assets into the economy.

Dependency Approaches and Regional Integration

By the 1960s, some proponents of structuralism became even more vocal, arguing that the industrialized world inevitably affected adversely the economic potential of developing nations. Dependency theory began to take shape as a school of thought that relied on the "center–periphery" dichotomy that had been expounded by CEPAL leaders. Its adherents asserted that forces beyond the control of Latin American leaders—such as economic policies of developed nations and inequalities inherent within the capitalist system—kept Latin America dependent on more industrialized and often larger countries. These theorists saw little benefit in the state-sponsored structuralist strategies put in place in earlier years because they believed center nations had naturally adapted to the periphery's attempts at industrialization; new forms of dependency followed as Latin American nations came to rely on the developed world for capital and heavy machinery. A deep sense of pessimism characterized the most ardent dependency theorists; some suggested that only a socialist revolution and a complete elimination of the capitalist system would allow the periphery to break free from the exploitative economic system. Marxists and other leftist-oriented leaders in Latin America often found dependency theory to be compelling, further escalating concerns in the United States, where a Cold War mentality made such ideas appear particularly dangerous.

Some CEPAL economists began to back away from a zealous industrialization approach and instead advocated a mixed model of state intervention. This prescription advocated diversifying exports and moving toward regional economic integration in combination with import substitution strategies. Nations with small economies found the regional integration approach particularly compelling as they struggled to compete with larger nations and hoped that combining markets and resources would give them a competitive edge. CEPAL's prescription for integration called for lowering internal tariffs within the regional market, maintaining a common external tariff, and coordinating trade and economic policies among member nations.

Central American nations launched a common market in 1960, lowering tariffs and other barriers to trade among its participants. The accord allowed members of the Central American Common Market to diversify manufacturing and exports; trade within the region increased from $33 million to more than $1 billion within two decades. At the same time, the Treaty of Montevideo created the Latin American Free Trade Agreement to facilitate economic integration among Mexico, Brazil, Argentina, Colombia, Chile, Ecuador, and Bolivia. Between 1960 and 1973, intraregional trade among the signatories nearly doubled.

Despite the seeming success of expanding trade, attempts at regional integration quickly began to fizzle. The Central American Common Market did not create sufficient industrial diversification and some member nations benefited more than others. Honduras withdrew from the common market in 1969 after economic and social tensions with El Salvador escalated into the Four-Day Soccer War; regional cooperation in Central America languished for nearly two decades. Latin American Free Trade Agreement members also struggled to make regional integration work as the larger nations of Mexico, Brazil, and Argentina were less reliant on their smaller neighbors for economic growth and internal dissent arose among member nations. Chile, Colombia, Peru, Ecuador, and Bolivia attempted to create a subregional market with the establishment of the Andean Pact in 1969. None of these early attempts at regional integration produced the desired outcomes, and the rise of military dictatorships and economic crises in the coming decades disrupted the trend toward coordinated trade blocs. Nevertheless, the foundations of regional integration remained and eventually became a part of neoliberal economic strategies in the 1990s.

CONSUMERS AND CULTURE AT MID-CENTURY

Import substitution policies brought some short-term benefits, primarily to the wealthy and the middle classes in the immediate postwar era. Consumers saw their purchasing power and their standard of living rise as national governments privileged manufacturing and protected locally produced goods from foreign imports. In Argentina, Juan Perón's 1946 Five-Year Plan favored the production of textiles, electrical appliances, and automotive parts. Under his tenure, the number of industrial plants more than doubled, primarily in the provinces. Employment increased dramatically in various sectors, including textile and electrical appliance manufacturing. The number of workers in the electrical appliance industry increased by 151 percent; and the number of refrigerators produced increased from 12,000 units in 1947 to 152,000 in 1955. Representing a transition from luxury to necessity, refrigerators represented half of all electrical appliances manufactured at this time, and the electricity supply struggled to keep up with both industry and consumer demand. Under Perón's economic policies, production of capital goods increased by 102 percent.

Women played a preeminent role in the purchasing decisions for large durable goods (such as automobiles and major appliances) and were responsible for the majority of day-to-day household shopping. Advertising agents and the government recognized the power working-class women had as consumers. Magazines in Argentina peddled the importance of beauty to women, especially to the young and newly married. Such publications communicated the message that maintaining a pleasant appearance through the right clothes, makeup, and hairstyle would allow women to keep themselves attractive and help them to keep their husbands content.

The growing number of employees in factories and other working-class occupations increased their participation as consumers during the postwar era. Thanks to installment payment plans, low-income purchasers could afford home appliances. Furthermore, increases in disposable income allowed workers to spend money on movies and other entertainment. Advertisers noted the expanding purchasing power of the working classes and many ad campaigns targeted this ascending consumer group. The Peronista government enacted education campaigns to instruct these new buyers on how to recognize fair pricing practices to make good purchasing decisions and also to report unscrupulous retailers to the police.

The U.S.-based retailer Sears opened its first location in Mexico City in 1947, following a religious procession and blessing led by that country's top-ranking Catholic official. Aware of the importance of religious culture, Sears's officials adapted some of their business practices to suit local preferences and appealed to Mexican nationalism. Shoppers responded favorably with $1 million in purchases in the first two weeks after the store's opening.

Advertising and Broadcasting

Marketing campaigns targeted the growing middle class as both the manufacturing and the retail sectors expanded under ISI. Advertisers relied heavily on print media, but also increasingly used radio broadcasting to reach their intended audience. Partnerships between Latin American entrepreneurs and U.S. radio companies developed in the 1920s and strengthened during World War II. The large listening audiences drawn to the popular *radionovelas* attracted the attention of marketers, and advertising spots for consumer goods became commonplace during *novela* broadcasts.

The first major television networks appeared in Cuba, Mexico, and Brazil in 1950, and in the following years broadcasts appeared in other Latin American nations as well. U.S. broadcasters such as NBC and CBS and equipment manufacturers such as RCA and General Electric supplied equipment, technical assistance, and programming guidance. As in radio and film, national industries emerged in Latin American television, but the United States played a vital role in the early years. In Argentina, Juan Perón set up a state monopoly over radio and television broadcasting that ended with his overthrow in 1955, but the military maintained firm control over the industry until the end of the decade. Dictatorial regimes in Colombia and Venezuela oversaw the early television industries in those countries, but private-sector interests quickly began making inroads. Throughout the 1950s and 1960s, most Latin American networks became commercial enterprises reliant on advertising revenue. As a result, large-scale marketing of consumer products developed hand in hand with the emerging broadcasting industry.

Fierce competition characterized the birth of Mexican television as radio moguls Rómulo O'Farrill Silva and Emilio Azcárraga Vidaurreta lobbied the government for the first broadcast concessions. O'Farrill used his close friendship with President Miguel Alemán Valdés to obtain authorization and his station XHTV transmitted the president's address to the nation on September 1, 1950. Azcárraga launched his station, XEW-TV, in January 1952 by broadcasting a baseball game. Other competing stations began operating soon afterward. Early television programming included coverage of national events such as Día de la Independencia and religious holidays like Los Reyes Magos (Three Kings' Day). News stories about industry and commerce often took on a decidedly pro-business tone. Broadcasts of sporting events such as boxing, soccer, and baseball also became popular.

The radio entrepreneur Francisco de Assis Chateaubriand Bandeira de Melo founded Brazil's first television station. TV Tupi Difusora began transmitting on September 18, 1950, in São Paulo, and other stations soon followed. National stations formed a network of independent broadcasters known as the Rede de Emissoras Independentes. As in other areas, programming depended on the popular sponsorship model whereby advertisers produced content for entertainment. Other sponsored programs included the *O Repórtero Esso*, produced by the eponymous U.S. oil company with news from CBS and UPI.

Television in Argentina debuted on October 17, 1951, with a broadcast of the celebration of *Día de la Lealtad Peronista* (Peronist Loyalty Day) on *Canal 7*. During the first few years of the station's existence, it broadcast live for only several hours a day. The station began transmitting a U.S.-produced series in 1955, and the military coup that year brought changes to the national broadcast landscape. The introduction of the *Ley Nacional de Radiodifusión y Televisión* set up a system of both state-owned and privately owned television stations.

Telenovelas made their debut in Cuba in the early 1950s and quickly became one of the most popular types of program in Latin America. The U.S.-based Colgate–Palmolive produced the first *telenovelas* as a way to market soap to Cuban consumers. Similar to their U.S. counterpart, the soap opera, *telenovelas* emerged as serialized dramas, but the Latin American versions offered a finite number of episodes, with runs of six to nine months. Colgate used this model throughout the region, as did Lever, Ford, and the European company Nestlé. The radio and television entrepreneur Goar Mestre helped to pioneer the new genre on his station CMQ with assistance from the NBC network in the United States. In the 1960s, he went to South America and, in partnership with CBS and Time Life, invested in the television industries in Argentina, Venezuela, and Peru.

The *telenovela* genre quickly spread throughout Latin America and its roots in serialized radio plays were readily apparent. Colgate sponsored an early Mexican show, *Senda Prohibida*, billed as "your Colgate novella" and one of the first Brazilian *telenovelas*, *Em Busca da Felicidade*, originated from a popular Colgate promotional campaign. With a predominantly female target audience, these programs embraced gendered themes intended to appeal to Latin American women. Plotlines featured social and class issues, including class differences, social mobility, inequality, and poverty. The protagonist, generally a young woman from a humble background, frequently experienced a reversal of fortune through an event such as winning the lottery or receiving an inheritance from a long-lost relative. Other plot points included mistaken identity and amnesia; supporting characters included villains who attempted to thwart the protagonist in her quest for love and various ancillary characters with their own subplots. Latin American audiences found comfort in the logic of the *telenovela*, which dictated that the protagonist would finally be united with the love of her life, would be reunited with a child or parent, or would achieve the wealth and status due her. The eventual plot resolution always included punishment for evil as the villain or villains received their comeuppance.

In these early years, the high costs of television sets prohibited many Latin American families from owning one. People often gathered outside store windows or congregated inside bars to watch soccer matches or other shows. Public viewings became an early form of television consumption and a forum for building a sense of community and identity. For those able to afford them, televisions quickly grew to be a status symbol and a way to demonstrate middle-class modernity. By the mid-1950s, nationally produced television sets became available to consumers in Mexico, Argentina, and Brazil. A steady and strong economy eventually made television sets more affordable and easier to obtain, but the consumer market remained limited.

The relatively high cost of televisions and the limited pool of potential consumers affected the market for advertising. Fewer viewers meant less incentive for advertisers to buy airtime, and television station operation costs remained high. Instead of competing against each other for advertising revenue, three Mexico City channels merged in 1955, forming Telesistema Mexicano. Led by Azcárraga and O'Farrill, the station expanded its broadcast coverage to include northern states and tailored each of its channels' programming for different audiences. Among its programming successes, Telesistema Mexicano helped popularize the *telenovela* nationwide and contributed to a further standardizing of entertainment and popular culture symbols across the country. The invention of videotape technology during the 1950s enabled the station to import programming from the United States and export its own programming to the rest of Latin America. Mexican-produced *telenovelas* proved to be one of the country's most successful media exports.

COLD WAR SECURITY AND POLITICS

Direct economic aid from the U.S. government to Latin America declined considerably after World War II, but investment from the country's retailers and manufacturers served to fill much of the void for private enterprise. The United States offered military equipment and training to regimes friendly to U.S. goals after

1945. Such aid for security and strategic purposes expanded as these goals increasingly came to encompass strong anticommunist strategies. U.S. leaders worked to create institutions and policies that foreshadowed growing ideological conflict throughout the Cold War. In 1946, the School of the Americas in the Panama Canal Zone opened its doors. As a training facility for Latin American military personnel, the School of the Americas specialized in teaching counterinsurgency techniques to be used against suspected leftist subversives.

The following year, U.S. and Latin American leaders signed the Inter-American Treaty for Reciprocal Assistance. Also known as the Rio Pact, the agreement marked a formal continuation of the commitment to hemispheric security that had emerged during World War II. But in the postwar environment, U.S. leaders saw the new treaty as a way to coalesce a hemispheric alliance against the spread of Soviet communism. Although the treaty reaffirmed a commitment to nonintervention in U.S.–Latin American affairs, it also established strong formal links between U.S. and Latin American military forces. The School of the Americas became one of the first vehicles for the regional military cooperation established in the treaty, and other institutions strengthened these connections as the Cold War progressed. Although they disavowed direct intervention in Latin American affairs, U.S. leaders still exerted enormous influence in the new inter-American security system established through the Rio Pact. U.S. leaders used the lure of military aid to pressure Latin American governments into suppressing the activities of leftist groups, including labor unions, leftist political parties, and peasant activist organizations. Furthermore, the formal military links between the United States and Latin American armed forces paved the way for a large degree of indirect intervention, while allowing policy makers to deny direct involvement.

Guatemala

Guatemala became the site of the first demonstration of U.S. Cold War policy in Latin America and it eventually served as a model for subsequent anticommunist strategies. In many ways, Guatemala was a typical Latin American nation in the middle decades of the twentieth century. The onset of the Great Depression paved the way for the rise of Jorge Ubico, who took power under the banner of bringing stability in the midst of economic crisis. He touted a strong anticommunist message and introduced a series of laws that allowed large landowners to exploit rural peasants. Ubico supported policies that favored the United Fruit Company; it enjoyed a reduced tax obligation and low-cost agrarian labor. As a result of its favorable relationship with the long-term dictator, the U.S.-based agricultural firm became the largest single landholder in Guatemala and also came to control most of the country's transportation and communications infrastructure.

In 1944, national unrest against Ubico began to mount as students, professionals, and workers resorted to vocal protests and public demonstrations against the dictator. Junior military officers eventually joined the opposition and in June, Ubico resigned and eventually fled into exile. New elections later that year heralded the promise of a democratic opening as the reformer and philosopher Juan

José Arévalo won the presidency. A new constitution, passed in 1945 and based on the Mexican constitution of 1917, introduced sweeping reform. It sought to impose greater social and political equality by expanding the electorate and giving women the right to vote. It also introduced social reforms in education and health care, supporting a governing philosophy that Arévalo referred to as "spiritual socialism." In the context of Cold War concerns, his reference to socialism captured the attention of the United States, and although the new president did not identify with Soviet-style communism, his policies came under intense scrutiny. Significantly, Guatemala's constitution guaranteed the rights of organized labor and called for extensive agrarian reforms to break the dominance of large landowners and end exploitation of the rural peasantry—reforms that further raised the suspicions of U.S. leaders.

Arévalo proved to be a savvy president who understood fully the precariousness of his reform agenda, both in the context of U.S. Cold War concerns and in the face of significant conservative opposition within Guatemala. He implemented reforms cautiously and somewhat gradually, yet still faced 22 attempted coups during his tenure. Nevertheless, he finished his term and new elections brought Jacobo Árbenz to power in 1950. A consummate reformer, Árbenz received more than 65 percent of the vote in possibly the most democratic election in Guatemala's history.

Árbenz proved much less patient and cautious than his predecessor, immediately initiating a vigorous reform agenda. He legalized communism, paving the way for the rise of the Partido Guatemalteco del Trabajo (Guatemalan Labor Party), which alarmed U.S. policy makers. He also began large-scale infrastructure projects that would allow the government to compete with the United Fruit Company's control of transportation, communications, and utilities. He invited several communist-affiliated individuals into his administration and continued social welfare programs, winning notable accolades from the Partido Guatemalteco del Trabajo. In 1952, he passed the Agrarian Law, which allowed the government to expropriate portions of large estates that were not being used productively. The law exempted any agricultural lands under cultivation at the time and called for compensation to owners based on the most current reported taxable value. Árbenz intended to distribute 42.5-acre plots to landless peasants in an effort to create an economy of small, family-sized farms. In the immediate years after its passage, the Agrarian Law facilitated the distribution of more than 1.5 million acres to 100,000 families.

Árbenz's sweeping reform program riled conservative opposition within Guatemala, particularly among the nation's landed aristocracy, whose properties frequently became targets of the Agrarian Law. But the most serious opposition came from the United States as the Guatemalan government expropriated hundreds of thousands of acres of idle land owned by the United Fruit Company. The U.S.-based corporation protested on the basis of inadequate compensation and demanded $75 per acre in restitution. Árbenz's administration offered $2.99 per acre, the taxable value self-reported by company executives. The U.S. government

An airplane dropping leaflets on a crowd of Guatemalans listening to Col. Carlos Castillo Armas' speech after the coup deposing President Jacobo Árbenz. Leaflet drops, along with other propaganda tactics, were used to foment public opinion against the Árbenz administration.

backed the company, despite its obvious record of tax fraud, protested the expropriations, and condemned many of Árbenz's reforms as Soviet-style communism.

Guatemala's experiment with democracy and social reform came to an abrupt end as a result of covert U.S. intervention supporting an opposition movement led by Colonel Carlos Castillo Armas, who had gone into exile when Árbenz took power. Aided by the Central Intelligence Agency, Castillo Armas assembled an armed force in Honduras and in June 1954 initiated a revolt against the government. In less than two weeks, Árbenz had resigned and fled into exile. Castillo Armas took power, received immediate recognition by the U.S. government, and quickly reversed the Agrarian Law and other controversial social programs.

The Legacy of Guatemala

This episode in Guatemala serves as an important barometer of the tenor of anti-communism in Latin America throughout the last half of the twentieth century. The 1954 coup destroyed the political center in the country. The Castillo Armas regime began decades of right-wing military rule, characterized by brutal repression and relentless human rights abuses in an attempt to annihilate any vestiges of communism. Guatemalans endured decades of civil war as only the extreme right and left remained and often violently competed to steer the nation's future.

U.S. actions in Guatemala also became a harbinger of later Cold War policies. Árbenz's program of social reform was the first test of U.S. hegemony in Latin America after World War II, when the pretext of anticommunism came to dominate hemispheric relations. By stifling Árbenz's social reform agenda and protecting the interests of U.S. businesses in the region, U.S. leaders sent a strong message to all of Latin America that they would not tolerate any policies that could be linked however imaginatively to Soviet-style socialism. The covert strategies used to overthrow Árbenz also served as a model for later U.S. interventions in Latin America carried out in the name of stopping the spread of communism.

The coup in Guatemala marked the starting point of decades of U.S. support for right-wing dictators in the name of fighting communism during the Cold War. Latin American militaries had become involved in politics in response to the onset of the Great Depression and their alliance with the United States during World War II often strengthened their position. By the early 1950s, military regimes controlled most Latin American countries and the United States often rewarded military leaders for anticommunist efforts by granting them large aid packages.

The Latin American general public often reacted to U.S. policies with understandable indignation. Marcos Pérez Jiménez became the dictator of Venezuela in 1952 and used that country's considerable oil wealth to modernize the capital city with lavish skyscrapers, extravagant hotels, and costly transportation projects. This seemingly impressive infrastructure expansion came at the cost of education and other social services, as the dictator diverted government resources into modernizing projects that proved to be little more than window dressing. He reined in opposition and silenced the left through censorship and brutal oppression. These same tactics allowed him and his supporters to line their own pockets, as the despot accumulated a personal fortune estimated at $250 million. But his vocal disdain for communism won him the admiration of the United States and President Dwight Eisenhower awarded him the Legion of Merit medal in 1954—an act perceived by many Latin Americans to be tacit endorsement of his cruel and exploitative tactics. When Vice President Richard Nixon visited Caracas in 1958, he barely escaped a riot in the streets as angry mobs surrounded his motorcade, spat at his car, and pelted it with stones. U.S. leaders imaginatively attributed the violent scene to communist agitators and the episode further convinced them that Latin America was at great risk for communist infiltration.

Between 1945 and 1959, Latin American Cold War realities took shape. With little economic assistance coming from the U.S. government, national leaders and regional economists in CEPAL looked increasingly to state-sponsored structuralism and import substitution industrialization to facilitate an expansion in manufacturing, trade, and commerce. Those policies supported the growth of a middle-class consumer market in the region, but they also created the illusion of economic advancement that would eventually prove to be limited to a few and unsustainable in the long term. Cold War security concerns came to dominate the attention of Latin America leaders, driven largely by the United States. Covert intervention by

Primary Source

The Central Intelligence Agency studied the political climate in 1952 and concluded that communist sympathies posed a grave threat to U.S. interests. Their assessment specifically placed the United Fruit Company at the heart of Cold War policy in Latin America.

SOURCE: Document I. Central Intelligence Agency, "Present Political Situation in Guatemala and Possible Development During 1952," NIB-62, March 11, 1952, in U.S. Department of State, *Foreign Relations of the United States*, 1952–1954, *Guatemala* (Washington, DC: U.S. Government Printing Office, 2003), 6–9.

The Problem

To analyze the present political situation in Guatemala and possible developments during 1952.

Conclusions

1. The Communists already exercise in Guatemala a political influence far out of proportion to their small numerical strength. This influence will probably continue to grow during 1952. The political situation in Guatemala adversely affects US interests and constitutes a potential threat to US security.

2. Communist political success derives in general from the ability of individual Communists and fellow travelers to identify themselves with the nationalist and social aspirations of the Revolution of 1944. In this manner, they have been successful in infiltrating the Administration and the pro-Administration political parties and have gained control of organized labor upon which the Administration has become increasingly dependent.

3. The political alliance between the Administration and the Communists is likely to continue. The opposition to Communism in Guatemala is potentially powerful, but at present it lacks leadership and organization . . .

4. Future political developments will depend in large measure on the outcome of the conflict between Guatemala and the United Fruit Company. This conflict is a natural consequence of the Revolution of 1944, but has been exacerbated by the Communists for their own purposes.

5. If the Company should submit to Guatemalan demands the political position of the Árbenz Administration would be greatly strengthened. It is probable that in this case the Government and the unions, under Communist influence and supported by national sentiment, would exert increasing pressure on other US interests, notably the Railway.

   . . .

9. In the longer view, continued Communist influence and action in Guatemala will gradually reduce the capabilities of the potentially powerful anti-Communist forces to produce a change. The Communists will also attempt to subvert or neutralize the Army in order to reduce its capability to prevent them from eventually taking full control of the Government.

the Central Intelligence Agency to overthrow the Árbenz government in Guatemala was only the foreshadowing of a long era of intimidation and violence in the name of fighting communism. In 1959, Cold War anxieties shifted to Cuba, and events on the island would eventually have major repercussions throughout Latin America.

SUGGESTIONS FOR FURTHER READING

Ameringer, Charles D. *The Socialist Impulse: Latin America in the Twentieth Century.* Gainesville: University Press of Florida, 2009.

Bulmer-Thomas, Victor, John Coatsworth, and Roberto Cortes-Conde. *The Cambridge Economic History of Latin America: Volume 2, The Long Twentieth Century.* Cambridge: Cambridge University Press, 2006.

Di Tella, Torcuato S. *History of Political Parties in Twentieth-Century Latin America.* New Brunswick, NJ: Transaction, 2005.

Dosman, Edgar J. *The Life and Times of Raúl Prebisch, 1901–1986.* Montreal: McGill–Queen's University Press, 2008.

Dwyer, John J. *The Agrarian Dispute: The Expropriation of American-Owned Rural Land in Postrevolutionary Mexico.* Durham, NC: Duke University Press, 2008.

Gill, Lesley. *The School of the America: Military Training and Political Violence in the Americas.* Durham, NC: Duke University Press, 2004.

Milanesio, Natalia. *Workers Go Shopping in Argentina: The Rise of Popular Consumer Culture.* Albuquerque: University of New Mexico Press, 2013.

Moreno, Julio. *Yankee Don't Go Home!: Mexican Nationalism, American Business Culture, and the Shaping of Modern Mexico, 1920–1950.* Chapel Hill: University of North Carolina Press, 2003.

O'Toole, Gavin. *Politics in Latin America.* 2nd ed. New York: Pearson, 2010.

Paige, Jeffery M. *Coffee and Power: Revolution and the Rise of Democracy in Central America.* Cambridge, MA: Harvard University Press, 1997.

Rivera, Salvador. *Latin American Unification: A History of Political and Economic Integration Efforts.* Jefferson, NC: McFarland, 2014.

Schlesinger, Stephen, and Stephen Kinzer. *Bitter Fruit: The Story of the American Coup in Guatemala.* Cambridge, MA: Harvard University Press, 2005.

Schwartzberg, Steven. *Democracy and U.S. Policy in Latin America during the Truman Years.* Gainesville: University Press of Florida, 2003.

CHAPTER 22

Cuban Revolution

April 1959	Fidel Castro visits the United States and meets with Vice President Richard Nixon; Castro denies any affiliation with the Communist Party
May 1959	First Agrarian Reform Law forbids foreign ownership of property and places limits on size of landholdings
February 1960	Cuba and the Soviet Union sign trade agreement for guaranteed sales of Cuban sugar and credit for Soviet industrial goods
July 1960	Cuba signs trade agreement with China; United States stops all sugar imports from Cuba
August 1960	Cuba nationalizes all U.S. companies and agricultural and business interests
October 1960	United States imposes economic embargo on all exports to Cuba except food and medicine
April 1961	U.S.-encouraged/supported Cuban dissidents stage failed invasion at the Bay of Pigs (Playa Girón); more than 1,200 rebels captured by Cuban forces
October 1962	Cuban Missile Crisis; Castro, to protect Cuba from the United States, allows Soviet nuclear missiles to be placed on the island; the Soviets and the United States resolve the crisis, with the Soviets agreeing to remove the missiles in exchange for the United States removing its missiles from Turkey
October 1967	Che Guevara is executed by Bolivian forces in La Higuera; Guevara had arrived the year prior to help foment revolution in that country

There must never be another Cuba. These words became the foundation of U.S. foreign policy in Latin America after 1959. The fall of the U.S.-backed Cuban government under the dictatorship of Fulgencio Batista to Fidel Castro's revolutionary forces symbolized a fundamental challenge to the role the United States had traditionally played throughout Latin America. The island nation's long history of close economic and political connections to its powerful neighbor had made Cuba an archetype of a well-behaved nation falling under U.S. hegemony. Countenanced by provisions in the Cuban constitution, the U.S. military intervened repeatedly in the early twentieth century to quell internal dissent and to protect American business interests on the island. Economic relations strengthened as U.S.-owned enterprises opened on the island and the majority of Cuban exports—primarily of agricultural goods such as sugar and citrus fruit—went to the United States.

Such close economic and political connections underscored the centrality of U.S. interests in Cuba. And the island's proximity—only 90 miles from U.S. soil—strengthened these connections and made it a symbol of the unequal power relationship U.S. leaders sought with all of Latin America. The Cuban revolution ended this cozy relationship. Moreover, it highlighted hemispheric realities that leaders in Washington preferred to ignore: democracy and political reform would not be sustainable without also solving problems such as illiteracy, disease, and unemployment—the faithful associates of poverty and underdevelopment. The ideal of ending these long-standing ills drove Castro's revolutionaries in 1959 and eventually earned the movement the label of communism. In an era of Cold War anxieties, tensions with the United States were destined to escalate.

INTERVENTIONS AND DICTATORSHIP

U.S. involvement in Cuban independence at the turn of the twentieth century set the stage for a contentious relationship between the two nations. The insistence by U.S. leaders that the Cuban constitution include the provisions set out in the Platt Amendment created a climate ripe for numerous military interventions in the coming decades. At the same time, U.S. citizens became increasingly involved in the island's economy; by 1925, U.S. planters owned more than half of all Cuban sugar estates, and roughly 95 percent of the total sugar crop was exported to the United States. Peasants and small farmers who had previously owned modest plots that allowed them to grow their own food and participate in the sugar economy found themselves working as exploited wage laborers on large U.S.-owned sugar estates. Poverty and political corruption became rampant and anti-American antagonisms flourished. These tensions converged after the onset of the Great Depression to end the dictatorship of Gerardo Machado in 1933.

The Rise of Batista

In the immediate aftermath of Machado's overthrow, Ramón Grau San Martín became president. An ardent nationalist and defender of leftist policy, he championed workers' rights, female suffrage, and land reform. He also declared that the Cuban government no longer recognized the Platt Amendment. Taken together, Grau's reform measures reflected the prevailing atmosphere of anti-Americanism, but he had little time to implement his nationalist vision. A significant challenge came from the emerging alliance between the U.S. assistant secretary of state Sumner Welles and Fulgencio Batista, one of Cuba's top military leaders. Grau resigned after only four months in office and a series of figurehead presidents served between 1934 and 1940.

Batista remained the true power behind the scenes, strengthening his relationship with the United States through reciprocal trade agreements and development loans. In 1934, U.S. leaders abrogated the Platt Amendment in accordance with the Good Neighbor Policy, indicating that the Roosevelt administration viewed the Batista political machine with favor. The Cuban leader seemed to fit the mold of the authoritarian populist, particularly in matters of social justice. He emphasized the need to help "*los humildes*," or the humble ones, in reference to workers and peasants who suffered the most during the Great Depression. Batista backed policies that created health programs for the poor and working class and supported initiatives to control consumer prices. He introduced modest agrarian reform and extended the vote to women. By the end of the decade, the government had gained considerable popular support. This backing expanded in 1940 when Batista endorsed a new constitution, which institutionalized many of those reforms. He won the presidency in that same year in relatively fair and open elections.

Batista rode a wave of popularity into the 1940s while Cuba's political and economic systems stabilized. His presidency coincided with the nation's involvement in World War II, which resulted in agreements with the United States regarding trade, financial programs, and military defense. The Cuban economy grew and the production of sugar alone increased more than 55 percent. The U.S. presence heightened as the favorable economic climate attracted investors in various industries.

Batista withdrew from executive leadership after Ramón Grau and the Auténtico Party defeated his handpicked successor in the 1944 presidential election. But the Auténtico leader began losing popular support as a consequence of political corruption and economic decline. As the 1952 presidential election approached, Batista orchestrated a coup and took control of the government. To consolidate power, he updated military facilities and invested in new equipment and weaponry. He also filled high-ranking military positions with individuals who were loyal to him and strategically appointed army officers to serve as governors and mayors in select provinces. Unlike his earlier presidency, Batista's rule after 1952 was neither democratic nor progressive. Like despots elsewhere, he cited corruption and growing instability to justify his dictatorial rule.

Many Cubans felt considerable antipathy toward the outgoing government and looked to Batista to end corruption and restore order. He promised to hold new elections and did so in 1954, running uncontested and winning in a highly questionable electoral process. Political opposition denounced him for corruption and lack of transparency, but Batista did improve Cuba's infrastructure. He invited U.S. investments in the mining and steel industries and initiated efforts to upgrade highways, ports, and city streets. Other projects included the construction of schools, hospitals, and water purification systems. Enjoying the support of laborers at first, Batista employed a combination of bribery and intimidation to keep union leaders under control.

On the surface, Cuba seemed to be thriving under Batista's leadership. Most Cubans lived in urban areas and the standard of living in cities indicated economic prosperity. A growing middle class could purchase televisions, radios, and automobiles. Nearly 90 percent of the urban population had access to education, social services, and reliable public utilities. The dictator and many of his supporters pointed to these signs of Cuba's apparent prosperity. But the cosmetic improvements Batista showcased to outsiders and to the national elite disguised underlying inequalities and fundamental cracks in the system. Batista based numerous decisions on his desire to increase his own wealth and elevate his social status. He oversaw the expansion of Havana's tourism industry by inviting figures within the U.S. mafia to open casinos, brothels, and other entertainment venues in the capital city. While cosmetic changes gave Cuba an aura of modernity and success, the dictator found ways to accumulate a personal fortune.

Growing Dissent

Despite signs of prosperity, Cuba's economy remained tied to a one-crop monoculture in which sugar production accounted for approximately 80 percent of foreign earnings. Even minor variations in the staple's price on the global market could have a profound impact on the Cuban economy. Although trade agreements with the United States guaranteed favorable prices for most of the island's sugar exports, many Cubans worried that this arrangement was creating a system of inequality and dependency that would ultimately weaken the nation. Sugar plantations occupied half of Cuba's cultivable lands and U.S. investors owned most of them. Rural employment on those estates remained a constant source of contention because of pay disparity between American and Cuban workers. Furthermore, the seasonal nature of sugar cultivation frequently led to high rates of unemployment that affected roughly 25 percent of the workforce tied to the industry. With Cuba's share of the world market falling in the 1950s, the economic stagnation caused by structural weaknesses led to an 18 percent decline in real income between 1952 and 1954 as wages failed to keep up with the increased cost of living.

Some of the most serious social and economic problems in Cuba arose from the growing disparities in income between the rich and the poor. Cubans living below the poverty line comprised a large portion of the rural population as well as residents in shantytowns on the outskirts of large cities. With the country's economic situation deteriorating in the 1950s, large numbers of rural workers abandoned sugar estates and relocated to urban areas. These waves of migration produced a glut of manual laborers, drove down wages, and created overcrowding in urban slums. Many lived in meager dwellings that lacked electricity and running water. The poor suffered higher rates of illiteracy rates and few had access to reliable medical care.

Many would-be opponents to the Batista regime fell silent in the immediate aftermath of the 1952 coup, fearing recrimination and reprisal as the dictator began targeting and imprisoning potential enemies. Among these critics was Fidel Castro, a 26-year-old law student and social activist who had planned to run for congress before Batista canceled the 1952 elections. Castro came from a landowning family in the Oriente Province and had demonstrated a keen sense of social awareness from a young age. As a teenager, he attempted to organize a work stoppage among the agricultural laborers on his father's sugar plantation—an act that foreshadowed his revolutionary ideology in later years. He joined the Ortodoxo Party, which opposed the dictatorship. From this party emerged a youth movement of idealistic university students who sought ways to correct social inequalities, mitigate poverty, end economic dependence, and curtail government corruption.

As Batista became increasingly authoritarian, Castro and his cronies in the Ortodoxo Youth Movement concluded that only armed insurrection could restore democracy and resolve Cuba's social problems. On July 26, 1953, Castro, his brother Raúl, and 120 other insurgents attacked the Moncada military barracks in an attempt to confiscate weapons and other supplies for future use. Outnumbered and outgunned, the rebels' action failed miserably; Cuban military forces captured and immediately executed many of the insurgents. Castro initially escaped, but was apprehended and imprisoned shortly thereafter. At his trial, the young radical seized the opportunity to denounce the government and publicize his demands for reform in his "History Will Absolve Me" speech. The court sentenced him to 15 years in prison, where he continued to write manifestos articulating a revolutionary ideology.

As opposition to Batista intensified, the dictator faced potential uprisings not only from Castro's youth movement, but also from other groups. The increasing public demonstrations against the regime often turned violent, and the dictator responded to the growing tension and the Moncada attack with increased repression. He suspended the constitution of 1940, which initially had been lauded as one of the most progressive charters in Latin America. New decrees allowed the dictator to suspend civil liberties—such as freedom of speech, freedom of the press, and the right to assembly—for up to 45 days for virtually any reason. He outlawed political parties and eventually extended the ban to any organized political activity; and he dissolved the congress and replaced it with a consultative body made up of loyal supporters.

Opponents of the regime countered Batista's despotism by amplifying public protests. Castro's supporters published anti-Batista propaganda and held clandestine meetings to plan continued resistance. Women played a crucial role at this point; Haydée Santamaría, Melba Hernández, and others formed vital alliances with other resistance groups such as the Martí Women's Civic Front and the Association of United Cuban Women. In an attempt to quiet dissent and appease critics, Batista declared a general amnesty for political prisoners in 1955 and Castro was released after serving only two years of his sentence.

The July 26th Movement

Castro and other leaders of the resistance movement held firm in their belief that only armed rebellion could end the Batista dictatorship and bring meaningful change to Cuba. But they also understood that the autocrat would closely monitor their activities. To escape surveillance, they retreated to Mexico to plan a large-scale rebellion. On a hacienda on the outskirts of Mexico City, the rebels formally founded the 26th of July Movement (M-26-7), named for the date of the failed Moncada Barracks attack two years earlier. The movement's leaders articulated their demands for reform, which included a return to democracy and a vast expansion of public education. They also insisted on extensive economic and social changes, particularly land redistribution to benefit rural peasants and the nationalization of vital industries and public services.

Castro secured some financial and logistical support in Mexico and began to train his small group for a new attack in Cuba. He also met Ernesto "Che" Guevara, an Argentine medical student who had toured Latin America and had become radicalized by the vast inequalities he had witnessed. Che found himself in Guatemala in 1953 and witnessed the coup against Jacobo Árbenz the following year. His experiences there convinced him that the United States was the main source of the poverty and other development problems in all of Latin America, and he advocated armed revolution to confront the evils of imperialism. By the time he joined M-26-7 in Mexico, he had become idealistic and extremely revolutionary. He eventually became Castro's second in command, providing a sense of intense militancy to the movement; he exhibited little tolerance for dissent and often brutally punished perceived enemies of the revolution.

While Castro's followers trained in guerrilla tactics in Mexico, anti-Batista groups in Cuba continued to pressure the regime. The Revolutionary Directorate, a secret student organization organized by José Echeverría dedicated to overthrowing the dictator, orchestrated student strikes and public demonstrations, many of which turned into violent riots. The government tried to crack down on the increasing disturbances and security forces killed many students in clashes throughout 1956. But other signs of dissent were beginning to surface, even among traditional Batista supporters. After discovering a potential conspiracy among members of the military, the dictator began to designate political loyalists to oversee sections of the armed forces.

Importantly, at this point Batista still had strong support from the United States. With profitable U.S. businesses on the island, his pro-U.S. and anticommunist predilections made him an ideal Cold War ally. Additionally, proximity and ease of travel made Cuba an idyllic vacation destination for U.S. tourists, who frequented the casinos and resorts that gave the illusion of a thriving and ascendant society. Indeed, many private citizens and government leaders alike saw Cuba as a virtual extension of the United States—a perception rooted in the two countries' unique relationship that had evolved following the War of 1898. Moreover, Cuban leaders had traditionally catered to U.S. concerns, often at the expense of national interests. As tensions escalated and Castro prepared to launch a new attempt at revolution, policy makers in the United States failed to understand the political dynamic within Cuba. They underestimated the popularity of opposition groups and discounted the urgency behind their demands for reform. And the recent experience in Guatemala led many in Washington to conclude that supporting right-wing military leaders would be an effective anticommunist strategy in all of Latin America.

REVOLUTION

By November 1956, Castro and the members of M-26-7 were prepared to launch a new attack on the Batista government. The group purchased a small, barely seaworthy yacht named the *Granma*. The overcrowded vessel landed in the Oriente Province on December 2, poetically at the same site of José Martí's 1895 rebellion that initiated the war for independence from Spain. The beginning of the revolution grew out of careful coordination between M-26-7 and other opposition groups. Indeed, in 1956 it was not at all clear that Castro would emerge as the revolution's main leader and much of his eventual success resulted from the collusion of other resistance groups. In Havana, the Revolutionary Directorate had instigated numerous student demonstrations and public riots to distract government troops and create a general feeling of unrest. Castro hoped that a surprise landing in the provinces would give the revolution a springboard to success. But his force of 82 ran into Batista troops almost immediately and only 11 men escaped into the mountains of the Sierra Maestra.

Under the leadership of the Castro brothers and Che Guevara, the remaining M-26-7 members regrouped and began small but effective attacks on military outposts. This strategy enabled them to acquire weapons and other vital supplies. Che used his medical training to provide health care to rural peasants and implemented his belief that winning the local population's loyalty was vital for the revolution to succeed. He later related these experiences in *Guerrilla Warfare*, which quickly became a guide to fighting imperialist and authoritarian regimes. After some small successes, the rebels began building momentum. Initially out of necessity and practicality, they stopped shaving their facial hair and thereby established a revolutionary identity; they quickly became known as "*los barbudos*" because their beards provided a symbol of the revolution's strength. Eventually, Castro required beards of all M-26-7 leaders and vowed not to shave his own until the revolution succeeded. Few observers considered Castro's guerrillas a significant threat in the early days, but their small numbers allowed them to remain mobile and difficult for government forces to find. As the rebellion strengthened, Batista responded with increasingly brutal repression; his forces routinely tortured and executed the insurgents they captured.

The United States continued its support of Batista even as the small band of revolutionaries gained momentum in Oriente Province. With high sugar prices, maintaining close ties with Cuba remained profitable for U.S. business interests. When rumors circulated in early 1957 that Castro had been killed and the revolution was faltering, Castro sought to boost morale and call broader attention to the movement by inviting the *New York Times* columnist Herbert Matthews to his rebel camp. The reporter published a three-part series showcasing the revolution and depicting it as a serious threat to the Batista regime. The story brought

Fidel Castro in the Sierra Maestra with nurses of the M-26-7, Castro's rebel army. The rebel movement attracted both men and women to join Castro's forces in Cuba's eastern mountains.

renewed energy to Castro's camp and further legitimized his effort among many Cubans. The coverage also drew attention to the bourgeoning revolution by introducing U.S. readers to its charismatic and idealistic leader. Other interviews followed and the *New York Times* piece became a model for publicizing the cause of the M-26-7. Che also brought attention to the rebellion by starting Radio Rebelde, a network of clandestine radio transmissions that disseminated revolutionary propaganda, provided news of rebel activities, and allowed guerrilla leaders to communicate.

Castro attracted additional support throughout 1957. He received reinforcements and aid from strategic allies, including Huber Matos and Celia Sánchez, who eventually became leaders in the movement. As mass public demonstrations continued in the cities, Batista's repression began to turn both Cuba's middle class and some U.S. observers against him. Some military garrisons in rural provinces mutinied, and Raúl Castro opened a second front in early 1958. Although rebel forces remained small and armed insurgents never numbered more than a few hundred, their strategic planning and coordinated efforts proved increasingly effective. Furthermore, political leaders in Washington started to withdraw support for Batista, ending weapons shipments in March 1958. Since U.S. military aid had kept the dictator's forces well armed in the face of the rebellion, this reversal in policy strongly indicated that his despotic regime was crumbling.

Castro's final offensive in late 1958 followed many of Batista's missteps. The dictator had sent more than 10,000 troops to the Sierra Maestra several months earlier, but increasingly they defected. Castro seized on the army's low morale. He publicized widely the contrast between his humane treatment of captives and the government's brutality toward apprehended rebels. When a fraudulent election in November allowed a close Batista ally to claim the presidency, even more Cubans concluded that violence offered the only way to rid their country of its dictator. In December, rebels opened four fronts of attack and brought the major cities of Santa Clara and Santiago to the verge of falling. In the early morning hours of January 1, 1959, Batista fled Cuba; rebel troops entered Havana the following day.

NEW GOVERNMENT AND INITIAL U.S. REACTION

Revolutionary forces installed Manuel Urrutia as president and Fidel Castro became prime minister, a post he held until 1976 and which gave him tremendous influence. Many of his closest revolutionary allies also secured cabinet positions; Raúl became the minister of defense and Che became the minister of industry. The revolutionary leadership immediately reinstated the constitution of 1940, but delayed elections for two years to allow political parties to form and define their platforms. During the early months after the rebel victory, executions followed public trials of many Batista loyalists. The U.S. government viewed Castro cautiously, but recognized the new government immediately. Although the prime minister's revolutionary platform embraced nationalization, he initially showed few signs of favoring wholesale communism.

Serious revolutionary reform began in the spring of 1959. In May, the new government passed the First Agrarian Reform Law, based on land reform provisions in the constitution of 1940. With few exceptions, it limited property holdings to 1,000 acres and forbade foreign ownership. The regime purchased surplus lands and either distributed them to individuals or converted them into government-run cooperatives. New labor legislation strengthened the power of unions and raised wages while urban housing reforms lowered rents up to 50 percent. Additionally, the government pushed through a series of laws targeting gambling, prostitution, and other vices.

Nationalizations also began immediately, starting with the U.S.-owned Cuban Telephone Company. This action and the expropriation of agricultural properties elicited vocal protests among U.S. businesses and began to raise concerns among leaders in Washington. Cuban reformers followed the same strategy that had been used by Jacobo Árbenz and compensated companies for the reported taxable value of assets. Like in Guatemala, corruption within the Batista regime and the dictator's pandering to U.S. interests had allowed business to underreport property values by a considerable amount. U.S. leaders grew even more concerned as the new government expropriated the assets of major steel companies and quickly raised the tax obligation of foreign oil companies; the rate reached 60 percent by the end of 1959. It is important to recognize that these early revolutionary reforms remained extremely popular among most Cubans. Indeed, the presence of U.S. companies had become a symbol of the superpower's hegemony over the island nation. Castro often reacted to complaints from U.S. entrepreneurs with his signature nationalist rhetorical flair, which only amplified the popular support he enjoyed among the masses.

In April 1959, Castro visited the United States at the invitation of the American Society of Newspaper Editors. His natural charisma and general likeability drew large crowds and complimentary coverage in the press. But U.S. political leaders voiced displeasure with the nature of Cuba's reforms. Vice President Richard Nixon, a staunch anticommunist, lectured the revolutionary on the benefits of democracy and capitalism during a three-hour meeting. He urged Castro to hold elections immediately and to welcome U.S. business investments. Prominent politicians in Washington had been closely monitoring Cuba's revolutionary reforms, and the question of communism surfaced repeatedly during Castro's trip. After his repeated denials of any affiliation with the Communist Party, analysts from the Central Intelligence Agency concluded that he was not a communist. Nevertheless, policy makers grew concerned at the bold measures contained in the Agrarian Law and other nationalization efforts.

As U.S. pressure on Castro escalated in the second half of 1959, the revolutionary leader increasingly interpreted anticommunist sentiment as an affront to nationalism and moved ever closer to embracing communism formally. At the same time, Cuban experts in the State Department and the Central Intelligence Agency began looking for ways to remove him from power. By the end of the year, the United States had already implemented sanctions that gradually reduced trade between the two nations and threatened to impose a complete embargo. Castro reacted by initiating negotiations with the Soviet Union. He hoped that strengthening

ties with the Soviet Union would provide his revolutionary government with necessary economic support and deter U.S. intervention. In February 1960, he signed
a formal trade agreement in which the USSR guaranteed minimum purchases of
Cuban sugar and offered a $100 million credit to allow the island nation to purchase
Soviet wheat, oil, and industrial goods. A similar accord with China followed in July.

Deteriorating Relations with the United States

Castro's turn to a Soviet economic alliance dismayed policy makers in the United
States. The new partnership seemed to confirm their worst fears that communist
infiltration in the Western Hemisphere was not only possible, but also likely. They
interpreted the loss of Cuba to communism as a serious failure of Cold War strategy, especially because the United States' visible role in Cuban history had fostered
the illusion that country was particularly beholden to its superpower neighbor.
Many U.S. leaders concluded that if Cuba could so easily turn communist, the rest
of Latin America was also vulnerable. The policy response to the emergence of
communism in the Cuban Revolution reflected this sense of alarm and informed
future U.S. Cold War efforts in the rest of Latin America.

Attempts at negotiation between the United States and Cuba failed and relations between the two nations worsened over the course of 1960. The Eisenhower
administration sought to put pressure on Castro by refusing to allow U.S. refineries
to process Soviet oil. Additionally, in July the United States terminated all sugar
imports from Cuba; the Soviet Union in turn agreed to increase its sugar imports.
By August, Cuba had nationalized all U.S. companies—including retailers such as
Sears and Coca-Cola—along with agricultural interests, sugar mills, numerous factories, banks, and public utilities. Tightening the economic embargo, by October
the United States had restricted exports to Cuba to only food and medicine.

Driven by Cold War desperation, U.S. leaders began formulating a scheme to
oust Castro and replace him with a U.S.-friendly regime. Modeled after the covert
plan that successfully overthrew Árbenz in Guatemala, the Cuba strategy involved
providing covert support to Cubans who opposed the dictator. Moderates within
Castro's revolutionary circle generally resisted the turn toward communism. Of
those who spoke out against the regime, many suffered imprisonment; others
fled and sought asylum in the United States. In the summer of 1960, dissidents
resident in both the United States and Cuba formed the Frente Revolucionario
Democrático, a group dedicated to destabilizing the Castro regime. U.S. leaders eventually collaborated with the armed wing of the Frente Revolucionario
Democrático when planning the April 1961 Bay of Pigs invasion that attempted
to overthrow the dictator. But unlike the intervention in Guatemala, the Cuban
effort failed dismally. Cuban forces captured more than 1,200 counterrevolutionaries and the regime subjected them to public trials.

Although it failed to bring down Castro, the Bay of Pigs fiasco proved an important watershed in U.S. policy toward Cuba. U.S. intelligence and security officials became consumed with Castro as a symbol of Latin American communism.
In the coming decades, various agencies participated in numerous destabilization

schemes intended to discredit, overthrow, or even assassinate the Cuban dictator. Collectively known as Operation Mongoose during the administration of John F. Kennedy, plans to collect intelligence, interfere in the Cuban economy, encourage revolt, and strain Cuban–Soviet relations shared a single objective: to get rid of Fidel Castro. Some farfetched ideas never made it past the drawing board, and those attempted uniformly failed. Indeed, their effect was to make the dictator appear larger than life and even legendary. For his part, Castro grew increasingly paranoid and cracked down on dissidents. With the opposition silenced and imprisoned, Cuba witnessed a surge of nationalism and support for the dictatorial government as it successfully fought off intervention by its much larger and richer adversary.

The failed Bay of Pigs attack also affected the relationship between Cuba and the Soviet Union. Seeing the United States discredited and criticized on the international stage for its role in the Bay of Pigs emboldened Nikita Khrushchev to establish closer ties with Castro. Cuba's victory over the invaders indicated that the revolution could potentially succeed, and the Soviets felt assured that the United States would not openly attempt to oust Castro in the short term. Khrushchev saw an opportunity to strengthen ties with Cuba as well as to alter the balance of power that had defined the USSR's Cold War relations with the United States.

Soviet military aid to Cuba increased throughout 1962 both to protect the Castro regime and to deter further U.S. interference. The strengthened military ties eventually evolved to include a nuclear component that Khrushchev hoped would tip the weapons advantage in favor of the Soviets. In October, U.S. intelligence officials discovered through reconnaissance photos that medium-range ballistic missiles had reached Cuba. President Kennedy immediately condemned the introduction of Soviet nuclear arms in the Western Hemisphere. He ordered a naval quarantine to intercept any offensive armaments while the Soviets refused to back down from plans to install atomic weapons facilities in Cuba. For nearly two weeks, tensions escalated between the two superpowers and the possibility of a full-scale nuclear confrontation seemed likely. Secret negotiations between U.S. and Soviet intermediaries ended the standoff. The final agreement stipulated that the USSR would remove all missiles from Cuba in exchange for the removal of U.S. missiles from Turkey and a guarantee that the United States would not invade Cuba.

LEGACY OF THE CUBAN REVOLUTION

The resolution of the Cuban Missile Crisis concluded overt U.S. attempts to overthrow the Castro regime and to destabilize the revolution. But the Central Intelligence Agency and other security agencies continued to sponsor clandestine operations aimed at assassinating, overthrowing, or discrediting the revolutionary leader and bringing an end to the communist threat in the Western Hemisphere. In response, the Cuban government maintained close ties to the Soviet Union and developed a sophisticated security and intelligence network. Castro frequently used the threat of U.S. intervention to justify autocratic actions, such as censoring the press, restricting individual liberties, and cracking down on dissidents.

Within Cuba, Castro's priorities turned to ensuring the revolution's survival. He united the various groups of participants in the revolution under an umbrella organization that eventually became the official Communist Party. Since its founding, Fidel and Raúl Castro were its leading figures; subsequent legal restrictions on competing political entities ensured its continued dominance. Government policies sought to reduce the island's reliance on sugar exports while overtly socialist measures fashioned new social and economic realities. Castro aimed to spread the revolution's benefits to all Cubans by establishing universal access to free education, health care, and social security. Simultaneously, the government nationalized small businesses and eliminated most private property. State-run farms became the foundation of the agricultural sector and most Cubans received "voluntary work" assignments on them as a contribution to the national good. The new shape of the economy often resulted in shortages of basic goods as a misallocation of the skilled workforce combined with the flight of many trained business people to the United States and the continued U.S. restrictions on trade. The embargo not only remained in place, but also expanded over time, eventually restricting nearly all travel and economic exchange. Symbolically, Castro attempted to instill the notion of the "New Socialist Man," defined by commitment to an egalitarian society.

Social Changes through Revolution

The Batista era had reinforced Cuba's traditional racial inequality, an injustice that the revolutionary government eventually sought to correct. Before 1959, law and common practice had allowed segregated schools, housing, and public spaces; black Cubans made up the bulk of low-wage laborers and substantial differences in income followed racial lines. To reverse these trends, revolutionary leaders promoted communist egalitarianism. This concept insisted that reforms designed to create an overall system of greater equality would also stamp out racism. Although many socialist measures undeniably improved the lives of Cuba's poorest citizens, critics charged that racially based economic and social inequalities persisted, accusing government leaders of ignoring these lingering problems.

Cuban leaders adopted a similar approach to gender equality in the early years of the revolution. Women had provided important leadership in movements opposed to the Batista regime and also contributed during the guerrilla warfare that preceded the dictator's departure. They continued to participate in the spirit of the revolution after 1959 by forming brigades to train and educate women in professional skills. Additionally, they comprised militias and defense committees, particularly as tensions with the United States escalated. Revolutionary leaders came to view feminism through the lens of Marxism and argued that women's lives would improve as social conditions in general improved. Changes to civil laws called for equality in the workforce and in the home as a new family code ostensibly required men to contribute to housework and child care, although enforcement remained problematic.

Policies on homosexuality offer another view of the evolving and often contradictory social assumptions implanted by Castro's regime. The state defined homosexuality as illegal prior to the revolution, and such intolerance went unchanged in the early years. Gay Cubans suffered arrest and imprisonment; many received sentences to labor in agricultural work camps known as Military Units to Aid Production. In 1975, official policy began to change when the courts banned discrimination based on sexual orientation in the workplace. Four years later, new legislation decriminalized homosexuality in private, but bias and bigotry persisted. Openly gay individuals often faced intolerance on the job, and national health officials quarantined persons afflicted with HIV. In the 1990s, the government outlawed discrimination based on sexual orientation and initiated educational programs intended to foster respect and acceptance of homosexuality.

Postrevolutionary Cultural Production

> "Within the revolution, everything. Against the revolution, nothing."
> —Fidel Castro at a meeting of Cuban writers and intellectuals at the
> Biblioteca Nacional, June 1961

Cuban officials after 1959 encouraged writers, intellectuals, and artists to participate in a revolutionary dialogue. Inspired in part by the Bolshevik and Mexican revolutions, artists created posters promoting a variety of government programs, including literacy campaigns. Their works often endorsed the ruler's political ideology and celebrated the turn toward communism. The Communist Party encouraged this creative output, arguing that writers had a responsibility to support the revolution and discard bourgeois traditions.

Some artists attempted to keep their work separate from the government's revolutionary message. Haydée Santamaría founded the Casa de las Américas to promote cultural expression; in its early days, it provided a welcoming environment to artists and writers who did not wholeheartedly embrace the revolution in their work. Nevertheless, as the Castro regime became more entrenched, cultural institutions like Casa de las Américas began to toe the party line.

Migration and Exiles

Some Cubans accepted the tenets of the new revolutionary society, but others sought to escape the hardships of their new reality. Roughly 250,000 Cubans, mostly of the middle and upper classes, fled to the United States in the first three years of the revolution. That number includes thousands of unaccompanied minors whose parents sent them to the United States in a secretive program orchestrated by the Central Intelligence Agency and the Catholic Church known as Operation Pedro Pan.

A second wave of refugees entered the United States between 1965 and 1974 after U.S. immigration reform laws made it easier for exiles already in the United States to sponsor visas for family members. But during that time, the Cuban government enacted strict regulations and denied exit visas to persons with desirable professional skills. As a result, the majority of these refugees came from the working class and arrived with less wealth than their predecessors.

A third wave occurred in 1980 when a downturn in the Cuban economy resulted in large numbers of people seeking asylum in foreign embassies on the

Primary Source

Fidel Castro made use of the U.S. media while fighting the revolution and in the months following Batista's overthrow. He outlined his plan for revolutionary reform in an interview with *The Wall Street Journal.*

SOURCE: Ed Cony, "Castro Describes His Plans for Cuba," *The Wall Street Journal,* April 22, 1959, http://lanic.utexas.edu/project/castro/db/1959/19590422.html.

In contrast to the cheerful confusion prevailing elsewhere in his party (his car is loaded with bearded bodyguards and clean-shaven U.S. security agents mingling with Cuban cabinet officers and wives), Dr. Castro seems cool and collected in the privacy of his drawing room as he continues to expound on his economic beliefs. Casually flicking scraps of cigar onto the bed, he says he has no intention of confiscating Cuban Telephone Co., an affiliate of International Telephone & Telegraph Corp., which has been operated for the past couple of months by a government "intervenor" who is looking into the utility's costs and rates. Does the government plan to buy the phone? "We have not talked about it; we have more urgent uses for our money," he says airily. He claims further that people have misinterpreted a remark of his in a recent speech which indicated he intended to abolish both the lower and upper economic classes and put everyone into a level middle class. "We do hope to raise the standard of living of everyone to what the middle class now has," he says. But he insists he has no thought of taking money away from any wealthy individual who invests in industry. "Industry owners will still make money," he promises. He is considerably less sympathetic, however, toward people who have invested in real estate and apartments. He defends vigorously his rent decree which slashed rents by April 1 by 30% to 50%. He maintains Cuba does not need this type of "non-productive" investment. Asked if his rent reduction hasn't frightened all investors, including those who might put up the industrial plants he wants so much, he concedes that many potential investors "are worried." But he claims manufacturers in Cuba "are happy."

island. Fidel Castro responded by opening the port of Mariel and allowing anyone wanting to migrate to do so. In the famous Mariel Boatlift, 125,000 Cubans fled via flotilla to Miami. Many of the *marielitos* were poor and uneducated; others had a criminal record or a history of mental illness. U.S. immigration officials held most of them in large detention centers while conducting background checks; the system struggled to accommodate the large influx of refugees. Approximately half of the Mariel migrants stayed permanently in the Miami area and changed the social and cultural energy of the city during the 1980s.

A fourth wave of migration took place after the fall of the Soviet Union in 1989 with new arrivals known as *balseros.* The withdrawal of Soviet aid created numerous economic crises in Cuba and the number of people attempting to escape the island on *balsas,* or rafts, increased substantially. A major antigovernment demonstration in the summer of 1994 escalated to a near riot as desperate Cubans hijacked ferries and boats in an attempt to flee to Miami. The following year, U.S. leaders changed the existing immigration law that had granted asylum to nearly all Cubans who attempted to escape to the United States. The new "Wet Foot, Dry Foot" regulation stipulated that only Cuban refugees who made it to U.S. soil would be given the opportunity to immigrate legally. Cubans intercepted at sea would be sent back to the island.

The consolidation of the Cuban revolution and Fidel Castro's turn to communism had important repercussions on the island nation's relationship with the United States. Leaders in Washington interpreted these revolutionary policies as an affront to U.S. inclinations and as a grave threat to Western Hemisphere security in the midst of the Cold War. Decade after decade, relations between the two countries worsened. U.S. agencies repeatedly pursued covert operations to destabilize the Castro regime or to eliminate the problematic leader altogether. Cuban leaders strengthened ties with the Soviet Union and eventually sought ways to export the spirit of the revolution beyond the island. The trade embargo and travel restrictions tightened, and diplomacy seemed to reach a stalemate. Even the dissolution of the Soviet Union did not lead to the downfall of the Castro regime; the island experienced a period of hardship with the end of Soviet aid, but Cuban communism survived.

Events in Cuba also had wider consequences throughout Latin America as U.S. Cold War policy became increasingly reactionary. Fear mounted that Castro's revolution would become a model for other leftist insurrections in the region and the imperative of preventing such actions took precedence in U.S. strategies. In the coming decades, Washington leaders supported right-wing, authoritarian regimes that resorted to a wide range of repression and human rights abuses in the name of stamping out the left.

SUGGESTIONS FOR FURTHER READING

Benjamin, Jules R. *The United States and the Origins of the Cuban Revolution: An Empire of Liberty in an Age of National Liberation*. Princeton, NJ: Princeton University Press, 1990.

Chase, Michelle. *Revolution within the Revolution: Women and Gender Politics in Cuba, 1952–1962*. Chapel Hill: University of North Carolina Press, 2015.

Chomsky, Aviva. *A History of the Cuban Revolution*. 2nd ed. Malden, MA: Wiley–Blackwell, 2015.

Farber, Samuel. *Cuba since the Revolution of 1959: A Critical Assessment*. Chicago: Haymarket, 2011.

García Luis, Julio (ed.) *Cuban Revolution Reader: A Documentary History of Fidel Castro's Revolution*. Minneapolis, MN: Ocean Press, 2008.

Guerra, Lillian. *Visions of Power in Cuba: Revolution, Redemption, and Resistance, 1959–1971*. Chapel Hill: University of North Carolina Press, 2012.

Kumaraswami, Par, and Antoni Kapcia. *Literary Culture in Cuba: Revolution, Nation-Building, and the Book*. Manchester: Manchester University Press, 2012.

Masud-Piloto, Felix Roberto. *From Welcomed Exiles to Illegal Immigrants: Cuban Migration to the U.S., 1959–1995*. Lanham, MD: Rowman & Littlefield, 1996.

Paterson, Thomas G. *Contesting Castro: The United States and the Triumph of the Cuban Revolution*. Oxford: Oxford University Press, 1995.

Sweig, Julia. *Inside the Cuban Revolution: Fidel Castro and the Urban Underground*. Cambridge, MA: Harvard University Press, 2002.

Wright, Thomas C. *Latin America in the Era of the Cuba Revolution*. Revised ed. Westport, CT: Praeger, 2001.

CHAPTER 23

National Security State
and Dirty Wars

In the late 1950s and early 1960s, ostensibly democratic governments were taking root in Latin America. Many of these civilian regimes cultivated images as defenders of social justice and popular reform. In Brazil, regular democratic elections between 1945 and 1960 provided a sense of legitimacy to the ISI-inspired economic policies that were defining the country. Although short lived, the popularly elected and socialist-oriented government of Jacobo Árbenz that gained power in Guatemala in 1951 also exemplified this trend. In Ecuador, the social reformer and former president José María Velasco Ibarra won the presidency once again in 1952 and pursued a socially oriented program that included land reform, high levels of government spending, and friendly relations with Cuba after the revolution. Juan Bosch won election as president in the Dominican Republic following decades of rule by dictators. He led a social-democratic government concerned with land reform, labor rights, and social welfare. In 1970, Chileans elected as president Salvador Allende, a founder of the nation's Socialist Party, as part of an alliance among leftist political parties. All of these governments relied on democratic elections to legitimize social justice measures and engaged in increasingly aggressive leftist rhetoric.

This democratic trend collapsed between 1964 and the 1980s, as a series of military coups replaced freely elected governments throughout Latin America. But the resulting authoritarian regimes lacked powerful and charismatic leaders common among the region's earlier *caudillos* and military dictators. Instead, the military as an institution became an authority figure that justified seizing power by force and retaining it because of alleged threats to the country's safety. During this era of the National Security State, military regimes made the doctrine of national security their foundation, often at the expense of individual liberties and social equality. The results included egregious human rights abuses and close alliance with the United States in defense against communism.

NATIONAL SECURITY STATE DEFINED

Unlike individual military dictatorships, National Security State regimes insisted their rule would last only until they had transformed economic and political systems. Most recognized the deleterious consequences of inflation, economic stagnation, and fiscal crises that had accompanied the ISI policies of earlier decades. Some of the new governments imposed rigid conservative economic systems in an effort to reverse the problems of ISI. Many identified leftist policies and popular revolutionary movements as their main political problems. In the name of anti-communism, the National Security State regimes routinely and heinously violated human rights.

Although a country's particular circumstances shaped the path toward power, National Security State regimes tended to exhibit some common characteristics. With the exception of Chile, nearly all followed a military coup that quickly ousted a civilian government and seized power in a matter of 24–48 hours and with little bloodshed.

Map 23.1 Dirty Wars in South America

Immediately invoking repressive authoritarian practices, the new right-wing leaders dissolved legislative bodies, censored the press, disallowed political parties, and took other measures to silence opposition. They presented themselves as anti-Marxist in general and anti-Cuba in particular. Thus, they cloaked their actions as preemptively preventing "another Cuba."

In most cases, the new governments addressed economic problems with conservative fiscal and monetary policies. They attacked inflation and cut government spending, particularly for social programs. They encouraged private investment as a strategy for diminishing government involvement in business ventures; they lowered tariffs and other trade barriers to create a more open environment for global exchange. These approaches often won them support from the middle and upper classes, particularly in the buildup to the coup and in its immediate aftermath.

The military governments showcased their actions as the best option to protect their countries' security and economic stability and managed to achieve some semblance of stability and progress. But their efforts came at a high price because their authoritarian practices quickly began to violate human rights. Claiming justification in the name of national well-being, security forces aggressively silenced the opposition—both real and perceived. They detained not only suspected dissidents, but also their family members, friends, and acquaintances. After their arrests— often made in the middle of the night—many prisoners suffered lengthy detention, torture, and even death, their bodies discarded in clandestine graves or tossed to sea. The secrecy shielding these tactics added to the grief of friends and family members left behind. Government officials frequently denied involvement in these cases and the victims augmented the growing number of "disappeared."

THE UNITED STATES AND NATIONAL SECURITY DOCTRINE

The United States fomented the National Security Doctrine as part of its strategy to prevent the Cuban Revolution from spreading to other parts of the hemisphere. The U.S.-operated School of the Americas trained more than 16,000 troops between 1961 and 1964 alone, developing techniques in counterinsurgency and weeding out leftist rebels. Bristling at the CEPAL's promotion of dependency theory and state-sponsored structuralism, U.S. leaders used aid programs and other inducements to encourage more conservative economic policies. To destabilize democratically elected leftist regimes and to disrupt daily life, the CIA covertly coordinated local agitators and repeatedly provided strategic support and indirect assistance to leaders of military coups.

Alliance for Progress

In March 1961, the administration of John F. Kennedy introduced an innovative plan to transform radically the social order of Latin America without violent revolution. Under his Alliance for Progress, the United States pledged billions of dollars in loans and aid. In exchange, Latin American nations pledged to correct social injustices and promote economic growth. The program encouraged land reform and changes in tax laws to alter the general framework of wealth and income distribution. In some countries, it supported building new homes and schools for the poor as well as health and sanitation initiatives. Largely a response to the Cuban

Revolution, Kennedy's Alliance for Progress sought to prevent future upheavals while promoting democracy and capitalist development.

To be successful, the new program needed the cooperation and support of the masses in Latin America as well as national leaders who would promote its vision and implement its provisions. The U.S. Information Agency used radio, film, and print media to publicize the way the program helped local communities. Alliance organizers also sponsored exchange and private aid programs between the United States and Latin America to establish educational and support networks across the hemisphere. In 1961, Kennedy also launched the Peace Corps program that sent thousands of idealistic youth to Latin America and around the world to provide assistance in impoverished areas and to participate in cultural exchange. Many of those volunteers returned after their Peace Corps tenure and entered graduate programs in Latin American studies. These strategies marked a continuation of those put in place by the OCIAA and other U.S. offices to enhance cultural relations during World War II. But complicated loan procedures overwhelmed the common people and failed to generate enthusiasm.

The Alliance for Progress eventually failed. It faced bureaucratic and insurmountable funding challenges in the United States as foreign policies shifted following Kennedy's assassination. Even more troublesome, Latin American leaders eschewed the types of structural social changes the Alliance advocated. As beneficiaries of land tenure systems that favored latifundia and perpetuated the exploitation of the poor, the economic and political elite opposed any attempt at serious reform. But the program spawned more ominous consequences by providing military aid to U.S.-friendly regimes.

After 1963, the administration of Lyndon Johnson increasingly shifted assistance from economic programs to those benefiting Latin American armed forces. Thus, the United States poured money into Víctor Paz Estenssoro's repressive regime in Bolivia as he faced growing challenges from leftist workers. U.S. cash also flowed to Nicaragua's national guard under the right-wing rule of the Somoza family. In the 1970s, officers at the School of the Americas became part of a brutal strategy to combat a leftist uprising in the country.

THE EMERGENCE OF NATIONAL SECURITY STATE TRENDS

Early signs of U.S. intervention and the National Security State doctrine emerged immediately following the overthrow of Jacobo Árbenz in Guatemala in 1954 and became more firmly entrenched after the Cuban Revolution in 1959. What started as individual instances of U.S. collusion in government repression against the Latin American left gave rise to a more coordinated region-wide authoritarian wave.

Ecuador

In 1960, the populist leader José María Velasco Ibarra won the presidency in Ecuador. Although he was not a communist, his toleration of leftist activists and refusal to sever ties with Cuba quickly caused concern among U.S. leaders. They responded with strategies to destabilize his administration while simultaneously undermining leftist groups. Covert action in Ecuador became a model for subsequent U.S. interventions in Latin America. Intelligence officials infiltrated political organizations to encourage social unrest and provoke a military response. They bribed newspaper editors to publish stories indicating the president lacked widespread support. U.S.-backed labor unions and other political organizations competed with and undermined the influence of legitimate local groups. In this increasingly unstable political atmosphere, demands for the president's removal followed.

As if following a script, the military ousted Velasco and two years later deposed his successor. In power through the 1970s, the military government outlawed communism, detained suspected leftists, and tortured perceived enemies. In 1977, the leftist labor union in the Aztra sugar mill went on strike, demanding wage increases and adherence to a collective contract. Armed security forces violently dispersed a crowd of workers, their wives, and children. Union leaders claimed that 120 people died in the "Aztra massacre"; however, government officials acknowledged the deaths of only 25 agitators.

Dominican Republic

The Caribbean island nation experienced decades of dictatorial rule under Rafael Trujillo, notorious for silencing political opposition while amassing a personal fortune. His hardline tactics eventually eroded U.S. support and alienated Dominican military leaders orchestrated his assassination in 1961. His successor, the social democrat Juan Bosch, backed reforms that included land redistribution, public works, low-rent housing, increased rights for labor, and some nationalization of businesses. Both local business leaders and the U.S. ambassador equated this social reform program to an endorsement of communism. President Kennedy cut off the country from Alliance for Progress aid and the CIA worked to undermine Bosch's local support. After the military overthrew Bosch in 1963, turmoil and civil war led to armed intervention by U.S. Marines. New elections in 1966 placed Joaquín Balaguer in the presidency. He followed the National Security Doctrine and used authoritarian rule to persecute political opponents and censor the press.

Paraguay and Bolivia

In Paraguay, Alfredo Stroessner seized power following a coup in 1954. A staunch anticommunist, he accepted U.S. aid and ruled through repression and terror for more than three decades. In response to almost immediate guerrilla resistance, the dictator declared a state of siege. Citing general chaos in the country as justification, he censored the press and imprisoned and tortured suspected opponents. Many fled into exile. The rise of military dictatorships in neighboring countries bolstered Stroessner's regime throughout the 1960s and he continued to rule despotically until his violent overthrow in 1989.

In 1964, a U.S.-supported coup started an 18-year repressive military dictatorship in Bolivia. During that time, the government arrested, tortured, and exiled approximately 5,000 suspected leftists; it killed or disappeared hundreds more. The situation in Bolivia attracted the attention of Che Guevara, who saw an opportunity to export the Cuban Revolution to South America. He led a small guerrilla force for almost a year, but government forces killed him in October 1967 with CIA assistance.

BUREAUCRATIC AUTHORITARIANISM

In an effort to understand the rise of military regimes and their distinct type of autocratic rule, the Argentinian scholar Guillermo O'Donnell introduced the concept of "bureaucratic authoritarianism" in 1973. He argued that rapid industrialization under ISI combined with social and political tensions that arose out of populist reform to create conditions ripe for this new form of despotism. In the bureaucratic authoritarian model, military juntas relied on expanded bureaucracies with civilian "technocrats" assigned to devise economic policy to encourage capitalist development. Thus, the ruling committees protected the interests of the economic elites while attempting to maintain social control. These more systematic, professionalized, and institutionalized military dictatorships contrasted with the personalism and volatility of earlier autocrats who exhibited remnants of caudillismo.

Political observers initially applied O'Donnell's term to the autocratic rule that emerged in Brazil, Argentina, Chile, and Uruguay from the 1960s to the 1980s. And although Mexico escaped any military coups during this period, its institutionalized one-party authoritarianism resembled the martial versions in many ways. Bureaucratic authoritarian regimes emphasized modernization and economic growth, often borrowing heavily from abroad to fund the expansion of infrastructure and state-owned industrial enterprises. Foreign debt also helped to pay the ever-increasing numbers of civilian bureaucrats. The governments believed such strategies would promote development, attract new investors, and boost the private sector.

The economic policies instituted by bureaucratic authoritarian regimes had a lasting impact in Latin America, notably in increased indebtedness that eventually led to near economic collapse after 1982. But the social consequences of military rule devastated many sectors of the population even more. Governments halted the redistributive and social justice reforms that the earlier populist regimes had implemented. Security forces suppressed the labor movement and other forms of social activism with terror and brutality, often justifying these measures as a way to stamp out leftist agitators who threatened national stability. In many countries civilians responded with a sense of powerlessness.

Socially active and politically aware university students and other young adults often became primary targets of a military regime's suppression of suspected dissidents. Their activism coincided with a rise in student movements around the world. College and even some high school students embraced an interpretation of history that privileged a sense of anti-imperialism and at times turned militant. Young people throughout Latin America, many inspired by the Cuban Revolution, organized themselves into social movements, committees, and brigades. They demanded an end to the exploitation and systems of widespread inequality that had long characterized Latin American society. Their movements became almost a festival full of music, street theater, and other artistic expressions, a momentary inversion of power.

Brazil

Brazil maintained a strong democratic tradition for nearly two decades following World War II. Civilian leaders embraced ISI policies and initially the economy appeared to thrive. But by the 1960s the effects of economic mismanagement had become obvious. Between 1962 and 1966, inflation rose more than 500 percent, while industrial production declined. At the same time, U.S. leaders scrutinized the reactions of Brazilian and other Latin American counterparts to the Cuban Revolution. Vice President João Goulart assumed Brazil's presidency in 1961 after Jânio Quadros resigned. The new president initially enjoyed the support of U.S. leaders, who hoped he would oppose communism and protect U.S. Cold War interests in the Western Hemisphere. But Goulart began pursuing suspect policies such as labor and land reform. Furthermore, he allied with the Brazilian Communist Party and refused to sever ties with Cuba and the Soviet Union. In response, the United States began to withhold economic aid and exert pressure on his administration. In 1964, a military coup—widely suspected of having CIA backing—overthrew the president and ushered in two decades of repression under the National Security State model.

Brazilian security forces targeted suspected leftists and engaged in a brutal campaign to weed out dissidents. Kidnappings, torture, and murder of political opposition created an environment of fear. A 2014 Truth Commission report—commissioned by President Dilma Rousseff, a victim of military repression—revealed a host of human rights abuses, including 191 deaths and more than 200 disappearances of suspected leftists.

Brazil's military coup and the onset of its National Security State regime had important repercussions. Much like the earlier overthrow of the Árbenz government in Guatemala, Brazil provided a model for other Latin American nations. Indeed, similar coups spread to the surrounding areas as other military leaders ousted civilian governments under the banner of national security. The establishment of the Brazilian military regime also set the stage for the emergence of a type of military brotherhood. Cooperation among neighboring military regimes often became a fundamental component of National Security States, particularly in the Southern Cone.

Mexico

In Mexico a youth movement emerged in the 1960s in response to rising poverty in large urban areas, labor issues, and concerns that government security forces were overstepping their boundaries. In summer 1968, university students in Mexico City went on strike to protest the vast government expenditures to host the upcoming Olympic Games. They also demanded the release of a jailed labor leader and called for abolition of the extralegal security forces known as the *granaderos*.

Many participants in the student movement came from middle-class families; their parents were educated beneficiaries of new government programs. But the young demonstrators represented a growing rejection of the government's typical rhetoric and policy changes that favored industrialization and capitalist growth over programs of redistribution for social justice. Import substitution strategies and state-sponsored structuralism had created short-term economic expansion evident in 6 percent annual gross domestic product growth and other macroeconomic measures; both the middle class and the major cities grew as population migrated to urban areas. But these changes occurred at the expense of the poor and rural sectors.

The movement began with strikes among students in Mexico City's two main universities and evolved into barricades in buildings, protest marches, and even street theater. Female students often participated and some even played leadership roles. As a result, the student movement introduced a call for more inclusive democracy and paved the way for a strong feminist movement in subsequent years.

As student protests gained momentum, the government response toughened. A large demonstration in Mexico City's prominent Tlatelolco Plaza on October 2, 1968, turned tragic when government forces opened fire on a crowd of approximately 5,000. Chaos ensued as demonstrators attempted to flee and security forces detained hundreds of young people. Press accounts downplayed the violence and repeated the official, and inaccurate, government account that foreign agitators had attacked police, resulting in 4 deaths. The actual toll was likely 200 to 300. Following Tlatelolco, the government cracked down on dissent—apprehending and torturing opponents of the Institutional Revolutionary Party, which remained the dominant political party. Faced with rising government repression, small-armed guerrilla groups formed in many rural areas. Their presence led to even more heavy-handed responses. A dirty war ensued as paramilitary units detained student activists and suspected guerrilla leaders in secretive and often extralegal operations.

Chile

Chile had enjoyed a long democratic experience throughout the twentieth century because a stable constitutional system had enabled it to avoid the military rule dominant elsewhere. But its relatively unique tradition did not immunize the country from the rise of the National Security State. Indeed, in the 1950s and 1960s the nation suffered from an array of socioeconomic inequalities: high rates of infant mortality, inadequate housing for the urban and rural poor, and a power imbalance based on workers' exploitation by the landowning elite under the system of latifundia. Chile had also experimented with ISI. The result forced the nation to begin importing food as the agricultural sector declined in favor of manufacturing. Despite efforts to diversify and shift the production of vital resources to national control, the copper industry and other large and profitable sectors remained under U.S. ownership.

In 1970, Salvador Allende won the presidency through an alliance of Chile's leftist parties behind a platform calling for sweeping reform to foment equality and social justice. His proposed changes included housing reforms, workers' rights, access to health care, improvements to the nation's legal system, and a system of milk distribution to combat infant mortality. Once in office, the president began to implement his ambitious agenda.

Allende's efforts to fulfill his campaign commitments came as no surprise. But the immediate impact of some policies angered many Chileans, particularly those in the middle and upper classes. Price freezes and mandated higher wages to increase poor Chileans' purchasing power reduced manufacturers' profits, so many stopped producing; shortages of some consumer goods followed. When the government rationed the distribution of milk and other foodstuffs based on need rather than ability to buy, middle- and upper-class mothers denounced the policy as well as other egalitarian reforms that erased social privilege.

Allende also faced serious challenges from the United States. Concerned that Chile's socialist-oriented solutions in the midst of the Cold War set a dangerous precedent, policy makers in Washington ordered the CIA to engage in covert de-stabilization strategies, similar to those employed in Ecuador in the early 1960s. In addition, the United States restricted trade with Chile, cut off aid, and blocked access to foreign credit. A declining price for copper created more problems since the Chilean economy relied heavily on mining exports. Copper workers and other labor unions went on strike, some at the instigation of U.S. covert agitators.

Allende's opposition expected the congressional election of 1973 to provide enough seats to allow a majority coalition to impeach the president. When they failed to win by a sufficient margin, many opponents concluded that only a military-backed coup could remove Allende from office.

On September 11, 1973, the Chilean military overthrew Allende's government. Fighter planes bombed the presidential palace as ground troops surrounded and then occupied the building. After several hours of fighting, Allende's personal security force was overrun; the president eventually committed suicide rather than surrender. A military junta assumed power and eventually General Augusto Pinochet became president, a position he held until 1990.

In the aftermath of the coup, military leaders anticipated popular resistance. They cracked down violently on Allende supporters and suspected leftist sympathizers, arresting, torturing, and often killing leaders of socialist and communist groups. The new government detained in 1973 alone an estimated 150,000 people of a total population of 10 million. Some of the early arrests resulted in public execution. Other detainees simply disappeared. For nearly two decades, many Chileans lived under a shroud of secrecy and fear. As family members searched for loved ones, security officials offered few answers.

Government censorship and the threat of repression kept many family members from speaking out. But some mothers, sisters, and wives of the disappeared turned to each other for support. Many gathered regularly in informal workshops to create tapestries, or *arpilleras*, specifically embroidered to portray scenes of military repression, poverty, and the desperate attempt to search for the disappeared. Catholic charities smuggled the tapestries out of the country and sold them abroad. For many embroiderers, the money earned was their sole source of income.

Chilean soldiers burning Marxist literature, including a poster with the image of Che Guevara, in the streets of Santiago after the coup deposing President Salvador Allende. The military dictatorship under General Augusto Pinochet initiated a period of repression in Chile that lasted until 1990.

The Pinochet regime worked hard to hide the true extent of its repression. Rumors circulated about security forces apprehending "subversives," but many middle- and upper-class Chileans remained unaware of the violent measures the government used in secret detention facilities. The government killed or disappeared an estimated 3,500 to 4,000 Chileans in the name of national security.

Argentina

Argentina's experience with a National Security State related to the legacy of Peronism. Forced out of office in 1955, Perón spent nearly two decades in exile while government control alternated between civilian Peronist activists and military leaders. In 1973, Perón returned to Argentina. Although he was elected president once again, he found that his delicate populist coalition had fractured. The extreme leftist branch had coalesced in the Montoneros, an increasingly militant urban guerrilla group engaged in violent attacks against the right-wing arm of the Peronist movement. The aging president denounced the Montoneros and tensions between the left and right Peronist factions continued to build.

When Perón died at the age of 78 after only one year in office, Isabel, his third wife and vice president, replaced him. Inheriting a tumultuous situation, she quickly proved unprepared for the responsibility, leaving all major decisions to her main advisor, José López Rega. Within two years, inflation had reached nearly 1,000 percent amid escalating violence among extremist groups. In March 1976, the military deposed her in a relatively quiet coup d'état and Jorge Videla assumed power.

Videla's military dictatorship invoked the National Security State doctrine to justify suppressing dissidents and suspected leftists throughout the country. Because of the secrecy surrounding Argentina's Dirty War, the precise number of victims questioned, tortured, and killed is uncertain, but subsequent human rights investigations estimates range between 10,000 and 30,000. Efforts to flee dictatorial repression in Argentina and elsewhere proved futile; military regimes throughout South America collaborated to investigate and hunt down dissidents who had sought refuge in other countries. Right-wing leaders in Argentina, Chile, Paraguay, Bolivia, Uruguay, and Brazil devised Operation Condor to exchange intelligence and pursue suspected leftists across borders—much of this carried out with the knowledge of U.S. officials. The former Chilean foreign minister Orlando Letelier and U.S. citizen Ronni Moffitt were two high-profile individuals targeted and killed by a car bomb in Washington, DC.

As elsewhere in Latin America, gender became an important component of the Dirty War. Torture tactics often included sexual assault, particularly against females. Young women who were pregnant when arrested—or became pregnant while detained—often gave birth in prison and suffered immediate separation from their child. Many of these mothers were eventually killed and the babies were adopted by unquestioning families friendly to the military regime.

Family members of detainees had few options in searching for loved ones and standing up to the military regime. One exception was the collective actions of mothers of the disappeared who began meeting as a small group to provide each other support and solace. As their numbers grew, the Madres de la Plaza de Mayo eventually held weekly public demonstrations in Buenos Aires' main public square. Identifiable by their white headscarves, the mothers generally marched in silence, but their somber protests began to attract national and international attention. Although members of the Madres at times fell victim to harassment, the military government generally refrained from interfering in their activities. The group proved instrumental in raising enough opposition to bring down the military government.

Dictatorial rule lasted until 1983. Sensing a decline in public support, the military had launched an ill-advised invasion of the Malvinas or Falkland Islands— a British possession off the coast of Argentina that had been the source of jurisdictional conflict since the 1830s. Argentina's humiliating defeat combined with growing popular animosity to return the country to civilian rule. In recent years, grandmothers of babies born in detention centers have rallied together as the Abuelas de la Plaza de Mayo. Leading a public campaign of DNA testing, they have successfully reunited with their biological families more than 100 of an estimated 500 children of the disappeared.

CULTURAL EXPRESSION UNDER AUTHORITARIANISM

Music

Folk and protest-inspired genres characterized new musical styles during the era of the National Security State. In Argentina, neofolklore combined traditional rural music with sophisticated arrangements. Artists included the singer Atahualpa Yupanqui and groups like Los Chalchaleros. Neofolk influenced music in both Catholic and Protestant church services in Latin America, in no small part because of the popularity of folk masses like Ariel Ramírez's *Misa criolla*. In other areas, a style known primarily as *nueva canción* (New Song) featured songs that addressed issues such as economic exploitation, North American imperialism, social inequality, and an implicit pan-Americanism. Artists included Amparo Ochoa and Los Folkloristas (Mexico), Silvio Rodriguez (Cuba), Mercedes Sosa (Argentina), Víctor Jara (Chile), Violeta Parra (Chile), Atahualpa Yupanqui (Argentina), and Daniel Viglietti (Uruguay).

The New Song movement in Chile took on a special character because of its association with leftist social movements and the regime of Salvador Allende. The singer, songwriter, poet, and theater director Víctor Jara (1934–1973) emerged as one of the most popular figures. Committed to recovering folk music and eschewing the overproduction of songs characteristic of more commercial neofolklore music, *nueva canción* in Chile included traditional instruments like the *charango*, a small Andean lute that features a resonator made with an armadillo shell.

Jara had experienced rural and urban poverty firsthand as a child and his music became an invective against hardship and social inequalities that he tied to conservative elements in Chile. As a supporter of Salvador Allende, Jara wrote "Venceremos" (We Will Triumph"), the theme song of the president's Unidad Popular movement. Jara became one of the first to be arrested in the immediate aftermath of the military coup in September 1973. In a particularly cruel display of torture, soldiers broke his hands and obliged him to play; he was later executed in

Santiago's Chile Stadium. Subsequently, the musician's memory became a symbol of resistance against the Pinochet regime, although the dictatorship effectively silenced his music until the 1990s.

U.S. and British rock and roll and international pop music trends also influenced Latin America popular music during the 1960s and 1970s. In Mexico, Spanish-language *rocanrol* groups like Los Teen Tops and Los Locos del Ritmo performed Spanish-language cover versions, known as *refritos*, of popular English-language songs by U.S artists like Elvis and Little Richard. *Rocanrol* appealed primarily to middle-class youth in urban areas. The same audience in the mid-1960s adopted English-language artists like the Rolling Stones and the Beatles. Leftist critics, however, denounced imported English-language rock music as part of U.S. cultural imperialism.

A countercultural movement known as *La Onda*, or "the wave," emerged in Mexico in the 1960s. Like their U.S. counterparts, *onderos* used music, clothing, and hairstyles as tools of social protest to challenge society's patriarchal structure. Young men eschewed traditional ideas of masculinity through long or unkempt hair and young women pushed the boundaries of dress with the miniskirt.

After the student massacre at Tlatelolco, a new generation of counterculture Mexican rock bands emerged, labeled as *La Onda Chicana*, with protest and politically tinged songs performed in English. In 1971, a local version of the Woodstock music festival took place in Valle de Bravo, two hours northwest of Mexico City. The state-approved Avándaro music festival attracted tens of thousands of mostly young males, reflecting the country's prevailing gender norms that generally circumscribed young women's mobility. Bands like Los Dug Dugs and Three Souls in My Mind performed and, like its U.S. counterpart, the Avándaro festival experienced crowds, rain, and mud. Unlike Woodstock, soldiers surrounded the Mexican music festival, lest it turn into a political rally.

Those on the far left criticized Avándaro as indicative of the cooptation of Mexican youth movement, since no mass gathering could happen without government approval and involvement. Others chastised participants for allowing themselves to be colonized by imperialist cultural forms. Conservatives denounced the festival for its perceived drug use, nudity, and other challenges to traditional Mexican values. The government blunted Avándaro's cultural impact by banning songs and images related to the festival, lest a political movement build around it.

Literature

During the 1960s and 1970s, the Latin American novel captured world attention in a literary movement known as the "Boom." A focus on Latin American identity and experimentation with form characterized the works of Gabriel García Márquez (Colombia), Carlos Fuentes (Mexico), Julio Cortázar (Argentina), Mario Vargas Llosa (Peru), Guillermo Cabrera Infante (Cuba), and Juan Carlos Onetti (Uruguay). Cortázar's *Rayuela* (1963), the first Boom novel to achieve international acclaim, uses a stream-of-consciousness narrative to produce a nonlinear reading. García Márquez's *Cien años de soledad* (1967) employs magical realism to reinterpret Latin America history through the story of the small town of Macondo. Carlos Fuentes's existential *La Muerte de Artemio Cruz* uses the life of its dying protagonist as a metaphor to explore the failures of the Mexican Revolution.

Several regional trends gave rise to the Boom. The economic policies of import substitution of the 1950s contributed to the formation of a larger, university-educated urban middle class whose sense of nationalism turned their literary tastes toward native authors. The Cuban Revolution drew attention to the region and fomented artistic imaginations across Latin America. Moreover, translations of Boom novels gave Latin American writers a global audience. The Boom, in a sense, created its own supply and demand as both Latin American and foreign readers gravitated toward García Márquez's village of Macondo and Fuentes's dying revolutionary Artemio Cruz. Boom authors have been recognized for their contributions to the world of letters. Fuentes, Onetti, Vargas Llosa, and Cabrera Infante have all received the Premio de Literatura en Lengua Castellana Miguel de Cervantes (the Miguel Cervantes Prize), one of the highest honors in Spanish letters. García Márquez and Vargas Llosa received the Nobel Prize in Literature in 1983 and 2010, respectively. Many of the Boom writers remain popular today, with García Márquez's *Cien años de soledad* a perennial favorite among readers.

Television

The television industry expanded and matured during the 1960s and 1970s. Several broadcasters rose to hemispheric prominence as audiences grew and programming became more sophisticated.

Under Brazil's military regime, television entered a nationalist phase (1964–1975) with the introduction of TV Globo, which began broadcasting in 1964. Aided by assistance and investment from Time Life, Inc., TV Globo set up a U.S.-style commercial operation that relied primarily on ad sales. The network also adopted U.S. management practices and uniform programming patterns for all of its stations across the country.

Live variety shows dominated much of the early programming. *Chacrinha* starred José Abelardo de Barbosa Medeiros as the eponymous clown, whose antics and interaction with audience members contributed to his popularity. In addition to comedy, dances, and games, *Chacrinha* often featured musicians known for criticizing the military government. The unpredictability and spontaneity of live television suffered with the imposition of prior censorship of all media. TV Globo complied by canceling *Chacrinha* in 1972 and replacing it with a more controlled and preproduced show called *Fantastico* in 1973.

Telenovelas became one of the most popular programming genres for Brazil's other networks. TV Globo aimed to produce a higher-quality version of the serial compared to its competitors and developed a sophisticated production operation. The network hired writers from cinema and theater and crafted its own star system to nurture talent. Its popular *telenovelas* included *Gabriela* and *Esclava Isaura*, adapted from the nineteenth-century novel by the abolitionist Bernardo Guimarães and showcasing issues of race, class, and gender. Set in nineteenth-century Brazil before the abolition of slavery, it featured the daughter of a black slave and a white man who escaped and lived as a free woman. Because of its immense popularity, a dubbed version later aired in other South American markets. *Esclava Isaura* would go on to be one of the first international *telenovelas*, eventually showing in more than 80 countries.

Like TV Globo, the Mexican broadcaster Televisa produced its own programming and came to dominate the local television market. Formed from the merger in 1973 between Telesistema Mexicano and Televisión Independiente de México (based in Monterrey, Nuevo León), the network faced little competition. It segmented its programming by channel and developed its own nascent star system through its *telenovelas*. Nationally produced movies, sports, and children's shows aired alongside dubbed U.S. programs such as *Kojak* and *The Streets of San Francisco*. Variety shows included *Siempre en Domingo*, which showcased singing, dancing, and an array of novelty acts. The beloved children's program *El Chapulín Colorado* starred the actor and comedian Roberto Gómez Bolaños as the eponymous bumbling superhero whose powers were a figment of his imagination. Many Televisa-produced programs proved popular throughout Latin America.

Latin American networks also developed transnational programming in local versions of the highly successful U.S. children's educational show *Sesame Street*, which debuted as *Vila Sésamo* in 1972. The show featured Brazilian characters and dubbed programming from the United States. A Mexican version first aired in 1972 on Televisa. *Plaza Sésamo* featured Muppet characters designed for the Latin American market, including Paco, a grouchy green parrot, and Beto and Enrique, based on Bert and Ernie. The Mexican government capitalized on Beto and Enrique's popularity, using the characters to help promote a vaccination campaign in 1975. By the mid-1970s, *Plaza Sésamo* aired in 17 Spanish-speaking countries.

By the mid-1970s, military dictatorship or some other type of bureaucratic authoritarian regime held power in every Latin American country except Costa Rica, Colombia, and Venezuela. Instead of moving away from the ISI models that had started showing weaknesses or addressing inequality and poverty, these governments began borrowing extensively from abroad. Some of the money went into military spending; a portion supported enormous state enterprises. Chile proved the sole exception to this trend; after 1975, the Pinochet regime devalued the national currency and eliminated protectionist trade barriers. Those measures led to a decline in industrial production, which served to weaken Pinochet's political opposition in the labor sector. The dictatorship refocused the nation's export sector on the "three F's:" fruit, fish, and forest products. Despite its alternate economic path, Chile did not escape the fiscal fate that befell the rest of Latin America as poor policy planning during the 1970s eventually gave way to a major debt crisis for the entire region.

Primary Source

The official government account of the violent confrontation between Mexican students and security forces in October 1968 blamed leftist agitators and minimized the casualty figures. The journalist Elena Poniatowska interviewed victims, witnesses, and family members and published a book of their firsthand accounts.

SOURCE: Elena Poniatowska, *Massacre in Mexico*, trans. Helen R. Lane (New York: Viking Press, 1975), 210–13.

They're dead bodies sir. . . .

A soldier, to José Antonio del Campo, reporter for El Día

I'll never forget one poor youngster, about sixteen or so, who crawled around the corner of the building, stuck his deadly pale face out, and made a V-for-Victory sign with two fingers. He didn't seem to have the least idea what was happening: he may have thought the men shooting were also students. Then the men in the white gloves yelled at him, "Get the hell out of here, you dumb bastard! Can't you see what's happening? Clear out of here!" The kids got to his feet and started walking toward them, as though he didn't have a care in the world. They fired a couple of shots at his feet, but the kid kept right on coming. He obviously didn't have the slightest idea what was going on, and they shot him in the calf of his leg. All I remember is that the blood didn't immediately spurt out; it just started slowly trickling down his leg. Meche and I started screaming at the guys with the white gloves like a couple of madwomen: "Don't kill him! Don't kill him! Don't kill him!" We ran to the door, but the kid had disappeared. I have no idea whether he managed to escape despite his wound, whether they killed him, or what happened to him.

Margarita Nolasco, anthropologist

. . .

Ever since then, whenever I see a helicopter, my hands start trembling. For many months after I'd seen that helicopter fire on the crowd like that—as I was sitting there in my car—I couldn't write, my hands trembled so.

Marta Zamora Vértiz, secretary

SUGGESTIONS FOR FURTHER READING

Arditti, Rita. *Searching for Life: The Grandmothers of the Plaza de Mayo and the Disappeared Children of Argentina*. Berkeley: University of California Press, 1999.

Brands, Hal. *Latin America's Cold War*. Cambridge, MA: Harvard University Press, 2010.

Carassai, Sebastián. *The Argentine Silent Majority: Middle Classes, Politics, Violence, and Memory in the Seventies*. Durham, NC: Duke University Press, 2014.

Carey, Elaine. *Plaza of Sacrifice: Gender, Power, and Terror in 1968 Mexico*. Albuquerque: University of New Mexico Press, 2005.

Cohn, Deborah N. *The Latin American Literary Boom and U.S. Nationalism during the Cold War*. Nashville, TN: Vanderbilt University Press, 2012.

Ensalco, Mark. *Chile under Pinochet: Recovering the Truth*. Philadelphia: University of Pennsylvania Press, 2000.

Esparza, Marcia, Henry R. Huttenbach, and Daniel Feierstein (eds.). *State Violence and Genocide in Latin America: The Cold War Years*. Hoboken, NJ: Taylor & Francis, 2009.

Feitlowitz, Marguerite. *A Lexicon of Terror: Argentina and the Legacies of Torture*. Revised ed. Oxford: Oxford University Press, 2011.

Field, Thomas C., Jr. *From Development to Dictatorship: Bolivia and the Alliance for Progress in the Kennedy Era*. Ithaca, NY: Cornell University Press, 2014.

Finchelstein, Federico. *The Ideological Origins of the Dirty War: Fascism, Populism, and Dictatorship in Twentieth-Century Argentina*. Oxford: Oxford University Press, 2014.

Garrard-Burnett, Virginia, Mark Atwood Lawrence, and Julio E. Moreno. *Beyond the Eagle's Shadow: New Histories of Latin America's Cold War*. Albuquerque: University of New Mexico Press, 2013.

Gonzalez de Bustamante, Celeste. *Muy Buenas Noches: Mexico, Television, and the Cold War*. Lincoln: University of Nebraska Press, 2012.

Grandin, Greg. *The Last Colonial Massacre Latin America in the Cold War*. Updated ed. Chicago: University of Chicago Press, 2011.

Guzman Bouvard, Marguerite. *Revolutionizing Motherhood: The Mothers of the Plaza de Mayo*. Lanham, MD: Rowman & Littlefield, 1994.

Harmer, Tanya. *Allende's Chile and the Inter-American Cold War*. Chapel Hill: University of North Carolina Press, 2011.

McSherry, J. Patrice. *Predatory States: Operation Condor and Covert War in Latin America*. Lanham, MD: Rowman & Littlefield, 2005.

O'Donnell, Guillermo A. *Bureaucratic Authoritarianism: Argentina, 1966–1973, in Comparative Perspective*. Berkeley: University of California Press, 1988.

Pensado, Jaime. *Rebel Mexico: Student Unrest and Authoritarian Political Culture during the Long Sixties*. Stanford, CA: Stanford University Press, 2013.

Poniatowska, Elena. *Massacre in Mexico*. Reprint ed. Columbia: University of Missouri Press, 1991.

Power, Margaret. *Right-Wing Women in Chile: Feminine Power and the Struggle against Allende, 1964–1973*. University Park: Pennsylvania State University Press, 2002.

Rabe, Stephen G. *The Most Dangerous Area in the World: John F. Kennedy Confronts Communist Revolution in Latin America*. Chapel Hill: University of North Carolina Press, 1999.

Rock, David. *Authoritarian Argentina: The Nationalist Movement, Its History and Its Impact*. Berkeley: University of California Press, 1993.

Sinclair, John. *Latin American Television: A Global View*. Oxford: Oxford University Press, 1999.

Stites Mor, Jessica (ed.). *Human Rights and Transnational Solidarity in Cold War Latin America*. Madison: University of Wisconsin Press, 2013.

Taffett, Jeffrey. *Foreign Aid as Foreign Policy: The Alliance for Progress in Latin America*. New York: Routledge, 2007.

Taylor, Diana. *Disappearing Acts: Spectacles of Gender and Nationalism in Argentina's "Dirty War."* Durham, NC: Duke University Press, 1997.

Wright, Thomas C. *State Terrorism in Latin America: Chile, Argentina, and International Human Rights*. Lanham, MD: Rowman & Littlefield, 2007.

Zolov, Eric. *Refried Elvis: The Rise of the Mexican Counterculture*. Berkeley: University of California Press, 1999.

CHAPTER 24

Debt and the Lost Decade

1996	U.S. Congress passes Helms–Burton Act, which penalizes foreign companies doing business in Cuba
1997	Chile's economy enters five years of stagnation
1998	Argentina sees a run on bank deposits, sparking a four-year depression
1999	Brazil currency stabilization plan fails and Brazil *real* loses two-thirds of value
2002	Argentina abandons Convertibility Plan
2002	Uruguay suffers banking crisis
2004	Cuba ends use of U.S. dollar and introduces dual currency system
2013	Cuba announces plans to end dual currency system

Throughout the 1960s and 1970s, many Latin American governments accumulated enormous international debt. During a first wave of borrowing, anticommunist regimes drew heavily on the World Bank. After 1973, in a second wave, they secured funds from private creditors; large economies under bureaucratic authoritarian regimes took out huge loans with little accountability for how they spent the money. Mexico, Argentina, and Brazil proved the worst offenders, but nearly all Latin American countries eventually followed their example. A debt crisis followed by the early 1980s as governments began to default on foreign loans and nearly crippled international financial markets. Securing recovery assistance from international institutions required dismantling state-sponsored development strategies and reversing the ISI model. For nearly a decade, Latin American nations suffered economic stagnation, high inflation, and skyrocketing rates of poverty. The consequences of such devastation disproportionately affected the working class and the poor. By the mid-1990s, governments had transformed their countries' economies and a system of regional and global integration was beginning to emerge.

DEBT CRISIS

U.S. attitudes toward Latin American economic development in the last half of the twentieth century influenced the larger trends that unfolded. Immediately after World War II, U.S. leaders repeatedly disregarded Latin American appeals for policies that would secure a market for their goods. The administrations of Harry Truman and Dwight Eisenhower rejected pleas to lower U.S. tariffs and to stabilize commodity prices on Latin American goods; instead, they urged leaders in the region to improve the overall commercial climate and attract private foreign investment. Such policies gave Latin Americans the unmistakable impression that their countries' economic development was of secondary importance to the United States, particularly in the context of Cold War security concerns. The resulting antagonism fueled arguments surrounding dependency theory, and the move toward state-sponsored structuralism in the 1950s proved a foundation for ISI policies in Latin America.

Aid Programs

The hard stance taken by U.S. leaders softened briefly under John F. Kennedy's Alliance for Progress in the early 1960s. In response to both the Cuban Revolution and a widespread and growing resentment in Latin America, Kennedy began to consult with Raúl Prebisch and other economists who had urged greater economic collaboration. The short-lived Alliance for Progress offered assistance to Latin American countries in exchange for their implementation of meaningful social and economic reforms. U.S. aid took the form of long-term capital assistance and commodity price stabilization. Latin American reforms included structural changes that affected land tenure, education, and tax reform.

Many Latin American economists praised the fledgling Alliance for Progress, but Kennedy's death in 1963 initiated the new program's eventual demise as the administration of Lyndon Johnson placed considerably less emphasis on Latin America. Under Johnson, U.S. economic policy was there to serve a broad anticommunist agenda. The president's limited approach fell under the "Mann Doctrine," which aimed to promote economic growth and protect U.S. private investment in the hemisphere. In a significant change from the Alliance for Progress, the doctrine took a neutral stance on social reform; additionally, it showed no preference for democratic rather than authoritarian institutions.

The Mann Doctrine helped Latin American nations sustain ISI during a time when that approach's limitations were starting to become evident. Under the doctrine, the United States offered infrastructure and capital investment in exchange for support in the fight against communism. Several important consequences affected Latin America for decades. First, the doctrine removed any requirement of structural change and political democracy for receiving U.S. aid. This allowed U.S. leaders to support right-wing military dictators who rose to power as part of the National Security State strategy in the 1960s and 1970s. Second, it failed to address any trade or development issues raised by Latin American economists. As a result, influential Latin American intellectuals continued to feel abandoned by the United States on economic policy. Finally, leaders in Washington began to encourage U.S.-based transnational banks to participate in foreign lending. This trend accelerated throughout the 1970s and eventually led to a deep economic crisis in the 1980s.

Latin American Debt

Prior to the 1970s, most indirect foreign investment had occurred through public, state-to-state loans or outright aid. Individual banks generally saw foreign lending as too risky, especially to the developing world. But in the 1970s, private lenders increasingly allowed Latin American countries to borrow large amounts of money; indeed, many aggressively sought out potential borrowers with enticing loan offers that cash-strapped government leaders found difficult to resist. This turn to private lending marked an important shift in the international financial system and increased the investors' risk. Any default on foreign loans from private banks could have a ripple effect that would touch individual clients in the United States. Thus, these banks intricately tied the financial well-being of U.S. citizens to Latin American debt.

The shift to transnational private lending in the 1970s resulted primarily from new developments in the global petroleum market. In 1960, oil-producing countries, primarily in the Middle East, joined together as the Organization of the Petroleum Exporting Countries (OPEC) and began collaborating to control the price of oil in the world market. By the 1970s, the oil cartel's influence enabled it to limit production and drive up prices. Rising earnings flooded OPEC nations with cash, which they stashed in U.S.-based transnational banks. Looking for ways to profit from large deposits of "petro-dollars," these banks sought new borrowers. Latin American nations offered a relatively untapped market for foreign loans and the elevated risk associated with developing economies allowed private banks to charge high interest rates. A steep rise in petroleum prices in 1973 because of OPEC's oil embargo further exacerbated this trend. Oil-producing countries transferred even more petro-dollars to transnational banks and lenders became increasingly desperate to convert these deposits into profitable loans. The rising oil prices put Latin American nations at a distinct disadvantage, since most of them relied on imported petroleum for energy, transportation, and manufacturing needs. This created a repetitive cycle of increased borrowing and growing external debt.

Throughout the 1970s, the external debt of developing nations rose by 21 percent per year and by the end of the decade the debt-to-gross national product ratio had reached 28 percent. As a region, Latin America's total external debt ballooned from $21 billion in 1970 to more than $300 billion by 1982. Although governments did the majority of borrowing during the 1970s, lending to private enterprises also expanded rapidly. Furthermore, banks demonstrated a clear preference for larger countries; Argentina, Mexico, Brazil, and Chile received the most attention. The smaller nations in the Caribbean and Central America (with the exception of Costa Rica) attracted less private bank money but still took on substantial encumbrances through assistance programs and other official capital transfers.

Hindsight makes clear that continued borrowing was not sustainable and that both the banks and the Latin American nations were engaging in reckless behavior. Many banks lent irresponsibly by aggressively selling high-priced loan packages to nations previously excluded from the international credit market. The high interest rates that compensated for elevated Latin American risk quickly added to the total owed and accelerated the debt cycle. The apparent health of larger economies like Mexico and Brazil lulled many lenders into a sense of false confidence that Latin America as a whole was economically sound. Such assumptions were also problematic since they rested on lenders' belief that the economies of oil-producing countries in Latin America were particularly strong. By the end of the 1970s, Mexico and Venezuela were taking on debt based on the prospect of future oil profits, and banks willingly overlooked their irresponsibly high rates of borrowing. To make matters worse, many lenders paid scant attention to the foolish ways that Latin American leaders spent loans in the heyday of the ISI economies. Flagrant corruption and poor policy planning abounded, and many loans financed expensive and inefficient state-owned industries.

Table 24.1 Total Annual Debt of Select Latin American Countries (in Billions of U.S.$)

COUNTRY	1978	1980	1981	1982	1983	1984	1985	1986	1987	1988	1989	1990	1991	1992	1993
Bolivia	1.778	2.34	2.653	2.803	3.176	3.208	3.294	3.536	4.162	4.066	3.492	3.779	3.628	3.774	3.900
Colombia	4.060	6.805	8.518	10.269	11.458	12.350	14.053	15.950	17.047	17.359	17.007	17.556	16.957	16.779	17.120
Ecuador	2.975	4.167	5.272	5.365	7.381	7.596	8.111	9.063	10.320	10.581	11.322	11.856	12.271	12.122	12.635
Mexico	33.946	50.700	74.900	87.600	93.800	96.700	97.800	100.500	102.400	100.900	95.100	101.900	114.900	114.000	125.000
Peru	9.324	9.595	9.606	11.465	12.445	13.338	13.721	14.477	15.373	16.493	18.536	19.762	20.735	21.333	21.685
Venezuela	16.568	29.606	32.100	32.050	34.712	33.862	34.302	33.838	34.833	34.684	33.195	33.092	34.036	36.000	37.000
Argentina	12.496	27.162	35.671	43.634	45.069	46.191	49.326	51.422	58.324	58.473	63.314	60.973	63.700	65.000	68.000
Brazil	53.614	70.957	80.373	92.812	98.269	105.254	105.126	111.045	121.174	113.469	115.096	122.200	123.910	130.200	131.700
Chile	7.011	11.207	15.591	17.159	18.037	19.659	20.403	20.829	20.660	18.960	17.520	18.576	17.371	18.926	19.915
Paraguay	.689	.861	.948	1.203	1.469	1.654	1.772	1.855	2.043	2.002	2.027	1.695	1.666	1.279	1.350
Uruguay	1.240	2.138	3.112	4.238	4.572	4.671	4.900	5.238	5.888	6.330	6.994	7.383	7.166	7.697	7.900
Costa Rica	1.870	2.209	2.687	3.188	3.532	3.925	4.140	4.079	4.384	4.470	4.488	3.930	4.016	4.022	4.200
El Salvador	.986	1.176	1.608	1.710	1.890	1.949	1.980	1.928	1.880	1.913	2.169	2.226	2.216	2.338	2.015
Guatemala	.821	1.053	1.385	1.639	2.156	2.495	2.694	2.674	2.700	2.599	2.731	2.602	2.561	2.582	2.480
Honduras	.960	1.388	1.588	1.986	2.162	2.392	3.034	3.366	3.773	3.810	3.374	3.547	3.174	3.538	3.595
Nicaragua	1.251	1.825	2.566	3.139	3.788	4.362	4.936	5.760	6.270	7.220	9.741	10.504	10.312	10.806	10.910
Panama	1.875	2.271	2.430	2.917	3.145	3.181	3.642	3.835	3.731	3.771	3.814	3.714	3.699	3.548	3.500
Dominican Republic	1.331	2.173	2.549	2.966	3.313	3.536	3.720	3.812	3.899	3.683	4.090	4.482	4.572	4.426	4.500

CEPAL ECONOMIC FIGURES.

Irresponsible lending, escalating debt, and gross misspending in the 1970s created a perfect storm; a crippling economic crisis ensued in the 1980s. Despite lower prices for Latin American exports in the late 1970s and early 1980s, governments sought to maintain spending levels and cover interest payments by borrowing even more money. Latin America's foreign debt rose to $159 billion in 1978 and then to the enormous sum of $327 billion just four years later. Plunging oil prices in 1982 had a devastating effect on Mexico, whose economy depended heavily on petroleum exports. In August of that year, Mexican leaders announced the country could no longer make its foreign-debt payments. As panic spread throughout the hemisphere, private banks slashed lending to the rest of Latin America as well. Within a year, 16 Latin American nations had defaulted.

The "Lost Decade"

Being cut off from foreign lending shocked Latin American countries. Moreover, it contributed to escalating economic crises throughout the 1980s. During this "Lost Decade," deep recession plagued nation after nation. Per capita gross domestic product (GDP) declined about 1 percent per year, unemployment rose, and real wages deteriorated. Governments accustomed to enormous budget deficits throughout the 1970s had relied on loans to cover the shortfall between expenditures and income. As access to additional capital disappeared, they tried to offset their deficits by increasing the money supply, a fiscal expedient that produced rampant hyperinflation throughout the 1980s. By 1990, inflation throughout Latin America exceeded 18 percent. In two of the most extreme cases, Argentina and Brazil, hyperinflation topped out at nearly 5,000 percent and 1,800 percent, respectively, in 1989. Peru's inflation exceeded 7,600 percent in 1990; Nicaragua's surpassed 33,500 percent in 1988, a staggering figure that was owed in large part to the U.S.-backed Contra war and accompanying economic pressures. The only exception to this inflationary trend was Panama, where the U.S. dollar was legal tender and whose currency had been pegged to it since 1904. The expansionary trends in fiscal policies devastated national economies throughout the region. As consumer prices rose virtually overnight, the purchasing power of the population dropped substantially.

Recovery efforts during Latin America's debt crisis fell under the auspices of the International Monetary Fund (IMF), an organization established in 1945 to promote fiscal and economic stability at the global level. The IMF worked with the World Bank and private lenders to provide emergency debt relief and eventually to restructure foreign loan payments. In exchange for this assistance, Latin American governments had to balance spending and eliminate budget deficits. National leaders initially met these requirements by imposing austerity measures that, for example, slashed spending on health, housing, general welfare, and education. State expenditures in these social assistance programs declined by approximately 25 percent across Latin America during the Lost Decade. According to CEPAL estimates, the number of households living in poverty increased from 40 percent to 48 percent. By the end of the decade, roughly half of all nonagricultural jobs

Table 24.2 Inflation Rates in Select Latin American Countries

	1980–1985	1985–1990	1990–1995	1995–2000
Argentina	322.6	583.8	32.2	-0.1
Bolivia	610.9	46.5	11.9	6.3
Brazil	146.2	673.0	736.9	7.5
Chile	21.3	19.4	13.8	5.1
Costa Rica	34.8	17.0	19.2	12.7
Cuba	-4.0	0.7	10.4	0.5
Dominican Republic	16.4	30.1	14.5	6.5
Ecuador	27.5	45.7	39.1	45.9
El Salvador	14.7	23.5	12.9	3.9
Guatemala	7.5	21.8	14.5	7.6
Haiti	9.1	4.3	26.0	14.7
Honduras	6.9	8.6	20.5	16.0
Mexico	60.7	69.7	17.6	19.1
Nicaragua	54.4	3005.4	122.2	11.3
Panama	3.2	0.5	1.2	1.2
Paraguay	15.2	27.8	18.3	8.8
Peru	102.1	823.8	78.4	6.9
Uruguay	44.8	78.2	60.9	13.5
Venezuela	11.1	36.9	44.3	42.4

ADAPTED FROM VICTOR BULMER-THOMAS, *THE ECONOMIC HISTORY OF LATIN AMERICA SINCE INDEPENDENCE*, 3RD ED. (NEW YORK: CAMBRIDGE UNIVERSITY PRESS, 1995), 416.

were in the informal sector, a figure that reflected extraordinarily high rates of underemployment.

The IMF also demanded economic measures intended to increase national income by expanding exports and to lessen inflation and thus allow Latin American economies to stabilize and grow. Structural reforms drastically altered the foundations of Latin American fiscal and commercial institutions. The emphasis on reduced state spending led government leaders to eliminate numerous employees in some state-owned industries and simply sell others. A wave of privatizations resulted as government-owned enterprises that had defined the era of ISI went on the chopping block. Often, foreign firms stepped in to purchase them; in other cases, partnerships between national and foreign private interests emerged. As a result, a new opening to the global market replaced the economic nationalism that had characterized Latin American trade and commerce following the Great Depression. Latin America stood in the center of the globalization trend that emerged in the latter decades of the twentieth century. Many critics have argued that the consequence was to expose these nations to new systems of exploitation.

The social consequences of the Lost Decade affected Latin Americans at all levels. Consumers reduced spending not only for leisure goods and activities, but also for basic needs including food and health care. In some of the most desperate cases, young children dropped out of school to work in the informal sector and contribute to family income. By some estimates, the consequence of the Lost

Decade hit women the hardest. Particularly in low-income families, wives often increased work hours or entered the informal labor sector to supplement family income or to replace the wages of an unemployed spouse.

Neoliberalism

As Latin American nations turned away from state-sponsored structuralism, policy makers began to embrace neoliberalism as the basis for economic development. Championed by faculty at the University of Chicago and other prestigious institutions in the United States where many influential economists from Latin America (mostly Chile) studied before becoming advisors for various South American regimes, neoliberalism became a new orthodoxy. Dubbed the "Chicago Boys," these economists helped to guide Latin American countries away from the earlier ISI models by promoting deregulation and greater involvement in the global market. Neoliberalism complemented the structural reforms put in place by the IMF at the onset of the debt crisis. The United States and other industrialized nations pressed Latin American nations to implement what became known as the "Washington Consensus." This called for reversing protectionism by reducing or eliminating tariffs, quotas, and other barriers to international trade. It also advocated tax reform and easing labor regulations in an attempt to attract foreign investment. Neoliberal policy makers throughout Latin America adopted this prescription and diminished the government's role in national economies by cutting subsidies, selling off state-owned enterprises, and moving away from currency regulation.

A vital aspect of neoliberalism and the Washington Consensus was the expansion of regional and global trade, particularly through multilateral free trade agreements. Experiments with regional trade blocks that had surfaced in the 1960s and 1970s gave way to a complex system of trade pacts emboldened by neoliberal tenets. In 1991, Argentina, Brazil, Uruguay, and Paraguay formed the Mercado Común del Sur (MERCOSUR); Venezuela joined in 2012 and other South American nations have become associate members with more limited rights and tariff obligations. In 2004, the MERCOSUR entered into an agreement with the Andean Community to allow a gradual elimination of trade restrictions and to create a single integrated trade zone. Caribbean and Central American nations formed the Association of Caribbean States in 1994. Also in that year, the North American Free Trade Agreement (NAFTA) took effect, merging the United States, Mexico, and Canada into a regional trade bloc. Neoliberals embraced trade agreements, arguing that freer movement of goods and services would ultimately encourage growth to the benefit of all countries involved. And between 1990 and 1996, Latin American exports increased by 73 percent, whereas imports grew by 127 percent. But critics insisted that simply considering the growth in trade masked underlying problems. NAFTA in particular was highly controversial because opponents argued that a treaty of that magnitude between unequal trading partners would only exacerbate inequality. Labor groups in the United States feared that lower wages in Mexico would entice U.S. manufacturers to relocate operations south of the border. Environmental activists predicted that lax regulations in Mexico would lead to devastating ecological consequences.

Export Processing Zones

Even before moving fully toward neoliberalism, many Latin American countries had looked for ways to attract foreign investment. In particular, they had sought large manufacturers to set up plants, provide jobs, and increase exports. In the 1940s, Panama set up a free zone adjacent to the Panama Canal where companies could assemble materials, repackage merchandise, store goods in transit, and reexport products without paying customs duties. Other Latin American nations established similar free trade areas close to borders and coastal ports in the 1960s. Export processing zones (EPZs) popped up in Mexico, Brazil, Colombia, and the Dominican Republic. Laws favorable to manufacturing and exporting attracted foreign-owned companies—many of them from the United States—that established assembly plants and other value-added operations that employed the local population. Often referred to as *maquiladoras*, the facilities in these zones took advantage of low wages to cut costs while expanding production of textiles, electronics, and other consumer goods.

Latin American nations created the free zones as way to boost exports and promote economic growth. The Mexican government implemented the Border Industrialization Program in the early 1960s to encourage manufacturing along the northern border. Leaders hoped that employment opportunities in new factories would offset an expected deluge of low-wage workers who were to repatriate after the United States ended the two-decade Bracero Program. As Latin American countries adopted trade liberalization policies following the onset of the debt crisis in the 1980s, EPZs proliferated.

Undisputable evidence confirms that EPZs contributed to a growth in exports for Latin American countries. One CEPAL study found that the value of Latin American exports increased from $104 billion in 1987 to $279 billion just 10 years later. But although many economic and political leaders emphasize EPZs' enormous benefits to local and national economies, other observers contend that the free zones have created a host of problems. For example, inadequate ecological and labor protections create the potential for abuse and exploitation. Environmental watch groups point to the inevitable increase in industrial waste and the upsurge of CO_2 emissions that necessarily accompany manufacturing in popular EPZ sectors, such as electronics, petrochemicals, auto parts, plastics, and rubber.

In the wake of NAFTA's passage, environmental activists drew much attention to the effects of export manufacturing along the U.S.–Mexico border, particularly in the cities of Tijuana, Mexicali, Ciudad Juarez, and Laredo. Illegal dumping of hazardous materials in some areas contaminated the water supply and caused rising levels of air pollutants. The rapid population growth in *maquila* areas strained local infrastructure and municipal services. During the 1980s, the population of border towns increased from 2.8 million to 3.8 million. Already in the mid-1990s, an estimated 25 million tons of raw sewage was flowing into the

Emergency workers carrying a rescued patient from the rubble of Juarez Hospital in Mexico City. The 8.0-magnitude earthquake on the morning of September 20, 1985, destroyed numerous buildings and caused deaths in the tens of thousands in the Mexican capital. It was the worst natural disaster in Mexican history.

Río Grande in the Laredo area alone. By 1998, *maquiladoras* employed more than 800,000 people—a figure equivalent to roughly 15 percent of Mexico's manufacturing workforce at the time. In 2015, more than 5,000 *maquiladoras* operated in Mexico, employing around 2.2 million people. *Colonias* (shantytowns) cropped up as new arrivals moved into hastily built structures in urban centers along the border. The poorest neighborhoods often lacked paved roads, running water, sewage facilities, and other basic sanitation services.

Mexico's *maquila* sector is the most well known, but developing EPZs became a primary strategy for increasing manufacturing in other countries as well. In Costa Rica, the number of export-oriented factories increased from 10 in 1986 to 186 by 1995. By 2007, 342 companies were operating in Honduras, employing 134,000 people. By 2005, EPZs accounted for 922,000 workers in Central America and produced 80 percent of exports in Nicaragua, 77 percent in the Dominican Republic, and 67 percent in Panama.

In addition to environmental concerns, the rise of EPZs has generated vocal criticism regarding injustices in labor practices. Facilities owned by companies from the United States or other industrialized countries employ a largely unskilled labor force and often pay a fraction of what comparable workers receive in more advanced economies. Activists argue that the cost of living in even the poorest neighborhoods often exceeds those meager wages. Rampant poverty limits opportunity for social mobility in these areas. Despite laws restricting child labor, the need to contribute to the family income lures many young people away from school and into the workforce. Central American *maquiladoras* aroused international attention in the 1990s when investigative journalists discovered that some of them employed teenagers, 15 years of age or younger. Offering wages of around $.50 per hour, those facilities manufactured clothes for mainstream U.S. retailers such as Gap and J. C. Penney.

Occasionally, *maquila* workers have resisted exploitation by attempting to unionize; some have reported labor and environmental abuses to government agencies or nongovernmental organization watch groups. But more often, *maquila* owners pushed back and fended off those efforts. Most factories have successfully prevented workers from unionizing. Some have even closed shop and relocated to skirt demands for reform and to continue maximizing profits.

In most EPZs, women make up a substantial majority of workers. Those with few skills and little education often find the stability and working conditions of *maquila* employment preferable to the grueling demands of the agricultural or informal sector. Early factories showed a preference for hiring young, single females, perhaps reflecting a cultural assumption that they would be more docile and thus more easily managed. This trend, although still prevalent, has begun to shift in recent years. In Mexico, border factories increasingly hire married women. And whereas female employees constituted 80 percent of the workforce there in the 1980s, that proportion had declined to less than 60 percent by 2006. A masculinization of the Central American *maquiladora* population has also occurred, although to a lesser degree.

Historically, women in the EPZ sector have earned considerably less than men and many have faced an objectionable degree of sexual harassment. Labor watch groups have called attention to a host of discriminatory and exploitative practices. Particularly in the early years of *maquiladora* growth, female employees in some factories might lose their jobs if they married or became pregnant. Moreover, supervisors often had the prerogative to censure or blacklist those who objected to abuses.

High rates of crime in bourgeoning *maquila* cities tended to put women at risk, especially since many of them walked to and from work, often late at night. In the most extreme example, Ciudad Juarez experienced a scourge of abductions, rapes, and murders starting in the early 1990s and peaking in 2009–2010. Inept investigations into the crimes yielded few suspects. Without adequate cooperation from law enforcement authorities, human rights groups can only estimate that over a period of two decades the number of victims ranges from 300 to 600 murders, but hundreds more women remain missing.

CHALLENGES TO NEOLIBERALISM

At the end of the 1980s, economic observers largely lauded Latin American leaders' use of neoliberalism to reverse the devastating effects of the debt crisis. The restructuring of foreign loans continued when the U.S. Treasury secretary introduced the Brady Plan in 1989. This initiative specified additional rescheduling of payments and resulted in international lenders forgiving roughly one-third of the total developing world debt, an amount at the time equal to $61 billion. After a decade of stagnation or declining productivity, the economies of most Latin American nations had stabilized by 1992 and the region as a whole began seeing average annual GDP growth of around 5 percent. Nevertheless, a new fiscal shock struck Mexico in 1994 and then spread to other countries.

The Mexican Peso Crisis of 1994

Mexico's economy seemed strong by 1990. Despite the crushing effects of default on debt compounded with the devastating consequences of the 1985 earthquake in the capital city, the nation appeared poised to join the industrialized world in terms of stability and economic growth. Taking office in 1988, President Salinas de Gortari extended wage and prices freezes in place since the beginning of the crisis. He strengthened a state-mandated pact between industry and labor intended to combat inflation put in place by his predecessor; and he launched the National Program for Social Solidarity (Programa Nacional de Solidaridad) to combat poverty by allocating resources to destitute rural areas. The government sold CONASUPO, the state agency that oversaw subsidies of consumer goods. In 1992, Salinas declared the success of the Mexican Revolution and amended the 1917 constitution to eradicate the communal land reform measures, considering them no longer necessary. Under his administration, Mexico entered into

A man in a Clinton mask during anti-NAFTA protests at gates near the U.S. Embassy in Mexico City. Protestors blamed the trade agreement for a host of ills plaguing the Mexican economy during the late 1990s.

the NAFTA with the United States and Canada. As Salinas approached his final year in office, it appeared that the Washington Consensus and free market reform had begun to yield the desired results.

Nevertheless, a series of upheavals undermined those efforts and eventually forced the devaluation of the Mexican peso. The government had maintained the value of national coinage by accumulating U.S. dollars as foreign currency reserves. By 1994, the Central Bank held more than $25 billion and maintained the peso at artificially high levels. In January of that year, a resistance movement rose up in the southern state of Chiapas. Taking the name Zapatista Army of National Liberation, the group called on the memory of the revolutionary hero Emiliano Zapata to protest globalization, the end of land reform, and the implementation of NAFTA. The Mexican army contained the rebellion, but the use of the media by its leader, Subcomandante Marcos, brought international attention to the insurrection and called into question the strength of the country's economic and political systems. In the following months, the assassination of Donaldo Colosio, the Institutional Revolutionary Party's leading presidential candidate, along with kidnappings and murders of other high-profile individuals, further shook confidence in Mexico's stability.

With each crisis, the international financial community distanced itself ever further from the country, which put pressure on the value of the peso. But instead of allowing the value of the currency to fall, the Mexican treasury cashed in currency reserves to maintain its worth. By March, the $25 billion that had backed the peso just two months earlier had already dwindled to roughly $16 billion. In December, just weeks after the newly elected president Ernesto Zedillo took office, reserves had fallen to around $6 billion. Authorities attempted a "controlled devaluation," but depleted dollar reserves forced them to allow the peso to fall freely. Within a month, it had lost nearly 70 percent of its value, plunging from 3.4 to 5.7 pesos to the dollar.

For the next two years, Mexico suffered devastating consequences from the currency crisis. Recent changes in the structure of government bonds made the catastrophe even worse. Throughout 1994, fiscal authorities had changed Mexico's peso-denominated bonds to ones that guaranteed investors' repayment in dollars. That modification and the subsequent devaluation meant that the government increased its total outstanding bond debt by approximately two-thirds virtually overnight. A substantial bailout loan from the United States helped avert further disaster, but it came with concessions that quickly sent Mexico into a recession. Once again, the Mexican government had to cut expenditures, raise taxes, and decrease government subsidies. Interest rates skyrocketed to more than 50 percent in 1995, and economic growth measured in GDP fell more than 6 percent.

Economic Decline in South America

Mexico's currency devaluation took the global market by surprise and an even more unexpected shock struck when the peso crisis seemed to spread to other developing countries. Emerging economies all over the world in Asia, Turkey, and Poland felt the effects, but other Latin American nations suffered some of the most drastic consequences. In what became known as the "tequila effect," currency decline and fiscal mismanagement in Mexico caused uncertainty to spread to seemingly healthy economies. Two months after Mexico's initial devaluation, stock markets in Peru, Argentina, and Brazil had fallen by roughly 30 percent. By March 1995, the value of Chile's stock market had begun to slide as well.

Of all countries that suffered the tequila effect, Argentina fared the worst. In an attempt to correct the catastrophic realities of the Lost Decade, President Carlos Menem had launched what amounted to Latin America's most drastic neoliberal reform measures. In addition to privatizing parastatals and attracting foreign investment, he introduced the Convertibility Plan in 1991. The ambitious policy fixed the exchange rate at one peso to the dollar and required the Central Bank to maintain sufficient currency reserves to support that rate. The panic that followed Mexico's devaluation led to a run on Argentine bank deposits and a depletion of currency reserves. A recession ensued, only abating after additional IMF relief and a renewal of austerity measures. But economic stability proved unsustainable, and in 1998 the country entered a crushing four-year depression. By 2002, GDP had fallen 28 percent, inflation had reached 41 percent, and unemployment skyrocketed to more than 23 percent. Eventually the government had to abandon the Convertibility Plan and the peso lost nearly 75 percent of its value.

Other seemingly stable economies struggled as well. After growing at an average rate of more than 7 percent annually since 1984, the Chilean economy entered a five-year period of stagnation in 1997. In 1999, Brazil's currency stabilization plan failed and the *real* lost two-thirds of its value. Economic growth contracted, unemployment rose to 25 percent, and average income fell by roughly 50 percent. The ravages of Argentina's depression also eventually spread to Uruguay, where a banking crisis in 2002 provoked rioting in the streets. These economic and fiscal shocks, punctuated in particular by the Argentine crisis, prompted many to denounce the underlying principles of neoliberalism and the Washington Consensus.

THE CUBAN EXCEPTION TO NEOLIBERALISM

The Soviet Union had provided Cuba financial assistance and favorable trade conditions that helped to finance many of the socialist reforms championed by Fidel Castro in the early decades of the revolution. But the superpower began to falter in the mid-1980s and adopt its own form of neoliberal economic reform. As the Soviet bloc eventually crumbled by the end of the decade, many experts expected the socialist orientation of the Cuban Revolution to collapse as well. But instead of embracing the policies of economic liberalism under way in the Soviet Union, Castro defied expectations and took steps to reshape the revolution on Cuban terms.

Rectification
Through a strategy known as "rectification," Cuban leaders refocused the pillars of the revolution to promote four main initiatives. First, the government placed

a renewed emphasis on volunteerism by creating minibrigades to work on community projects. A second initiative incorporated a new sense of internationalism into the Cuban Revolution. Castro sent construction workers to the developing world to work on infrastructure projects, and he sent health-care workers all over the world to train local doctors and promote preventative medicine. Of considerable concern to the United States, Cuban military advisors began providing logistical and technical assistance to leftist revolutionaries in Central America. A third set of initiatives included campaigns to combat corruption and eliminate black markets in an effort to promote greater economic stability. Finally, rectification strategies also quietly invited private investors into targeted sectors of the Cuban economy, such as construction, basic manufacturing, and tourism.

Special Period

As the Cold War drew to a close, the economic security that Cuba had once enjoyed through its commerce with the Soviet Union declined considerably. The island nation saw approximately 80 percent of its trade disappear; the Soviets slashed imports of sugar and Cuba lost a vital source of petroleum and foodstuffs. Throughout the 1990s, Cubans experienced a severe economic crisis known as the "special period." In the first three years of that decade, Cuba's GDP fell by more than 30 percent.

Before the collapse of the Soviet Union, the average monthly income in Cuba was 180 pesos, or roughly $225. Since the government provided basic necessities, Cubans had disposable income for modest leisure activities, such as hotel stays at the Havana Libre for 15 pesos a night or vacations in Varadero or Viñales for 100 pesos a week. But in the 1990s, inflation caused the value of Cuban currency to drop from 1.25/dollar to a low of 150/dollar. With stagnant incomes, Cubans lost purchasing power as, for example, the price of durable goods like washing machines increased to three times the average yearly income. Castro attempted to weather these economic difficulties through a variety of measures. The need to pay for foreign imports in hard currency compelled government leaders to legalize the dollar in 1993, and U.S. currency became the basis of many transactions for Cubans at so-called "dollar stores." One Havana department store, La Epoca, priced its goods only in dollars. The government also introduced the convertible peso in 1994, with a value roughly equivalent to the dollar.

Cuba's drastic economic decline produced major shortages and rationing. Oil and energy supply became the most immediate concern, affecting transportation, construction, and public works. Scarcity of consumer goods, particularly food and medicine, also afflicted the island. Some Cubans turned to the black market and informal networks to obtain household necessities such as soap, cooking oil, and meat. Expensive household goods like electrical appliances and building materials like tile and cement were often only available through informal markets and almost always required U.S. dollars. Despite the government *libreta*, or ration book, for basics like rice and sugar, ordinary Cubans saw the black market as a necessary tool for surviving the special period.

As the situation worsened, U.S. leaders capitalized on a minor skirmish that erupted when the Cuban military shot down a Miami-based airplane dropping propaganda materials on the island. In 1996, Congress passed the Helms–Burton legislation, which attempted to strengthen the U.S. trade embargo by calling for penalties on foreign companies doing business in Cuba. Other nations protested the law, claiming it violated national sovereignty; that measure was never fully enforced. Most important, a lesser-known provision of the decree codified the trade embargo in U.S. law. Until Helms–Burton, trade restrictions with Cuba had been established through a series of executive decrees and the U.S. president could change them unilaterally. After 1996, any changes to the embargo required congressional approval; and the legislation stipulated that lifting the embargo would be conditional on democratization and an abandonment of communism in Cuba.

Despite the draconian measures put in place by the Helms–Burton legislation, the Cuban economy experienced a gradual recovery by the end of the decade. Government policy began to favor sustainability—incorporating bicycles and animals into transportation strategies, investigating alternative sources of energy, and promoting urban gardens and other forms of sustainable agriculture. The government also attracted foreign investors in various sectors.

In 2004, the Cuban government reformed its monetary policy in response to U.S. sanctions, making the dollar no longer legal tender on the island. It introduced a dual currency system, requiring foreign visitors to use the convertible peso, whereas Cuban citizens conducted business in the *moneda nacional*. Workers in tourism and related industries benefited from the access to convertible pesos through tips, since the government allowed citizens to convert them to *moneda nacional*. The system also favored Cubans with access to dollars through family. Sex workers specializing in the tourist trade, private taxi drivers, and others working in the black market also had ready access to convertible pesos. The dual currency economy produced more societal inequality, and in 2013 Cuba announced plans for a gradual phase-out of the convertible peso.

CULTURAL PRODUCTION IN THE LOST DECADE AND THE SPECIAL PERIOD

More open trade and investment policies intended to combat the debt crisis had a notable impact on expressions of popular culture in Latin America. Access to affordable radios and televisions, for example, expanded for the middle class; as economic recovery began to set in, consumers took advantage of newly available goods. The number of television sets in the region as a whole more than doubled between 1980 and 1990 and video recordings also saw major growth. Watching television and renting popular movies became a leading source of cultural identification, and television networks' influence over public opinion grew enormously.

Economic changes also brought a drastic shift in the nature of broadcasting as deregulation and privatization placed networks under new management. Military regimes had controlled mass media and had censored the production of cultural messages throughout the 1960s and 1970s. Authoritarian regimes had also subsidized the broadcast industry and funded investments in new technologies, which allowed for impressive growth and development. Economic liberalization in the 1980s opened the door to foreign investment, and the Latin American television industry expanded rapidly. TV Globo in Brazil and Televisa in Mexico grew to become the fourth and fifth largest networks in the world in the 1990s. The expansion of the broadcast industry also included an internationalization of Latin American media. Television and radio industries exported locally produced programs throughout the world and found that *telenovelas* in particular generated wide appeal. These Spanish-language serials attracted a growing audience among the Latino population in the United States; TV Globo's *Isaura the Slave* became a hit in Italy and its popularity eventually spread to the rest of Europe as well.

Cultural Production in Cuba
The fall of the USSR and the loss of Soviet support profoundly affected cultural production in Cuba. Resources such as paper and art supplies became scarce; despite such shortages, intellectual activity continued. Artists, writers, and performers practiced their crafts, but often with an altered message. The revolutionary rhetoric so prevalent during the previous three decades began to give way to expressions of disillusionment. A new generation of novels, in particular, reflected the economic and social realities of 1990s Cuba. Leonardo Padura Fuentes's detective fiction criticizes corruption within the system and challenges the political rhetoric of the revolution. Other writers, like Zoé Valdés, use humor and sexuality to pan Cuban sensibilities.

LATIN AMERICAN TOURISM

By the 1990s, tourism had become a major industry in many Latin American countries. Mexican leaders had implemented policies to develop beach resorts and historic areas in the years immediately following World War II. Acapulco became a popular vacation destination in the 1940s and 1950s, facilitated by the construction of new hotels, the opening of a local airport, and the expansion of the highway from Mexico City. Additional government initiatives spurred the development of tourism in Cancun, Los Cabos, and Huatulco starting in the 1970s. Public works projects such as drainage, insect fumigation, road construction, and the installation of electricity, telephone, and potable water services attracted private investors who build hotels, restaurants, shops, and other attractions. Cancun quickly grew to become Mexico's most popular vacation destination; in 2013, it hosted roughly 4 million tourists in some 27,000 hotel rooms.

Other Latin American countries catered to national travelers as the middle class expanded during the era of economic expansion in the 1950s and 1960s. But the onset of the National Security State and the rise of military regimes stifled the

Primary Source

In the 1990s, investigative journalists revealed that many high-profile U.S. retailers were sourcing textiles and other manufactured consumer goods from "sweatshops" in Latin America and other developing nations. Their news stories brought intense public scrutiny and launched important discussions about labor exploitation.

SOURCE: Larry Rohter, "Hondurans in 'Sweatshops' See Opportunity," *International New York Times*, July 18, 1996.

What residents of rich country like the United States see as exploitation can seem a rare opportunity to residents of a poor country like Honduras, where the per capita income is $600 a year and unemployment is 40 percent. Such conflicts of standards and perceptions have become increasingly common as the global economy grows more intertwined, and have set off a heated debate about international norms of conduct and responsibility.

The recent controversy involving the television personality Kathie Lee Gifford and a line of clothing made here that bears her name provides a widely publicized case in point.

To critics in the United States, the apparel assembly plants here, known in Spanish as maquiladoras, are merely "monstrous sweatshops of the New World Order," to use the phrase of the National Labor Committee, the New York–based group that originally accused Mrs. Gifford of turning a blind eye to Hondurans working for "slave wages."

The National Labor Committee, a non-profit group, is largely financed by foundations but also receives money from labor unions in the United States.

After the attacks on her, Mrs. Gifford has now endorsed efforts to monitor and improve conditions in apparel plants around the world. But the debate over what constitutes adequate wages, what minimum working conditions should be required and at what age it becomes permissible for minors to work continues here and in other developing countries that have eagerly welcomed assembly plants as a source of employment for their poor.

Whether workers think they are better off in the assembly plants than elsewhere is not the real issue, argues Charles Kernaghan, executive director of the National Labor Committee. Employers, he said, have a moral obligation to pay not merely what the market will bear, but a wage they know to be just.

---

growth of tourism, particularly in South America and the Caribbean. The economic crisis of the Lost Decade along with the continuation of political uncertainties discouraged tourism investors and travelers from considering most areas of Latin America as a vacation destination. Nevertheless, the structural economic reforms introduced in the wake of the debt crisis combined with a turn toward democracy in most regions generated new interest in Latin America and tourism emerged as a main economic sector.

Tropical beaches, rain forests, historic architecture, and pre-Columbian sites provide an eclectic array of attractions for vacationers in Latin America; and economic and political stability allowed many countries to expand the tourism industry. Foreign companies built beach resorts in Mexico, the Dominican Republic, and Costa Rica in particular; many began marketing "all-inclusive" packages that proved popular with vacationers. U.S. travelers have driven much of the growth of tourism in those countries, and Brazil and Cuba have attracted large numbers of Europeans. Between 1995 and 2007, annual tourists to Latin America increased by 49 percent and tourist spending rose by 61 percent.

The debt crisis of the 1980s forced significant changes in economic and fiscal foundations throughout Latin America. IMF assistance demanded a drastic retreat from state-sponsored development and encouraged neoliberal policies. The resulting economic contraction and high rates of inflation created new hardships in an era that became known as the Lost Decade. By the 1990s, leaders in the region had adopted alternate economic models, and Latin American nations increasingly forged larger regional and global trade networks. In some areas, EPZs emerged as foreign investors sought to take advantage of lower manufacturing costs in Latin America, but they also presented the potential for new forms of exploitation and inequality. Tourism industries grew in Mexico and the Caribbean as economies stabilized and travel to South America began to increase as well.

SUGGESTIONS FOR FURTHER READING

Berger, Dina, and Andrew Grant Wood. *Holiday in Mexico: Critical Reflections on Tourism and Tourist Encounters*. Durham, NC: Duke University Press, 2010.

Brenner, Phillip, Marguerite Rose Jiminez, John M. Kirk, and William M. Leo Grande (eds.). *A Contemporary Cuba Reader: Reinventing the Revolution*. Lanham, MD: Rowman & Littlefield, 2008.

Bulmer-Thomas, Victor. *The Economic History of Latin America since Independence*. Cambridge: Cambridge University Press, 1994.

Bulmer-Thomas, Victor. *Regional Integration in Latin America and the Caribbean: The Political Economy of Open Regionalism*. London: University of London Press, 2001.

Crandall, Russell. *The United States and Latin America after the Cold War*. Cambridge: Cambridge University Press, 2008.

Dabène, Olivier. *The Politics of Regional Integration in Latin America: Theoretical and Comparative Explorations*. New York: Palgrave, 2009.

Devlin, Robert. *Debt and Crisis in Latin America: The Supply Side of the Story*. Princeton, NJ: Princeton University Press, 1989.

Domínguez, Jorge I. (ed.). *Economic Strategies and Policies in Latin America*. New York: Garland, 1994.

Franko, Patrice M. *The Puzzle of Latin American Economic Development*. 3rd ed. Lanham, MD: Rowman & Littlefield, 2007.

Gillespie, Richard (ed.). *Cuba after Thirty Years: Rectification and the Revolution*. London: Frank Cass, 1990.

Hershberg, Eric, Fred Rosen, and North American Congress on Latin America. *Latin America after Neoliberalism: Turning the Tide in the 21st Century?* New York: New Press: NACLA: Distributed by W. W. Norton, 2006.

Massey, Douglas S., Magaly Sanchez R., and Jere R. Berhman (eds.). *Chronicle of a Myth Foretold: The Washington Consensus in Latin America*. Thousand Oaks, CA: Sage, 2006.

Merrill, Dennis. *Negotiating Paradise: U.S. Tourism and Empire in Twentieth-Century Latin America.* Chapel Hill: University of North Carolina Press, 2009.

Nelson, Brian A., and Ebrary, Inc. *The Silence and the Scorpion: The Coup against Chávez and the Making of Modern Venezuela.* New York: Nation Books, 2009.

Petras, James F., and Henry Veltmeyer. *Social Movements in Latin America Neoliberalism and Popular Resistance.* New York: Palgrave Macmillan, 2011.

Robinson, William I. *Latin America and Global Capitalism: A Critical Globalization Perspective.* Baltimore: Johns Hopkins University Press, 2008.

Thorp, Rosemary. *Progress, Poverty and Exclusion: An Economic History of Latin America in the Twentieth Century.* Washington, DC: Johns Hopkins University Press and the Inter-American Development Bank, 1998.

Tufte, Thomas. *Living with the Rubbish Queen: Telenovelas, Culture, and Modernity in Brazil.* Bedfordshire: University of Luton Press, 2000.

Valdés, Juan Gabriel. *Pinochet's Economists: The Chicago School in Chile.* Cambridge: Cambridge University Press, 2008.

Walker, Louis. *Waking from the Dream: Mexico's Middle Classes after 1968.* Stanford, CA: Stanford University Press, 2013.

CHAPTER 25

Violence and Security in the Late Twentieth Century

October 1979   U.S.-supported coup overthrows General Carlos Romero in El Salvador; military junta led by José Napoleón Duarte takes power

1980   "Year of Literacy" declared by FLSN

1980   Peru becomes nominally democratic

March 1980   Archbishop Oscar Romero assassinated as he says mass in San Salvador

December 1980   Four U.S. nuns are kidnapped, raped, and murdered by members of the National Guard of El Salvador; two land reform advisers are also murdered

December 1980   Leftists unite under aegis of the Farabundo Martí Front for National Liberation; civil war breaks out in El Salvador, claiming 75,000 lives over 12 years

As Latin America experienced the Lost Decade during the 1980s, security concerns posed additional challenges in many areas. Leftist rebels rose up against the exploitation and persistent inequalities associated with long-established right-wing regimes in Central America. The resulting violence devastated the region for most of the decade. Additionally, the illicit drug trade in Mexico and the Andean region of South America morphed from the small and localized networks that had arisen in earlier decades to become increasingly vicious and sophisticated operations earning enormous profits. The extent of U.S. intervention in these hemispheric security concerns also expanded, but levels of violence and instability grew as well.

CIVIL WAR IN GUATEMALA

Right-wing military regimes held power in Guatemala following the U.S.-backed overthrow of the democratically elected leftist president Jacobo Árbenz in 1954. Like in other areas of Central America, military dictatorships clashed with groups made up of guerrilla rebels and indigenous rural peasants who wanted political and social change. By the 1970s, government-sponsored death squads were pursuing a brutal campaign of eliminating such leftist opposition by detaining, torturing, and disappearing tens of thousands of dissidents. In the 1980s, the violence escalated even further, especially during the 17-month rule of General José Efraín Ríos Montt (1982–1983), who declared rural Mayan peasants to be the internal enemy of the right-wing government and implemented a program of systematic extermination. Later, United Nations investigations estimated that approximately 200,000 Guatemalans perished during the 36-year civil war and that government forces were responsible for more than 90 percent of these deaths.

To escape the violence, hundreds of thousands of Mayan peasants fled their villages. Some escaped to other areas of Guatemala, whereas others sought refuge abroad. Rigoberta Menchú Tum, an activist who played a leading role in indigenous rights groups, went into hiding after members of her family were killed in the early 1980s. She eventually published her life story in *I, Rigoberta Menchú*, which brought considerable international attention to the plight of the Maya in Guatemala's civil war. Menchú won the Nobel Peace Prize in 1992 for her outspoken support of indigenous rights.

OTHER VIOLENCE IN CENTRAL AMERICA

Protracted violence and unrest in Central America gave way to destructive civil wars in the 1980s as the United States attempted to impose a broad anticommunist agenda across the hemisphere. When a Marxist-inspired uprising toppled the long-standing Somoza regime in Nicaragua in 1979, U.S. leaders interpreted the victory as an expansion of the Cuban Revolution. Their policy priorities turned to destabilizing the new government and preventing the spread of similar rebellions to neighboring Central American countries. But the surge of U.S. military assistance and the advent of covert counterinsurgency forces served to provoke leftist guerrillas in other countries and to destabilize the region further.

Nicaragua Revolution

Nicaragua endured decades of authoritarian rule under the Somoza dynasty dating from the 1930s. Although the economy grew in the 1950s under his policies to favor foreign investment, Anastasio Somoza García suppressed organized labor and allowed high levels of worker exploitation in new export sectors, including cotton, bananas, and other commodities. Nicaragua developed some modest manufacturing in the 1960s by following the precepts of ISI, but the limited expansion and the focus on industry and foreign investment only served to exacerbate inequality. In the countryside, a small group of elite controlled most arable land in latifundia that displaced and exploited the peasants. Workers' status deteriorated while a small but growing middle class emerged with rising expectations for improvements in its standard of living.

After Somoza García's assassination in 1956, power passed to his son, Luis. Although somewhat less dictatorial than his father, the new leader embraced right-wing policies that kept him in favor with the United States. For example, he offered logistical support to the U.S.-backed Bay of Pigs Invasion that failed to topple Fidel Castro in 1961. He discretely ruled through puppet presidents until his death in 1967, when the family dynasty continued under his brother, Anastasio Somoza Debayle. Whereas Luis had ruled somewhat pragmatically, Anastasio reinstated a level of repression reminiscent of his father's dictatorship. He manipulated the constitution to remain in power, circumventing laws that prohibited immediate reelection.

In 1972, Managua suffered a severe earthquake that destroyed much of the city and killed approximately 10,000. Added to his outright exploitation of the population, Somoza's failure to handle the crisis created growing discontent. Accusations surfaced that the dictator was plundering emergency funds for his own benefit, while the city languished in disrepair and the population suffered. Numerous opposition groups rallied in an attempt to force him out of office. The Catholic Church, small business owners, liberal and conservative political groups, and Somoza's own Independent Liberal Party formed the Nicaraguan Democratic Movement. Traditional elites supported the journalist Pedro Joaquín Chamorro, the son of a prominent newspaper publisher who had criticized the Somoza regime.

Perhaps the most visible opposition came from the Sandinista National Liberation Front (FSLN) founded in 1962 by a group of university students who wanted to oust the Somoza regime and end U.S. influence in Nicaragua. The FSLN took its name from Augusto Sandino, the nationalist revolutionary of the 1920s who had been assassinated by Somoza for defying the U.S.-backed dictatorship. Its commitment to socialist ideals earned immediate antipathy from the United States.

The FSLN had been waging guerrilla war since the 1960s, but its efforts intensified and became more successful in the 1970s after obtaining advice and assistance from Fidel Castro. In 1978, several events contributed to the eventual fall of the Somoza regime. Chamorro, who had exposed the government's corruption after the 1972 earthquake, was assassinated in January. His supporters and other anti-Somoza groups put increasing pressure on the dictator to resign; in August, FSLN militants took over the National Palace. U.S. President Jimmy Carter ended all U.S. military assistance to Somoza, citing human rights violations. On July 19, 1979, Somoza fled Nicaragua and FSLN leaders took over the government.

Leaders of different FSLN factions formed a reconstruction committee (Junta of National Reconstruction). As the government moved farther to the left, non-Marxists resigned, including Violeta Chamorro, the widow of the slain journalist. Under the leadership of Daniel Ortega, the Sandinistas declared the Government of National Reconstruction and began implementing extensive reforms that included the nationalizations of railroads, mining, and banks as well as the confiscation of Somoza family properties. Emphasizing social reform, Sandinistas proclaimed 1980 the "Year of Literacy" and implemented one of the largest literacy programs in the world. The government made public health a major priority and initiated programs of preventive care. Sandinista ideology emphasized gender equality and a women's movement emerged out of the revolution as well. New programs attempted to correct gender inequalities by giving women greater access to education and health care, and they responded enthusiastically to government encouragement to take an active public role in many social reform initiatives. Women comprised the majority of teachers in the national literacy campaign and also served as public health advocates in the Sandinista's national vaccination campaign.

El Salvador

Like Nicaragua, El Salvador suffered for many years under repressive right-wing military regimes during the twentieth century (1932–1982). Paramilitary forces imposed a perilous sense of order, targeting peasant groups and leftist agitators through violations of individual rights and other abuses. Decades of oppression and exploitation maintained socioeconomic inequalities that allowed a small landed elite to monopolize the nation's wealth and resources at the expense of the peasantry. Ruthless dictators often operated in close collaboration with the United States, particularly during the Cold War, when its desire for anticommunist allies in Latin America trumped concerns for democracy and human rights. Persecution of the leftist opposition intensified in El Salvador after the Cuban Revolution. In the 1970s, these groups turned increasingly militant in response to the rise of "death

Daniel Ortega, head of Nicaragua's Sandanista government, meeting Pope John Paul II during the Pontiff's visit to Managua in 1983. John Paul was critical of the Nicaraguan clergy's support of the Sandinistas and publicly admonished priests known to be sympathetic to the government.

squads" and government forces' growing use of violence. Accusations of officials' corruption and indiscriminate brutality mounted; several public demonstrations turned deadly as paramilitary squads fired on unarmed civilians.

El Salvador became an important site of manifestations of liberation theology, a doctrine that began to take shape in the 1960s. Its adherents articulated one of the first clear statements of purpose at the 1968 Conference of Latin American Bishops held in Medellín, Colombia. They saw a correlation between centuries of capitalist development and the region's economic and social inequalities. They viewed the systematic exploitation of Latin America's poor as a societal sin and argued that those who failed to resist inequality, injustice, and oppression actively were also sinners. This message found a receptive audience among many leftist revolutionaries who challenged right-wing, capitalist-friendly regimes in the 1960s and 1970s, although most liberation theologians did not self-identify as Marxists. Both philosophies stemmed from a belief in the inherent abuses of class-based exploitation and its pernicious effects on the poor; liberation theology exhorted members of the church to effect social change.

Some church leaders who subscribed to liberation theology became militant and took up arms in insurgencies against military dictatorships. Others played a more peaceful, yet public role as leaders and activists. Archbishop Oscar Romero was the latter. The Salvadoran cleric became radicalized by the extreme poverty and social injustices he witnessed in his country, particularly among the rural poor. He offered asylum to victims of state-sponsored violence and used the pulpit to speak out against the brutality of paramilitary death squads in his weekly sermons. Under a regime that exercised widespread censorship of the media, Romero used church newsletters and radio broadcasts to report grisly details of disappearances, torture, and executions.

After the success of the Sandinista Revolution in neighboring Nicaragua, concerns escalated that a similar outcome might follow in El Salvador. In October 1979, a coup supported by the United States overthrew the corrupt and ruthless regime of General Carlos Romero. A junta government, led by José Napoleón Duarte, promised a wide array of social and political reforms, but human rights abuses continued as violence escalated. In March 1980, Archbishop Romero was gunned down while saying mass; one week later, demonstrators and mourners faced further military brutality at the archbishop's funeral.

In the following months, other high-profile atrocities followed. These included the rape and murder of four U.S. nuns and the killing of two land reform advisers who had recently arrived from Washington. By the end of 1980, leftist opposition had united under the Farabundo Martí Front for National Liberation—its name paid tribute to the slain leader of the ill-fated 1932 peasant uprising. As guerrilla forces hardened their opposition under this front, a full-scale civil war ensued, eventually claiming the lives of approximately 75,000 people—many of them civilians—over a 12-year period. Despite such widespread bloodshed, much of the world remained unaware of the full scope of the violence. An attack by military forces on the small rural village of El Mozote in December 1981 left approximately 900 men, women, and children dead. And although some mainstream journalists initially attempted to report the incident in the United States, a comprehensive account of the massacre did not surface until more than a decade later.

THE UNITED STATES AND THE CONTRAS

U.S. leaders monitored the escalating violence throughout Central America with increasing concern and different administrations tried various strategies to mitigate the recurrent crises. In the late 1970s, President Jimmy Carter attempted to make global protection of democracy and human rights a cornerstone of U.S. diplomacy. He encouraged the Organization of American States to mediate a peaceful transition to democratic rule in Nicaragua, but Somoza rejected the overtures. With the success of the Sandinista Revolution, the United States shifted to using economic and military aid to influence events in Central America. As the Marxist momentum threatened to spill over the border into El Salvador, Carter committed more than $100 million in direct aid to its military government. Although he withdrew U.S.

assistance briefly in response to reports of egregious abuses of human rights, soon he resumed aid payments, using economic incentives to push for human rights reforms. Ultimately, like other U.S. leaders throughout the Cold War, Carter accepted right-wing military leaders as a tolerable buffer against the spread of communism.

The perceived urgency of anticommunism intensified in the 1980s as President Ronald Reagan looked for ways to combat it by supporting local movements throughout Central America. He was particularly concerned that the Marxist-leaning Sandinista government in Nicaragua had started supplying arms to the Salvadoran Farabundo Martí Front for National Liberation, often transporting them through neighboring Honduras. An administration plan of December 1981 provided $20 million to create a small paramilitary force to engage in counterrevolutionary operations in the three Central American nations. Modeling the program on the successful Guatemala coup of 1954, U.S. security specialists recruited exiled Nicaraguans who opposed the new Sandinista government. Trained by Argentine advisers, the Contras operation represented the troublesome culmination of cooperation between National Security State–style Latin American regimes operating with U.S. support through the School of the Americas. The initial 500-person force known as the "Contras" launched strategic offensives immediately in Central America. These prompted the Sandinista government in Nicaragua both to amplify its own military presence and simultaneously to suppress internal opposition and to suspend individual liberties. The size and scope of Contra operations expanded concomitantly; their numbers reached 5,000 by the end of 1982 and 15,000 by the end of 1988.

As the Contras ramped up their attacks against the Sandinistas, some members of Congress grew increasingly uneasy about the nature of U.S. support to armed rebels in Central America. Starting in 1982, lawmakers passed a series of measures known as the Boland Amendments to restrict the Reagan administration's ability to arm the Contras. With each new amendment, administration officials sought ways to circumvent the legal prohibition. Those machinations eventually led to the complex and ignominious Iran–Contra affair, a clandestine and illegal scheme that nearly brought down the Reagan presidency. It began in 1984 with a coalition of administration officials, private citizens, and foreign governments who colluded to channel money to the Contras. A convoluted strategy emerged in which U.S. officials illegally brokered the sale of weapons to Iran, defying the administration's own highly publicized arms embargo. They hoped to improve U.S. standing in the Middle East and eventually to persuade Iranian militants to release U.S. hostages being held in Lebanon. Huge profits from these illicit arms deals were then funneled into Swiss bank accounts that funded Contra operations. Suspicions of conspiracy reported in the media eventually led to congressional investigations and the full scope of the administration's scheme became public knowledge.

A Latin American Peace Plan

Significantly, covert funding of the Contras in Central America failed to topple the Sandinista government in Nicaragua. And the civil wars in neighboring El Salvador and Guatemala continued to escalate throughout the 1980s, despite regional efforts to broker peace. In 1983, the leaders of Colombia, Mexico, Venezuela, and Panama formed the Contadora Group (Contadora Four) and worked to find a diplomatic solution. The group attempted to formalize a peace plan that would end the civil wars and bring democracy to the region. But the 1984 Contadora Act failed to win the approval of U.S. leaders who expected Contra activities to destabilize the Marxist government and rejected the plan's recognition of the Sandinista regime.

By 1986, the Contadora efforts seemed to be deadlocked and the civil wars in the region had reached a stalemate. But as the full extent of the Iran–Contra scheme became known, many observers questioned the legitimacy of U.S. intentions in the region. The Costa Rican president Oscar Arias Sánchez bypassed the United States and sponsored peace talks with the heads of state of other Central American countries. Known as Esquipulas I, those talks yielded promising results; subsequent meetings eventually delivered the Esquipulas II Peace Accord of 1987. Negotiated without the involvement of the United States and signed by all Central American leaders, the agreement represented a high point in regional diplomacy. Each nation agreed to end hostilities and to hold free elections. The accord also called for an end to the use of irregular forces and created a path to amnesty for the Contras. U.S. leaders spurned the peace plan, arguing that diminishing the military pressure in Nicaragua would only embolden the Sandinista government. But despite these admonitions, the FSLN held true on its promise to allow open elections. In 1990, Violeta Chamorro—the widow of the assassinated journalist Pedro Joaquín Chamorro—won the presidency and became the first female elected head of state in Latin America. Oscar Arias was awarded the Nobel Peace Prize in 1987 in recognition of his role in mediating the Esquipulas Accord.

DEMOCRATIZATION AND THE END OF COLD WAR

Even as right-wing regimes tightened their grip in Central America throughout the 1980s, a shift away from military dictatorship was evident elsewhere in Latin America. In many cases, that transition resulted from the deepening economic crises that afflicted the region. State-sponsored structuralism and heavy foreign borrowing proved unsustainable. And neoliberal economic reforms that accompanied international financial bailout programs in the 1980s were more compatible with democracy and financial institutions in a liberal state. Disillusionment with the social costs of military regimes had also grown as government repression many times targeted not only leftist dissidents and the poor, but also the middle and upper classes. Furthermore, the tensions of the Cold War began to abate as the United States and the Soviet Union moved toward rapprochement. The eventual dissolution of the Soviet Union in 1991 eliminated the need for ardently anticommunist military regimes. Indeed, U.S. leaders had already withdrawn support for right-wing dictators in Latin America, an action that reflected the public backlash to the Iran–Contra episode.

As the shift to democracy began, local civic organizations emerged in many areas. Some, like the *arpillera* workshops in Chile and the Madres of the Plaza de

Mayo in Argentina, initially formed as social and economic support networks in the midst of government repression. In other instances, such groups mobilized to help the poor meet their daily needs in a time of economic crisis. In Mexico City, the government's inability to respond to tens of thousands of displaced residents after the 1985 earthquake prompted a wave of neighborhood activism, as neighbors helped each other by providing food, shelter, and other basic services to those in need. For years, a masked superhero known as "Super Barrio" patrolled the streets, protecting poor neighborhoods from the effects of poverty. With a cape and red tights, Super Barrio adopted the style of Mexico's popular *lucha libre* wrestlers and helped to spearhead civic organization by leading rallies, advocating for workers' rights, and acting as a champion against corrupt landlords.

Women in Lima began forming common kitchens as a form of popular activism and community assistance. Formal organizations emerged, often in collaboration with local Catholic churches. As the economic decline of the Lost Decade worsened in Peru, the number of community kitchens grew to more than 5,000 by 1991. Even as the economy improved, the number of kitchens and sense of solidarity surrounding them did not decline. Polls in 2003 estimated that the kitchens still fed approximately 7 percent of the city's population.

A wave of democratic restoration began in Ecuador with the promulgation of a new constitution in 1978 and the election of Jaime Roldós to the presidency the following year. By 1985, democratic elections had brought civilian rule to Bolivia, Argentina, Brazil, Uruguay, and Honduras. By the end of the decade, Augusto Pinochet had stepped down in Chile, and dictators in Panama and Paraguay had been overthrown. The transition to democracy took root more gradually in some countries. Guatemala implemented a new constitution in 1985, opening the door for civilian rule. But civil war continued there until 1996. Peru became nominally democratic in 1980, although clashes between military forces and insurgent guerrillas combined with the heavy-handed rule of Alberto Fujimori in the 1990s constrained individual freedoms for two more decades. Mexico's case was also problematic; one-party rule had dominated the presidency since 1929 even as regular elections took place every six years. In the 1980s, the opposition National Action Party began winning some municipal and state elections and challenged the Institutional Revolutionary Party's dominance. The Party of the Democratic Revolution, a leftist opposition party, formed after disaffected members of the Institutional Revolutionary Party protested the results of the 1988 presidential election. In 2000, the National Action Party candidate Vicente Fox won the presidency, a moment many observers considered a major triumph for democracy.

THE ILLEGAL DRUG TRADE

In the late twentieth century, economic pressures and social dislocation fed the growth of the illegal drug trade in the Western Hemisphere. Trafficking illicit substances expanded in response to growing demand in the United States—first for marijuana and opium and later for cocaine and other drugs. Although U.S.

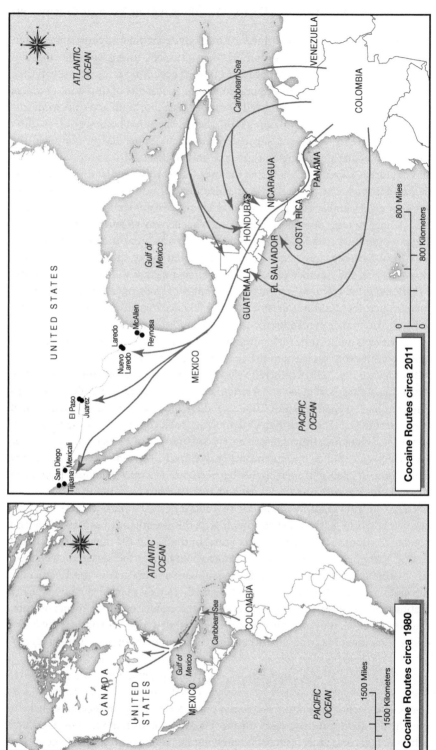

Map 25.1 Changes in Cocaine Trafficking Routes

drug enforcement leaders sought to sway Latin American governments' actions through aid programs and interdiction policies, these efforts proved hopelessly ineffective. In South America and Mexico, powerful drug cartels emerged that eventually proved capable of challenging formal state authority in terms of both wealth and influence. Particularly after 1980, their activities complicated governments' attempts to democratize and achieve economic stability.

The Criminalization of Drugs in Historical Context

The use of psychotropic substances in Latin America preceded the arrival of the Spaniards. Indigenous religious, medicinal, and cultural practices often incorporated tobacco, peyote, and coca leaves. The Spanish introduced cannabis production in select regions of Mexico, primarily for the cultivation of hemp fiber, but some indigenous workers on haciendas recognized the plant's medicinal uses. Andeans had a long tradition of chewing coca leaves for their nutritional and health benefits. In leaf form, coca provides a mild stimulant effect similar to caffeine and can combat fatigue, aid in digestion, and alleviate altitude sickness. It is nutritionally rich, providing calcium, potassium, protein, and a number of vitamins. Whereas some *hacendados* and mine owners encouraged the use of coca leaves to boost the stamina of indigenous workers, it was perhaps more common for workers to demand coca leaves before beginning a day's grueling labor.

In the nineteenth century, scientists took an interest in the medicinal uses of various substances. Morphine—derived from opium—became a widely used pain reliever, particularly in the U.S. Civil War. In the 1860s, a German scientist isolated the alkaloid in the coca leaf that provides the stimulant effect. Through chemical alteration, he produced cocaine, a much stronger "upper" that quickly became marketed as a miracle cure for nearly any ailment. Increasingly popular patent medicines and mystery elixirs in the late nineteenth century frequently contained unspecified amounts of one or more of these substances.

U.S. leaders began encouraging global eradication of mind-altering substances as early as 1905. The Harrison Narcotics Act of 1914 regulated the distribution and use of cocaine and opiates, and the Marijuana Tax Act effectively criminalized cannabis in 1937. Nevertheless, recreational drug use grew in the United States throughout the twentieth century, soaring in the 1960s and beyond. Latin America's economic travail of the 1970s and 1980s coincided with an ever-increasing demand for illicit drugs in the United States. As U.S. leaders devised drug-control policies, they began to expand their operations throughout Latin America. In 1968, the Bureau of Narcotics and Dangerous Drugs was established. One year later, that office oversaw Operation Intercept—a complete closure of the Mexican border as security officials subjected all traffic to search and seizure. The three-week operation created major bottlenecks and strained relations between the United States and Mexico. The Nixon administration created the Drug Enforcement Administration in 1973 to replace and consolidate the efforts of previous drug-control offices. The agency increased U.S. operations in Mexico throughout the 1970s, targeting traffickers in opium, heroin, and marijuana.

The Emergence of Mexican Cartels

The networks in Latin America that organized the production and distribution of illegal drugs became increasingly sophisticated as the volume and value of drug trafficking increased in the last half of the twentieth century. In Mexico, an initial framework of drug infrastructure emerged in the 1960s in the northwestern state of Sinaloa, in the production of first opium and later marijuana. Rising demand in the United States encouraged smugglers to expand their operations to other Mexican states, fragmenting the early structure. Rafael Caro Quintero, Ernesto Fonseca Carrillo, Miguel Ángel Félix Gallardo (known as "El Padrino"), and Joaquín Guzmán (known as "El Chapo") came out of the inchoate Sinaloa enterprise and later formed the Guadalajara Cartel in the nearby state of Jalisco. El Padrino, in particular, contributed to transforming the drug trade into a corporate-style enterprise. He began dividing the cartel's plaza, or turf, into subterritories where he allowed lower-level traffickers to operate as long as they bought their supply from his network. And although smugglers had a long history of close ties to local government and law enforcement, Félix Gallardo spearheaded efforts to secure the cooperation of federal officials, an expansion that helped the Guadalajara organization to dominate the nation's drug trafficking. By the 1980s, a type of "gentlemen's agreement" had emerged in which authorities allowed cartels to operate with relative impunity as long as they restrained violence and kept bribes flowing.

A major transition occurred in the 1980s when the Guadalajara Cartel began transporting cocaine. The group's shipments eventually accounted for 90 percent of the supply entering the United States and brought in an estimated $5 billion a year. This shift to cocaine coincided with the onset of Mexico's debt crisis and the subsequent economic crash. The rampant poverty that accompanied the Lost Decade made the drug trade an attractive form of employment for growing numbers of people. Cartel leaders exploited this widespread desperation; with promises of financial gain, they easily enlisted low-level recruits and procured the loyalty of entire towns.

The new torrent of cocaine trafficking attracted the attention of the U.S. Drug Enforcement Administration, whose activities in Mexico had expanded considerably. Violence escalated as profits rose and cartels pushed back against mounting pressure from U.S. law enforcement. The kidnapping and murder of agent Enrique Camarena in 1985 brought the full force of U.S. authorities to bear in Mexico.

The Camarena episode contributed to the present-day drug conflict. First, it guaranteed that U.S. drug enforcement in Mexico would remain prominent and resources to fight the "drug war" would increase substantially. Second, it brought intense scrutiny to widespread corruption in Mexican law enforcement and political circles. Mexican officials arrested Quintero and Fonseca, in what many considered a perfunctory response. Dissatisfied U.S. agents imposed their own form of justice by abducting a suspected accomplice from his home. Bypassing official extradition proceedings, they transported him under cover of night to the United States to stand trial.

Most important, the arrest of key figures in the Guadalajara Cartel led to its eventual downfall. Smuggling operations began to disperse into smaller rings in Tijuana,

Juárez, and Matamoros. The capture of El Padrino in 1989 consummated the organization's fragmentation and laid the foundation for the structure of the ultraviolent syndicates that have plagued Mexico in recent years.

Drug Cartels in South America

After World War II, the United States intensified efforts to eradicate global narcotics trafficking. Capitulating to pressure from the Federal Bureau of Narcotics and the United Nations, South American countries agreed to criminalize cocaine—Peru in 1948 and Bolivia in 1961. But an illicit drug trade quickly emerged in those two countries and came to dominate South American cocaine trafficking until 1970. Small-scale smuggling networks operated, often through intermediaries in Cuba, Chile, Argentina, and Brazil. In the midst of the Cold War, right-wing regimes friendly to the United States in both Peru and Bolivia attempted to crack down on illicit enterprises sprouting up in their countries. But repressive law enforcement along with the promise of generous financial reward drove increasing numbers of poor peasants into ever more remote jungle regions, where the drug trade began to flourish.

Nevertheless, during those formative years the illicit cocaine industry did not constitute a sophisticated network of organized crime. Oftentimes it existed alongside the South American marijuana trade. But more exorbitant profits, fueled by relentless demand in the United States, turned many traffickers exclusively to cocaine. After Fidel Castro rose to power in Cuba, Havana drug lords fled to South America, where they professionalized the industry. A major Chilean mafia also emerged that by 1959 likely accounted for at least half of the cocaine shipped to the United States. But following Pinochet's 1973 military coup, Chilean law enforcement cracked down on crime, often in brutal and repressive ways. Authoritarian armed forces broke up distribution networks from Peru and wiped out the Chilean mafia. Much of South America's coca cultivation, however, remained in the central Andean highlands, whereas cocaine processing and trafficking shifted to Colombia.

By the 1980s, the cartels in Medellín and Cali had firmly entrenched themselves as the main suppliers of South American cocaine. Their networks stretched through the Caribbean and into the United States via Miami and New York. Under Pablo Escobar's magnetic leadership, the Medellín ring administered approximately 80 percent of Colombian cocaine trafficking until the early 1990s. He and competing drug bosses extended their influence by funding services for the poor and donating to charities, universities, and churches. Escobar even invested in Colombia's national soccer team, which garnered him considerable popular support while serving as a front for money laundering. Ultimately, however, the rise of cocaine trafficking had a devastating effect on the country. Violence among competing cartels escalated; and when bribes failed to entice, "narcoterrorists" often coerced cooperation by kidnapping or assassinating politicians, journalists, law enforcement officials, or their friends and family. The growing partnership between cartels and guerrilla groups in the drug trade along with attempts by the Drug Enforcement Administration and the Colombian government to stamp out their activities intensified the bloodshed even further.

Drugs and Democratization in Panama

By the end of the 1980s, U.S. leaders' anxiety over the War on Drugs had supplanted concern about the evils of communism in the Western Hemisphere. The deescalation of the Cold War brought a corresponding realignment in attention and resources as eradicating the Latin American drug trade assumed pride of place. These shifting priorities became most evident in Panama, where Manuel Noriega had opened the country to money laundering for drug profits. The dictator's close ties to Colombian drug cartels allowed him to accumulate massive wealth; his staunch support for anticommunist policies in Central America had prompted Washington leaders to ignore his illegal activities. But in 1988, the United States severed ties with Noriega and federal prosecutors named him on drug charges. The indictment coincided with fraudulent elections and accusations of corruption against the dictator. U.S. forces invaded from bases in the Canal Zone the following year; after just a few weeks, they captured Noriega. He stood trial in the United States and has since served consecutive prison sentences in the United States, France, and Panama.

SOCIAL AND CULTURAL IMPACT OF VIOLENCE

Artistic and cultural expression through cinema had suffered during the era of National Security State regimes. Filmmakers often fell victim to repressive military governments and many fled into exile to escape persecution. But the demise of right-wing governments in the 1980s provided new opportunities for filmmakers to react to the era of dictatorship. Their cinematic expressions often proved cathartic for the audience as well. Luis Puenzo's *La Historia Oficial* (*The Official Story*) told a dramatic tale based on clandestine adoptions of children of Argentina's disappeared. It reached international acclaim and won the Academy Award for Best Foreign Language Film in 1986. In Brazil, Bruno Barreto's *O Que É Isso Companheiro?* (*Four Days in September*, 1997) portrayed the 1969 kidnapping of the U.S. ambassador by the leftist urban guerrilla group, MR-8. One year later, Walter Salles's *O Central do Brasil* (*Central Station*) earned a nomination for the Academy Award for Best Foreign Language Film; the leading lady Fernanda Montenegro became the first Brazilian to be nominated for the Academy Award for Best Actress.

Issues of gender and sexuality achieved cinematic prominence throughout the region. The Argentine director María Luisa Bemberg released a number of films featuring strong female protagonists, including *Camila* in 1984 and *Yo, la peor de todas* (*I, the Worst of All*) in 1990. The 1991 film adaptation of Laura Esquivel's novel *Como agua para chocolate* (*Like Water for Chocolate*) met critical acclaim in Mexico's national movie industry and became one of the most popular Latin American films of its time in the United States as well. Tomás Gutiérrez Alea's *Fresa y chocolate* (*Strawberry and Chocolate*, 1994) brought attention to issues of homosexuality.

Testimonio

A new literary genre that relied on testimonial narrative emerged in late twentieth-century Latin America. *Testimonios* often document the experiences of an eye-witness, or *testimonialista*, who comes from a marginalized group of society and has experienced injustice or oppression at the hands of the state or other forces in power. A sympathetic interlocutor generally records and transcribes the *testimonio*; the edited account provides a riveting portrayal of dictatorship, oppression, and exploitation. Literary figures began using the *testimonio* to represent the experiences of marginalized groups and as repudiation of the status quo and repression. *Testimonios* also challenged the official version of events and offered a different point of view, usually from a group that lacks social or economic leverage.

Elena Poniatowska provided one of the first high-profile *testimonios* in 1971 when she recorded eyewitness accounts of the 1968 student massacre at Tlatelolco. Published in Spanish as *La noche de Tlatelolco* and translated into English as *Massacre in Mexico*, Poniatowska's *testimonio* confronted the official government narrative of events and gave voice to hundreds of victims. She used a similar strategy in her account of the 1985 Mexico City earthquake, *Nada, nadie: Las voces del temblor*, which highlights the struggles and rescue efforts of ordinary Mexicans in the wake of natural disaster and government incompetence. The exclusion of interviews and testimony from government officials in *Nada, nadie* is an indictment against the government for its failure to endorse building codes, its poor disaster planning, and its treatment of the impoverished citizens in Mexico City.

The journalist and newspaper publisher Jacobo Timerman documented his imprisonment and torture at the hands of the Argentine military government in his 1981 book, *Prisoner without a Name, Cell without a Number*. Arrested in 1977, Timerman spent more than a year in secret prisons, during which time security officials interrogated and tortured him with horrific beatings and electrical shocks to his genitals. He suffered extended periods in solitary confinement and after his release spent 17 months under house arrest. The military government never gave Timerman a reason for his detention and treatment other than vague references to a conspiracy to settle part of Argentina as a second Jewish state. Cleared of the charges against him by three separate judicial bodies, Timerman's case drew world-wide attention, including from the Vatican, the Organization of American States, and President Jimmy Carter. On his release, the military government stripped the journalist of his citizenship, confiscated his newspaper and assets, and put him on a plane to Israel. Timerman remained in exile until 1983, when Argentina elected a democratic government to replace the one headed by disgraced military officers.

Rigoberta Menchú's autobiography and indictment of the right-wing regime in Guatemala fits also within the genre of the *testimonio* and drew international attention to the victims of Central America's civil wars in the 1980s. Other authors combined *testimonio* narrative with historical fiction, using the oppression and exploitation inherent in recent dictatorships as the foundation for heart-wrenching plot lines. In 1982, Isabel Allende, cousin to the ousted Chilean president Salvador Allende, wrote *Casa de los espíritus* (*The House of Spirits*), in which a military regime arrests, tortures, and disappears the opposition. Similarly, Julia Alvarez's *In the Time of the Butterflies* (1994) portrays the brutality of the Trujillo dictatorship in the Dominican Republic.

Developments in Television

Because of the spread of satellite dishes linked to repeater transmitters, television's reach in Latin America extended into rural areas during the 1980s, allowing networks to expand social influences even further. Rural and low-income people treated television viewing as a communal experience, often watching in public places or at the home of a friend. Networks like Mexico's Televisa and Brazil's Globo increased their audience to become truly national networks. By 1982, Globo's share of viewers averaged 75 percent during peak viewing hours. Television's popularity continued into the 1990s.

The state continued to play a role in the development of mass media during the 1980s. In Mexico, Televisa's Emilio Azcárraga Milmo responded to President Miguel de la Madrid's 1982 constitutional charge to turn over all domestic satellite

Table 25.1 Television and Radio Receivers in Select Latin American Countries, 1992 (per 1,000 Households)

	TELEVISION RECEIVERS	RADIO RECEIVERS
Argentina	219.3	673
Bolivia	98.4	574
Brazil	203.6	373
Chile	200.6	340
Colombia	108.1	167
Costa Rica	136.1	259
Cuba	203.4	343
Dominican Republic	81.9	168
Ecuador	82.3	314
El Salvador	87.1	403
Guatemala	44.7	64
Haiti	4.5	42
Honduras	70.3	384
Mexico	126.8	242
Nicaragua	61.4	247
Panama	164.6	222
Paraguay	48.2	169
Peru	94.6	251
Uruguay	227.2	600
Venezuela	156.0	432

ADAPTED FROM *WORLD MEDIA HANDBOOK, 1992–1994* (NEW YORK: UNITED NATIONS DEPARTMENT OF PUBLIC INFORMATION); RICHARD R. COLE, *COMMUNICATION IN LATIN AMERICA: JOURNALISM, MASS MEDIA, AND SOCIETY* (WILMINGTON, DE: SR BOOKS, 1996), 31–32.

development to the state by basing Televisa's own international satellite system in the United States. Launched in 1988, Empresa de Comunicaciones Orbitales transmitted programming to Europe, parts of Africa, and North and South America, ushering in a new era of international broadcasting. Despite the friction between Televisa and the de la Madrid administration over satellite transmission, the network continued to support the state through partisan coverage of the Institutional Revolutionary Party, Mexico's ruling party. In 1986, the network ignored the controversial reversal of the opposition National Autonomist Party's election victory in Chihuahua. The Institutional Revolutionary Party also enjoyed partisan coverage of the 1988 presidential election, with Azcárraga declaring himself among the party faithful. The Mexican state continued to operate its own national network, known as Imevisión, and UNAM in Mexico City maintained its channel of cultural programming.

From the 1950s to the 1980s, Argentina's television system operated under a unique system in which the state regulated content, whereas television and radio stations were managed commercially. No large national networks existed like those in Mexico and Brazil. The 1980s saw the privatization of television, with cable and satellite technologies the preferred modes of distribution and a mix of international and national programming.

In Brazil, Globo complied with the government's severe censorship laws and toed the party line through its programming and management of public opinion, which in turn helped legitimize the state's antilabor union and antipopulist stance. By 1980, it dominated the market as the only truly national network. Fearing its power as a virtual monopoly, the administration of João Figueiredo (president general, 1979–1985) opened concessions to other broadcasters friendly to the military regime. Granting new licenses to competitors altered the relationship between the government and Globo and resulted in the latter's more favorable coverage of the opposition during the debt crisis and election of 1984.

Thanks to a decrease in production costs during the 1980s, the number of networks and independent stations increased throughout Latin America, as did the number and kind of program genres. Popular *telenovelas* displaced imported U.S. programs from prime-time evening hours, and the serials expanded their plotlines to include contemporary social issues and concerns. Brazilian *telenovelas* dealt with political themes like corruption, nepotism, and land reform. By the late 1980s, *telenovelas* had become one of the top entertainment exports from the region to North America and Europe. The first successful Venezuelan *telenovela* export was the rags-to-riches story *Cristal* (1986), which became wildly popular in Spain. Other *telenovela*-exporting countries include Mexico, Argentina, and Colombia.

The variety show also continued its dominance on Latin American airwaves during the 1980s. Notable examples include *Siempre en Domingo* (*Always on Sunday*) in Mexico and Brazil's *Domingão do Faustão* (*Big Fausto's Big Sunday*). These shows featured a charismatic host who interacted with the audience. The entertainment on the show included musical acts, games, comedy acts, magicians, and interviews.

The 1980s was a decade of transition for most Latin American nations. The economic crisis that formed the basis of the Lost Decade propelled drastic changes in fiscal and trade policies. Security concerns shifted from the remnants of Cold War anticommunist rhetoric to the growing threat of powerful drug traffickers. Through those economic and security developments, the United States remained a constant presence as leaders in Washington attempted to impose solutions that often created new hardships. Two notable results emerged from this era of transition. First, disillusionment with U.S. hegemony would propel a new wave of leftist populism in the coming decades. And second, the region found itself increasingly absorbed into globalization trends that have begun to materialize. Both developments have had important repercussions for Latin Americans into the twenty-first century.

Primary Source

The Costa Rican president Oscar Arias Sánchez surprised the world when he orchestrated a Central American peace plan in 1987 in defiance of the United States. In that same year, he won the Nobel Peace Prize for his efforts at ending violence in Central America.

SOURCE: Oscar Arias Sánchez's Acceptance Speech, on the occasion of the award of the Nobel Peace Prize in Oslo, December 10, 1987. http://nobelpeaceprize.org.

We seek in Central America not peace alone, not peace to be followed some day by political progress, but peace and democracy, together, indivisible, an end to the shedding of human blood, which is inseparable from an end to the suppression of human rights. . . . We believe that justice and peace can only thrive together, never apart. A nation that mistreats its own citizens is more likely to mistreat its neighbors.

To receive this Nobel Prize on the 10th of December is for me a marvelous coincidence. My son Oscar Felipe, here present, is eight years old today. I say to him, and through him to all the children of my country, that we shall never resort to violence, we shall never support military solutions to the problems of Central America. It is for the new generation that we must understand more than ever that peace can only be achieved through its own instruments: dialogue and understanding; tolerance and forgiveness; freedom and democracy.

I know well you share what we say to all members of the international community, and particularly to those in the East and the West, with far greater power and resources than my small nation could never hope to possess, I say to them, with the utmost urgency: let Central Americans decide the future of Central America. Leave the interpretation and implementation of our peace plan to us. Support the efforts for peace instead of the forces of war in our region. Send our people ploughshares instead of swords, pruning hooks instead of spears. If they, for their own purposes, cannot refrain from amassing the weapons of war, then, in the name of God, at least they should leave us in peace.

SUGGESTIONS FOR FURTHER READING

Boullosa, Carmen, and Mike Wallace. *A Narco History: How the United States and Mexico Jointly Created the "Mexican Drug War."* New York: OR Books, 2015.

Burgos-Debray, Elizabeth (ed.). *I, Rigoberta Menchu: An Indian Woman in Guatemala.* 2nd ed. London: Verso, 2009.

Carey, Elaine. *Women Drug Traffickers: Mules, Bosses, and Organized Crime.* Albuquerque: University of New Mexico Press, 2014.

Campos, Isaac. *Home Grown: Marijuana and the Origins of Mexico's War on Drugs.* Chapel Hill: University of North Carolina Press, 2012.

Danner, Mark. *The Massacre at El Mozote: A Parable of the Cold War.* London: Granta Books, 2005.

Gootenberg, Paul. *Andean Cocaine: The Making of a Global Drug.* Chapel Hill: University of North Carolina Press, 2009.

Hart, Stephen M. *A Companion to Latin American Film.* Rochester, NY: Tamesis, 2004.

Horton, Lynn. *Peasants in Arms: War and Peace in the Mountains of Nicaragua, 1979–1994.* Athens, OH: Ohio University for International Studies, 1998.

Kampwirth, Karen. *Women and Guerrilla Movements: Nicaragua, El Salvador, Chiapas, Cuba.* University Park: Pennsylvania State University Press, 2002.

LaFeber, Walter. *Inevitable Revolutions: The United States in Central America.* 2nd ed. New York: W. W. Norton, 1993.

Manz, Beatriz. *Paradise in Ashes: A Guatemalan Journey of Courage, Terror, and Hope.* Berkeley: University of California Press, 2004.

Russo, Eduardo A. *The Film Edge: Contemporary Filmmaking in Latin America.* Buenos Aires: Teseo, 2010.

Tombs, David. *Latin American Liberation Theology.* Leiden: Brill Academic, 2003.

Wald, Elijah. *Narcocorrido: A Journey into the Music of Drugs, Guns, and Guerrillas.* New York: Rayo/Harper Collins, 2001.

Weld, Kirsten. *Paper Cadavers: The Archives of Dictatorship in Guatemala.* Durham, NC: Duke University Press, 2014.

CHAPTER 26

Latin America in the Twenty-First Century

2000	National Autonomist Party candidate Vicente Fox wins presidency in Mexico, ending 70 years of rule by the Institutional Revolutionary Party
2003	Luiz Inácio Lula da Silva wins presidential elections in Brazil
2003	Néstor Kirchner elected president in Argentina
2005	Evo Morales, former coca-growers union leader, wins the presidency in Bolivia
2005	Tabaré Vázquez wins presidency in Uruguay
2007	Cristina Fernández de Kirchner elected as president and succeeded her husband, Néstor Kirchner
2007	Rafael Correa elected to the presidency in Ecuador
2007	Former Sandinista Daniel Ortega elected president
2007	Mexican president Felipe Calderón signs Mérida Initiative with the United States in effort to combat drug violence
2008	Fernando Lugo, a former Catholic bishop, elected president in Paraguay
2010	José Mujica, former Tupamaro imprisoned by the military, elected president in Uruguay; known for his austere lifestyle while in office
2010	Costa Rican Supreme Court declares Internet a basic human right
2012	Institutional Revolutionary Party candidate Enrique Peña Nieto wins presidential election in Mexico
2012	Honduras, Guatemala, El Salvador see high levels of violence
2012	Rise of #yosoy132 movement on Twitter and other social media in protest against Institutional Revolutionary Party candidate Enrique Peña Nieto
2013	30 percent of foreign-born nationals in United States are from Mexico
2014	43 students from the Ayotzinapa Rural Teachers' College disappear after confrontation with police in Iguala, Guerrero
2014	Central American refugees, many of them children, spark immigration crisis on U.S.–Mexico border
2015	Joaquín "El Chapo" Guzmán, head of the Sinaloa Cartel, escapes prison
2015	Peru's Shining Path reemerges as drug trade organization
2015	29 Latino representatives in the U.S. House and 3 in the U.S. Senate
2016	Rio de Janeiro hosts Summer Olympic Games
2016	Brazilian Senate votes to impeach President Dilma Roussef
2016	Colombian government reaches peace deal with FARC
2016	Donald Trump elected president of the United States
2016	Fidel Castro dies at the age of 90
2017	President Barack Obama ends wet foot, dry foot policy that gave Cuban migrants expedited residency
2017	"El Chapo" Guzmán extradited from Mexico to the United States

A new century has drawn Latin America more fully into a globally assimilated system in terms of economic structures, security concerns, migration patterns, and cultural expression. By the end of the 1990s, many Latin Americans had grown wary of the Washington Consensus. Open markets and strict controls on government spending had caused widespread social dislocation and growing poverty. These combined with the poor performances of economies that had whole-heartedly embraced neoliberalism to create a pervasive sense of disillusionment and to provide an opening for alternative visions. Political shifts accompanied these economic frustrations and a new generation of populist-style leaders emerged. At the same time, security trends shifted as the Cold War drew to a close and global attention turned to the continued escalation of drug violence in the region. Culturally, Latin Americans have integrated themselves into an increasingly global world through migration and digital communication.

THE TURN "LEFT"

The downfall of communism and neoliberalism's bolstering of free market ideas seemed to portend the demise of the left in Latin America. But as the Cold War drew to a close and security trends shifted, a new populist tide swept the region, drawing global attention. Particularly after 2000, leftist leaders rose to power in numerous countries through democratic elections. Their policies largely broke away from the free market reforms urged by the Washington Consensus. But members of this "new left" also set themselves apart from the ardently national-ist orientation of their predecessors in the early twentieth century. Most notably, they advocated regionalism as a way of breaching the persistent hegemony of the United States regarding hemispheric security and economic practices.

The concurrence of military dictatorship and open market reform altered the framework of leftist thought in Latin America, starting as early as the 1960s and ac-celerating toward the end of the century. Following the Cuban Revolution, National Security States stifled the democratic process and socialist-leaning groups found themselves on the fringes of political participation. In many countries guerrilla movements emerged as the principal alternative for promoting and defending the popular agenda. But their actions often provoked retaliation by U.S.-backed right-wing regimes that resulted in escalating violence. The Bolivian military executed Che Guevara in 1967 as the revolutionary ideologue was attempting to unite resistance movements throughout South America. In the 1970s, military regimes in the South-ern Cone justified their brutality as the most effective weapon against urban guerrillas, namely the Tupamaros in Uruguay, the Montoneros and the People's Revolutionary Army in Argentina, and, to a lesser extent, the National Liberator Alliance in Brazil. Central American opposition to right-wing military repression in the 1980s also took the form of guerrilla movements, with the Sandinistas in Nicaragua, the FMLN in El Salvador, and the Guerrilla Army of the Poor, among others, in Guatemala.

The demise of military regimes in the 1980s stimulated a restructuring of left-ist groups and notable shifts in their strategies. Some militant guerrilla groups, including those in Brazil and Argentina, disbanded. Others transitioned into more conventional political parties. As the Contra threat abated, the Sandinistas in Nicaragua began to demilitarize and opened the country to democracy. The Tupamaros in Uruguay established the Movement of Popular Participation, which later formed part of a powerful leftist coalition in the Frente Amplio.

Electoral Shifts
The economic shocks in Argentina, Brazil, and elsewhere at the turn of the century fueled disillusionment with the Washington Consensus and stimulated the resur-gence of parties and political coalitions on the left. The first and most palpable

case of dismantling open market policies occurred in Venezuela. After leading two failed coup attempts against the neoliberal president Carlos Andrés Pérez in 1992, the socialist candidate Hugo Chávez won the presidency through a democratic election in 1998. He insisted on a more socially inclusive economic program and immediately began rebuking what he called the imperialism of the United States. Eventually, he nationalized the holdings of foreign oil companies; profits from petroleum funded expansion in health, education, and other social programs. During his 14 years in office, Chávez provided billions of dollars in financial assistance to Cuba, at a time when aid from the former Soviet Union had dried up.

In subsequent years, leftist and populist leaders gained power throughout Latin America. Evo Morales, a former leader of the coca-growers' union, won the presidency of Bolivia in 2005. A descendent of Aymara natives, he has vigorously advocated for the nation's indigenous population. Often likened to Chávez, Morales nationalized the oil industry and devoted substantial government money to combatting poverty. Both leaders opened themselves to criticism by amending their respective constitutions to strengthen executive power and to institutionalize nationalist economic policies.

Other left-of-center populist leaders include Luiz Inácio Lula da Silva, who took office in Brazil in 2003. The Peronist adherent Néstor Kirchner inherited the aftermath of Argentina's economic crisis in 2003; four years later, his wife, Cristina Fernández de Kirchner, succeeded him and continued left-leaning and populist policies often referred to as "Kirchnerismo." Tabaré Vázquez of the Frente Amplio governed Uruguay starting in 2005; his successor, José Mujica, became known as "the world's poorest president" because of his austere lifestyle. The former Tupamaro, prone to peppering his public addresses with expletives, became most known for increasing government spending, drastically reducing poverty, and legalizing both marijuana and gay marriage. Daniel Ortega returned to the presidency in Nicaragua in 2007, although many observers have labeled him leftist in name only. The former Sandinista continues to espouse the rhetoric of socialism and anti-imperialism. Although his administration increased social spending, its economic policies have tended to embrace an open market strategy. Ecuador's Rafael Correa, who came to power in 2007, enjoyed widespread popularity largely as a result of expanding social spending and reducing poverty. But increasingly critics have chided him for bolstering executive power and censoring the press. In Paraguay, the former Catholic bishop Fernando Lugo defeated the Colorado Party candidate in 2008, ending more than 60 years of right-wing rule.

As politics have shifted in Latin America, women have gained greater access to public office. Between 1970 and 2016, eight served as president of a Latin American nation—accounting for 25 percent of all female heads of state in the world during that time. Michelle Bachelet was president of Chile from 2006 to 2010 and won election again in 2013. Laura Chinchilla held the Costa Rican presidency from 2010 to 2014, and Dilma Rousseff became Brazil's first female head of state in 2011; she was suspended early in 2016 and her impeachment trial coincided with Brazil's hosting of the Olympic Games. In addition to presidential leadership, Latin American women enjoy a larger proportion of representation in national legislatures, accounting for roughly one-fourth of all congressional seats in the region. This total benefits from quota requirements in a number of countries: Costa Rica, Bolivia, and Panama require an equal gender balance among all candidates, and other countries stipulated slightly lower ratios of female candidates. Costa Rica leads the region on electoral results, with women holding nearly 40 percent of all congressional positions in 2015.

The changing political atmosphere has also led to new efforts to investigate and prosecute the worse perpetrators of human rights abuses during the era of military dictatorship. In 2009, Alberto Fujimori of Peru was sentenced to 25 years in prison. Prosecutors tried to charge Luis Echeverría with genocide for his role in Mexico's 1968 student massacre, but a federal court ruled that the former president could not stand trial for lack of evidence. Guatemala's Efraín Ríos Montt was convicted of genocide in 2013, but the courts threw out that ruling immediately afterward. They later determined he was mentally incompetent and could not be sentenced. Chilean courts attempted to charge Augusto Pinochet with kidnapping, murder, and other human rights violations while jurists debated his health and mental capacity; he died in 2006 before resolution of any charges. Hundreds of prosecutions and convictions related to the Dirty War took place in Argentina during the Kirchner administration.

The deescalation of the Cold War and the rise of leftist politicians throughout Latin America only recently translated into a rapprochement between the United States and Cuba. Indeed, the Helms–Burton legislation, which tightened the embargo and created new obstacles for lifting it, passed a full five years after the fall of the Soviet Union. The administration of George W. Bush tightened travel and shipping restrictions even further in 2003. But in December 2014, U.S. and Cuban leaders announced an agreement to regularize diplomatic relations and to ease restrictions on trade and travel between the two nations. The surprise announcement provoked considerable outrage among Cuban émigrés in the United States, but many of their children and grandchildren celebrated the move toward reconciliation. Although the reestablishment of ties was set to occur gradually, the U.S. Embassy reopened in Havana in August 2015 after being closed for 54 years.

REGIONAL INTEGRATION

Into the twenty-first century, a new type of regionalism guided the way Latin American nations structured trade and economic policies. This model generally bypassed the United States and other Western powers, allowing Latin American leaders greater autonomy in commercial affairs. The left-of-center leaders who came to power in the late 1990s and after have embraced this strategy as an alternative to the failures of the Washington Consensus in the wake of the Lost Decade. Subregional and bilateral agreements have characterized the new regionalism; individual nations and trading blocs alike signed trade pacts in Asian and European markets.

Free Trade Area of the Americas

The turn toward a new type of regionalism first became evident in the debates surrounding the proposed Free Trade Area of the Americas (FTAA) that would have created a free trade zone encompassing all of the countries of the Western Hemisphere. Introduced at the 1994 Summit of the Americas and modeled after the NAFTA, the FTAA called for a broad reduction in trade restrictions to start in 2005. But challenges to the FTAA quickly surfaced through a combination of grassroots, popular protests and newly elected leftist leaders. Initially, only Venezuela's Hugo Chávez voted against the FTAA, and in 2001 he proposed the Bolivarian Alliance for the Americas (ALBA) as an alternative to a U.S.-dominated trade bloc. ALBA envisions regional integration less as a forum for trade and commerce and more as a relationship of solidarity to combat poverty and social inequality while ensuring mutually beneficial development of member nations. In 2004, Venezuela and Cuba joined forces under the new regional organization and by 2012 it had eight member nations. As Latin American leaders united under ALBA, energy for the FTAA fizzled by 2005. In that same year, the Dominican Republic–Central America Free Trade Agreement passed among the United States, Guatemala, El Salvador, Honduras, Nicaragua, Costa Rica, and the Dominican Republic. Two-way trade between the United States and other member nations totaled more than $50 billion in 2015. But critics have charged that the agreement has exacerbated inequality and exploitation and that it has strengthened U.S. hegemony in the region.

Other alternative regional organizations formed in the aftermath of the FTAA's demise. The Union of South American Nations brought together the member nations of the MERCOSUR and the Andean Community in 2008. The Community of Latin American and Caribbean States formed in 2010, with 33 member nations. Both organizations exclude the United States and Canada because their goals include reducing U.S. hegemony in hemispheric affairs and giving greater autonomy to Latin American nations.

Most recently, Mexico, Peru, Colombia, and Chile signed an agreement establishing the Pacific Alliance. Formally created in 2012, the participants aim to facilitate integration between member nations and countries of the Asia-Pacific region. Like ALBA, the Union of South American Nations, and the Community of Latin American and Caribbean States, the Pacific Alliance represents an attempt by Latin American nations to bypass the economic hegemony traditionally exercised by the United States in the Western Hemisphere. But the Pacific Alliance deviates from the approach taken by other recent trade pacts by embracing globalization rather than rejecting commercial linkages outside a narrow alliance of Latin American nations.

NEW DEVELOPMENTS IN DRUG TRAFFICKING

In the 1990s, drug violence escalated as a result of growing competition among cartels. Attempts by the United States and Latin American law enforcement to stamp out trafficking networks further worsened the bloodshed. As government leaders devoted more attention and resources to combatting drug smuggling and distribution, the structure of cartels and other groups shifted and organized crime syndicates grew stronger. Powerful cartels emerged in Mexico, and militant guerrilla groups became involved in South America's drug trade.

Some early government efforts had focused on the eradication of crops and the destruction of processing facilities. As early as 1975, U.S.–Mexican agencies collaborated in Operation Condor to target opium and marijuana plants through the use of defoliants. Their actions disrupted cultivation temporarily, but producers simply relocated to other states. In 1986, the Drug Enforcement Administration's Operation Blast Furnace financed and supported jungle raids in Bolivia to destroy coca-processing facilities. The Peruvian government began regulating coca production in the 1960s and initiated measures in the 1980s to destroy illegal coca plantations. In 1992, the Peruvian president Alberto Fujimori carried out an "autogolpe," suspending the constitution and declaring martial law. He cited the growing threat of drug traffickers and affiliated guerrilla movements as justification.

Shining Path

As cocaine trafficking in South America shifted to Colombian cartels, drug rings in Bolivia and Peruvian players turned to coca cultivation, with those in the latter group accounting for 65 percent of the illicit production of the plant in the 1980s. Remote jungle operations carried out a crude extraction process and shipped the resulting "coca paste" to Colombia, where cartel facilities purified it and produced cocaine. Peru's ascension as the main provider of coca paste coincided with an escalating war between revolutionary guerrillas of the Shining Path (Sendero Luminoso) and the Peruvian government. The Marxist rebels relied on revenues from the illegal drug trade to fund a protracted and violent insurgency against the state.

The Shining Path originally formed as a small group of Maoist-inspired, leftist revolutionaries united under Abimael Guzmán. They sought to challenge the nation's ruling elite and to defend the interests of rural peasants in Ayacucho and surrounding areas. Feeble land reform efforts introduced in 1969 had failed to improve their condition; most remained poor, isolated, and mired in a seemingly perpetual pattern of exploitation and inequality. Neoliberal policies introduced after 1978 cut social spending and hit Peru's poor population particularly hard. Leaders also reversed the meager attempts at agrarian reform. In the 1980s, Guzmán coalesced isolated and sporadic pockets of guerrilla rebels into the Shining Path.

The rebel group maintained a central goal of bring down the Peruvian government. Members used violence to destabilize the country by disrupting the economy and preventing the government from carrying out social programs. Women comprised up to 35 percent of its leadership and its founding principles emphasized the need for equality, including in the area of gender. Funding for the Shining Path's activities came in part from taxing transports of coca leaves and coca paste through territories under its control. It also resorted to kidnapping for ransom and other forms of extortion, but drug revenue brought in at least $10 million per year in the late 1980s and early 1990s.

The Tupac Amaru Revolutionary Movement formed in 1984 employed a similar strategy of using illicit drug trafficking revenue to fund guerrilla insurrection. The group took its name from Tupac Amaru II, the martyred indigenous head of a major late eighteenth-century rebellion. Its leaders attempted, unsuccessfully, to compete for turf with the Shining Path. The latter held a prevailing command over coca shipments to Colombia and posed the greater threat to the Peruvian government. Alberto Fujimori cracked down on guerrilla activities when he took power in 1990 and two years after his auto-golpe government forces captured many leaders of the Tupac Amaru Revolutionary Movement and the Shining Path. The arrest of Guzmán was the most high profile and Fujimori touted this as a great success of his administration; his critics disparaged his near indiscriminate human rights abuses.

The Colombian Drug Trade

As coca growing came under increasing pressure in Peru and Bolivia, cultivation of the plant shifted to Colombia. The Medellín Cartel benefited the most, becoming a powerful, vertically integrated operation that controlled every stage of cocaine production in South America. But the growing dominance of Colombia's organized cartels provoked a heightened response from the Drug Enforcement Administration. In 1993, the agency scored a major victory when a U.S.-equipped police unit located Pablo Escobar and killed him in a gunfight. The death of the powerful kingpin precipitated the swift collapse of the Medellín Cartel. The Cali Cartel briefly advanced as the prevailing drug syndicate, but the arrest of its leaders in 1995 signaled its demise.

The collapse of the powerful cartels led to a substantial shake-up in Colombia's drug trade as the large production and transportation networks splintered into smaller operations. Local drug gangs emerged from the junior ranks of the former cartels. But new actors also appeared as militant guerrilla groups increasingly turned to the drug trade to finance terrorist operations. The rural-based FARC and the urban-based National Liberation Army arose in the 1960s in the aftermath of *La Violencia*, a 10-year civil war that resulted in more than 200,000 deaths between 1948 and 1958. Drug connections also helped to finance the April 19th Movement (M-19), formed in 1970. Of these groups, the FARC has posed the greatest threat to Colombia. Initially formed to protect leftist peasants from government repression, the guerrillas quickly broadened their agenda to include regime change and the adoption of Marxism at the national level.

In the early 1980s, the FARC began imposing a "tax" on the production and transport of coca, marijuana, and opium in remote rural areas under its control. In the early 1990s, the Peruvian government's offensive against coca shipments into Colombia pushed growers even further into FARC territory. As large cartels were crumbling, the militant guerrillas expanded their reach into the drug trade. The group's growing wealth and influence allowed it to recruit even more followers. Poor peasants frequently saw no other option to joining the militants; FARC members increased from around 6,000 in 1982 to some 20,000 two decades later. But the ascendancy of the FARC also prompted a pushback; some landowners and rival drug gangs formed right-wing militias that coalesced as the United Self-Defense Forces of Colombia. Initially claiming to protect civilians from the ruthlessness of leftist guerrillas, the group soon began engaging in the drug trade as well.

By 2000, violence had reached appalling levels and U.S. intelligence officials warned that the FARC could topple the Colombian government. Congress responded by approving a multi–billion dollar assistance package to combat drug trafficking in South America. Plan Colombia funded eradication efforts as well as counternarcotics military operations that often targeted the FARC. The program produced mixed results. The Colombian government significantly limited FARC profits and captured or killed many of the group's prominent leaders. Security heightened in much of the country as homicides, kidnappings, and terrorist attacks decreased. But drug producers often simply relocated to other areas and the volume of Colombian cocaine entering the United States has remained the same. Furthermore, a total of roughly $9 billion in aid over 15 years did little to curb the corruption and human rights abuses that often accompanied counternarcotics and security operations. Four years of negotiations finally produced a peace agreement between FARC rebels and the Colombian government in 2016.

Evolution in Mexico's Drug Violence

The ever-expanding drug trade in South America and law enforcement's efforts to suppress it created a spillover effect into Mexico. In the 1980s, the Drug Enforcement Administration began extensive operations in the Caribbean, which served as a transit point for South American cocaine headed to the United States. Those efforts drove Colombian cartel leaders to seek alternate routes through Central America and to establish partnerships with Mexican kingpins. Félix Gallardo (El Padrino) took the lead in expanding this enterprise and other traffickers followed suit. Mexican cartels' sophisticated network of alliances with political leaders and law enforcement officials facilitated this transition and profits from cocaine shipping skyrocketed. Estimates indicate that by the mid-1990s, the transport of South American cocaine brought Mexican traffickers more revenue than the earnings generated in the country's legal petroleum industry. In 1989, approximately one-third of the cocaine in the United States entered via Mexico; 10 years later, that number had jumped to nearly 85 percent.

New access to such exorbitant profits coincided with the organizational breakdown of Mexico's early cartel structure after the murder of the U.S. agent Enrique Camarena and subsequent arrest of major bosses. The subtraffickers that had operated under El Padrino split into the Juárez and Tijuana cartels, and El Chapo Guzmán entrenched his enterprise in a more structured Sinaloa Cartel. Bloodshed escalated as the competing syndicates challenged each other for turf, employing ever-growing levels of brutality. The Tijuana operation fell under the leadership of Amado Carrillo Fuentes, the predominant force behind much of Mexico's drug trade in the 1990s. Known as the "Lord of the Skies" for his use of airplanes to transport cocaine from South America, Carrillo Fuentes had become the nation's most powerful kingpin before he died in 1997 during a botched cosmetic surgery.

The Gulf Cartel in northeastern Mexico also underwent a transformation when it turned to cocaine transport in the 1980s. Its armed wing broke away in the late 1990s and formed the Zetas, a group known for its overt, widespread, and highly visible savagery. As the profits from trafficking South American cocaine skyrocketed, so too did the competition for turf and the violence among competing cartels. But law enforcement efforts heightened as well. In 1998, the United States and Mexico entered into a Binational Drug Control Strategy that provided nearly $400 million in funding for interdiction campaigns, security strategies, and money-laundering investigations.

The defeat of the Institutional Revolutionary Party in the 2000 presidential election fundamentally altered the long-standing pact between the government and drug organizations. The administration of Vicente Fox opened a new era in Mexico's drug war as the president began to go after some of the most powerful cartel leaders. His successor, Felipe Calderón, amplified those efforts in 2006; in an attempt to combat rampant corruption among poorly paid local police forces, he relied increasingly on military troops. In 2007, he signed the Mérida Initiative, securing even higher levels of assistance from the United States. Between 2008 and 2010, Mexico received $1.5 billion to combat drug violence. Law enforcement efforts caused many of the large and powerful cartels to fragment into as many as 80 smaller gangs that have been even more ruthless and difficult to control. Moreover, as cartels responded to a growing military presence, the death toll rose to unprecedented levels. Some estimates suggest that drug violence accounted for as much as 60 percent of the 120,000 homicides during Calderón's six years in office—a figure that represents a twofold increase over such violence during his predecessor's term.

Rising frustrations over Calderón's failed drug enforcement initiatives may partially explain the victory of the Institutional Revolutionary Party candidate Enrique Peña Nieto in the 2012 presidential election. But a populace hoping for an alleviation of drug violence has been left disappointed. Drug trafficking has adapted to include increasing amounts of heroin and methamphetamines. Furthermore, smaller and more mobile criminal gangs branched out from extortion, kidnapping, and drug activities to include human trafficking, petroleum theft, and other forms of racketeering. In the face of seeming state impotence, vigilante militias known as *autodefensas* have formed in many rural areas to defend the local population against cartel violence. In the first two years of Peña Nieto's administration, federal forces captured several high-profile cartel leaders.

Despite the seeming successes of the government's efforts to combat drug violence, deeply rooted problems remain in Mexico. In 2014, 43 normal school students from Ayotzinapa went missing after violent confrontations with local police in Iguala, Guerrero. Government leaders came under scrutiny as subsequent investigations indicated a likely collusion between police and drug gangs in the area. Less than a year later, the escape of El "Chapo" Guzmán from Mexico's maximum-security federal prison further reduced the public's confidence in the government's competence. Journalists reporting incidents of organized crime or conducting investigations into drug-related corruption have increasingly fallen victim to the rising violence. Between 2000 and 2014, 127 journalists were killed in Mexico, making it one of the deadliest countries for reporters.

Recent Trends in Central and South America

Growing pressure by law enforcement on organized crime in Mexico and Colombia has produced a ripple effect in other areas of Latin America. In Peru, the Shining Path resurfaced as a major force in the drug trade and in 2015 the United States declared the group a narcotrafficking threat. Furthermore, transit routes shifted to Central America where gang violence has intensified; the notorious MS-13 (Mara Salvatrucha) and Barrio 18 compete for turf in the poorest neighborhoods of urban areas. In 2012, Honduras, El Salvador, and Guatemala ranked in the top five most dangerous countries in the world. Honduras's homicide rate was roughly 15 times the global average; and El Salvador exceeded the world average nearly sevenfold. Desperate Central American parents began sending young children, many of them unaccompanied, on the dangerous journey to the United States in hopes of saving them from brutal violence and rampant poverty. In the first half of 2014, U.S. border patrol agents intercepted roughly 60,000 child refugees and almost as many families from Central America. For many migrants, that dangerous voyage involves traversing Mexico on top of cargo trains. Some are maimed or killed after falling onto the tracks as the trains move at high speeds; others fall victim to extortion, rape, and other types of gang violence. The perilous nature of the journey has earned the train the nickname "La Bestia."

The Cultural Impact of Drug Violence

Escalating drug violence throughout Latin America has taken an enormous human toll as rates of murders and other crimes have risen. The near-constant coverage of cartel-related kidnappings, robberies, and deaths in the Latin American media has kept the matter in the spotlight. Security concerns have affected businesses and economic activity in local areas hardest hit by drug violence. In some instances, drug gangs have overrun entire towns, causing significant migration as people attempted to flee. Large corporations have adapted by beefing up security, but many small entrepreneurs in problem areas have gone out of business.

Even as cartel violence has created economic and security challenges, many people have embraced new trends in popular culture that glorify the lifestyle of drug traffickers. The celebration of "narco-culture" is evident in the fame of popular saints in Mexico. Many low-level dealers pay homage to Jesús Malverde and Santa Muerte, believing the cult figures will help to ensure safe passage on drug trafficking missions. *Narcocorridos* have become a popular musical genre, particularly in regions with a strong cartel presence. The folk ballads follow the structure of traditional *corridos* that were used to disseminate news and other information throughout the country in the absence of mass media. But *narcocorridos* have taken on an ominous tone, frequently glorifying the violent lifestyle of drug traffickers and making heroes of the most notorious kingpins.

Other forms of popular culture idolize cartel members and their lifestyles. Fashion trends in some areas of Mexico have followed the garb of the nation's most wanted drug criminals. Photos of the arrests of several high-profile cartel leaders wearing collared jerseys with the Ralph Lauren label helped propel the popularity of "narco-polos." T-shirts and baseball hats with the image of El Chapo Guzmán became hot-ticket items after his infamous prison escape in 2015.

Standards of beauty for women have shifted in many locales as well; the image of the exotic bombshell on the arm of a cartel leader has become a trope. In Colombia, Pablo Escobar popularized the concept of the "narco-novia," as he surrounded himself with young, beautiful women who had undergone extensive plastic surgery to erase any minor imperfections. Many Colombian women embraced the trend and cosmetic surgery has become commonplace in the country. Often, the *novias* of cartel members find themselves pulled into the dangerous lifestyle. In 2014, María José Alvarado was killed not long after being crowned Miss Honduras. She and her sister fell victim to a jealous rage by the boyfriend of the latter, who was also the leader of a local drug gang. Women are also starting to assume leadership positions within cartel frameworks. Melissa Margarita Calderón Ojeda, known as "La China," and Enedina Arellano Félix, known as "La Jefa," have been identified as bosses of Mexican cartels. And some of the most violent syndicates have started recruiting young women assassins, who have earned the nickname "La Flaca" or "Skinny Girl."

Narco-culture entered into literary expression when a new genre emerged in Colombia that became known as *sicaresca*. Fernando Vallejo published the first of these with *La virgin de los sicarios* (*Our Lady of the Assassins*, 1994), which tells the story of fictionalized hit men of the Medellín Cartel. Élmer Mendoza introduced the genre to Mexico in 1999 with *Un asesino solitario* (*A Solitary Assassin*). Narco-fiction through novels spurred similar types of cultural expression in film and television, and many screen adaptations featured storylines that targeted a female audience. A film based on Jorge Franco's novel *Rosario Tijeras* premiered in 2005 and became wildly popular with audiences there and around the world. A television series by the same name aired in 2010.

Colombian broadcasting companies have taken the lead in popularizing the narco-drama—a *telenovela* with the drug cartel lifestyle as a central theme. This trend became particularly prevalent after the 1990s when the most dangerous era of the nation's drug violence had passed. *Sin senos no hay paraíso* (*Without Breasts There Is No Paradise*), based on a book by Gustavo Bolívar, first aired in 2006 and portrays the culture of plastic surgery that has developed among narco-novias. It later aired throughout Latin America and in Europe as well. *El cartel de los sapos* (*The Snitch Cartel*) debuted in 2008 as a television series and a film version premiered in 2011.

Colombia's narco-drama industry has expanded into Mexico. *La reina del sur* (*The Queen of the South*, 2011), based on a novel by Arturo Pérez-Riverte, narrates the story of a woman who becomes a powerful drug trafficker in a plot that crosses the Atlantic Ocean to Spain. Kate del Castillo starred in the telenovela and she paired up with Sean Penn to orchestrate a meeting with El Chapo Guzmán shortly before he was recaptured by law enforcement. A bizarre interview between the Hollywood actor and the drug boss appeared in *Rolling Stone* magazine in January 2016. Other recent programs from both countries depict the lives of some of the most high-profile real-life kingpins. Colombia's *Pablo Escobar: Patrón del mal* (2012) is an account of the Medellín Cartel leader's life; in Mexico, *El Señor de los Cielos* is based on the Juárez boss's life.

IMMIGRATION

Debates regarding Latino immigration have dominated much of Latin America's recent relationship with the United States. In 2013, foreign-born people made up roughly 13 percent of the U.S. population. Within that group, nearly half were of Latin American origin, and nearly 30 percent were born in Mexico. By contrast, in 1970, Mexicans made up less than 8 percent of the immigrant population. The rapid growth of the Latino demographic in recent decades has had a significant impact on the United States.

Latino immigration to the United States has a long history, dating back to the boundary shift outlined in the 1848 Treaty of Guadalupe Hidalgo. The transfer of an immense expanse of territory following the U.S.–Mexican War created the first sizeable Mexican American population, virtually overnight. The treaty granted U.S. citizenship to as many as 100,000 Mexicans living on the ceded land. It also defined the new population as "white" and provided property protections for land grants issued prior to the war. With the presence of the new "Mexican American" ethnic group in the U.S. Southwest, a Latino culture emerged. But early signs of systematic discrimination also appeared, particularly as increasing numbers of so-called "real" white settlers migrated to western states. Local officials rejected 27 percent of Mexican American land grant claims in California and 76 percent of those in New Mexico. Prejudicial education programs also arose. Starting in 1850, Texas and California enforced "English-only" policies in public schools in an attempt to compel cultural assimilation. Such measures eventually gave rise to formal segregation through separate classrooms or entire schools.

The arrival of new Latino immigrants remained limited until the economic boom at the end of the nineteenth century, when employers dealt with a labor shortage by recruiting across the border. Facing language and cultural barriers, newly arrived workers often endured exploitative conditions and low wages in agriculture, industry, and railroad construction. Social dislocation spawned by the Mexican Revolution led to a dramatic increase in migration at a time when few legal restrictions existed to limit it. By 1930, the number of Mexican-born people in the United States had reached more than 600,000, and the population of Mexican descent totaled approximately 1.5 million. Nevertheless, persistent discrimination remained; laws to protect U.S. citizens subjected hundreds of thousands of recently arrived Latino immigrants to massive repatriation campaigns during the Great Depression of the 1930s.

Two policies in particular shaped the trajectory of Latino immigration in the twentieth century. First, the Bracero Program prompted an immigration boom starting in the 1940s. Initiated during World War II to supplement the U.S. workforce with temporary Mexican "braceros," the program continued until 1964. During that time, more than 4.5 million contracts provided a legal mechanism for low-wage guest workers to find employment across the United States. The program appealed to underprivileged Mexicans, many of whom lacked the resources or patience to follow official bureaucratic channels. A parallel pattern emerged of undocumented Mexican laborers who migrated temporarily to the United States. According to some estimates, the number of unauthorized immigrant workers entering the United States during these years was roughly equivalent to the number of licensed braceros.

The Immigration and Naturalization Act passed in 1965 enshrined a second major policy of lasting impact on the U.S. Latino population. The law intended to eliminate the overt preference for white Europeans stipulated in earlier immigration law. But it also established a legal mechanism for migrants in the United States to sponsor family members, a provision that has resulted in a massive increase in legal immigration. Since 1965, people of Mexican descent have constituted the majority of migrants to the United States, arriving through both legal and unauthorized channels. But immigrants from other countries as well have contributed to the growing number of Latinos. Following the Cuban Revolution, waves of exiles escaped to Miami and New York, creating a vibrant local culture and exerting enormous political influence. The Cuban Adjustment Act of 1966 provided a foundation for preferential residency status for Cubans migrating to the United States. A revision known as the wet foot, dry foot policy passed in 1995 and stipulated that the United States would no longer welcome Cubans who were intercepted at sea; those who made it to dry land qualified for expedited permanent residency. In an unexpected move, Barack Obama ended the policy just one week before leaving office in 2017. Cuban Americans currently make up 3.5 percent of the U.S. Latino population.

After 1970, the civil wars in Guatemala, El Salvador, and Nicaragua also inspired large waves of mostly poor and undocumented Central Americans to migrate. In the 1980s alone, an estimated 1 million such refugees fled to the United States; many sought protection under a new asylum law. In a bit of cruel irony, however, U.S. officials generally considered those from El Salvador and Guatemala merely economic migrants, whereas Nicaraguan migrants could seek political refugee status to escape the leftist Sandinista regime. By 1984, immigration courts had approved less than 3 percent of political asylum cases from Central America. In response, many churches and religious organizations formed a Sanctuary Movement, providing vital assistance to undocumented refugees. Most asylum seekers did not receive legal protection from the U.S. government until the early 1990s. By that time, their population totaled approximately 1.3 million.

Economic displacement and other consequences of the debt crisis further stimulated migration to the United States. Although the 1980s became known as the Lost Decade in Latin America, many commentators in the United States referred to it as the "decade of the Hispanic." As a demographic block, the population of Latin American descent grew to unprecedented numbers and observers began to acknowledge their potential political and economic influence. In 1980, only one-third of the eligible Latino population was registered to vote, and only 30 percent of those registered actually participated in elections. The Southwest Voter Registration Education Project began in 1974 as the first program to target the Latino population. Just 20 years later, the initiative had registered 20 million new voters. In 1975, Congress passed an expansion of the Voting Rights Act, requiring language assistance at polling stations. As a result, Latino participation in the electorate increased substantially. Today, more than 24 million Latinos are eligible to vote in the United States. They have tended to support Democratic candidates; more than 70 percent backed Barack Obama for president in 2012. And although disparate exit polls showed wide discrepancy, Hillary Clinton won between 65 and 79 percent of the Latino vote in 2016. Furthermore, the Latino population—formerly concentrated in a handful of Southwestern states—has dispersed to other parts of the country. In 2015, there were 29 Latinos serving in the U.S. House of Representatives and 3 in the Senate; 2 of the senators campaigned for the Republican nomination for the presidency in 2016.

People of Latin American descent exercise increasing economic muscle in the United States as laborers and as consumers. The number of Hispanic workers grew

Singer Ricky Martin performing at the iHeart Radio Fiesta Latina in Inglewood, California. Martin's popularity among U.S. and international audiences represents the ascendancy of Latin American and Latino culture on the world stage.

from 9 million in 1988 to 23 million in 2011; it is expected to exceed 30 million by 2020. By 2013, a majority of Latino workers were U.S. born. And although many work in low-skill and low-wage industries, the population as a whole is become more educated and moving into higher-paying jobs. Between 1990 and 2014, their share of buying power in the consumer market has grown from 9 percent to nearly 17 percent. As the Latino labor force grows, so too will Hispanics' influence as consumers. Retailers and advertisers have taken note and marketing campaigns targeting the Spanish-speaking consumer demographic have become common.

The decade of the Hispanic also launched an era of Latino cultural ascendancy. Films and music celebrating a multicultural yet deeply Hispanic heritage entered the mainstream with examples such as *La Bamba* (1987) at the box office and the popular boy-band Menudo on the airwaves. The latter helped launch the careers of Robi Draco Rosa and Ricky Martin, two superstars of Latin pop who continue to enjoy enormous success in the United States and throughout Latin America. Latino authors often used autobiography to depict the cultural tensions that children of immigrant families faced growing up in the United States. Sandra Cisneros's *The House on Mango Street* published in 1984 set a standard for this type of literature.

GLOBALIZATION

The neoliberal turn in the 1990s created an environment that allowed transnational connections to flourish. The abrupt removal of barriers to trade and production, the growing mobility of people, and continuing improvements in transportation and communications technologies contributed to the rise of globalization in Latin America in recent decades. Economic and social transformations have resulted; and U.S. commercial and cultural pursuits have largely dominated the accompanying process of assimilation. Virtually unheard of before the 1980s, transnational retailers, fast food restaurants, and manufacturing firms have moved into the region and supplanted local enterprises. Global agribusinesses replaced many small producers with industrial farms, exporting soy from South America and a wide variety of fruits and vegetables from Mexico. New factories in EPZs and a vast expansion in manufacturing resulted in a fivefold increase in the value of *maquiladora* output in Central America alone between 1993 and 2003. By 2000, transnational retailers' share of the Latin American market had burgeoned to 60 percent, up from just 10 percent a decade earlier. New construction by large hotel and restaurant chains, along with the development of recreation spaces (beaches, golf courses, and eco-adventures), has fostered massive growth in the tourism industry. Already in 2004, tourism accounted for 12 percent of foreign revenue in Latin America as a whole and more than 30 percent for many countries in Central America and the Caribbean.

Digital Technology
The rapid growth in access to digital media in recent decades has driven profound social transformations in Latin America. In 2014, nearly 400 million people—approximately two-thirds of the population—used mobile phones. In that same

year, Internet penetration reached roughly 310 million. That figure accounts for just over half of the population and marks an increase of nearly 10 percent over the previous year, placing Latin America second in the world in terms of growth. Usage among young people partially explains this digital surge, with social media sites dominating data usage. Latin Americans account for 20 percent of Facebook users and 38 percent of subscribers to the data-based messaging service WhatsApp. Online retailers are making rapid gains in the Latin American market as well.

Since 2000, several Latin American governments have adopted universal access policies intended to expand the availability of digital telecommunications to rural and low-income populations. In 2010, a Costa Rican Supreme Court decision declared access to the Internet a basic human right and the nation embarked on an ambitious program of digital inclusion. Brazil, Chile, Colombia, and Argentina have also experienced notable success in expanding Internet access and digital literacy to impoverished people. Many of these programs provide information and communication technology to educational institutions. Furthermore, government-operated telecenters often complement the rapid growth of private subscriber access in the broadband, wireless, and mobile data markets.

Digital inclusion has the potential to bring about a major paradigm shift in Latin American society, particularly as access to information and new technologies expands beyond the elite and reaches even the working class and the poor. Information obtained through blogs, news sites, and personal contacts can have a democratizing effect and could encourage greater civic participation. As early as the 1990s, activist groups began using the Internet to reach a larger audience and to coordinate action. The Zapatista Army of National Liberation in southern Mexico was one of the first to incorporate the Internet and a rudimentary version of social media. Subsequent activist movements have turned to digital media in ever-expanding ways; as new technologies emerged, their strategies evolved to include new tools. Facebook and Twitter have become standard resources for disseminating information and recruiting supporters. In 2006, social media enabled the mobilization of 600,000 students in a demonstration against the Chilean president Michelle Bachelet. In the 2012 Mexican presidential election, the Twitter hashtag #yosoy132 gave rise to a protest movement, primarily of university students, who united to challenge bias and a lack of transparency in politics and journalism. As Brazil prepared to host the 2016 Olympic Games, protestors increasingly turned to social media to call attention to their grievances and to organize public demonstrations.

Latin American leaders understand the powerful reach of the Internet as well. Both new twenty-first century populists and senior politicians now use social media to connect with supporters more directly. Fidel Castro launched a Twitter account in 2010 to supplement his prolific writings in print media; within a year it surpassed 100,000 followers, becoming the first Cuba-based account to reach that milestone. Hugo Chávez also became an avid Twitter user and, like Castro, often used social media to taunt the United States. Among the masses, Internet usage has been limited and tightly controlled in Cuba, and the Venezuelan government has been accused of restricting Internet service as well. A vigilante group made up

Primary Source

El Chigüire Bipolar is a satirical news site, similar to the U.S.-based digital media organization, *The Onion*. In April 2010, its writers seized on the extensive media coverage of Hugo Chávez's first tweet and subjected the Venezuelan leader to the site's biting satire.

SOURCE: *El Chigüire Bipolar*, "Tras cámaras del primer Tweet presidencial," http://www.elchiguirebipolar .com/2010/04/tras-camaras-del-primer-tweet.html.

Behind the scenes of Chavez's first Tweet

Our exclusive spy system Directv 2000, installed in the president's office, has granted us exclusive behind the scenes access to what happened before President Hugo Chavez sent his first tweet under the username @chavezcandanga. Unfortunately, we do not have video because a doily given to the President by a grandmother covered our hidden camera, but we have audio, transcribed as follows:

. . .

"What appears onscreen, Mr. President?"

"A little bird talking . . . and text saying . . . hold on . . . uh, "Everything about Twitter" Oh, I see . . . I wrote Twitter with a 'U.'"

. . .

"Well, if you click "Sign In," up there. . . . It's on the paper that Diosdado gave you."

"Username: hugocandanga. Password: Fidel1234. Now what?"

"Click 'Sign In . . .'"

". . . What do I do now?

"Write! Write whatever you want . . . but it cannot be more than 140 characters, Mr. President. I recommend you summarize, and be brief and organized with your ideas, Mr. President."

"Summarize? What is that?"

"Nah, forget it. . . . You can now write, just try not to talk so much."

The President: "OK. Now, what do I write?. . . . *A Bolivarian and revolutionary greeting, let the ideals of Bolivar ignite the interwebs of Twitter, another weapon in our relentless fight against the Evil Empire that oppresses us. They will not return! . . . Too long . . . Well, better I put: Hey, how are you? I'm here at midnight as promised. I'm off to Brazil. I'm very happy to work for Venezuela. We will overcome!! Ha, I'm on a roll . . . now I'll really mess with you emaciated twits . . . surely you will not rest."*

of orthographic enthusiasts in Ecuador attracted unwanted attention when they extended their activities beyond correcting grammatical mistakes in public graffiti and went after errors in one of President Correa's tweets.

The twenty-first century has already been a time of enormous change for Latin America as the region has adapted to changing security concerns with the end of the Cold War as well as new realities tied to globalization. Centuries of indigenous presence, racial mixture, European rule and economic exploitation, the challenges of political independence, and a kaleidoscope of religious and other cultural changes have shaped the region into what it is today: the sum of individual countries with their own unique stories and character, but guided by numerous shared experiences that have informed their development. Iberian institutions established during three centuries of European rule laid the foundation for development patterns, political systems, and cultural responses that continue to shape Latin America today. Just as inequalities and exploitation originated both internally and from outside interventions, so too did solutions to challenges and strategies for a path forward.

SUGGESTIONS FOR FURTHER READING

Bagley, Bruce M., and Magdalena Defort (eds.). *Decline of U.S. Hegemony? A Challenge of ALBA and a New Latin American Integration of the Twenty-First Century*. Lanham, MD: Lexington Books, 2015.

Benavides, O. Hugo. *Drugs, Thugs, and Divas: Telenovelas and Narco-Dramas in Latin America*. Austin: University of Texas Press, 2008.

Borjas, George J. (ed.). *Mexican Immigration to the United States*. Chicago: University of Chicago Press, 2007.

Bowden, Mark. *Killing Pablo: The Hunt for the World's Greatest Outlaw*. New York: Atlantic Monthly Press, 2001.

Brittain, James J., and James Petras. *Revolutionary Social Change in Colombia: The Origin and Direction of the FARC-EP*. London: Pluto Press, 2010.

Campbell, Howard. *Drug War Zone: Frontline Dispatches from the Streets of El Paso and Juarez*. Austin: University of Texas Press, 2009.

Cannon, Barry. *Hugo Chavez and the Bolivarian Revolution: Populism and Democracy in a Globalized Age*. Manchester: Manchester University Press, 2009.

Corchado, Alfredo. *Midnight in Mexico: A Reporter's Journey through a Country's Descent into Darkness*. London: Penguin Books, 2014.

Edberg, Mark Cameron. *El Narcotraficante: Narcocorridos & the Construction of a Cultural Persona on the U.S.–Mexico Border*. Austin: University of Texas Press, 2004.

Edwards, Sebastian. *Left Behind: Latin America and the False Promise of Populism*. Chicago: University of Chicago Press, 2010.

Flores-Macías, Gustavo A. *After Neoliberalism? The Left and Economic Reforms in Latin America*. Oxford: Oxford University Press, 2012.

Foley, Neil. *Mexicans in the Making of America*. Cambridge, MA: Harvard University Press, 2014.

Guerin-González, Camille. *Mexican Workers and American Dreams: Immigration, Repatriation, and California Farm Labor, 1900–1939*. New Brunswick, NJ: Rutgers University Press, 1996.

Nelson, Marcel. *A History of the FTAA: From Hegemony to Fragmentation in the Americas*. New York: Palgrave, 2015.

Suárez-Orozco, Marcelo M., and Mariela Páez (eds.). *Latinos: Remaking America*. Berkeley: University of California Press, 2009.

Taylor, Lewis. *Shining Path: Guerrilla War in Peru's Northern Highlands, 1980–1997*. Liverpool: Liverpool University Press, 2006.

Epilogue

As this book goes to press, major developments in Latin America and around the world could signal a new shift in the trajectory of the region's history. Economic hardships and political scandals in many countries have left them on shaky footing. Brazil's senate voted to impeach the president, Dilma Rousseff, in August 2016, spotlighting the nation's fractured and tumultuous political system. Voters in Colombia narrowly rejected a negotiated peace accord between the government and FARC rebels. One month later, the congress ratified a modified version, the success or failure of which may dictate the country's political future. Low oil prices, hyperinflation, and a currency crisis have brought Venezuela to the brink of collapse as shortages of food, medicine, and other basic commodities afflict the population. As these and other crises unfold, half of the nations of Latin America will hold elections in 2017 and 2018. Many observers will interpret the outcomes as a referendum on the status quo.

But perhaps the most significant harbinger of an imminent shift for Latin America is Donald Trump's victory in the 2016 U.S. presidential election. Having campaigned on promises to build a wall between Mexico and the United States, restrict immigration, and withdraw from the NAFTA treaty, the new president immediately doubled down on an "America first" rhetoric. Undocumented immigrants who had sought protection under the Deferred Action for Childhood Arrivals policy face a precarious future. Talk of imposing a tariff on Mexican imports to pay for a border wall generated a nationalist outcry in Mexico, complete with campaigns to boycott U.S. companies. The U.S. election, moreover, cast doubt on the normalization of relations between the United States and Cuba, even after Fidel Castro's death on November 25, 2016, and Raúl Castro's announcement that he would step down in 2018.

In the midst of intense uncertainty, Latin American leaders have called for unity against the new U.S. president. Analysts are already predicting that U.S. economic nationalism, if implemented, would spur China to fill the resulting trade void in the Western Hemisphere. Potentially even more dire for the United States is the escalating anti-*yanqui* rhetoric evident as Latin American politicians and citizens respond to the implications of Trump's economic threats. Resistance has moved to the fore.

Glossary

Aguardiente—An alcoholic beverage distilled from wine.

Aguardiente de caña—An alcoholic beverage distilled from sugar cane.

Alcabala—A sales tax.

Alcalde or *alcalde ordinario*—A local magistrate, usually elected.

Alcalde mayor—An administrator of a province or district, especially in New Spain.

Aldeias—In Brazil, recongregated Indian communities associated with Christian conversion.

Altepetl—Indigenous city-state in central Mexico.

Alternativa—The rotation of clerical offices, especially in regular orders, between peninsulars and creoles.

Arpilleras—Tapestries depicting scenes of military repression, created by female relatives of disappeared victims during Chile's Dirty War in the 1970s.

Audiencia—A high court and advisory body to a regional chief executive in the Spanish colonies; similar to a *relaçao* in Brazil. Also the territorial jurisdiction of such a court.

Auto de fé—An act of faith; a public or private event at which the Inquisition decreed punishment of transgressions.

Autodefensas—Vigilante militias formed by local populations to protect against drug cartel violence.

Avándaro—Woodstock-like music festival in Mexico in 1971.

Ayllu—The basic kin groups in the Andean region; family units claiming ties to a common ancestor.

Ayuntamiento—A municipal council, also known as a *cabildo*.

Balsas—Rafts used by Cuban migrants attempting to reach the United States.

Balseros—Cuban refugees who migrated to the United States via raft.

Barrio—An urban neighborhood or district.

Batab—A term for a native chieftain in Yucatan.

Boland Amendments—A series of three legislative amendments passed by Congress between 1982 and 1984, prohibiting U.S. funding to Contra rebels in Central America.

Boom—Literary movement of the 1960s and 1970s.

Bozales—Slaves born in Africa.

Cabareteras—A film set in a dance hall.

Cabildo—A municipal council, also known as an *ayuntamiento*.

Cabildo abierto—An extraordinary meeting of *cabildo* attended by representatives of the Church, other governmental institutions, and members of the economic elite.

Cacica—Wife or daughter of a *cacique;* also a female chieftain.

Cacique—An Indian chieftain, usually hereditary. Known as a *kuraka* in the Andes and a *batab* in the Mayan region.

Café com leite (coffee with milk)—A political alliance and power-sharing arrangement between the elite of São Paulo and Minas Gerais, Brazil. Named after the prominent agricultural products of each region.

Cafetaleros—Elite owners of coffee estates who emerged as a powerful ruling bloc in Costa Rica in the nineteenth century.

Calidad—A putatively racial category assigned to an individual based on culture, place of residence, wealth, honor, lineage, and other characteristics that together made up total reputation.

Calpolli—Subunits of an ethnic city-state in Central Mexico.

Candomblé—An African-based religion popular in Brazil.

Carnaval—Public celebration common in Roman Catholic in the days prior to the onset of lent.

Casta—A person of mixed racial background, which included African ancestry or the suspicion of it because of illegitimacy.

Caudillo—A strongman leader, primarily in the nineteenth century, who used a combination of charisma and coercion to maintain control.

Centralism—System of government in which political authority is concentrated under a strong central government.

Charango—A small Andean lute.

Chasquis—Inka couriers.

Chicha—An Andean alcoholic beverage often made from corn.

Cielito—A folkloric music and dance genre in nineteenth-century Argentina.

Científicos—Advisors to Porfirio Díaz, who adhered to the tenets of positivism in late nineteenth-century Mexico.

Clientelism—Strategy employed by many populist leaders of offering personal favors in return for political loyalty.

Cofradía—A lay religious brotherhood.

Colegio—A secondary school in the Spanish colonies and Brazil.

Colonia—Neighborhood. Often used to refer to unincorporated shantytowns.

Coloniaje—A deprecatory term introduced in the 1820s, it referred to the three centuries of Spanish rule in the Americas.

Colonos—European immigrants who worked as agricultural colonists in late nineteenth-century Brazil.

Comarca—A territorial jurisdiction in Brazil.

Comedia ranchera—A comedic film set on a ranch. Common in Mexican cinema in the mid-twentieth century.

Compadrazgo—(Sp) Godparentage; *Compadrio* (Port).

Comparative advantage—A nation's ability to produce a type of good comparatively well relative to another nation.

Comuneros—Supporters of a popular revolt. In Spanish America, rebels in Paraguay in 1720s and 1730s and in New Granada in 1780.

Concertaje—A system of debt peonage in Ecuador.

Congregación—Also known as a *reducción* or, in Brazil, an *aldeia*. A resettlement of Indians by Spaniards to aid in the Indians' conversion to Christianity.

Conservatism—A nineteenth-century ideology that favored maintaining colonial traditions, including a strong central government, retaining legal privileges (*fueros*) for corporate bodies, and ensuring the strength of the Catholic Church.

Consulado—A merchant guild.

Contadora Group—Made up of diplomatic leaders of Mexico, Venezuela, Colombia, and Panama who unsuccessfully attempted to mediate a peaceful solution to Central American civil wars in the 1980s.

Contras—U.S.-financed rebels who fought against the leftist Sandinista government of Nicaragua in the 1980s.

Contribución única—A type of tribute collected by the Peruvian government in the decades following independence.

Conventillo—A type of urban tenement or slum.

Converso—A convert to Christianity; usually applied to a converted Jew or a "New Christian."

Corregidor—A magistrate and chief administrative officer for a provincial jurisdiction. In much of Spanish America, the Spanish official charged with the administration of Indian communities.

Corregimiento—An administrative province or district.

Corridos—A form of epic lyric poetry in Mexico.

Cortes—A type of parliament.

Costumbrista—A literary and artistic genre of the late nineteenth century that emphasized local customs and daily life.

Creole (criollo)—A Spaniard or, less frequently, a black born in the New World.

Descamisados—Literally "shirtless ones." The term used by Juan and Eva Perón to describe the impoverished Argentines whose support they sought.

Dirty War—Refers to government-sponsored oppression in an attempt to subdue leftist subversives common throughout Latin America between 1960 and the 1980s.

Doctrina—An Indian parish.

Don, Doña—Lord, lady; a title rare in the Conquest but subsequently more commonly used.

Ejidos—A communal system of land tenure in Mexico.

Encomendero—The holder of an *encomienda* (q.v.).

Encomienda—A grant of authority over a group of Indians. It carried the obligation to Christianize and protect them in exchange for labor services and/or tribute.

Engenho (Sp. ingenio)—The Portuguese term for sugar mill. Refers to the complete operation, including the physical plant, land, and slaves.

Escribano—Notary or scribe.

Esquipulas I and II—Peace treaties authored by the Costa Rican president Oscar Arias Sánchez to end civil wars in Central America in the 1980s.

Estado Novo—Authoritarian government of Getúlio Vargas in Brazil from 1937 to 1945.

Estampa—Lithographic print.

Estancia See Hacienda.

Faitorias—Armed Portuguese trading posts.

Familiares—Lay agents of the Inquisition.

Favela—Brazilian slum.

Fazenda—The Brazilian term for *hacienda* (q.v.).

Federalism—System of government that maintains local or regional autonomy and a relatively weak central government.

Filibuster—U.S. mercenaries who claimed lands in Latin America on behalf of the United States in the nineteenth century.

Fiscal de iglesia—A native village's most important parish office other than that of priest; held by an Indian fluent in Castilian.

Flota—The fleet that sailed from Spain to Veracruz.

Forastero—An outsider; a person residing in a region other than where he or she was born.

Fueros—Special judicial privileges enjoyed by a particular group—for example, ecclesiastical *fueros*.

Fútbol—Soccer.

Galeones—The convoy (galleons) that sailed from Spain to Cartagena and Panama.

Gaucho—A cowboy, usually of mixed ancestry, in the Río de la Plata. Known as *llanero* in Venezuela and *vaqueiro* in the Brazilian backlands.

Golpe—Coup d'état.

Granaderos—Extralegal security force in 1960s Mexico.

Guano—Excrement of bats or seabirds used in natural fertilizers.

Hacendado—The owner of an *hacienda* (q.v.).

Hacienda—Generally a large estate, also known as an *estancia* in some locations, devoted to livestock raising or agricultural activities. Known as a *fazenda* in Brazil.

Hidalgo (fidalgo in Portuguese)—An untitled noble.

Hidalguía—A Castilian aristocratic ideal of nobility.

Huaca—A native Andean god; often thought of as an ancestor. Commonly represented as hills, stones, water, or mummies.

Indigenismo—The celebration of select characteristics of indigenous culture and heritage that became prominent in the first half of the twentieth century.

Indio—Indian.

Ingenio—See *engenho*.

Jefe político superior—The highest colonial administrative officer in the reorganized system created in the constitution of 1812, replacing the viceroy.

Khipus—Multicolored knotted strings that served as memory aids in preconquest Peru. Also known as *quipus*.

Kuraka—See *cacique*.

Ladino—The Central American term for *mestizo;* also applied more broadly to Indians who spoke fluent Spanish.

Laissez-faire—Economic model, common in the nineteenth century, that implied freedom from government regulation and interference.

La Matanza—Massacre of El Salvadoran peasants by government forces in 1932.

La Mazorca—A violent, extralegal enforcement squad used by Juan Manuel de Rosas to maintain order in nineteenth-century Argentina.

La Onda—Mexican countercultural youth movement of the 1960s.

La Reforma—The period from 1854 to 1857 when liberal leaders in Mexico ushered in sweeping reforms, culminating in the constitution of 1857 and eventually leading to civil war with conservatives.

Latifundia—System of land ownership in which control of large estates is concentrated in the hands of a few.

Latifundio—Large landed estate under the system of *latifundia*.

Lavradores de cana—In Brazil, sugar cultivators who depended on an *engenho* for *processing*. Many were sharecroppers.

Letrados—University trained lawyers, men of letters.

Liberalism—A nineteenth-century ideology that rejected colonial traditions and sought to diminish the power of corporate bodies, such as the Catholic Church.

Libreta—Ration book in issued in Cuba to manage shortages after the revolution.

Limpieza de sangre—Blood purity; the absence of Jewish or Muslim ancestors.

Llanero—See *gaucho*.

Llanos—The southern plains of Venezuela.

Los barbudos—Literally "the bearded ones." Term used to describe Fidel Castro and his small band of guerrilla fighters who refused to shave their beards during the Cuban Revolution.

Lucha libre—A form of professional wrestling in Mexico.

Lunfrado—A type of Italian slang introduced by immigrants in early twentieth-century Buenos Aires.

Mameluco—The offspring of Portuguese and Indian parents.

Manikongo—Ruler of the Kingdom of Kongo.

Maquiladora—Assembly plants that operate in tariff free zones.

Marielitos—Cuban refugees who migrated to the United States as part of the Mariel boatlift in 1980.

Mayorazgo—An entailed estate.

Mestizaje—The celebration of race mixing.

Mestizo—The offspring of Spanish and Indian parents.

Miserables—The "wretched poor".

Mita—The colonial forced labor draft that provided Indian workers on a rotational basis—most common in mining in Peru. Adapted from an Inka precedent.

Mitayo—An Indian forced to serve in *mita*.

Mitmaq—The Indian colonizers in Andean Peru sent to exploit an ecological zone or to help secure a conquered region.

Modernismo—Literary genre of the late nineteenth century that emphasized the beauty of natural landscapes to critique the harshness of the modern world.

Moneda nacional—National currency in Cuba.

Montoneros—Leftist urban guerrilla group in Argentina active in the 1970s.

Mulatto—Offspring of black and white parents and, in some regions, black and Indian parents.

Narcocorrido—A folk song in Mexico that tells the story of drug dealers or narcotrafficking.

Native son—Here a creole in the *audiencia* district or diocese of his birth.

Neofolklore—An Argentine musical genre that emerged in the late twentieth century as a combination of traditional and modern styles.

Neoliberalism—Economic theory popular in the late twentieth century that calls for deregulation, free trade through formal treaties, and an end to government ownership of industry.

Novia—Girlfriend.

Nueva canción—Musical style of the late twentieth century that addressed social inequality and exploitation.

Oba—King of Benin.

Obraje—A primitive factory commonly used to produce textiles in Spanish colonies. Usually dependent on forced labor.

Obrerismo—Strategy used by Hipólito Yrigoyen in Argentina to build a political coalition of Argentine-born workers and second-generation immigrants.

Oidor—A judge on an *audiencia*.

Oligarchy—Rule by a small group, generally of the elite.

Operation Condor—Cooperative strategy employed by military governments in South America to exchange intelligence and pursue suspected leftist sympathizers across borders during the era of Dirty War. Also refers to a partnership between Mexico and the United States to eradicate opium and marijuana crops in the 1970s.

Padroado—The Portuguese crown's patronage over the Church; analogous to the *patronato real* of the Spanish crown.

Pampa—The plains of Río de la Plata.

Parastatal—A government-owned industry.

Pardo—A mulatto; person with some African ancestry.

Patronato—A type of apprenticeship that was part of gradual emancipation of slaves in Cuba in the 1880s.

Patronato real—Royal patronage over the Church. The right to nominate for Church offices and supervise Church administration.

Pecho—A direct tax in Castile paid only by commoners.

Pelado—A working-class male character in Mexican cinema, often portrayed as drunk and unkempt.

Peninsular—A Spaniard born in Iberia.

Peso—A coin and monetary unit in Spanish America. The silver peso was valued at eight *reales* of silver.

Pipiltin—Hereditary Mexica nobility.

Plan of Iguala—An 1821 agreement between Agustín de Iturbide and insurgent leaders that called for Mexican independence under a constitutional monarch while preserving the power of the Catholic Church.

Plaza mayor—A rectangular plaza at the heart of a Spanish city or town.

Pochteca—Long-distance merchants in Aztec Mexico.

Populism—Political movements of the twentieth century that sought to appeal to the needs of the masses.

Porfiriato—Period from 1876 to 1910 when Mexico was under the authoritarian rule of Porfirio Díaz.

Positivism—Philosophy popular in the late nineteenth century, which argued that logic, reason, and empiricism should form the basis of knowledge.

Presidio—A frontier garrison.

Pronunciamiento—A type of military coup common in the nineteenth century.

Pueblo—Indian village.

Pulque, pulquería—An alcoholic beverage made from maguey, popular in Mexico before and after the conquest; a tavern that sold *pulque*.

Radicado—A Spaniard long resident in the colonies. The term suggests someone who is well connected with local interests through marriage, friendship, and business associations.

Radionovela—A serialized radio play common in the early days of radio throughout Latin America.

Reales—Small coins of which 8 of silver equaled 1 peso.

Recogimiento—House of refuge or seclusion for women.

Recôncavo—The area surrounding Bahia's Bay of All Saints.

Reducciónes—New villages in Peru created by forced relocation of natives from prior settlements; the process of relocating was the Peruvian equivalent to congregation in Mexico.

Refritos—Spanish-language cover versions of songs made popular by U.S. rock and roll stars of the 1950s and 1960s.

Relação—High court of appeals in Brazil; similar to an *audiencia* in the Spanish colonies.

Repartimiento—The allocation of an Indian chieftain and his people to a Spaniard to provide labor; a forced labor draft (known as *mita* in Peru).

Repartimiento de bienes—The forced sale of merchandise to Indians by Spanish officials.

Resguardo—Communally owned indigenous lands, primarily in Colombia.

Residencia—The judicial review of an official's conduct in office.

Revista—A popular periodical.

Rocanrol—Hispanicized word for "rock & roll".

Rurales—Special security force used to bring order and stability to the countryside in late nineteenth-century Mexico.

Senado da câmara—Municipal council in Brazil.

Sertão—The backland of Brazil.

Sicaresca—Crime narratives that emerged in the late twentieth century around themes of drug violence. They often combine personal testimonio with the crime novel genre.

Social Darwinism—Theory that applies the biological notion of "survival of the fittest" to society.

Soldaderas—Female soldiers who fought in the Mexican Revolution.

Tambo—Inka rest area and storehouse.

Teatro bufo—A satirical style of clown theater that became popular in nineteenth-century Cuba.

Teatro gauchesco—A genre of theater in Argentina that romanticized the life of the *gaucho*.

Telenovela—A serialized television drama with daily episodes that run for six months to one year.

Testimonio—Literary style in the late twentieth century characterized as a testimonial narrative, usually telling the story of personal or social crisis.

Tlatoani—An indigenous "ruler" or *cacique* in central Mexico.

Traza—The rectilinear core of a colonial city.

Vecino—A citizen of a municipality.

Visita—An official inspection into the conduct of bureaucrats, usually unscheduled and unexpected.

Waranqa—A group of *ayllus* in the Andes during Inka rule.

Yana—Andean commoners who had left their *ayullus* and labored for the Inka empire and its nobles.

Yanacona—A post-Conquest native retainer or laborer bound to an overlord in the Andean region.

Yerba maté—An herbal tea indigenous to Paraguay.

Zambo—Offspring of black and Indian parents; often called a "mulatto" in New Spain.

Acronyms

ALBA—Bolivarian Alliance for the Americas
CEPAL—Comisión Económica para América Latina y el Caribe (ECLAC in English)
CIA—Central Intelligence Agency
ECLAC—Economic Commission for Latin America and the Caribbean (CEPAL in Spanish)
EPZ—export-processing zone
FARC—Revolutionary Armed Forces of Colombia
FSLN—Sandinista National Liberation Front (Nicaragua)
FTAA—Free Trade Area of the Americas
IMF—International Monetary Fund
ISI—import substitution industrialization
M-19—April 19th Movement (Colombia)
M-26-7—26th of July Movement (Cuba)
MERCOSUR—Mercado Común del Sur
NAFTA—North American Free Trade Agreement
OCIAA—Office of the Coordinator of Inter-American Affairs
OPEC—Organization of the Petroleum Exporting Countries

Credits

p 8: Mancco Ccpac I, Inca del Peru, Peru, late 19th Century, Denver Art Museum Collection: Gift of Dr. Belinda Straight, 1977, 1977.45.1, Photograph courtesy of the Denver Art Museum.

p 8: Mama Ocollo Huacco I Ccoya del Peru, Peru, late 19th Century, Denver Art Museum Collection: Gift of Dr. Belinda Straight, 1977, 1977.45.2, Photograph courtesy of the Denver Art Museum.

p 12: Plaque, Benin, Nigeria, 1550-1650, Denver Art Museum Collection: Native Arts acquisition fund, 1955.317. Photograph © the Denver Art Museum.

p 35: D. Francisco Pizarro Conquistador del Peru, Peru, late 19th century, Denver Art Museum Collection: Gift of Dr. Belinda Straight, 1977, 1977.45.16. Photograph courtesy of the Denver Art Museum.

p 75: St. Ignatius Loyola (San Ignacio Loyola), Augustin del Pino, c. 1700, Denver Art Museum Collection: Gift of Frederick and Jan Mayer, 2013.302. Photograph courtesy of Denver Art Museum.

p 76: Inca Noblewoman, Cuzco, Peru, early 1800s. Denver Art Museum Collection: Gift of Dr. Belinda Straight by exchange and New World Department Acquisition Funds, 1996.18. Photograph courtesy of the Denver Art Museum.

p 119: Portrait of Don Francicso de Orense y Moctezuma, Conde de Villalobos, Anonymous Artist, Mexican Schoo, 1761. Denver Art Museum Collection: Gift of Frederick and Jan Mayer, 2011.427. Photograph courtesy of the Denver Art Museum.

p 126: Rendering of a Mulatta (Diceno de Mulata), attributed to Manuel de Arellano, 1711. Denver Art Museum: Collection of Frederick and Jan Mayer. Photograph courtesy of the Denver Art Museum.

p 131: Portrait of Joachim Sanchez Pareja Narvaez y la Torre as an army cadet, unknown artist, August 28, 1773. Denver Art Museum: Collection of Frederick and Jan Mayer. Photograph courtesy of the Denver Art Museum.

p 139: Young Woman with a Harpsichord, unknown Artist, Mexican Schoo, early 1700s. Denver Art Museum: Collection of Frederick and Jan Mayer. Photograph courtesy of the Denver Art Museum

p 143: De Barsino y Mulata, China, Francisco Clapera, c. 1785. Denver Art Museum Collection: Gift of Frederick and Jan Mayer, 2011.428.13. Photograph courtesy of the Denver Art Museum.

p 147: Death Portrait of Don Thomas Maria Joachim Villasenor y Gomez, unknown artist, 1760. Denver Art Museum Collection: Gift of Frederick and Jan Mayer, 2013.316. Photograph courtesy of the Denver Art Museum.

p 197: Planter and his wife: From the New York Public Library, b11723219

p 223: Theatre in St. Iago: From the New York Public Library, b16044202

p 224: Santa Anna declining: Courtesy of the Library of Congress, LC-USZ62-13650 DLC

p 246: Courtesy of Archivo General de la Nación Argentina, 1908, via Wikimedia Commons

p 271: Christmas on the Isthmus: Courtesy of the Library of Congress, LC-DIG-ppmsca-25807 DLC

p 285: Emiliano Zapata: Courtesy of the Library of Congress, Bain Collection, LC-USZ62-73425

p 301: Courtesy of National Archives and Records Administration, RG229, E1, Box 4

p 306: AP Photo

p 327: AP Photo

p 338: AP Photo

p 357: AP Photo

p 374: AP Photo/Jack Smith

p 376: AP Photo/Jose Luis Magana

p 389: AP Photo/Arturo Mari, pool

p 418: Chris Pizzello/Invision/AP, file

INDEX

Note: Page numbers in *italics* indicate figures or illustrations; *t* after a page number denotes a table.